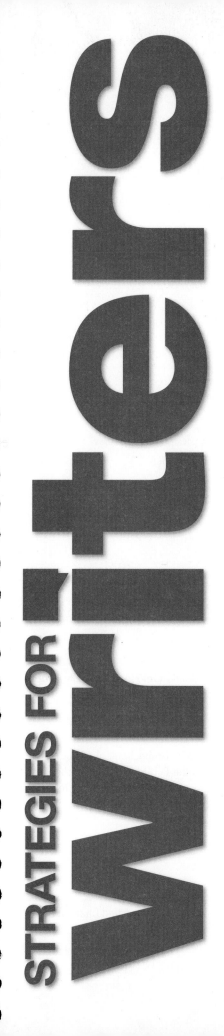

STRATEGIES FOR writers

Teacher Edition 6

Senior Author
Rebecca Bowers Sipe, Ed.D.
Eastern Michigan University

Consulting Authors
Julie Coiro, Ph.D.
University of Rhode Island

Amy Humphreys, Ed.M., NBCT
Educational Consultant

Sara B. Kajder, Ph.D.
University of Pittsburgh

Mark Overmeyer, M.A.
Cherry Creek School District, Colorado

Senior Consultant
James Scott Miller, M.Ed.
National Writing Consultant

ZB **Zaner-Bloser**

Program Reviewers

Zaner-Bloser wishes to thank these educators who reviewed portions of this program and provided comments prior to publication.

ISBN 978-0-7367-7274-7

Credits
Photo credits: Cover and title page: © Liane Carey/age fotostock; Z4: © iStockphoto.com/Sean Locke; Z7: © Jamie Grill/Iconica/Getty Images; Z8: author supplied; Z10: author supplied; Z12: author supplied; Z16: © George C. Anderson; Z18: author supplied; Z19: author supplied

Zaner-Bloser, Inc.
1-800-421-3018
www.zaner-bloser.com

Printed in the United States of America   11 12 13 14 15 19840 5 4 3 2 1

Certified Chain of Custody
Promoting Sustainable
Forest Management
www.sfiprogram.org

This SFI label applies to the text paper.

Table of Contents

21st Century Writing Instruction for 21st Century Students

Strategies for Writers is a complete writing and grammar program that prepares all students to be confident, proficient, and effective 21st century writers, ready for college and/or career.

With this program's cutting-edge technology tools, students' digital literacy and engagement in writing increases.

CCSS
Meets 100% of the Common Core State Standards for Writing and Language

Ease of Use

- **Clear, concise lessons** simplify instruction to enhance students' writing skills and produce the results they need for success in college and career.

- ***Strategies for Writers*** **Online Writing Center** provides a comprehensive digital writing and grammar classroom experience, allowing students to complete and submit their assignments online.

- **Consistent, Common Core State Standards terminology** facilitates improved peer-to-peer, peer-group, and teacher-led conferences. **CCSS**

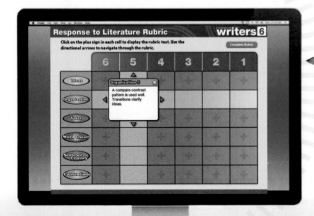

Genre-Specific and Interactive Rubrics

- **Genre-specific rubrics** give students a clear understanding of the expectations for each writing form as they deconstruct models and interactive anchor papers and as they write.

- **Online interactive rubrics** allow students to explore the point-by-point qualities of genre-specific characteristics for the six traits of writing on a four-, five-, or six-point scale.

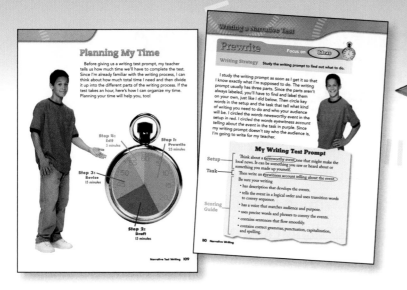

Test Preparation and Assessment

- **A dedicated test-writing chapter** in each unit improves students' confidence and performance on high-stakes writing tests.

- **Online interactive Grammar Assessments** include automatic scoring to provide immediate student feedback and formative assessment data for teachers.

Complete Grammar Instruction ▷ and Practice

- **100% coverage of the CCSS for Language** in the Student Edition ensures students learn the grammar skills they need for success in college and career.

- **Online games and interactive whiteboard activities** get students excited about grammar, usage, and mechanics.

Online Essay Grader and Writing Tutor

Powered by Vantage Learning's MY Access!®, this tool gives students

- **immediate, ongoing, sentence-by-sentence feedback**.

- **helpful suggestions** to improve their draft.

- **a holistic score and a trait-specific score** on their final draft.

- **unlimited response submissions** to the prompts.

21st Century Writing Instruction for 21st Century Teachers

With *Strategies for Writers'* dynamic, versatile mix of print and digital resources, teachers can easily accommodate students' varying learning styles and abilities and customize writing instruction to be fully digital, completely print-based, or a blend of digital and print resources.

This program gives all teachers—from novice to expert—the tools they need to confidently deliver effective, rigorous instruction that meets 100% of the CCSS for Writing and Language.

Complete Online Writing Instruction

- **Online Writing Center** allows teachers to make differentiated assignments and review students' work digitally.
- **Student and Teacher Dashboards** house all of the program's technology tools in one easy-to-manage location.

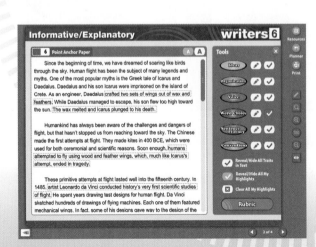

Flexible Instruction

- **Narrative, Informative/Explanatory, Opinion or Argument, and Descriptive Writing units** can be taught in any order to suit any teacher's needs.
- **Choice of four-, five-, and six-point rubrics** is integrated into all aspects of instruction.

Common Core State Standards **CCSS** ▷

- *Strategies for Writers* covers 100% of the CCSS for Writing and Language, so teachers can be confident that their students are prepared to be effective writers in every mode: Narrative, Informative/Explanatory, and Opinion or Argument, and Descriptive.

- Only *Strategies for Writers* references the CCSS at point-of-use in the Teacher Edition (print and eBook) to make planning easier.

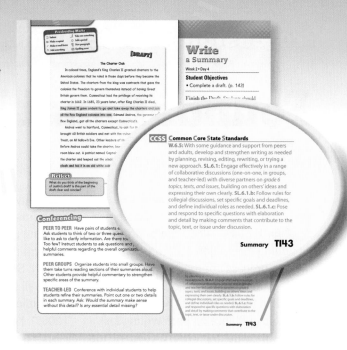

72 additional Writing Across the Curriculum prompts per grade!

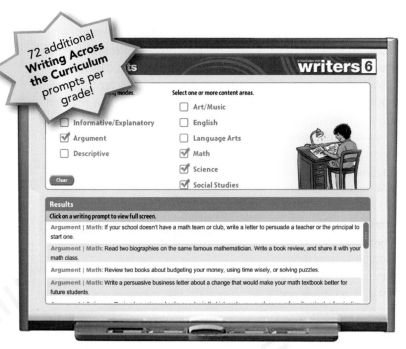

Differentiation and English Language Learner Support ▽

- **Enrichment and Reinforcement activities and tips for four levels of English Language Learners** allow teachers to meet the needs of each student.

- **The program's abundance of grammar, usage, and mechanics resources and activities** provide differentiated skill instruction and practice.
  - ‣ Interactive whiteboard grammar games and proofreading activities
  - ‣ Online grammar games and proofreading activities
  - ‣ Grammar lessons embedded in the Student Edition
  - ‣ Additional Grammar Practice in Appendix A of the Student Edition
  - ‣ Grammar, Usage & Mechanics Student Practice Book
  - ‣ Grammar Practice Masters

◁ Interactive Whiteboard Resources

- **Provide interactive presentation resources and activities** for whole- and small-group interactive whiteboard instruction:
  - ‣ interactive anchor papers
  - ‣ proofreading practice and grammar games
  - ‣ writing process videos
  - ‣ interactive graphic organizers and more
  - ‣ cross-curricular writing prompts and more

Free Online Resources ▽

The *Strategies for Writers* Online free resources website includes

- customizable presentations.
- four-, five-, and six-point rubrics.
- graphic organizers.
- minilesson videos
- and more!

www.sfw.z-b.com

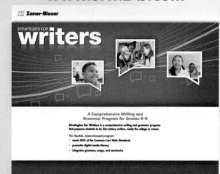

Foundational Research

by Rebecca Bowers Sipe, Ed.D.

Based on 30 years of solid research in writing development, *Strategies for Writers* reflects the best practices of writing instruction: It combines a writing process approach with a focus on strategy and skills development. Rubrics based on the six traits of writing give students guidance on each writing task as well as provide them with a concrete tool for self-assessment for all four modes of writing. *Strategies for Writers* balances a skills-based and process approach and contains the key elements of successful instruction identified by the national *Writing Next* report (Graham & Perin, 2007).

> *Strategies for Writers is based on best practices and the Common Core State Standards.*

Process Writing and Writing Strategies

Since the 1970s, the process approach to writing has been used increasingly as the base instructional model in language arts (Pritchard & Honeycutt, 2006). With this approach, teachers identify and model the stages of writing (prewriting, drafting, editing, revising, proofreading, and publishing) and engage students in collaborative activities. The process approach is also embedded in the Common Core State Standards (CCSS) for English Language Arts (Common Core State Standards Initiative, 2010; see especially standards under "Production and Distribution of Writing").

Strategy instruction explicitly and systematically teaches the steps of the writing process and has a dramatic effect on writing quality (Graham & Perin, 2007). Strategy instruction seems to help all students improve their writing, regardless of their starting point (Graham, 2008). Key strategic behaviors within the writing process, for example, planning and revising, are important ingredients in writing development. Skilled writers plan and revise better than unskilled writers do, and planning and revising behavior predicts writing performance. Research has thus demonstrated conclusively that "teaching developing writers how to plan or revise has a strong and positive impact on their writing" (Graham & Harris, 2009, 61).

Rubrics and Assessment in Writing

Researchers find that the process approach to generating writing should be coupled with an additional focus on the product of writing to attain greater student improvement (Honeycutt & Pritchard, 2005). Rubrics based on the six traits of writing help students to identify their writing goals during the process as well as to assess their writing products. In addition, as some researchers suggest (NWREL, n.d.; De La Paz, 2009), rubrics can be turned into heuristics that help students prepare for standardized testing, in which they are most often asked to write on demand (Gregg, Coleman, Davis, & Chalk, 2007; Mayer, 2010).

Because it addresses each of the modes in each grade, at grade-appropriate levels of sophistication, *Strategies for Writers* also correlates to the CCSS focus on the range of text types and purposes in writing.

Mode-based lessons incorporate rubrics that are specific to that mode, which can be used for self-assessment as part of the revising process. Recent research suggests that giving students clear goals and expectations for a writing product helps improve their revision process and result in better writing (Butler & Britt, 2011).

Butler, J. A., & Britt, M. A. (2011). Investigating instruction for improving revision of argumentative essays. *Written Communication, 28* (1), 70–96.

Common Core State Standards Initiative. (2010). *Common core state standard for English language arts & literacy in history/social studies, science, and technical subjects.* Retrieved from www.corestandards.org.

De La Paz, S. (2009). Heuristics for developing writing strategies. *Assessment for Effective Intervention, 34*(3), 134–146.

Graham, S., & Perin, D. (2007). *Writing next: Effective strategies to improve writing of adolescents in middle and high schools—A report to Carnegie Corporation of New York.* Alliance for Excellent Education.

Graham, S. (2008). Strategy instruction and the teaching of writing. In C. A. MacArthur, S. Graham, J. Fitzgerald (Eds.), *Handbook of Writing Research.* Guilford, 187–207.

Graham, S., & Harris, K. R. (2009). Almost 30 years of writing research: Making sense of it all with *The Wrath of Khan. Learning Disabilities Research & Practice, 24* (2), 58–68.

Gregg, N., Coleman, C., Davis, M., & Chalk, J. C. (2007). Timed essay writing: Implications for high-stakes tests. *Journal of Learning Disabilities, 40,* 306–318.

Honeycutt, R. L., & Pritchard, R. J. (2005). Using a structured writing workshop to help good readers who are poor writers. In G. Rijlaarrsdan, H. van den Bergh, & M. Couzijin (Eds.), *Studies in Writing* (2nd ed., vol. 4). Kluwer, pp. 141–150.

Mayer, M. (2010). *Two roads diverged and I took both: Meaningful writing instruction in an age of testing.* AuthorHouse (self-published).

Northwest Regional Educational Laboratory. (n.d.) *About 6+1 trait writing.* Retrieved February 18, 2011, from http://educationnorthwest.org/resource/949.

Pritchard, R. J., & Honeycutt, R. L. (2006). The process approach to writing instruction: Examining its effectiveness. In C.A. MacArthur, S. Graham, J. Fitzgerald (Eds.), *Handbook of Writing Research.* Guilford, 275–290.

Please visit **www.sfw.z-b.com** for the complete research report and cited references.

Traits and the Writing Process

by Rebecca Bowers Sipe, Ed.D.

The six traits of writing and the writing process are essential elements of effective writing instruction. While they may be taught and understood separately, they should be viewed as parts of a coherent and complete instructional whole. The traits define and support the writing process, simplify instruction, and facilitate a clear understanding among students of what makes writing work. To demonstrate the relationship between traits and process, let's discuss and define each separately.

Steps of the Writing Process

The writing process is cyclical, recursive, and composed of five steps: **Prewriting, Drafting, Revising, Editing,** and **Publishing.** Instructionally, we must take care to recognize that these steps are not necessarily sequential. During the development of a composition, a proficient writer will certainly employ each of these steps, but the organic evolution of the writing itself will determine the sequence and manner in which the steps are negotiated. In teaching the steps of the writing process explicitly, we help students to understand how good writers go about crafting their work.

Writing Traits

If the writing process is the "how" of excellent writing, then the traits of writing represent the "what." The traits are the specific elements that writers focus upon in each step of the process. They are the six observable, assessable, revisable, and editable features that characterize all writing. The traits comprise a comprehensive way of looking at writing. This model also simplifies our understanding of writing because it allows us to focus our attention upon the

Writing Traits

Ideas represents the concepts, thoughts, insights, assertions, and details that the author wishes to express to the reader.

Organization relates to the effectiveness of the "blueprint" that the author uses to sequence and arrange ideas for the reader.

Voice is closely related to the tone established by the author and the affective mood that results from the way the writing is crafted. Voice also reflects the personality, attitude, and enthusiasm of the author.

Word Choice influences Voice. Excellent Word Choice results when a writer uses exactly the right words to carry the message. Typically, this means that nouns and verbs are clear and precise, carrying the author's message with support from a few carefully chosen modifiers.

Sentence Fluency may be described as the rhythm or flow of sentences that results from variations in length, structure, and beginnings.

Conventions includes grammar, usage, and mechanics. A talented writer may even control Conventions in creative or unique ways to convey or underscore meaning with extreme effectiveness.

individually manageable traits themselves: **Ideas, Organization, Voice, Word Choice, Sentence Fluency,** and **Conventions.**

Traits and Process

In the final analysis, traits and process may be taught and understood separately, but their true partnership and power comes from their interplay during authentic writing. For example, in **Prewriting,** a writer selects ideas and organizes them according to the needs of a specific audience; envisioning one's audience helps the writer establish a stronger voice. In **Drafting,** a writer supports ideas with good word choice, writing these words into sentences that flow, contributing to good sentence fluency. A writer may **Revise** for ideas, organization, voice, word choice, or sentence fluency, then **Edit** for conventions. During **Publishing,** a writer might pay special attention to the conventions that make the work correct and neat.

Ultimately, the relationship between traits and process is clear: In every step of the writing process, a good writer skillfully and purposefully manages some combination of traits. *Strategies for Writers* fully incorporates the traits of writing within each step of the writing process. Students who use *Strategies for Writers* will learn, practice, and apply writing strategies that support this model in every step of every lesson.

Rubric-Based Instruction

by James Scott Miller, M.Ed.

What is good writing? More specifically, what qualities of writing cause readers to be entertained, persuaded, enlightened, or informed?

Excellent rubrics answer these questions by capturing the essence of a reader's expectations. Rubrics clearly articulate these expectations and provide a scale to measure the extent to which they are accomplished in a piece of writing. The best rubrics speak clearly from reader to writer, almost as if to say, "Here's exactly what I'm looking for in your writing." In fact, the words of a well-crafted and familiar rubric may almost sound to a writer like advice from a trusted friend.

Rubrics Drive Revision and Editing

Since authors write to a variety of audiences and for a variety of purposes, the most common rubrics are specific to either a writing mode (Narrative, Descriptive, Informative/Explanatory, Opinion or Argument), or to a writing genre (like a cause-and-effect essay or a book report). In either case, the greatest value of the instrument lies in its formative properties i.e., its ability to drive effective revision and editing within the writing process. Rubrics may also be used in a summative manner when the writing process is completed. When objective scores and defensible grades are required (as they are in most classrooms), excellent rubrics render scores that are trustworthy.

Effective Rubrics

To be effective, a rubric must have a sufficient number of levels (or "points") to be sensitive to incremental improvements in the writing. Six-point rubrics are perhaps the most common among

formative rubrics. Thoughtfully crafted four- and five-point rubrics may also be used effectively where fewer score points are desired. For very young writers in kindergarten and first grade, it may be appropriate to further reduce the number of levels to three.

Trait-Specific Rubrics

The usefulness of a rubric is based upon the characteristics of writing it seeks to assess. So what exactly should rubrics seek to measure? There are essentially six characteristics, or "traits", evident in all writing: Ideas, Organization, Voice, Word Choice, Sentence Fluency, and Conventions. Presentation is an outgrowth of the Conventions trait, but is often identified separately to emphasize the importance of neatness and appearance. Taken together, these traits constitute the observable, assessable, and revisable features of all writing, so they make an ideal foundation for the development of quality rubrics.

Benefits of Rubrics

The benefits of using trait-specific rubrics are many. To begin with, these rubrics provide a common writing language that helps define clear composition goals. This keeps us focused and honest, challenging our preconceived notions of proficiency and keeping us "balanced" in our analysis of writing. It's important to understand that the goal of rubrics is not to remove all subjectivity from assessment, but to hold us accountable to defensible criteria that reflect the overall quality of the written message (rather than more arbitrary criteria, such as length, ink color, or neatness).

Trait-specific rubrics also clarify, simplify, and accelerate scoring. Like

interchangeable lenses, these instruments allow teachers to assess any number of traits within a given composition. By scoring multiple traits, teachers are able to identify comparative strengths and weaknesses in students' writing and deliver targeted feedback and instruction. Through explicit instruction and consistent modeling of trait-based assessment, teachers accomplish perhaps the most important goal, which is to transfer assessment proficiency to the students themselves. While all six traits should be explicitly instructed and assessed repeatedly throughout the year, rarely is it necessary or recommended to assess all six at once. Over time, as teachers and students use a common set of trait-specific rubrics, a kind of automaticity develops, leading to faster assessment and more consistent and meaningful scores.

Rubrics Support Writers and Teachers

To summarize, quality, trait-specific rubrics help students and teachers to go far beyond simply evaluating the "correctness" (Conventions) of text. These indispensible tools enable writers to focus on the most impactful elements of composition as they prewrite, draft, revise, edit, and publish excellent writing. Trait-specific rubrics also support rapid, precise scoring, making formative and summative assessment easier and more meaningful. For these reasons and many more, *Strategies for Writers* incorporates exemplary trait-based, mode-and-genre-specific rubrics to support the development and assessment of student writing in every lesson.

Multifaceted Assessment

In order to help students progress, teachers must be able to gauge each student's progress. And in order to improve, each student must understand his or her unique strengths and challenges. Without assessment, there can be no progress. That is why *Strategies for Writers* provides a variety of ways to measure progress and guide instruction.

Rubrics Guide Self-Assessment

In *Strategies for Writers,* assessment begins with the rubric.

Each chapter in *Strategies for Writers* presents a genre-specific six-point rubric. This rubric—based on the writing traits of Ideas, Organization, Voice, Word Choice, Sentence Fluency, and Conventions— guides instruction throughout the chapter. That guidance begins as the Student Writing Partner walks the student through using the rubric to assess a successful piece of writing. In this way, the Student Writing Partner models how to assess good writing as he or she explains what good writing looks like in this particular genre.

Throughout each chapter, the genre-specific rubric guides instruction as the Student Writing Partner uses the rubric to model how to create writing that excels in each of the six traits. At the same time, the Student Writing Partner is modeling good self-assessment.

At the end of the chapter, the student is invited to use the genre-specific rubric to assess the Student Writing Partner's final product as well as the student's own writing.

Rubrics to Match a Variety of Needs

The genre-specific rubric in each chapter provides six levels of accomplishment in each trait. A six-point rubric is utilized in many states and allows for more focused assessment in each area.

In addition to the rubrics focused on specific genres, more global rubrics are provided in the back of each Student and Teacher Edition. Based on a single writing mode (i.e., Narrative, Informative/Expository, Opinion or Argument, and Descriptive), these rubrics can be used to assess any type of writing within the targeted mode. For additional flexibility, each mode-specific rubric is available in a four-, five-, or six-point version.

Writing to Take a Test

The real "test" of writing instruction takes place when students must complete writing on demand in test-taking situations. Writing in a testing situation places unique demands upon students, demands that they may not encounter when completing a writing assignment in class over a number of days or weeks. When they write on demand, students must not only be mindful of their writing. They must be mindful of:

- Understanding the writing prompt *(What am I being asked to write?)*

- The unique requirements of the writing prompt *(Am I writing what I am being asked to write?)*

- The limitations of time *(How much time should I spend drafting? How much time should I spend revising?)*

- Staying calm *(What will happen to me if I do poorly on this test?)*

In order to prepare students for these potentially stressful situations, *Strategies for Writers* includes four Test Writing chapters in each grade level (Grades 2 through 8). Each Test Writing chapter focuses on one writing mode (Narrative, Informative/Expository, Opinion or Argument, Descriptive) and provides instruction in how to succeed in a writing-on-demand situation. In addition, these chapters serve as a review of writing strategies that have been presented in previous chapters.

Digital Resources

Strategies for Writers also provides assessment vehicles through its digital resources. A variety of anchor papers are available for projection via an interactive white board, and an online essay grader for specific writing prompts is also available.

Differentiating Instruction
With Strategies for Writers Extensions Online

by Amy Humphreys, Ed.M., National Board Certified Teacher

Our Goal

Maximize student achievement. As classroom educators, our job is to teach in ways that fit learners, rather than forcing students to adjust to our instructional preferences. So how do we do that? It's called Differentiated Instruction (DI). Through DI we deliberately offer multiple avenues through which students can master essential skills and knowledge. This strategic way of planning for student success challenges both regular division and gifted learners. And it is exactly the kind of prescriptive instruction necessary to support at-risk learners under Response to Intervention (RTI).

The Basics of DI

In a differentiated classroom, the learning standards provide the foundation, and the teacher, students, and their parents must share a clear understanding of those targets. Add to that

- a research-based curriculum,

- effective formative assessment practices that guide instructional decisions,

- flexible and strategic use of time, resources, and instructional groupings, and

- a commitment to growth for all learners,

and you have the essential ingredients for a differentiated learning environment that maximizes achievement.

Strategies for Writers Extensions Online

While many teachers recognize the value of DI, it is demanding to meet a wide range of learner needs on a daily basis. Help is here. Evidence-based understandings about writing and ways in which students learn best have been translated into each *Strategies for Writers* Extensions Online making them appropriate for varied readiness levels and learning profiles. Every activity uses a combination of visual, written, oral, and kinesthetic elements and deliberately leverages the power of collaboration and conversation so students learn to think like writers in fun and engaging ways. By strategically using the core lessons and extensions, you are providing consistently differentiated learning opportunities that encourage deeper understanding of essential writing skills among all the learners you teach. It is a perfect recipe for student success.

Using the Extensions

Each of the *Strategies for Writers* Extensions Online activities addresses multiple writing traits and can be revisited several different times throughout the year. In fact, you can even incorporate authentic writing, vocabulary, and skills you want to target with your students into many of the activities. That means you provide greater instructional precision for individual students and thereby achieve better results overall.

Although the directions for the Extensions are simple, it is important to briefly discuss them with students and to do some modeling to insure essential learning targets are clear, to maximize time-on-task, and to facilitate smooth transitions into and out of the activities.

Teaching tips are provided for each Extension so you can easily adapt many of the games and activities for either whole or small group settings. Suggestions for providing additional support or challenges are also given regularly to ensure you have other easy-to-implement ideas to extend your DI efforts and boost students' achievement.

And since we know you're busy, we've designed each Extension so it requires little or no advanced preparation other than copying and cutting apart task cards and placing items in zip bags for easy use and storage.

Ready, Set, Differentiate

Please take a few minutes to preview the different *Strategies for Writers* Extensions Online available as PDFs at **www.sfw.z-b.com**. By printing and keeping the Extension Overview Chart next to your plan book and Teacher Edition, you can see at a glance the games that correspond to the skills and concepts you are currently addressing. Use assessment results to determine the learning needs of your students. Then choose an appropriate Extension, print, and play. With *Strategies for Writers* Extensions Online, the engaging differentiated learning options your students deserve are just a mouse click away.

Reinforcement and Enrichment

You'll find additional suggestions for differentiating instruction in the *Strategies for Writers* Teacher Edition. Every unit contains a number of Reinforcement activities to help students better understand the targeted skills and concepts, and Enrichment activities that provide additional challenges for your more proficient students.

Working With
English Language Learners

Writing Process and ELLs

The process approach to writing instruction helps English Language Learners refine their reading and oral language skills as well as their writing skills, and enables them to explore a variety of forms and functions of academic or "school" language.

Activities for ELLs

Look for tips for English Language Learners throughout each unit of the *Strategies for Writers* Teacher Edition. These tips focus on writing vocabulary and include individual, partner, and whole-group activities that illustrate various writing concepts taught in the unit. Examples include using graphic organizers, using transition words, understanding fact and opinion, using varied sentence lengths, identifying more vivid words, and so on.

ELL Levels to Differentiate Instruction

Strategies for Writers provides suggestions to differentiate instruction based on four levels of English Language Learners. See the box at right for a description of the characteristics of each ELL level.

General Guidelines for Working with ELLs

When introducing a vocabulary word or writing concept, use the following routine as much as possible:

- Introduce the word or concept.
- Model pronunciation or demonstrate meaning.
- Have students repeat.
- Check students' understanding by asking questions, first to the group and then to each student.
- Have each student say the word or demonstrate the concept one more time.

Provide multiple opportunities for repetition as each word or concept is introduced.

If a student makes a mistake, do not ignore it, but do not criticize it. Model the correct pronunciation or wording, and have the student repeat it correctly.

Maximize time for practicing English, both spoken and written, by having students work in pairs in small groups. You might also provide opportunities for higher-level ELLs to work with lower-level ELLs in a "peer teaching" situation.

Levels of English Language Learners

ELL LEVEL	CHARACTERISTICS
Beginning ELLs	• Can draw, point, say *yes* and *no*, and use a few key words • May use only present tense • Will need frequent repetition, visual cues, and other assistance • May not ask for help and may remain silent as they wait for more clues to context and meaning
Intermediate ELLs	• Have a limited vocabulary, which they tend to overuse • Frequently misunderstand • Are beginning to produce simple sentences
Advanced ELLs	• Usually understand English • Are beginning to extend the language beyond the simple present tense and can speak and write some complex sentences • Make mistakes that are often repeated
Advanced High ELLs	• Are beginning to blend in with their English-speaking peers • Are synthesizing information with minimal support • Are growing their social and academic vocabulary, and it may now be comparable to that of their peers

Writer's Workshop

What Is a Writer's Workshop?

Writer's Workshop is a highly effective format for process writing instruction that incorporates authentic practices within a consistent structure. As students write within the Workshop model, they have an array of choices that may include (but are not limited to) topic, genre, ideas, organization, and tone. Students then move freely and at a comfortable pace through the writing process. Some students might move through the steps sequentially. Others might forge their own path, skipping or repeating steps in a unique progression. In the Writer's Workshop classroom, this is normal, natural, and encouraged.

In such an environment, it is common for one student to be prewriting while another is drafting (and yet another may be revising). The Writer's Workshop helps teachers oversee and support each student's writing process while also facilitating sharing and feedback in a variety of groups, such as peer-to-peer, peer-groups, and teacher-led conferences. How is this extraordinary combination of authenticity, flexibility, and oversight possible? The secret to Writer's Workshop lies in its unique structure and routines.

Common Elements of a Writer's Workshop

Time

The craft of writing takes time, so students should be allowed to work at predictable times and for predictable durations so that they can practice and internalize the steps of the writing process. A successful Writer's Workshop is far more process-oriented than product-oriented, so it is expected that students will take varying amounts of time to complete writing projects. When students can't complete an assignment by a deadline, they typically put their unfinished work into a folder to revisit and complete at a later time. Students who finish early may return to previously unfinished pieces from their writing folders, or they may choose to begin the writing process anew with a fresh topic. The Writer's Workshop provides ample time for all writers.

Space

Effective arrangement of space within the Workshop classroom is essential. Desks, chairs, and other furniture should be arranged for comfort, safety, and access to materials (paper, pencils, and writing folders). It's also important to plan for students' frequent movement around the classroom as they group for sharing and conferencing. In a Writer's Workshop, even wall space is carefully planned, featuring a variety of student work samples and helpful reference materials (such as charts and signs featuring workshop routines, the writing process, the six traits, or writing strategies).

Mini-lessons and Focus Lessons

Mini-lessons are short (about 10 minutes) and focus on a specific writing skill. In a typical mini-lesson, the teacher will:

- Activate students' prior knowledge
- Directly instruct a skill
- Model the skill
- Engage students in discussing or practicing the skill
- Connect the skill to other learned writing skills

Focus lessons are similar but are used to introduce larger, more complex topics. For example, a focus lesson may be used to introduce students to a new mode, genre, or trait of writing.

Models

As students learn to write, it is critical that they view, analyze, discuss, and emulate a variety of writing models. One type of modeling occurs as the teacher becomes a writer in full view of the class by composing and thinking aloud. This is perhaps the most important and indispensible form of modeling. Other kinds of models include mentor text— quality literature and student writing models—which may be used to teach how specific traits, genres, strategies, or steps of the writing process function in published text.

Choice

In a Writer's Workshop, teachers may gently guide students' choices, but topics are not "assigned." Depending upon the nature of the task and the mini-lessons provided, students may also choose how to manage a wide range of writing variables such as genre, main idea, supporting details, theme, organizational structure, and tone. Choice is encouraged and supported in the Writer's Workshop model.

Conferences

In a Writer's Workshop, students will confer frequently with a variety of readers. Conferencing supports the writer with authentic responses that may help shape and develop the composition. When writers conference, they learn to listen to the wants and needs of the reader—an important skill that leads to excellent ideation, precise word choice, and appropriate organization and voice. A few common types of conferences that take place during a Writer's Workshop include:

Teacher-led conferences typically occur during independent writing time. During this conference, the teacher meets individually with students for approximately two-to-three minutes each. One main goal of teacher-led conferences is to help students reflect upon their work and consider revisions to make the writing more effective.

Peer-group conferences take place throughout the writing process. While groups may vary in size, three-to-five students is considered ideal.

Peer-to-peer conferences may also occur throughout the writing process. During these conferences, students share their work with individual classmates and receive authentic feedback.

Whole-Group Sharing

While conferencing certainly incorporates an element of sharing, it is important to also provide an opportunity for writing to be celebrated. (Some teachers use an "Author's Chair" for whole-class sharing.) While it is perfectly acceptable for members of the student audience to comment and ask questions, the main purpose of this type of sharing is to validate and praise the author's accomplishments.

A Typical Schedule

A Writer's Workshop lesson unfolds in three parts:

Mini-lesson and Status of the Class (10–15 minutes)

Following the mini-lesson (described above), the teacher and students take a moment to note where students are in their individual writing processes and to determine what students will work on.

Independent Writing Time (30–40 minutes)

Students work independently. Teacher conferences also take place during this time.

Sharing (5–10 minutes)

Students participate in peer-to-peer or peer-group conferences. Whole-group sharing may also take place.

Strategies for Writers Supports Writer's Workshop

Time

Students can work at their own pace in *Strategies for Writers*. Student Writing Partners are introduced at the beginning of each unit and speak directly to your students in a friendly, first-person voice, guiding them through the steps of the writing process.

Space

***Strategies for Writers* digital resources and posters** include useful reference material to display in your Writer's Workshop classroom.

Mini-lessons and Focus Lessons

Each lesson features:

- **Explicit instruction** for all steps of the writing process and for each of the six traits
- **A clear, trait-specific writing goal** supported by a clearly explained writing strategy
- Trait-specific revising and editing strategies for **targeted mini-lessons**, including multiple mini-lessons for conventions

Models

Accessible student writing models are provided and annotated for genre-specific composition strategies. Each lesson rubric helps students identify the trait-specific strengths in the writing models. **Mentor text exemplars** for each mode and genre are listed in the Teacher Edition.

Choice

Flexible lesson prompts allow students to choose their own topics. Authentic purposes for writing are established to increase student engagement with the writing task. "Apply" sections encourage students to use what they've learned as they continue to work on their own compositions.

Conferences

Students develop a common writing language for conferences as they work with the student-friendly rubrics before they start writing. "Reflect" sections provide questions that students can ask and answer during peer-to-peer and peer-group conferences. Suggestions for peer-to-peer, peer-group, and teacher-led conferences are included in the Teacher Edition.

Whole Group

A variety of **publishing and presentation suggestions** promote creative options for students to share their work with the class or other audiences.

Test Prep in a Writer's Workshop

In *Strategies for Writers*, even test preparation writing lessons support the Writer's Workshop model. Test writing lessons use the same workshop-supporting features described above. They also contain direct instruction to help students analyze writing prompts and scoring guides like the ones on high-stake assessments. **Each test-writing lesson contains full writing process instruction and results in an authentic composition.**

Mentor Texts

Strategies for Writers Senior Author Becky Sipe points out that students cannot produce good writing in the various modes and genres if they do not have the appropriate "mental models." A mental model is a good example of a finished product. Whether it's a personal narrative, a letter to the editor, or a report on a science experiment, students need examples to show them the way.

Strategies for Writers integrates these mental models in four ways.

Exemplar Texts

Each chapter begins with an exemplar text in the targeted mode. The chapter's Student Writing Partner expands upon that piece of writing by explaining in detail why this model is a good model. This explanation is based on the six traits of writing, so students have a clear understanding of how each trait should be represented in this writing genre.

Student Writing Partner's Text

After examining the exemplar text, the Student Writing Partner begins his or her own piece of writing. As the Student Writing Partner moves through the chapter, he or she provides a step-by-step model of what to do and what not to do to create successful writing in this genre. In addition to writing the text and referring to the six traits as exemplified in the chapter's genre-specific rubric, the Student Writing Partner thinks out loud about what he or she is doing. By example and explanation, the Student Writing Partner provides a road map for the student writer to create his or her own piece of writing.

Examples From Literature

The Teacher Edition provides a list of related texts from literature. These text exemplars, many recommended by the Common Core State Standards, can be shared with students to provide additional models of good writing in the targeted genre and examples of the use of specific traits in literature.

Writing Across the Curriculum

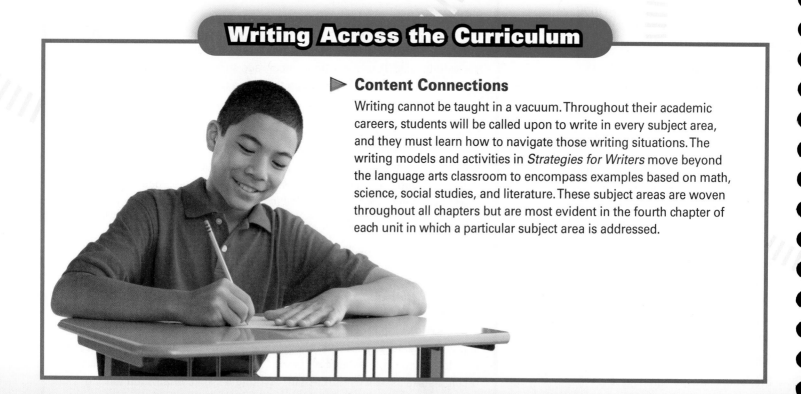

▶ **Content Connections**

Writing cannot be taught in a vacuum. Throughout their academic careers, students will be called upon to write in every subject area, and they must learn how to navigate those writing situations. The writing models and activities in Strategies for Writers move beyond the language arts classroom to encompass examples based on math, science, social studies, and literature. These subject areas are woven throughout all chapters but are most evident in the fourth chapter of each unit in which a particular subject area is addressed.

Integrated Grammar Instruction
Relevant and Related Skills...Paired With Right Practice

Relevant Skills

Grammar instruction is not an end but a means to successful writing. Clear writing demands a keen understanding of important conventions.

Strategies for Writers includes instruction in key grammar, usage, and mechanics (GUM) skills as part of the editing instruction, tied to the Conventions trait, in every chapter. The Student Writing Partner ties the skill to a writing strategy statement and explains how he or she used the skill in his or her writing. In addition, a clear explanation of the skill is provided in a Writer's Term box. The Student Writing Partner puts the skill immediately into practice, and an optional page of practice on that skill follows.

Related Skills

Targeting GUM in Conventions instruction is only one facet of grammar instruction in *Strategies for Writers*. Instruction and practice in an additional skill is also included in the body of each chapter. This skill relates to and expands upon the targeted skill. For example, in Grade 4, the targeted GUM skill in Writing a Play is commas in a series. The related skill is commas after introductory phrases. In Grade 7, for example, the targeted GUM skill in Writing a Personal Narrative is avoiding sentence fragments and run-on sentences. The related skill is coordinating conjunctions.

Additional practice in both the targeted and the related skill appears in the back of the Student Edition in Appendix A: Grammar Practice.

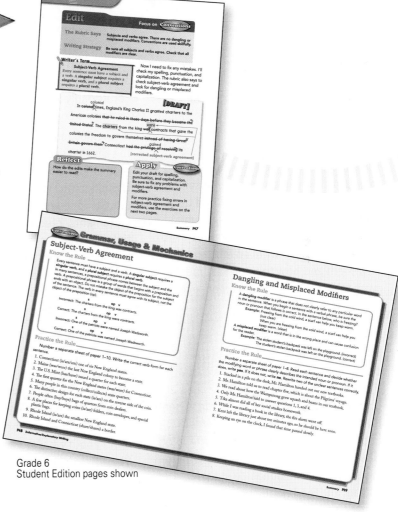

Grade 6
Student Edition pages shown

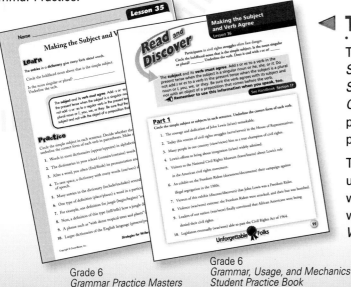

Grade 6
Grammar Practice Masters

Grade 6
Grammar, Usage, and Mechanics
Student Practice Book

The Right Practice

Two additional resources build upon this foundation. The *Strategies for Writers Grammar, Usage, and Mechanics Student Practice Book* and the *Strategies for Writers Grammar Practice Masters* each provides additional practice pages in a variety of skills related to sentence structure, parts of speech, usage, grammar, and mechanics.

These resources combine to make instruction in grammar, usage, and mechanics skills relevant to the writing task while expanding students' overall knowledge of important writing conventions. Tied to the right practice, *Strategies for Writers* will put your students on the right grammar track!

21st Century Literacies
Technology, Digital Media, and Writing

by Julie Coiro, Ph.D., and Sara Kajder, Ph.D.

Teaching readers and writers situates us deeply in the texts that our students navigate, compose, and share with others. In addition to journal prompts, written drafts, and polished pieces of writing, the landscape of digital media expands our thinking about authentic writing to include practices such as creating digital stories, listening to podcasts, and interacting with screen casts of peer reviews. Surrounded by these rapidly evolving digital literacy practices, teaching writing requires us to know both how to write an effective thesis statement and how to publish students' work for an engaged, networked, even global audience.

New Technologies

While the writing technology of ink on paper remains, the reality is that the landscape of tools for writers has changed. The changes have come faster than we can possibly learn each tool, and the creation of new tools is changing moment to moment. As a result, writing teachers must sit alongside student writers and learn together.

In addition, teachers of 21st century writers need to be thoughtful. We need strategies for how to navigate what's new and how to best equip our writers to be flexible, purposeful, and effective. We also need to remember that we come to these moments for learning with a great deal of expertise in knowing what it means to be a writer. We aren't starting over. We're just thinking in newer, more open ways.

Digital Literacy Practices

This isn't about learning the "hottest" new technology tool (though you'll find several discussed throughout this Teacher Edition).

The goal is to think about the literacy practices that emerging tools, writing spaces, and digital media make possible, and then to consider how these sit comfortably within your current practices or demand new thinking.

A core document that has led our thinking as teachers navigating digital media right alongside you is the "NCTE Definition of 21st Century Literacies (2008)." (See **www.ncte.org/positions/statements/21stcentdefinition**.) We have tinkered with the framework, aligned the literacy practices it mentions with the genres in each chapter of *Strategies for Writers*, and anchored each section of the text with a "21st Century Literacy Practice."

Effective Technology Use

Each of these practices allows us to look across the range of tools available and make very specific, intentional selections in where we pay attention and why. The goal is to think less about the tool and more about what we want writers to do. Simply put, the practices live significantly beyond the shelf life of a tool, and they value and affirm the knowledge that each of us brings to this work as writing teachers (more than techies).

Technology Support for Teachers

To support your thinking about digital media and writing, you'll find two features in this Teacher Edition. First, each unit begins with a full page that provides core ideas about how to use a range of digital tools, websites, and instructional strategies to foster online inquiry about new topics or inspire creative writing ideas in a particular mode of writing. The second support appears in each chapter as specific teaching tips. Imagine that we're sitting next to you as you read and plan your classes. When opportunities appear, we will use this space to share an idea, a suggestion, or a little "nudge" meant to open your thinking (and teaching) to what we're calling "21st Century Literacies."

Mode/Genre	21st Century Literacy Practice
Narrative	Creating and responding to multimodal texts
Informative/Explanatory	Organizing, evaluating, analyzing, and using online information
Argument/Opinion	Engaging effectively with a connected audience
Descriptive	Designing and creating content for purposeful use

Common Core State Standards
for Writing and Language

by Mark Overmeyer, M.A.

A Unique Opportunity

The advent of the Common Core State Standards provides a unique opportunity for educators in America: the chance to work together to create a meaningful, world-class curriculum for our students. We have not had national standards before. Although organizations such as the National Council of Teachers of English and the International Reading Association have published guidelines for best practices when designing curriculum, this is the first time national standards have been proposed on a grade level basis.

When I first heard of the initiative, I will admit I was worried. At the time, I was volunteering to rewrite the Colorado State standards, and I was concerned that no national standards could truly represent the thinking that goes on in each state. I also worried about some of the unintended consequences of the standards movement itself: long lists of skills and sub-skills students must master at each grade level. The standards movement has encouraged some districts to develop checklists of skills that can be routinely marked as "finished" once they are taught. Without care, standards can create an assembly-line atmosphere in the classroom and the feeling that we need to just cover certain material rather than think deeply about student learning.

Strong, Meaningful Verbs

Upon examination, I have found that the Common Core can easily lead us beyond checklists in a meaningful direction, particularly when we examine the verbs in the Writing and Language Standards documents. In the Writing Standards, students in grade K–12 are asked to **compose** opinion pieces, **defend** their reasoning, **research** topics, and **develop** narratives. In the Language Standards, students are asked to **apply** their knowledge of grammar and mechanics when they **speak** and **write**. These strong verbs create an image of students actually generating texts, researching ideas, and revising and editing for clarity. As a result, students will be thinking critically, writing, and reflecting instead of completing a series of worksheets to demonstrate they have "mastered" a particular standard.

Apply Knowledge

When we actually ask students to apply their knowledge of grammar and mechanics, we are finally following the research about grammar instruction. The standards do not ask students to "know and understand" the conventions of English, but instead to "form and use" correctly written and spoken English. This is an important distinction. The 2007 Carnegie Report *Writing Next* by Graham and Perin, a document that describes research-based writing practices, states: "Grammar instruction in the studies reviewed involved the explicit and systematic teaching of the parts of speech and structure of sentences... but surprisingly, the effect was negative. Teaching students to focus on *the function and application of grammar within the context of writing* (versus teaching grammar as an independent activity) *produced strong and positive effects on students' writing*" (emphasis added mine). The Common Core follows this research directly: Students write and apply their knowledge of grammar to improve their writing.

Becoming Writers and Teachers

The message in the Common Core is clear across all grade levels: Students must write to become better writers. Students must use and apply their knowledge of grammar to demonstrate their skill as writers and thinkers.

Of course even the Common Core State Standards, as strong as they are, appear in a list. All standards do. But because the Core Standards require students to compose and edit their own work, the standards can only be met by asking students to think and write authentically. Such standards cannot just be "covered," but can be met through meaningful practice, especially if teachers require students to write in increasingly more volume as they progress through grade levels.

Beyond Skills

As teachers, we have always known about the importance of practice. We know our students are apprentices on their writing journeys, but if standards are reductive and become a list of knowledge-level skills, it is easy to get lost in the mire of just covering by teaching skills. Because of its high standards, the Common Core will not create a reductive classroom environment, but rather a place where students think, draft, revise, and edit frequently. Because of this, we should welcome the Common Core. It provides much-needed guidance and expectation for all of us who care about the education of our students.

STANDARD	CORRELATION

WRITING Text Types and Purposes

Anchor Standard 1: Write arguments to support claims in an analysis of substantive topics or texts, using valid reasoning and relevant and sufficient evidence.

Standard 1: Write arguments to support claims with clear reasons and relevant evidence.

1a: Introduce claim(s) and organize the reasons and evidence clearly.	**Student Edition:** 252, 254, 258, 262, 266, 278, 280, 284, 290, 300, 302, 306, 310, 322, 324, 329, 333, 348, 358 **Teacher Edition:** T252, T254, T258, T262, T266, T270, T278, T280, T284, T290, T300, T302, T306, T310, T322, T324, T329, T333, T348, T358 **Optional Revising Lessons:** Opinion 21 **Grammar, Usage, and Mechanics:** *Student Practice Book:* 16, 112; *Teacher Edition:* T18, T48
1b: Support claim(s) with clear reasons and relevant evidence, using credible sources and demonstrating an understanding of the topic or text.	**Student Edition:** 252, 254, 258, 262, 266, 278, 280, 284, 300, 302, 306, 314, 322, 324, 328, 332, 336, 348 **Teacher Edition:** T252, T254, T258, T262, T266, T278, T280, T284, T294, T300, T302, T306, T314, T322, T324, T328, T332, T336, T348, T362 **Optional Revising Lessons:** Opinion 23, 29 **Grammar, Usage, and Mechanics:** *Student Practice Book:* 16, 112; *Teacher Edition:* T18, T48
1c: Use words, phrases, and clauses to clarify the relationships among claim(s) and reasons.	**Student Edition:** 252, 260, 264, 265, 270, 278, 286, 293, 302, 308, 315, 324, 330, 334, 349, 362 **Teacher Edition:** T252, T260, T264, T265, T270, T278, T281, T286, T290, T293, T302, T308, T315, T324, T325, T330, T334, T338, T349, T362 **Optional Revising Lessons:** Opinion 28 **Grammar, Usage, and Mechanics:** *Student Practice Book:* 16; *Teacher Edition:* T18
1d: Establish and maintain a formal style.	**Student Edition:** 254, 259, 269, 280, 285, 292, 300, 302, 307, 312, 349, 361 **Teacher Edition:** T254, T259, T269, T280, T285, T292, T300, T302, T307, T312, T316, T349, T361 **Optional Revising Lessons:** Opinion 26
1e: Provide a concluding statement or section that follows from the argument presented.	**Student Edition:** 254, 285, 290, 302, 307, 324, 329, 333, 348 **Teacher Edition:** T254, T285, T290, T294, T302, T307, T316, T324, T329, T333, T348 **Optional Revising Lessons:** Opinion 24, 25

Anchor Standard 2: Write informative/explanatory texts to examine and convey complex ideas and information clearly and accurately through the effective selection, organization, and analysis of content.

Standard 2: Write informative/explanatory texts to examine a topic and convey ideas, concepts, and information through the selection, organization, and analysis of relevant content.

2a: Introduce a topic; organize ideas, concepts, and information, using strategies such as definition, classification, comparison/contrast, and cause/effect; include formatting (e.g., headings), graphics (e.g., charts, tables), and multimedia when useful to aiding comprehension.	**Student Edition:** 126, 128, 135, 144, 154, 158, 164, 165, 166, 167, 176, 178, 204, 206, 211, 215, 242, 243, 370, 375, 380, 384, 392, 394, 404, 405 **Teacher Edition:** T126, T128, T135, T144, T154, T158, T164, T165, T166, T167, T176, T178, T204, T206, T211, T215, T242, T243, T370, T375, T380, T384, T392, T394, T404, T405 **Grammar, Usage, and Mechanics:** *Student Practice Book:* 10, 31, 38, 42, 58, 83, 98, 100, 130, 135, 136; *Teacher Edition:* T17, T22, T25, T26, T30, T38, T43, T44, T53, T54
2b: Develop the topic with relevant facts, definitions, concrete details, quotations, or other information and examples.	**Student Edition:** 128, 134, 138, 139, 142, 143, 144, 152, 154, 162, 163, 176, 184, 194, 204, 206, 210, 215, 218, 232, 370, 375, 392, 394, 398, 422 **Teacher Edition:** T128, T134, T138, T139, T142, T143, T144, T146, T152, T154, T162, T163, T170, T176, T184, T194, T204, T206, T210, T215, T218, T232, T246, T370, T375, T392, T394, T398, T422 **Optional Revising Lessons:** Informative/Expository: 11, 13, 19 **Grammar, Usage, and Mechanics:** *Student Practice Book:* 10, 31, 38, 42, 58, 83, 98, 100, 130, 135, 136; *Teacher Edition:* T17, T22, T25, T26, T30, T38, T43, T44, T53, T54
2c: Use appropriate transitions to clarify the relationships among ideas and concepts.	**Student Edition:** 154, 159, 178, 206, 211, 219, 232, 244, 392, 394, 398, 524 **Teacher Edition:** T154, T159, T170, T178, T206, T211, T219, T232, T244, T392, T394, T398, T408 **Optional Revising Lessons:** Informative/Expository: 14; Descriptive: 34 **Grammar, Usage, and Mechanics:** *Student Practice Book:* 31, 58; *Teacher Edition:* T22, T30
2d: Use precise language and domain-specific vocabulary to inform about or explain the topic.	**Student Edition:** 146, 154, 160, 169, 176, 178, 186, 195, 204, 206, 212, 216, 217, 233, 246, 375, 386, 392, 394, 400, 407, 416, 418, 424 **Teacher Edition:** T146, T154, T155, T160, T169, T176, T178, T179, T186, T195, T204, T206, T207, T212, T216, T217, T220, T233, T246, T375, T377, T386, T392, T394, T395, T400, T407, T416, T418, T419, T424 **Optional Revising Lessons:** Informative/Expository: 17 **Grammar, Usage, and Mechanics:** *Student Practice Book:* 31, 38, 42, 58, 83, 98, 135; *Teacher Edition:* T22, T25, T26, T30, T38, T43, T54

STANDARD	CORRELATION
Writing Standard 2 continued 2e: Establish and maintain a formal style.	**Student Edition:** 135, 145, 206, 211 **Teacher Edition:** T135, T145, T206, T211, T220 **Optional Revising Lessons:** Informative/Expository: 18 **Grammar, Usage, and Mechanics:** *Student Practice Book:* 42, 135, 136; *Teacher Edition:* T26, T54
2f: Provide a concluding statement or section that follows from the information or explanation presented.	**Student Edition:** 154, 164, 165, 176, 178, 185, 204, 206, 211, 215, 404, 405 **Teacher Edition:** T154, T164, T165, T176, T178, T185, T196, T204, T206, T211, T215, T404, T405 **Optional Revising Lessons:** Informative/Expository: 15 **Grammar, Usage, and Mechanics:** *Student Practice Book:* 42, 136; *Teacher Edition:* T26, T54

Anchor Standard 3: Write narratives to develop real or imagined experiences or events using effective technique, well-chosen details, and well-structured event sequences.

Standard 3: Write narratives to develop real or imagined experiences or events using effective technique, relevant descriptive details, and well-structured event sequences.

3a: Engage and orient the reader by establishing a context and introducing a narrator and/or characters; organize an event sequence that unfolds naturally and logically.	**Student Edition:** 4, 6, 11, 15, 18, 30, 37, 41, 42, 54, 56, 60, 61, 64, 65, 76, 78, 84, 89, 92, 106, 111, 115, 116, 117, 428, 429, 440 **Teacher Edition:** T4, T6, T11, T15, T18, T30, T37, T41, T42, T46, T54, T56, T60, T61, T64, T65, T70, T76, T78, T84, T89, T92, T106, T111, T115, T116, T117, T428, T429, T440 **Optional Revising Lessons:** Narrative: 4, 5 **Grammar, Usage, and Mechanics:** *Student Practice Book:* 14, 20, 24, 31, 32, 44, 50, 52, 57, 60, 78, 84, 86, 114, 118, 122, 128; *Teacher Edition:* T18, T19, T20, T22, T27, T28, T29, T30, T32, T37, T38, T40, T49, T50, T51, T52
3b: Use narrative techniques, such as dialogue, pacing, and description, to develop experiences, events, and/or characters.	**Student Edition:** 4, 6, 10, 14, 15, 16, 17, 20, 28, 30, 36, 41, 54, 56, 60, 61, 65, 68, 78, 84, 85, 89, 106, 120, 444, 445, 452, 464, 474, 475, 478 **Teacher Edition:** T4, T6, T10, T14, T15, T16, T17, T20, T28, T30, T36, T41, T54, T56, T60, T61, T65, T68, T70, T78, T84, T85, T89, T106, T112, T120, T444, T445, T452, T454, T464, T470, T474, T475, T478 **Optional Revising Lessons:** Narrative: 6, 9; Descriptive: 38, 39 **Grammar, Usage, and Mechanics:** *Student Practice Book:* 14, 20, 24, 31, 32, 44, 50, 52, 57, 60, 78, 84, 86, 114, 118, 122, 128; *Teacher Edition:* T18, T19, T20, T22, T27, T28, T29, T30, T32, T37, T38, T40, T49, T50, T51, T52
3c: Use a variety of transition words, phrases, and clauses to convey sequence and signal shifts from one time frame or setting to another.	**Student Edition:** 30, 37, 42, 56, 78, 85, 93, 106, 111, 115, 118, 120, 524 **Teacher Edition:** T30, T37, T42, T56, T78, T85, T93, T106, T111, T115, T118, T120 **Optional Revising Lessons:** Narrative: 10 **Grammar, Usage, and Mechanics:** *Student Practice Book:* 31, 44; *Teacher Edition:* T22, T27
3d: Use precise words and phrases, relevant descriptive details, and sensory language to convey experiences and events.	**Student Edition:** 6, 7, 11, 12, 18, 20, 30, 38, 45, 56, 62, 69, 78, 86, 90, 107, 111, 115, 120, 382, 386, 403, 438, 446, 450, 451, 465, 478 **Teacher Edition:** T6, T7, T11, T12, T18, T20, T30, T31, T38, T45, T56, T57, T62, T69, T78, T79, T86, T90, T94, T107, T111, T115, T120, T382, T386, T403, T438, T441, T446, T450, T451, T464, T465, T478 **Optional Revising Lessons:** Narrative: 8; Descriptive: 31 **Grammar, Usage, and Mechanics:** *Student Practice Book:* 14, 24, 31, 44, 50, 52, 57, 84, 86, 114; *Teacher Edition:* T18, T20, T22, T27, T28, T29, T30, T38, T40, T49
3e: Provide a conclusion that follows from the narrated experiences or events.	**Student Edition:** 6, 11, 15, 30, 37, 41, 42, 56 **Teacher Edition:** T6, T11, T15, T30, T37, T41, T42, T56 **Grammar, Usage, and Mechanics:** *Student Practice Book:* 44, 114; *Teacher Edition:* T27, T49

WRITING Production and Distribution of Writing

Anchor Standard 4: Produce clear and coherent writing in which the development, organization, and style are appropriate to task, purpose, and audience.

Standard 4: Produce clear and coherent writing in which the development, organization, and style are appropriate to task, purpose, and audience.

	Student Edition: 14, 15, 16, 17, 18, 19, 20, 21, 22, 23, 24, 25, 26, 27, 40, 41, 42, 43, 44, 45, 46, 47, 48, 49, 50, 51, 52, 53, 64, 65, 66, 67, 68, 69, 70, 71, 72, 73, 74, 75, 88, 89, 90, 91, 92, 93, 94, 95, 96, 97, 98, 99, 100, 101, 110, 112, 113, 114, 115, 116, 117, 118, 119, 120, 121, 122, 123, 138, 139, 140, 141, 142, 143, 144, 145, 146, 147, 148, 149, 150, 151, 162, 163, 164, 165, 166, 167, 168, 169, 170, 171, 172, 173, 174, 175, 188, 189, 190, 191, 192, 193, 194, 195, 196, 197, 198, 199, 200, 201, 202, 203, 214, 215, 216, 217, 218, 219, 220, 221, 222, 223, 224, 225, 226, 227, 236, 237, 238, 239, 240, 241, 242, 243, 244, 245, 246, 247, 248, 249, 262, 263, 264, 265, 266, 267, 268, 269, 270, 271, 272, 273, 274, 275, 276, 277, 288, 289, 290, 291, 292, 293, 294, 295, 296, 297, 298, 299, 310, 311, 312, 313, 314, 315, 316, 317, 318, 319, 320, 321, 332, 333, 334, 335, 336, 337, 338, 339, 340, 341, 342, 343, 352, 353, 354, 355, 356, 357, 358, 359, 360, 361, 362, 363, 364, 365, 378, 379, 380, 381, 382, 383, 384, 385, 386, 387, 388, 389, 390, 391, 402, 403, 404, 405, 406, 407, 408, 409, 410, 411, 412, 413, 414, 415, 426, 427, 428, 429, 430, 431, 432, 433, 434, 435, 436, 437, 448, 449, 450, 451, 452, 453, 454, 455, 456, 457, 458, 459, 468, 469, 470, 471, 472, 473, 474, 475, 476, 477, 478, 479, 480, 481 **Teacher Edition:** T14, T15, T16, T17, T18, T19, T20, T21, T22, T23, T24, T25, T26, T27, T40, T41, T42, T43, T44, T45, T46, T47, T48, T49, T50, T51, T52, T53, T64, T65, T66, T67, T68, T69, T70, T71, T72, T73, T74, T75, T88, T89, T90, T91, T92, T93, T94, T95, T96, T97, T98, T99, T100, T101, T110, T112, T113, T114, T115, T116, T117, T118, T119, T120, T121, T122, T123, T138, T139, T140, T141, T142, T143, T144, T145, T146, T147, T148, T149, T150, T151, T162, T163, T164, T165, T166, T167, T168, T169, T170, T171, T172, T173, T174, T175, T188, T189, T190, T191, T192, T193, T194, T195, T196, T197, T198, T199, T200, T201, T202, T203, T214, T215, T216, T217, T218, T219, T220, T221, T222, T223, T224, T225, T226, T227, T236, T237, T238, T239, T240, T241, T242, T243, T244, T245, T246, T247, T248, T249, T262,

STANDARD	CORRELATION
Writing Standard 4 continued	T263, T264, T265, T266, T267, T268, T269, T270, T271, T272, T273, T274, T275, T276, T277, T288, T289, T290, T291, T292, T293, T294, T295, T296, T297, T298, T299, T310, T311, T312, T313, T314, T315, T316, T317, T318, T319, T320, T321, T332, T333, T334, T335, T336, T337, T338, T339, T340, T341, T342, T343, T352, T353, T354, T355, T356, T357, T358, T359, T360, T361, T362, T363, T364, T365, T378, T379, T380, T381, T382, T383, T384, T385, T386, T387, T388, T389, T390, T391, T402, T403, T404, T405, T406, T407, T408, T409, T410, T411, T412, T413, T414, T415, T426, T427, T428, T429, T430, T431, T432, T433, T434, T435, T436, T437, T448, T449, T450, T451, T452, T453, T454, T455, T456, T457, T458, T459, T468, T469, T470, T471, T472, T473, T474, T475, T476, T477, T478, T479, T480, T481

Optional Revising Lessons: Narrative: 1, 2, 3, 4, 5, 6, 7, 8, 9, 10; Expository/Informative: 11, 12, 13, 14, 15, 16, 17, 18, 19, 20; Opinion: 21, 22, 23, 24, 25, 26, 27, 28, 29, 30; Descriptive: 31, 32, 33, 34, 35, 36, 37, 38, 39, 40

Grammar, Usage, and Mechanics: *Student Practice Book:* 8, 10, 14, 16, 20, 24, 31, 32, 38, 42, 44, 50, 52, 57, 58, 60, 62, 68, 78, 84, 84, 86, 92, 94, 98, 100, 112, 114, 118, 122, 126, 128, 130, 135, 136; *Teacher Edition:* T16, T17, T18, T19, T20, T22, T25, T26, T27, T28, T29, T30, T32, T33, T34, T37, T38, T40, T42, T43, T44, T48, T49, T50, T51, T52, T53, T54

Anchor Standard 5: Develop and strengthen writing as needed by planning, revising, editing, rewriting, or trying a new approach.

Standard 5: With some guidance and support from peers and adults, develop and strengthen writing as needed by planning, revising, editing, rewriting, or trying a new approach.

Student Edition: 14, 15, 16, 17, 18, 19, 20, 21, 22, 23, 24, 25, 26, 27, 40, 41, 42, 43, 44, 45, 46, 47, 48, 49, 50, 51, 52, 53, 64, 65, 66, 67, 68, 69, 70, 71, 72, 73, 74, 75, 88, 89, 90, 91, 92, 93, 94, 95, 96, 97, 98, 99, 100, 101, 110, 112, 113, 114, 115, 116, 117, 118, 119, 120, 121, 122, 123, 138, 139, 140, 141, 142, 143, 144, 145, 146, 147, 148, 149, 150, 151, 162, 163, 164, 165, 166, 167, 168, 169, 170, 171, 172, 173, 174, 175, 188, 189, 190, 191, 192, 193, 194, 195, 196, 197, 198, 199, 200, 201, 202, 203, 214, 215, 216, 217, 218, 219, 220, 221, 222, 223, 224, 225, 226, 227, 236, 237, 238, 239, 240, 241, 242, 243, 244, 245, 246, 247, 248, 249, 262, 263, 264, 265, 266, 267, 268, 269, 270, 271, 272, 273, 274, 275, 276, 277, 288, 289, 290, 291, 292, 293, 294, 295, 296, 297, 298, 299, 310, 311, 312, 313, 314, 315, 316, 317, 318, 319, 320, 321, 332, 333, 334, 335, 336, 337, 338, 339, 340, 341, 342, 343, 352, 353, 354, 355, 356, 357, 358, 359, 360, 361, 362, 363, 364, 365, 378, 379, 380, 381, 382, 383, 384, 385, 386, 387, 388, 389, 390, 391, 402, 403, 404, 405, 406, 407, 408, 409, 410, 411, 412, 413, 414, 415, 426, 427, 428, 429, 430, 431, 432, 433, 434, 435, 436, 437, 448, 449, 450, 451, 452, 453, 454, 455, 456, 457, 458, 459, 468, 469, 470, 471, 472, 473, 474, 475, 476, 477, 478, 479, 480, 481

Teacher Edition: T14, T15, T16, T17, T18, T19, T20, T21, T22, T23, T24, T25, T26, T27, T40, T41, T42, T43, T44, T45, T46, T47, T48, T49, T50, T51, T52, T53, T64, T65, T66, T67, T68, T69, T70, T71, T72, T73, T74, T75, T88, T89, T90, T91, T92, T93, T94, T95, T96, T97, T98, T99, T100, T101, T110, T112, T113, T114, T115, T116, T117, T118, T119, T120, T121, T122, T123, T138, T139, T140, T141, T142, T143, T144, T145, T146, T147, T148, T149, T150, T151, T162, T163, T164, T165, T166, T167, T168, T169, T170, T171, T172, T173, T174, T175, T188, T189, T190, T191, T192, T193, T194, T195, T196, T197, T198, T199, T200, T201, T202, T203, T214, T215, T216, T217, T218, T219, T220, T221, T222, T223, T224, T225, T226, T227, T236, T237, T238, T239, T240, T241, T242, T243, T244, T245, T246, T247, T248, T249, T262, T263, T264, T265, T266, T267, T268, T269, T270, T271, T272, T273, T274, T275, T276, T277, T288, T289, T290, T291, T292, T293, T294, T295, T296, T297, T298, T299, T310, T311, T312, T313, T314, T315, T316, T317, T318, T319, T320, T321, T332, T333, T334, T335, T336, T337, T338, T339, T340, T341, T342, T343, T352, T353, T354, T355, T356, T357, T358, T359, T360, T361, T362, T363, T364, T365, T378, T379, T380, T381, T382, T383, T384, T385, T386, T387, T388, T389, T390, T391, T402, T403, T404, T405, T406, T407, T408, T409, T410, T411, T412, T413, T414, T415, T426, T427, T428, T429, T430, T431, T432, T433, T434, T435, T436, T437, T448, T449, T450, T451, T452, T453, T454, T455, T456, T457, T458, T459, T468, T469, T470, T471, T472, T473, T474, T475, T476, T477, T478, T479, T480, T481

Optional Revising Lessons: Narrative: 1, 2, 3, 4, 5, 6, 7, 8, 9, 10; Expository/Informative: 11, 12, 13, 14, 15, 16, 17, 18, 19, 20; Opinion: 21, 22, 23, 24, 25, 26, 27, 28, 29, 30; Descriptive: 31, 32, 33, 34, 35, 36, 37, 38, 39, 40

Grammar, Usage, and Mechanics: *Student Practice Book:* 27, 53, 79, 105, 131, 134; *Teacher Edition:* T21, T29, T37, T45, T53, T54

Anchor Standard 6: Use technology, including the Internet, to produce and publish writing and to interact and collaborate with others.

Standard 6: Use technology, including the Internet, to produce and publish writing as well as to interact and collaborate with others; demonstrate sufficient command of keyboarding skills to type a minimum of three pages in a single sitting.

Student Edition: 24, 98, 120, 187, 200, 224, 298

Teacher Edition: T2C, T24, T25, T50, T51, T74, T75, T90, T98, T99, T120, T124C, T137, T151, T161, T175, T187, T192, T200, T201, T213, T216, T224, T225, T250C, T261, T274, T275, T298, T299, T309, T320, T321, T343, T366C, T377, T390, T401, T412, T413, T425, T436, T437, T447, T458, T459

Grammar, Usage, and Mechanics: *Student Practice Book:* 42, 130, 136; *Teacher Edition:* T26, T53, T54

WRITING   Research to Build and Present Knowledge

Anchor Standard 7: Conduct short as well as more sustained research projects based on focused questions, demonstrating understanding of the subject under investigation.

Standard 7: Conduct short research projects to answer a question, drawing on several sources and refocusing the inquiry when appropriate.

Student Edition: 40, 41, 88, 89, 126, 138, 139, 140, 152, 162, 163, 170, 188, 189, 190, 191, 192, 193, 194, 195, 196, 197, 198, 199, 200, 201, 202, 203, 214, 288, 336

Teacher Edition: T40, T41, T46, T88, T89, T126, T138, T139, T140, T152, T162, T163, T170, T188, T189, T190, T191, T192, T193, T194, T195, T196, T197, T198, T199, T200, T201, T202, T203, T214, T288, T336, T404

Optional Revising Lessons: Narrative: 3

Grammar, Usage, and Mechanics: *Student Practice Book:* 38, 58, 98, 130, 136; *Teacher Edition:* T25, T30, T43, T53, T54

STANDARD	CORRELATION

Anchor Standard 8: Gather relevant information from multiple print and digital sources, assess the credibility and accuracy of each source, and integrate the information while avoiding plagiarism.

Standard 8: Gather relevant information from multiple print and digital sources; assess the credibility of each source; and quote or paraphrase the data and conclusions of others while avoiding plagiarism and providing basic bibliographic information for sources.

	Student Edition: 40, 41, 46, 88, 89, 112, 113, 138, 139, 140, 162, 163, 176, 188, 189, 190, 191, 214, 215, 239, 262, 288, 289, 311, 355, 380, 381, 426, 427, 448, 470 **Teacher Edition:** T40, T41, T46, T88, T89, T112, T113, T138, T139, T140, T162, T163, T176, T188, T189, T190, T191, T214, T215, T239, T262, T288, T289, T311, T355, T380, T381, T426, T427, T448, T470 **Optional Revising Lessons:** Narrative: 3

Anchor Standard 9: Draw evidence from literary or informational texts to support analysis, reflection, and research.

Standard 9: Draw evidence from literary or informational texts to support analysis, reflection, and research.

9a: Apply grade 6 Reading standards to literature (e.g., "Compare and contrast texts in different forms or genres [e.g., stories and poems; historical novels and fantasy stories] in terms of their approaches to similar themes and topics").	**Student Edition:** 252, 253, 254, 255, 256, 257, 258, 259, 260, 261, 262, 263, 264, 265, 266, 267, 268, 269, 270, 271, 272, 273, 274, 275, 276, 277 **Teacher Edition:** T252, T253, T254, T255, T256, T257, T258, T259, T260, T261, T262, T263, T264, T265, T266, T267, T268, T269, T270, T271, T272, T273, T274, T275, T276, T277 **Grammar, Usage, and Mechanics:** *Student Practice Book:* 21, 135; *Teacher Edition:* T20, T54
9b: Apply grade 6 Reading standards to literary nonfiction (e.g., "Trace and evaluate the argument and specific claims in a text, distinguishing claims that are supported by reasons and evidence from claims that are not").	**Student Edition:** 278, 279, 280, 281, 282, 283, 284, 285, 286, 287, 288, 289, 290, 291, 292, 293, 294, 295, 296, 297, 298, 299 **Teacher Edition:** T278, T279, T280, T281, T282, T283, T284, T285, T286, T287, T288, T289, T290, T291, T292, T293, T294, T295, T296, T297, T298, T299 **Grammar, Usage, and Mechanics:** *Student Practice Book:* 135; *Teacher Edition:* T54

WRITING Range of Writing

Anchor Standard 10: Write routinely over extended time frames (time for research, reflection, and revision) and shorter time frames (a single sitting or a day or two) for a range of tasks, purposes, and audiences.

Standard 10: Write routinely over extended time frames (time for research, reflection, and revision) and shorter time frames (a single sitting or a day or two) for a range of discipline-specific tasks, purposes, and audiences.

	Student Edition: 14, 15, 16, 17, 18, 19, 20, 21, 22, 23, 24, 25, 26, 27, 40, 41, 42, 43, 44, 45, 46, 47, 48, 49, 50, 51, 52, 53, 64, 65, 66, 67, 68, 69, 70, 71, 72, 73, 74, 75, 88, 89, 90, 91, 92, 93, 94, 95, 96, 97, 98, 99, 100, 101, 110, 112, 113, 114, 115, 116, 117, 118, 119, 120, 121, 122, 123, 138, 139, 140, 141, 142, 143, 144, 145, 146, 147, 148, 149, 150, 151, 162, 163, 164, 165, 166, 167, 168, 169, 170, 171, 172, 173, 174, 175, 188, 189, 190, 191, 192, 193, 194, 195, 196, 197, 198, 199, 200, 201, 202, 203, 214, 215, 216, 217, 218, 219, 220, 221, 222, 223, 224, 225, 226, 227, 236, 237, 238, 239, 240, 241, 242, 243, 244, 245, 246, 247, 248, 249, 262, 263, 264, 265, 266, 267, 268, 269, 270, 271, 272, 273, 274, 275, 276, 277, 288, 289, 290, 291, 292, 293, 294, 295, 296, 297, 298, 299, 310, 311, 312, 313, 314, 315, 316, 317, 318, 319, 320, 321, 332, 333, 334, 335, 336, 337, 338, 339, 340, 341, 342, 343, 352, 353, 354, 355, 356, 357, 358, 359, 360, 361, 362, 363, 364, 365, 378, 379, 380, 381, 382, 383, 384, 385, 386, 387, 388, 389, 390, 391, 402, 403, 404, 405, 406, 407, 408, 409, 410, 411, 412, 413, 414, 415, 426, 427, 428, 429, 430, 431, 432, 433, 434, 435, 436, 437, 448, 449, 450, 451, 452, 453, 454, 455, 456, 457, 458, 459, 468, 469, 470, 471, 472, 473, 474, 475, 476, 477, 478, 479, 480, 481 **Teacher Edition:** T14, T15, T16, T17, T18, T19, T20, T21, T22, T23, T24, T25, T26, T27, T40, T41, T42, T43, T44, T45, T46, T47, T48, T49, T50, T51, T52, T53, T64, T65, T66, T67, T68, T69, T70, T71, T72, T73, T74, T75, T88, T89, T90, T91, T92, T93, T94, T95, T96, T97, T98, T99, T100, T101, T110, T112, T113, T114, T115, T116, T117, T118, T119, T120, T121, T122, T123, T138, T139, T140, T141, T142, T143, T144, T145, T146, T147, T148, T149, T150, T151, T162, T163, T164, T165, T166, T167, T168, T169, T170, T171, T172, T173, T174, T175, T188, T189, T190, T191, T192, T193, T194, T195, T196, T197, T198, T199, T200, T201, T202, T203, T214, T215, T216, T217, T218, T219, T220, T221, T222, T223, T224, T225, T226, T227, T236, T237, T238, T239, T240, T241, T242, T243, T244, T245, T246, T247, T248, T249, T262, T263, T264, T265, T266, T267, T268, T269, T270, T271, T272, T273, T274, T275, T276, T277, T288, T289, T290, T291, T292, T293, T294, T295, T296, T297, T298, T299, T310, T311, T312, T313, T314, T315, T316, T317, T318, T319, T320, T321, T332, T333, T334, T335, T336, T337, T338, T339, T340, T341, T342, T343, T352, T353, T354, T355, T356, T357, T358, T359, T360, T361, T362, T363, T364, T365, T378, T379, T380, T381, T382, T383, T384, T385, T386, T387, T388, T389, T390, T391, T402, T403, T404, T405, T406, T407, T408, T409, T410, T411, T412, T413, T414, T415, T426, T427, T428, T429, T430, T431, T432, T433, T434, T435, T436, T437, T448, T449, T450, T451, T452, T453, T454, T455, T456, T457, T458, T459, T468, T469, T470, T471, T472, T473, T474, T475, T476, T477, T478, T479, T480, T481 **Optional Revising Lessons:** Narrative: 1, 2, 3, 4, 5, 6, 7, 8, 9, 10; Expository/Informative: 11, 12, 13, 14, 15, 16, 17, 18, 19, 20; Opinion: 21, 22, 23, 24, 25, 26, 27, 28, 29, 30; Descriptive: 31, 32, 33, 34, 35, 36, 37, 38, 39, 40 **Grammar, Usage, and Mechanics:** *Student Practice Book:* 8, 10, 14, 16, 20, 24, 31, 32, 38, 42, 44, 50, 52, 57, 58, 60, 62, 68, 78, 84, 84, 86, 92, 94, 98, 100, 112, 114, 118, 122, 126, 128, 130, 135, 136; *Teacher Edition:* T16, T17, T18, T19, T20, T22, T25, T26, T27, T28, T29, T30, T32, T33, T34, T37, T38, T40, T42, T43, T44, T48, T49, T50, T51, T52, T53, T54

STANDARD	CORRELATION

LANGUAGE Conventions of Standard English

Anchor Standard 1: Demonstrate command of the conventions of standard English grammar and usage when writing or speaking.

Standard 1: Demonstrate command of the conventions of standard English grammar and usage when writing or speaking.

Standard	Correlation
1a: Ensure that pronouns are in the proper case (subjective, objective, possessive).	**Student Edition:** 63, 71, 72, 73, 171, 172, 295, 296, 297, 298, 493, 494, 495, 517 **Teacher Edition:** T63, T71, T72, T73, T171, T172, T281, T295, T296, T297, T298, T493, T494, T495 **Grammar, Usage, and Mechanics:** *Student Practice Book:* 35, 36, 37, 38, 55, 57, 59, 60, 61, 62, 63, 64, 71, 72, 81, 83, 84, 85, 86, 87, 88, 89, 90, 91, 92, 93, 94, 202, 203; *Teacher Edition:* T25, T30, T32, T33, T35, T38, T40, T41, T42 **Grammar Practice Masters:** 29, 30, 31, 32, 67, 68, 69, 70, 71, 72, 73, 74
1b: Use intensive pronouns (e.g., myself, ourselves).	**Student Edition:** 63, 501, 517, 518 **Teacher Edition:** T63, T71, T72, T501 **Grammar, Usage, and Mechanics:** *Student Practice Book:* 35, 36, 57, 203; *Teacher Edition:* T25, T30 **Grammar Practice Masters:** 29, 30
1c: Recognize and correct inappropriate shifts in pronoun number and person.	**Student Edition:** 63, 71, 72, 73, 171, 172, 287, 295, 296, 297, 298, 493, 494, 495, 517 **Teacher Edition:** T63, T71, T72, T73, T171, T172, T281, T287, T295, T296, T297, T298, T493, T494, T495 **Grammar, Usage, and Mechanics:** *Teacher Edition:* T32, T33, T35 **Grammar Practice Masters:** 29, 30, 31, 32, 67, 68, 69, 70, 71, 72
1d: Recognize and correct vague pronouns (i.e., ones with unclear or ambiguous antecedents).	**Student Edition:** 63, 71, 72, 73, 171, 172, 287, 295, 296, 297, 298, 493, 494, 495, 517 **Teacher Edition:** T63, T71, T72, T73, T171, T172, T281, T287, T295, T296, T297, T298, T493, T494, T495 **Grammar Practice Masters:** 71, 72
1e: Recognize variations from standard English in their own and others' writing and speaking, and identify and use strategies to improve expression in conventional language.	**Student Edition:** 119, 502, 520 **Teacher Edition:** T118, T119, T220, T316, T502 **Grammar, Usage, and Mechanics:** *Student Practice Book:* 83; *Teacher Edition:* T38 **Optional Revising Lessons:** Informative/Expository: 18; Opinion: 26 **Grammar Practice Masters:** 47, 48, 49, 50, 51, 52, 53, 54, 55, 56, 57, 58, 59, 60, 61, 62, 63, 64, 65, 66, 73, 74, 77, 78

Anchor Standard 2: Demonstrate command of the conventions of standard English capitalization, punctuation, and spelling when writing.

Standard 2: Demonstrate command of the conventions of standard English capitalization, punctuation, and spelling when writing.

Standard	Correlation
2a: Use punctuation (commas, parentheses, dashes) to set off nonrestrictive/parenthetical elements.	**Student Edition:** 21, 22, 23, 47, 49, 273, 294, 388, 511, 513, 523 **Teacher Edition:** T21, T22, T23, T47, T48, T49, T272, T273, T294, T309, T388, T409, T511, T513 **Grammar, Usage, and Mechanics:** *Student Practice Book:* 21, 22, 205; *Teacher Edition:* T20 **Grammar Practice Masters:** 21, 22, 99, 100
2b: Spell correctly.	**Student Edition:** 6, 13, 21, 30, 47, 50, 56, 63, 71, 74, 79, 86, 98, 104, 108, 111, 115, 121, 128, 137, 147, 150, 154, 161, 171, 178, 187, 197, 200, 206, 213, 221, 230, 234, 241, 247, 254, 261, 271, 274, 280, 287, 295, 302, 309, 317, 320, 324, 331, 339, 342, 350, 363, 370, 377, 387, 390, 394, 409, 412, 418, 433, 436, 440, 447, 455, 458, 466, 479 **Teacher Edition:** T6, T7, T13, T21, T30, T31, T47, T50, T56, T57, T63, T71, T74, T79, T86, T98, T104, T108, T111, T115, T121, T128, T137, T147, T150, T154, T155, T161, T171, T174, T178, T179, T187, T197, T200, T206, T207, T213, T221, T224, T230, T234, T241, T247, T254, T255, T261, T271, T274, T280, T281, T287, T295, T298, T302, T303, T309, T317, T320, T324, T325, T331, T339, T342, T350, T363, T370, T371, T377, T387, T390, T394, T395, T409, T412, T418, T419, T433, T436, T440, T441, T447, T455, T458, T466, T479 **Grammar, Usage, and Mechanics:** *Student Practice Book:* 27, 53, 79, 105, 131; *Teacher Edition:* T21, T29, T37, T45, T53 **Grammar Practice Masters:** 7, 28, 35, 36

LANGUAGE Knowledge of Language

Anchor Standard 3: Apply knowledge of language to understand how language functions in different contexts, to make effective choices for meaning or style, and to comprehend more fully when reading or listening.

Standard 3: Use knowledge of language and its conventions when writing, speaking, reading, or listening.

Standard	Correlation
3a: Vary sentence patterns for meaning, reader/ listener interest, and style.	**Student Edition:** 6, 12, 21, 22, 23, 30, 38, 46, 56, 62, 70, 86, 94, 104, 108, 111, 115, 128, 136, 154, 160, 170, 178, 186, 196, 206, 212, 220, 230, 234, 241, 254, 260, 280, 286, 294, 302, 308, 316, 324, 330, 338, 350, 370, 376, 394, 400, 408, 418, 424, 432, 440, 446, 454, 466, 483, 486, 487, 506, 514, 515, 521 **Teacher Edition:** T6, T7, T12, T20, T21, T22, T23, T30, T31, T38, T46, T56, T57, T62, T70, T86, T94, T104, T108, T111, T115, T128, T129, T136, T146, T154, T155, T160, T170, T178, T179, T186, T196, T206, T207, T212, T220, T230, T234, T241, T246, T254, T255, T260, T270, T280, T281, T286, T294, T302, T303, T308, T316, T324, T325, T330, T338, T350, T362, T370, T371, T376, T386, T394, T395, T400, T408, T418, T419, T424, T432, T440, T441, T446, T454, T466, T478, T483, T486, T487, T506 **Grammar, Usage, and Mechanics:** *Student Practice Book:* 11, 112; *Teacher Edition:* T48 **Optional Revising Lessons:** Narrative: 1; Informative/Expository: 12, 20; Opinion: 22, 30; Descriptive: 32, 40 **Grammar Practice Masters:** 8, 10, 11, 12, 14, 20, 22, 23, 24, 26, 28, 30, 34, 36, 38, 40, 42, 44, 48, 50, 52, 54, 56, 58, 60, 62, 64, 66, 68, 70, 74, 76, 78, 80, 82, 84, 88, 90, 94, 96, 98, 100, 102, 104, 106

STANDARD	CORRELATION
Language Standard 3 continued 3b: Maintain consistency in style and tone.	**Student Edition:** 11, 56, 78, 85, 104, 107, 111, 115, 206, 259, 269, 285, 300, 349, 361, 394, 399, 406, 418, 440, 445, 477 **Teacher Edition:** T11, T13, T56, T70, T78, T85, T104, T107, T111, T115, T200, T206, T259, T269, T285, T300, T349, T361, T394, T399, T406, T418, T432, T440, T445, T477 **Grammar, Usage, and Mechanics:** *Student Practice Book:* 8, 10, 14, 16, 20, 24, 31, 32, 38, 42, 44, 50, 52, 57, 58, 60, 62, 68, 78, 84, 84, 86, 92, 94, 98, 100, 112, 114, 118, 122, 126, 128, 130, 135, 136; *Teacher Edition:* T16, T17, T18, T19, T20, T22, T25, T26, T27, T28, T29, T30, T32, T33, T34, T37, T38, T40, T42, T43, T44, T48, T49, T50, T51, T52, T53, T54 **Optional Revising Lessons:** Narrative: 5; Informative/Expository: 18; Descriptive: 36

LANGUAGE Vocabulary Acquisition and Use

Anchor Standard 4: Determine or clarify the meaning of unknown and multiple-meaning words and phrases by using context clues, analyzing meaningful word parts, and consulting general and specialized reference materials, as appropriate.

Standard 4: Determine or clarify the meaning of unknown and multiple-meaning words and phrases based on grade 6 reading and content, choosing flexibly from a range of strategies.

4a: Use context (e.g., the overall meaning of a sentence or paragraph; a word's position or function in a sentence) as a clue to the meaning of a word or phrase.	**Student Edition:** 38, 45, 154, 160, 169, 178, 186, 195, 206, 212, 330, 334 **Teacher Edition:** T38, T45, T154, T155, T160, T169, T178, T186, T195, T200, T206, T212, T330, T334, T338 **Grammar, Usage, and Mechanics:** *Student Practice Book:* 10, 11, 12, 14, 16, 18, 20, 32, 57, 59, 63, 64, 67, 70, 75, 76, 78, 84, 89, 90, 96, 97, 104, 111, 113, 115, 119, 121, 124; *Teacher Edition:* T17, T18, T19, T22, T26, T30, T32, T33, T34, T35, T36, T37, T38, T41, T43, T45, T48, T49, T50, T51 **Optional Revising Lessons:** Informative/Expository: 17; Opinion: 28
4b: Use common, grade-appropriate Greek or Latin affixes and roots as clues to the meaning of a word (e.g., audience, auditory, audible).	**Grammar, Usage, and Mechanics:** *Teacher Edition:* T35
4c: Consult reference materials (e.g., dictionaries, glossaries, thesauruses), both print and digital, to find the pronunciation of a word or determine or clarify its precise meaning or its part of speech.	**Teacher Edition:** T90 **Grammar, Usage, and Mechanics:** *Student Practice Book:* 212, 213
4d: Verify the preliminary determination of the meaning of a word or phrase (e.g., by checking the inferred meaning in context or in a dictionary).	**Grammar, Usage, and Mechanics:** *Student Practice Book:* 212

Anchor Standard 5: Demonstrate understanding of figurative language, word relationships, and nuances in word meanings.

Standard 5: Demonstrate understanding of figurative language, word relationships, and nuances in word meanings.

5a: Interpret figures of speech (e.g., personification) in context.	**Student Edition:** 440, 446, 450, 451, 465 **Teacher Edition:** T386, T425, T440, T446, T450, T451, T454, T465 **Optional Revising Lessons:** Descriptive: 31, 38
5b: Use the relationship between particular words (e.g., cause/effect, part/whole, item/category) to better understand each of the words.	**Grammar, Usage, and Mechanics:** *Student Practice Book:* 43, 45, 67,68, 73, 74, 75, 76; *Teacher Edition:* T27, T34, T36
5c: Distinguish among the connotations (associations) of words with similar denotations (definitions) (e.g., stingy, scrimping, economical, unwasteful, thrifty).	**Grammar, Usage, and Mechanics:** *Teacher Edition:* T34 **Grammar Practice Masters:** 81, 82

STANDARD	CORRELATION
Anchor Standard 6: Acquire and use accurately a range of general academic and domain-specific words and phrases sufficient for reading, writing, speaking, and listening and the college and career readiness level; demonstrate independence in gathering vocabulary knowledge when encountering an unknown term important to comprehension or expression.	
Standard 6: Acquire and use accurately grade-appropriate general academic and domain-specific words and phrases; gather vocabulary knowledge when considering a word or phrase important to comprehension or expression.	

	Student Edition: 15, 20, 21, 41, 47, 65, 66, 69, 70, 89, 95, 141, 144, 146, 147, 162, 164, 171, 189, 190, 192, 197, 215, 218, 264, 266, 268, 271, 289, 290, 293, 295, 311, 312, 317, 333, 336, 337, 338, 339, 380, 382, 384, 397, 403, 409, 428, 431, 433, 449, 450, 455
	Teacher Edition: T15, T20, T21, T41, T47, T65, T66, T67, T69, T70, T89, T94, T95, T141, T144, T146, T147, T162, T164, T170, T171, T189, T190, T192, T196, T197, T215, T218, T264, T265, T266, T268, T270, T271, T289, T290, T293, T294, T295, T311, T312, T317, T333, T336, T337, T338, T339, T380, T381, T382, T384, T386, T397, T403, T408, T409, T428, T431, T433, T449, T450, T455
	Grammar, Usage, and Mechanics: *Student Practice Book:* 10, 11, 12, 14, 16, 18, 20, 32, 57, 59, 63, 64, 67, 70, 75, 76, 78, 84, 89, 90, 96, 97, 104, 111, 113, 115, 119, 121, 124; *Teacher Edition:* T17, T18, T19, T22, T26, T30, T32, T33, T34, T35, T36, T37, T38, T41, T43, T45, T48, T49, T50, T51
	Optional Revising Lessons: Narrative: 2, 5, 7; Informative/Expository: 11, 14, 15; Opinion: 21, 23; Descriptive: 31, 34

SPEAKING AND LISTENING Comprehension and Collaboration	
Anchor Standard 1: Prepare for and participate effectively in a range of conversations and collaborations with diverse partners.	
Standard 1: Engage effectively in a range of collaborative discussions (one-on-one, in groups, and teacher led) with diverse partners on grade 6 topics, texts, and issues, building on others' ideas and expressing their own clearly.	

1a: Come to discussions prepared, having read or studied required material; explicitly draw on that preparation by referring to evidence on the topic, text, or issue to probe and reflect on ideas under discussion.	**Student Edition:** 4, 5, 6, 7, 8, 9, 10, 11, 12, 13, 27, 28, 29, 30, 31, 32, 33, 34, 35, 36, 37, 38, 39, 53, 54, 55, 56, 57, 58, 59, 60, 61, 62, 63, 75, 76, 77, 78, 79, 80, 81, 82, 83, 84, 85, 86, 87, 101, 102, 103, 104, 105, 106, 107, 108, 109, 122, 123, 126, 127, 128, 129, 130, 131, 132, 133, 134, 135, 136, 137, 151, 152, 153, 154, 155, 156, 157, 158, 159, 160, 161, 175, 176, 177, 178, 179, 180, 181, 182, 183, 184, 185, 186, 187, 202, 204, 205, 206, 207, 208, 209, 210, 211, 212, 213, 226, 228, 229, 230, 231, 232, 233, 234, 235, 248, 249, 252, 253, 254, 255, 256, 257, 258, 259, 260, 261, 277, 278, 279, 280, 281, 282, 283, 284, 285, 286, 287, 299, 300, 301, 302, 303, 304, 305, 306, 307, 308, 309, 321, 322, 323, 324, 325, 326, 327, 328, 329, 330, 331, 343, 344, 345, 346, 347, 348, 349, 350, 351, 364, 365, 368, 369, 370, 371, 372, 373, 374, 375, 376, 377, 391, 392, 393, 394, 395, 396, 397, 398, 399, 400, 401, 415, 416, 417, 418, 419, 420, 421, 422, 423, 424, 425, 437, 438, 439, 440, 441, 442, 443, 444, 445, 446, 447, 459, 460, 461, 462, 463, 464, 465, 466, 467, 480, 481 **Teacher Edition:** T4, T5, T6, T7, T8, T9, T10, T11, T12, T13, T26, T27, T28, T29, T30, T31, T32, T33, T34, T35, T36, T37, T38, T39, T52, T53, T54, T55, T56, T57, T58, T59, T60, T61, T62, T63, T75, T76, T77, T78, T79, T80, T81, T82, T83, T84, T85, T86, T87, T100, T101, T102, T103, T104, T105, T106, T107, T108, T109, T122, T123, T126, T127, T128, T129, T130, T131, T132, T133, T134, T135, T136, T137, T151, T152, T153, T154, T155, T156, T157, T158, T159, T160, T161, T175, T176, T177, T178, T179, T180, T181, T182, T183, T184, T185, T186, T187, T202, T203, T204, T205, T206, T207, T208, T209, T210, T211, T212, T213, T226, T227, T228, T229, T230, T231, T232, T233, T234, T235, T248, T249, T252, T253, T254, T255, T256, T257, T258, T259, T260, T261, T276, T277, T278, T279, T280, T281, T282, T283, T284, T285, T286, T287, T299, T300, T301, T302, T303, T304, T305, T306, T307, T308, T309, T321, T322, T323, T324, T325, T326, T327, T328, T329, T330, T331, T343, T344, T345, T346, T347, T348, T349, T350, T351, T364, T365, T368, T369, T370, T371, T372, T373, T374, T375, T376, T377, T391, T392, T393, T394, T395, T396, T397, T398, T399, T400, T401, T414, T415, T416, T417, T418, T419, T420, T421, T422, T423, T424, T425, T437, T438, T439, T440, T441, T442, T443, T444, T445, T446, T447, T459, T460, T461, T462, T463, T464, T465, T466, T467, T480, T481 **Grammar, Usage, and Mechanics:** *Student Practice Book:* 8, 10, 16, 24, 26, 32, 38, 42, 44, 46, 50, 57, 58, 60, 62, 64, 66, 68, 72, 76, 78, 83, 86, 88, 92, 94, 96, 100, 110, 112, 114, 116, 118, 122, 128, 130; *Teacher Edition:* T16, T17, T18, T19, T20, T21, T22, T24, T25, T26, T27, T28, T29, T30, T32, T33, T34, T35, T36, T37, T38, T40, T41, T42, T43, T44, T45, T46, T48, T49, T50, T51, T52, T53
1b: Follow rules for collegial discussions, set specific goals and deadlines, and define individual roles as needed.	**Student Edition:** 4, 5, 6, 7, 8, 9, 10, 11, 12, 13, 27, 28, 29, 30, 31, 32, 33, 34, 35, 36, 37, 38, 39, 53, 54, 55, 56, 57, 58, 59, 60, 61, 62, 63, 75, 76, 77, 78, 79, 80, 81, 82, 83, 84, 85, 86, 87, 101, 102, 103, 104, 105, 106, 107, 108, 109, 122, 123, 126, 127, 128, 129, 130, 131, 132, 133, 134, 135, 136, 137, 151, 152, 153, 154, 155, 156, 157, 158, 159, 160, 161, 175, 176, 177, 178, 179, 180, 181, 182, 183, 184, 185, 186, 187, 202, 204, 205, 206, 207, 208, 209, 210, 211, 212, 213, 226, 228, 229, 230, 231, 232, 233, 234, 235, 248, 249, 252, 253, 254, 255, 256, 257, 258, 259, 260, 261, 277, 278, 279, 280, 281, 282, 283, 284, 285, 286, 287, 299, 300, 301, 302, 303, 304, 305, 306, 307, 308, 309, 321, 322, 323, 324, 325, 326, 327, 328, 329, 330, 331, 343, 344, 345, 346, 347, 348, 349, 350, 351, 364, 365, 368, 369, 370, 371, 372, 373, 374, 375, 376, 377, 391, 392, 393, 394, 395, 396, 397, 398, 399, 400, 401, 415, 416, 417, 418, 419, 420, 421, 422, 423, 424, 425, 437, 438, 439, 440, 441, 442, 443, 444, 445, 446, 447, 459, 460, 461, 462, 463, 464, 465, 466, 467, 480, 481 **Teacher Edition:** T4, T5, T6, T7, T8, T9, T10, T11, T12, T13, T26, T27, T28, T29, T30, T31, T32, T33, T34, T35, T36, T37, T38, T39, T52, T53, T54, T55, T56, T57, T58, T59, T60, T61, T62, T63, T75, T76, T77, T78, T79, T80, T81, T82, T83, T84, T85, T86, T87, T100, T101, T102, T103, T104, T105, T106, T107, T108, T109, T122, T123, T126, T127, T128, T129, T130, T131, T132, T133, T134, T135, T136, T137, T151, T152, T153, T154, T155, T156, T157, T158, T159, T160, T161, T175, T176, T177, T178, T179, T180, T181, T182, T183, T184, T185, T186, T187, T202, T203, T204, T205, T206, T207, T208, T209, T210, T211, T212, T213, T226, T227, T228, T229, T230, T231, T232, T233, T234, T235, T248, T249, T252, T253, T254, T255, T256, T257, T258, T259, T260, T261, T276, T277, T278, T279, T280, T281, T282, T283, T284, T285, T286, T287, T299, T300, T301, T302, T303, T304, T305, T306, T307, T308, T309, T321, T322, T323, T324, T325, T326, T327, T328, T329, T330, T331, T343, T344, T345, T346, T347, T348, T349, T350, T351, T364, T365, T368, T369, T370, T371, T372, T373, T374, T375, T376, T377, T391, T392, T393, T394, T395, T396, T397, T398, T399, T400, T401, T414, T415, T416, T417, T418, T419, T420, T421, T422, T423, T424, T425, T437, T438, T439, T440, T441, T442, T443, T444, T445, T446, T447, T459, T460, T461, T462, T463, T464, T465, T466, T467, T480, T481 **Grammar, Usage, and Mechanics:** *Student Practice Book:* 57, 58, 92, 110; *Teacher Edition:* T20, T21, T25, T26, T29, T30, T32, T33, T35, T36, T41, T42, T43, T44, T46, T48

STANDARD	CORRELATION
Speaking and Listening Standard 1 continued **1c:** Pose and respond to specific questions with elaboration and detail by making comments that contribute to the topic, text, or issue under discussion.	**Student Edition:** 27, 53, 75, 101, 122, 123, 151, 175, 202, 226, 248, 249, 277, 299, 321, 343, 364, 365, 391, 415, 437, 459, 480, 481 **Teacher Edition:** T26, T27, T52, T53, T75, T100, T101, T122, T123, T151, T175, T202, T203, T226, T227, T248, T249, T276, T277, T299, T321, T343, T364, T365, T391, T414, T415, T437, T459, T480, T481 **Grammar, Usage, and Mechanics:** *Student Practice Book:* 38, 57, 110; *Teacher Edition:* T20, T25, T30, T32, T33, T40, T42, T46
1d: Review the key ideas expressed and demonstrate understanding of multiple perspectives through reflection and paraphrasing.	**Student Edition:** 27, 53, 75, 101, 122, 123, 151, 175, 202, 226, 248, 249, 277, 299, 321, 343, 364, 365, 391, 415, 437, 459, 480, 481 **Teacher Edition:** T26, T27, T52, T53, T75, T100, T101, T122, T123, T151, T175, T202, T203, T226, T227, T248, T249, T276, T277, T299, T321, T343, T364, T365, T391, T414, T415, T437, T459, T480, T481 **Grammar, Usage, and Mechanics:** *Student Practice Book:* 50, 57, 58, 83, 110; *Teacher Edition:* T16, T17, T18, T19, T20, T21, T24, T25, T26, T27, T28, T29, T30, T32, T33, T34, T35, T36, T37, T38, T40, T41, T42, T43, T44, T46, T49, T50, T51

Anchor Standard 2: Integrate and evaluate information presented in diverse media and formats, including visually, quantitatively, and orally.

Standard 2: Interpret information presented in diverse media and formats (e.g., visually, quantitatively, orally) and explain how it contributes to a topic, text, or issue under study.

	Student Edition: 4, 5, 6, 7, 8, 9, 10, 11, 12, 13, 27, 28, 29, 30, 31, 32, 33, 34, 35, 36, 37, 38, 39, 53, 54, 55, 56, 57, 58, 59, 60, 61, 62, 63, 75, 76, 77, 78, 79, 80, 81, 82, 83, 84, 85, 86, 87, 101, 102, 103, 104, 105, 106, 107, 108, 109, 122, 123, 126, 127, 128, 129, 130, 131, 132, 133, 134, 135, 136, 137, 151, 152, 153, 154, 155, 156, 157, 158, 159, 160, 161, 175, 176, 177, 178, 179, 180, 181, 182, 183, 184, 185, 186, 187, 202, 204, 205, 206, 207, 208, 209, 210, 211, 212, 213, 226, 228, 229, 230, 231, 232, 233, 234, 235, 248, 249, 252, 253, 254, 255, 256, 257, 258, 259, 260, 261, 277, 278, 279, 280, 281, 282, 283, 284, 285, 286, 287, 299, 300, 301, 302, 303, 304, 305, 306, 307, 308, 309, 321, 322, 323, 324, 325, 326, 327, 328, 329, 330, 331, 343, 344, 345, 346, 347, 348, 349, 350, 351, 364, 365, 368, 369, 370, 371, 372, 373, 374, 375, 376, 377, 391, 392, 393, 394, 395, 396, 397, 398, 399, 400, 401, 415, 416, 417, 418, 419, 420, 421, 422, 423, 424, 425, 437, 438, 439, 440, 441, 442, 443, 444, 445, 446, 447, 459, 460, 461, 462, 463, 464, 465, 466, 467, 480, 481 **Teacher Edition:** T4, T5, T6, T7, T8, T9, T10, T11, T12, T13, T26, T27, T28, T29, T30, T31, T32, T33, T34, T35, T36, T37, T38, T39, T52, T53, T54, T55, T56, T57, T58, T59, T60, T61, T62, T63, T75, T76, T77, T78, T79, T80, T81, T82, T83, T84, T85, T86, T87, T100, T101, T102, T103, T104, T105, T106, T107, T108, T109, T122, T123, T126, T127, T128, T129, T130, T131, T132, T133, T134, T135, T136, T137, T151, T152, T153, T154, T155, T156, T157, T158, T159, T160, T161, T175, T176, T177, T178, T179, T180, T181, T182, T183, T184, T185, T186, T187, T202, T203, T204, T205, T206, T207, T208, T209, T210, T211, T212, T213, T226, T227, T228, T229, T230, T231, T232, T233, T234, T235, T248, T249, T252, T253, T254, T255, T256, T257, T258, T259, T260, T261, T276, T277, T278, T279, T280, T281, T282, T283, T284, T285, T286, T287, T299, T300, T301, T302, T303, T304, T305, T306, T307, T308, T309, T321, T322, T323, T324, T325, T326, T327, T328, T329, T330, T331, T343, T344, T345, T346, T347, T348, T349, T350, T351, T364, T365, T368, T369, T370, T371, T372, T373, T374, T375, T376, T377, T391, T392, T393, T394, T395, T396, T397, T398, T399, T400, T401, T414, T415, T416, T417, T418, T419, T420, T421, T422, T423, T424, T425, T437, T438, T439, T440, T441, T442, T443, T444, T445, T446, T447, T459, T460, T461, T462, T463, T464, T465, T466, T467, T480, T481 **Grammar, Usage, and Mechanics:** *Student Practice Book:* 57, 68, 94; *Teacher Edition:* T16, T17, T18, T19, T25, T28, T30, T33, T34, T42, T45, T49

SPEAKING AND LISTENING **Presentation of Knowledge and Ideas**

Anchor Standard 3: Evaluate a speakers' point of view, reasoning, and use of evidence and rhetoric.

Standard 3: Delineate a speaker's argument and specific claims, distinguishing claims that are supported by reasons and evidence from claims that are not.

	Teacher Edition: T142, T166, T287 **Grammar, Usage, and Mechanics:** *Student Practice Book:* 50, 57; *Teacher Edition:* T28, T30, T33, T40

Anchor Standard 4: Present information, findings, and supporting evidence such that listeners can follow the line of reasoning and the organization, development, and style are appropriate to task, purpose, and audience.

Standard 4: Present claims and findings, sequencing ideas logically and using pertinent descriptions, facts, and details to accentuate main ideas or themes; use appropriate eye contact, adequate volume, and clear pronunciation.

	Student Edition: 98, 200, 334 **Teacher Edition:** T98, T142, T166, T287, T334, T342, T390, T391 **Grammar, Usage, and Mechanics:** *Student Practice Book:* 57, 83; *Teacher Edition:* T20, T27, T28, T30, T33, T37, T38, T45

Anchor Standard 5: Make strategic use of digital media and visual displays of data to express information and enhance understanding of presentations.

Standard 5: Include multimedia components (e.g., graphics, images, music, sound) and visual displays in presentations to clarify information.

	Student Edition: 87, 98, 187, 200, 224, 331, 458 **Teacher Edition:** T24, T50, T63, T87, T98, T99, T151, T161, T187, T200, T201, T213, T216, T224, T225, T274, T298, T331, T342, T343, T390, T401, T412, T413, T425, T436, T437, T458, T459 **Grammar, Usage, and Mechanics:** *Teacher Edition:* T28, T33, T34, T51

STANDARD	CORRELATION
Anchor Standard 6: Adapt speech to a variety of contexts and communicative tasks, demonstrating command of formal English when indicated or appropriate.	
Standard 6: Adapt speech to a variety of contexts and tasks, demonstrating command of formal English when indicated or appropriate.	

Student Edition: 4, 5, 6, 7, 8, 9, 10, 11, 12, 13, 27, 28, 29, 30, 31, 32, 33, 34, 35, 36, 37, 38, 39, 53, 54, 55, 56, 57, 58, 59, 60, 61, 62, 63, 75, 76, 77, 78, 79, 80, 81, 82, 83, 84, 85, 86, 87, 101, 102, 103, 104, 105, 106, 107, 108, 109, 122, 123, 126, 127, 128, 129, 130, 131, 132, 133, 134, 135, 136, 137, 151, 152, 153, 154, 155, 156, 157, 158, 159, 160, 161, 175, 176, 177, 178, 179, 180, 181, 182, 183, 184, 185, 186, 187, 202, 204, 205, 206, 207, 208, 209, 210, 211, 212, 213, 226, 228, 229, 230, 231, 232, 233, 234, 235, 248, 249, 252, 253, 254, 255, 256, 257, 258, 259, 260, 261, 277, 278, 279, 280, 281, 282, 283, 284, 285, 286, 287, 299, 300, 301, 302, 303, 304, 305, 306, 307, 308, 309, 321, 322, 323, 324, 325, 326, 327, 328, 329, 330, 331, 343, 344, 345, 346, 347, 348, 349, 350, 351, 364, 365, 368, 369, 370, 371, 372, 373, 374, 375, 376, 377, 391, 392, 393, 394, 395, 396, 397, 398, 399, 400, 401, 415, 416, 417, 418, 419, 420, 421, 422, 423, 424, 425, 437, 438, 439, 440, 441, 442, 443, 444, 445, 446, 447, 459, 460, 461, 462, 463, 464, 465, 466, 467, 480, 481

Teacher Edition: T4, T5, T6, T7, T8, T9, T10, T11, T12, T13, T26, T27, T28, T29, T30, T31, T32, T33, T34, T35, T36, T37, T38, T39, T52, T53, T54, T55, T56, T57, T58, T59, T60, T61, T62, T63, T75, T76, T77, T78, T79, T80, T81, T82, T83, T84, T85, T86, T87, T100, T101, T102, T103, T104, T105, T106, T107, T108, T109, T122, T123, T126, T127, T128, T129, T130, T131, T132, T133, T134, T135, T136, T137, T151, T152, T153, T154, T155, T156, T157, T158, T159, T160, T161, T175, T176, T177, T178, T179, T180, T181, T182, T183, T184, T185, T186, T187, T202, T203, T204, T205, T206, T207, T208, T209, T210, T211, T212, T213, T226, T227, T228, T229, T230, T231, T232, T233, T234, T235, T248, T249, T252, T253, T254, T255, T256, T257, T258, T259, T260, T261, T276, T277, T278, T279, T280, T281, T282, T283, T284, T285, T286, T287, T299, T300, T301, T302, T303, T304, T305, T306, T307, T308, T309, T321, T322, T323, T324, T325, T326, T327, T328, T329, T330, T331, T343, T344, T345, T346, T347, T348, T349, T350, T351, T364, T365, T368, T369, T370, T371, T372, T373, T374, T375, T376, T377, T391, T392, T393, T394, T395, T396, T397, T398, T399, T400, T401, T414, T415, T416, T417, T418, T419, T420, T421, T422, T423, T424, T425, T437, T438, T439, T440, T441, T442, T443, T444, T445, T446, T447, T459, T460, T461, T462, T463, T464, T465, T466, T467, T480, T481

Grammar, Usage, and Mechanics: *Student Practice Book:* 122, 128, 130; *Teacher Edition:* T48, T51, T52, T53

STRATEGIES FOR Writers

6

Senior Author
Rebecca Bowers Sipe, Ed.D.
Eastern Michigan University

Consulting Authors
Julie Coiro, Ph.D.
University of Rhode Island

Amy Humphreys, Ed.M., NBCT
Educational Consultant

Sara B. Kajder, Ph.D.
University of Pittsburgh

Mark Overmeyer, M.A.
Cherry Creek School District, Colorado

Senior Consultant
James Scott Miller, M.Ed.
National Writing Consultant

ZB **Zaner-Bloser**

Program Reviewers

Zaner-Bloser wishes to thank these educators who reviewed portions of this program and provided comments prior to publication.

Joe Anspaugh
Shelbyville Middle School
Shelbyville, IN

Michele Barto, Ed.D.
Fairleigh Dickinson University
Madison, NJ

Jackie Blosser
Lima City Schools
Lima, OH

Kim Bondy
South Arbor Academy
Ypsilanti, MI

Kelly Caravelli
Meadowbrook Middle School
Poway, CA

Cathy Cassy
St. Louis Public Schools
St. Louis, MO

Penny Clare
Educational Consultant
Lee, NH

Mary Dunton
Literacy Consultant
Sparks, NV

Emily Gleason
Beaverton School District
Beaverton, OR

Denise Gray, Ed.D.
Whiteriver Elementary School
Whiteriver, AZ

Laura Hall
Walton Charter Academy
Pontiac, MI

Donna Jett
Rockwood South Middle School
Fenton, MO

Christine Johnson, Ed.D.
Boonton Public Schools
Boonton, NJ

Dr. Roma Morris
Columbia School District
Columbia, MS

Rosanne Richards
Southern Nevada Regional
Professional Development
Program
North Las Vegas, NV

Sharlene E. Ricks
Alpine School District
American Fork, UT

Debbie Rutherford
Independent National Consultant
Omaha, NE

Melinda Springli
Lawton Public Schools
Lawton, OK

Kerry Stephenson
Pendleton County School District
Butler, KY

Photography: Cover © Purestock/age fotostock; Interior models, Tom Dubanowich; Stopwatch image © Royalty-Free/Corbis; p. 3 © Strauss/Curtis/Corbis; p. 33 © Marvin E. Newman/Getty Images; p. 81 © Bettmann/Corbis; pp. 99–101 © iStockphoto.com/sonia_ai; p. 101 © iStockphoto.com/Graffizone and © Corbis; p. 125 © George Ostertag/Superstock Inc/Photolibrary; p. 138 © Burstein Collection/Corbis; p. 139 Quarter-dollar coin images from United States Mint; p. 227 © iStockphoto.com/Mark Stay; p. 227 © iStockphotocom/essxboy; p. 251 © iStockphoto.com/David Liu; p. 367 © Comstock/Photolibrary; p. 371 © Mike Dobel/Masterfile; pp. 378, 379, 381, 391 © Dave Robertson/Masterfile

Art Credits: pp. 4, 28, 54, 126, 152, 176, 227, 252, 278, 300, 368, 392, 416 Illustrated by Alaskan Moose Studio; pp. 395, 399, 414 Sandy Joncas; p. 233 Tammie Lyon; pp. 76, 204, 322, 438, 441 Chris Vallo

Literature Credits: pp. 129–131 *A Touch of Genius* by Patricia Millman © 2000 by Highlights for Children, Inc., Columbus, Ohio; pp. 138–139 *The Tree That Saved History* by Jane Sutliffe © 2000 by Highlights for Children, Inc. Columbus, Ohio

ISBN 978-0-7367-7281-5

Copyright © 2013 Zaner-Bloser, Inc.

Zaner-Bloser, Inc.
1-800-421-3018
www.zaner-bloser.com

Printed in the United States of America   11 12 13 14 15   19840 5 4 3 2 1

SUSTAINABLE FORESTRY INITIATIVE

Certified Chain of Custody
Promoting Sustainable
Forest Management
www.sfiprogram.org

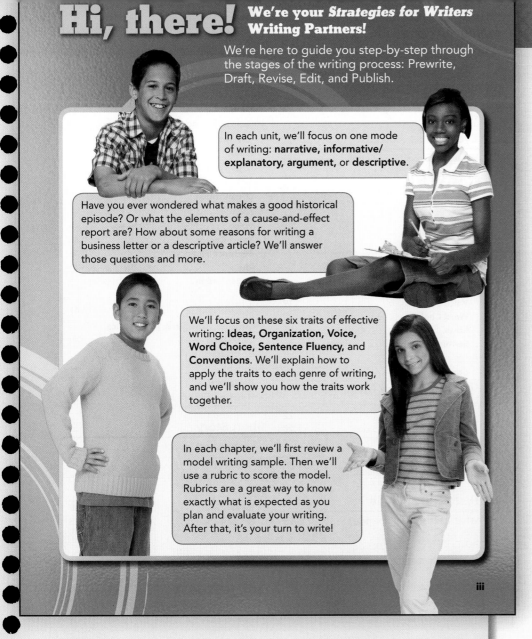

Hi, there!

We're your *Strategies for Writers* Writing Partners!

We're here to guide you step-by-step through the stages of the writing process: Prewrite, Draft, Revise, Edit, and Publish.

In each unit, we'll focus on one mode of writing: **narrative, informative/explanatory, argument,** or **descriptive**.

Have you ever wondered what makes a good historical episode? Or what the elements of a cause-and-effect report are? How about some reasons for writing a business letter or a descriptive article? We'll answer those questions and more.

We'll focus on these six traits of effective writing: **Ideas, Organization, Voice, Word Choice, Sentence Fluency,** and **Conventions**. We'll explain how to apply the traits to each genre of writing, and we'll show you how the traits work together.

In each chapter, we'll first review a model writing sample. Then we'll use a rubric to score the model. Rubrics are a great way to know exactly what is expected as you plan and evaluate your writing. After that, it's your turn to write!

iii

About the Cover

Although writing is viewed as a language arts skill, it crosses subject areas and genres. Writers tell stories and communicate about history, science, the arts, areas of personal interest, and the mundane. The image on the cover is intended to depict a possible writing subject and the text box shows the beginning of a piece of student writing. You may wish to have students read the text in the text box and discuss how the text relates to the picture.

Introduce the Writing Partners

An important element of becoming a writer is viewing oneself as a writer. In order to help students "see themselves as writers," *Strategies for Writers* introduces all instruction through a **Writing Partner**. Each of the four students pictured on this page will guide your students through one *Strategies for Writers* unit. The **Writing Partners** will

- introduce the genre of writing in each chapter.
- help students deconstruct the writing model.
- develop their own piece of writing based on the model.

Through the **Writing Partner**, your students will see a new piece of writing evolve. As the **Writing Partner** explains his/her writing strategy and "thinks aloud" about what he/she is writing, your students will have a window into the mind of a young writer like themselves.

To ensure students understand the **Writing Partner's** role,

- invite students to take turns reading the **Writing Partners'** comments on this page.
- use the first two pages in each unit to introduce the unit **Writing Partner.**
- encourage students to discuss the **Writing Partner's** comments and explanations throughout the unit.

Narrative writing

Table of Contents

Tv

Informative/Explanatory writing

Table of Contents

Tvii

Argument writing

Table of Contents

Tix

Descriptive writing

Table of Contents

Appendices

Appendix A: Grammar Practice

Table of Contents

Narrative writing

Eyewitness Account

Pages T4A–T27

This genre opens the door to narrative writing by encouraging students to write about something that happened in real life.

Prewrite   Choose an incident and record details to help answer the 5 W's.
Make a 5 W's Chart to organize the notes.

Draft   Use the best details to describe the event and keep readers interested.

Revise   Write a strong beginning and ending.
Share your feelings about the topic.
Choose words and phrases to convey ideas precisely.

Edit   Fix sentence fragments, run-on sentences, and comma splices.

Publish   Use neat handwriting or word processing.

Historical Episode

Pages T28A–T53

This genre gives students an opportunity to weave fact and fiction together and create a story based on an actual time, place, event, or person in history.

Prewrite   Use several sources to take notes on a historical event.
Make a Story Map to organize the notes.

Draft   Make sure your writing has a clear organization.

Revise   Express knowledge and caring about the topic.
Explain the meanings of any unfamiliar words.
Vary sentence patterns for meaning, reader interest, and style.

Edit   Check the use of quotation marks and commas.

Publish   Include a title, writer's name, and page numbers.

Short Story

Pages T54A–T75

As they write a short story, students use their imagination to come up with interesting plots and believable characters.

Prewrite   Brainstorm characters and events to use in the story.
Make a Storyboard to organize the ideas.

Draft   Use first-person point of view and dialogue.

Revise   Add sensory details to build suspense.
Replace overused words with more exact words.
Use active voice to strengthen sentences.

Edit   Recognize and correct inappropriate shifts in pronoun number and person.

Publish   Indent every paragraph.

Unit Overview

SOCIAL STUDIES CONNECTION

Biography

Pages T76A–T101

Students will demonstrate their knowledge of a historical figure by writing a biography, the story of a person's life.

Prewrite Choose an interesting subject and decide on what part of the subject's life to focus.
Make a Biography Map to organize the notes.

Draft Replace ordinary words and weak verbs.

Revise Find details that are new to readers.
Use transition words and phrases.
Vary the length of the sentences.

Edit Recognize and correct inappropriate shifts in verb tense.

Publish Use visuals that illustrate the life and times of the subject.

Narrative Test Writing

Pages T102A–T123

Students will learn and practice how to read a narrative test prompt and how to plan their time. They will also learn and practice writing strategies for successful test writing in the narrative mode.

Prewrite Study the writing prompt to find out what to do.
Respond to the task. Choose a graphic organizer.
Check the graphic organizer against the scoring guide.

Draft Use specific, related details.

Revise Use transition words to guide the reader. Use a casual tone.
Use precise words and phrases.

Edit Check the grammar, punctuation, capitalization, and spelling.

Online Writing Center

Interactive Whiteboard Ready

Complete Digital Writing Instruction!

- My Writing Pad
- Interactive Rubrics
- Anchor Papers
- Graphic Organizers

- Content Area Writing Prompts
- Grammar Games
- Proofreading Activities
- Instructional Videos

- Virtual File Cabinet
- eBooks
- Assessments

For information, go to www.sfw.z-b.com

Also available: **Online Essay Grader and Writing Tutor**, powered by Vantage Learning's MY Access®.

21st Century Literacies
Technology, Digital Media & Writing

by **Julie Coiro, Ph.D.**, University of Rhode Island & **Sara Kajder, Ph.D.**, University of Pittsburgh

 INSPIRE Websites to Spark Ideas

Inspiring Ideas for Writing Historical Episodes

The Internet connects students to a wide range of multimedia information about significant events and people throughout history. Many websites may spark ideas for students not quite sure what to write about for a historical fiction story or for those simply looking for more information about a particular person or event around which to base their stories.

- **American Memory (http://memory.loc.gov/ ammem/index.html)** provides free and open access to written and spoken words, sound recordings, still and moving images, prints, maps, and sheet music that document the American experience. Students may find the photographs and audio clips particularly helpful for inspiring writing ideas for a historical fiction story.

- **New York Times Learning Network (http://www. nytimes.com/learning/index.html)** or current news releases from news websites, such as **PBS Newshour (http://www.pbs.org/newshour/)**, **BBC World News (http://news.bbc.co.uk/1/hi/world/ default.stm)** or **CNN World News (http://www. cnn.com/WORLD/)**, provide information for students interested in basing their historical fiction stories on current events.

- **EASE History (http://www.easehistory.org/ index2.html)** provides access to hundreds of historical videos and photographs searchable by theme, keyword, or classroom topic in an Experience Accelerated Supportive Environment (EASE) created by professors at Michigan State University.

Writing Biographies

Many websites can spark ideas for students who are not quite sure whom to write about for a biography or for those simply looking for more information about a particular person. These websites offer opportunities for students to link their writing to topics such as science, math, social studies, and art. Here are a few online biography collections your students may wish to visit:

- **Biographies for Kids: Famous Leaders for Young Readers (http://gardenofpraise.com/leaders)** includes stories of presidents, inventors, athletes, educators, scientists, business men and women presented to inspire students to follow their examples of courage, determination, and honesty.

- **Exploreres of the Millennium (http://library. thinkquest.org/4034/)** is an award-winning Thinkquet Junior website designed by fourth and fifth graders in Illinois. Its Hall of Fame features 29 explorers along with an Explorer Quiz and Timeline.

- **Women of the Century (http://school. discoveryeducation.com/schooladventures/ womenofthecentury/)**, sponsored by Discovery Education, features a collection of biographies about inspirational females in space, science, arts, government, sports, and exploration.

- **Mr. Nussbaum's Famous People Biographies For Kids (http://www.mrnussbaum.com/bio2. htm)** was designed by a teacher in Fairfax County, Virginia. It also features biographies and other interactive games about famous athletes throughout history.

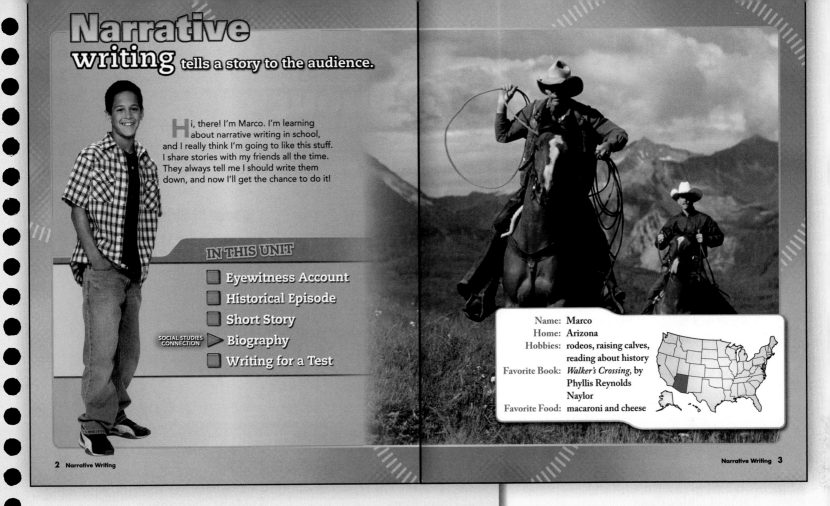

Narrative
writing tells a story to the audience.

Hi, there! I'm Marco. I'm learning about narrative writing in school, and I really think I'm going to like this stuff. I share stories with my friends all the time. They always tell me I should write them down, and now I'll get the chance to do it!

IN THIS UNIT

- Eyewitness Account
- Historical Episode
- Short Story

SOCIAL STUDIES CONNECTION ▶ Biography
- Writing for a Test

Name: Marco
Home: Arizona
Hobbies: rodeos, raising calves, reading about history
Favorite Book: *Walker's Crossing*, by Phyllis Reynolds Naylor
Favorite Food: macaroni and cheese

Meet Your Writing Partner, Marco

The writing partner for this unit is Marco, a boy from Arizona. You may wish to discuss with students how Marco's background, interests, and personality help him choose topics to write about. Tell students that, like Marco, they will use what they already know as they choose topics for their narratives. Each student has unique and authentic stories to tell. Encourage students to draw on their background knowledge, interests, and personalities to write their narratives, as Marco does.

To differentiate instruction and maximize student achievement, use the Extensions Online activities available at **www.sfw.z-b.com.**

Created by Amy Humphreys, Ed.M., these engaging activities can be used to meet a wide range of learner needs. Each activity uses a combination of visual, written, oral, and kinesthetic elements, and deliberately leverages the power of collaboration and conversation so students learn to think like writers in fun and engaging ways. For more information on Differentiated Instruction, see page Z12.

Eyewitness Account Planner

WEEK 1

Day 1
Introduce an Eyewitness Account

Student Objectives
- Review the elements of an eyewitness account.
- Consider purpose and audience.
- Learn the traits of narrative writing.

Student Activities
- Read and discuss **What's in an Eyewitness Account?** (p. 4)
- Read and discuss **Why write an Eyewitness Account?** (p. 5)
- Read **Linking Narrative Writing Traits to an Eyewitness Account.** (p. 6)

Day 2
Analyze Read an Eyewitness Account

Student Objectives
- Read a model eyewitness account.

Student Activities
- Read **"The Great Circus Parade."** (p. 7)

Day 3
Analyze Introduce the Rubric

Student Objectives
- Learn to read a rubric.

Student Activities
- Review **"The Great Circus Parade."** (p. 7)
- Read and discuss the **Eyewitness Account Rubric.** (pp. 8–9)

WEEK 2

Day 1
Write Prewrite: Ideas

Student Objectives
- Read and understand a prewriting strategy.

Student Activities
- Read and discuss **Prewrite: Focus on Ideas.** (p. 14)
- Apply the prewriting strategy.

Day 2
Write Prewrite: Organization

Student Objectives
- Create a 5 W's Chart to organize the notes.

Student Activities
- Read and discuss **Prewrite: Focus on Organization.** (p. 15)
- Reflect on the model 5 W's Chart.
- Apply the prewriting strategy to create a 5 W's Chart.
- Participate in a peer conference.

Day 3
Write Draft: Ideas

Student Objectives
- Begin writing, choosing the best details to keep writers interested.

Student Activities
- Read and discuss **Draft: Focus on Ideas.** (p. 16)
- Apply the drafting strategy by using a 5 W's Chart to write a draft.

WEEK 3

Day 1
Write Revise: Voice

Student Objectives
- Revise to share personal feelings about the topic.

Student Activities
- Read and discuss **Revise: Focus on Voice.** (p. 19)
- Participate in a peer conference.

Day 2
Write Revise: Word Choice

Student Objectives
- Revise to use words and phrases that convey ideas precisely.

Student Activities
- Read and discuss **Revise: Focus on Word Choice.** (p. 20)

Note: Optional Revising Lessons appear on the *Strategies for Writers* CD-ROM.

Day 3
Write Edit: Conventions

Student Objectives
- Edit to fix sentence fragments, run-on sentences, and comma splices.

Student Activities
- Read and discuss **Edit: Focus on Conventions.** (p. 21)

Note: Teach the Conventions mini-lessons (pp. 22–23) if needed.

Day 4	Day 5
Analyze Ideas, Organization, and Voice	**Analyze** Word Choice, Sentence Fluency, and Conventions
Student Objectives • Read a model eyewitness account. • Use the eyewitness account rubric. • Use the model eyewitness account to study Ideas, Organization, and Voice. **Student Activities** • Review **"The Great Circus Parade."** (p. 7) • Review the rubric. (pp. 8–9) • Read and discuss **Using the Rubric to Study the Model.** (pp. 10–11)	**Student Objectives** • Read a model eyewitness account. • Use the eyewitness account rubric. • Use the model eyewitness account to study Word Choice, Sentence Fluency, and Conventions. **Student Activities** • Review **"The Great Circus Parade."** (p. 7) • Review the rubric. (pp. 8–9) • Read and discuss **Using the Rubric to Study the Model.** (pp. 12–13)

Day 4	Day 5
Write Draft	**Write** Revise: Organization
Student Objectives • Complete a draft. **Student Activities** • Finish the draft. (p. 17) • Participate in a peer conference.	**Student Objectives** • Revise for a strong beginning and ending. **Student Activities** • Read and discuss **Revise: Focus on Organization.** (p. 18) • Reflect on a model draft. • Apply the revising strategy.

Day 4	Day 5
Write Publish: +Presentation	**Write** Publish: +Presentation
Student Objectives • Discuss preparation for publishing and presentation. • Use a final editing checklist to publish their work. **Student Activities** • Read and discuss **Publish: +Presentation.** (p. 24) • Apply the publishing strategy.	**Student Objectives** • Use an eyewitness account rubric. • Share a published eyewitness account. **Student Activities** • Share their work. • Use the rubric to reflect upon and evaluate the model and their own writing. (pp. 8–9, 25–27)

To complete the chapter in fewer days, combine the learning objectives and activities in a way that supports students as they write.

Resources at-a-Glance

Grammar, Usage & Mechanics

Differentiating Instruction

For additional Differentiating Instruction activities, see Strategies for Writers *Extensions Online at* **www.sfw.z-b.com.**

English Language Learners

Conferencing

Technology Tip

 Connection Letter
Reproducible letter (in English and Spanish) appears on the *Strategies for Writers* CD-ROM and at **www.sfw.z-b.com.**

Online Writing Center

Provides IWB resources, interactive games and practice activities, videos, eBooks, and a virtual file cabinet.

 Strategies for Writers Online
Go to **www.sfw.z-b.com** for free online resources for students and teachers.

Introduce
an Eyewitness Account

Student Objectives

- Review the elements of an eyewitness account. *(p. 4)*
- Consider purpose and audience. *(p. 5)*
- Learn the traits of narrative writing. *(p. 6)*

What's an Eyewitness Account?

Ask a student to describe an event that he or she saw during the past week. Prompt him or her to provide details. Explain that the student just gave an eyewitness account. Point out that when people describe something they witnessed in real life, they are using the eyewitness account genre.

What's in an Eyewitness Account?

Read and discuss the elements of an eyewitness account on page 4. Explain that these elements can also be found in news stories heard on television or found in newspapers or magazines. Ask a volunteer to provide you with a current event. Guide students to understand how each of these elements might be present in a story about that current event.

Strategies for Writers Online

Go to **www.sfw.z-b.com** for additional online resources for students and teachers.

What's an Eyewitness Account?

It's a true report of something that happened in real life. I think this kind of writing is fun because I can pretend I'm a newspaper reporter!

What's in an Eyewitness Account?

Narrator
That's me! The narrator is the person who tells about something he or she saw. I've seen a lot of things that I'd like to report on, so now I'll tell my audience about one of them!

Order
This is the order in which I saw things happen. I'll describe the events as they really happened because I want my reader to understand the big picture.

Tone
This is how I want my story to sound and how I want my readers to feel. I can change the tone depending on what I'm writing. I can use short sentences to build suspense, powerful verbs to create drama, or descriptive words to create a serious, sad, or funny mood.

The 5 W's
These are the details of *who, what, when, where,* and *why* in my account. I'll use all of these, but I'll have to remember to keep each detail accurate and true!

4   Narrative Writing

Narrative Text Exemplars (Eyewitness Account)

Douglass, Frederick. *Narrative of the Life of Frederick Douglass, an American Slave: Written by Himself.* **Bedford/St. Martin's, 2003.** CCSS In this groundbreaking autobiography, Frederick Douglass recounts his life as a slave. He describes the fear and brutality he faced, and his dramatic escape to freedom in the North.

Santiago, Esmeralda. *When I Was Puerto Rican.* **Da Capo Press, 2006.** *When I Was Puerto Rican* recounts Santiago's childhood in Puerto Rico and her teenage years in New York City. It describes the hardships Santiago faced with language and culture when she moved to the United States.

Why write an **Eyewitness Account?**

There are many reasons to write an eyewitness account. I listed some here, since I'm still thinking about why I want to write.

Entertainment
Entertaining the reader is one good reason to write an eyewitness account. When I see something that is funny, exciting, or sad, I just want to share it with someone else.

Personal Reflection
Reflecting can help me understand how I've been affected by something I've seen. Writing helps me reflect, or make sense out of the things I see.

Information
I can write my account to educate, instruct, or inform my reader. He or she might find useful or interesting new information in my account.

Summarize
Sometimes the events I see are long and complicated. Often, there are smaller details that lead up to one main event, so it's important for me to summarize only the details my reader really needs to know. It's also good practice to use my summarization skills, especially since I'll use them a lot in school.

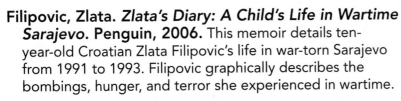

Why write an Eyewitness Account?

Read and discuss the reasons for writing an eyewitness account. Point out that all writing has a purpose and that writers write for a variety of reasons and audiences. Explain that these authentic purposes help shape the writing. For example, someone writing to entertain might use a tone that conveys humor or excitement. A writer who is writing for personal reflection might focus on feelings and thoughts. When writing to inform, a person might include many facts and explanations to educate, instruct, or inform the reader. Ask students to discuss topics they think would fit each purpose for writing an eyewitness account. Encourage students to reflect upon and elaborate on other students' ideas.

Filipovic, Zlata. *Zlata's Diary: A Child's Life in Wartime Sarajevo*. Penguin, 2006. This memoir details ten-year-old Croatian Zlata Filipovic's life in war-torn Sarajevo from 1991 to 1993. Filipovic graphically describes the bombings, hunger, and terror she experienced in wartime.

Vogel, Carole G. *Nature's Fury: Eyewitness Reports of Natural Disasters*. Scholastic, Inc. 2000. *Nature's Fury: Eyewitness Reports of Natural Disasters* is an eye-opening account of 13 disasters, including earthquakes, tornados, and flash floods. The author also includes interviews with several survivors of the disasters.

CCSS **C**ommon **C**ore **S**tate **S**tandards

SL.6.1: Engage effectively in a range of collaborative discussions (one-on-one, in groups, and teacher-led) with diverse partners on *grade 6 topics, texts, and issues,* building on others' ideas and expressing their own clearly. **SL.6.1.b:** Follow rules for collegial discussions, set specific goals and deadlines, and define individual roles as needed. **SL.6.1.c:** Pose and respond to specific questions with elaboration and detail by making comments that contribute to the topic, text, or issue under discussion.

Introduce
an Eyewitness Account

Linking Narrative Writing Traits to an Eyewitness Account

Explain to students that they will follow Marco as he models using the writing process and the traits together. As they follow Marco through the writing process, students will see how the Narrative Writing Traits have been adapted and applied to writing an eyewitness account. They will see that an eyewitness account has many factors in common with other types of narrative writing. However, the particular audience and purpose of an eyewitness account determine how the traits are used.

Linking Narrative Writing Traits to an Eyewitness Account

In this chapter, you will write about something that happened in real life. This type of narrative writing is called an eyewitness account. Marco will guide you through the stages of the writing process: Prewrite, Draft, Revise, Edit, and Publish. In each stage, Marco will show you important writing strategies that are linked to the Narrative Writing Traits below.

Narrative Writing Traits

Ideas	• a focused topic, experience, or series of events • engaging, accurate details that develop and describe the topic, experience, or series of events
Organization	• logically sequenced events, often in chronological order • an interesting beginning and a satisfying ending • transitions that signal the sequence of events as well as shifts in time or setting
Voice	• a voice and tone that are appropriate for the purpose and audience • dialogue that, if used, fits the characters
Word Choice	• precise, descriptive words and phrases
Sentence Fluency	• a variety of sentences that flow and are a pleasure to read aloud
Conventions	• no or few errors in grammar, usage, mechanics, and spelling

Before you write, read Joe Torelli's eyewitness account on the next page. Then use the eyewitness account rubric on pages 8–9 to decide how well he did. (You might want to look back at What's in an Eyewitness Account? on page 4, too!)

6 Narrative Writing

Narrative Writing Traits in an Eyewitness Account

 **Ideas** The writer focuses on one appropriately sized experience and answers all 5 W's to paint a complete picture of the event. Interesting, descriptive details are used to help the reader visualize the account.

 **Organization** The narrative starts with an attention-grabbing lead and closes with an ending that reflects back on the event. Details are presented in a logical, natural sequence. The writer uses effective transitions to guide the reader through the events of the story, as well as to link related ideas.

 **Voice** The writer uses a voice that is expressive, engaging, and appropriate for both the subject and the audience.

THE GREAT CIRCUS PARADE

by Joe (Bongo the Clown) Torelli

Narrator

Last week I was amazed, astounded, flabbergasted, and stupefied! I saw wild animals, dozens of circus wagons and bands, hundreds of horses, and thousands of people in costumes. I, Bongo the Clown, fell under the spell of the Great Circus Parade.

Why As a professional clown, I had to see the parade. *Who* *What* *When* Every July, it winds three miles through downtown Milwaukee, Wisconsin. From near and far, people come to see the spectacle. *Where* *5 W's*

The day I attended was cloudless and bright; a faint breeze floated in from Lake Michigan. A drum troop at the start of the parade stirred up *Order* the crowd. Following close behind, young men in knickers pedaled high-wheeled bicycles, and mounted police waved from their saddles. By the time the clown snake charmers arrived, the parade was in full swing.

The clowns were funny, but I was more impressed by the historic circus wagons. Each one showed off a dazzling color scheme. As the wheels turned, yellow and orange webbing between the spokes swirled like sunbursts. Huge draft horses with fancy brass harnesses hauled most of the wagons, some weighing more than a ton.

Magnificent bandwagons carried musicians playing grand old tunes. One bandwagon stood out. Sparkling with gold mermaids and swans, it was like something from a fairy tale. *Tone*

The cage wagons displayed exotic animals, including a pygmy hippo, a buffalo, and a giraffe. I even saw a liger (a cross between a lion and a tiger).

Most splendid were the tableau wagons. Filled with carved and painted wooden figures, they are historical scenes on wheels. A woman dressed as Cleopatra rode a tableau pulled by camels. A two-headed green dragon roared from the top of a tableau that celebrated the age of knights and castles.

At the end of the parade were lumbering elephants and a steam calliope. Belching out plumes of smoke and hooting old-time melodies, the calliope bid farewell to the satisfied crowd. I smiled all the way home, thinking about those sunburst wheels. I'm still smiling. Maybe I should run off to join the circus parade.

Eyewitness Account 7

Word Choice The writer uses plenty of descriptive and sensory language to help the reader picture the event. The reader should feel as if he or she witnessed the event, too.

Sentence Fluency A variety of sentence types and structures is used in a good narrative to give the writing energy and flow. Different sentence beginnings vary the pace and create interest.

Conventions A good writer carefully edits his or her work prior to publishing. Mistakes in spelling, punctuation, capitalization, and grammar will confuse the reader and obscure the author's purpose.

Analyze the Model

Week 1 • Day 2

Student Objectives

- Read a model eyewitness account. *(p. 7)*

Read the Model

Have students read "The Great Circus Parade" on page 7. Remind students to watch for the writing traits outlined on page 6.

Elements of an Eyewitness Account

Use the notes on the model to discuss each of the elements described in What's in an Eyewitness Account? on page 4. Ask:

- How did Joe pull the reader in right away? (Possible answer: The words *amazed*, *astounded*, *flabbergasted*, and *stupefied* are exciting and eye-catching.)

- What kind of tone did Joe use? How did that affect you as you read his story? (Possible response: The words and phrases Joe used showed how excited he was to see the parade. It helped me feel excited, too.)

- How does the ending reflect back on the event? (Possible response: The very last line mentions the circus parade, which is what the account began with.)

CCSS **C**ommon **C**ore **S**tate **S**tandards
R/Lit.6.1: Cite textual evidence to support analysis of what the text says explicitly as well as inferences drawn from the text. **SL.6.1.a:** Come to discussions prepared, having read or studied required material; explicitly draw on that preparation by referring to evidence on the topic, text, or issue to probe and reflect on ideas under discussion. **SL.6.1.d:** Review the key ideas expressed and demonstrate understanding of multiple perspectives through reflection and paraphrasing.

Analyze the Model

Week 1 • Day 3

Student Objectives

• Learn to read a rubric. *(pp. 8–9)*

Use the Rubric

Explain the Rubric Explain that a rubric is a tool that helps you plan, improve, and evaluate a piece of writing. A rubric also helps a writer focus on key elements, or traits, in writing (**Ideas, Organization, Voice, Word Choice, Sentence Fluency, Conventions,** and **Presentation**).

The 6-point rubric on pages 8 and 9 is based on the Narrative Writing Traits that students read on page 6. Draw students' attention to the six columns to explain how the scoring system works. Explain that the column under the numeral 6 describes a very good eyewitness account, one that has received the highest score in all categories. This is what students should strive for in their own writing.

Discuss the Rubric Guide the students in a discussion of the rubric. Read the descriptors that go with each trait. Note how the descriptors vary as you move from column to column. Remind students to keep the rubric in mind when they write their own eyewitness account and again when they revise it.

Online Writing Center

Provides a variety of **interactive rubrics,** including 4-, 5-, and 6-point models.

Rubric

Use this 6-point rubric to plan and score an eyewitness account.

	6	5	4
Ideas	The narrator uses the 5 W's to establish a context for the event. Strong details engage the reader and develop the event.	The narrator answers the 5 W's. Details engage the reader and develop the event.	The writer answers most of the 5 W's. Details are mostly engaging and develop the event.
Organization	An engaging lead introduces the event; the ending follows from the narrated event.	The lead introduces the event, and the ending follows from the narrated event.	The lead introduces the event, but the ending could be stronger.
Voice	The voice is expressive and engages the reader throughout.	The voice is expressive most of the time. The writing connects with the reader.	The voice is sometimes inconsistent. The writer sometimes seems unaware of the audience.
Word Choice	Descriptive and sensory language helps the reader create a precise picture of the event.	Descriptive and sensory words strengthen the writing.	Words are usually clear and sensory but not always the best choice.
Sentence Fluency	Variety in sentence beginnings makes the writing interesting to the reader.	Most sentences begin in different ways. The writing is easy to read.	There is some variety in sentence beginnings. The report isn't always smooth to read.
Conventions	All the sentences are correct and complete.	A few minor errors with sentences are difficult to spot.	Some sentences are incorrect or incomplete and distract the reader.
＋Presentation	The eyewitness account is legible and neat.		

8 Narrative Writing

CCSS Common Core State Standards

Eyewitness Account

As students learn to write an eyewitness account, they will receive instruction based on the Common Core State Standards (CCSS) for Narrative writing, as well as several Speaking & Listening, Language, and Reading/Literature CCSS standards for grade 6.

The rubric and writing strategies for Ideas and Word Choice reflect standards **W.6.3, W.6.3.a, W.6.3.b,** and **W.6.3.d,** which encourage the writer to develop one topic using strong, descriptive, and sensory details, including details that answer the 5 W's, to develop and enliven the story. The rubric and writing strategies for Organization incorporate standards **W.6.3** and **W.6.3.a,** which emphasize the use of a strong

3	2	1	
Several of the 5 W's are missing. Several details are weak, irrelevant, or missing.	It is not clear what event the writer is describing. Details are sketchy and not engaging.	The writing does not attempt to describe an event. Details seem to have been included for no reason.	**Ideas**
The lead is present but does not pull the reader in. The ending does not follow from the event or is missing.	The organization is hard to follow. The lead and ending need work.	The writing is not organized. The lead and ending are missing.	**Organization**
The voice is sometimes dull and unengaging.	The voice is wrong for this piece of writing. It does not draw the reader in.	The writing is dull and has no voice.	**Voice**
Some of the words are unclear and misused. They don't help the reader get a clear picture.	The writer's words are ordinary and repetitive.	The writing doesn't make sense. The words are confusing.	**Word Choice**
Sentence beginnings are repeated in places, creating patches that are dull or hard to read.	Many sentences begin the same way, making the report hard to read.	Sentences are incomplete or run-on. The report is very hard to read.	**Sentence Fluency**
Several noticeable errors with sentences slow down the reader.	Errors with sentences are frequent and get in the way of reading the writing.	Many errors with sentences make the writing very difficult to read.	**Conventions**

See Appendix B for 4-, 5-, and 6-point narrative rubrics.

Apply the Rubric

Assign Groups Divide students into six groups. Assign each group a trait. Have students search the model on page 7 for strong examples of the assigned trait as described by the rubric.

Reassemble the Class Bring the class together and ask one person from each group to report the group's findings to the class. Remind students that the point of this exercise is less to score the model than it is to further their understanding of the traits and to practice identifying them within a piece of writing.

Additional Rubrics Appendix B includes 4-, 5-, and 6-point rubrics that can be used with any piece of narrative writing. The rubrics are also available as blackline masters in the back of this Teacher Edition, beginning on page T525.

beginning and logical, satisfying ending. The rubric and writing strategies for Voice reflect standards **W.6.3** and **W.6.3.b,** which stress the use of narrative technique to develop experiences. The rubric and writing strategies for Sentence Fluency are grounded in Language standard **L.6.3.a,** which focuses on varying sentence patterns for meaning and reader interest.

Standards **L.6.1** and **L.6.2** are clearly reflected throughout the editing pages of the chapter. Standard **W.6.6,** which outlines the requirement for students to take full advantage of resources offered on the Internet and in the word processing programs, resonates throughout the entire Narrative unit.

CCSS Common Core State Standards

SL.6.1: Engage effectively in a range of collaborative discussions (one-on-one, in groups, and teacher-led) with diverse partners on *grade 6 topics, texts, and issues,* building on others' ideas and expressing their own clearly. **SL.6.1.a:** Come to discussions prepared, having read or studied required material; explicitly draw on that preparation by referring to evidence on the topic, text, or issue to probe and reflect on ideas under discussion. **SL.6.1.c:** Pose and respond to specific questions with elaboration and detail by making comments that contribute to the topic, text, or issue under discussion.

Analyze
the Model

Week 1 • Day 4

Student Objectives

- Read a model eyewitness account. *(p. 7)*
- Use the eyewitness account rubric. *(pp. 8–9)*
- Use the model eyewitness account to study Ideas, Organization, and Voice. *(pp. 10–11)*

Study the Model

Assess the Model Have students turn to pages 10–11. Explain that these pages show how the model on page 7 uses the writing traits described in the rubric. Read each section with students. Use questions such as the following to discuss the sections. Be sure students can back up their answers with examples from the model.

- Why is it effective that Joe answered several of the 5 W's right away? (Possible response: By answering the 5 W's at the beginning, Joe gives the reader a clear idea of what the account is about.)

Strategies for Writers Online
Go to **www.sfw.z-b.com** for additional online resources for students and teachers.

Eyewitness Account
Using the Rubric
to Study the Model

Did you notice that the model on page 7 points out some key elements of an eyewitness account? As he wrote "The Great Circus Parade," Joe Torelli used these elements to help him tell about a real-life event. He also used the 6-point rubric on pages 8–9 to plan, draft, revise, and edit the writing. A rubric is a great tool to evaluate writing during the writing process.

Now let's use the same rubric to score the model. To do this, we'll focus on each trait separately, starting with Ideas. We'll use the top descriptor for each trait (column 6), along with examples from the model, to help us understand how the traits work together. How would you score Joe on each trait?

Ideas

- **The narrator uses the 5 W's to establish a context for the event.**
- **Strong details engage the reader and develop the event.**

Joe answers the 5 W's early on to set the scene of his event. Strong, vivid details like *faint breeze* and *high-wheeled bicycles* keep me interested and wanting to know more.

[from the writing model]

The day I attended was cloudless and bright; a faint breeze floated in from Lake Michigan. A drum troop at the start of the parade stirred up the crowd. Following close behind, young men in knickers pedaled high-wheeled bicycles, and mounted police waved from their saddles.

10 Narrative Writing

English Language Learners

BEGINNING

Sequencing Using pictures, tell a short story to students. Post the pictures on the board in random order. Hold up one finger and ask, *Which happened first?* Have a student write *First* or *1* next to the first picture. Model the sentence *This happened first.* Continue for the remaining pictures using words such as *second, then, next, last,* and *finally.*

INTERMEDIATE

The 5 W's Tell students, *Let's plan a party!* Draw a blank party invitation on the board with *Party!* at the top. Ask students, *What kind of party will we have?* If students say, for example, *a birthday party,* write *What: birthday* on the invitation. Repeat for the remaining 5 W's.

Organization

- An engaging lead introduces the event; the ending follows from the narrated event.

Joe's lead paragraph pulls me in immediately. I need to know more about this amazing event! I also like the way Joe's ending ties into the astounded feelings he describes in the lead. This helps the account feel well-rounded and complete.

> [from the writing model]
>
> Last week I was amazed, astounded, flabbergasted, and stupefied! I saw wild animals, dozens of circus wagons and bands, hundreds of horses, and thousands of people in costumes.

> [from the writing model]
>
> I smiled all the way home, thinking about those sunburst wheels. I'm still smiling. Maybe I should run off to join the circus parade.

Voice

- The voice is expressive and engages the reader throughout.

Joe uses an enchanting tone to describe the parade. His use of the words *magnificent*, *grand*, and *sparkling* remind me of the way a ringmaster describes a circus.

> [from the writing model]
>
> Magnificent bandwagons carried musicians playing grand old tunes. One bandwagon stood out. Sparkling with gold mermaids and swans, it was like something from a fairy tale.

Eyewitness Account **11**

- How has Joe organized the events of his story? (in a natural, chronological order)

- Is Joe's voice appropriate for the subject? Why or why not? (Possible response: Yes, because the circus parade is an exciting, colorful, and whimsical event, and Joe uses a voice that shows how much he enjoys it all.)

ADVANCED

Sequencing Read a short story that clearly answers the 5 W's and follows a logical order. After you read the story once, give students 3 minutes to work quietly with a partner to fill out a Sequence Chain graphic organizer. After 3 minutes, read the story again. Have partners revise their Sequence Chains as necessary. Have students review as a group.

ADVANCED HIGH

Identifying the 5 W's Give each student a language-level-appropriate narrative to read. It can be a newspaper article or a decodable book or leveled reader from a reading program. After students have read their piece, have them fill in a 5 W's chart. They may use other clues, such as pictures, to gather information. Then have them trade selections and 5 W's charts with a partner who should read the selection and review the chart for mistakes.

CCSS Common Core State Standards

R/Lit.6.1: Cite textual evidence to support analysis of what the text says explicitly as well as inferences drawn from the text. **R/Lit.6.3:** Describe how a particular story's or drama's plot unfolds in a series of episodes as well as how the characters respond or change as the plot moves toward a resolution. **SL.6.1.a:** Come to discussions prepared, having read or studied required material; explicitly draw on that preparation by referring to evidence on the topic, text, or issue to probe and reflect on ideas under discussion.

Analyze
the Model

Week 1 • Day 5

Student Objectives

- Read a model eyewitness account. *(p. 7)*
- Use the eyewitness account rubric. *(pp. 8–9)*
- Use the model eyewitness account to study Word Choice, Sentence Fluency, and Conventions. *(pp. 12–13)*

Continue Discussing the Traits

Now use pages 12 and 13 to discuss **Word Choice, Sentence Fluency,** and **Conventions**. Ask students to paraphrase their classmates' ideas to ensure that they understand them. Ask questions such as these:

- Find some descriptive words or sensory language that Joe uses to bring his account to life. (Possible responses: *cloudless; knickers; dazzling color scheme; splendid; lumbering; belching out plumes of smoke*)

- How does Joe keep his sentences energetic and flowing? (Possible response: He uses a variety of structures. He begins some sentences with prepositional phrases.)

- How would the reader be affected by several spelling, grammar, or punctuation mistakes? (Possible response: Lots of errors would leave the reader feeling frustrated. They would muddle the images of the circus parade and detract from the reader's experience.)

Strategies for Writers Online

Go to **www.sfw.z-b.com** for additional online resources for students and teachers.

Word Choice
- Descriptive and sensory language helps the reader create a precise picture of the event.

Interesting and colorful sensory language helps me picture what's happening. For example, the elephants don't just walk, they *lumber*. And the smoke doesn't just come out of the calliope, it *belches* out in *plumes*. Joe's excellent use of description is truly inspiring!

[from the writing model]

At the end of the parade were lumbering elephants and a steam calliope. Belching out plumes of smoke and hooting old-time melodies, the calliope bid farewell to the satisfied crowd.

Sentence Fluency
- Variety in sentence beginnings makes the writing interesting to the reader.

Joe uses many different sentence beginnings and patterns to help his writing flow. This variety not only makes the reading easier for me, but it also helps keep me interested the whole way through.

[from the writing model]

Most splendid were the tableau wagons. Filled with carved and painted wooden figures, they are historical scenes on wheels. A woman dressed as Cleopatra rode a tableau pulled by camels. A two-headed green dragon roared from the top of a tableau that celebrated the age of knights and castles.

12 Narrative Writing

Technology Tip for 21st Century Literacies

Ask students to take on the role of citizen journalist, telling the stories that emerge from their experiences in school, in the community, or at home. Citizen journalists use digital images, audio recordings, and video to capture events from a participant's perspective. Compile these multimodal texts into a series of slides on a tool like Present.Me to share, cross-comment, and publish outside of the classroom. The key 21st century skill here is to use multimodal content to share events/story/perspective to engage, inform, or motivate others.

See **www.sfw.z-b.com** for further information about and links to these websites and tools.

Conventions

- All the sentences are correct and complete.

I went back and checked Joe's account to see if there were any mistakes. There aren't any sentence fragments or run-ons because every sentence has a subject and a verb. Joe also uses coordinating conjunctions such as *but* to join shorter sentences. None of the words are misspelled, and all sentences are capitalized and punctuated correctly.

[from the writing model]

The clowns were funny, but I was more impressed by the historic circus wagons. Each one showed off a dazzling color scheme. As the wheels turned, yellow and orange webbing between the spokes swirled like sunbursts.

+ Presentation The eyewitness account is legible and neat.

My Turn!

I'm going to write an eyewitness account of something that I have seen. I'll follow the rubric and use good writing strategies. Read on to see how I do it!

Presentation Explain that Presentation is just as important as any other trait. Emphasize the importance of neat handwriting or accurate typing, as well as the efficient use of white space (side/top/bottom margins and between paragraphs) to help organize the text on the page. Text that is easy on the eyes is also easier to read.

Think About the Traits Now ask students which traits they think are most important in an eyewitness account. Explain that all traits are important in every piece of writing, but some stand out more in some genres than in others. Some students may feel that the trait of **Ideas** is very important—after all, telling someone about the topic is the point of an eyewitness account. Others may think that **Word Choice** is important because the details and sensory language help the reader experience the events of the story.

Differentiating Instruction

ENRICHMENT

Explore Tone Explain that the feelings a writer expresses toward a situation help create tone, which is a part of the writer's voice. For example, the opening line *Last week I was amazed, astounded, flabbergasted, and stupefied!* from the model helps Joe express his awe of the circus parade. Have students choose a different tone, such as anger, boredom, or humor, and rewrite all or part of the model to reflect that tone.

REINFORCEMENT

Support Sentence Fluency Read the following version of the model aloud: *The clowns were funny. I was impressed by the historic circus wagons. Each showed a dazzling color scheme.* Then read the actual passage. Guide a discussion about which sentences are smoother and why.

CCSS Common Core State Standards
R/Lit.6.1: Cite textual evidence to support analysis of what the text says explicitly as well as inferences drawn from the text. **SL.6.1.c:** Pose and respond to specific questions with elaboration and detail by making comments that contribute to the topic, text, or issue under discussion. **SL.6.1.d:** Review the key ideas expressed and demonstrate understanding of multiple perspectives through reflection and paraphrasing.

Write
an Eyewitness Account

Week 2 • Day 1

Student Objectives

• Read and understand a prewriting strategy. *(p. 14)*

Prewrite

Focus on Ideas

Choose an Experience Discuss how Marco chose to write about the rodeo in Cody. Ask students how Marco's topic choice relates to the hobbies he lists on page 3. Review Marco's notes and talk about how they relate to the 5 W's. Discuss as a class how these details will help Marco write a descriptive account of his memory.

Now have students take a moment to choose an experience they wish to write about. Remind them to draw on their own interests, as Marco did. Once they have chosen a memory, instruct them to record as many details as possible. Remind them that they will remember more details as they begin to write but that they might decide not to include every detail in the writing. Being selective about which details to include is part of good writing.

Online Writing Center

Provides **interactive graphic organizers** as well as a variety of graphic organizers in PDF format.

Prewrite — Focus on Ideas

The Rubric Says	The narrator uses the 5 W's to establish a context for the event.
Writing Strategy	Choose an incident and record details to help answer the 5 W's.

I knew what I wanted to write about as soon as my teacher announced the assignment: the rodeo I saw last summer in Cody, Wyoming. There are so many details I remember. I think I'll jot down what I remember while keeping the 5 W's in mind. Using details to answer *who, what, where, when,* and *why* will help my reader better experience the event. It's amazing how vivid the sights, sounds, and smells of the rodeo still are in my mind.

My Notes on the Cody Stampede Rodeo
- ✔ every year during July 1–4, in Cody, Wyoming (when/where)
- ✔ smells like animal sweat and dust
- ✔ noisy: announcer, crowd cheering, buzzers, animals banging against fences
- ✔ Grand Entry parade: flag colors, 4th of July
- ✔ timed events: calf roping, barrel racing—fast cowgirl event
- ✔ bulldogging (steer wrestling): invented in early 1900s by Will Pickett, an African American cowboy (what)
- ✔ rough stock events: bareback, saddle bronc, bull riding—8 seconds and one hand (what)
- ✔ rodeo clowns: protect bull riders from bulls (who)
- ✔ pickup men: protect bronc riders from broncs (who)
- ✔ winners get prize money and rodeo buckle (why)

Apply

Choose an event you've witnessed. Then record what you remember, keeping in mind the 5 W's.

14 Narrative Writing

English Language Learners

BEGINNING/INTERMEDIATE

Sensory Details Prepare a set of index cards with sensory words associated with a place, such as a train station, for example, *rumble, smoke, whistle, people pushing,* and so on. Draw a web graphic organizer with the label *Train Station.* Label the outer circles with the five senses. Introduce a word on the index cards and ask students to tell which category the word belongs with. A word may fit in more than one category.

ADVANCED/ADVANCED HIGH

Sensory Details Briefly review the five senses. Present students with an object or idea, such as *a train.* Have partners list sensory details about it, making sure to include one idea for each of the five senses, if applicable. Prompt them to think about the sounds they hear in the train or at the station, the smells on the train, the colors they see, the special foods they might eat, and how the movement of the train feels.

Prewrite

Focus on **Organization**

The Rubric Says	An engaging lead introduces the event; the ending follows from the narrated event.
Writing Strategy	Make a 5 W's Chart to organize the notes.

✏ Writer's Term

5 W's Chart

A **5 W's Chart** organizes information according to what happened, who was there, why it happened, when it happened, and where it happened.

Now I need to organize my notes into a 5 W's chart. The chart will help me as I write my draft. With all my details organized, it'll be easier to write a strong, interesting lead and solid ending.

5 W's Chart

What **happened?** Buffalo Bill Cody Stampede Rodeo, bronc rider bucked high, bull rider thrown over horns, sharpshooter act

Who **was there?** my dad and I, cowboys and cowgirls, crowd, rodeo announcers and judges, clowns, animals, sharpshooter

Why **did it happen?** so cowboys and cowgirls can show off their skills and entertain people

When **did it happen?** July 1–4 last summer (and annually)

Where **did it happen?** Cody, Wyoming

Reflect
How will Marco's 5 W's chart help him write his draft?

Apply
Organize your ideas by using your notes to make a 5 W's Chart.

Eyewitness Account **15**

Conferencing

PEER TO PEER Have pairs exchange 5 W's Charts. Students should ask themselves: *Is all the important information here? Have all 5 W's been answered?* Students inform each other of any missing information.

PEER GROUPS Have students pass their 5 W's Charts around the group. Each student records on an index card one question he or she would like answered or a detail that seems misplaced. The index card and chart are then returned to the student to make any additions or adjustments.

TEACHER-LED Meet with students who are struggling to fill out their 5 W's Charts. Review the 5 W's, what information falls under each W, and why this information is important in an eyewitness account. Guide each student to see where additional information is needed.

Student Objectives

• Create a 5 W's Chart to organize the notes. *(p. 15)*

Prewrite

Focus on **Organization**

Make a 5 W's Chart Explain that good writers start by gathering their information and then organizing it. The organized information then guides the writing. Point out that a graphic organizer can help the writer notice if any essential information is missing. For example, if any rows were empty, Marco would have realized that he was missing information and filled it in prior to writing his draft. Have students use their notes to create 5 W's Charts of their own.

✏ Writer's Term

5 W's Chart One category that is sometimes added to the 5 W's is *H* for *How.* If the manner in which something was done is important to a narrative, writers may choose to create a chart that answers *Who, What, Why, When, Where,* and *How.*

CCSS Common Core State Standards

W.6.3: Write narratives to develop real or imagined experiences or events using effective technique, relevant descriptive details, and well-structured event sequences. **W.6.3.a:** Engage and orient the reader by establishing a context and introducing a narrator and/or characters; organize an event sequence that unfolds naturally and logically.

Write
an Eyewitness Account

Week 2 • Day 3

Student Objectives

• Begin writing, choosing the best details to keep writers interested. *(p. 16)*

Draft

Focus on Ideas

Begin a Draft Make sure students understand the difference between a draft and a final copy. Explain that the main goal when writing a draft is to get ideas down on paper. Assure students that there will be time for revising and editing later.

One purpose of writing an eyewitness account is to describe the event, so descriptive—and, perhaps, unique—details are important. Emphasize that the details must be fresh and engaging; readers will become bored if the details are very ordinary and already known by the readers.

Have students use their 5 W's Charts to begin drafting their accounts. Remind them to select the best details to help readers imagine the event. Encourage students to refer to the rubric often as they write, just as Marco does.

Online Writing Center

Provides student eBooks with an **interactive writing pad** for drafting, revising, editing, and publishing.

Draft
Focus on **Ideas**

The Rubric Says	Strong details engage the reader and develop the event.
Writing Strategy	Use the best details to describe the event and keep readers interested.

Now I'll use my 5 W's Chart to write my draft. According to the rubric, I need to use strong details to engage my reader and develop the event. I've included lots of details in my 5 W's chart, but I'll be sure to use only the most vivid and descriptive details in my writing. Vague or incomplete details will only weaken my account and bore or confuse my readers. The rodeo was so exciting—I want my audience to feel that excitement, too!

I think I'll open with the announcer welcoming folks to the rodeo. That will be a really engaging lead! I'll begin writing and see how it goes. I'll do my best with spelling and grammar, but I won't worry too much about mistakes right now. I can always fix those later!

16 Narrative Writing

Differentiating Instruction

ENRICHMENT
Include Dialogue Encourage students to include at least one passage of dialogue between two characters to enliven their eyewitness accounts. The dialogue should help expose some of the 5 W's for readers and contain interesting descriptive details.

REINFORCEMENT
Practice Sensory Details Explain that sensory details appeal to the five senses and can be used to create vivid descriptions. Choose a location in the school or community with which students are familiar. Write the headings *Sight, Sound, Taste, Smell*, and *Touch* on the board. Have students think of sensory details about the location for each of the senses and write them on the board. Together, compose a paragraph to describe the location.

[DRAFT]

[engaging lead]   **Ride 'em, Cowboy!**

"Welcome, folks! Welcome to the annual Buffalo Bill Cody Stampede Rodeo in Cody, Wyoming!" the announcer's voice blared from the loudspeakers. "Let the Grand Entry begin!"

My dad and I yelled as the cowboys and cowgirls came by [detail] wearing colorful western clothes. Some of them wore patriotic colors because the rodeo took place over the Fourth of July.

We had been to the stampede three times before. Last year we sat in the Buzzard's Roost, the best seats in the arena. [detail] I could take in everything from up there. It was dusty, and I could smell animal sweat and hear the gates banging and see the cowboys hanging out. It was like a big stable.

Timed events were first on the program. Mainly ropeing and racing against the clock. Calf ropeing shows off ranching skills. I was watching to learn more about ropeing, I had to feel for the calves. A calf would take off from the shoot. Then suddenly it would be on the ground with a rope tied in a half hitch around three legs.

Reflect

What do you think of Marco's lead? Is it engaging? Has he included interesting details to hold his readers' attention?

Apply

Use your 5 W's chart to help you write a draft of your account. Include engaging details to hold your readers' interest.

Eyewitness Account **17**

Conferencing

PEER TO PEER Pairs exchange drafts and 5 W's Charts. Each student looks to see that all critical information from the chart is not only used, but used in the beginning of the account to help the reader understand the narrative. Partners offer suggestions for clarifying the 5 W's in the draft.

PEER GROUPS Small groups of students take turns reading their drafts aloud. After each draft is read, each group member notes a detail he or she found especially helpful in picturing the story, and then suggests one area where more details are needed.

TEACHER-LED Meet with pairs of students. As one student reads his or her draft aloud, the other listens for vivid, descriptive details. Coach students in offering constructive suggestions for commenting on each other's narratives.

Write
an Eyewitness Account

Week 2 • Day 4

Student Objectives

- Complete a draft. (p. 17)

Finish a Draft Read Marco's draft on page 17 aloud as students refer to his 5 W's Chart on page 15. Ask:

- Do the details Marco has included so far paint a vivid and clear image of the rodeo? (yes)

- What senses has Marco described so far? (sight, sound, smell)

Point out how Marco took the details from his 5 W's Chart and expanded on them, using his memory to fill in the gaps. Assure students that more details will come to them as they write their drafts, too.

Remind students that Marco is not worried about making mistakes in spelling and grammar at this time. He knows this is the time to get his ideas down clearly and in order. Assure students that there will be plenty of time later on to fix any mistakes they might make.

CCSS **C**ommon **C**ore **S**tate **S**tandards

W.6.3.b: Use narrative techniques, such as dialogue, pacing, and description, to develop experiences, events, and/or characters. **W.6.3.d:** Use precise words and phrases, relevant descriptive details, and sensory language to convey experiences and events. **W.6.10:** Write routinely over extended time frames (time for research, reflection, and revision) and shorter time frames (a single sitting or a day or two) for a range of discipline-specific tasks, purposes, and audiences.

Write
an Eyewitness Account

Week 2 • Day 5

Student Objectives

- Revise for a strong beginning and ending. *(p. 18)*

Revise

Focus on Organization

Write a Strong Beginning and Ending Explain that writing a strong beginning is like using just the right bait when fishing—you want to "hook" your reader's attention and hold it for the entire narrative. Add that writing a strong ending—an ending that wraps up all loose ends, answers questions, and reflects back on the story—is just as important. There is nothing more disappointing than reading an exciting story, only to find that the ending is weak, abrupt, or disconnected from the rest of the story.

Then direct students' attention to Marco's draft excerpt. Read aloud the versions before and after the revision. Discuss as a class how the revised sentence reflects back on the story and wraps up Marco's impressions of the rodeo. Instruct students to revise their own writing for a strong beginning and ending.

 Strategies for Writers Online
Go to **www.sfw.z-b.com** for additional online resources for students and teachers.

Revise — Focus on **Organization**

The Rubric Says	An engaging lead introduces the event; the ending follows from the narrated event.
Writing Strategy	Write a strong beginning and ending.

After I wrote my draft, I checked the beginning again and decided that it is strong. It's interesting and engages the reader. But my ending needs work. I want my reader to take away the idea that the rodeo experience was fun and memorable. I think I'll add details to the last sentence.

> **[DRAFT]**
>
> On the last night, the winners got to take home prize money and a rodeo trophy: a belt buckle. ~~It was late and I went home tired.~~ I took home a new rodeo poster and a saddlebag of memories.

Apply

Try adding details to your account that make the beginning and ending strong and engaging.

18 Narrative Writing

English Language Learners

BEGINNING/INTERMEDIATE

Feelings Demonstrate various feelings using gestures and facial expressions, such as happiness, sadness, fear, and so on. Write each word as you introduce it. Tell students these are *feelings*. Write the word and have students repeat. As students' abilities allow, introduce ways to describe certain feelings in their writing; for example, *A tear ran down my face.*

ADVANCED/ADVANCED HIGH

Varied Sentence Beginnings Write the following sentence on the board: *The frog quickly jumped into the lake as I got closer to it.* Challenge partners to work together to determine how the sentence can be changed so the beginning is different but the point of the sentence remains the same. If students need help, prompt them with new sentence starters, such as *As I got closer, Quickly, In an instant,* and so on.

Revise

Focus on Voice

The Rubric Says	The voice is expressive and engages the reader throughout.
Writing Strategy	Share your feelings about the topic.

One way I can be expressive is by using words and phrases that let my reader know how I feel, such as *Let the grand entry begin!* and *the best seats in the arena.* If I reveal a variety of feelings, I'll help the reader share my experience. Take a look at how I changed the sentences below to convey how scary it was to see a cowboy almost get hurt.

[DRAFT]

At the stampede, I saw a Brahma Bull ~~come out of~~ the shoot
explode from
, twisting like a tornado   flipped over the bull's horns and flopped
~~and twist around a lot.~~ The rider ~~fell off the bull and landed at~~

its feet.

Reflect

How do Marco's changes help you as a reader share his feelings?

Apply

Add expressive words and phrases that show your feelings about what is happening.

Eyewitness Account **19**

Conferencing

PEER TO PEER Student pairs exchange and read each other's drafts. Students should focus on the beginning and ending. Does the opening grab the reader's attention? Does the ending satisfy? Students then offer ways to strengthen either.

PEER GROUPS Divide students into small groups. Each student takes a turn reading his or her draft aloud. Each listening student then points out one strength in either the beginning or ending and makes one suggestion on how to strengthen either.

TEACHER-LED Meet with individual students. Have each student listen as you read his or her draft aloud. Together, discuss any weaknesses your or the student noticed in the beginning or ending as you read. Help the student think of ways to improve the beginning and ending.

Write
an Eyewitness Account

Week 3 • Day 1

Student Objectives

- Revise to share personal feelings about the topic. *(p. 19)*

Revise

Focus on Voice

Share Your Feelings Explain that readers would rather have a writer *show* them how he or she is feeling about an event than simply tell them. For example, the phrase *I shook from my head to my toes in anticipation* is much more expressive than *I was so excited I was shaking.* Explain that when writers share how they feel about a topic in a creative way, readers stay interested in the writing and find it easier to share in those emotions.

Have a volunteer read the draft excerpt aloud, first without the revisions, and then with the revisions. Discuss as a class how the revised text helps readers better understand and share in Marco's feelings. Now have students revise their own writing to find ways to share their feelings about their topics.

CCSS Common Core State Standards

W.6.3.a: Engage and orient the reader by establishing a context and introducing a narrator and/or characters; organize an event sequence that unfolds naturally and logically. **W.6.3.b:** Use narrative techniques, such as dialogue, pacing, description, to develop experiences, events, and/or characters. **W.6.3.d:** Use precise words and phrases, relevant descriptive details, and sensory language to convey experiences and events. **W.6.3.e:** Provide a conclusion that follows from the narrated experiences or events.

Eyewitness Account **T19**

Write
an Eyewitness Account

Week 3 • Day 2

Student Objectives

- Revise to use words and phrases that convey ideas precisely. *(p. 20)*

Revise

Focus on  Word Choice

Use Descriptive Words On the board, write *Walking around, I watched out the window for the bus.* To show how precise language can pull the reader into the writing, write the revised sentence, *Pacing back and forth, I peered eagerly out the window for the bus.* Ask:

- How do the two sentences differ? (Possible responses: The first sentence gives basic information. The second sentence describes the scene more clearly.)

Discuss how each of Marco's revisions paints a clear picture. Instruct students to revise their own writing, replacing vague, common words with precise ones.

Writer's Term

Common Words Some common adjectives to watch out for are *interesting, bad, happy,* and *sad.* Common nouns include *things* and *stuff.* Common verbs that can often be replaced include *say, be,* and *get.*

Online Writing Center

 Provides **interactive proofreading activities** for each genre.

Revise

Focus on Word Choice

The Rubric Says	Descriptive and sensory language helps the reader create a precise picture of the event.
Writing Strategy	Choose words and phrases to convey ideas precisely.

The rubric encourages me to use descriptive sensory language. I know that I enjoy reading descriptions that help me create images in my mind. I'll be sure to choose my words carefully so that I can help readers "see" and "hear" the rodeo in their own minds.

Writer's Term

Common Words

Common words are plain and boring. Their meanings are so general that they do not create a clear picture in the reader's mind. Words such as **nice, good, big,** and **beautiful** are examples of common words.

[DRAFT]

whooped   paraded past, decked out in
My dad and I ~~yelled~~ as the cowboys and cowgirls ~~came by~~
                 shirts, hats, belts, boots, and chaps
~~wearing~~ colorful western ~~clothes~~.

[replaced common words]

Apply

Replace common words with descriptive sensory language to help your readers clearly picture your event.

20 Narrative Writing

Optional Revising Lessons

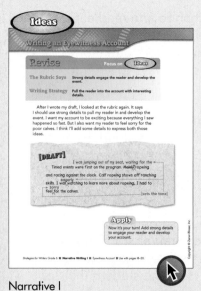

Narrative 1

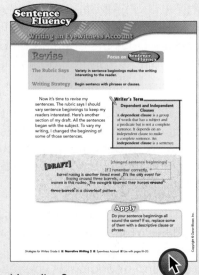

Narrative 2

 Go to **Strategies for Writers Grade 6 CD-ROM**

Edit

Focus on Conventions

The Rubric Says	All the sentences are correct and complete.
Writing Strategy	Fix sentence fragments, run-on sentences, and comma splices.

✏️ Writer's Term

Sentence Fragments/Run-Ons
A **sentence fragment** is a group of words that begins with a capital letter and ends with a period or other end punctuation but does not state a complete thought. A **run-on sentence** and a comma splice are made up of two simple sentences that are run together and are not joined properly by a conjunction or a semicolon.

I need to check my spelling, punctuation, and capitalization. The rubric also says that all sentences should be correct and complete. That means there should be no sentence fragments, run-on sentences, or comma splices. A sentence fragment is missing a subject or a predicate. A run-on sentence and a comma splice string thoughts together without a conjunction or a semicolon.

[DRAFT]

[fixed capitalization and spelling]

Cowboys called "pickup men" protect the bronc riders from the
, and
broncs rodeo clowns protect the bull riders from the bulls.

At the stampede, I saw a Brahma Bull explode from the chute
shoot, twisting like a tornado.

[joined compound sentence correctly]

Reflect

Is Marco's account free of sentence fragments, run-on sentences, and comma splices? Are the sentences correct and easy to follow?

Apply — Conventions

Edit your draft for spelling, punctuation, and capitalization. Be sure to fix sentence fragments, run-ons, and comma splices.

For more practice fixing fragments, run-ons, and comma splices, use the exercises on the next two pages.

Eyewitness Account **21**

Related Grammar Practice _____

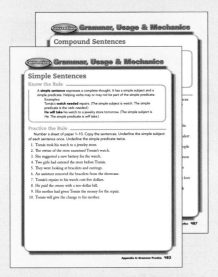

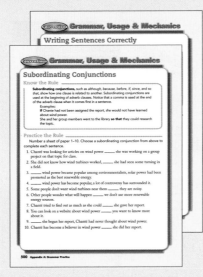

Student Edition pages 483, 487, 500, 506

Go to ▷ **Appendix A: Grammar Practice**

Write
an Eyewitness Account

Week 3 • Day 3

Student Objectives

• Edit to fix sentence fragments, run-on sentences, and comma splices. *(p. 21)*

Edit

Focus on Conventions

Use Complete Sentences Remind students that a complete sentence has a subject and a verb and is a complete thought. A run-on sentence or comma splice can be fixed by breaking the sentence into two sentences or by joining the two ideas with a semicolon or a comma and a conjunction.

Teach the mini-lessons on T22 and T23 and have students complete the exercises on pages 22 and 23.

✏️ Writer's Term _____

Sentence Fragments/Run-ons
To determine if a sentence is a fragment, ask yourself: *Who* is doing *what*? If you cannot answer either who or what, then you most likely have a fragment. If you read the sentence aloud and it sounds like it needs a pause, it is most likely a run-on.

CCSS Common Core State Standards
W.6.3.d: Use precise words and phrases, relevant descriptive details, and sensory language to convey experiences and events. **L.6.1:** Demonstrate command of the conventions of standard English grammar and usage when writing or speaking. **L.6.2:** Demonstrate command of the conventions of standard English capitalization, punctuation, and spelling when writing. **L.6.2.b:** Spell correctly.

Eyewitness Account **T21**

Conventions

Mini-Lesson

Student Objectives

• Learn to identify and correct sentence fragments, run-ons, and comma splices. *(p. 22)*

Sentence Fragments, Run-ons, and Comma Splices

Emphasize that a sentence must contain a subject and a predicate.

Write the following on the board: *My twin sisters, Tina and Rosa.*

Ask if this is a complete sentence or a sentence fragment. (sentence fragment) What is missing? (predicate) Ask for suggestions on how to make the fragment a complete sentence. (Possible response: My twin sisters, Tina and Rosa, graduated from high school.)

Run-on sentences and comma splices are two simple sentences that run together and are not joined correctly or clearly.

Write the following on the board: *Hybrid cars are fuel-efficient their engines rely on both gasoline and electric power.* Ask if this is a compound sentence or run-on. (run-on) What is missing? (a comma and a conjunction or semicolon) Ask for suggestions on how to correct it. (Possible response: Hybrid cars are more fuel-efficient; their . . .)

 Strategies for Writers Online

Go to **www.sfw.z-b.com** for additional online resources for students and teachers.

T22 *Narrative Writing*

Sentence Fragments, Run-ons, and Comma Splices

Know the Rule

A sentence that is missing a subject or a predicate is called a **fragment**.
> **Fragment:** Looked forward to the rodeo. (subject missing)
> **Fragment:** A clown on the fence. (predicate missing)

When you join two sentences as a **compound sentence,** put a comma followed by a conjunction between them. You can also join them with a semicolon. Sentences that are not joined correctly are called **run-ons** or **comma splices**.
> **Run-on:** Rodeo clowns look funny they take their work seriously.
> **Comma splice:** Rodeo clowns look funny, they take their work seriously.
> **Correct:** Rodeo clowns look funny, but they take their work seriously.
> **Correct:** Rodeo clowns look funny; they take their work seriously.

Practice the Rule

Number a sheet of paper 1–10. Identify the problem with each item below. Write the problem on your paper. Then rewrite sentences 8–10 correctly.

1. Gripping the reins tightly. fragment
2. Bulls with names like Turbo and Jackhammer. fragment
3. Streaked from the chute like a shot from a cannon. fragment
4. The announcer named the winners, the crowd cheered for each one. comma splice
5. Some people protest the use of animals in rodeos rodeo animals are treated well. run-on
6. Compete for money and prizes. fragment
7. Rodeo performers work hard, they enjoy their work. comma splice
8. The cowboy hit the ground hard the crowd gasped. run-on
9. Was handed the grand prize as the crowd clapped and cheered. fragment
10. Fearless Frank, last year's champion. fragment

Possible answers:
8. The cowboy hit the ground hard, and the crowd gasped.
9. The champion was handed the grand prize as the crowd clapped and cheered.
10. Fearless Frank, last year's champion, won the rodeo again.

Related Grammar Practice

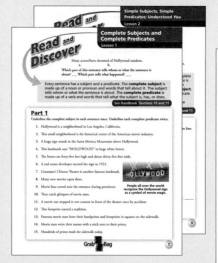

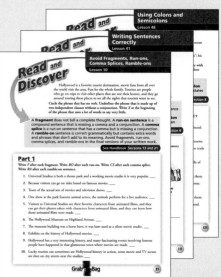

Pages 7, 9, 25, III, 125

Go to ⟹ **G.U.M. Student Practice Book**

Coordinating Conjunctions

Know the Rule

> **Coordinating conjunctions** (*and, but, or*) connect words or groups of words (including independent clauses) that are similar. They can be used to fix run-on sentences, sentence fragments, and comma splices.
>
> **Examples:** Elephants decorated with jewels paraded down Main Street, and two camels pulled a fancy circus wagon.
>
> The clowns are funny, but some people like the trapeze artists better.
>
> You can see the main act in the Big Top, or you can go to the smaller carnival acts.

Practice the Rule

Number a sheet of paper 1–10. Use coordinating conjunctions to correct the sentence fragments, run-on sentences, and comma splices. Then write the complete sentences on a separate piece of paper.

1. At the rodeo you can sit in the stands, *or* you can walk around and buy food at the stalls.
2. Steer wrestling is one of the fastest rodeo events, *and* it often takes only three or four seconds.
3. Two cowboys try to rope the head of a cow, *but* in team roping they can rope the legs.
4. In barrel racing, a horse and rider race around barrels set in a pattern, *but* this event is about speed.
5. You can see calf roping, *and* you can also see bull riders.
6. A rodeo cowboy competes in rodeo events, *and* he earns more money when he wins.
7. The saddles used in saddle bronc riding are lightweight, *and* they have no saddle horn.
8. The pickup men at a rodeo rescue riders from their horses, *and* they manage horses and bulls.
9. This year I'm taking Grandpa Jack, *and* we'll celebrate his birthday at the rodeo.
10. He's always wanted to go, *but* he's always been too busy to attend.

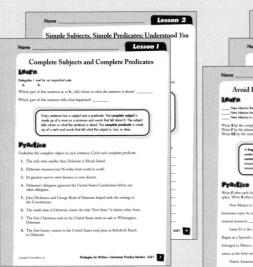
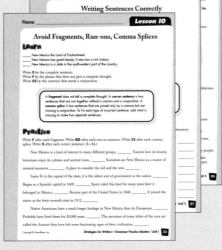

Pages 7, 9, 25, 87, 101

Go to ▷ Grammar Practice Masters

Mini-Lesson

Student Objectives

- Learn to use coordinating conjunctions correctly. *(p. 23)*

Coordinating Conjunctions

Have students read the Know the Rule box. Write the following coordinating conjunctions on the board: *and, but, or*. Explain that *and* is used when linking similar ideas together, *but* is used when discussing an exception, and *or* is used when only one of two or more ideas applies.

Write the following on the board:

I would love to go to the movies, _____ I have not finished my homework. (but)

Tonight's dinner was delicious, _____ the dessert was great, too! (and)

Charlie can choose to sleep over at Liam's house _____ he can come with us to Grandma's instead. (or)

Call on volunteers to determine which coordinating conjunction best joins the clauses above. If necessary, use examples similar to these to continue the lesson. Have students complete page 23. Then review the answers together.

CCSS **C**ommon **C**ore **S**tate **S**tandards

L.6.1: Demonstrate command of the conventions of standard English grammar and usage when writing or speaking. **L.6.2:** Demonstrate command of the conventions of standard English capitalization, punctuation, and spelling when writing. **L.6.3:** Use knowledge of language and its conventions when writing, speaking, reading, or listening.

Write an Eyewitness Account

Week 3 • Day 4

Student Objectives

- Discuss preparation for publishing and presentation. *(p. 24)*
- Use a final editing checklist to publish their work. *(p. 24)*

Publish ✛Presentation

Publishing Strategy Ask students if they like Marco's choice for sharing his eyewitness account. Tell the class that his choice is not the only option for publishing his work. Invite students to name other ways they could publish their own eyewitness accounts. Encourage students to share copies of their eyewitness accounts with friends and relatives, especially those who may have shared the experience with them.

Review Marco's final checklist. Have each student make a checklist of his or her own, based on Marco's checklist but tailored to his or her own writing.

Online Writing Center

 Provides **interactive grammar games** and **practice activities** in student eBook.

Publish ✛Presentation

Publishing Strategy	Add your account to a class journal.
Presentation Strategy	Use neat handwriting or word processing.

Now it's time to publish my eyewitness account. There are a lot of ways to publish my work, but I've decided to put my account into my class journal. I want my account to be easy to read, so I need to make sure I use neat handwriting and watch the letter and word spacing. Or I could choose a couple of clear readable fonts on the computer. Before publishing my work, I want to read through it one last time to make sure it includes all the items on my final checklist.

My Final Checklist

Did I—

- ✔ check for sentence fragments, run-on sentences, and comma splices?
- ✔ use neat handwriting or a couple of clear fonts on the computer?
- ✔ check spelling, capitalization, and punctuation?

Apply
Check your eyewitness account against your own checklist. Then make a final copy to publish.

24 Narrative Writing

Differentiating Instruction

ENRICHMENT

Multimedia Presentation Suggest students collect short videos, audio recordings, or photographs relating to their eyewitness accounts to display along with the text. The items can come from students' personal collections, or students can gather related images online.

REINFORCEMENT

Support Word-Processing Skills Pair students who need guidance with word-processing skills with more computer-literate students. Features to be reviewed are using the tab key; setting margins; selecting a font; and saving, retrieving, and printing a file.

RIDE 'EM, COWBOY!

by Marco

"Welcome, folks! Welcome to the annual Buffalo Bill Cody Stampede Rodeo in Cody, Wyoming!" the announcer's voice blared from the loudspeakers. "Let the Grand Entry begin!"

My dad and I whooped as the cowboys and cowgirls paraded past, decked out in colorful western shirts, hats, belts, boots, and chaps. Some wore red, white, and blue because the rodeo took place over the Fourth of July.

We had been to the Stampede three times before, but this time we sat in the Buzzard's Roost, the best seats in the arena. From up there, I could take in the entire scene. I could smell animal sweat, hear the gates banging, and see the cowboys hanging out. It was like a big, dusty stable.

Timed events were first on the program. I was jumping out of my seat, waiting for the roping and racing against the clock. Calf roping shows off ranching skills. I was eagerly watching to learn more about roping, but I had to feel sorry for the calves. One second a calf was running from the chute, and less than 30 seconds later it was on the ground bawling, with a rope tied in a half hitch around three legs.

Eyewitness Account 25

Technology Tip for 21st Century Literacies

Have students identify a compelling need in the community and then create a blog to communicate the need through words, images, and audio to share the message, recruit support, and so on. Share the blog's URL through Twitter or a school e-mail list. Encourage students to create a multimodal text (i.e., the blog) that will tell a story and mobilize action.

See **www.sfw.z-b.com** for further information about and links to these websites and tools.

Write
an Eyewitness Account

Week 3 • Day 5

Student Objectives

- Use an eyewitness account rubric. *(pp. 8–9)*
- Share a published eyewitness account. *(pp. 25–27)*

Presentation Strategy Discuss the importance of the appearance of a piece of writing. Messy handwriting or inaccurate typing will frustrate readers and drive them away. Encourage students to take advantage of computer features to make an attractive presentation. They should use the header-footer feature to label pages with page numbers, and the tab key to make uniformly indented paragraphs. There should be one clear font for the body text and a display font for the title.

CCSS Common Core State Standards

W.6.5: With some guidance and support from peers and adults, develop and strengthen writing as needed by planning, revising, editing, rewriting, or trying a new approach. **W.6.6:** Use technology, including the Internet, to produce and publish writing as well as to interact and collaborate with others; demonstrate sufficient command of keyboarding skills to type a minimum of three pages in a single sitting. **SL.6.5:** Include multimedia components (e.g., graphics, images, music, sound) and visual displays in presentations to clarify information.

Reflecting on an Eyewitness Account

Have students use the rubric on pages 8 and 9 to assess how well Marco did. What score would students give Marco for each trait? Be sure students can support their answers with specific examples from the text. Encourage students to refer to the rubric to assess their own narratives.

Then have students think back on this assignment as a whole. Encourage students to share how they feel about the experience. You might ask:

- How effective was the use of a 5 W's Chart as a guide? Is there a different graphic organizer you could use the next time you write an eyewitness account?

- How was writing an eyewitness account different from writing a personal narrative or short story?

- What trait is the strongest in your writing? What makes it strong?

Have students record their answers in a writing journal or discuss them as a class or in small groups.

 Strategies for Writers Online
Go to **www.sfw.z-b.com** for additional online resources for students and teachers.

Barrel racing is another timed event. If I remember correctly, it's the only event for women in this rodeo. Racing around three barrels, the cowgirls spurred their horses in a cloverleaf pattern. Skillfully, they avoided knocking down any barrels.

Almost 100 years ago, an African American cowboy named Will Pickett invented steer wrestling—my favorite timed event. Leaning off the side of his horse, he seized a steer by its horns and slid to the ground. Then he dug in his boot heels and twisted the steer over onto its side. Pickett called it "bulldogging." At the Stampede, the steers were dropping like flies.

Rough stock is the tough stuff: bareback riding, saddle bronc riding, and bull riding. To qualify for the next round in rough stock events, a cowboy has to hang on to a bucking beast with one hand and hold out for at least eight seconds. The first bareback rider flew so high you could see daylight between him and the horse. Yee haw! If the rider's free hand touches anything, the judges disqualify him. Then the announcer always remarks, "Let's give him a hand, folks. It may be all he's taking home tonight."

Rodeo is downright dangerous. Broken bones, cuts and bruises, pulled muscles, and concussions are common. Riders are sometimes trampled. Cowboys called "pickup men" protect the bronc riders from the broncs, and rodeo clowns protect the bull riders from the bulls. At the Stampede, I saw a Brahma bull explode from the chute, twisting like a tornado. The rider flipped over the bull's horns and flopped at its feet. In a flash, a red-nosed rodeo clown distracted the bull, and the cowboy sprang up and scrambled over the fence to safety.

The Stampede always has a famous specialty act. One year, it was a trained buffalo. Last summer, it was a sharpshooter who also did tricks with a bullwhip and a lasso. He snapped a target from his own mouth with the whip! Crrrrack!

On the last night, the winners got to take home prize money and a rodeo trophy: a belt buckle. I took home a new rodeo poster and a saddlebag of memories.

Reflect

What do you think? Did Marco use all the traits of a good eyewitness account in his writing? Does your writing have all the traits of a good eyewitness account? Be sure to check it against the rubric.

Eyewitness Account 27

CCSS **Common Core State Standards**

SL.6.1.c: Pose and respond to specific questions with elaboration and detail by making comments that contribute to the topic, text, or issue under discussion. **SL.6.1.d:** Review the key ideas expressed and demonstrate understanding of multiple perspectives through reflection and paraphrasing.

Historical Episode Planner

WEEK 1

Day 1
Introduce
a Historical Episode

Student Objectives
- Review the elements of a historical episode.
- Consider purpose and audience.
- Learn the traits of narrative writing.

Student Activities
- Read and discuss **What's in a Historical Episode?** (p. 28)
- Read and discuss **Why write a Historical Episode?** (p. 29)
- Read **Linking Narrative Writing Traits to a Historical Episode.** (p. 30)

Day 2
Analyze
Read a Historical Episode

Student Objectives
- Read a model historical episode.

Student Activities
- Read **"Conquest of the Stratosphere."** (pp. 31–33)

Day 3
Analyze
Introduce the Rubric

Student Objectives
- Learn to read a rubric.

Student Activities
- Review **"Conquest of the Stratosphere."** (pp. 31–33)
- Read and discuss the **Historical Episode Rubric.** (pp. 34–35)

WEEK 2

Day 1
Write
Prewrite: Ideas

Student Objectives
- Read and understand a prewriting strategy.

Student Activities
- Read and discuss **Prewrite: Focus on Ideas.** (p. 40)
- Apply the prewriting strategy.

Day 2
Write
Prewrite: Organization

Student Objectives
- Create a Story Map to organize story elements.

Student Activities
- Read and discuss **Prewrite: Focus on Organization.** (p. 41)
- Reflect on the model Story Map.
- Apply the prewriting strategy to create a Story Map.
- Participate in a peer conference.

Day 3
Write
Draft: Organization

Student Objectives
- Use a Story Map to begin writing.

Student Activities
- Read and discuss **Draft: Focus on Organization.** (p. 42)
- Apply the drafting strategy by using a Story Map to write a draft.

WEEK 3

Day 1
Write
Revise: Word Choice

Student Objectives
- Revise to explain the meanings of any unfamiliar words.

Student Activities
- Read and discuss **Revise: Focus on Word Choice.** (p. 45)
- Participate in a peer conference.

Day 2
Write
Revise: Sentence Fluency

Student Objectives
- Revise to vary sentence patterns for meaning, reader interest, and style.

Student Activities
- Read and discuss **Revise: Focus on Sentence Fluency.** (p. 46)

Note: Optional Revising Lessons appear on the *Strategies for Writers* CD-ROM.

Day 3
Write
Edit: Conventions

Student Objectives
- Edit to ensure quotation marks and commas are used correctly.

Student Activities
- Read and discuss **Edit: Focus on Conventions.** (p. 47)

Note: Teach the Conventions mini-lessons (pp. 48–49) if needed.

Day 4	Day 5
Analyze Ideas, Organization, and Voice	**Analyze** Word Choice, Sentence Fluency, and Conventions

Student Objectives
- Read a model historical episode.
- Use the historical episode rubric.
- Use the model historical episode to study Ideas, Organization, and Voice.

Student Activities
- Review **"Conquest of the Stratosphere."** *(pp. 31–33)*
- Review the rubric. *(pp. 34–35)*
- Read and discuss **Using the Rubric to Study the Model.** *(pp. 36–37)*

Student Objectives
- Read a model historical episode.
- Use the historical episode rubric.
- Use the model historical episode to study Word Choice, Sentence Fluency, and Conventions.

Student Activities
- Review **"Conquest of the Stratosphere."** *(pp. 31–33)*
- Read and discuss **Using the Rubric to Study the Model.** *(pp. 38–39)*

Day 4	Day 5
Write Draft	**Write** Revise: Voice

Student Objectives
- Complete a draft.

Student Activities
- Finish the draft. *(p. 43)*
- Participate in a peer conference.

Student Objectives
- Revise to show knowledge and caring about the topic.

Student Activities
- Read and discuss **Revise: Focus on Voice.** *(p. 44)*
- Reflect on a model draft.
- Apply the revising strategy.

Day 4	Day 5
Write Publish: +Presentation	**Write** Publish: +Presentation

Student Objectives
- Discuss preparation for publishing and presentation.
- Use a final editing checklist to publish their work.

Student Activities
- Read and discuss **Publish: +Presentation.** *(p. 50)*

Student Objectives
- Use a historical episode rubric.
- Share a published historical episode.

Student Activities
- Share their work.
- Use the rubric to reflect upon and evaluate the model and their own writing. *(pp. 34–35, 51–53)*

To complete the chapter in fewer days, combine the learning objectives and activities in a way that supports students as they write.

Resources at-a-Glance

Grammar, Usage & Mechanics

Differentiating Instruction
For additional Differentiating Instruction activities, see Strategies for Writers *Extensions Online at* **www.sfw.z-b.com.**

English Language Learners

Conferencing

Technology Tip

 Connection Letter
Reproducible letter (in English and Spanish) appears on the *Strategies for Writers* CD-ROM and at **www.sfw.z-b.com.**

Online Writing Center
Provides IWB resources, interactive games and practice activities, videos, eBooks, and a virtual file cabinet.

 Strategies for Writers Online
Go to **www.sfw.z-b.com** for free online resources for students and teachers.

Introduce
a Historical Episode

Week 1 • Day 1

Student Objectives

- Review the elements of a historical episode. *(p. 28)*
- Consider purpose and audience. *(p. 29)*
- Learn the traits of narrative writing. *(p. 30)*

What's a Historical Episode?

Discuss with students the definition of a historical episode. Ask students whether any of them have ever read a fictional narrative with a plot that took place during a historical era. Ask for volunteers to share a quick synopsis of the books. Point out that any time writers base stories on actual historical events, they are using the historical episode genre.

What's in a Historical Episode?

Read and discuss with students the various elements of a historical episode as outlined on page 28. Ask volunteers which elements are also common to other forms of writing. (Possible responses: Setting— fiction, memoir; Characters—short story, folktale; Accuracy—opinion essay, scientific report; Interest— poetry, adventure story) Discuss why each element is important in a historical episode.

 Strategies for Writers Online
Go to **www.sfw.z-b.com** for additional online resources for students and teachers.

What's a Historical Episode?

It's a story that's based on an actual time, place, event, or person in history. Both fact and fiction can be woven together. I like this kind of writing because I can be creative while making history come alive.

What's in a Historical Episode?

Setting
This is the time and place of my story. I want to make sure my readers understand the historical period I'm writing about.

Characters
I can write about real people from history or make up fictional characters. I just need to be sure my characters act like real people from the past.

Accuracy
This is important for the true parts of my story. I don't want to give my readers incorrect information, so I'll research my facts very carefully.

Interest
My story won't bring history to life if it's just a list of facts. I need to focus on an exciting problem or a fascinating event. I'll use an interesting beginning and clear details to keep my readers involved.

Narrative Text Exemplars (Historical Episode)

Yep, Lawrence. *Dragonwings.* HarperCollins, 1977.
CCSS A young Chinese boy joins his father in San Francisco at the turn of the twentieth century. The boy and his father experience prejudice as they work toward making a flying machine.

Park, Linda Sue. *A Single Shard.* Sandpiper, 2011.
Tree-ear is an orphan boy in twelfth-century Korea. After he accidentally breaks a pot, the boy embarks on a long and dangerous journey that will pay for the damaged pot and change his life forever.

Why write a Historical Episode?

Since I'm interested in history, I enjoy this kind of writing. There are many other reasons for writing a historical episode. I've listed some here.

Information
My readers can learn more about familiar topics or find out something completely new about history. I can share real information about historical people and events.

Entertainment
History is really interesting! It's fun to read about how people in the past lived, what they thought, and how they coped with life. I want to share that with my readers.

Research Skills
Even though a historical episode is partly fiction, I have to do a lot of research before writing. Practicing my research skills is important since I'll use them throughout my education.

Why write a Historical Episode?

Direct students to read and discuss the reasons for writing a historical episode on page 29. Point out that all writing has a purpose and is aimed at a specific audience. These authentic purposes help authors shape their writing. Ask a volunteer to read the Information box aloud. Then have students discuss other reasons someone might write a historical episode for information purposes. Repeat this process for the Entertainment and Research Skills boxes. Then have students brainstorm purposes for writing a historical episode that are not listed on page 29. Encourage students to ask their classmates questions to help clarify their ideas. Explain that students should think about their own reasons for writing a historical episode and how these reasons will affect the tone and focus of their writing.

Lowry, Lois. *Number the Stars.* **Sandpiper, 2001.**
In 1943, Annemarie and her best friend Ellen experience many hardships during the German occupation of Denmark. When the Jews in Denmark are relocated, Ellen moves in with Annemarie's family. Annemarie must do all she can to help shelter her Jewish friend from the Nazis.

Giff, Patricia Reilly. *Lily's Crossing.* **Bantam Doubleday Dell, 1999.** Every summer, Lily and her father and grandmother vacation at a beach house in New York's Rockaways. After her father enlists in the army to fight in World War II, Lily befriends a Hungarian refugee. Together, the two friends share their hopes, fears, and adventures.

CCSS Common Core State Standards

SL.6.1: Engage effectively in a range of collaborative discussions (one-on-one, in groups, and teacher-led) with diverse partners on *grade 6 topics, texts, and issues*, building on others' ideas and expressing their own clearly. **SL.6.1.b:** Follow rules for collegial discussions, set specific goals and deadlines, and define individual roles as needed. **SL.6.1.c:** Pose and respond to specific questions with elaboration and detail by making comments that contribute to the topic, text, or issue under discussion.

Introduce
a Historical Episode

Linking Narrative Writing Traits to a Historical Episode

Help students understand that they will follow Marco as he models using the writing process and the traits together. As they follow Marco through the writing process, students will see how the Narrative Writing Traits have been adapted and applied to writing a historical episode. They will see that a historical episode, which is a story, has many factors in common with other types of narrative writing. However, the particular audience and purpose of a historical episode determine how the traits are used.

Linking Narrative Writing Traits to a Historical Episode

In this chapter, you will write a story that takes place in a specific time period. This type of narrative writing is called a historical episode. Marco will guide you through the stages of the writing process: Prewrite, Draft, Revise, Edit, and Publish. In each stage, Marco will show you writing strategies that are linked to the Narrative Writing Traits below.

Narrative Writing Traits

 Ideas
- a focused topic, experience, or series of events
- engaging, accurate details that develop and describe the topic, experience, or series of events

 **Organization**
- logically sequenced events, often in chronological order
- an interesting beginning and a satisfying ending
- transitions that signal the sequence of events as well as shifts in time or setting

 Voice
- a voice and tone that are appropriate for the purpose and audience
- dialogue that, if used, fits the characters

 Word Choice
- precise, descriptive words and phrases

 Sentence Fluency
- a variety of sentences that flow and are a pleasure to read

 **Conventions**
- no or few errors in grammar, usage, mechanics, and spelling

Before you write, read Kim Lee's historical episode on the next three pages. Then use the rubric on pages 34–35 to decide how well she did. (Look back at What's in a Historical Episode? on page 28, too!)

Narrative Writing Traits in a Historical Episode

 Ideas The writer focuses on one historical event so as not to confuse the reader. The setting, characters, and events are accurate and vividly described; the reader finds the story believable and engaging.

 **Organization** The writer presents events in a logical, natural order. The beginning, middle, and ending are clearly defined and linked with helpful transitions.

 **Voice** The writer's voice is engaging and easy to connect with. It also clearly shows the writer's knowledge of the historical facts, lending additional credibility to the narrative.

Conquest of the Stratosphere

by Kim Lee

Setting

Characters

Two men sat across from each other on a train chugging through the Swiss Alps. They had met only an hour earlier, but they were enjoying each other's company. Auguste Piccard, the elder one, was a long-limbed professor. A wreath of wild hair encircled his balding crown. Small round glasses perched on his long slender nose. His mustache wiggled as he talked. Paul Kipfer, the younger man, had sandy hair and soft blue eyes. He didn't talk much. Instead, he listened intently as Auguste described his research on cosmic rays in the atmosphere.

After a pause in the conversation, Auguste asked Paul, "Are you married?"

"No," Paul replied.

Interesting beginning →

"Good," Auguste said eagerly. "Are you engaged?"

"No," said Paul, puzzled by Auguste's questions.

"Ah, wonderful!" Auguste exclaimed. "Would you like to go up into the stratosphere in a balloon with me? We could study the cosmic rays!"

In 1930, this was a dangerous proposal. The stratosphere begins six to eight miles above Earth's surface. It is deadly cold and lacks enough oxygen for survival. Paul knew that no one had ever been up there and returned alive. Balloons had only open-air baskets. Even airplanes did not yet have pressurized cabins to hold in oxygen.

← Accurate historical details

Auguste knew it was risky, too. That was why he wanted an assistant without a wife and family. Auguste's family accepted his determination to make the hazardous trip. Paul also felt the force of that determination. He listened to Auguste's plan. By the time the train arrived in Brussels, Belgium, where Auguste lived, Paul had agreed to be his assistant. *Setting*

Word Choice The writer uses plenty of vivid, sensory language to paint a complete image of the characters, setting, and events. All unfamiliar words are defined.

Sentence Fluency A good variety of sentence lengths, types, and structures gives the writing energy and flow. The historical episode is a joy to read or listen to.

Conventions The writing has been carefully edited for spelling, grammar, punctuation, and capitalization errors. All dialogue has been accurately punctuated, which helps the reader follow conversations between two or more characters.

Analyze
the Model

Week 1 • Day 2

Student Objectives

• Read a model historical episode. *(pp. 31–33)*

Read the Model

Have students read "Conquest of the Stratosphere" on pages 31–33. Before they read, remind students to refer to the elements of a historical episode on page 28, as well as the writing traits outlined on page 30.

Elements of a Historical Episode

Use the notes on the model to point out and discuss each of the elements of a historical episode. Ask:

• How would you feel about the story if Kim did not include dialogue? (Possible response: The story would be boring and difficult to follow.)

• What if the setting was unclear? (Possible response: It would be very hard to picture the action. Knowing the location and time in history is important in helping the reader get situated in the story.)

Ask students to talk about how each underlined element contributes to the narrative. Explain that each element must be present to create a solid, engaging historical episode.

CCSS Common Core State Standards
R/Lit.6.1: Cite textual evidence to support analysis of what the text says explicitly as well as inferences drawn from the text. SL.6.1.a: Come to discussions prepared, having read or studied required material; explicitly draw on that preparation by referring to evidence on the topic, text, or issue to probe and reflect on ideas under discussion. SL.6.1.d: Review the key ideas expressed and demonstrate understanding of multiple perspectives through reflection and paraphrasing.

Auguste took care of every detail. The giant balloon was made of rubberized cotton. Attached to it was a pressurized cabin. It consisted of an airtight aluminum sphere with portholes as windows. It included a system that recycled oxygen so it would last longer. No lightweight crash helmets were available in those days, so Auguste created some out of upside-down sewing baskets. He added seat cushions for padding. Accurate historical details

Accurate historical facts

On the morning of May 27, 1931, Paul and Auguste prepared for take-off in Augsburg, Germany. As the balloon was being inflated, Auguste imagined all he would learn on this scientific adventure. Suddenly, a gust of wind rolled the cabin off its platform, and it crashed to the ground. It had only slight damage, so the launch continued as scheduled.

A few minutes later, however, the men heard a hissing sound. The cabin was leaking air. Auguste patched the leak with petroleum jelly and waited with his fingers crossed.

Communication with the ground crew would be impossible. Radio was only in its infancy, and satellite technology was decades in the future. Like the early explorers, the scientists sailed alone into an uncharted world.

By afternoon, the balloon had safely risen nearly ten miles, well into the stratosphere. Auguste and Paul made some observations and measurements. Then they prepared for their descent, but something went wrong. The ropes that release the gas from the balloon had become tangled. The two men were stuck in the stratosphere!

Hours passed. The sun's heat raised the temperature inside the cabin to over 90 degrees. Sweating, the men eyed the gauges on the oxygen tanks in their silver bubble. Accurate historical facts

Auguste was certain that at nightfall the air in the balloon would cool, and they would start to descend. Yet even after the sun went down, the balloon did not. Around 6:00 A.M., Auguste wrote in his log, "We have oxygen left for only four hours."

Books for Professional Development

Urquhart, Vickie, and Monett McIver. *Teaching Writing in the Content Areas.* Alexandria, VA. ASCD, 2005. This book shows how to quickly integrate writing assignments into content areas by using strategic, practical tools. Included in the book are 35 classroom strategies that will help teachers guide students through the steps of preparing written assignments, getting their thoughts down, and refining their work.

Kendall, Juli, and Outey Khoun. *Writing Sense: Integrated Reading and Writing Lessons for English Language Learners K–8.* Portland, ME. Stenhouse, 2006. The prospect of teaching writing to a classroom full of students can be quite a challenge, even more so if those students learning English are at different levels. *Writing Sense* includes 68 classroom-tested lessons that integrate writing and reading instruction to help English language learners become stronger writers.

 Strategies for Writers Online
Go to **www.sfw.z-b.com** for additional online resources for students and teachers.

In the meantime, people around the world waited for each day's newspaper to learn about the fate of the scientists. Readers were troubled by headlines that the balloon was out of control. In the midst of a worldwide economic depression, people craved hope and heroes.

Finally, the balloon started to float slowly down. Auguste and Paul landed the next night on top of a glacier—but where? They crawled from the cramped cabin. Unprepared for a freezing climate, they wrapped themselves in the balloon fabric to stay warm. At dawn, they picked their way down the ice slope. A rescue party soon caught up with them.

Shivering, Auguste asked a round man with a pointed wool hat, "Wh—wh—what country are we in?"

"Austria," the man answered. "We're near a village called Obergurgl."

Auguste Piccard and Paul Kipfer had spent 16 hours inside the sphere. They had ascended 51,775 feet, a height no one had reached before. Not only did they gather valuable scientific data, but they also proved that people could survive in pressurized cabins high above Earth. Their conquest of the stratosphere paved the way for future air and space travel.

Wood, Karen D., and Janis M. Harmon. *Strategies for Integrating Reading and Writing in Middle and High School Classrooms*. Westerville, OH. NMSA, 2001. These easy-to-use, research-based strategies are designed to improve students' performance and interest in course content by increasing the time they spend reading and writing. Each chapter addresses a topic relevant to middle school and high school literacy and offers sample lessons to illustrate the application to various subject areas.

Graves, Donald H. *A Fresh Look at Writing*. Portsmouth, NH. Heinemann, 1994. This classic book is an informative and useful guide for teachers who want to implement classroom strategies to help students strengthen their writing skills. It explains how the use of strategies such as the author's chair and portfolios can help students practice and take pride in their writing.

CCSS **C**ommon **C**ore **S**tate **S**tandards

R/Lit.6.1: Cite textual evidence to support analysis of what the text says explicitly as well as inferences drawn from the text. **SL.6.1.a:** Come to discussions prepared, having read or studied required material; explicitly draw on that preparation by referring to evidence on the topic, text, or issue to probe and reflect on ideas under discussion. **SL.6.1.d:** Review the key ideas expressed and demonstrate understanding of multiple perspectives through reflection and paraphrasing.

Analyze the Model

Week 1 • Day 3

Student Objectives

- Learn to read a rubric.
  (pp. 34–35)

Use the Rubric

Explain the Rubric Explain that a rubric is a tool that helps you plan, improve, and evaluate a piece of writing. Tell students that a rubric helps a writer focus on key elements, or traits, in writing (**Ideas, Organization, Voice, Word Choice, Sentence Fluency, Conventions,** and **Presentation**).

The 6-point rubric on pages 34 and 35 is based on the Narrative Writing Traits on page 30. Draw attention to the six columns to explain how the scoring system works. Explain that the column under the 6 describes a historical episode that has received the highest score in all categories. This is what students should strive for in their own writing.

Discuss the Rubric Guide the students in a discussion of the rubric. Read the descriptors that go with each trait. Note how the descriptors vary as you move from column to column. Remind students to keep the rubric in mind when they write their own historical episode and again when they revise it.

Online Writing Center

Provides a variety of **interactive rubrics,** including 4-, 5-, and 6-point models.

Rubric

Use this 6-point rubric to plan and score a historical episode.

	6	5	4
Ideas	The episode focuses on one historical event. Details and quotes are credible, accurate, and interesting.	The writing focuses mainly on one event. Details and quotes are accurate and credible.	The writing sometimes strays from the historical event. Some details are vague or inaccurate.
Organization	The sequence of events in the episode unfolds naturally. Transitions guide the reader smoothly from the beginning to the end. There is a clear beginning, middle, and end.	The sequence of events is logical. Transitions guide the reader. There is a clear beginning, middle, and end.	The events are mostly easy to follow. Several transitions are used. There is a beginning, middle, and end.
Voice	The writer's voice is knowledgeable and connects with the audience throughout the episode.	The writer's voice is knowledgeable and engaging throughout most of the episode.	The writer's voice starts out strong and engaging but fades as the episode goes on.
Word Choice	Unfamiliar words are clearly defined for the reader.	Unfamiliar words are defined for the reader.	Some unfamiliar words are poorly defined, forcing the reader to stop and reread.
Sentence Fluency	There is great variety in length and structure of sentences. The writing is enjoyable to read.	Variety in sentence length and structure makes the writing easy to read.	There is some variety in sentence length and structure. The writing is easy to read.
Conventions	Quotation marks and commas are used correctly. The episode is easy to read and understand.	A few errors with quotation marks and commas do not distract the reader.	Some noticeable errors in quotation marks don't confuse the reader.
⁺Presentation	All the pages are labeled and numbered.		

34 Narrative Writing

CCSS Common Core State Standards

Historical Episode

As students learn to write a historical episode, they will receive instruction based on the Narrative writing standards, as well as several Speaking & Listening, Language, and Reading/Literature standards for grade 6.

The rubric and writing strategies for Ideas are based on standards **W.6.3, W.6.3.a, W.6.3.b,** and **W.6.3.d,** which encourage the writer to develop one topic and use narrative techniques such as the use of details to develop experiences, events, and/or characters. The rubric and writing strategies for Organization have a foundation in standards **W.6.3, W.6.3.a, W.6.3.c** and **W.6.3.e,** which outline the need for naturally sequenced events, an engaging beginning, an ending that reflects back on the narrative, and the use of

3	2	1	
It is not always clear which event is being described. Details may be lacking, and some are vague.	The episode does not focus on one event. The details are weak or incorrect.	The episode does not attempt to tell about an event. Details are missing or unrelated.	**Ideas**
Some of the events are out of order. More transitions would help the reader follow the story. The beginning or the end is weak and needs work.	The events are difficult to follow. Very few transitions are used. Both the beginning and the end need work.	The reader feels lost with the writer's list of random details. The beginning and the end are missing.	**Organization**
Sometimes the voice is present; sometimes it disappears. There is little connection to the reader.	The writer's voice is weak and does not engage with the reader.	The writer's voice is absent from the writing.	**Voice**
Several unfamiliar words are not defined or are poorly defined, making it hard for the reader to understand the episode.	The writer does not bother defining unfamiliar words, leaving the reader in the dark.	Words are incorrectly used, and definitions are missing.	**Word Choice**
Sentences are repetitive in beginnings and similar in length. The writing is choppy in places.	There are many choppy or incomplete sentences and very little variety in length or beginnings.	Many sentence problems make the writing a challenge to read.	**Sentence Fluency**
Many errors in the use of quotation marks and commas interfere with meaning.	The writing has many errors with quotation marks, commas, and other conventions that get in way of the message.	The writing has not been edited and is very difficult to read.	**Conventions**

See Appendix B for 4-, 5-, and 6-point narrative rubrics.

Apply the Rubric

A Show of Hands Have students reread "Conquest of the Stratosphere" on pages 31–33 and refer to the rubric on pages 34–35. When they have finished reading, ask students to review the descriptors for the trait of Ideas. Ask:

• Who would give Kim a six for Ideas? A five?

Continue through the row, counting and recording on the board the number of hands raised for each score. For visual clarity, record the information in a chart that mimics the rows and columns of the rubric. Repeat this process for the remaining five traits. Discuss the results, focusing on scores that are two or more points apart. Why is there such disparity in the scores? Ask students to defend their scores and then take a recount.

Additional Rubrics Appendix B includes 4-, 5-, and 6-point rubrics that can be used with any piece of narrative writing. The rubrics are also available as blackline masters in the back of this Teacher Edition, beginning on page T525.

effective transitions to guide the reader from one time frame to another. The rubric and writing strategies for Voice also reflect standards **W.6.3** and **W.6.3.b,** as this trait incorporates dialogue and description. The rubric and writing strategies for Sentence Fluency are grounded in Language standard **L.6.3.a,** which focuses on varying sentence patterns for meaning and reader interest.

Standards **L.6.1** and **L.6.2** are clearly reflected throughout the editing pages of the chapter, while standard **W.6.6** resonates throughout the entire Narrative unit, as students are encouraged to take full advantage of word-processing programs and to use a wide range of resources found on the Internet.

CCSS **C**ommon **C**ore **S**tate **S**tandards

SL.6.1.a: Come to discussions prepared, having read or studied required material; explicitly draw on that preparation by referring to evidence on the topic, text, or issue to probe and reflect on ideas under discussion.
SL.6.1.c: Pose and respond to specific questions with elaboration and detail by making comments that contribute to the topic, text, or issue under discussion.

Analyze
the Model

Week 1 • Day 4

Student Objectives

- Read a model historical episode. (pp. 31–33)
- Use the historical episode rubric. (pp. 34–35)
- Use the model historical episode to study Ideas, Organization, and Voice. (pp. 36–37)

Study the Model

Assess the Model Explain that pages 36–37 show how the model on pages 31–33 uses the writing traits described in the rubric. Read each section with students. Use questions such as the following to discuss each section.

- Why didn't Kim write about the years of research Auguste must have performed prior to the moment he met Paul? How would a story of that size affect this narrative? (Possible response: That would have been too large a story to fit into a narrative of this size. Important information would have been excluded, or too many details would have been clustered together in a confusing way.)

Strategies for Writers Online
Go to **www.sfw.z-b.com** for additional online resources for students and teachers.

Historical Episode
Using the Rubric to Study the Model

Did you notice that the model on pages 31–33 points out some key elements of a historical episode? As she wrote "Conquest of the Stratosphere," Kim Lee used these elements to help her describe an event in history. She also used the 6-point rubric on pages 34–35 to plan, draft, revise, and edit the writing. A rubric is a great tool to evaluate writing during the writing process. Now let's use the same rubric to score the model.

To do this, we'll focus on each trait separately, starting with Ideas. We'll use the top descriptor for each trait (column 6), along with examples from the model, to help us understand how the traits work together. How would you score Kim on each trait?

Ideas
- The episode focuses on one historical event.
- Details and quotes are credible, accurate, and interesting.

Kim focuses on one historical event throughout the episode. She includes details about the people and the event that are interesting and accurate. Her quotes sound like real conversation.

[from the writing model]

Auguste Piccard, the elder one, was a long-limbed professor. A wreath of wild hair encircled his balding crown. . . .

"Ah, wonderful!" Auguste exclaimed. "Would you like to go up into the stratosphere in a balloon with me?"

English Language Learners

BEGINNING

Parts of a Story On the board, draw three stick people on one side and a house on the other. Read a simple story. Make sure the story has characters and an obvious setting. After you finish reading, say the name of the character(s) (for example, Snow White) in the story you read. Ask, *Is Snow White a person or a place? Is the seven dwarfs' house a person or a place?* Introduce the terms *character* and *setting*. Write them on the board and have students repeat.

INTERMEDIATE

Parts of a Story Have a volunteer tell a favorite story, either from childhood or from a book they have recently read. Ask other students to listen carefully and identify the characters, setting, and basic plot of the story. Discuss as a class.

Organization

- The sequence of events in the episode unfolds naturally.
- Transitions guide the reader smoothly from the beginning to the end.
- There is a clear beginning, middle, and end.

Kim sequences the episode's events in chronological order, which makes sense. She uses transitions, such as *In the meantime* and *Suddenly*, to help the reader follow along. It's easy to tell which parts of the story are the beginning, middle, and end.

[from the writing model]

As the balloon was being inflated, Auguste imagined all he would learn on this scientific adventure. Suddenly, a gust of wind rolled the cabin off its platform, and it crashed to the ground.

Voice

- The writer's voice is knowledgeable and connects with the audience throughout the episode.

Kim's voice makes it easy for the reader to stay connected to the events of the balloon ride. In this paragraph, Kim describes the beginning of the men's descent. Notice how she draws the audience in with an exclamation about the danger the men are in.

[from the writing model]

Then they prepared for their descent, but something went wrong. The ropes that release the gas from the balloon had become tangled. The two men were stuck in the stratosphere!

Historical Episode 37

- Kim has presented events in the order in which they happened. Why is this important? (Possible responses: Chronological order allows the reader to follow the story from start to finish. Chronological order is often used in narratives.)

- How does Kim make her voice sound knowledgeable? (Possible response: She includes a lot of accurate facts about the science and history of the time.)

ADVANCED

Historical Settings Draw a chart of the board with the last 10 decades as column heads, for example *1910s, 1920s,* and so on. Set the following row heads: *Airplanes, Cars, Bicycles, Trains, Spacecraft, Motorcycles.* Have students work with a partner to determine if the items in each row—cars, for example—were widely used in each decade. They should use print or online encyclopedias to find unknown information. Tell students they will need to use such resources when researching the historical time periods for their historical episodes.

ADVANCED HIGH

Accurate and Credible Review the Ideas rubric on page 36. Point out the second bulleted item. Have volunteers explain the terms *accurate* and *credible.* Check students' understanding that they mean "correct" and "believable," respectively.

CCSS **Common Core State Standards**

R/Lit.6.1: Cite textual evidence to support analysis of what the text says explicitly as well as inferences drawn from the text. **R/Lit.6.3:** Describe how a particular story's or drama's plot unfolds in a series of episodes as well as how the characters respond or change as the plot moves toward a resolution. **SL.6.1.a:** Come to discussions prepared, having read or studied required material; explicitly draw on that preparation by referring to evidence on the topic, text, or issue to probe and reflect on ideas under discussion.

Analyze
the Model

Week 1 • Day 5

Student Objectives

- Read a model historical episode. *(pp. 31–33)*
- Use the historical episode rubric. *(pp. 34–35)*
- Use the model historical episode to study Word Choice, Sentence Fluency, and Conventions. *(pp. 38–39)*

Continue Discussing the Traits

Now use pages 38 and 39 to discuss how **Word Choice, Sentence Fluency,** and **Conventions** were used in the historical episode. Use the following questions:

- How would the reader's reaction to Kim's story be affected if she did not define unfamiliar terms? (Possible response: The story would be harder to understand; the reader might have to interrupt reading to look up words in a dictionary.)

- Choose a passage and explain why it flows well. (Possible response: *Kim starts the sixth paragraph on page 32 with a short, dramatic sentence and makes effective use of a verbal to begin the third sentence.*)

- Why is it important to punctuate dialogue accurately? (Possible responses: Otherwise, you never know who is speaking when. Missing quotation marks make it hard to know what is dialogue.)

Strategies for Writers Online
Go to **www.sfw.z-b.com** for additional online resources for students and teachers.

Word Choice
- Unfamiliar words are clearly defined for the reader.

Kim makes sure her readers know the meanings of unfamiliar words, such as *stratosphere* and *pressurized cabin*, so they can fully understand the story.

> [from the writing model]
>
> The stratosphere begins six to eight miles above Earth's surface. It is deadly cold and lacks enough oxygen for survival.

> [from the writing model]
>
> The giant balloon was made of rubberized cotton. Attached to it was a pressurized cabin. It consisted of an airtight aluminum sphere with portholes as windows. It included a system that recycled oxygen so it would last longer.

Sentence Fluency
- There is great variety in length and structure of sentences. The writing is enjoyable to read.

Kim varies her sentences to make her writing flow and to keep it lively. Read the following paragraph. Do you see how Kim uses sentences of different lengths? Some of her sentences start with a subject, and others start with a phrase. She even ends one sentence with a question!

> [from the writing model]
>
> Finally, the balloon started to float slowly down. Auguste and Paul landed the next night on top of a glacier—but where? They crawled from the cramped cabin. Unprepared for a freezing climate, they wrapped themselves in the balloon fabric to stay warm. At dawn, they picked their way down the ice slope. A rescue party soon caught up with them.

38 Narrative Writing

Technology Tip for 21st Century Literacies

Ask students to compile a series of digital images that either capture a historical episode or represent some aspect of the event. Assemble the images into a collage with a tool such as Shape Collage to communicate on two levels: through the individual images that are included and through the shape collage forms. Pair this with a reflective writing task so students articulate the reasoning behind their selections. How do the images work together to communicate what students know about the historical episode?

See **www.sfw.z-b.com** for further information about and links to these websites and tools.

Conventions

• Quotation marks and commas are used correctly. The episode is easy to read and understand.

Kim really knows how to use quotes. Every time a character speaks in this story, his exact words have quotation marks around them. She even uses dashes to help the reader understand how the character is speaking. It's a little unusual, but it's very effective!

[from the writing model]

Shivering, Auguste asked a round man with a pointed wool hat, "Wh—wh—what country are we in?"
"Austria," the man answered. "We're near a village called Obergurgl."

+Presentation All the pages are labeled and numbered.

My Turn!
Now I'm going to use the rubric to help me write a historical episode. Read along and see how I do it.

Historical Episode 39

Differentiating Instruction

ENRICHMENT
Expand Story Elements Challenge students to choose one existing element from "Conquest of the Stratosphere" and expand it in their own creative way. For example, students could establish a more detailed setting and describe the Swiss Alps or the village Obergurgl. Or perhaps they could use dialogue between the men to uncover more about Auguste's or Paul's past.

REINFORCEMENT
Support Ideas Some students may benefit from a closer examination of how the author blends fact and fiction in "Conquest of the Stratosphere." On the board, write the headings *Fact* and *Fiction*. Then work with a small group to review the story, asking for examples of each.

Presentation Point out that the appearance of a piece of writing is important. Remind students that producing neat and legible work is one way a writer shows respect for not only his or her own hard work but also the reader who is taking the time to enjoy the finished product. Explain that as historical episodes tend to be more than one page when finished, it is very important that students label and number each page in case the pages get separated.

Think About the Traits Ask students which traits they think are most important in a historical episode. Explain that all traits are important in every piece of writing, but some of the traits stand out more in some genres than in others. Some may feel that the trait of **Ideas** is important, as the topic, or experience, is at the heart of any narrative. Others may think that **Voice** is very important because the writer's voice is the element that makes a connection to the reader.

CCSS **Common Core State Standards**
R/Lit.6.1: Cite textual evidence to support analysis of what the text says explicitly as well as inferences drawn from the text. SL.6.1.c: Pose and respond to specific questions with elaboration and detail by making comments that contribute to the topic, text, or issue under discussion. SL.6.1.d: Review the key ideas expressed and demonstrate understanding of multiple perspectives through reflection and paraphrasing.

Write a Historical Episode

Week 2 • Day 1

Student Objectives

- Read and understand a prewriting strategy. *(p. 40)*

Prewrite

Focus on Ideas

Research Your Topic Ask students what they'll need to know before developing a plot for their historical episodes. (Possible responses: historical facts and events, people involved with the episode) Discuss the importance of using several sources to research a topic. For example, encyclopedias are useful for general information, such as dates and the names of locations and people, but biographies or websites may offer more details about a historical event or person.

Ask students to name several resources they might use to help get background information. (Possible responses: encyclopedias, history textbooks, history magazines, the Internet) Discuss Marco's notes. Point out that he recorded a mixture of facts, quotes, and details that will help him write an interesting account. Emphasize the importance of using reliable sources and of keeping track of them for proper citation.

Online Writing Center

 Provides **interactive graphic organizers** as well as a variety of graphic organizers in PDF format.

Prewrite
Focus on **Ideas**

The Rubric Says The episode focuses on one historical event.

Writing Strategy Use several sources to take notes on a historical event.

I found out about the Cardiff Giant hoax online. I was fascinated! When my teacher asked us to write a historical episode, I decided to write about the Giant.

First, I read an overview of the event in an encyclopedia. Then I looked at a library book and some reliable websites on the topic. Here are some of the notes I took.

My Notes on the Cardiff Giant

- ✔ 1866: George Hull heard some people talk about giants on Earth—he got an idea
- ✔ 1868: Hull sent a chunk of gypsum from Ft. Dodge to Chicago
- ✔ stonecutters made 10-foot man, twisted body, calm face—acid to make it look old
- ✔ Hull buried statue near Cardiff, NY, on farm of William Newell, his relative who was in on hoax
- ✔ Oct. 16, 1869: well diggers found giant, Newell put up tent, charged 300–500 people daily to see statue
- ✔ people say they saw Hull and wagon with box the year before—Hull admits hoax on Dec. 10
- ✔ "We'll make a fortune off the fools."—Hull's partner
- ✔ giant stored, exhibited at fairs, bought by Farmers' Museum in Cooperstown, NY, in 1947
- ✔ period: after Civil War, mid-Victorian Age—growth in business, science, and technology (no cars or phones)

Apply

Choose an interesting historical event. Gather information from reliable sources, and take notes.

40 Narrative Writing

English Language Learners

BEGINNING/INTERMEDIATE

Create a Story Map Introduce or review the terms *character, setting, plot, conflict,* and *resolution.* Give students a story idea, such as *a ride on a waterfall.* Have partners use a Story Map to plan a story. Make sure they include characters' names, a description of the setting, a problem (conflict), plot events, and a resolution. They may use just a few words to describe each.

ADVANCED/ADVANCED HIGH

Story Map Review the elements of a story. Ask, *What can you find in a story?* Students should be able to answer questions such as *What is a character/setting/plot?* Students should know that the *conflict* in the story is the problem, and the *resolution* is the solution. Have partners brainstorm ideas for a play and complete a Story Map as a prewriting activity.

Prewrite

Focus on **Organization**

The Rubric Says	The sequence of events in the episode unfolds naturally.
Writing Strategy	Make a Story Map to organize the notes.

Writer's Term

Story Map
A **Story Map** organizes the setting, characters, problem, plot, and ending of a story.

The rubric reminds me to order events naturally. A historical episode is a story, so the events should unfold logically. A Story Map will help me organize the events into a natural sequence so my audience can easily follow along.

Story Map

Setting Time 1866–1869   **Place** farm near Cardiff, NY

Characters George Hull, William Newell, well diggers, scientist

Problem Hull has to convince people that a stone sculpture is a giant fossilized prehistoric man and get them to pay to see it.

Plot/Events Hull learns about the giant story, comes up with a hoax, has a stone sculpture made, and has it buried on a relative's farm. It's discovered, people pay to see it, and Hull sells part ownership of it. People start to doubt Hull's claims and check into them.

Ending (Resolution) Hull admits the hoax. The giant is moved around for years. It finally ends up in a NY museum.

Reflect

Think about Marco's Story Map. Are the events organized in a clear and natural way?

Apply

Organize your ideas by using your notes to make a Story Map.

Historical Episode **41**

Conferencing

PEER TO PEER Have pairs of students exchange Story Maps. Students should review all the elements and point out any places where they believe important information may have been left out.

PEER GROUPS Divide students into groups of four or five. Each student gets a turn sharing his or her Story Map, describing story events to the group. The listening group members can then provide helpful and supportive feedback regarding event sequence, possible missing information, and clarity.

TEACHER-LED Meet with individual students. Have the student summarize his or her episode as you follow along in the student's Story Map. Discuss any elements in the student's summary that should be added to or expanded on in the Story Map.

Write
a Historical Episode

Week 2 • Day 2

Student Objectives

- Create a Story Map to organize story elements. *(p. 41)*

Prewrite

Focus on **Organization**

Create a Story Map Review Marco's Story Map with students. Point out what is featured in each section (Setting, Characters, Problem, Plot/Events, Ending). Ask:

- Has Marco already determined how his historical episode will end? (yes)

- Why is it helpful to know the ending before starting to write? (Possible response: It helps a writer stay on track and include all the details that will lead to the ending.)

Have students create a Story Map of their own using the notes they took earlier.

Writer's Term

Story Map It is possible to create a more detailed Story Map in which each event is listed in a separate box. This helps ensure that the plot has no gaps in logic.

CCSS Common Core State Standards
W.6.3: Write narratives to develop real or imagined experiences or events using effective technique, relevant descriptive details, and well-structured event sequences. **W.6.3.a:** Engage and orient the reader by establishing a context and introducing a narrator and/or characters; organize an event sequence that unfolds naturally and logically. **W.6.3.e:** Provide a conclusion that follows from the narrated experiences or events.

Write
a Historical Episode

Week 2 • Day 3

Student Objectives

• Use a Story Map to begin writing. *(p. 42)*

Draft

Focus on Organization

Begin a Draft Review the difference between a draft and a final copy. Encourage students to focus on getting their ideas down on paper while drafting.

Discuss the importance of a clear beginning, middle, and ending. Ask:

• What is the easiest way to help your readers understand when the time frame or setting shifts? (use effective transitions)

Discuss the transitions Marco mentions. Have students suggest other effective transitions. (Possible responses: *Many years later, After a week, Just before midnight, In 1866*)

Instruct students to begin drafting their historical episodes. Remind them to use their Story Maps throughout the drafting process. Point out that Marco often refers to the rubric as he writes; encourage students to do the same. Refer them to the list of transitions on page 524.

Online Writing Center

 Provides student eBooks with an **interactive writing pad** for drafting, revising, editing, and publishing.

Draft

Focus on **Organization**

The Rubric Says	Transitions guide the reader smoothly from the beginning to the end. There is a clear beginning, middle, and end.
Writing Strategy	Make sure your writing has a clear organization.

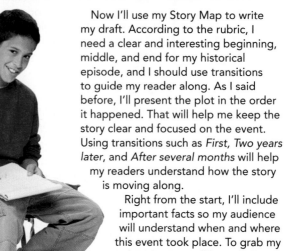

Now I'll use my Story Map to write my draft. According to the rubric, I need a clear and interesting beginning, middle, and end for my historical episode, and I should use transitions to guide my reader along. As I said before, I'll present the plot in the order it happened. That will help me keep the story clear and focused on the event. Using transitions such as *First, Two years later,* and *After several months* will help my readers understand how the story is moving along.

Right from the start, I'll include important facts so my audience will understand when and where this event took place. To grab my readers' interest, I'll hint at what's to come but leave them wondering for a while. This is my draft, so I'll just write now and worry about spelling and grammar later.

42 Narrative Writing

Differentiating Instruction

ENRICHMENT

Experiment With Organization Explain that some stories "begin at the end" to grab the reader's attention and then circle back to tell the story in chronological order. Then challenge students to rewrite a brief version of the model using this organization. Have students share their finished stories with their peers.

REINFORCEMENT

Narrow the Topic Model how to narrow the scope of a historical episode. Say: *I'm interested in ancient Egypt, so I'll list what I already know about this topic. I'll use an encyclopedia as a guide. I'm most interested in the Sphinx. I'll write about an ordinary person who helped construct the Sphinx. I'll research to find out what it's made of, when and why it was built, who the laborers were, and what the work was like.*

[DRAFT]

[places readers into the historical period]

[clear beginning introduces historical event]

The Cardiff Giant

In 1866, the Civil War had just ended, and the nation was looking towards a bright future. George Hull of Binghamton, New York, was visiting his sister in Iowa. During his visit, he learned that some people believed there were giants on Earth long ago. That gave Hull an idea. Hull began to make plans to put his own giant on Earth.

[hint of what's to come]

Two years later, Hull returned to Iowa. He sent a block of gypsum from a quarry near Fort Dodge to Chicago. Then he hired stonecutters to carve it into a man. Hull wanted it to look like a prehistoric man, so he "aged" it with acid. To create the look of skin pores, he poked the stone with darning needles.

When the sculpture was completed, Hull shipped it to the farm of William Newell, a relative who was in on the skeem. Newell lived near Cardiff, New York, south of Syracuse Together they buried the giant behind Newell's barn.

[grabs audience interest and makes readers wonder what will happen next]

Reflect

Does the beginning of the story make the historical period clear? Is it interesting enough to get the audience's attention?

Apply

Write a draft using your Story Map as a guide. Make your beginning clear so your readers are placed right into the historical period.

Historical Episode 43

Conferencing

PEER TO PEER Have pairs of students exchange drafts and Story Maps. Students discuss if any vital information is missing, events are out of order, or the ending is confusing or leaves questions unanswered.

PEER GROUPS Divide students into small groups. Each student gets a turn reading his or her draft aloud. Each listening student then describes one strength in the draft and gives one suggestion for where strengthening is needed. Areas to focus on include the beginning, the setting, the sequence of events, and the ending.

TEACHER-LED Meet with pairs of students. Have each student read his or her draft aloud while the other looks at the Story Map. Guide students to point out where the writing strays from the Story Map and offer suggestions on how to revise the writing for focus and clarity.

Write
a Historical Episode

Week 2 • Day 4

Student Objectives

• Complete a draft. *(p. 43)*

Finish the Draft Have students read the draft excerpt on page 43 and refer to Marco's Story Map on page 41. Ask:

• Does Marco clearly introduce the characters from his Story Map? (yes, two of the most important ones)

• Does he paint a clear picture of the setting? (He gives the date and location.)

• Does his beginning pull you in? Why? (Possible response: Yes, because clearly George Hull has a trick in mind, and I want to see if he can pull it off.)

Allow time for students to complete their drafts. Remind them to continue to refer to both the rubric and their Story Maps as they write. Proofreading marks are provided on page 43 for students' reference. They will be useful when students revise and edit their writing.

CCSS Common Core State Standards

W.6.3.b: Use narrative techniques, such as dialogue, pacing, and description, to develop experiences, events, and/or characters. **W.6.3.c:** Use a variety of transition words, phrases, and clauses to convey sequence and signal shifts from one time frame or setting to another. **W.6.3.d:** Use precise words and phrases, relevant descriptive details, and sensory language to convey experiences and events. **W.6.3.e:** Provide a conclusion that follows from the narrated experiences or events.

Write
a Historical Episode

Week 2 • Day 5

Student Objectives

• Revise to show knowledge and caring about the topic. (p. 44)

Revise

Focus on Voice

Create a Writer's Voice Explain to students that revising is different from editing. When a writer revises, he or she makes changes to strengthen specific aspects of the writing, such as **Voice** or **Word Choice**. Editing is the process of fixing spelling, punctuation, or grammatical errors.

Remind students that audience and purpose always inform the writer's voice. Based on the audience and purpose, the writer selects certain ideas, chooses certain words to express the ideas, and arranges the ideas into sentences. These factors combine to create the writer's voice. The writer's voice, in turn, determines whether the reader will be interested in the writing.

Discuss as a class how the added sentences in Marco's excerpt help him sound like he understands and cares about his topic. Instruct students to revise their drafts to strengthen the trait of **Voice**.

 Strategies for Writers Online
Go to **www.sfw.z-b.com** for additional online resources for students and teachers.

Revise
Focus on (Voice)

The Rubric Says	The writer's voice is knowledgeable and connects with the audience throughout the episode.
Writing Strategy	Sound like I know and care a lot about the topic.

I know that a historical episode can both inform and entertain. If I want my reader to believe me, I have to sound knowledgeable about my topic. To connect with and entertain my audience, I'll write as if I'm speaking directly to my readers. See where I added information to sound more knowledgeable.

[DRAFT]

Geology was a new science in the mid-1800s, but paleontologists knew that flesh could not be turned to stone.
Most scientists were certain it was a fake. This judgment led
to another theory . . .

Apply
Make sure your voice connects with the audience. Does it sound like you know your topic and care about it?

English Language Learners

BEGINNING/INTERMEDIATE

Quotation Marks Explain that quotation marks separate dialogue in text. Ask, *Where do you live?* On the board, write *The teacher asked Where do you live?* Review correct punctuation placement. Then write a student's answer in this way: *The student said I live in Houston.* Have a student insert quotes and a comma. Have partners create their own correctly punctuated dialogues and read them to the class.

ADVANCED/ADVANCED HIGH

Unfamiliar Words Ask a student to define *familiar*. Ask other students to give examples of things that are familiar. Repeat for *unfamiliar*. If students use a word that is unfamiliar in their writing, they should explain the word more fully. Review the use and construction of appositive phrases. Also point out that an extra sentence can be added to give more information about the unfamiliar word or idea.

Revise

Focus on *Word Choice*

The Rubric Says	Unfamiliar words are clearly defined for the reader.
Writing Strategy	Explain the meanings of any unfamiliar words.

After I wrote my draft, I looked at the rubric again. It says that I should explain any domain-specific vocabulary that is specific to my topic. I see some words like that in my draft. I think I'll add some phrases to make their meaning more clear.

[DRAFT]

Two years later, Hull returned to Iowa. He sent a block of
, a soft, light-colored mineral, ← [explains meaning of gypsum]
gypsum from a quarry near Fort Dodge to Chicago. Then he hired

stonecutters to carve it into a man. Hull wanted it to look like a

prehistoric man, so he "aged" it with acid. To create the look of

skin pores, he poked the stone with darning needles.

[explains meaning of darning needles]

These long needles were usually used for mending holes in knitted clothing, not for creating fake fossils!

Reflect

What do you think? Does Marco sound knowledgeable about his subject? How do his explanations strengthen his writing?

Apply

Add words or phrases that will explain any difficult vocabulary in your episode.

Historical Episode 45

Conferencing

PEER TO PEER Have student pairs exchange drafts. Tell them to circle in pencil any words that they do not fully understand or that they think other readers will not understand.

PEER GROUPS Each student takes a turn reading his or her draft aloud. Listening students should focus on the voice and tone of the writing. After the draft is read, each listening student points out where the writer could revise the text to sound more enthusiastic and informed about the subject.

TEACHER-LED Meet with pairs of students. Have the students read their drafts aloud to each other. Guide students in offering praise for passages that show a knowledgeable and enthusiastic voice and in offering constructive suggestions about how the voice can be strengthened.

Write
a Historical Episode

Week 3 • Day 1

Student Objectives

• Revise to explain the meanings of any unfamiliar words. *(p. 45)*

Revise

Focus on *Word Choice*

Explain Unfamiliar Words Explain that when readers come upon an unfamiliar term that is not defined, they may become confused.

Have a volunteer read the draft excerpt aloud both with and without the revisions. Compare the versions. Ask:

• How do the revisions strengthen the writing? (Possible response: They clarify the meaning.)

• How do the explanations help you enjoy and appreciate Marco's historical episode? (Possible response: They create a complete picture of the action.)

Instruct students to revise their papers to explain any unfamiliar words, using a dictionary if necessary.

CCSS **Common Core State Standards**
W.6.3.b: Use narrative techniques, such as dialogue, pacing, and description, to develop experiences, events, and/or characters. **W.6.3.d:** Use precise words and phrases, relevant descriptive details, and sensory language to convey experiences and events. **SL.6.1:** Engage effectively in a range of collaborative discussions (one-on-one, in groups, and teacher-led) with diverse partners on *grade 6 topics, texts, and issues*, building on others' ideas and expressing their own clearly. **L.6.4.c:** Consult reference materials (e.g., dictionaries, glossaries, thesauruses), both print and digital, to find the pronunciation of a word or determine or clarify its precise meaning or its part of speech.

Write
a Historical Episode

Week 3 • Day 2

Student Objectives

- Revise to vary sentence patterns for meaning, reader interest, and style. (p. 46)

Revise

Focus on  Sentence Fluency

Use a Variety of Sentences Explain that good writing should flow smoothly and have energy that keeps the reader interested. When several sentences in a row all follow the same pattern, readers can easily lose interest. A good way to ensure that writing has energy and flow is to use a variety of sentence lengths, structures, and beginnings.

The best way to check for good flow is to read a passage aloud. Read aloud Marco's draft, first without the revisions and then with them. Discuss how each revision energized this excerpt and helped the writing flow better. Point out that beginning a sentence with a participial phrase that describes the subject is a great way to strengthen sentence fluency. Caution students, however, that a participial phrase that does not appear near the word(s) it modifies is a dangling modifier and can confuse readers. Instruct students to revise their own writing to include a variety of sentence patterns.

Online Writing Center

Provides **interactive proofreading activities** for each genre.

Revise Focus on Sentence Fluency

The Rubric Says	There is great variety in length and structure of sentences. The writing is enjoyable to read.
Writing Strategy	Vary sentence patterns for meaning, reader interest, and style.

Time to check sentence fluency. The rubric says I should use different sentence lengths and structures to make my writing enjoyable to read. Let's look at another section of my draft. All the sentences here began with the subject, and most were about the same length. But look how I changed some of the sentences to vary my writing. Now this section reads much more smoothly.

[DRAFT]

After clearing away the rest of the dirt,
~~He cleared away the rest of the dirt and~~ the workman ran to fetch Newell.
Rubbing his beard,
Newell peered down into the pit ~~and rubbed his beard~~. A silent stone giant stared back. It's body was twisted as if in pain, but it's face had a peaceful expression. Newell said ride into town boys and tell them what we've got here. [added introductory phrases]

Apply

Do your sentences all sound the same? If so, add some descriptive phrases or rewrite some sentences into different patterns.

46 Narrative Writing

Optional Revising Lessons

Ideas

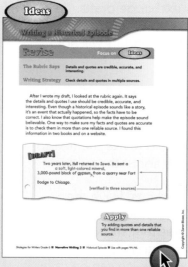

Narrative 3

Organization

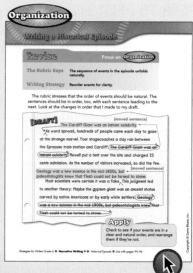

Narrative 4

Go to ⇨ Strategies for Writers Grade 6 CD-ROM

Edit

Focus on  **Conventions**

The Rubric Says	Quotation marks and commas are used correctly. The episode is easy to read and understand.
Writing Strategy	Check the use of quotation marks and commas.

Writer's Term

Quotation

A **quotation** restates the exact words of a speaker or writer. A quotation is placed within quotation marks and is credited to the speaker or writer.

Now I need to check my draft for errors. I will check my spelling, grammar, and capitalization. I will pay special attention to punctuation. If quotations are not punctuated correctly or if commas are out of place, the reader will be confused.

[DRAFT]

[punctuated quotes correctly]

When the sculpture was completed, Hull shipped it to the farm of
scheme
William Newell, a relative who was in on the ~~skeem~~. Newell lived near

Cardiff, New York, south of Syracuse. Together they buried the

giant behind Newell's barn. Wiping the dirt from his hands, Hull said,

"We'll make a fortune off the fools, but we must wait until the time is

right."

Reflect

How did Marco's sentence structure revisions improve the flow of his writing? How do his edits help you better understand his historical episode?

Apply

Conventions

Edit your draft for spelling, punctuation, and capitalization. Be sure quotations are punctuated correctly and commas are correct.

For more practice correcting quotation and comma errors, use the exercises on the next two pages.

Historical Episode 47

Related Grammar Practice

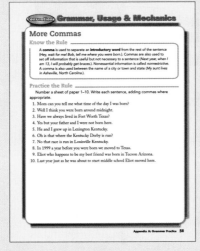

Student Edition pages 510, 511

Go to ▷ **Appendix A: Grammar Practice**

Student Objectives

• Edit to ensure quotation marks and commas are used properly. (p. 47)

Edit

Focus on Conventions

Check for Errors Have students read the page. Then discuss each of Marco's edits. Have students explain how the corrections make Marco's writing easier to understand. Then have students edit their own drafts for all errors; remind them to pay close attention to dialogue punctuation.

If any students are having trouble understanding how to punctuate dialogue, you may wish to teach the mini-lessons on pages T48 and T49. Then have students complete the exercises on pages 48 and 49. Review the answers as a class.

✏ Writer's Term

Quotation In addition to punctuating dialogue accurately, writers must remember to start a new line each time the speaker changes in text. This visual cue helps the reader keep track of who is saying what.

CCSS Common Core State Standards

L.6.1: Demonstrate command of the conventions of standard English grammar and usage when writing or speaking. **L.6.2:** Demonstrate command of the conventions of standard English capitalization, punctuation, and spelling when writing. **L.6.2.b:** Spell correctly. **L.6.3.a:** Vary sentence patterns for meaning, reader/listener interest, and style.

Conventions

Mini-Lesson

Student Objectives

- Learn to punctuate quotations correctly. *(p. 48)*

Quotations

Have students read the Know the Rule box. Then write the following on the board: *I'll be home around five o'clock she said.*

Ask students if the sentence is punctuated correctly. (**no**) Ask volunteers to punctuate the sentence correctly. (*"I'll be home around five o'clock," she said.*)

Explain that the end punctuation should be inside the closing quotation mark.

Write the following sentences on the board:

- *He yelled, "Stay away from that door"!*

- *"When you get home," said Mom. "please start dinner."*

Ask students how to edit the quotations so that they are correct. (*He yelled, "Stay away from that door!" "When you get home," said Mom, "please start dinner."*)

Point out that the second example is tricky because the speaker tag interrupts the sentence. Use examples similar to these if you feel students need more practice.

Online Writing Center

 Provides **interactive grammar games** and **practice activities** in student eBook.

Quotations

Know the Rule

A **quotation** is the exact words of a speaker or a writer. Quotations can add interest to nearly every piece of writing. Quotations must be punctuated correctly.

Use **quotation marks** at the beginning and end of a quote. Use a comma to separate the speaker's words from the rest of the sentence. If a quotation is a complete sentence, begin it with a capital letter. Add the correct end punctuation before the last quotation mark.

> **Examples:** "Will people believe us?" asked Newell.
> Hull said, "Of course they will!"

Practice the Rule

Correct the punctuation of each quotation below. Then write the correct sentences on a separate piece of paper.

1. To the people at the quarry, Hull said, "The stone is for a patriotic statue."
2. One article said, "Hull was the model for the giant's face."
3. Newell asked, "Should I dig up the giant myself or have it dug up by others?"
4. "What is it? Who carved it? How old is it? Why was it buried?" everyone asked.
5. People began telling each other, "The giant is a Goliath!"
6. At least one scientist exclaimed, "This has to be a fake!"
7. One of Newell's neighbors asked, "Didn't we see Hull bring a large crate last year?"
8. "I sold shares of the giant just in time," Hull admitted.
9. "Whatever happened to the Cardiff Giant?" people wondered years later.
10. "Grandpa said, "I think it's in a museum in New York."

Related Grammar Practice

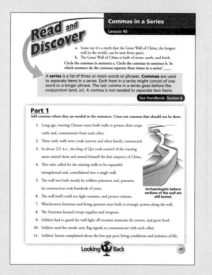

Page 121

Page 127

 Go to G.U.M. Student Practice Book

Commas

Know the Rule

A **comma** tells a reader where to pause, such as the point where a **compound sentence** is connected with a coordinating conjunction.

> **Example:** People found out that the Cardiff Giant was a hoax, **but** they still go to see it at the Farmers' Museum.

A comma is used to separate an **introductory word or phrase** from the rest of the sentence.

> **Example: When they first saw the sculpture,** many people believed it was really a petrified man.

A comma is also used to separate a **noun of direct address** from the rest of a sentence. A noun of direct address names a person who is being spoken to.

> **Example: "William,** we can make a lot of money from this sculpture if we wait until the time is right."

Practice the Rule

Number a sheet of paper 1–8. Rewrite the following sentences with the correct punctuation.

1. There have been dozens of world fairs, but the Chicago World's Fair in 1893 was one of the best of its day.
2. For the arts and architecture, this fair had a strong influence.
3. Frederic Law Olmsted was a famous architect, and he designed the fairgrounds.
4. In the Court of Honor, buildings were constructed out of white stucco.
5. This area was called the White City, and it was lighted at night with street lights.
6. In Katharine Lee Bates's poem "America the Beautiful," the phrase "alabaster cities" came from the White City.
7. Next door to the fair, Buffalo Bill put on his Wild West show to entertain people.
8. Someone might have said to the mayor of Chicago, "Mr. Harrison, this exhibition is truly an inspiration!"

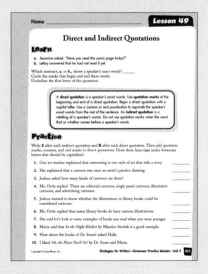

Page 97   Page 103

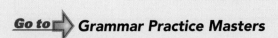 **Grammar Practice Masters**

Mini-Lesson

Student Objectives

- Learn how to use commas correctly. *(p. 49)*

Commas

Explain that punctuation functions the same way for a reader as road signs function for a driver. Different punctuation marks tell readers to do something or think something different. Commas, for example, tell readers when to pause. They group together related information.

Write the following sentences on the board:

- *You could wait until tomorrow to do your homework or you could just get it over with tonight.*
- *Just down the street there is a great deli.*
- *John Alexandra is here to see you.*

Ask students to direct you in placing a comma correctly in each sentence. (before *or*; after *street*; after *John*) Have students explain why each comma should be placed as it is. (Sentence 1: The comma comes before the coordinating conjunction *or*. Sentence 2: The comma comes after the introductory phrase. Sentence 3: The comma comes after the noun of direct address.)

CCSS Common Core State Standards

L.6.1: Demonstrate command of the conventions of standard English grammar and usage when writing or speaking. **L.6.2:** Demonstrate command of the conventions of standard English capitalization, punctuation, and spelling when writing. **L.6.3:** Use knowledge of language and its conventions when writing, speaking, reading, or listening.

Write
a Historical Episode

Week 3 • Day 4

Student Objectives

- Discuss preparation for publishing and presentation. *(p. 50)*
- Use a final editing checklist to publish their work. *(p. 50)*

Publish ⁺Presentation

Publishing Strategy As a class, brainstorm different ways to publish students' historical accounts. For example, the class could use a three-ringed binder to compile a class history book, and a copy of each historical account could be placed into the binder in chronological order.

Review Marco's final checklist with students. Ask:

- How will this checklist help Marco produce the best possible final copy? (Possible response: It reminds him to check for certain details that are often overlooked when writing, such as punctuating quotations and labeling/numbering all pages.)

Have students make a checklist of their own to use when writing their final copy. Encourage students to share copies of their historical episodes with friends and relatives who might be interested in reading about what they wrote.

 Strategies for Writers Online
Go to **www.sfw.z-b.com** for additional online resources for students and teachers.

T50 Narrative Writing

The Cardiff Giant

by Marco

It was 1866. The Civil War had just ended, and the nation was looking toward a brighter future. George Hull of Binghamton, New York, was visiting his sister in Iowa. During his visit, he learned that some people believed there were giants on Earth long ago. That gave Hull an idea for a new business venture. On the long trip home by steamboat and train, Hull began to hatch a plan to put a giant on Earth.

Two years later, Hull returned to Iowa. He shipped a 3,000-pound block of gypsum, a soft, light-colored mineral, from a quarry near Fort Dodge to Chicago. Then he hired stonecutters to secretly carve the hunk of rock into the shape of a man more than ten feet tall.

Hull wanted the statue to look like a petrified prehistoric man, so he "aged" it with acid. To create the appearance of skin pores, he pounded the stone with darning needles. These long needles were usually used for mending holes in knitted clothing, not for creating fake fossils!

When the sculpture was completed, Hull shipped it to the farm of William Newell, a relative who was in on the scheme. Newell lived near Cardiff, New York, south of Syracuse. Together they buried the giant

Historical Episode 51

Technology Tip for 21st Century Literacies

Convert the written text into an audio text using Audioboo or another web-based audio capture and publishing tool. This not only allows student writers to think about the ways in which their words sound (and engage) when read aloud, but it encourages publishing their work for an audience that reaches outside the classroom. Publishing a collection of students' audio historical episodes also makes this a "higher stakes" (and often more relevant and motivating) task for student writers. Real writers write to be read—or, in this case, to be heard.

See **www.sfw.z-b.com** for further information about and links to these websites and tools.

Write
a Historical Episode

Week 3 • Day 5

Student Objectives

- Use a historical episode rubric. (pp. 34–35)
- Share a published historical episode. (pp. 51–53)

Presentation Strategy Placing information on each page that identifies the page as part of a larger paper is a courtesy to the reader. Explain that word-processing programs have a header-footer feature that will label and number each page automatically. Remind students that although they may be careful to turn in each page of their narrative, there are times when a page becomes misplaced or out of order.

CCSS **Common Core State Standards**

W.6.5: With some guidance and support from peers and adults, develop and strengthen writing as needed by planning, revising, editing, rewriting, or trying a new approach. **W.6.6:** Use technology, including the Internet, to produce and publish writing as well as to interact and collaborate with others; demonstrate sufficient command of keyboarding skills to type a minimum of three pages in a single sitting. **SL.6.5:** Include multimedia components (e.g., graphics, images, music, sound) and visual displays in presentations to clarify information.

Reflecting on a Historical Episode

Have students think back on this assignment as a whole. Encourage students to turn to a partner to share how they feel about the experience. Ask:

- Which part of the process was most challenging for you? Why?

- Which part of the process was easiest for you? Why?

- Did you succeed in your goal of writing for a particular purpose and audience? What makes your writing successful?

Have students write their responses in a writing journal or discuss them as a class or in small groups.

behind Newell's barn. Wiping the dirt from his hands, Hull said, "We'll make a fortune off the fools, but we must wait until the time is right."

A year later, a large bed of fossils was discovered nearby. Hull sent a mysterious telegram to Newell. It read, "Strike while the iron is hot."

On October 16, 1869, Newell hired two men to dig a well at a certain spot near the barn. A few feet down, their shovels clanked against something. "I declare, someone has been buried here!" said one of the workmen as he uncovered a stone foot.

After clearing away the rest of the dirt, the workman ran to fetch Newell. Rubbing his beard, Newell peered down into the pit. A silent stone giant stared back. Its body was twisted as if in pain, but its face had a peaceful expression. Newell said, "Ride into town, boys, and tell them what we've got here."

The Cardiff Giant was an instant celebrity. As word spread, hundreds of people came each day to gaze at the strange marvel. Four stagecoaches a day ran between the Syracuse train station and Cardiff. Newell put a tent over the site and charged 25 cents admission. As the number of visitors increased, so did the fee.

At first, many thought the sculpture really was a petrified man from an earlier time. After all, the region was known for its fossils. Recent advances in science and technology made the public believe that almost anything was possible.

Marco Page 2

52 Narrative Writing

Strategies for Writers Online
Go to **www.sfw.z-b.com** for additional online resources for students and teachers.

Most scientists were certain it was a fake. Geology was a new science in the mid-1800s, but paleontologists knew that flesh could not be turned to stone. This judgment led to another theory: Maybe the gypsum giant was an ancient statue carved by Native Americans or by early white settlers.

Hull suspected his hoax would soon be revealed. He sold part ownership of the giant to a group of local businesspeople. It was moved to Syracuse and then toured other cities in New York.

In the meantime, an investigation was started. Local people remembered they had seen Hull traveling with a large wooden crate on a wagon the year before. On December 10, Hull admitted the hoax. One of Hull's partners commented, "What a bunch of fools!"

The Cardiff Giant toured for a while and then went into storage. Later it appeared at fairs in Iowa and New York. It was even stored in a child's playroom for a while. In 1947, the Farmers' Museum in Cooperstown, New York, bought the giant.

Today, visitors to the museum stand under a tent just like the first visitors did in 1869. There, they ponder the Cardiff Giant, America's greatest hoax.

Reflect

Did Marco use all the traits of a good historical episode? Check his writing against the rubric. Be sure to check your own story against the rubric too.

Marco Page 3

CCSS Common Core State Standards

W.6.4: Produce clear and coherent writing in which the development, organization, and style are appropriate to task, purpose, and audience. **W.6.5:** With some guidance and support from peers and adults, develop and strengthen writing as needed by planning, revising, editing, rewriting, or trying a new approach. **W.6.6:** Use technology, including the Internet, to produce and publish writing as well as to interact and collaborate with others; demonstrate sufficient command of keyboarding skills to type a minimum of three pages in a single sitting.

Short Story Planner

WEEK 1

Day 1
Introduce
a Short Story

Student Objectives
- Review the elements of a short story.
- Consider purpose and audience.
- Learn the traits of narrative writing.

Student Activities
- Read and discuss **What's in a Short Story?** (p. 54)
- Read and discuss **Why Write a Short Story?** (p. 55)
- Read **Linking Narrative Writing Traits to a Short Story.** (p. 56)

Day 2
Analyze
Read a Short Story

Student Objectives
- Read a model short story.

Student Activities
- Read **"Loser!"** (p. 57)

Day 3
Analyze
Introduce the Rubric

Student Objectives
- Learn to read a rubric.

Student Activities
- Review **"Loser!"** (p. 57)
- Read and discuss the **Short Story Rubric.** (pp. 58–59)

WEEK 2

Day 1
Write
Prewrite: Ideas

Student Objectives
- Read and understand a prewriting strategy.

Student Activities
- Read and discuss **Prewrite: Focus on Ideas.** (p. 64)
- Apply the prewriting strategy.

Day 2
Write
Prewrite: Organization

Student Objectives
- Create a Storyboard to organize ideas.

Student Activities
- Read and discuss **Prewrite: Focus on Organization.** (p. 65)
- Reflect on the model Storyboard.
- Apply the prewriting strategy to create a Storyboard.
- Participate in a peer conference.

Day 3
Write
Draft: Voice

Student Objectives
- Begin writing, using first-person point of view and dialogue.

Student Activities
- Read and discuss **Draft: Focus on Voice.** (p. 66)
- Apply the drafting strategy by using a Storyboard to write a draft.

WEEK 3

Day 1
Write
Revise: Word Choice

Student Objectives
- Revise to replace overused words with more exact words.

Student Activities
- Read and discuss **Revise: Focus on Word Choice.** (p. 69)
- Reflect on the model draft.
- Apply the revising strategy.
- Participate in a peer conference.

Day 2
Write
Revise: Sentence Fluency

Student Objectives
- Revise to use active voice.

Student Activities
- Read and discuss **Revise: Focus on Sentence Fluency.** (p. 70)
- Reflect on the model draft.
- Apply the revising strategy.

Note: Optional Revising Lessons appear on the *Strategies for Writers* CD-ROM.

Day 3
Write
Edit: Conventions

Student Objectives
- Edit to correct inappropriate shifts in pronoun number and person.

Student Activities
- Read and discuss **Edit: Focus on Conventions.** (p. 71)
- Reflect on the model draft.
- Apply the editing strategy.

Note: Teach the Conventions mini-lessons (pp. 72–73) if needed.

Day 4	Day 5

Analyze
Ideas, Organization, and Voice

Student Objectives
- Read a model short story.
- Use the short story rubric.
- Use the model short story to study Ideas, Organization, and Voice.

Student Activities
- Review **"Loser!"** (p. 57)
- Review the rubric. (pp. 58–59)
- Read and discuss **Using the Rubric to Study the Model.** (pp. 60–61)

Analyze
Word Choice, Sentence Fluency, and Conventions

Student Objectives
- Read a model short story.
- Use the short story rubric.
- Use the model short story to study Word Choice, Sentence Fluency, and Conventions.

Student Activities
- Review **"Loser!"** (p. 57)
- Review the rubric. (pp. 58–59)
- Read and discuss **Using the Rubric to Study the Model.** (pp. 62–63)

Day 4	Day 5

Write
Draft

Student Objectives
- Complete a draft.

Student Activities
- Finish the draft. (p. 67)
- Participate in a peer conference.

Write
Revise: Ideas

Student Objectives
- Revise to add sensory details and build suspense.

Student Activities
- Read and discuss **Revise: Focus on Ideas.** (p. 68)
- Reflect on a model draft.
- Apply the revising strategy.

Day 4	Day 5

Write
Publish: +Presentation

Student Objectives
- Discuss preparation for publishing and presentation.
- Use a final editing checklist to publish their work.

Student Activities
- Read and discuss **Publish: +Presentation** (p. 74)

Write
Publish: +Presentation

Student Objectives
- Use a short story rubric.
- Share a published short story.

Student Activities
- Share their work.
- Use the rubric to reflect upon and evaluate the model and their own writing. (pp. 58–59, 75)

To complete the chapter in fewer days, combine the learning objectives and activities in a way that supports students as they write.

Resources at-a-Glance

Grammar, Usage & Mechanics
Personal and Possessive Pronouns T72
Indefinite Pronouns T73
Grammar Practice T71–T73

Differentiating Instruction
Using the Rubric T63
Draft T66
Publish T74
For additional Differentiating Instruction activities, see Strategies for Writers *Extensions Online at* **www.sfw.z-b.com.**

English Language Learners
Using the Rubric T60–T61
Prewrite T64
Revise T68

Conferencing
Peer to Peer T65, T67, T69
Peer Groups T65, T67, T69
Teacher-Led T65, T67, T69

Technology Tip
Using the Rubric T62
Publish T75

School Home Connection Letter
Reproducible letter (in English and Spanish) appears on the *Strategies for Writers* CD-ROM and at **www.sfw.z-b.com.**

Online Writing Center
Provides IWB resources, interactive games and practice activities, videos, eBooks, and a virtual file cabinet.

 Strategies for Writers Online
Go to **www.sfw.z-b.com** for free online resources for students and teachers.

Introduce
a Short Story

Student Objectives

- Review the elements of a short story. *(p. 54)*
- Consider purpose and audience. *(p. 55)*
- Learn the traits of narrative writing. *(p. 56)*

What's a Short Story?

Discuss the definition of a short story with students. Talk about the difference between a novel and a short story. (A short story has fewer characters, a simpler plot, and is much shorter in length.) Ask:

- What other genres are similar to a short story? (Possible responses: mystery, historical episode, adventure, folktale)

What's in a Short Story?

Explain that all short stories contain specific elements as outlined on page 54. Ask a student volunteer to tell the class about his or her favorite short story. Have the student provide a short summary of what happens in the story. Then have the class identify the elements described on page 54 in the student's story. Ask the student volunteer what made the story feel realistic to him or her and have other students respond by expanding on what lends realism to a story.

 Strategies for Writers Online
Go to **www.sfw.z-b.com** for additional online resources for students and teachers.

What's a Short Story?

A short story is a story that may or may not be true. It has only a few characters, and it focuses on one problem or conflict. I like using my imagination to do this kind of writing!

What's in a Short Story?

Protagonist
This is the main character in the story, the person who has the problem. I want my readers to relate to my protagonist, so I need to make his or her personality come alive.

Point of View
A short story can be written in either first person or third person. Third person works well for most stories, but sometimes nothing beats being right inside the protagonist's head!

Plot
To make my story exciting, I'll think of an interesting problem for my protagonist. Then I'll tell the events of the story in a logical order while building tension. My readers will love the climax, or high point, of my story!

Realism
Even if my story is made up, it has to seem real. My readers want to feel as if they are living the story! I need to use strong writing to capture the interest of my audience and keep them involved all the way through the story.

54 Narrative Writing

Narrative Text Exemplars (Short Story)

Hamilton, Virginia. "The People Could Fly." *The People Could Fly: American Black Folktales.* **Knopf Books for Young Readers, 2009.** CCSS "The People Could Fly" is one of 24 short stories in Virginia Hamilton's book *The People Could Fly: American Black Folktales.* This particular tale describes how many people escaped slavery by flying away, while others were forced to stay and endure the oppressive conditions of servitude.

Soto, Gary. *Baseball in April and Other Stories.* **Sandpiper, 2000.** *Baseball in April and Other Stories* is a collection of short stories set in California. The stories deal with the normal problems of adolescence and growing up that young people face everywhere.

Why write a Short Story?

I can think of a lot of reasons to write a short story! Here are some of my ideas.

Personal Enjoyment
It's a lot of fun to write something as creative as a short story. I like making up my own characters and imagining what happens to them.

Writing Skills
Writing a short story uses a lot of important skills that I need to practice. I can get better at organizing my thoughts, writing sentences, and spelling and punctuating correctly while I do something interesting and fun!

Entertainment
Everybody enjoys a good story! I can share my short story with my family and friends and other people, too. For just a while, my readers can take a break from their real lives and experience my imagination!

Understanding
Writing my own stories can help me understand the stories I read. I can see how authors construct their stories when I've been through the process myself. And I can really appreciate the way good writers bring life into their writing!

Why write a Short Story?

Discuss each of the reasons for writing a short story on page 55. Explain that the purpose and audience of a story are closely linked to its theme. For example, if a writer wants to make readers laugh and forget their worries for a while, the theme of the story will likely be lighthearted and humorous. Other times, a writer may wish to help readers understand a difficult or interesting topic, such as a specific disease, or help readers work through a difficult issue.

Challenge students to brainstorm different reasons for writing a short story. Ask them to consider short stories they have read in the past and determine what purpose the writer had in mind while writing each. Remind students that every writer also keeps the audience in mind while writing. This helps the writer stay on task and use an appropriate voice to convey the theme.

Cisneros, Sandra. "Eleven." *Woman Hollering Creek and Other Stories.* Random House, 1991. **CCSS**
"Eleven" is a short story about a young girl who has an awful experience on her eleventh birthday. However, as she fights to be understood, she shows a maturity well beyond her years.

Bambara, Toni Cade. *Raymond's Run.* Creative Education, 1990. "Raymond's Run" is the story of Hazel, known in the neighborhood as Squeaky, who takes care of her disabled brother, Raymond. After winning a race against her rival, Squeaky learns that her brother shares a passion for running. She decides to retire from running in order to train him.

CCSS **C**ommon **C**ore **S**tate **S**tandards
SL.6.1: Engage effectively in a range of collaborative discussions (one-on-one, in groups, and teacher-led) with diverse partners on *grade 6 topics, texts, and issues,* building on others' ideas and expressing their own clearly. **SL.6.1.b:** Follow rules for collegial discussions, set specific goals and deadlines, and define individual roles as needed. **SL.6.1.c:** Pose and respond to specific questions with elaboration and detail by making comments that contribute to the topic, text, or issue under discussion.

Introduce
a Short Story

Linking Narrative Writing Traits to a Short Story

Help students understand that they will follow Marco as he models using the writing process and the traits together. As they follow Marco through the writing process, students will see how the Narrative Writing Traits have been adapted and applied to writing a short story. They will see that a short story has many factors in common with other types of narrative writing. However, the particular audience and purpose of a short story determine how the traits are used.

Linking Narrative Writing Traits to a

In this chapter, you will write a story that has only one problem or conflict. This type of narrative writing is called a short story. Marco will guide you through the stages of the writing process: Prewrite, Draft, Revise, Edit, and Publish. In each stage, Marco will show you important writing strategies that are linked to the Narrative Writing Traits below.

Narrative Writing Traits

Ideas	• a focused topic, experience, or series of events • engaging, accurate details that develop and describe the topic, experience, or series of events
Organization	• logically sequenced events, often in chronological order • an interesting beginning and a satisfying ending • transitions that signal the sequence of events as well as shifts in time or setting
Voice	• a voice and tone that are appropriate for the purpose and audience • dialogue that, if used, fits the characters
Word Choice	• precise, descriptive words and phrases
 **Sentence Fluency**	• a variety of sentences that flow and are a pleasure to read aloud
Conventions	• no or few errors in grammar, usage, mechanics, and spelling

Before you write, read Ivan Phillips's short story on the next page. Then use the short story rubric on pages 58–59 to decide how well he did. (You might want to look back at What's in a Short Story? on page 54, too!)

Narrative Writing Traits in a Short Story

 **Ideas** The writer uses vivid details to paint the clearest picture of both the characters and the events. Carefully chosen details also build suspense as the story unfolds.

 Organization The writer paces events in a way that moves the story along. Events occur in a logical sequence; tension builds towards the climax and falls as the story reaches its resolution.

 **Voice** The writer uses a voice that is appropriate for the subject and easy for readers to connect with. The voice is energetic and engaging and brings the entire story to life.

Loser!

by Ivan Phillips

Protagonist

Third-person point of view

"What are you doing here?" demanded David.

Stephanie hopped off her bike and looked at the other club members. Everyone stood beside a sleek, high-tech bicycle that made her rusty clunker look prehistoric. "I . . . I came for the marathon," she replied.

"But you just joined the club two days ago!" cried Jenna.

"Everybody else has trained for months," added Miller. **← Realism**

They were saying she couldn't handle such a long ride. But Stephanie liked challenges. "I really want to try this," she said quietly.

David snorted. "Well, we really want to win. So don't expect us to hold back for you." *Plot—protagonist's problem*

As the marathon began, Stephanie kept up with the others in her club. But soon everybody else shot ahead. "See you later, loser!" someone called back.

She tried to catch up, pumping hard until her legs ached, but the others quickly became colorful blobs in the heat waves far down the road. Then they disappeared. *Plot—building tension* →

After that, Stephanie slowed to a steady pace. For a while, other bikers zoomed by, their wheels whizzing smoothly on the pavement. Then she biked on alone with just the rumbling of the support van's engine behind her. She must be the very last biker!

Realism

When the enormous hill appeared ahead, Stephanie was already exhausted from riding so long. Her lungs burned with every breath, and her rubbery legs quivered. She wouldn't give up now. She couldn't! *Plot—building tension*

The bike crept upwards, rocking side-to-side as Stephanie strained against the pedals. The higher she rose, the harder she struggled. Grunting out the last of her breath, she finally felt the pedals ease beneath her. She had reached the top!

Below her stretched a golden valley of corn waving in the breeze. The flags of the finish line flapped beside a barn less than a mile away! *Plot—climax*

Realism

Stephanie coasted downhill and then pedaled with new energy. Only a few people waited at the finish line, so she knew she was terribly late. Still, she lifted her arms in victory as she sailed under the flags. So what if she came in last? Completing the marathon made her feel like a real winner.

Word Choice Creative and precise language creates vivid images for the reader. The setting, characters, and action are clearly depicted and easy to visualize.

Sentence Fluency A variety of sentence lengths and structures gives the writing flow. Sentences in active voice lend clarity and energy to the story.

Conventions The writer has taken the time to edit the writing. There are no spelling, grammar, punctuation, or capitalization errors in the short story.

Analyze
the Model

Week 1 • Day 2

Student Objectives

• Read a model short story. *(p. 57)*

Read the Model

Have students read "Loser!" on page 57. Remind them to look for the elements discussed in class. You may wish to have them look back at What's in a Short Story? on page 54.

Elements of a Short Story

Use the notes and highlighted text in the model to discuss elements of a short story. Ask these questions to help students better understand how each element is used in a short story:

• **What tells you that the story is told in third-person point of view?** (The writer uses third-person nouns and pronouns—*Stephanie, her*—to refer to the protagonist.)

• **How does Ivan build some realism into the story?** (Possible response: He includes believable details about how Stephanie feels and what she sees as she races.)

• **How do the highlighted passages build tension?** (Possible response: They make the reader wonder whether or not Stephanie will finish the race.)

CCSS **C**ommon **C**ore **S**tate **S**tandards

R/Lit.6.1: Cite textual evidence to support analysis of what the text says explicitly as well as inferences drawn from the text. **SL.6.1.a:** Come to discussions prepared, having read or studied required material; explicitly draw on that preparation by referring to evidence on the topic, text, or issue to probe and reflect on ideas under discussion. **SL.6.1.d:** Review the key ideas expressed and demonstrate understanding of multiple perspectives through reflection and paraphrasing.

Analyze
the Model

Student Objectives

• Learn to read a rubric. (pp. 58–59)

Use the Rubric

Explain the Rubric Explain that a rubric is a tool that helps you plan, improve, and evaluate a piece of writing. Tell students that a rubric helps a writer focus on key elements, or traits, in writing (**Ideas, Organization, Voice, Word Choice, Sentence Fluency, Conventions,** and **Presentation**).

The 6-point rubric on pages 58 and 59 is based on the Narrative Writing Traits that students read on page 56. Draw students' attention to the six columns to explain how the scoring system works. Explain that the column under the numeral 6 describes a very good short story, one that has received the highest score in all categories. This is what students should strive for in their own writing.

Discuss the Rubric Guide the students in a rubric discussion. Read the descriptors that go with each trait. Note how the descriptors vary as you move from column to column. Remind students to keep the rubric in mind when they write their own short story.

Online Writing Center

Provides a variety of **interactive rubrics,** including 4-, 5-, and 6-point models.

Rubric

Use this 6-point rubric to plan and score a short story.

	6	5	4
Ideas	Vivid details describe and develop the events and characters. Suspense moves the plot along.	Strong details develop the events and characters. Suspense is present in the story.	Some interesting details are used to develop events and characters. There are moments of suspense.
Organization	Events are paced so that tension builds to the climax and resolves at the end in a satisfying way.	Most of the events build tension to the climax. The story ends in a satisfying way.	The story has a climax and resolution. The reader feels tension only at times. The resolution may not be satisfying.
Voice	The writer's voice connects with the reader and brings the topic to life.	The writer is speaking to the reader, and the reader feels engaged in the story.	Sometimes the writer's voice fades, but some moments grab the reader.
Word Choice	Precise words and memorable phrases create strong images for the reader.	Precise words and phrases create pictures for the reader.	Some precise words and phrases are used well. Some moments create images for the reader.
Sentence Fluency	The story contains strong sentences written in active voice.	Most of the sentences are clear and written in active voice.	Some sentences are written in passive voice, making the writing weak in places.
Conventions	Personal, possessive, and indefinite pronouns are used correctly. The writing is easy to read.	A few errors with personal, possessive, and indefinite pronouns require careful review to spot.	Noticeable errors with personal, possessive, and indefinite pronouns don't interfere with the meaning.
⁺Presentation	All paragraphs are indented.		

CCSS Common Core State Standards

Short Story

As students learn to write a short story, they will receive instruction based on the Narrative writing standards, as well as several Speaking & Listening, Language, and Reading/Literature standards for grade 6.

The rubric and writing strategies for Ideas are based on standards **W.6.3, W.6.3.b,** and **W.6.3.d,** which outline the need for plenty of vivid, descriptive details to develop events and characters. The rubric and writing strategies for Organization reflect standards **W.6.3, W.6.3.a, W.6.3.b,** and **W.6.3.e,** which outline the need for well-organized, logically sequenced events that are paced effectively and end the story in a satisfying way. The rubric and writing strategies for Voice

3	2	1	
Plot and character details are general and not developed. The reader rarely feels suspense.	Characters are not developed, and the plot is vague. There is no feeling of suspense.	The characters and plot are hard to discern. There is no suspense because the plot is impossible to follow.	**Ideas**
The climax is hard to discern. The story has a resolution, but it is not satisfying.	The climax or resolution is missing entirely. The reader has trouble staying interested in the story.	There is no plot structure to hold the writing together, and the writing doesn't make sense.	**Organization**
The writer's voice comes and goes. The writer lacks confidence in the story.	The writer's voice is weak. The writing lacks details.	The writer's voice is absent. The reader is not sure who is telling the story.	**Voice**
Some vague or general words (*nice, fun, good*) are used. The reader has to work to form images.	Many words are vague or unclear. Verbs are weak.	Words are vague. There are no strong verbs. The writer struggled to find words.	**Word Choice**
Several sentences in a row are in passive voice, making reading dull in places.	Many sentences are weak, passive, or incorrect. The story is dull for the reader.	Sentences are incomplete or run-on. The story is almost impossible to read out loud.	**Sentence Fluency**
Noticeable errors with personal, possessive, and indefinite pronouns interfere with meaning.	Many errors with personal, possessive, and indefinite pronouns make reading a challenge.	The writing is filled with errors with personal, possessive, and indefinite pronouns that make reading difficult.	**Conventions**

See Appendix B for 4-, 5-, and 6-point narrative rubrics.

Apply the Rubric

Assign Traits Divide the class into small groups. Assign each group one trait to focus on. Each group should assign a score based on how well Ivan used that trait in the model. Students should be prepared to support the score with examples from the model.

Reveal Scores Call on one volunteer from each group to share the score his or her group gave Ivan for their assigned trait. Record each group's score on the board. Discuss as a class how well each trait was used in the short story.

Remind students that the point of this discussion is less to score the model than it is to practice identifying and evaluating the traits within a piece of writing.

Additional Rubrics Appendix B includes 4-, 5-, and 6-point rubrics that can be used with any piece of narrative writing. The rubrics are also available as blackline masters in the back of this Teacher Edition, beginning on page T525.

are also based on standards **W.6.3** and **W.6.3.b**. The rubric and writing strategies for Word Choice are clearly rooted in standard **W.6.3.d,** which stresses the use of precise words. The rubric and writing strategies for Sentence Fluency embody language standard **L.6.3.a,** which focuses on varying sentence patterns for meaning and reader interest.

Language standards **L.6.1** and **L.6.2** are clearly reflected throughout the editing pages of the chapter, while standard **W.6.6** resonates throughout, as students are encouraged to take full advantage of word-processing programs and use a wide range of resources found on the Internet.

CCSS **C**ommon **C**ore **S**tate **S**tandards

SL.6.1.a: Come to discussions prepared, having read or studied required material; explicitly draw on that preparation by referring to evidence on the topic, text, or issue to probe and reflect on ideas under discussion.
SL.6.1.c: Pose and respond to specific questions with elaboration and detail by making comments that contribute to the topic, text, or issue under discussion.

Analyze
the Model

Week 1 • Day 4

Student Objectives

- Read a model short story. *(p. 57)*
- Use the short story rubric. *(pp. 58–59)*
- Use the model short story to study Ideas, Organization, and Voice. *(pp. 60–61)*

Study the Model

Assess the Model Have students turn to pages 60–61. Explain that these pages show how the model on page 57 uses the writing traits described in the rubric. Read each section with students. Use questions such as the following to discuss each section. Be sure students can back up their answers with examples from the model. Encourage students to respond to each other's ideas in a constructive way.

- How does Ivan create a sense of suspense? (Possible response: Images like *exhausted* and *her lungs burned with every breath* create a sense of suspense.)

Strategies for Writers Online
Go to **www.sfw.z-b.com** for additional online resources for students and teachers.

Using the Short Story Rubric to Study the Model

Did you notice that the model on page 57 points out some key elements of a short story? As he wrote "Loser!" Ivan Phillips used these elements to help him tell a story. He also used the 6-point rubric on pages 58–59 to plan, draft, revise, and edit the writing. A rubric is a great tool to evaluate writing during the writing process. Now let's use the same rubric to score the model.

To do this, we'll focus on each trait separately, starting with Ideas. We'll use the top descriptor for each trait (column 6), along with examples from the model, to help us understand how the traits work together. How would you score Ivan on each trait?

Ideas

- Vivid details describe and develop the events and characters.
- Suspense moves the plot along.

Ivan's vivid details give depth to the characters and the plot. The story has lots of suspense, and the dialogue also helps to move the plot along. Look at how the details and the dialogue make you wonder what will happen next.

[from the writing model]

They were saying she couldn't handle such a long ride. But Stephanie liked challenges. "I really want to try this," she said quietly.

David snorted. "Well, we really want to win. So don't expect us to hold back for you."

English Language Learners

BEGINNING

Point of View Write the following sentence frame on the board: _____ *made a big mistake.* As you insert different subjects into the sentence, have students tell whether the sentence is told from the first- or the third-person point of view. Use the following subjects: *I, Diego and Maya, The baseball team, We, Our family, Mr. Smith, My sisters and I.*

INTERMEDIATE

Characters and Plot Ask students to think about some of the (real or fictional) heroes they know about. List them on the board. Discuss the problem each hero faced and the dangers or risks each had to take in order to solve the problem. Did the hero have any enemies? What were his or her strengths? Weaknesses? Have students use this information to develop their characters and plot.

Organization

- Events are paced so that tension builds to the climax and resolves at the end in a satisfying way.

Things seem to get worse and worse for Stephanie! First, the club members leave her behind. Then the other bikers pass her by. She bikes until she's exhausted. You really wonder if she's going to make it! Finally she crosses the finish line in the exciting climax below.

[from the writing model]

Stephanie coasted downhill and then pedaled with new energy. Only a few people waited at the finish line, so she knew she was terribly late. Still, she lifted her arms in victory as she sailed under the flags.

Voice

- The writer's voice connects with the reader and brings the topic to life.

The reader is drawn into Ivan's narrative voice. I found the action and characters in the story realistic—they really came to life for me! Look at how Ivan describes the beginning of the marathon.

[from the writing model]

As the marathon began, Stephanie kept up with the others in her club. But soon everyone else shot ahead. "See you later, loser!" someone called back.

She tried to catch up, pumping hard until her legs ached, but the others quickly became colorful blobs in the heat waves far down the road. Then they disappeared.

Short Story 61

- Does the story end in a satisfying way? Why or why not? (Possible responses: Yes. There are no questions left unanswered, no events left unexplained. Stephanie fought hard to finish the race, and she succeeded in a way that made her happy.)

- How does Ivan use voice to connect with his readers? (Possible response: Ivan uses a casual, energetic voice that is appropriate for the subject to engage readers and hold their attention throughout the whole story.)

ADVANCED

Realism Ask a student to define the word *real*. Discuss synonyms for *real*, such as *accurate*, *actual*, or *genuine*. Tell students that *realism* is a quality about their writing that makes it seem real. Check students' understanding of the word by asking questions such as *Is there realism in my story if it has a talking frog? What about a sixth-grade teacher?*

ADVANCED HIGH

Protagonist Explain that a protagonist is the main character in a story. Read the Protagonist bubble on page 54 as a class. Teach the meanings of the following: *the person who has the problem, I want my readers to relate to my protagonist,* and *make his or her personality come alive.*

CCSS **Common Core State Standards**

R/Lit.6.1: Cite textual evidence to support analysis of what the text says explicitly as well as inferences drawn from the text. **R/Lit.6.3:** Describe how a particular story's or drama's plot unfolds in a series of episodes as well as how the characters respond or change as the plot moves toward a resolution. **SL.6.1.a:** Come to discussions prepared, having read or studied required material; explicitly draw on that preparation by referring to evidence on the topic, text, or issue to probe and reflect on ideas under discussion.

Analyze
the Model

Week 1 • Day 5

Student Objectives

- Read a model short story. (p. 57)
- Use the short story rubric. (pp. 58–59)
- Use the model short story to study Word Choice, Sentence Fluency, and Conventions. (pp. 62–63)

Continue Discussing the Traits

Ask questions such as the following to use the model to discuss **Word Choice, Sentence Fluency,** and **Conventions:**

- Point out some precise nouns and memorable phrases in the story that helped you visualize the action. (Possible responses: *sleek, high-tech bicycle; rusty clunker; quickly became colorful blobs; wheels whizzing smoothly*)

- Choose a sentence from the model and restate it in the passive voice. How is it different from the active-voice sentence? (Possible response: *She had reached the top!/The top had been reached by her!* The passive-voice sentence is clunky and awkward, and it doesn't sound as energetic.)

- How does Ivan's careful editing affect your experience with his short story? (Possible response: I was able to read the story easily, because there are no errors.)

Strategies for Writers Online

Go to **www.sfw.z-b.com** for additional online resources for students and teachers.

Word Choice
- Precise words and memorable phrases create strong images for the reader.

Ivan chooses his words carefully. Instead of writing with overused words, he uses precise words that make the story come alive. He could have written something like this: "The bike *went* upwards, *moving* side-to-side as Stephanie *pushed* against the pedals. The higher she *went*, the harder she *worked*." Just look at the precise, vivid words he uses instead.

[from the writing model]

The bike *crept* upwards, *rocking* side-to-side as Stephanie *strained* against the pedals. The higher she *rose*, the harder she *struggled*.

Sentence Fluency
- The story contains strong sentences written in active voice.

A verb is in active voice if the subject of the sentence is doing the action. A verb is in passive voice if the subject of the sentence is not doing the action. Sometimes passive voice works well, but usually sentences are stronger if they're written in active voice.

Obviously, Ivan knew that! He could have written sentences such as "Stephanie had been exhausted by the long ride" or "Her lungs were burned by every breath." But look how he used active voice to make the following paragraph strong.

[from the writing model]

When the enormous hill appeared ahead, Stephanie was already exhausted from riding so long. Her lungs burned with every breath, and her rubbery legs quivered. She wouldn't give up now. She couldn't!

62 Narrative Writing

Technology Tip for 21st Century Literacies

As an alternate short story prompt, challenge student writers to work from an image on the Dear Photograph website. The prompt for this website is to "take a photo from the past into the present." Have students either write from one of the images posted on the site or create their own "Dear Photograph" image. Discuss what it means to integrate an image (in this case, one from the past) into an image (in this case, one from the present). How does the image communicate in ways that only words might not?

See **www.sfw.z-b.com** for further information about and links to these websites and tools.

Conventions

- Personal, possessive, and indefinite pronouns are used correctly. The writing is easy to read.

I checked Ivan's story for mistakes, but I don't see any, do you? He has spelled, capitalized, and punctuated everything correctly. And he knows how to use personal, possessive, and indefinite pronouns correctly, too. You can tell that from the paragraph below.

[from the writing model]

As the marathon began, Stephanie kept up with the others in her club. But soon everybody else shot ahead. "See you later, loser!" someone called back.

⁺Presentation All paragraphs are indented.

My Turn!

I'm going to write my own short story! I'll follow the rubric and use good writing strategies. You can read along and see how I do it.

Differentiating Instruction

ENRICHMENT
Illustrate Key Events Have students choose which key events should be illustrated in the model short story. Encourage students to explain how they chose the events and details that could be illustrated. Tell them to remember this kind of planning when they write (and illustrate) their own short stories.

REINFORCEMENT
Support Organization On the board, write *rising action, climax, falling action, resolution*. Draw a mountain-shaped plot diagram beside the words. Describe each term and write it in the appropriate place on the plot diagram. For example, *rising action* is placed ascending the mountain, while *climax* is at the peak. Ask students to tell you where the other terms should go after you define them.

Presentation Explain to students that the greatest story in the world cannot be enjoyed if it is too messy to read. Remind them that people choose to read short stories for many reasons, but ultimately will put the story down if the print is messy, full of mistakes, or hard on their eyes. Explain that good writers understand this and use white space to make the text easier to read. Side margins should be neat, text should be double-spaced, and all paragraphs should be indented. Writers show respect for themselves and their readers by producing neat, legible work.

Think About the Traits Ask students which trait they feel is the most important when writing a short story. Explain that all traits are important in every piece of writing, but in each genre, certain traits are more important than others. For a short story, some may feel that the trait of **Ideas** is important, as the plot and characters are the heart of any good story. Others may think **Sentence Fluency** is important because smooth, flowing sentences make for good storytelling.

CCSS Common Core State Standards

R/Lit.6.1: Cite textual evidence to support analysis of what the text says explicitly as well as inferences drawn from the text. **SL.6.1.c:** Pose and respond to specific questions with elaboration and detail by making comments that contribute to the topic, text, or issue under discussion. **SL.6.1.d:** Review the key ideas expressed and demonstrate understanding of multiple perspectives through reflection and paraphrasing.

Write
a Short Story

Week 2 • Day 1

Student Objectives

- Read and understand a prewriting strategy. *(p. 64)*

Prewrite

Focus on Ideas

Brainstorm Ideas Point out that Marco understands that the main character and conflict must be determined before writing begins. Explain that a writer writing a short story without figuring out these major details runs the risk of writing a confusing and non-directional story. Having a game plan prior to writing is essential.

Now read Marco's brainstorming notes aloud. Guide a discussion regarding each of his ideas. Ask:

- Which ideas seem too big or vague for a short story? (Possible response: All the ideas could be too big for a short story if they are not narrowed down to a specific event or aspect.)

- What must Marco do to select a topic? (Possible response: He has to find an interesting part or aspect of an event around which he can develop a story.)

Remind them that it is helpful to choose a topic they know something about. Even so, they may need to do research in order to write realistically.

▶ Online Writing Center

Provides **interactive graphic organizers** as well as a variety of graphic organizers in PDF format.

Prewrite — Focus on Ideas

The Rubric Says	Vivid details describe and develop the events and characters.
Writing Strategy	Brainstorm characters and events to use in the story.

Ever since our teacher asked us to write a short story, I've been kicking around some ideas. To develop the plot and characters, I need to decide who the main character is and what his or her problem will be. Here are the notes I jotted down about possible characters and events for my story.

Notes

Characters:
- brave firefighter
- boy my age who's afraid of something
- cowboy
- girl my age who likes sports

Events:
- mountain-climbing expedition
- school play
- skydiving lesson
- sleepover
- camping trip

I decided I'd like to write a story about a boy my age, so I chose the boy who's afraid of something as my protagonist. I don't want him to be afraid of something obvious such as skydiving or seeing an alien, so I think I'll make him afraid of something at a sleepover. Maybe the sleepover can be held at a scary, creepy, old house. He will have to pretend he's not scared in front of his friends. Hey, I think I have a good idea for my story!

Apply

Brainstorm some ideas for characters and events for your story. Jot down your ideas and put your imagination to work!

64 Narrative Writing

English Language Learners

BEGINNING/INTERMEDIATE

Brainstorming Ideas Write *Outdoor Jobs* on the board and ask, *Who works outside?* Quickly write their answers on the board and encourage them to keep the ideas coming. Tell them this is called *brainstorming* and that all ideas are good ideas when they are brainstorming. Then have partners choose a job and brainstorm reasons that they would like to have that job.

ADVANCED/ADVANCED HIGH

Vivid Details Introduce vivid details. Write: *There are many fish in our aquarium. Many brightly colored fish swished through the swaying grasses and clear water inside our aquarium.* Ask, *Which sentence gives vivid detail? Which is more vague?* Write another example of a sentence with vague wording and have partners work together to add vivid details to it.

Prewrite

Focus on Organization

The Rubric Says	Events are paced so that tension builds to the climax and resolves at the end in a satisfying way.
Writing Strategy	Make a Storyboard to organize the ideas.

Writer's Term

Storyboard
A **Storyboard** can help you plot the main parts of a story in chronological order. Each frame in the Storyboard represents a part of the story. Words and/or pictures can be used in a Storyboard.

Now that I've decided on my protagonist and his problem, I have to plan my story. I will organize the events to build tension toward the climax. I can use a Storyboard to help me. See what I did below.

STORYBOARD

EVENT 1
Chris and his best friend arrive at a creepy house for a sleepover. Chris is scared and has to hide his fear.

EVENT 2
Chris and his friend go in and find that the party is normal. Chris has a good time.

EVENT 3
At bedtime, Chris gets scared again and can't go to sleep.

EVENT 4
Chris hears footsteps and thinks someone is hurting his best friend!

EVENT 5—CLIMAX
Even though he's scared, Chris tries to save his friend. He jumps on the figure and knocks him down!

EVENT 6
It was just the host of the party sleepwalking, but Chris feels good that he handled his fear.

Reflect
How will Marco's Storyboard help him build tension in the story?

Apply
Use a Storyboard to organize the events of your short story.

Short Story 65

Student Objectives

• Create a Storyboard to organize ideas. *(p. 65)*

Prewrite

Focus on Organization

Create a Storyboard Explain that a Storyboard will help students organize the key events. Plotting each event of the story helps a writer ensure that the rising action, climax, and resolution are clear and logical. Creating a Storyboard is like building a bridge of stepping stones across a stream. The "stones," or key events, are then in place to help the writer easily "step" from event to event. Now instruct students to create a Storyboard for their own short stories.

Writer's Term

Storyboard Storyboards mimic the graphic boards used by filmmakers to plot out scenes in movies. Like a film storyboard, this graphic organizer can be filled in with illustrations, text, or both.

CCSS Common Core State Standards
W.6.3: Write narratives to develop real or imagined experiences or events using effective technique, relevant descriptive details, and well-structured event sequences. W.6.3.a: Engage and orient the reader by establishing a context and introducing a narrator and/or characters; organize an event sequence that unfolds naturally and logically. W.6.3.d: Use precise words and phrases, relevant descriptive details, and sensory language to convey experiences and events. W.6.3.e: Provide a conclusion that follows from the narrated experiences or events.

Conferencing

PEER TO PEER Student pairs review each other's Storyboards to ensure that events are logically sequenced and that the rising action/climax/falling action is clear and makes sense.

PEER GROUPS Have students pass their Storyboards around the group. Each member reads the Storyboard and then, on a scrap of paper or an index card, records where an additional event is needed or an already existing event needs clarification or reordering. Comments are returned to the writer for future reference.

TEACHER-LED Meet with individual students. Review the student's Storyboard with him or her and discuss how the student plans to build suspense in the course of the events listed.

Write
a Short Story

Week 2 • Day 3

Student Objectives

- Begin writing, using first-person point of view and dialogue. (p. 66)

Draft

Focus on  Voice

Use First Person Remind students that a draft is an early form of a piece of writing. It is not expected to be error free. Students should focus on getting their ideas down while writing a draft; there will be time later to fix any mistakes.

Have students read page 66. Explain that using first-person point of view helps the writer establish an immediate connection with the audience. The story now feels as though it is about someone they might know—or a friend. Words such as *I, we,* and *me* all imply personal connection. Readers tend to engage easily with stories told in the first person.

Instruct students to use their Storyboards to begin drafting their short stories. Point out that Marco refers often to the rubric as he writes and that they should do the same.

Online Writing Center

 Provides student eBooks with an **interactive writing pad** for drafting, revising, editing, and publishing.

Writing a Short Story

Draft
Focus on **Voice**

The Rubric Says	The writer's voice connects with the reader and brings the topic to life.
Writing Strategy	Use first-person point of view and dialogue.

> **Writer's Term**
>
> **Point of View**
> **Point of view** helps the reader know who is telling the story. In **first person,** the story is told from the protagonist's point of view using words such as **I** and **me** throughout. In **third person,** the writer or narrator tells the story. The writer uses words such as **he, she,** and **they** when writing in third person.

Now I'll use my Storyboard to write my draft. I know that a good way to draw the reader into the action is for the narrator to speak in first-person point of view. Then, to move the plot along and build some tension about how scared Chris is of the creepy house, I can include dialogue. I know that what my characters say may be in a different point of view so the reader will know who is talking to whom. That way the dialogue will also sound realistic.

I can't wait to start writing! I'm going to be very careful to use only complete sentences in my story—no fragments or run-ons! For now, I'll just do my best with spelling, punctuation, capitalization, and grammar while I'm getting my story down on paper. I'll fix any mistakes later!

66 Narrative Writing

Differentiating Instruction

ENRICHMENT

Experiment With Voice Challenge students to rewrite part of the model using either second- or third-person point of view. Discuss how the different points of view alter the narrative and change the reader's experience of the story.

REINFORCEMENT

Support Point of View Write the following on the board: *I'm in the mood to make spaghetti! I'll find a recipe and get cooking. I can't wait to dig in!* Circle each pronoun. Explain that these sentences are written in first person. Ask a volunteer to change the sentences to second person, using the pronoun *you.* Ask another student to do the same, but this time using third person. Discuss how different points of view affect the reader's experience with the writing.

Creepover!   [DRAFT]

by Marco

"Isn't this great, Chris?" asked my best friend, Og.

"Sure," I lied.

We stood outside the castle-sized door of the old Evans manshun. When this house was empty, everyone talked about its eerie glowing windows and strange moaning sounds. Now Roger, the new kid, lived here—and he'd invited the guys to a sleepover! I was afraid of that creepy place, but somehow I had to hide my fear from my friends.

After Og banged the iron nocker a few times, Roger opened the door with a creek and let us in. He took us to the huge, paneled room where somebody was hanging out. Any of the guys roasted marchmallows in the stone fireplace? He played cards or video games. It looked like a normal sleepover!   [first-person point of view]◄

For a while, I actually enjoyed myself. But when we spread our sleeping bags on the floor and Roger turn off the lights, I got nervous again. I just couldn't relax.

Reflect

How does Marco build tension in the story? How does first-person point of view help you connect with the protagonist?

Apply

Write a draft using your Storyboard as a guide. Be sure to build tension throughout the story, leading up to an exciting climax.

Short Story 67

Conferencing

PEER TO PEER Pairs exchange drafts. Instruct each student to use a pencil to underline any areas where first-person point of view or additional dialogue would be helpful.

PEER GROUPS Divide students into small groups. Each student takes a turn reading his or her draft aloud. Listening students point out one strength and one area where more dialogue is needed to help the reader stay connected.

TEACHER-LED Meet with pairs of students. Have students read each other's drafts. Then coach them on how to give and receive constructive feedback about point of view and dialogue by prompting them with questions and ideas.

Write
a Short Story

Week 2 • Day 4

Student Objectives

• Complete a draft. *(p. 67)*

Finish a Draft Ask for volunteers to point out specific examples of first-person point of view in Marco's draft. Discuss how the story would sound different if told in third-person point of view.

Allow time in class for students to finish their drafts. Point out the proofreading marks on page 67 for future reference.

Writer's Term

Point of View First-person point of view allows the writer to address the reader directly and forge an intimate connection. It is, however, limited because everything is filtered through the narrator. Third-person point of view allows the reader to view the characters from the outside, without the writer's explicit bias. In limited third-person point of view, the reader still has access to the thoughts of only one character. In omniscient third-person, the reader learns the thoughts of multiple characters.

CCSS Common Core State Standards

W.6.3.b: Use narrative techniques, such as dialogue, pacing, and description, to develop experiences, events, and/or characters. **W.6.3.d:** Use precise words and phrases, relevant descriptive details, and sensory language to convey experiences and events. **W.6.10:** Write routinely over extended time frames (time for research, reflection, and revision) and shorter time frames (a single sitting or a day or two) for a range of discipline-specific tasks, purposes, and audiences.

Write
a Short Story

Week 2 • Day 5

Student Objectives

• Revise to add sensory details and build suspense. (p. 68)

Revise

Focus on Ideas

Add Sensory Details Write the five senses on the board: *sight, touch, smell, taste, hearing.* Under the word *sight,* write this sentence: *Through the fog, I spotted a large figure, bigger than any person I'd ever seen before.* Tell students that writing about what they see appeals to the reader's sense of sight. Have student volunteers come up with sentences for each of the additional words on the board. Encourage students to think of sentences that focus on sensory details and also include an element of suspense, for example, *I heard a soft hissing sound coming from the grass at my feet.*

Focus on the draft excerpt and discuss as a class how Marco's revision strengthened his writing and added suspense to his story. Instruct students to turn to their own stories and add sensory details to help the reader fully experience the action.

 Strategies for Writers Online
Go to **www.sfw.z-b.com** for additional online resources for students and teachers.

Revise

Focus on Ideas

The Rubric Says Suspense moves the plot along.

Writing Strategy Add sensory details to build suspense.

After I wrote my draft, I read it through and noticed that I needed to build more suspense in the story. I want my reader to feel Chris's tension about the house where the sleepover is. Adding sensory details will help my readers feel what the narrator feels.

[DRAFT]

For a while, I actually enjoyed myself. But when we spread our sleeping bags on the floor and Roger turn off the lights, I got nervous again. ~~I just couldn't relax~~

[added sensory details]

The dying fire cast strange shadows, and a dreary moan blew around the house. I burrowed into my downy sleeping bag, but I couldn't relax.

Apply
Try adding some sensory details to make your story come alive.

68 Narrative Writing

English Language Learners

BEGINNING/INTERMEDIATE

Suspense Write the following sentences on the board: *I heard glass break outside. I looked out the window. It was very dark outside. Then I heard a woman scream!* Explain any words students do not know. Ask, *Do you want to know what happens next in the story?* Tell them that the details in the sentences create suspense. Write *suspense,* say it, and have students repeat.

ADVANCED/ADVANCED HIGH

Using Exact Words Identify a few vague words that students wrote in their drafts, for example, *change* or *help.* Challenge partners to come up with more precise words, for example, *adjust* or *offer assistance.* Then have each student revise their charts and drafts to replace vague words with stronger ones.

Revise

Focus on Word Choice

The Rubric Says	Precise words and memorable phrases create strong images for the reader.
Writing Strategy	Replace overused words with more exact words.

Writer's Term

Overused Words
Overused words have been used so often by writers and speakers that they have become bland and boring. Overused words carry meaning but are not precise.

Now it's time to look at my word choices. I looked at my draft again, and I have to say there are some parts that are full of overused words. The rubric tells me to use precise words and memorable phrases. Check out how I changed the paragraph below by taking out some overused words and replacing them with clearer, more precise words.

[DRAFT]

[replaced overused words]

scrambled   jumped onto threatening   towered
I got to my feet and ran at the dark figure that stood over Og.
     wrestled   realized
I pulled it to the floor before I saw the figure was Roger!

"Was I sleepwalking again?" he mumbled.

Reflect
How do the new word choices make Marco's writing more lively and interesting?

Apply
Replace any overused words in your draft with precise words and memorable phrases.

Short Story 69

Conferencing

PEER TO PEER Have student pairs read each other's drafts. Using a pencil, students circle any words they feel are overused or vague. After returning the drafts, students discuss possible replacements for each circled word.

PEER GROUPS Have students pass their drafts around the group. Students look for areas in the drafts where sensory details are needed to create more realistic and vivid images or build suspense. Suggestions are recorded on an index card, which is returned to the writer with his or her draft.

TEACHER-LED Meet with pairs of students. Have each student read his or her draft aloud. You and the other student should ask questions about any plot points that need clarification or where suspense could be increased. Coach students in thinking of ways to build suspense.

Write
a Short Story

Week 3 • Day 1

Student Objectives

• Revise to replace overused words with more exact words. (p. 69)

Revise

Focus on Word Choice

Replace Overused Words Write these words from Marco's original draft on the board: *got, ran at, dark, stood, pulled, saw.* Tell students that while these words are correct and work in the places where Marco used them, his replacement words are much more vivid. Ask students to come up with other words or phrases that could replace the words on the board.

Now instruct students to apply this technique to their own stories. Have them replace each overused word with a more precise or descriptive word or phrase.

Writer's Term

Overused Words Overused words such as *got* and *said* tend to become "invisible" over time. They pass unnoticed without making an impression on the reader. Because they are not wrong, they are hard to spot in one's own writing. Having a third party check for overused words can be useful.

CCSS **Common Core State Standards**
W.6.3.b: Use narrative techniques, such as dialogue, pacing, and description, to develop experiences, events, and/or characters. **W.6.3.d:** Use precise words and phrases, relevant descriptive details, and sensory language to convey experiences and events.

Write
a Short Story

Week 3 • Day 2

Student Objectives

• Revise to use active voice. *(p. 70)*

Revise

Focus on

Use Active Voice Write this sentence on the board: *The customer was thanked by the cashier.* Ask if the sentence is active or passive. **(passive)** Ask a volunteer to change the sentence from passive to active. **(The cashier thanked the customer.)** Tell students that often the verb *be* and the word *by* are good clues that a sentence is in the passive voice.

Have students read page 70. Discuss as a class how active voice affected Marco's writing and the story's energy as a whole. Instruct students to look for places where active voice is needed in their own short stories.

✏ Writer's Term_____

Active Voice and Passive Voice
Although the passive voice is often avoided on purpose, it can be useful. Sometimes, the writer wants to emphasize that the subject received the action (e.g., *The dog was attacked by a group of coyotes.*). Sometimes, the instigator of the action is unknown (e.g., *The cake had already been eaten when I got home!*).

▶ Online Writing Center

 Provides **interactive proofreading activities** for each genre.

Revise
Focus on Sentence Fluency

The Rubric Says	The story contains strong sentences written in active voice.
Writing Strategy	Use active voice to strengthen sentences.

✏ Writer's Term_____

Active Voice and Passive Voice
A verb is in **active voice** if the subject of the sentence is doing the action. A verb is in **passive voice** if the subject of the sentence is receiving or being affected by the action.

My short story is really coming along! The rubric says to write my sentences in active voice. That's because active voice almost always sounds stronger than passive voice.

I see one paragraph in my draft that has a lot of passive voice. I'm going to change the passive voice to active voice and make those sentences stronger!

[changed to active voice]

[DRAFT]

I still tried to save my friend
Even though I was frightened, ~~my friend had to be saved!~~ So what he didn't actually need my help?
if ~~my help wasn't really needed.~~ I ~~still hadn't been controlled by my~~ had controlled my fear,
~~fears~~ and that was what mattered!

Apply

Are any of your sentences written in passive voice? If they are, change them to active voice to make them stronger.

Optional Revising Lessons_____

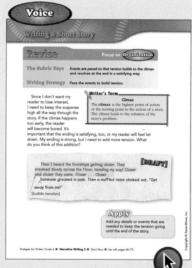

Narrative 5

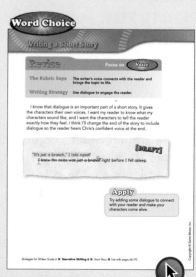

Narrative 6

 Go to ➡ *Strategies for Writers Grade 6 CD-ROM*

Edit — Focus on **Conventions**

The Rubric Says Personal, possessive, and indefinite pronouns are used correctly. The writing is easy to read.

Writing Strategy Recognize and correct inappropriate shifts in pronoun number and person.

Writer's Term

Indefinite Pronouns
Indefinite pronouns refer to persons or things that are not identified as individuals.

Now I need to check my spelling, punctuation, and capitalization. The rubric also says I need to use different kinds of pronouns correctly. Sometimes indefinite pronouns are confusing, and it looks like that happened in the paragraph below!

[DRAFT]

— [corrected indefinite pronouns] —

After Og banged the iron ^k nocker a few times, Roger opened the
        creak
door with a ~~creek~~ and let us in. He took us to the huge, paneled
        everybody   Some
room where ~~somebody~~ was hanging out. Any of the guys roasted
marshmallows
~~marshmallows~~ in the stone fireplace. ~~He~~ played cards or video games.
                              Others

It looked like a normal sleepover!

Reflect
Look at all the pronouns in the draft. Does Marco need to make any more corrections?

Apply — **Conventions**
Edit your draft for spelling, punctuation, and capitalization. Be sure to fix any problems with pronouns.

For more practice using pronouns correctly, use the exercises on the next two pages.

Short Story 71

Related Grammar Practice

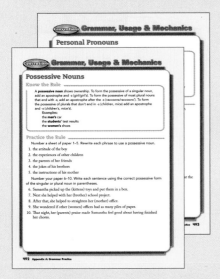

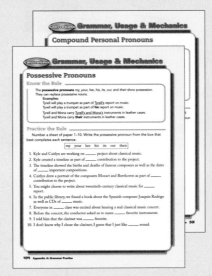

Student Edition pages 492, 493, 494, 501

Go to ➡ Appendix A: Grammar Practice

Student Objectives

• Edit to correct inappropriate shifts in pronoun number and person. *(p. 71)*

Edit

Focus on **Conventions**

Use Pronouns It is now time for students to correct any mistakes they have made in their stories. Ask volunteers to give examples of indefinite pronouns. Then go through the draft and discuss Marco's edits, focusing on the correct use of indefinite pronouns. Instruct students to edit their writing for all mistakes.

If any students are having trouble with pronouns, teach the mini-lessons on pages T72 and T73. Then have students do the exercises on pages 72 and 73.

Writer's Term

Indefinite Pronouns Common indefinite pronouns include *someone, everyone, some, anyone,* and *nobody.* Some indefinite pronouns take a singular verb. (*Someone is knocking at the door.*) Some take a plural verb, as this very sentence illustrates.

CCSS Common Core State Standards
L.6.1: Demonstrate command of the conventions of standard English grammar and usage when writing or speaking. **L.6.1.c:** Recognize and correct inappropriate shifts in pronoun number and person. **L.6.2:** Demonstrate command of the conventions of standard English capitalization, punctuation, and spelling when writing. **L.6.2.b:** Spell correctly.

Conventions

Student Objectives

- Learn how to use personal and possessive pronouns correctly. (p. 72)

Personal and Possessive Pronouns

Write the following words on the board and have students tell you whether each one is a personal or a possessive pronoun: *it* (personal), *I* (personal), *you* (personal), *his* (possessive), *her* (personal or possessive), *us* (personal), *their* (possessive), *its* (possessive), *they* (personal), *my* (possessive), *your* (possessive), *we* (personal).

Write some practice sentences on the board and have students choose the correct pronoun to complete each one:

- *On the last day of class _____ (we/our) had a picnic.*
- *We had relay races, and _____ (me/my) class won!*
- *Mrs. Sanchez brought _____ (she/her) guitar and played.*
- *The kids in the choir sang along; _____ (they/their) sounded amazing!*

Ask volunteers to make up original sentences using personal and possessive pronouns.

Online Writing Center

Provides **interactive grammar games** and **practice activities** in student eBook.

Conventions **Grammar, Usage & Mechanics**

Personal and Possessive Pronouns

Know the Rule

A **pronoun** can take the place of a noun.
Use the **personal pronouns** *I*, *me*, *we*, and *us* to speak or write about yourself. Use the personal pronouns *she*, *her*, *it*, *he*, *him*, *you*, *they*, and *them* to refer to other people and things.
The **possessive pronouns** *her*, *his*, *its*, *our*, *their*, *my*, and *your* show possession.

Practice the Rule

Number a sheet of paper 1–10. Rewrite each sentence with the correct pronoun(s).

1. Last year (me/my) friends gave me a surprise birthday party.
2. They blindfolded (I/me) and took me to my favorite restaurant.
3. Cara brought (she/her) camera and took pictures of all of (we/us) eating dinner.
4. Then (we/us) went to see a scary movie at the neighborhood movie theater.
5. Would (you/your) believe I was so tired that I fell asleep during the scariest part?
6. I woke up when all (me/my) friends screamed in fear.
7. My friends said (they/their) were glad I missed that part of the movie.
8. (They/Them) know I sometimes get really scared at the movies.
9. After the movie, all of (we/us) went out for ice cream.
10. That night, back in (me/my) own bedroom, I slept like a baby.

72 Narrative Writing

Related Grammar Practice

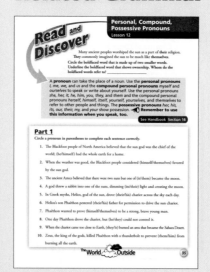

Page 35

Page 37

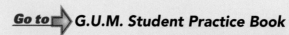

Go to G.U.M. Student Practice Book

Indefinite Pronouns

Know the Rule

An **indefinite pronoun** refers to persons or things that are not identified as individuals. Indefinite pronouns include *all, any, anybody, anything, both, each, either, everybody, everyone, everything, few, many, most, nobody, no one, nothing, one, several, some,* and *someone.*

Practice the Rule

Number a sheet of paper 1–10. Rewrite each sentence by writing an indefinite pronoun from the Word Bank. Remember to capitalize any words that begin a sentence. Some sentences could have more than one correct answer. Some words may be used more than once.

Word Bank

one	many	everyone	some
no one	somebody	most	any
someone	anybody	something	several

1. _____ has lived in the Evans mansion for years. **No one**
2. Maybe that's why so _____ of us find the old house mysterious. **many**
3. I don't believe _____ of the stories about the Evans mansion. **any**
4. Still, _____ about that old house creeps me out. **something**
5. _____ say they have seen strange lights glowing in its windows. **Some**
6. _____ of my friends claim to have heard eerie noises around there. **Some**
7. I think _____ of the weirdest things about the house is its enormous front door. **one**
8. _____ houses today don't have doors that look like they belong on a castle! **Most**
9. People say that _____ once robbed a bank and hid the loot in the house. **someone**
10. _____ around here has heard the story. **Everyone**

Short Story 73

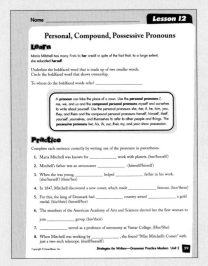

Page 29

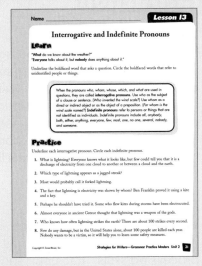

Page 31

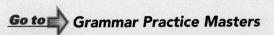

Go to ➡ *Grammar Practice Masters*

Conventions

Mini-Lesson

Student Objectives

- Learn how to use indefinite pronouns correctly. *(p. 73)*

Indefinite Pronouns

Explain that indefinite pronouns do not specify a specific person or thing, gender, or number, with some exceptions, such as *none, nobody,* and *no one.*

Write the word *everybody* on the board. Then ask:

- How many people does this word signify? (unknown)
- Are the people female, male, or a mix of both? (That cannot be determined.)

Explain that all that can be determined from the word *everybody* is that more than one person is being discussed.

Now write the following on the board: *The whole team* is sick. Ask students to change the phrase *the whole team* into an indefinite pronoun. (Possible response: *All are sick.*)

Ask for volunteers to name more indefinite pronouns. (Possible answers: *anyone, anybody, somebody, either, neither, all, any, some, none*) Point out that students will have to be careful about subject-verb agreement when the subject is an indefinite pronoun.

CCSS **Common Core State Standards**
L.6.1: Demonstrate command of the conventions of standard English grammar and usage when writing or speaking. **L.6.1.c:** Recognize and correct inappropriate shifts in pronoun number and person. **L.6.2:** Demonstrate command of the conventions of standard English capitalization, punctuation, and spelling when writing. **L.6.3:** Use knowledge of language and its conventions when writing, speaking, reading, or listening.

Write
a Short Story

Week 3 • Day 4

Student Objectives

- Discuss preparation for publishing and presentation. *(p. 74)*
- Use a final editing checklist to publish their work. *(p. 74)*

Publish +Presentation

Make a Final Copy Have students read Marco's remarks on page 74. Discuss his publishing decision as a class. Challenge students to think of other ways to publish their short stories. Encourage them to pursue their preferred publishing methods by allowing time in class to research online magazines or websites that feature student writing. Students may also wish to compile the class's short stories into one bound book to be displayed somewhere in the classroom or library.

Read through Marco's final checklist. Instruct students to follow Marco's checklist or to create their own, focusing on elements of writing that concern them most. Encourage them to share copies of their published work with friends and family members.

Strategies for Writers Online

Go to **www.sfw.z-b.com** for additional online resources for students and teachers.

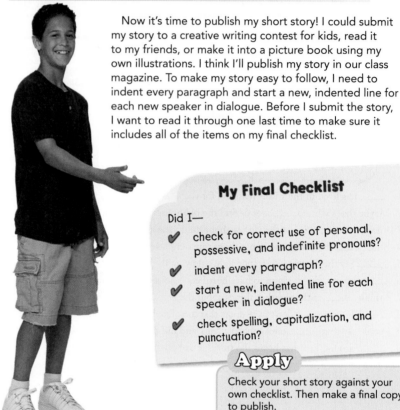

Publish +Presentation

Publishing Strategy	Publish your short story in a class magazine.
Presentation Strategy	Indent every paragraph.

Now it's time to publish my short story! I could submit my story to a creative writing contest for kids, read it to my friends, or make it into a picture book using my own illustrations. I think I'll publish my story in our class magazine. To make my story easy to follow, I need to indent every paragraph and start a new, indented line for each new speaker in dialogue. Before I submit the story, I want to read it through one last time to make sure it includes all of the items on my final checklist.

My Final Checklist

Did I—

✓ check for correct use of personal, possessive, and indefinite pronouns?

✓ indent every paragraph?

✓ start a new, indented line for each speaker in dialogue?

✓ check spelling, capitalization, and punctuation?

Apply

Check your short story against your own checklist. Then make a final copy to publish.

74 Narrative Writing

Differentiating Instruction

ENRICHMENT

Make a Recording Encourage students to make a podcast or recording of their stories, complete with sound effects (such as footsteps, howling wind, creaking doors) and appropriate music. Remind students to alter their voices for each character and to use a narrator's voice for non-dialogue text. Students may work in groups, with one providing the narrative voice and others reading the dialogue parts or providing sound effects.

REINFORCEMENT

Word-Processing Practice Pair a struggling student with a student who already has strong computer and word-processing skills. Each pair should practice using various word-processing functions, as well as creating, saving, retrieving, and printing a file.

Creepover!

by Marco

"This is going to be so great, Chris," said my best friend, Og. "Don't you think?"

"Sure," I lied.

We stood outside the castle-sized front door of the old Evans mansion. When the house stood empty, everyone talked about its eerie glowing windows and the strange moaning that couldn't be just the wind. Now Roger, the new kid, lived here—and Og and I were invited to a sleepover in the creepiest house around. I was afraid of that place, but somehow I had to hide my fear for the whole night!

After Og banged the heavy iron knocker a few times, Roger opened the door with a creak and let us in. He took us to the huge, paneled room where everybody was hanging out. Some of the guys roasted marshmallows in the stone fireplace. Others played cards or video games. It looked like a normal sleepover!

For a while, I forgot where I was and just enjoyed myself. But when we spread our sleeping bags on the floor and Roger turned off the lights, I got nervous again. The dying fire cast strange shadows, and a dreary moan blew around the house. I burrowed into my downy sleeping bag, but I couldn't relax.

Then I heard the footsteps. They creaked slowly across the floor, heading my way! Closer and closer they came. Closer . . . Closer . . .

Someone groaned in pain. Then a muffled voice choked out, "Get away from me!"

It was Og! And he needed help!

I scrambled to my feet and jumped onto the threatening figure that towered over Og. I wrestled it to the floor before I realized the figure was Roger!

"Was I sleepwalking again?" he mumbled.

"Yeah," said Og. "You stepped right on me!"

"Sorry." Roger crawled back to his spot, closed his eyes, and started snoring.

"He scared me to death," said Og, settling back down.

"Yeah, me too." As I slid into my sleeping bag, I realized something. Even though I was frightened, I still tried to save my friend. So what if he didn't actually need my help? I had controlled my fear, and that was what mattered!

Finally, I nestled into my bag and took a deep breath. Something was scratching against the windowpane, but I closed my eyes anyway.

"It's just a branch," I told myself right before I fell asleep.

Reflect

Look at the story. Does it have all the traits of a good short story? Check it against the rubric. Then use the rubric to check your own story.

Technology Tip for 21st Century Literacies

The recent explosion of apps has led to the emergence of multiple platforms and spaces for multimodal composing. Encourage students to use the full range of tools and spaces to which they have access, including those on mobile devices. Students can use Storyrobe as a tool for recasting short stories into a multimodal format. Use this as an opportunity not only to discuss the "mobile" aspect of what students can compose, but also to talk about the difference between writing that uses images and words, as opposed to relying on a single mode.

See **www.sfw.z-b.com** for further information about and links to these websites and tools.

Write a Short Story

Week 3 • Day 5

Student Objectives

- Use a short story rubric. (pp. 58–59)
- Share a published short story. (p. 75)

Presentation Strategy Explain that indenting signals the beginning of a new paragraph and groups related information visually. If block paragraphs are used, there should be a line of space between paragraphs. Encourage students to format their stories on a computer.

Reflecting on a Short Story

Instruct students to use the rubric on pages 58 and 59 to evaluate "Creepover!" Ask the groups to present their scores to the class. Opinions should be supported with examples.

Ask students to reflect on their story-writing experience. Ask:

- How does writing a short story differ from other types of writing?

CCSS Common Core State Standards

W.6.5: With some guidance and support from peers and adults, develop and strengthen writing as needed by planning, revising, editing, rewriting, or trying a new approach. **W.6.6:** Use technology, including the Internet, to produce and publish writing as well as to interact and collaborate with others; demonstrate sufficient command of keyboarding skills to type a minimum of three pages in a single sitting. **SL.6.5:** Include multimedia components (e.g., graphics, images, music, sound) and visual displays in presentations to clarify information.

Biography Planner

WEEK 1

Day 1
Introduce
a Biography

Student Objectives
- Review the elements of a biography.
- Consider purpose and audience.
- Learn the traits of narrative writing.

Student Activities
- Read and discuss **What's in a Biography?** (p. 76)
- Read and discuss **Why write a Biography?** (p. 77)
- Read **Linking Narrative Writing Traits to a Biography.** (p. 78)

Day 2
Analyze
Read a Biography

Student Objectives
- Read a model biography.

Student Activities
- Read **"Mary McLeod Bethune."** (pp. 79–81)

Day 3
Analyze
Introduce the Rubric

Student Objectives
- Learn to read a rubric.

Student Activities
- Review **"Mary McLeod Bethune."** (pp. 79–81)
- Read and discuss the **Biography Rubric.** (pp. 82–83)

WEEK 2

Day 1
Write
Prewrite: Ideas

Student Objectives
- Read and understand a prewriting strategy.

Student Activities
- Read and discuss **Prewrite: Focus on Ideas.** (p. 88)
- Apply the prewriting strategy.

Day 2
Write
Prewrite: Organization

Student Objectives
- Create a Biography Map to organize notes.

Student Activities
- Read and discuss **Prewrite: Focus on Organization.** (p. 89)
- Reflect on the model Biography Map.
- Apply the prewriting strategy to create a Biography Map.
- Participate in a peer conference.

Day 3
Write
Draft: Word Choice

Student Objectives
- Begin writing, avoiding ordinary words and weak verbs.

Student Activities
- Read and discuss **Draft: Focus on Word Choice.** (p. 90)
- Apply the drafting strategy by using a Biography Map to write a draft.

WEEK 3

Day 1
Write
Revise: Organization

Student Objectives
- Revise to use transition words and phrases.

Student Activities
- Read and discuss **Revise: Focus on Organization.** (p. 93)
- Participate in a peer conference.

Day 2
Write
Revise: Sentence Fluency

Student Objectives
- Revise to vary the length of sentences.

Student Activities
- Read and discuss **Revise: Focus on Sentence Fluency.** (p. 94)

Note: Optional Revising Lessons appear on the *Strategies for Writers* CD-ROM.

Day 3
Write
Edit: Conventions

Student Objectives
- Edit to recognize and correct inappropriate shifts in verb tense.

Student Activities
- Read and discuss **Edit: Focus on Conventions.** (p. 95)

Note: Teach the Conventions mini-lessons (pp. 96–97) if needed.

Day 4	Day 5
Analyze Ideas, Organization, and Voice	**Analyze** Word Choice, Sentence Fluency, and Conventions

Student Objectives
- Read a model biography.
- Use the biography rubric.
- Use the model biography to study Ideas, Organization, and Voice.

Student Activities
- Review **"Mary McLeod Bethune."** (pp. 79–81)
- Review the rubric. (pp. 82–83)
- Read the discuss **Using the Rubric to Study the Model.** (pp. 84–85)

Student Objectives
- Read a model biography.
- Use the biography rubric.
- Use the model biography to study Word Choice, Sentence Fluency, and Conventions.

Student Activities
- Review **"Mary McLeod Bethune."** (pp. 79–81)
- Review the rubric. (pp. 82–83)
- Read and discuss **Using the Rubric to Study the Model.** (pp. 86–87)

Day 4	Day 5
Write Draft	**Write** Revise: Ideas

Student Objectives
- Complete a draft. (p. 91)

Student Activities
- Finish the draft.
- Participate in a peer conference.

Student Objectives
- Revise to use details that are new to readers.

Student Activities
- Read and discuss **Revise: Focus on Ideas.** (p. 92)
- Reflect on a model draft.
- Apply the revising strategy.

Day 4	Day 5
Write Publish: +Presentation	**Write** Publish: +Presentation

Student Objectives
- Discuss preparation for publishing and presentation.
- Use a final editing checklist to publish their work.

Student Activities
- Read and discuss **Publish: +Presentation.** (p. 98)

Student Objectives
- Use a biography rubric.
- Share a published biography.

Student Activities
- Share their work.
- Use the rubric to reflect upon and evaluate the model and their own writing. (pp. 82–83, 99–101)

To complete the chapter in fewer days, combine the learning objectives and activities in a way that supports students as they write.

Grammar, Usage & Mechanics

Action and Linking Verbs T96
Verb Tense T97
Grammar Practice T95–T97

Differentiating Instruction

Using the Rubric T87
Draft...................T90
Publish.....................T98
For additional Differentiating Instruction activities, see Strategies for Writers *Extensions Online at* **www.sfw.z-b.com.**

English Language Learners

Using the Rubric T84–T85
Prewrite T88
Revise T92

Conferencing

Peer to Peer T89, T91, T93
Peer Groups T89, T91, T93
Teacher-Led T89, T91, T93

Technology Tip

Using the Rubric T86
Publish.....................T99

 Connection Letter
Reproducible letter (in English and Spanish) appears on the *Strategies for Writers* CD-ROM and at **www.sfw.z-b.com.**

Online Writing Center

Provides IWB resources, interactive games and practice activities, videos, eBooks, and a virtual file cabinet.

 Strategies for Writers Online

Go to **www.sfw.z-b.com** for free online resources for students and teachers.

Introduce
a Biography

Student Objectives

- Review the elements of a biography. *(p. 76)*
- Consider purpose and audience. *(p. 77)*
- Learn the traits of narrative writing. *(p. 78)*

What's a Biography?

Discuss with students the definition of a biography. Ask students to name biographies they have read, either for school or on their own. Discuss what the biographies had in common and ask students what they did and did not like about the biographies they read.

What's in a Biography?

Read and discuss with students the various elements of a biography as outlined on page 76. Ask volunteers which elements are also common to other forms of writing. (Possible responses: Subject—historical episode, interview; Third-Person Point of View—magazine features, short stories; Accuracy—descriptive essay, how-to essay) Discuss why each element is important to writing a biography.

Strategies for Writers Online

Go to **www.sfw.z-b.com** for additional online resources for students and teachers.

What's a **Biography?**

A biography is a factual account of a person's life. However, it should be more than just a string of facts. A good biography tells a clear, engaging story about a person's life or some part of that life. A biography should not include made-up information.

What's in a **Biography?**

Subject
This is the person I am writing about. I want to be consistent and clear in identifying my subject. I should communicate the important facts about the person's life or about the part of his or her life that I'm focusing on.

Third-Person Point of View
I will use *he* or *she* because in a biography I am telling about the life of someone else. Third-person point of view is part of writing a biography.

Accuracy
I am responsible for providing accurate information about my subject from beginning to end. This means I should check figures in any dates I give. I should check spelling and facts about any names or places I mention.

Narrative Text Exemplars (Biography)

Partridge, Elizabeth. *This Land Was Made for You and Me: The Life and Songs of Woody Guthrie.* **Viking, 2002.** CCSS This biography chronicles the life of Woody Guthrie, a talented songwriter and folksinger who traveled across the country and experienced political and social conflicts. Many of these conflicts helped inspire some of his most memorable songs.

McGovern, Ann. *The Secret Soldier: The Story Of Deborah Sampson.* **Scholastic Paperbacks, 1990.** This book is the exciting true-life story of a woman who became a soldier during the Revolutionary War by dressing and acting like a man.

Why write a Biography?

When I wrote a biography last year, I remember it was challenging but also satisfying. I have listed some reasons why I would like to write biographies.

Information
I like to discover new information about people in history, and I enjoy sharing what I learned. I want others to know about these amazing lives.

Inspiration
When I read about someone who did something that inspires me, I want to pass that on to others, too. Sometimes I'm surprised about what inspires me. I might not know until I have read a lot about the person.

Personal Enjoyment
When I choose the subject for a biography, it's like choosing a friend I want to get to know better. I personally enjoy the time I spend reading and learning about someone I am curious about.

Why write a Biography?

Read and discuss with students the reasons for writing a biography. Point out that all writing has a purpose and is aimed at a specific audience. These authentic purposes help authors shape their writing. Ask a volunteer to read aloud each reason. Then have students explore purposes for writing a biography that are not listed on the page. Encourage students to think about their own reasons for writing a biography and how these reasons will affect the ideas and voice of their writing.

Smith Jr., Charles R. *Twelve Rounds to Glory: The Story of Muhammad Ali.* Candlewick Press, 2007.
In *Twelve Rounds to Glory: The Story of Muhammad Ali*, Smith uses rap-style language to describe the famous boxer's life, from the racism Ali encountered as a child to his lighting of the Olympic torch in 1996.

Petry, Ann. *Harriet Tubman: Conductor on the Underground Railroad.* HarperCollins, 1983. **CCSS**
This book describes how Harriet Tubman helped hundreds of slaves reach freedom by using the Underground Railroad. Harriet Tubman became a symbol of courage and hope to African Americans living in the South.

CCSS **C**ommon **C**ore **S**tate **S**tandards
SL.6.1: Engage effectively in a range of collaborative discussions (one-on-one, in groups, and teacher-led) with diverse partners on *grade* 6 *topics, texts, and issues*, building on others' ideas and expressing their own clearly. **SL.6.1.b:** Follow rules for collegial discussions, set specific goals and deadlines, and define individual roles as needed. **SL.6.1.c:** Pose and respond to specific questions with elaboration and detail by making comments that contribute to the topic, text, or issue under discussion.

Introduce
a Biography

Linking Narrative Writing Traits to a Biography

Explain to students that they will follow Marco as he models using the writing process and the traits together. As they follow Marco through the writing process, students will see how the Narrative Writing Traits have been adapted and applied to writing a biography. They will see that a biography has many factors in common with other types of narrative writing. However, the particular audience and purpose of a biography determine how the traits are used.

Linking Narrative Writing Traits to a Biography

In this chapter, you will write about a real person's life. This type of narrative writing is called a biography. Marco will guide you through the stages of the writing process: Prewrite, Draft, Revise, Edit, and Publish. In each stage, Marco will show you important writing strategies that are linked to the Narrative Writing Traits below.

Narrative Writing Traits

Ideas	• a focused topic, experience, or series of events • engaging, accurate details that develop and describe the topic, experience, or series of events
Organization	• logically sequenced events, often in chronological order • an interesting beginning and a satisfying ending • transitions that signal the sequence of events as well as shifts in time or setting
Voice	• a voice and tone that are appropriate for the purpose and audience • dialogue that, if used, fits the characters
Word Choice	• precise, descriptive words and phrases
Sentence Fluency	• a variety of sentences that flow and are a pleasure to read aloud
Conventions	• no or few errors in grammar, usage, mechanics, and spelling

Before you write, read Cindy Lyman's biography on the next three pages. Then use the biography rubric on pages 82–83 to decide how well she did. (You might want to look back at What's in a Biography? on page 76, too!)

Narrative Writing Traits in a Biography

 Ideas The writer focuses on one person's life, often narrowing the focus to one portion of that life. Plenty of memorable, descriptive details are used to create a clear picture of the person and the events of his or her life.

 **Organization** Events are presented in a logical, natural order; effective transitions are used to guide the reader from one event to the next and to show how ideas or events are related.

 Voice The writer uses third-person point of view to keep the spotlight on the subject. A respectful and engaging tone is used throughout, and direct quotations capture the essence of the subject.

Mary McLeod Bethune

by Cindy Lyman

Subject of biography

Mary McLeod Bethune, a great African American educator and leader, was born in 1875 on a farm in South Carolina, where she soon learned how to plant seeds and make them grow to their full value. All through her life, Mary McLeod Bethune planted other kinds of seeds—of learning, equal rights, hope, and change. With constant dedication and wisdom, she did everything in her power to make these grow to their full value for African Americans.

In her time, African Americans in the South were free from slavery, but they were not free in some other important ways. Because of segregation, which separated people by race, African Americans could not attend public schools for white students or go to hospitals for white people. Unfortunately, in many places there were no schools for black students or hospitals for black people. One of those places was Daytona, Florida. There, Mary McLeod Bethune started a school with five black students and developed it into a highly respected college for more than a thousand young men and women. Also in Daytona she opened a very small hospital and helped it grow into a large, important one. These were just two of her numerous accomplishments that improved education, health, and opportunity for African Americans.

What seeds were planted in Mary's early life that led to such accomplishments? Her parents, Samuel and Patsy McLeod, were born in slavery, and together they had fourteen children who were born before slavery was outlawed during the Civil War. Once they were free from slavery, the McLeods bought their own land, built their own home, and ran their own farm. Mary was their first child born in freedom. In that way she was special to her parents, although they trained her to pick cotton and do other hard work that all farm children were expected to do.

Accurate facts

Biography **79**

Word Choice The writer uses precise, descriptive language to bring the subject and events to life. Specific nouns, colorful adjectives, and strong verbs help listeners or readers get to know the person being described in the biography.

Sentence Fluency The writer keeps the writing lively by using a variety of clearly written sentences. The writing has energy and flow, which helps move the narrative along.

Conventions The biography has been carefully edited for errors. All verbs are used correctly, and the biography is a pleasure to read.

Analyze
the Model

Week 1 • Day 2

Student Objectives

• Read a model biography. (pp. 79–81)

Read the Model

Have students read "Mary McLeod Bethune" on pages 79–81. Remind them to listen for the writing traits outlined on page 78.

Elements of a Biography

Use the notes on the model to discuss the various elements of a biography. Ask:

• Why has Cindy organized the events of Mary's life in chronological order? (Possible response: The reader can see how the events of her life built on each other.)

• How is using third-person point of view appropriate when writing a biography? (A biography is about someone other than the writer.)

• How do the quotations affect your understanding of the subject? (Possible response: They help me understand how Mary really felt.)

Encourage students to respond to each other's ideas. You may wish to have students refer back to What's in a Biography? on page 76.

CCSS **C**ommon **C**ore **S**tate **S**tandards
R/Lit.6.1: Cite textual evidence to support analysis of what the text says explicitly as well as inferences drawn from the text. **SL.6.1.a:** Come to discussions prepared, having read or studied required material; explicitly draw on that preparation by referring to evidence on the topic, text, or issue to probe and reflect on ideas under discussion. **SL.6.1.d:** Review the key ideas expressed and demonstrate understanding of multiple perspectives through reflection and paraphrasing.

Third-person pronouns

Sometimes in a break from the hardest work, Mary's mother told amazing stories. Mary's grandmother also shared stories about her family's heritage in Africa. Mary loved to listen to these stories and was fascinated by the spoken words. In _her_ whole family, nobody could read or write because they were never given an opportunity to learn. Mary had looked at books in white people's homes, and _she_ desperately wanted to understand the printed words inside. But there were no schools for black children anywhere near _her_ home, so Mary could only hope something would change.

Third-person point of view →

Finally, one day, a young black woman in city clothes came to visit. Her name was Emma Wilson, and she was starting a mission school for black children. The McLeods could send only one child, and all agreed it would be Mary, who was then seven years old. Each day, Mary proudly walked five miles to Miss Wilson's school and then strode back eager to share the reading, writing, and math she had learned there. Later she wrote, "The whole world opened to me when I learned to read."

Mary was a serious student and a strong leader in Miss Wilson's school. When she graduated at age eleven, she hoped for further education, but in her region there were no higher schools for black students. Eventually, Miss Wilson was able to find a sponsor who paid for Mary to study at an academy in North Carolina and then at a missionary training institute in Chicago, where Mary was the only black student.

When she finished her studies, Mary dedicated herself to improving the lives of African Americans, especially in the South. Besides founding schools and hospitals, Mary McLeod Bethune formed and led organizations of black women, and she held important posts in national government as well. She advised presidents and oversaw programs for young people around the country. From age twenty until nearly seventy, she was always actively and effectively managing some major challenge to her community or her country.

Accurate facts ──┘

Books for Professional Development

Zarnowski, Myra. _History Makers: A Questioning Approach to Reading and Writing Biographies._ Portsmouth, NH. Heinemann, 2003. In this book, history students become biographers who read, discuss, research, and write books about their subjects, providing their own original interpretations of the facts. By digging into the past and reflecting on what they have learned, students get involved in the process.

Peha, Steve, and Margot Carmichael Lester. _Be a Better Writer: Power Tools for Young Writers!_ Bend, OR. The Leverage Factory, 2006. Packed with practical techniques to help young writers build a solid foundation, this fun guide is a comprehensive introduction to the world of the written word. Students will learn how to generate interesting ideas, how to use descriptive detail, and how to beat writer's block.

 Strategies for Writers Online

Go to **www.sfw.z-b.com** for additional online resources for students and teachers.

Certainly, one seed that grew to a towering tree in Mary's life was her love of words, in the songs and stories she learned from her family and then in the books she learned to read at Miss Wilson's school. The way she expressed herself in words became a key to her leadership and teaching. In formal speeches or friendly conversations, her confident, compelling voice convinced black people and white people to support the projects and causes she believed in. Her written words clearly conveyed her visions and convictions. Though Mary McLeod Bethune died in 1955, her words and her life story have continued to inspire others to carry on her work.

Subject of biography, summarized

Peregoy, Suzanne F., and Owen F. Boyle. *Reading, Writing and Learning in ESL: A Resource Book for K–12 Teachers.* 4th ed. Boston. Allyn & Bacon, 2004. This is an outstanding resource book for elementary and secondary teachers who work with ESL students.

National Writing Project. *Because Digital Writing Matters: Improving Student Writing in Online and Multimedia Environments.* San Francisco: Jossey-Bass, 2010. In this new book from the National Writing Project, the authors look at how educators, parents, and policymakers can promote technology development in schools to create learning environments that support digital literacy. *Because Digital Writing Matters* offers practical solutions and models for effectively finding, using, summarizing, evaluating, creating, and communicating information while using digital technologies.

CCSS **C**ommon **C**ore **S**tate **S**tandards
R/Lit.6.1: Cite textual evidence to support analysis of what the text says explicitly as well as inferences drawn from the text. **SL.6.1.a:** Come to discussions prepared, having read or studied required material; explicitly draw on that preparation by referring to evidence on the topic, text, or issue to probe and reflect on ideas under discussion. **SL.6.1.d:** Review the key ideas expressed and demonstrate understanding of multiple perspectives through reflection and paraphrasing.

Analyze the Model

Week 1 • Day 3

Student Objectives

- Learn to read a rubric. (pp. 82–83)

Use the Rubric

Explain the Rubric Explain that a rubric is a tool that helps you plan, improve, and evaluate a piece of writing. Tell students that a rubric helps a writer focus on key elements, or traits, in writing (**Ideas, Organization, Voice, Word Choice, Sentence Fluency, Conventions,** and **Presentation**).

The 6-point rubric on pages 82 and 83 is based on the Narrative Writing Traits that students read on page 78. Draw students' attention to the six columns to explain how the scoring system works. Explain that the column under the numeral 6 describes a very good biography, one that has received the highest score in all categories. This is what students should strive for in their own writing.

Discuss the Rubric Guide the students in a discussion of the rubric. Read the descriptors that go with each trait. Note how the descriptors vary as you move from column to column. Remind students to keep the rubric in mind when they write their own biographies.

Online Writing Center

Provides a variety of **interactive rubrics,** including 4-, 5-, and 6-point models.

Biography

Rubric

Use this 6-point rubric to plan and score a biography.

	6	**5**	**4**
Ideas	The biography is focused and developed. All details develop the subject and bring it to life.	The biography is focused. A few more details would help develop the subject.	The biography is focused. It lacks enough details to be well developed.
Organization	The events are organized in a way that unfolds naturally and logically. Smooth and effective transition words and phrases connect ideas and paragraphs.	The writing is organized. A few more transitions between paragraphs are needed.	The writing is organized. Not enough transitions are used to link ideas.
Voice	The writer uses an appropriate point of view consistently. Quotations add authenticity.	The writer uses an appropriate point of view. A few more quotations are needed.	The writer's point of view is somewhat inconsistent. Quotations don't work well with the surrounding text.
Word Choice	Precise language conveys the events and enlivens the writing.	Language is precise most of the time. A few words are weak or overused.	Some of the language is precise. Several words used are weak or overused.
Sentence Fluency	A variety of sentence structures links the ideas and moves the story along at a good pace.	Several sentences in a row share the same structure. The pace is good.	Many sentences begin the same way but vary in length. Parts of the story move along well.
Conventions	The writing has been carefully edited. Verbs are used correctly.	Minor errors are present but do not interfere with meaning. Verbs are used correctly.	A few errors cause confusion. One or two verbs or shifts in tense are problematic.
+Presentation	Visuals are thoughtfully integrated into the biography.		

CCSS Common Core State Standards

Biography

As students learn to write a biography, they will receive instruction based on the Narrative writing standards, as well as several Speaking & Listening, Language, and Reading/Literature standards for grade 6.

The rubric and writing strategies for Ideas are based on standards **W.6.3, W.6.3.b,** and **W.6.3.d,** which encourage the writer to focus on one subject and to use strong, descriptive details to develop the narrative and bring the subject to life. The rubric and writing strategies for Organization have a foundation in standards **W.6.3, W.6.3.a, W.6.3.c,** and **W.6.3.e,** which outline the need for naturally sequenced events and the use of effective transitions to connect ideas and guide the reader through the biography to the conclusion. The

3	2	1	
The biography is focused. Details seem undeveloped or unimportant.	The biography is not focused. Details may be unrelated.	The biography is not focused. Details are sketchy or merely listed.	**Ideas**
The writing is somewhat organized. Transitions are weak or ineffective.	Organization is unclear or inconsistent. Transitions are confusing or missing.	The writing is not organized. Transitions are not used.	**Organization**
The writer's point of view is inconsistent and confusing. Quotations may be inaccurate.	The writer's voice sounds far away or inconsistent. Quotations are not used.	The voice is weak or absent. Quotations are not used.	**Voice**
Most of the language is vague and imprecise. Overused words weaken the writing.	Ordinary and overused words make it hard for the reader to engage with the writing.	Many words are overused or used incorrectly. The writing is dull.	**Word Choice**
Most sentences share the same structure. The pace of the story is affected.	Sentences are too short. The pace is choppy.	Sentences are very basic in structure. Many are incomplete.	**Sentence Fluency**
Many errors are repeated and cause confusion. Some verbs are used incorrectly.	Serious errors interfere with meaning. Many verbs are used incorrectly.	The writing has not been edited.	**Conventions**

See Appendix B for 4-, 5-, and 6-point narrative rubrics.

Biography **83**

Apply the Rubric

Score the Model Draw a blank model of the rubric on the board, labeling each row and column. Beginning with Ideas, ask students to raise a hand if they feel the model should receive a 6. Record the number of votes in the corresponding cell. Continue the process for Ideas 5 down to 1 and then proceed with the remaining traits.

Tally the Scores Discuss the results with students. If any scores differ by two or more points, ask students to defend their scores. After a discussion, take a recount. Make sure students understand the purpose of this exercise is less to score the model than it is to practice identifying and evaluating the traits within a piece of writing.

Additional Rubrics Appendix B includes 4-, 5-, and 6-point rubrics that can be used with any piece of narrative writing. The rubrics are also available as blackline masters in the back of this Teacher Edition, beginning on page T525.

rubric and writing strategies for Voice reflect standard **L.6.3.b,** which calls for writers to use a consistent style and tone, and standards **W.6.3, W.6.3.b,** and **W.6.3.d,** which stress the use of effective technique, such as using effective pacing, direct quotations, and precise, descriptive, sensory language. These standards are also reflected in the rubric and writing strategies for Word Choice and Sentence Fluency.

Standards **L.6.1, L.6.2,** and **L.6.3** are clearly reflected throughout the editing pages, while standard **W.6.6** resonates throughout the entire Narrative unit, as students are encouraged to take full advantage of word-processing programs and use a wide range of resources found on the Internet.

CCSS **Common Core State Standards**

SL.6.1.a: Come to discussions prepared, having read or studied required material; explicitly draw on that preparation by referring to evidence on the topic, text, or issue to probe and reflect on ideas under discussion. **SL.6.1.c:** Pose and respond to specific questions with elaboration and detail by making comments that contribute to the topic, text, or issue under discussion.

Analyze
the Model

Week 1 • Day 4

Student Objectives

- Read a model biography. (*pp. 79–81*)
- Use the biography rubric. (*pp. 82–83*)
- Use the model biography to study Ideas, Organization, and Voice. (*pp. 84–85*)

Study the Model

Assess the Model Have students turn to pages 84–85. Explain that these pages show how the model on pages 79–81 uses the writing traits described in the rubric. Read each section with students. Use questions such as the following to discuss each section. Encourage students to back up their answers with examples from the model and to contribute to other students' responses.

- Which detail about Mary McLeod Bethune's life did you find especially intriguing or memorable? (Possible responses: She worked for 50 years to improve the lives of African Americans.)

Strategies for Writers Online
Go to **www.sfw.z-b.com** for additional online resources for students and teachers.

Biography
Using the ∧Rubric to Study the Model

Did you notice that the model on pages 79–81 points out some key elements of a biography? As she wrote "Mary McLeod Bethune," Cindy Lyman used these elements to help tell her subject's life story. She also used the 6-point rubric on pages 82–83 to plan, draft, revise, and edit the writing. A rubric is a great tool for evaluating writing during the writing process.

Now let's use the same rubric to score the model. To do this, we'll focus on each trait separately, starting with Ideas. We'll use the top descriptor for each trait (column 6), along with examples from the model, to help us understand how the traits work together. How would you score Cindy on each trait?

 **Ideas**

- The biography is focused and developed.
- All details develop the subject and bring it to life.

Cindy connects Mary McLeod Bethune's early life with her later accomplishments through the idea of planting seeds and making sure they grow to their full value. Then she uses details from Mary's childhood to help the reader understand the subject. Mary really came alive for me as I read!

[from the writing model]

Mary McLeod Bethune, a great African American educator and leader, was born in 1875 on a farm in South Carolina, where she soon learned how to plant seeds and make them grow to their full value. All through her life, Mary McLeod Bethune planted other kinds of seeds— of learning, equal rights, hope, and change.

84 Narrative Writing

English Language Learners

BEGINNING

Biography Write *biography*. Circle *bio* and underline *graph*. Tell students that *bio* means "life" and that *graph* means "to write." Then say, *So, the word* biography *means "to write about someone's life."* Have several books available that are good examples of biographies. If possible, try to find books about people whom students may know, such as Bill Gates, Barack Obama, or Queen Elizabeth.

INTERMEDIATE

Chronological Order Write *chronological* on the board. Underline *chrono-* and tell students that it means "time." Review the word *order*. Remind students that when they write about someone's life, they should write in chronological order. Say *chronological order* and have students repeat. Practice chronological order using a Timeline graphic organizer.

Organization

- The events are organized in a way that unfolds naturally and logically.
- Smooth and effective transition words and phrases connect ideas and paragraphs.

Cindy presents the events in Mary's life in a natural and logical way. It was interesting to read about some of Mary's accomplishments, and then look back at her early experiences to see how they influenced her life. Cindy uses a question to transition to Mary's early life. I had no problem following along.

[from the writing model]

What seeds were planted in her early life that led to such accomplishments? Her parents, Samuel and Patsy McLeod, were born in slavery, and together they had fourteen children who had been born before slavery was outlawed during the Civil War. Once they were free from slavery, the McLeods bought their own land, built their own home, and ran their own farm. Mary was their first child born in freedom.

Voice

- The writer uses an appropriate point of view consistently.
- Quotations add authenticity.

Because Cindy has written a biography, she uses *she, her,* and the subject's name throughout. Her third-person perspective is consistent and leaves no confusion about who her subject is. Cindy uses a quotation that shows Mary's voice, but it fits in with her own writing.

[from the writing model]

Each day, Mary proudly walked five miles to Miss Wilson's school and then strode back eager to share the reading, writing, and math she had learned there. Later she wrote, "The whole world opened to me when I learned to read."

Biography 85

- How does Cindy help you understand the passing of time? (Possible response: She uses transitions such as *In her time; Finally; Later she wrote.*)

- How does Cindy feel about Mary McLeod Bethune? How can you tell? (Possible response: It is clear she greatly admires her. Cindy uses language that reflects respect and admiration, such as *a serious student; her confident, compelling voice; her words and her life story have continued to inspire.*)

ADVANCED

Focused and Developed Review the Ideas rubric on page 84. Ask students what they think *focused and developed* means. Demonstrate *focus* using an overhead projector. Tell students that in writing, the content should be clear and should concentrate on one thing at a time. If writing is well *developed*, then each paragraph has a main idea that is supported by relevant details.

ADVANCED HIGH

Using Powerful Verbs After students have written their first drafts, have them circle all the verbs they used in the first paragraph. Then have them trade with a partner who will read the paragraph and change each of the circled verbs to a stronger one. Then have the partners discuss why they made each change. Monitor that students' changes were appropriate.

CCSS Common Core State Standards

R/Lit.6.1: Cite textual evidence to support analysis of what the text says explicitly as well as inferences drawn from the text. **R/Lit.6.3:** Describe how a particular story's or drama's plot unfolds in a series of episodes as well as how the characters respond or change as the plot moves toward a resolution. **SL.6.1.a:** Come to discussions prepared, having read or studied required material; explicitly draw on that preparation by referring to evidence on the topic, text, or issue to probe and reflect on ideas under discussion.

Analyze
the Model

Week 1 • Day 5

Student Objectives

- Read a model biography. (pp. 79–81)
- Use the biography rubric. (pp. 82–83)
- Use the model biography to study Word Choice, Sentence Fluency, and Conventions. (pp. 86–87)

Continue Discussing the Traits

Now use pages 86–87 to discuss **Word Choice, Sentence Fluency,** and **Conventions** in the model. Use the following questions:

- Point out some precise language that helped you picture Mary and the events of her life. (Possible responses: *great African American educator and leader; dedication and wisdom; segregation; numerous accomplishments; sponsor; missionary training institute*)

- Explain how sentence variety kept you interested and engaged with the writing. (Possible response: The variety in sentence lengths kept me from getting bored or distracted.)

- How would you have felt about reading the model if Cindy's writing was full of errors? (Possible response: I would have felt frustrated and tired while trying to read and understand her writing. I might not have finished the biography at all.)

 Strategies for Writers Online
Go to **www.sfw.z-b.com** for additional online resources for students and teachers.

Word Choice
- Precise language conveys the events and enlivens the writing.

Cindy uses precise, vivid language to describe Mary's response to her first school experience. Strong action verbs help express Mary's feelings and bring a sense of reality to the entire biography. Cindy really gave me a clear picture of what life was like for Mary.

[from the writing model]

She advised presidents and oversaw programs for young people around the country. From age twenty until nearly seventy, she was always actively and effectively managing some major challenge to her community or her country.

Sentence Fluency
- A variety of sentence structures links the ideas and moves the story along at a good pace.

In her paragraphs, Cindy varies the length of sentences, so the rhythm for the reader is more lively. Find the longest and shortest sentences and compare their lengths. You'll see how much variety Cindy created!

[from the writing model]

Unfortunately, in many places there were no schools for black students or hospitals for black people. One of those places was Daytona, Florida. There, Mary McLeod Bethune started a school with five black students and developed it into a highly respected college for more than a thousand young men and women.

Technology Tip  for 21st Century Literacies

As more complex information becomes available through the web, it is critical that students develop the skills needed to present that data in a clear, concise way. Infographics are visual texts that work to do this and require different reading skills to unpack the information depicted. Work with students to locate and unpack an infographic. An infographic pertaining to education in a digital age at **http://www. onlineeducation.net/internet-revolutionizing-education** is one example, but a quick online search will unearth many other options. Talk with students about how the infographic presents data and how the visual form aids and enhances communication.

See **www.sfw.z-b.com** for further information about and links to these websites and tools.

Conventions

- The writing has been carefully edited.
- Verbs are used correctly.

Of course, this biography is about someone who is no longer alive, so it is about the past. Still, it can sometimes be tricky to decide when to use past or present tense. Cindy was careful to use verb tenses correctly throughout her writing. She also did a great job with spelling, grammar, and punctuation. I couldn't find a single error!

[from the writing model]

In formal speeches or friendly conversations, her confident, compelling voice convinced black people and white people to support the projects and causes she believed in. Her written words clearly conveyed her visions and convictions. Though Mary McLoed Bethune died in 1955, her words and her life story have continued to inspire others to carry on her work.

⁺Presentation
Visuals are thoughtfully integrated into the biography.

Now I'm going to use the rubric to help me write a biography. Follow along to see how I do it!

Biography **87**

Differentiating Instruction

ENRICHMENT

Explore Organization Explain that sometimes writers open a narrative with the ending and then circle back around to the beginning of the story. This technique hooks readers, piquing their curiosity about how the subject came to this point in his or her life. Challenge students to rewrite or rethink the organization of the model using this method.

REINFORCEMENT

Support Topic Selection Help students who are struggling to think of a topic. Write on the board a list of people students have learned about in social studies. Ask students to contribute the facts they remember about each person and write them down. Help students choose a subject who interests them or whom they find admirable.

Presentation Explain to students that many writers choose to include some sort of visual with their biographies to give readers an even deeper understanding of the subject. Photographs or drawings of the subject, the subject's hometown, awards he or she has won, or even historical events that occurred during the subject's lifetime can help readers better connect with the subject and energize the overall finished report. Explain that any visuals that are used must be inserted in the appropriate places within the biography. Poorly placed visuals will only confuse the reader and detract power from the biography.

Think About the Traits Ask which traits students think are most important in a biography. Explain that while all traits are important, some stand out more in some genres than in others. Some may feel the trait of **Ideas** is important, because a biography cannot exist without a subject. Others may think that **Voice** is important because the writer needs to make it clear to the reader that he or she respects and cares about the subject.

CCSS **C**ommon **C**ore **S**tate **S**tandards
R/Lit.6.1: Cite textual evidence to support analysis of what the text says explicitly as well as inferences drawn from the text. **SL.6.1.c:** Pose and respond to specific questions with elaboration and detail by making comments that contribute to the topic, text, or issue under discussion. **SL.6.1.d:** Review the key ideas expressed and demonstrate understanding of multiple perspectives through reflection and paraphrasing.

Write
a Biography

Week 2 • Day 1

Student Objectives

• Read and understand a prewriting strategy. (p. 88)

Prewrite

Focus on **Ideas**

Choose a Subject Note that writing a biography is a way for students to demonstrate their content-area knowledge. Consider working with students' social studies teacher(s) to select appropriate topics.

Ask students to make a list of people they have studied and found interesting. Remind students that they will find writing the biography easier and more enjoyable if they have a personal or positive connection with the subject.

Once students have chosen their subjects, instruct them to take some time to gather information about the person from several sources, such as the Internet and the school library. Once again remind students how to evaluate the reliability of sources and to keep track of the sources for proper citation.

Online Writing Center

 Provides **interactive graphic organizers** as well as a variety of graphic organizers in PDF format.

T88 Narrative Writing

Prewrite   Focus on (Ideas)

| **The Rubric Says** | The biography is focused and developed. |
| **Writing Strategy** | Choose an interesting subject and decide on what part of the subject's life to focus. |

Our teacher asked us to write a biography about someone in United States history. She posted a long list to choose from. I chose Will Rogers because I like rodeos and I knew he was a cowboy, but I didn't know much more until I read some Web biographies and lots of funny quotes. He was also featured in a book of famous Native Americans. My notes show some things I learned about Will Rogers. Looking them over, I think I'll focus on his life as a performer.

My Notes on Will Rogers

✔ 1879–1935, born in Indian Territory that became Oklahoma, died in plane crash in Alaska

✔ mother and father were part Cherokee (father, Clem Rogers, fought in Civil War, became judge)

✔ loved horses, learned riding and roping skills from African American ranch hand

✔ 1901, traveled to England, Argentina, South Africa, and Australia, did cowboy and Indian acts in Wild West show and circus

✔ 1905, did rope tricks on stage in New York City and got steady work in show business

✔ 1908 married Betty Blake and settled in New York, started popular comedy act about whatever was in the daily newspaper

✔ 1918 starred in silent film, then in sound films after 1929; voted most popular actor in Hollywood, 1934

✔ wrote newspaper column and did regular radio show with funny comments on politics and other events of the times

Apply

Choose a subject and then do some research to decide what part of the subject's life you want to focus on.

88 Narrative Writing

English Language Learners

BEGINNING/INTERMEDIATE

Third-Person Point of View Review usage of the third-person pronouns. Give several simple examples, such as *She worked in the fields for most of her life. It was a difficult job.* Write other examples without pronouns. Have Beginning ELLs fill in the appropriate pronouns, and ask Intermediate ELLs to check for mistakes. Tell students they will write their biographies from a third-person point of view.

ADVANCED/ADVANCED HIGH

Transitions Write the following transitions on the board: *After winning the election, Surprisingly, Why was Mrs. Roosevelt so shy?* Have partners complete the sentences or answer the question in another sentence. Review that transition words, phrases, and even sentences can help the information flow more smoothly. Write *transitions* and have students repeat the word.

Prewrite
Focus on Organization

The Rubric Says	The events are organized in a way that unfolds naturally and logically.
Writing Strategy	Make a Biography Map to organize the notes.

✏️ **Writer's Term**_____

Biography Map
A **Biography Map** organizes the important events, actions, and accomplishments of a person's life, including a summary at the end.

The rubric reminds me to organize the events in the biography naturally and logically. I will use a Biography Map because it's a good way to show the logical sequence of important events and accomplishments in my subject's life.

Biography Map

Subject: William Penn Adair Rogers
Birth facts: born November 4, 1879 in Indian Territory, later became Oklahoma.

Actions, Accomplishments:
Riding and roping on family ranch, then in Wild West shows in Africa, Australia, and back in different parts of the U.S., with success in New York.

Actions, Accomplishments:
Writing newspaper columns and speaking on radio programs with funny, thoughtful comments about politics and current events.

Actions, Accomplishments:
Acting in silent films (1918) and then star roles in talking films (1929). Flying in planes allowed him to travel widely and write about his experiences.

Summary of Life: After sudden death in plane crash, August 15, 1935, reactions around the country showed how popular and important he was as a performer.

Reflect
How will the Biography Map help Marco write his biography?

Apply
Organize your ideas by using your notes to make a Biography Map.

Biography **89**

Conferencing

PEER TO PEER Have partners trade Biography Maps. Each student studies the map to ensure that chronological order is accurate and events are clearly recorded. Students discuss where there are discrepancies, contradictions, or details that are unclear.

PEER GROUPS Have students pass their Biography Maps around the group. Each student reads the map and records one helpful comment on a sticky note that is attached to the map. Details to focus on are missing events, detail clarity, accurate chronological order, and natural/logical sequence of events.

TEACHER-LED Meet with individual students. Review each student's Biography Map with him or her. Ask the student questions to clarify any details that are unclear or any gaps in the sequence of events.

Write
a Biography

Student Objectives

- Create a Biography Map to organize notes. (p. 89)

Prewrite

Focus on Organization

Create a Biography Map Remind students that the key to strong writing is organization. Marco chose to create a Biography Map to organize the important information and details for his biography.

Point out that Marco lists events in chronological order in his Biography Map. This is important because any misplaced events in the map might cause Marco to present events out of order in his draft.

✏️ **Writer's Term**_____

Biography Map Recording a summary of the subject's life in the last space of the Biography Map is important. Writers may leave some questions unanswered if they do not plan the summary in advance.

CCSS **C**ommon **C**ore **S**tate **S**tandards
W.6.3: Write narratives to develop real or imagined experiences or events using effective technique, relevant descriptive details, and well-structured event sequences. **W.6.3.a:** Engage and orient the reader by establishing a context and introducing a narrator and/or characters; organize an event sequence that unfolds naturally and logically. **W.6.3.e:** Provide a conclusion that follows from the narrated experiences or events. **W.6.8:** Gather relevant information from multiple print and digital sources; assess the credibility of each source; and quote or paraphrase the data and conclusions of others while avoiding plagiarism and providing basic bibliographic information for sources.

Biography **T89**

Write
a Biography

Week 2 • Day 3

Student Objectives

• Begin writing, avoiding ordinary words and weak verbs. *(p. 90)*

Draft

Focus on

Use Precise Language Remind students that drafting is a chance to get their ideas on paper without having to worry about making mistakes. Reassure them that they will have plenty of time later to fix any errors they have made.

Explain that it is a writer's job to paint the clearest, most interesting pictures of the subject and action. Using ordinary, run-of-the-mill nouns and weak, overused verbs will not help a reader visualize anything. If a writer uses precise and colorful language to describe a person and events, the pictures created for the reader are crisp, engaging, and lifelike.

Have students use their Biography Maps to begin writing. Remind them that they may circle ordinary words and phrases that they would like to revise later, just as Marco has done. Also, point out that Marco repeatedly refers to the rubric as he writes. Encourage students to do the same.

Draft

Focus on Word Choice

The Rubric Says	Precise language conveys the events and enlivens the writing.
Writing Strategy	Replace ordinary words and weak verbs.

I think the Biography Map has helped me see Will Rogers's life as a story or a series of connected stories. Now that the events of his life are organized into a natural and logical order, I can start writing.

The purpose of a biography is to tell the subject's story and also to give the reader as clear a picture as possible of what the person was like. To do that, I'll need to use precise, descriptive language that will add energy to my writing and bring the subject to life. Too-general or ordinary words won't help me convey Will Rogers's energy and humor. If I can't think of precise or strong words while writing my first draft, I will circle the places I want to revise. Then when I have time to reread my writing and look in a thesaurus, I can come up with better words to use.

As I write my draft, I won't worry too much about perfect grammar and spelling. I'll check for those things when I proofread my writing later.

90 Narrative Writing

Differentiating Instruction

ENRICHMENT

Evaluate Technology Encourage students to explore websites that are designed to help students become stronger writers. There are online writing labs, thesauruses, dictionaries, and encyclopedias. Have students write brief evaluations of one or two sites that their classmates can use when deciding whether to use the sites themselves. Evaluations should focus on accuracy, appearance, and ease of use.

REINFORCEMENT

Support Word Choice Write the following words on the board: *hoped, grew, learned, serious.* Have small groups of students look up each word in a thesaurus and record what they find. Point out that each suggestion means something slightly different. Emphasize how important it is to use words that convey the intended meaning.

[DRAFT]

Will Rogers

[Precise language]

Will Rogers, famous film star, humorist, writer, and stage performer, was born in 1879 on a ranch in a part of Indian Territory that would later become the state of Oklahoma. His parents, both proud of their Native American heritage, named him after a Cherokee leader, William Penn Adair. Will's father Clement Rogers, was a military and government leader who tried to keep Cherokee rights within the laws of the United States.

[Find better word]

Growing up on the family ranch, Will loved to ride horses and rope cattle. He learned and practiced many tricks with the lariat, or rope, and hoped for success. In contrast, he did not perform well in most school subjects, and he wasn't a serious student. Yet Will Rogers became nationally known for his writing and philosophy, as well as his acting and humor. His many talents grew at different times in his life.

One exciting time in his life began in 1901 when he set out from home for Argentina to find work on a cattle ranch. Though he did not find ranch work in Argentina, he got a job tending cattle and other animals on a big ship bound for South Africa.

Reflect

What do you think? How does Marco's precise language bring the subject to life? Can you find other weak words that could use replacing?

Apply

Write a draft using your Biography Map as a guide. Remember to use precise language to enliven your writing. Circle words or phrases that could use strengthening in your next draft.

Biography **91**

Conferencing

PEER TO PEER Have students exchange both Biography Maps and drafts. Each looks for instances where the draft leaves out important details from the map or where events are out of place.

PEER GROUPS Each student takes a turn reading his or her draft aloud to the group. Listening students then take turns expressing one strength and one area that needs strengthening. Specific areas to focus on are word choice and event sequence.

TEACHER-LED Meet with pairs of students. Have students exchange drafts and use a pencil to circle words they believe can be replaced with more precise or interesting terms. Guide students in discussing what words can be used to replace the circled ones.

Write
a Biography

Week 2 • Day 4

Student Objectives
• Complete a draft. *(p. 91)*

Finish the Draft Have students read the draft. Remind students that the goal of drafting is to capture ideas on paper. Point out the words that Marco circled. Ask:

• Why did Marco circle these words? (Possible response: He knows that they are not the best words to use, and he will find better ones later.)

• Where can Marco find ideas to replace these circled words? (Possible response: a thesaurus)

• Where has Marco defined a word that many readers might not know? Why would he do that? (He defined *lariat* to help readers fully understand and enjoy the biography.)

Point out the proofreading marks at the top of the page. Explain that these marks will be used for revising and editing. Remind students to refer often to both their Biography Maps and the rubric as they draft.

CCSS **C**ommon **C**ore **S**tate **S**tandards

W.6.3.b: Use narrative techniques, such as dialogue, pacing, and description, to develop experiences, events, and/or characters. **W.6.3.d:** Use precise words and phrases, relevant descriptive details, and sensory language to convey experiences and events. **W.6.10:** Write routinely over extended time frames (time for research, reflection, and revision) and shorter time frames (a single sitting or a day or two) for a range of discipline-specific tasks, purposes, and audiences.

Write
a Biography

Week 2 • Day 5

Student Objectives

• Revise to use details that are new to readers. (p. 92)

Revise

Focus on Ideas

Use New Details Point out that it is a writer's job to present a subject in a new and interesting way to keep readers engaged and help them see the subject in a fresh light. The easiest way to accomplish this is to include details that are not commonly associated with the subject. Sometimes, too, a writer may need to include information that is new to readers and that will help them understand some aspect of the subject's life. Remind students that this is why research is so important. The extra time one takes to research a subject yields interesting new tidbits of information that can transform a narrative from OK to outstanding.

As a class, discuss how Marco's revision strengthened the excerpt. Now instruct students to revise their own biographies to ensure they've used fresh and engaging details that offer insights into the subject's life.

 Strategies for Writers Online
Go to **www.sfw.z-b.com** for additional online resources for students and teachers.

Revise

Focus on **Ideas**

The Rubric Says All details develop the subject and bring it to life.

Writing Strategy Find details that are new to readers.

The rubric reminds me that all the details in my biography should help the reader see my subject as a living, breathing person. One way to interest my readers and bring my subject to life is to include information they don't know. I just added a detail about the Great Depression because our class hasn't studied this period in history yet. I want my readers to understand why it was so hard and why people valued what Will Rogers said.

[DRAFT]   [added detail to bring subject to life]

when large numbers of people were out of work and very poor,
Especially during the Great Depression, his words helped many
laugh and somehow feel hopeful. He was critical of Republican
presidents Calvin Coolidge and Herbert Hoover and much more
upbeat about Democrat Franklin D. Roosevelt. All three presidents
paid close attention to what he said.

Apply
Find places where you can add details that bring your subject to life.

92 Narrative Writing

English Language Learners

BEGINNING/INTERMEDIATE
Past-Tense Verbs Show students a picture of a child dancing. Ask, *What is the child doing?* After students respond, say and write on the board, *Today the child dances.* Then say and write on the board, *Yesterday the child danced.* Read and students repeat. Underline *ed.* Explain that if something happens before now, or in the past, we add *-ed* to the verb. Repeat with several regular verbs.

ADVANCED/ADVANCED HIGH
Using Quotations Tell students to think about the subject of their biography. Ask, *What interesting thing did the person say?* Tell students that the exact words a person says is called a *direct quote.* Have students repeat the phrase. Model using a direct quote. For example, *Mrs. Roosevelt said, "You must do the thing which you think you cannot do."* Review placement of the comma and quotations marks.

Revise

Focus on Organization

The Rubric Says	Smooth and effective transition words and phrases connect ideas and paragraphs.
Writing Strategy	Use transition words and phrases.

I need to look at the way I use words to connect ideas and make the transition from one idea to another. One way to create a smooth and effective transition between paragraphs is to repeat a word, a phrase, or an idea. I found a place where I could use repetition to make one paragraph flow better into the next. What do you think of my revision?

[DRAFT]

Later on, he used a similar approach to news of the day and conditions of the times when he spoke on the <u>radio</u> or wrote a regular newspaper column. In his <u>writing</u>, he could sum up the problems and progress of the nation in a few simple words. Over the years, he compiled his thoughts in books that sold very well.
In writing and on the radio,
∧ Will Rogers made fun of politics and government, but he also expressed his belief in American democracy and in ordinary human beings.

[words leading to transition]

[used repeated words/ideas for transition]

Reflect
How does the added phrase help the reader connect the ideas and make the transition between paragraphs?

Apply
Find places in your biography where you need to add transition words that connect ideas from paragraph to paragraph.

Biography 93

Conferencing

PEER TO PEER Have partners exchange drafts. Using light pencil marks, each student should draw an arrow or an asterisk where transitions are needed for clarity. Students then return the drafts and explain each mark they drew.

PEER GROUPS Each student reads his or her draft aloud to the group. Each listening student asks a question about a fact or detail he or she did not understand or that could use additional clarification.

TEACHER-LED Meet with individual students. Read the student's draft aloud, instructing him or her to listen for and visualize the sequence of events. When you are done reading, ask: *Were there any places where you couldn't follow the events? Were you able to follow how much time had passed between events?* Together, brainstorm different transitions that could be used to clarify the writing.

Write
a Biography

Student Objectives
• Revise to use transition words and phrases. *(p. 93)*

Revise

Focus on Organization

Use Transitions Explain that the most effective way to convey the passing of time, a change in setting, or a shift from one idea to the next is to use transition words and phrases. Give examples of common transition words and phrases, such as *furthermore, in addition, later, after, down the street, nearby.* Have students give more examples of time-order, location, or idea transition words. Refer students to the list of transitions on page 524.

Explain that sometimes transitions are made without using the conventional transition words. One way to make a transition is to repeat words or ideas from one paragraph in the next paragraph. Have students read page 93. Help students understand that Marco tied together two paragraphs by introducing the second paragraph with key words from the first. Instruct students to use effective transitions in their own writing, just as Marco has done.

CCSS **Common Core State Standards**
W.6.3.c: Use a variety of transition words, phrases, and clauses to convey sequence and signal shifts from one time frame or setting to another. **W.6.3.d:** Use precise words and phrases, relevant descriptive details, and sensory language to convey experiences and events.

Write
a Biography

Week 3 • Day 2

Student Objectives

• Revise to vary the length of sentences. (p. 94)

Revise

Focus on  Sentence Fluency

Vary Sentences Explain to students that using a variety of sentence structures and types is a great way to give their writing flow and energy. Everyone has experienced reading too many short or long sentences in a row. Either situation is tiring to read and may lead to confusion. Using a good mix of short and long sentences keeps the writing fresh and helps readers find it easier to stay engaged.

Challenge students to identify the variety of sentence structures that Marco uses. (an appositive, a prepositional phrase, a dependent clause) Point out that ending the paragraph with a short sentence gives a sense of finality to this section of the biography. Now have students revise their own writing to ensure they've used a good variety of sentence lengths.

Online Writing Center

 Provides **interactive proofreading activities** for each genre.

Revise
Focus on Sentence Fluency

The Rubric Says	A variety of sentence structures links the ideas and moves the story along at a good pace.
Writing Strategy	Vary the length of the sentences.

The rubric says that varying my sentence structure will link my ideas and help my writing flow well. I looked at my paragraphs to see whether each one had a good mix of sentence lengths, and I found one paragraph that was made up entirely of long sentences. It was simple to break one of the sentences into two shorter ones and give the paragraph a little more variety.

[DRAFT]

Will Rogers, sometimes called the Cherokee Kid, returned to Oklahoma in 1904, with skills that gave him opportunities to perform in other parts of the United States. In New York City, Will's quick action in one cowboy show made big news when he expertly roped a steer that had accidentally gotten loose into the audience. As his career in show business became more solid, he married a woman he had met in Oklahoma, and they settled in New York to raise a family. [broke long sentence into two short ones]

Apply

Check each of your paragraphs for variety in sentence lengths. Break up long sentences or combine short ones to create a good mix.

94   Narrative Writing

Optional Revising Lessons

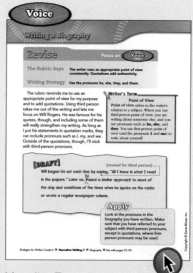

Voice

Narrative 7

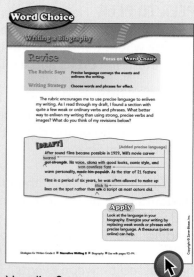

Word Choice

Narrative 8

Go to **Strategies for Writers Grade 6 CD-ROM**

Edit

Focus on Conventions

The Rubric Says The writing has been carefully edited. Verbs are used correctly.

Writing Strategy Recognize and correct inappropriate shifts in verb tense.

Writer's Term

Verb Tense
The **verb tense** tells the time of an action. Verbs show action that happened in the past, happens in the present, or will happen in the future. Verbs can also show that an action is ongoing.

Now I will check my draft and correct errors in spelling, capitalization, and punctuation. I'll also check the tenses of the verbs I used and correct any mistakes I made.

[DRAFT]

[corrected from present tense to past tense]

Besides newspaper and radio, film ~~is~~ **was** another medium that suited ~~suits~~ Will Rogers. He began as a cowboy star in silent films that were made in the New York area. When the film industry shifted location to California, Will eventually ~~moves~~ **moved** there with his wife and children.

Reflect

What are some reasons that using the correct tense can be challenging in writing a biography? How will Marco's edits help his readers better understand his writing?

Apply

Conventions

Edit your draft for spelling, punctuation, and capitalization. Be sure verb tenses are used correctly.

For more practice with verbs and verb tenses, use the exercises on the next two pages.

Biography 95

Related Grammar Practice

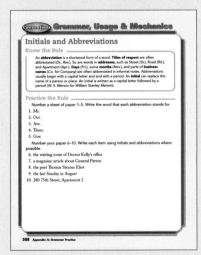

Conventions Grammar, Usage & Mechanics

Initials and Abbreviations

Know the Rule

An **abbreviation** is a shortened form of a word. **Titles of respect** are often abbreviated (Dr., Rev.). So are words in **addresses**, such as Street (St.), Road (Rd.), and Apartment (Apt.). **Days** (Fri.), some **months** (Nov.), and parts of **business names** (Co. for Company) are often abbreviated in informal notes. Abbreviations usually begin with a capital letter and end with a period. An **initial** can replace the name of a person or place. An initial is written as a capital letter followed by a period (W. S. Merwin for William Stanley Merwin).

Practice the Rule

Number a sheet of paper 1–5. Write the word that each abbreviation stands for.
1. Mr.
2. Oct.
3. Ave.
4. Thurs.
5. Gov.
Number your paper 6–10. Write each item using initials and abbreviations where possible.
6. the waiting room of Doctor Kelly's office
7. a magazine article about General Patton
8. the poet Thomas Stearns Eliot
9. the last Sunday in August
10. 280 75th Street, Apartment 2

508 Appendix A: Grammar Practice

Student Edition page 508

Go to ▷ **Appendix A: Grammar Practice**

Student Objectives

• Edit to recognize and correct inappropriate shifts in verb tense. *(p. 95)*

Edit

Focus on Conventions

Edit for Mistakes Direct students' attention to Marco's draft excerpt. Discuss each edit, making sure students understand why the original verb was incorrect. Instruct students to edit their own writing for spelling, grammar, punctuation, and capitalization.

If students are having trouble with action and linking verbs or verb tense, teach the mini-lessons on pages T96 and T97. Then have students complete the exercises on pages 96 and 77. Review the answers as a class.

Writer's Term

Verb Tense One of the most common mistakes in writing is inconsistent verb tense. Reading aloud one's work is a helpful way to hear if all verbs are used correctly and the tense is consistent.

CCSS Common Core State Standards

L.6.1: Demonstrate command of the conventions of standard English grammar and usage when writing or speaking. **L.6.2:** Demonstrate command of the conventions of standard English capitalization, punctuation, and spelling when writing. **L.6.2.b:** Spell correctly.

Mini-Lesson

Student Objectives

• Learn how to use action and linking verbs correctly. *(p. 96)*

Action and Linking Verbs

Lead a class discussion on the action and linking verbs to be sure that students have a firm grasp on the difference between the two. Then use the following exercises to solidify their understanding.

Write the sentences below on the board. Ask volunteers to identify which verbs are action verbs and which are linking verbs. Remind students that a linking verb acts like a chain that links a subject with either a predicate noun or a predicate adjective. In the sentence *The shirt is blue,* the verb *is* links *shirt* with *blue.*

• *Please sit by the fire and listen to this story.* (sit-AV/listen-AV)

• *Now I am tired. We'll extinguish the fire and climb into our tents for the night.* (am-LV/extinguish-AV/climb-AV)

Continue with additional sentences as needed.

Online Writing Center

Provides **interactive grammar games** and **practice activities** in student eBook.

Action and Linking Verbs

Know the Rule

An **action verb** shows action.
> **Example:** Marian Anderson's voice **enchanted** everyone who **heard** her singing.

A **linking verb** does not show action. Instead, a linking verb connects the subject of a sentence to one or more words that describe or rename the subject. Linking verbs are usually forms of *be;* some of these are *am, is, are, was, were,* and *will be. Become, seem, appear,* and *look* can also be used as linking verbs.
> **Examples:** She **was** a serious music student. She **became** a famous singer.

Practice the Rule

Number a separate sheet of paper 1–10. Write the verb or verbs in each sentence, adding the letter **A** for action verbs and the letter **L** for linking verbs.

1. Woody Guthrie was a singer and songwriter who lived from 1912 to 1967. **L**
2. At his birth in Oklahoma, his parents named him Woodrow Wilson Guthrie. **A**
3. Woody was not a trained musician, but he learned guitar from a family friend. **L, A**
4. His mother's illness, a dear sister's death, and a disastrous fire were some of the many difficulties of his childhood. **L**
5. Woody had little formal education, but he loved reading, writing, drawing, and singing. **L, A**
6. From library books, he learned many subjects. **A**
7. Woody became very creative with the sounds, rhythms, and feelings of words. **L**
8. As a young man, he traveled to different parts of the country on foot and in freight cars. **A**
9. "This Land is Your Land" is one of his best-known songs. **L**
10. Woody wrote more than three thousand songs, including many for and about his children. **A**

Related Grammar Practice

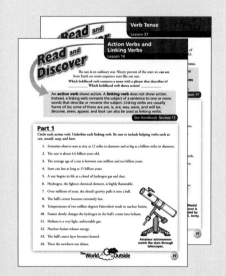

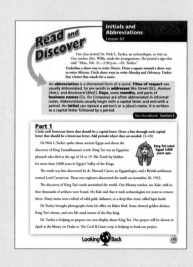

Pages 39, 97, 115

Go to G.U.M. Student Practice Book

Verb Tense

Know the Rule

All words in a sentence must work together to give an accurate sense of time. Make sure each **verb** is in the proper **tense** for the time period being discussed. Use dates, time, and other **time expressions** such as *last week, next week, yesterday, later,* or *during* to help show time.

> **Example: Last year,** I **wrote** a short biography of George Washington Carver, who **lived** from 1864 to 1943.
>
> **Example: Next week,** we **will write** biographies of friends or family members after we **interview** them about their lives.

Practice the Rule

Number a separate sheet of paper 1–10. Write the correct verb or verbs in parentheses to complete each sentence.

1. Cesar Chavez (was/is) born in Arizona on March 31, 1927, and died in 1993.
2. Since 2001 in California, his birthday (has been/will be) a state holiday called Cesar Chavez Day.
3. Arizona, Texas, and Colorado (are/were) some other states that now honor Cesar Chavez on this date.
4. After circulating petitions around the country, some groups hope that Cesar Chavez Day (became/will become) a national holiday.
5. Cesar Chavez (is/was) a farm worker, labor leader, and civil rights activist.
6. In 1962, he (founds/founded) the National Farm Workers Association that later (becomes/became) the United Farm Workers.
7. Besides organizing farm workers to strike against the unfair conditions of grape pickers, he (gets/got) people around the country to stop buying grapes until conditions improved.
8. Based on his childhood and adult experience as a farm worker, Cesar Chavez (was/is) deeply committed to ending unfair, unsafe, and unrewarding conditions.
9. Through nonviolent actions such as fasts and marches, Cesar Chavez (inspired/inspires) others to support the causes he stood for.
10. On the next Cesar Chavez Day, students in our school (participated/will participate) in community service projects.

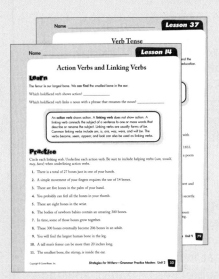
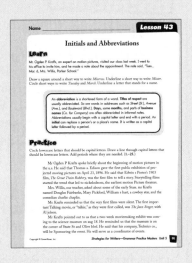

Pages 33, 79, 91

Go to ➡ *Grammar Practice Masters*

Conventions

Mini-Lesson

Student Objectives

- Learn how to use verb tenses consistently and accurately. *(p. 97)*

Verb Tense

Write the following sentences on the board:

- *Yesterday, I spoke to Alana and give her my new e-mail address.*
- *She thanks me and immediately copied it down in her notebook.*
- *Tomorrow, I will call her and invites her to my house for a sleepover.*

Ask a volunteer to read the first sentence aloud. Ask the student to first point out any words or phrases that indicate time. (Yesterday) Then ask him or her to point out the verb(s). (spoke/give) Ask:

- Do both verbs match the tense of the sentence? (no)
- How can you fix the sentence so that it makes sense? (Yesterday, I spoke to Alana and gave her my new e-mail address.)

Repeat this process with the remaining sentences. (sentence two—*thanked*; sentence three—*invite*.)

CCSS Common Core State Standards
L.6.1: Demonstrate command of the conventions of standard English grammar and usage when writing or speaking. **L.6.2:** Demonstrate command of the conventions of standard English capitalization, punctuation, and spelling when writing. **L.6.3:** Use knowledge of language and its conventions when writing, speaking, reading, or listening.

Write
a Biography

Student Objectives

- Discuss preparation for publishing and presentation. (p. 98)
- Use a final editing checklist to publish their work. (p. 98)

Publish +Presentation

Publishing Strategy Ask students how they feel about Marco's publishing choice. Ask:

- How else could you publish your finished biographies?

Write students' suggestions on the board. Encourage students to choose a publishing method that excites them and makes sense for this genre.

Read through Marco's final checklist. Instruct students to follow Marco's checklist or to create their own, focusing on elements of writing that concern them most. Encourage them to share copies of their published work with friends and family members.

► Strategies for Writers Online

Go to **www.sfw.z-b.com** for additional online resources for students and teachers.

Publish +Presentation

Publishing Strategy	Present your biography as a slide show.
Presentation Strategy	Use visuals that illustrate the life and times of the subject.

I've written and revised my biography, but I still have to plan how to present it in social studies class. Our teacher expects us to present a slide show and include visuals. Luckily there are many photos of Will Rogers because he was a performer and film star. I even found a website with videos of Will Rogers performing rope tricks. I would like to show a few minutes of that video clip as part of my presentation because it shows his skill and humor and gives us an idea of film technology in his time. I'll need to plan and time it to fit it in with my text and other visuals. I'll also want to use my final checklist to make sure I haven't overlooked anything.

My Final Checklist

Did I—

- ✔ check my spelling, punctuation, and capitalization carefully?
- ✔ use verb tenses correctly?
- ✔ find visuals that go with my subject?
- ✔ practice my presentation and the timing of my visuals?

Apply

Find visuals to go with the subject of your biography and plan an effective way to fit them in with the words of your presentation.

98 Narrative Writing

Differentiating Instruction

ENRICHMENT

Encourage Publishing Help writers submit their biographies for publication by offering guidance on how to write a query letter. Explain that a query letter introduces and explains the piece of writing to the editor, must be engaging and succinct, should be written in business letter format, and should include a self-addressed stamped envelope for a response.

REINFORCEMENT

Support Presentation Help students think of visuals they could use in their biographies. Begin a list of ideas on the board. Write *photographs* as the first item and elicit more ideas from students. Possible ideas include small images of an invention, artwork, or music the subject has created; an image of the subject's childhood home; and paintings of the subject.

Will Rogers
Rider, Roper, Writer, Actor

by Marco

Will Rogers, famous film star, humorist, writer, and stage performer, was born in 1879 on a ranch in a part of Indian Territory that would later become the state of Oklahoma. His parents, both proud of their Native American heritage, named him after a Cherokee leader, William Penn Adair. Will's father, Clement Rogers, was a military and government leader who tried to stand up for Cherokee rights within the laws of the United States.

Growing up on the family ranch, Will loved to ride horses and rope cattle. He learned and practiced many tricks with the lariat, or rope, and he dreamed of winning rodeo prizes. In contrast, he did not do well in most school subjects, and teachers called him a class clown. Yet Will Rogers became nationally known for his writing and wise sayings, as well as his acting and humor. His many talents developed at different times in his life.

One exciting time in his life began in 1901 when he set out from home for Argentina to find work on a cattle ranch. Though he did not find ranch work in Argentina, he got a job tending cattle and other animals on a big ship bound for South Africa. In South Africa Will was hired to perform rope tricks and other cowboy skills in a traveling Wild West show, where he gained confidence as a performer. After that he sailed to Australia, where he used his talents in a traveling circus. During his travels, he wrote letters that entertained his friends and family with humorous but thoughtful observations.

Biography 99

Technology Tip for 21st Century Literacies

Challenge students to create an infographic that presents some of their findings related to their written biography. Using a tool like Many Eyes will support the process by offering both model texts and a user-friendly environment in which students can compose and share. Talk with students about the added value of presenting their selected information in this way. This is also a rich opportunity for reflective writing as student writers are making several interesting choices throughout this process. Use reflection to make that thinking visible.

See **www.sfw.z-b.com** for further information about and links to these websites and tools.

Write
a Biography

Week 3 • Day 5

Student Objectives

- Use a biography rubric.
- Share a published biography. (pp. 82–83, 99–101)

Presentation Strategy Discuss how Marco's slide show will enhance readers' experience with his biography. Ask:

- What other visuals could students use to enliven their presentations? (Possible responses: a collage, a short film—either silent or with sound, a mock photo album, a mobile featuring major events, accomplishments, or details from the subject's life)

Encourage students to think of engaging visuals they can include in their final copies to enhance the reading experience for their audience. Encourage students to research their images online and in hard-copy sources.

CCSS Common Core State Standards

W.6.5: With some guidance and support from peers and adults, develop and strengthen writing as needed by planning, revising, editing, rewriting, or trying a new approach. **W.6.6:** Use technology, including the Internet, to produce and publish writing as well as to interact and collaborate with others; demonstrate sufficient command of keyboarding skills to type a minimum of three pages in a single sitting. **SL.6.5:** Include multimedia components (e.g., graphics, images, music, sound) and visual displays in presentations to clarify information.

Reflecting on a Biography

Ask students to return to the rubric on pages 82 and 83 to evaluate Marco's biography of Will Rogers. Have students work in groups to decide how to score the writing on each of the six traits and then ask the groups to present their scores to the class. Encourage students to support their opinions with examples.

Ask students to reflect on the experience of writing a biography. Ask:

- Were you surprised at any of the steps or methods for writing a biography?

- Did you enjoy the research process? Are there other resources you could use the next time you write a biography?

- What part of the writing process did you enjoy the most?

- What advice would you give to someone about how to write a biography?

Have students write their responses in a writing journal or discuss them as a class or in small groups.

 Strategies for Writers Online
Go to **www.sfw.z-b.com** for additional online resources for students and teachers.

Will Rogers, sometimes called the Cherokee Kid, returned to Oklahoma in 1904, with skills that gave him opportunities to perform in other parts of the United States. In New York City, Will's quick action in one cowboy show made big news when he expertly roped a steer that had accidentally gotten loose into the audience. As his career in show business became more solid, he married a woman he had met in Oklahoma. They settled in New York to raise a family.

For many years, Will Rogers continued to be a popular performer in major New York stage shows, where he perfected an act that included cowboy rope tricks and his own funny, clever comments on the daily news. Will began his act each time by saying, "All I know is what I read in the papers." Later on, he used a similar approach to news of the day and conditions of the times when he spoke on the radio or wrote a regular newspaper column. In his writing, he could sum up the problems and progress of the nation in a few simple words. Over the years, he compiled his thoughts in books that sold very well.

In writing and on the radio, Will Rogers made fun of politics and government, but he also expressed his belief in American democracy and in ordinary human beings. Especially during the Great Depression, when large numbers of people were out of work and very poor, his words helped many laugh and somehow feel hopeful. He was critical of Republican presidents Calvin Coolidge and Herbert Hoover and much more upbeat about Democrat Franklin D. Roosevelt. All three presidents paid close attention to what he said.

Besides newspaper and radio, film was another medium that suited Will Rogers. He began as a cowboy star in silent films that were made in the New York area. When the film industry shifted location to California, Will eventually moved there with his wife and children. After

100 Narrative Writing

sound films became possible in 1929, Will's movie career soared. His voice, along with good looks, comic style, and warm personality, won countless fans. As the star of 21 feature films in a period of six years, he was often allowed to make up lines on the spot rather than stick to a script as most actors did.

Though he gained wealth and stardom, Will Rogers never seemed to change his modest, friendly manner. One of his famous quotes was "No man is great if he thinks he is." Will never seemed to think he was great. Others thought he was. When his life ended in a plane crash on August 15, 1935, the sudden loss stunned people around the country. In remembering and honoring Will Rogers long after his death, people confirmed the greatness of his gentle humor, sensible words, and memorable performances.

Reflect

Which traits in this biography seemed strongest to you? After checking the biography against the rubric, do the same with the biography you have written.

CCSS **C**ommon **C**ore **S**tate **S**tandards

W.6.10: Write routinely over extended time frames (time for research, reflection, and revision) and shorter time frames (a single sitting or a day or two) for a range of discipline-specific tasks, purposes, and audiences.
SL.6.1.c: Pose and respond to specific questions with elaboration and detail by making comments that contribute to the topic, text, or issue under discussion.
SL.6.1.d: Review the key ideas expressed and demonstrate understanding of multiple perspectives through reflection and paraphrasing.

Narrative Test Planner

WEEK 1

Introduce
Narrative Test Writing

Student Objectives
- Learn the components of the writing prompt.

Student Activities
- Read and discuss **Read the Writing Prompt.** *(pp. 102–103)*

Analyze
Introduce the Scoring Guide

Student Objectives
- Recognize the relationship of the scoring guide to the rubric and the six traits of writing.
- Read a model writing test response.

Student Activities
- Read **Writing Traits in the Scoring Guide.** *(p. 104)*
- Read **"Bucky's Big Break."** *(p. 105)*

Analyze
Apply the Scoring Guide

Student Objectives
- Apply the scoring guide to the writing prompt response model.

Student Activities
- Read and discuss **Using the Scoring Guide to Study the Model.** *(pp. 106–107)*

WEEK 2

Write
Prewrite: Ideas

Student Objectives
- Read and understand a writing prompt for narrative writing.
- Apply the six traits of writing to the writing prompt.

Student Activities
- Read and discuss **Prewrite: Focus on Ideas.** *(pp. 110–111)*

Write
Prewrite: Ideas

Student Objectives
- Learn how to respond to the task in the writing prompt.

Student Activities
- Read and discuss **Prewrite: Focus on Ideas.** *(p. 112)*

Write
Prewrite: Organization

Student Objectives
- Learn how to choose a graphic organizer for the writing prompt.

Student Activities
- Read and discuss **Prewrite: Focus on Organization.** *(p. 113)*

WEEK 3

Write
Revise: Organization

Student Objectives
- Revise to use transitions to guide the reader.

Student Activities
- Read and discuss **Revise: Focus on Organization.** *(p. 118)*

Write
Revise: Voice

Student Objectives
- Revise to use a casual tone.

Student Activities
- Read and discuss **Revise: Focus on Voice.** *(p. 119)*

Write
Revise: Word Choice

Student Objectives
- Revise to use precise words and phrases.

Student Activities
- Read and discuss **Revise: Focus on Word Choice.** *(p. 120)*

Note: Optional Revising Lessons appear on the *Strategies for Writers* CD-ROM.

Day 4

Analyze
Apply the Scoring Guide

Student Objectives
- Continue to apply the scoring guide to a model test response.

Student Activities
- Read and discuss **Using the Scoring Guide to Study the Model.** *(p. 108)*

Day 5

Analyze
Time Management

Student Objectives
- Learn how to plan time during a writing test.

Student Activities
- Read and discuss **Planning My Time.** *(p. 109)*

Day 4

Write
Prewrite: Organization

Student Objectives
- Learn how to check the graphic organizer against the scoring guide.

Student Activities
- Read and discuss **Prewrite: Focus on Organization.** *(pp. 114–115)*

Day 5

Write
Draft: Ideas

Student Objectives
- Draft a writing test response, using specific, related details.

Student Activities
- Read and discuss **Draft: Focus on Ideas.** *(pp. 116–117)*
- Draft a narrative writing test response.
- Reflect on a model draft.

Day 4

Write
Edit: Conventions

Student Objectives
- Edit the writing test response for grammar, spelling, capitalization, and punctuation.

Student Activities
- Read and discuss **Edit: Focus on Conventions.** *(pp. 121–122)*

Day 5

Review
Test Tips

Student Objectives
- Review tips for writing for a test.

Student Activities
- Read and discuss **Test Tips.** *(p. 123)*

To complete the chapter in fewer days, combine the learning objectives and activities in a way that supports students as they write.

Differentiating Instruction

For additional Differentiating Instruction activities, see Strategies for Writers *Extensions Online at* **www.sfw.z-b.com.**

English Language Learners

School Home Connection Letter

Reproducible letter (in English and Spanish) appears on the *Strategies for Writers* CD-ROM and at **www.sfw.z-b.com**.

Online Essay Grader and Writing Tutor

Powered by Vantage Learning's MY Access!®, includes writing prompts and ongoing feedback for students as they write. Available for Grades 5–8.

Online Writing Center

Provides IWB resources, interactive games and practice activities, videos, eBooks, and a virtual file cabinet.

 Strategies for Writers Online

Go to **www.sfw.z-b.com** for free online resources for students and teachers.

Introduce
Narrative Test Writing

Week 1 • Day 1

Student Objectives

• Learn the components of the writing prompt. *(pp. 102–103)*

Read the Writing Prompt

Narrative Test Writing In this chapter, students will apply what they have learned about narrative writing to the challenge of taking a narrative writing test. Remind students that there will be times they will be expected to write on demand to complete an assignment or test. Tell students that when they write for a test, they will receive a writing prompt and a certain amount of time in which to write. Their finished writing will be evaluated, just as with any assignment or test. Assure students that they do not need to be anxious about writing a test; the skills they have been learning and using throughout this unit will help them do a good job. Then direct their attention to the three parts of the writing prompt.

Setup The setup does exactly what its name implies: It sets the writer up to do a good job. The setup helps writers to think about the writing topic in general before they choose a more specific topic.

 Strategies for Writers Online
Go to **www.sfw.z-b.com** for additional online resources for students and teachers.

Narrative
test writing

Read the Writing Prompt

When you take a writing test, you'll get a writing prompt. Most writing prompts have three parts:

Setup This part of the writing prompt gives you the background information you need to get ready to write.

Task This part of the writing prompt tells you exactly what you are supposed to write: an eyewitness account about a newsworthy event that you observed.

Scoring Guide This section tells how your writing will be scored. To do well on the test, you should make sure you do everything on the list.

> **R**emember the rubrics you used earlier in the unit? When you take a writing test, you don't always have all of the information that's on a rubric. But the scoring guide is a lot like a rubric. It lists everything you need to think about to write a good paper. Like the rubrics you've used in this unit, many scoring guides are based on these important traits of writing:

Ideas   Organization   Voice

Word Choice   Sentence Fluency   Conventions

Online Essay Grader and Writing Tutor

Powered by Vantage Learning's MY Access!®, this tool gives students

• immediate, ongoing, sentence-by-sentence feedback.

• helpful suggestions to improve their draft.

• a holistic score and a trait-specific score on their final draft.

• unlimited response submissions to the prompts.

Writing MODEL Prompt

Think about a newsworthy event, one that might make the local news. It can be something you saw or heard about or something you made up yourself.

Then write an eyewitness account telling about the event.

Be sure your writing
- uses descriptive details to develop the events.
- tells the event in a logical order and uses transition words to convey sequence.
- has a voice that matches audience and purpose.
- uses precise words and phrases to convey the events.
- contains sentences that flow smoothly.
- contains correct grammar, punctuation, capitalization, and spelling.

Task The task tells students not only what to write about but also what kind of writing to do: narrative, descriptive, explanatory/ informative, or opinion. Tell students that the best-written test will not receive a strong grade if it misses the topic or uses a form of writing other than the assigned form. Students must follow the instructions in the task.

Scoring Guide The scoring guide helps students plan and evaluate their writing. Tell students that the scoring guide is similar to the rubrics they have used in the past. They should read the scoring guide carefully before writing and refer to it as they draft and revise their tests. Help students understand how the scoring guide is similar to the rubrics by asking these questions:

- Which bullet focuses on the ideas in the writing? (the first bullet)

- Which bullet focuses on the organization of the writing? (the second bullet)

- Which bullet encourages you to improve your sentence fluency? (the fifth bullet)

CCSS Common Core State Standards

SL.6.1: Engage effectively in a range of collaborative discussions (one-on-one, in groups, and teacher-led) with diverse partners on *grade 6 topics, texts, and issues*, building on others' ideas and expressing their own clearly. **W.6.10:** Write routinely over extended time frames (time for research, reflection, and revision) and shorter time frames (a single sitting or a day or two) for a range of discipline-specific tasks, purposes, and audiences.

Analyze
the Scoring Guide

Week 1 • Day 2

Student Objectives

- Recognize the relationship of the scoring guide to the rubric and the six traits of writing. *(p. 104)*
- Read a model writing test response. *(p. 105)*

Writing Traits in the Scoring Guide

Scoring Guide as a Rubric

Remind students how they have used rubrics to guide, evaluate, and improve their writing in other narrative assignments. Point out that in a writing test, the scoring guide acts as a rubric. Read the scoring guide and discuss why each trait is important in good narrative writing.

Tell students they will sometimes use writing prompts that do not include guidance for each of the six traits by name. However, students can use their writing experience to remember the main requirements for narrative writing as listed on page 104.

Writing Traits in the Scoring Guide

The scoring guide in the prompt on page 103 has been made into this chart. Does it remind you of the rubrics you've used? Not all prompts include all of the writing traits, but this one does. Use them to do your best writing. Remember to work neatly and put your name on each page.

 **Ideas**
- Be sure your writing uses descriptive details to develop the events.

 **Organization**
- Be sure your writing tells the events in a logical order and uses transition words to convey sequence.

 **Voice**
- Be sure your voice matches the audience and purpose.

 **Word Choice**
- Be sure your writing uses precise words and phrases to convey the events.

 **Sentence Fluency**
- Be sure your writing contains sentences that flow smoothly.

 **Conventions**
- Be sure your writing contains correct grammar, punctuation, capitalization, and spelling.

Look at Olivia Mayes's story on the next page. Did she follow the scoring guide?

English Language Learners

BEGINNING

The Writing Process Review the steps in the writing process using simple words. Use the following words to substitute for *prewrite, draft, revise, edit,* and *publish: about/plan, write, change, fix,* and *show.* Remind students to follow all of these steps during a writing test.

INTERMEDIATE

Logical Order To help with organization during a narrative writing test, suggest students use a 5 W's Chart. Give partners a brief story to read. Have them complete a graphic organizer to track the events of the story. Then have them trade stories and 5 W's Charts with another pair who will read the story and verify the correct order of events.

Bucky's Big Break

by Olivia Mayes

I knew something was wrong the moment my mom turned onto our street Monday afternoon. Several of our neighbors were standing outside and so, I noticed, was another resident of Shelton Lane. Bucky, the 1,000-pound longhorn who lived in a field across the street from us, had escaped once again. The neighbors were banding together to bring him back home.

My mom rolled down her window. "Looks like Bucky is up to his old tricks again," she told Mr. Thatcher, Bucky's owner. Bucky had been known in the past to break through the fence of the Thatchers' yard in order to take a stroll through the neighborhood. Mr. Thatcher just shook his head.

Slowly, we drove by Bucky, who was standing in the Garcias' front yard, happily chomping on Mrs. Garcia's flowers, or what was left of her flowers! Bucky gazed up at us, oblivious to what was about to happen.

After we parked in our driveway, mom and I walked back to the front yard to witness the action. Kenny, Mr. Thatcher's teenage son, was hammering away at the fence, repairing the break that Bucky had used for his escape. "Okay, ready!" he called to his dad and the other neighbors. Lassoing this wandering longhorn and guiding him back to the field was a four-person effort!

Although Bucky was a gentle animal who mainly stayed in the yard, lazily eating and observing the neighborly goings-on, he was still a big animal. The men approached him cautiously.

"Okay, boy," Mr. Thatcher said, "time to come home."

Pausing from his afternoon snack, Bucky turned his head toward the men and seemed to realize the party was about to end. Quickly, he started to move away. The men trailed him, ready with the lasso. Bucky picked up his pace.

Then the men tossed the lasso over his head and tugged. Bucky stopped, appearing quite annoyed that his play time was ending. The men led him back to the open gate. Without missing a beat, Bucky resumed his eating, and the neighbors returned home knowing this wouldn't be the last time they'd have to bring Mr. Thatcher's wayward longhorn home again.

Narrative Test Writing 105

Read the Model

Writing Prompt Response Have students read "Bucky's Big Break." Tell them to keep in mind the requirements of the scoring guide as well as the traits outlined on page 104 as they read. When students are finished reading, ask questions such as the following:

- How did Olivia engage your interest in the beginning of the story? (Possible response: She made me curious as to what was "wrong" on Shelton Lane—and then I wanted to know more about Bucky.)

- How are the events in the narrative organized? (in chronological order)

- How did Olivia establish a casual and lighthearted tone in her narrative? (Possible response: By using words and phrases such as *up to his old tricks again; stroll; or what was left of her flowers,* she set an engaging and warm tone to the story.)

ADVANCED

Using Different Kinds of Sentences Tell students they can make their writing more interesting by varying the types of sentences they write. Write several plain sentences on the board, and have students suggest ways to make them more dramatic by using single words, phrases, questions, exclamations, or commands.

ADVANCED HIGH

Writing Traits Remind students that when writing for a test, they should know what is expected for each type of writing. A narrative piece, for example, should tell a story. The story should be told in order, have characters and a setting, and have a plot with a problem and a resolution. To test students' knowledge, have them create a scoring guide for a narrative writing test. They must include details for Ideas, Organization, Voice, Word Choice, Sentence Fluency, and Conventions.

CCSS **Common Core State Standards**

SL.6.1.a: Come to discussions prepared, having read or studied required material; explicitly draw on that preparation by referring to evidence on the topic, text, or issue to probe and reflect on ideas under discussion. **SL.6.1.c:** Pose and respond to specific questions with elaboration and detail by making comments that contribute to the topic, text, or issue under discussion.

Analyze
the Model

Student Objectives

- Apply the scoring guide to the writing prompt response model. (pp. 106–107)

Using the Scoring Guide to Study the Model

Review the Scoring Guide The scoring guide is the tool that an evaluator—a teacher or another professional—will use to score the writing tests. Students are given the scoring guide so they will know the criteria on which their writing will be judged. They should use the scoring guide as they write to make sure they meet all requirements.

Use the Scoring Guide Have students use the Writing Traits in the Scoring Guide on page 104 to evaluate "Bucky's Big Break." The chart is based on the scoring guide portion of the writing prompt.

Find More Examples Explain that pages 106–108 show how the writing model on page 105 meets all six writing traits. Have students read pages 106–107 and look for additional examples of **Ideas, Organization, Voice,** and **Word Choice** in the model.

 Strategies for Writers Online

Go to **www.sfw.z-b.com** for additional online resources for students and teachers.

Using the Scoring Guide to Study the Model

Now let's use the scoring guide to check Olivia's writing test, "Bucky's Big Break." We'll see how well her eyewitness account meets each of the six writing traits.

 Ideas
- The writing uses descriptive details to develop the events.

Olivia's narrative is full of vivid description that helps develop the events for me in my mind. In the paragraph below, I can really picture the size and usual gentleness of the longhorn, as well as the men walking up to him—very carefully.

> Although Bucky was a gentle animal who mainly stayed in the yard, lazily eating and observing the neighborly goings-on, he was still a big animal. The men approached him cautiously.

 **Organization**
- The writing tells the event in a logical order and uses transition words to convey sequence.

I found Olivia's story easy to follow because she tells what happens in chronological order. Notice how she uses the transition words *After* and *Then* in the sentences below to move the action along.

> After we parked in our driveway, Mom and I walked back to the front yard to witness the action. . . .
>
> Then the men tossed the lasso over his head and tugged.

Differentiating Instruction

ENRICHMENT

Expand Dialogue Even experienced writers find it challenging to write dialogue that sounds true to life and enhances the events in the narrative. Encourage students to challenge themselves by including extra dialogue in their writing, working to make it sound authentic. Have students set a goal for dialogue in their accounts (e.g., a minimum of three dialogue exchanges). Remind them to read aloud what they've written; it is much easier to hear awkward dialogue when it is read aloud.

Voice

- The voice matches the audience and purpose.

Right from the beginning, Olivia's voice appeals to the reader and creates interest. You know that her purpose is to tell a story. Look at these sentences that draw you into the event and make you want to read more.

> Bucky, the 1,000-pound longhorn who lived in a field across the street, had escaped once again. The neighbors were banding together to bring him back home.

Word Choice

- The writing uses precise words and phrases to convey the events.

I can tell when I read Olivia's story that she made careful and specific word choices to describe what happened. Olivia could have said the longhorn was *eating* flowers, but instead she used the word *chomping*. I think that's a much more precise way to describe how a 1,000-pound animal eats. She also says he *gazed up* at the men, instead of *looked up*. I'd say she definitely made the right word choices!

> Slowly, we drove by Bucky, who was standing in the Garcias' front yard, happily chomping on Mrs. Garcia's flowers, or what was left of her flowers! Bucky gazed up at us, oblivious to what was about to happen.

Narrative Test Writing 107

Think About the Traits Once students have thoroughly discussed the model narrative test, ask them which traits they think are most important in narrative writing. Of course, all the traits are important in every piece of writing, but some traits stand out more in some genres than in others. Students might say, for example, that **Organization** is very important because events must be told in a way that's easy to follow in order for readers to understand and enjoy the story. They may also say that **Word Choice** is important because vivid and precise descriptive language helps the reader visualize the characters and action.

REINFORCEMENT

Support Organization Write the following words on the board: *first, second, third, finally*. Explain that these words are transitions that help readers understand how events are ordered. Then challenge students to brainstorm additional time-order words and phrases. (**Possible responses:** *later that afternoon, after several deep breaths, as day was breaking, several hours later*) Point out that sometimes two events happen at the same time. Words such as *while* and *during* indicate simultaneous events.

CCSS **Common Core State Standards**

SL.6.1.c: Pose and respond to specific questions with elaboration and detail by making comments that contribute to the topic, text, or issue under discussion.
SL.6.1.d: Review the key ideas expressed and demonstrate understanding of multiple perspectives through reflection and paraphrasing.

Narrative Test Writing **T107**

Analyze
the Model

Week 1 • Day 4

Student Objectives

• Continue to apply the scoring guide to a model test response. (p. 108)

Analyze the Model Ask students to find other examples of passages in the model that have a good variety of sentence lengths. (Possible response: *Pausing from his afternoon snack, Bucky turned his head toward the men and seemed to realize the party was about to end. Quickly, he started to move away.*)

Ask:

• How does this sentence variety make the model more enjoyable to read? (Possible response: Using a variety of sentence lengths and types gives the writing good flow and helps keep the reader engaged.)

Remind students that using conventions correctly is crucial to making their writing accessible. The most interesting characters and events will be lost on readers if poor grammar and spelling make the writing difficult to understand. Ask students to think about areas of grammar, spelling, or punctuation in which they often make mistakes. Have them look for examples of those conventions used correctly in the model.

 Strategies for Writers Online
Go to **www.sfw.z-b.com** for additional online resources for students and teachers.

Using the Scoring Guide to Study the Model

 **Sentence Fluency**
• The writing contains sentences that flow smoothly.

The story really flowed naturally as I read it. I think it helps that Olivia uses a variety of sentences, including dialogue. In the last paragraph, she starts off with the transition *Then*. She also starts sentences with clauses and adverbs.

Then the men tossed the lasso over his head and tugged. Bucky stopped, appearing quite annoyed that his play time was ending. The men led him back to the open gate. Without missing a beat, Bucky resumed his eating, and the neighbors returned home knowing this wouldn't be the last time they'd have to bring Mr. Thatcher's wayward longhorn home again.

 **Conventions**
• The writing contains correct grammar, punctuation, capitalization, and spelling.

It looks as though Olivia didn't make any grammar or spelling mistakes. I know that's really important when you take a test. That's why it's a good idea to check for mistakes in your own work. Throughout the writing process, you should edit for correct grammar, punctuation, capitalization, and spelling. That way, you won't have any errors on your final test.

Planning My Time

Before giving us a writing test prompt, my teacher tells us how much time we'll have to complete the test. Since I'm already familiar with the writing process, I can think about how much total time I need and then divide it up into the different parts of the writing process. If the test takes an hour, here's how I can organize my time. Planning your time will help you, too!

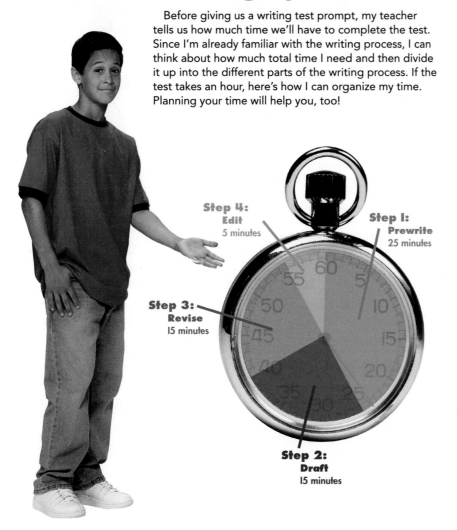

Step 4:
Edit
5 minutes

Step 1:
Prewrite
25 minutes

Step 3:
Revise
15 minutes

Step 2:
Draft
15 minutes

Narrative Test Writing **109**

Differentiating Instruction

REINFORCEMENT

Practice Time Passing Many students may feel anxious about too much time passing during one part of the assignment. You can help them feel more confident by practicing what it feels like to work through a set amount of time. Write the allotted times for each section on the board. (25 minutes for prewriting, 30 minutes for drafting and revising, 5 minutes for editing) Then tell students to work on a writing assignment for each of those time periods. Give them a verbal warning approximately five minutes before the end of each segment.

Analyze
Time Management

Week 1 • Day 5

Student Objectives

• Learn how to plan time during a writing test. *(p. 109)*

Planning My Time

Time Management Explain that when they write for a test, students must complete all the steps of the writing process quickly. Students may be surprised that the student guide, Marco, has allotted so much of the time—25 minutes out of 60—to prewriting. Explain that without a plan for writing, students might write a draft that does not respond to the task. Then they will not have time to write another draft.

Remind students that revising is part of the writing task, too. Drafting and revising together take almost the same amount of time—30 minutes—as prewriting; 5 minutes remain to edit. Tell students that when they have a shorter or longer time in which to write a test, they can use a similar time plan: about the same amount of time for prewriting and for drafting/revising, with a shorter time left for editing.

CCSS Common Core State Standards
W.6.10: Write routinely over extended time frames (time for research, reflection, and revision) and shorter time frames (a single sitting or a day or two) for a range of discipline-specific tasks, purposes, and audiences.

Narrative Test Writing **T109**

Write
a Narrative Test

Week 2 • Day 1

Student Objectives

• Read and understand a writing prompt for narrative writing. *(p. 110)*

• Apply the six traits of writing to the writing prompt. *(p. 111)*

Prewrite

Focus on Ideas

Study the Writing Prompt Discuss how Marco found and labeled the setup, task, and scoring guide prior to writing. Discuss other words in the prompt that students might want to circle or underline. Suggest that students similarly mark their scoring guides to highlight instructions they often overlook in their writing. Ask students to share which sections of the scoring guide they would choose to highlight. Remind students that when highlighting, only the key words should be marked.

> **Strategies for Writers Online**
> Go to **www.sfw.z-b.com** for additional online resources for students and teachers.

Prewrite   Focus on Ideas

Writing Strategy   Study the writing prompt to find out what to do.

I study the writing prompt as soon as I get it so that I know exactly what I'm supposed to do. The writing prompt usually has three parts. Since the parts aren't always labeled, you'll have to find and label them on your own, just like I did below. Then circle key words in the setup and the task that tell what kind of writing you need to do and who your audience will be. I circled the words *newsworthy event* in the setup in red. I circled the words *eyewitness account telling about the event* in the task in purple. Since my writing prompt doesn't say who the audience is, I'm going to write for my teacher.

My Writing Test Prompt

Setup — Think about a (newsworthy event,)one that might make the local news. It can be something you saw or heard about or something you made up yourself.

Task — Then write an (eyewitness account telling about the event.)
Be sure your writing

• has description that develops the events.

• tells the event in a logical order and uses transition words to convey sequence.

Scoring Guide — • has a voice that matches audience and purpose.

• uses precise words and phrases to convey the events.

• contains sentences that flow smoothly.

• contains correct grammar, punctuation, capitalization, and spelling.

110   Narrative Writing

English Language Learners

BEGINNING

Writing Prompt Give students a copy of the narrative test writing prompt. Have them look at each word in the prompt and circle the words they do not know. Then teach the most important words, such as *eyewitness account, newsworthy, logical order, transition*. You might have a higher-level ELL work with a lower-level ELL to review word meanings.

INTERMEDIATE

Writing Prompt Have students read the narrative writing prompt and write down words they do not know. Review how to ask for help, such as *What does* newsworthy *mean? Does* newsworthy *mean "interesting"?* Have them practice asking and answering with other students. Finally, ask students to write their answers. Review as a class.

You'll want to think about how the scoring guide relates to the writing traits you've studied in the rubrics. All of the traits might not be included in every scoring guide, but you need to remember them all to write a good essay.

Ideas
- Be sure your writing uses descriptive details to develop the events.

I want my reader to fully understand my account, so I'll use lots of descriptive details to develop the events.

Organization
- Be sure your writing tells the event in a logical order and uses transition words to convey sequence.

To make the story easy to follow, I'll tell what happens in chronological order and use transitions to move my story along.

Voice
- Be sure your voice matches the audience and purpose.

My voice should connect to my audience and create interest. My reader should know that my purpose is to tell a story.

Word Choice
- Be sure your writing uses precise words and phrases to convey the events.

My writing will be much more interesting if I make careful and precise word choices to describe what happened.

Sentence Fluency
- Be sure your writing contains sentences that flow smoothly.

I can use a variety of sentences with clauses or adverbs, as well as dialogue, to help my writing flow smoothly.

Conventions
- Be sure your writing contains correct grammar, punctuation, capitalization, and spelling.

It's really important to edit my story for correct grammar and mechanics!

Narrative Test Writing **111**

Have students take turns reading the bulleted text on page 111. Discuss Marco's responses and encourage students to add their own thoughts. For example, ask:

- How might you organize events in your account?

- What are a few different ways you could grab your reader's attention at the beginning of the narrative?

- What narrative techniques can you use to connect with your audience?

Take time to reinforce the connection between bullet points in the scoring guide and their corresponding writing traits. For instance, ask which writing trait corresponds to the first bullet point. (Ideas) Encourage students to ask any questions they have about the scoring guide and the traits. Call on volunteers to answer the questions before you provide answers yourself.

ADVANCED

Writing Prompt Make a few copies of the narrative writing prompt. Cut apart the sentences in the scoring guide. Have partners work together to assign the sentences to one of the rubric writing traits—Ideas, Organization, Voice, Word Choice, Sentence Fluency, and Conventions.

ADVANCED HIGH

Writing Prompt Have students read the narrative writing prompt and write down no more than three words in each part of the prompt that they think are most important. Then have them compare with a partner and discuss the differences.

CCSS **C**ommon **C**ore **S**tate **S**tandards
SL.6.1.a: Come to discussions prepared, having read or studied required material; explicitly draw on that preparation by referring to evidence on the topic, text, or issue to probe and reflect on ideas under discussion.
SL.6.1.b: Follow rules for collegial discussions, set specific goals and deadlines, and define individual roles as needed. **SL.6.1.c:** Pose and respond to specific questions with elaboration and detail by making comments that contribute to the topic, text, or issue under discussion.

Write
a Narrative Test

Week 2 • Day 2

Student Objectives

• Learn how to respond to the task in the writing prompt. *(p. 112)*

Prewrite

Focus on Ideas

Gather Information Remind students that they have written narrative pieces in the past and will be using writing strategies they've already practiced. Review the elements of an eyewitness account if you have taught it already (see pp. T4A–T27). Point out that the step on page 112 is similar to the first step in any other writing assignment—think about the topic and then generate a quick list of details about it. Ask:

• How did Marco prepare before writing? (He chose an experience he found exciting and then jotted down details he remembered.)

Direct students' attention to Marco's notes at the bottom of the page. Note that he does not need a long, detailed list of notes to begin writing. He has jotted down the key points— more details will come as he creates his graphic organizer and writes his account. Assure students that the same will happen for them. Instruct students to choose an event and then jot down some related details.

Online Writing Center

 Provides **interactive graphic organizers** as well as a variety of graphic organizers in PDF format.

Prewrite   Focus on   Ideas

Writing Strategy   Respond to the task.

Before I start writing, I'm going to gather some information and take notes. In a writing test, you can gather a lot of information right from the writing prompt. Look at the task to find out what you are supposed to write. Then think about how you'll respond to the task. That'll help save time since you won't have much time during a test!

The writing prompt for my test says to write an eyewitness account of a newsworthy event. I decided to write about the time I saw a construction crew lift a new pedestrian overpass over the freeway with a huge crane. I quickly jotted down some notes.

Task ———
Then write an eyewitness account telling about the event.

Notes

✓ Crews used a huge crane to move the overpass over the freeway.

✓ They had to shut down traffic on both sides.

✓ A bunch of people stopped to watch it.

Apply

Be sure to think about how you are going to respond to the task before you start writing. Then write down notes that will help you gather information.

112 Narrative Writing

Differentiating Instruction

ENRICHMENT

Explore Voice Challenge students to write their eyewitness account as a report by a TV journalist who is on the scene as the event unfolds. The journalist can provide a narration of what is happening and also interview eyewitnesses to provide dialogue and a variety of points of view. Each speaker will require a unique voice. After the test responses have been written, you may wish to have students convert their eyewitness accounts into scripts and act them out with classmates.

Prewrite

Focus on **Organization**

Writing Strategy   Choose a graphic organizer.

The writing prompt says my event should be told in a logical order. Using a 5 W's chart in the past has been helpful in ordering details or events, so I'll use one now.

First, I wrote down *who* was there. Then I wrote *what* I saw. I also included some interesting details, since the scoring guide says I should include details that help make the narrative real. Next, I wrote *when* it happened, *where* it happened, and *why* it happened.

Who **was there?** My cousin and I were watching the action.

What **happened?** The construction crew used a crane to put a pedestrian bridge across a freeway.

- They closed the freeway. There were no cars!
- The bridge was in two parts. The crane operator moved one part over the freeway. They put one side of it in the middle where the cement support was. Then they did the same thing with the other side.
- Then the crew went on to finish installing and connecting it.

When **did it happen?** Last summer. It was really early on a Saturday morning.

Where **did it happen?** On a freeway near Denver, where my cousin lives.

Why **did it happen?** They're putting in a new rail system near the freeway and had to put in a pedestrian bridge so people could cross the road.

Reflect

Does the chart answer *who, what, when, where,* and *why*?

Apply

Choose a graphic organizer that fits the type of writing you're doing. Here a 5 W's Chart worked best.

Narrative Test Writing **113**

REINFORCEMENT

Support Organization   Help students review how graphic organizers can help them structure their notes. Ask volunteers to name various types of graphic organizers, such as those they have used throughout this unit. **(Biography Map, Story Map, Storyboard)** Then ask students how they might decide which organizer to use on a test. Remind them to look for clues in the writing prompt to help them decide on the best organizer.

Write
a Narrative Test

Week 2 • Day 3

Student Objectives

- Learn how to choose a graphic organizer for the writing prompt. *(p. 113)*

Prewrite

Focus on **Organization**

Choose an Organizer   Once students have chosen an event and recorded some notes, have them take a moment to think about other graphic organizers they have used to organize narratives. Discuss Marco's choice of graphic organizer. Ask:

- How will a 5 W's Chart help Marco as he writes his story? (Possible response: It will help him remember to include all vital information.)

Now tell students to choose the organizer they feel is best for their purpose (a 5 W's Chart or other organizer) and complete it. Remind them that this organizer will function as a guide as they write, so it is very important that they record all the necessary information now.

CCSS Common Core State Standards

W.6.3: Write narratives to develop real or imagined experiences or events using effective technique, relevant descriptive details, and well-structured event sequences. **W.6.3.a:** Engage and orient the reader by establishing a context and introducing a narrator and/or characters; organize an event sequence that unfolds naturally and logically. **W.6.3.d:** Use precise words and phrases, relevant descriptive details, and sensory language to convey experiences and events.

Write
a Narrative Test

Week 2 • Day 4

Student Objectives

- Learn how to check the graphic organizer against the scoring guide. (pp. 114–115)

Prewrite

Focus on  Organization

Check the Graphic Organizer

Remind students that they will be checking their work against the scoring guide throughout the writing test. Have students read Marco's words at the top of page 114. Then direct students' attention to page 115. Discuss how Marco has checked the traits to be sure that his prewriting—gathering and organizing information—is on track. Ask:

- Does Marco's 5 W's Chart meet the setup and task requirements in the writing prompt? (yes)

- Does the information he's recorded clearly describe his topic? (yes)

- Has he organized the events in a logical, natural order? (yes)

Point out that Marco often refers to the scoring guide just as he would a rubric. Encourage students to do the same as they prepare to write.

 Strategies for Writers Online
Go to **www.sfw.z-b.com** for additional online resources for students and teachers.

Prewrite
Focus on **Organization**

Writing Strategy Check the graphic organizer against the scoring guide.

You won't have much time, if any, to revise when you take some tests. That's why prewriting is important! Before I start to write, I'll check my 5 W's Chart against the scoring guide in the writing prompt.

Who **was there?** My cousin and I were watching the action.

What **happened?** The construction crew used a crane to put a pedestrian bridge across a freeway.
- They closed the freeway. There were no cars!
- The bridge was in two parts. The crane operator moved one part over the freeway. They put one side of it in the middle where the cement support was. Then they did the same thing with the other side.
- Then the crew went on to finish installing and connecting it.

When **did it happen?** Last summer. It was really early on a Saturday morning.

Where **did it happen?** On a freeway near Denver, where my cousin lives.

Why **did it happen?** They're putting in a new rail system near the freeway and had to put in a pedestrian bridge so people could cross the road.

Ideas
- Be sure your writing uses descriptive details to develop the events.

I think the details in my chart will help me describe the events in a realistic and engaging way.

Organization
- Be sure your writing tells the event in a logical order and uses transition words to convey sequence.

I'll arrange the information from my chart to tell the story in chronological order, with the help of transition words.

Voice
- Be sure your writing voice matches the audience and purpose.

My voice should connect to my reader and create interest so he or she knows that my purpose is to tell a story.

Word Choice
- Be sure your writing uses precise words and phrases to convey the events.

Even though I have the details written down, I'll need to use precise, descriptive language and vocabulary as I write.

Sentence Fluency
- Be sure your writing contains sentences that flow smoothly.

As I write my draft, I'll use dialogue and pay attention to how my sentences are flowing.

Conventions
- Be sure your writing contains correct grammar, punctuation, capitalization, and spelling.

I'll check my writing closely for errors when I go back and edit my draft.

Reflect

The 5 W's Chart covers a lot of the points from the scoring guide. How will the chart help Marco write an engaging account?

Apply

You'll want to go back and reread the writing prompt one more time so you know just what to do when you start writing your draft.

Write
a Narrative Test

Prepare to Draft Discuss why Marco cannot yet check his work against all six writing traits. For example, be sure students understand that he will need to write a draft before he can check for variety in sentence lengths and correct spelling and grammar. Point out, however, that he has at least acknowledged the fact that he needs to use an engaging voice and good sentence fluency to create a well-written eyewitness account. Ask:

- Why has Marco stopped at this point to check his work against the scoring guide? (Possible response: He doesn't have much time to draft and has no time to start over, so he wants to be sure he's responding to the task correctly.)

Point out to students that by reviewing each of the writing traits again, Marco is also reminding himself of what to keep in mind as he writes his draft.

CCSS **Common Core State Standards**

W.6.3: Write narratives to develop real or imagined experiences or events using effective technique, relevant descriptive details, and well-structured event sequences. **W.6.3.a:** Engage and orient the reader by establishing a context and introducing a narrator and/or characters; organize an event sequence that unfolds naturally and logically. **W.6.3.d:** Use precise words and phrases, relevant descriptive details, and sensory language to convey experiences and events.

Write
a Narrative Test

Week 2 • Day 5

Student Objectives

• Draft a writing test response, using specific, related details. (pp. 116–117)

Draft

Focus on Ideas

Tips for Test Writing Prior to drafting, have students place their graphic organizers on their desks for easy referral. Remind them to look at their organizers often while drafting to ensure they stay on track and include all the important information. Also remind students to write on every other line so that there will be room to make revisions and edits.

Remind students that they will have fifteen minutes to draft their tests. Urge them to write as neatly as possible despite the time constraints. Then have students read Marco's words on page 116 and direct their attention to the draft on pages 116–117. Have students compare the draft to Marco's 5 W's Chart. Note that Marco added some details that were not included in the graphic organizer, but these details do relate to the central topic.

Online Writing Center

Provides student eBooks with an **interactive writing pad** for drafting, revising, editing, and publishing.

Draft

Focus on Ideas

Writing Strategy Use specific, related details.

The scoring guide says to use description to develop the events. I need to create scenes for the reader that sound like they really happened, even if the reader has never seen what I am describing. I also need to do it in a way that's not dull and boring. All the details have to be related to my topic. I'll bet not many people have seen a bridge being installed across a freeway.

[DRAFT]

The Day the Freeway Closed
by Marco

Have you ever wondered how contruction crews build a bridge across the top of a freeway. Well, I got to see it firsthand, and it was the coolest, most amazing thing to watch! You would not believe how they install a bridge it's almost unreal. Here's what happened one early morning last summer.

I got to go to visit my cousin. Xavier lives in Denver, where they are building a new rail system alongside a freeway that it will take people to and from downtown Denver. Xavier and his family lives near the freeway, and early one Saturday morning, his dad told us the freeway had been shut down. Imagine a whole freeway being closed? We had to go see it, so we took off on bikes to an open lot by the freeway.

116 Narrative Writing

English Language Learners

BEGINNING
Word Order On the board, write *crashed cars The*. Ask, *Is this a sentence?* Tell students that the words need to be rearranged. Ask partners to fix the order of words in the sentence: *The cars crashed.* Underline *cars* and circle *crashed*. Point out that this sentence has a subject and a verb, so it is complete.

INTERMEDIATE
Sentence Order Narrative writing tells a story in order of events. To practice this, have students write a four-sentence story about an accident. They should begin each sentence on a new line. Make sure students use appropriate words to signal order. Then have them cut apart their sentences and trade with another student. The second student should put the sentences in the proper order, using order words and context to do so.

When we got there, there wasn't a single car on the road, just a bunch of constructions workers and heavy equipment. Then we saw the crane start to move. Hanging from it was a bridge. "they're putting in a pedestrian bridge so people can walk to the new train station, Xavier told me.

The crane operator moved the bridge to the support structures that had been built on the side and in the middle of the freeway. I could tell now that this was only have of the bridge. The other half was still lying on the other side of the road.

The construction crew moved in to check things. They moved to the other bridge to help secure the crane to it. This took quite some time. The crane started moving again slowly. This part seemed even trickier, having to match up one part of the bridge with the other without crashing into it! There was man now standing on the part of the bridge that had been placed, watching closely as the crane moved.

Soon, the other half of the bridge was in place The crew on the ground moved in again, ready to begin checking and securiting the new bridge. With the heavy loading and moving done Xavier and I decided to leave.

Reflect

Do the details help develop the events? Do they sound real and related to the topic?

Apply

You'll want to draw your readers in from the very beginning, so be sure your first paragraph is interesting and exciting.

Narrative Test Writing 117

Write
a Narrative Test

Check for Related Details Ask students to point out details in the draft that Marco used to describe the setting, characters, and action. Remind students that vivid, descriptive details are the key to grabbing a reader's attention and bringing the story and characters to life.

Have students begin drafting their narrative essays. Remind them to include specific, related details to paint a clear picture of the setting, characters, and action. Students should keep the following in mind:

- Does each detail relate to my story?
- Does each detail help the reader experience the characters, setting, or action?
- Does each detail relate well to the other details in the paragraph?

Remind students that they are not obligated to include every detail that appears in their graphic organizers. As they write, they may find that some information they recorded earlier is not relevant after all.

ADVANCED
Using Exact Words After students have written their first drafts, have them circle all the adjectives and verbs they used in the first paragraph. Then have them trade with a partner who will read the paragraph and change each of the circled words to a more descriptive one. Then have the partners discuss why they made each change. Monitor that students' changes were appropriate.

ADVANCED HIGH
Peer Review After students have drafted their eyewitness accounts, have them trade with another student. Partners should review the draft and specifically look for details. Students should point out weak supporting sentences and suggest more vivid words their partners could use. As you monitor, identify two or three examples of weak words or sentences, and discuss ways to strengthen them as a class.

CCSS Common Core State Standards

W.6.3: Write narratives to develop real or imagined experiences or events using effective technique, relevant descriptive details, and well-structured event sequences. W.6.3.b: Use narrative techniques, such as dialogue, pacing, and description, to develop experiences, events, and/or characters. W.6.3.d: Use precise words and phrases, relevant descriptive details, and sensory language to convey experiences and events.

Write a Narrative Test

Week 3 • Day 1

Student Objectives

• Revise to use transitions to guide the reader. *(p. 118)*

Revise

Focus on  Organization

Use Transitions Have students read the page. Ask volunteers to think of additional helpful transitions that can be used to sequence events.

Then turn students' attention to the draft excerpt. Ask:

• How does Marco's revision clarify this scene? (Possible response: The transition clarifies exactly when he got to visit his cousin.)

Remind students that transitions can guide readers between ideas as well as between events. Review different types of transitions. On the board, write *Time Order, Cause and Effect, Opposition,* and *Comparison.* Have students call out transitions for each category, and write them on the board. (Possible responses: Time Order—later, that evening; Cause and Effect—because, therefore, as a consequence; Opposition—but, on the other hand, instead; Comparison—similarly, just like, unlike, in contrast) Tell students they can use the lists for inspiration as they think about transitions to guide readers through their eyewitness accounts.

 Strategies for Writers Online
Go to **www.sfw.z-b.com** for additional online resources for students and teachers.

Revise Focus on Organization

Writing Strategy Use transition words to guide the reader.

Now that I have written my draft, I reread it to see if I missed anything. The scoring guide says to use transition words to help my reader see the sequence of events. I can move smoothly from one paragraph to the next by repeating a word. I see where I can do that in the beginning of this paragraph. I'll also use the transition word *During* to show that my summer vacation and my visit to Xavier happened at the same time.

[DRAFT]

[Added transition words]
Here's what happened one early morning last summer.
▸During my summer vacation,
    I got to visit my cousin. Xavier lives in Denver, where they are building
    ∧
a new rail system alongside a freeway that it will take people to and

from downtown Denver.

Apply
When you're writing a story, use transition words to move smoothly from one paragraph to the next.

Differentiating Instruction

ENRICHMENT

Explore Tone Have students rewrite all or part of their eyewitness accounts in a very formal tone. Call on students to read both the formal and informal versions of their drafts to the group. Discuss what creates a formal or an informal tone in writing. (Possible responses: Formal—longer, more difficult words; no contractions; fewer expressions of emotion; often third-person point of view. Informal—more casual, everyday words; more short sentences; more contractions and use of first-person point of view) Discuss circumstances in which a more formal presentation of an eyewitness account would be appropriate. (Possible responses: in a court of law, in a newspaper)

Revise

Focus on Voice

Writing Strategy Use a casual tone.

Now to check my paper for voice. Since the purpose of writing a story is to share a personal experience, my tone can be casual and informal. I have already addressed the reader directly by using *you*. Look at how I added a more appealing ending to my story. Using the word *but* is not a typical way to start a sentence, but it fits the casual tone.

[DRAFT]

The crew on the ground moved in again, ready to begin checking and securing the new bridge. With the heavy loading and moving done Xavier and I decided to leave. But we sure had a story to tell.

Reflect

Does the story appeal to the reader with a casual tone?

Apply

When you share a personal experience, add words that have a casual and informal tone.

Narrative Test Writing **119**

REINFORCEMENT

Support Tone Help students understand the difference between a casual and a formal tone. Write the following sentence pairs on the board. *We're going to the mall tonight. We will shop at the mall this evening. Hi there, pleased to meet you! I am happy to make your acquaintance. Wow, that was an amazing experience! The experience made quite an impression on me.* Have students point out which sentence in each pair is casual and which one is formal. Discuss the differences between the sentences in each pair. Make sure students talk about how they react to each tone as readers.

Write
a Narrative Test

Student Objectives

• Revise to use a casual tone. (p. 119)

Revise

Focus on Voice

Use a Casual Tone Have a volunteer read the draft excerpt both before and after Marco's revision. Ask:

• How does this revision help Marco better connect with the reader? (Possible responses: When a writer uses a casual tone, I feel invited to share the story. It feels like a friend is telling me about an experience he or she had.)

Have students review their writing for a casual tone. Tell them to focus especially on the second half of their essays, where writers often lose track of the voice they established at the beginning and become inconsistent.

CCSS Common Core State Standards

W.6.3.a: Engage and orient the reader by establishing a context and introducing a narrator and/or characters; organize an event sequence that unfolds naturally and logically. **W.6.3.c:** Use a variety of transition words, phrases, and clauses to convey sequence and signal shifts from one time frame or setting to another. **L.6.3.b:** Maintain consistency in style and tone.

Write
a Narrative Test

Week 3 • Day 3

Student Objectives

- Revise to use precise words and phrases. *(p. 120)*

Revise

Focus on Word Choice

Use Precise Language List several vague words, such as *said, good, bad, big, little,* and *is.* Explain that while these words are sometimes perfectly appropriate, oftentimes they can and should be replaced by language that is more precise and concrete. Have students brainstorm words that could be used in place of the vague ones you listed. **(Possible responses: shouted, delicious, horrifying, monstrous, tiny, remains)**

Now have a volunteer read the draft excerpt both before and after Marco made his revisions. Discuss how the revisions help readers better visualize the construction site and the bridge. Instruct students to review their own writing to find vague words and phrases that should be replaced with language that is more precise and concrete.

Remind students to make their changes as neatly as possible. They should keep in mind that their writing must be legible so the evaluator can read it easily and accurately.

 Strategies for Writers Online
Go to **www.sfw.z-b.com** for additional online resources for students and teachers.

Revise   Focus on **Word Choice**

Writing Strategy   Use precise words and phrases.

The scoring guide says that I should use precise words and phrases to convey the events. I don't want my writing to seem dull or confusing! I found a few places where changing a word or adding a phrase would make a huge difference in how my story reads. I'll make my changes as neatly and carefully as I can.

[DRAFT]

—— [added precise words and phrases] ——

When we got there, there wasn't a single car on the road, just a ~~bunch of constructions workers~~ and heavy equipment. Then we saw the ~~huge~~ , slowly and cautiously   what looked like a long metal cage. crane start to move. Hanging from it was ~~a bridge~~ "they're putting in a pedestrian bridge so people can walk to the new train station, Xavier told me.

Reflect

Does Marco use the best words to describe things in his account?

Apply

Your word choices can make a huge difference. Replace dull and ordinary words with more precise words that fit your writing.

120   Narrative Writing

Optional Revising Lessons

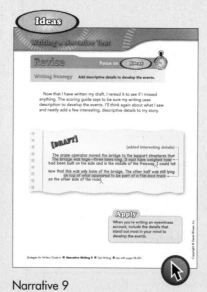

Narrative 9   Narrative 10

 Strategies for Writers Grade 6 CD-ROM

Writing Strategy   Check the grammar, punctuation, capitalization, and spelling.

I'm almost done—just one more step! The scoring guide says to use correct grammar, punctuation, capitalization, and spelling. That's very important, so I made sure to leave enough time.

[FINAL DRAFT]

The Day the Freeway Closed

by Marco

Have you ever wondered how ~~contruction~~ construction crews build a bridge across the top of a freeway? Well, I got to see it firsthand, and it was the coolest, most amazing thing to watch! You would not believe how they install a bridge; it's almost unreal. Here's what happened one early morning last summer.

During my summer vacation, I got to go to visit my cousin. Xavier lives in Denver, where they are building a new rail system alongside a freeway that it will take people to and from downtown Denver. Xavier and his family lives near the freeway, and early one Saturday morning, his dad told us the freeway had been shut down. Imagine a whole freeway being closed! We had to go see it, so we took off on bikes to an open lot by the freeway.

Apply

Don't forget to check your grammar, punctuation, capitalization, and spelling every time you write for a test.

Narrative Test Writing 121

Differentiating Instruction

ENRICHMENT

Early Finishers Some students finish tests early and fall into the habit of simply waiting for the testing period to be over. Advise students to make good use of the extra time by checking the prompt once again and rereading their tests very carefully.

Write
a Narrative Test

Week 3 • Day 4

Student Objectives

• Edit the writing test response for grammar, spelling, capitalization, and punctuation. *(pp. 121–122)*

Edit

Focus on **Conventions**

Edit the Test Ask students to recall how much time they will have for editing. (5 minutes) Explain that an eyewitness account written in one sitting over a short period of time will not be perfect. However, students should find and correct as many errors as they can despite the time limitations. Test evaluators look for evidence that students have made an effort to edit. For example, when they see misspelled words crossed out and correctly spelled words inserted, evaluators know that students are paying attention to editing.

Have students study the edited draft on pages 121 and 122. Discuss why Marco made each edit and used certain proofreading marks. Now have students edit their own writing for grammar, spelling, capitalization, and punctuation.

CCSS Common Core State Standards
L.6.1: Demonstrate command of the conventions of standard English grammar and usage when writing or speaking. **L.6.2:** Demonstrate command of the conventions of standard English capitalization, punctuation, and spelling when writing. **L.6.2.b:** Spell correctly.

Review
Test Tips

Week 3 • Day 5

Student Objectives

- Review tips for writing for a test. *(p. 123)*

Test Tips

Reviewing Test Writing Read and discuss each of the test tips with students. Incorporate the following thoughts:

- Remind students to always read the writing prompt carefully and completely, making no assumptions about what the prompt might require.

- Before writing, students should look for and label the three key parts of the prompt—the setup, task, and scoring guide.

- Stress that not all writing test prompts will include the six traits of good writing. Nevertheless, students should keep all the traits in mind as they write.

Remind students that a writing prompt may include an illustration. Urge students to use the illustration as another clue to understanding the task. In addition to circling key words in the task, encourage students to mark their scoring guides, highlighting instructions they often overlook in their writing.

Online Writing Center

Provides **interactive proofreading activities** for each genre.

[FINAL DRAFT]

When we got there, there wasn't a single car on the road, just a bunch of constructions workers and heavy equipment. Then we saw the huge crane start to move. Hanging from it was a bridge. , slowly and cautiously what looked like a long metal cage. "they're putting in a pedestrian bridge so people can walk to the new train station," Xavier told me.

The bridge was huge—three lanes long. It must have weighed tons! The crane operator moved the bridge to the cement support structures that had been built on the side and in the middle of the freeway. I could tell now that this was only half of the bridge. The other half was still lying on top of what appeared to be part of a flat-bed truck on the other side of the road.

With the bridge in place, The construction crew moved in to check things. Then They moved to the other bridge to help secure the crane to it. This took quite some time, but we weren't about to leave!

Finally, The crane started moving again slowly. This part seemed even trickier, having to match up one part of the bridge with the other without crashing into it! There was a man now standing on the part of the bridge that had been placed, watching closely as the crane moved.

Soon, the other half of the bridge was in place. The crew on the ground moved in again, ready to begin checking and securing the new bridge. With the heavy loading and moving done, Xavier and I decided to leave. But we sure had a story to tell.

Reflect

Is anything missing? Check Marco's draft against the scoring guide one last time. It's important to use the writing prompt's scoring guide to check your writing any time you take a test!

122 Narrative Writing

Differentiating Instruction

REINFORCEMENT

Support Editing Have students practice editing by writing sample sentences for correction on the board. Then ask them to take turns using the appropriate editing marks from page 475 to edit the sentences. Tailor the sentences to focus on the conventions that give students the most trouble.

Well, we're done. And it wasn't so bad, was it? Here are some helpful tips for when you write for a test.

TEST TIPS

1. **Study the writing prompt before you start to write.** Most writing prompts have three parts: the setup, the task, and the scoring guide. The parts probably won't be labeled. You'll have to figure them out for yourself!

2. **Make sure you understand the task before you start to write.**
   - Read all three parts of the writing prompt carefully.
   - Circle key words in the task part of the writing prompt that tell what kind of writing you need to do. The task might also identify your audience.
   - Make sure you know how you'll be graded.
   - Say the assignment in your own words to yourself.

3. **Keep an eye on the clock.** Decide how much time you will spend on each part of the writing process and try to stick to your schedule. Don't spend so much time prewriting that you don't have enough time left to write.

4. **Reread your writing. Compare it to the scoring guide at least twice.** Remember the rubrics you have used all year? A scoring guide on a writing test is like a rubric. It can help you keep what's important in mind.

5. **Plan, plan, plan!** You don't get much time to revise during a test, so planning is more important than ever.

6. **Write neatly.** Remember: If the people who score your test can't read your writing, it doesn't matter how good your essay is!

Narrative Test Writing 123

Tell students that while remaining aware of their time is important, they should focus primarily on the test itself. Advise them not to worry if some students seem to finish early. They should stay focused on their own work. Similarly, remind students who do finish early to use the time remaining to review their writing again and make any last-minute revisions/edits.

Finally, urge students who experience test anxiety to keep a positive attitude and to stay relaxed throughout the test. Remind them that they have been learning and practicing the skills necessary to complete the test successfully. If any students begin to feel nervous, suggest they sit back, take a few deep breaths, relax and refocus, and then resume the test. The benefits will be well worth the few seconds this takes.

CCSS **Common Core State Standards**

L.6.1: Demonstrate command of the conventions of standard English grammar and usage when writing or speaking. **L.6.2:** Demonstrate command of the conventions of standard English capitalization, punctuation, and spelling when writing. **W.6.10:** Write routinely over extended time frames (time for research, reflection, and revision) and shorter time frames (a single sitting or a day or two) for a range of discipline-specific tasks, purposes, and audiences.

Informative/Explanatory writing

Summary

Pages T126A–T151

By writing a summary, students demonstrate that they understand and can identify the main points of a nonfiction text.

Prewrite Read an article. Take notes on the main points.
Make a Spider Map to organize and connect details.

Draft Include only the most important ideas and details.

Revise Include an attention-grabbing detail in the opening paragraph.
Use third-person point of view plus facts.
Choose words carefully and replace wordy phrases with succinct language.

Edit Be sure all subjects and verbs agree and all modifiers are clear.

Publish Read the summary to the class.

Cause-and-Effect Report

Pages T152A–T175

The cause-and-effect structure is a common organization of nonfiction writing.

Prewrite Use the Internet to find credible sources of information on the topic.
Make a Cause-and-Effect Chain to organize the notes.

Draft Introduce the topic and present causes and effects in a logical order.

Revise Speak directly to the reader.
Use specific words. Define them, if necessary.
Rewrite long, confusing sentences.

Edit Make sure subject and object pronouns are used correctly and that irregular verbs are in the correct form.

Publish Add the report to the class binder.

Research Report

Pages T176A–T203

This genre gives students an opportunity to ask questions, conduct research to find answers, and share their discoveries.

Prewrite Use an encyclopedia and at least two other sources to research the topic.
Make an Outline to organize the information.

Draft Use the active voice.

Revise Take out unrelated details or facts.
Use and define domain-specific words correctly.
Use different sentence lengths and structures.

Edit Make sure proper nouns and proper adjectives are capitalized correctly.

Publish Include the report as part of a multimedia presentation to the class.

Unit Overview

MATH CONNECTION

Explanatory Essay
Pages T204A–T227

Students will demonstrate their understanding of a math concept by writing an explanatory essay.

Prewrite Choose and narrow a topic. Take notes.
Make a Fact Web to organize the notes.

Draft Make sure domain-specific vocabulary is used and defined correctly.

Revise Replace unnecessary or weak details with strong facts and details.
Use transition words or phrases to connect sentences and paragraphs.
Add prepositional phrases to sentences.

Edit Make sure all prepositions are correct.

Publish Present the essay as a multimedia slide show.

Informative/Explanatory Test Writing
Pages T228A–T249

Students will further develop their test-writing skills as they learn to read and analyze an informative/explanatory test prompt, plan time for the steps in the writing process, and write a test in the informative/explanatory mode.

Prewrite Study the writing prompt to find out what to do. Respond to the task.
Choose a graphic organizer.
Check the graphic organizer against the scoring guide.

Draft State the topic clearly.

Revise Use transition words to clarify connecting ideas.
Use active voice and first-person point of view.
Use specific words.

Edit Check grammar, spelling, capitalization, and punctuation.

Online Writing Center

Interactive Whiteboard Ready

Complete Digital Writing Instruction!

- My Writing Pad
- Interactive Rubrics
- Anchor Papers
- Graphic Organizers

- Content Area Writing Prompts
- Grammar Games
- Proofreading Activities
- Instructional Videos

- Virtual File Cabinet
- eBooks
- Assessments

For information, go to
www.sfw.z-b.com

Also available: **Online Essay Grader and Writing Tutor,** powered by Vantage Learning's MY Access®.

21st Century Literacies
Technology, Digital Media & Writing

by **Julie Coiro, Ph.D.,** University of Rhode Island & **Sara Kajder, Ph.D.,** University of Pittsburgh

 **INQUIRE** First Locate, Then Evaluate

Locating Resources: Reading Within Search Engine Results

As your students increasingly turn to the Internet for research, one of the most challenging aspects of online reading is understanding how to strategically evaluate a long list of search results to determine which link, if any, to pursue. Some strategies you might wish to share with students to determine which link is best:

- **Read the description, not just the link.** Some students only skim the blue underlined titles that appear in the beginning of a search list entry without realizing the description that follows contains helpful clues. Encourage students to stop, read, and notice that the keywords from their search are often bolded within the descriptions.

- **Know how to read the parts of a website address.** A great deal of information can be gleaned from the dots, slashes, abbreviations, and words contained in the web address that appears below descriptions in many lists of search results. Take a few minutes in class to show students how web addresses, or URL's, can be broken down into parts, with each part providing identification of the path leading to the website host, as follows:

http://	type of protocol
www.nytimes.com/	domain name, or host
learning/	path to the file
index.html	name and type of file

- **Use the clues to try a different search.** If nothing useful is found in the first 10 or 20 sites listed, try a new search with different keywords. Encourage students to think about words that appeared in the descriptions or within the websites they visited.

Critical Evaluation: Evaluating Reliability

As children begin using Internet websites as a source for information, it is important that they realize websites do not go through the same editing process as books. One important strategy to discuss with students involves evaluating the reliability of the information they find online.

For educational purposes, a reliable website is one created by a person or group of people with a reputation for publishing high-quality, truthful information for children. It is critical that students be prepared to investigate who created a website, why it was created, and what authority the person has to publish the information.

All quality websites should have an "About Us" page that tells more about the authors, their qualifications, contact information, and their purpose for creating the site. You can usually find this information at a link labeled "Who We Are" or "About Us" on the homepage of a website.

To begin, select two or three websites, using a digital projector to view each site with your students. Scroll up and down the site's homepage to look for the "About Us" link. Once you have found the link, then discuss the answers to questions such as these:

a) Who created the information?

b) What is the purpose of this website?

c) When was the information at this site updated?

d) What qualifications does the author have?

e) Is the information at this website worthy of being used in your own expository writing? Why or why not?

Encourage students to consider this series of questions each time they visit a website.

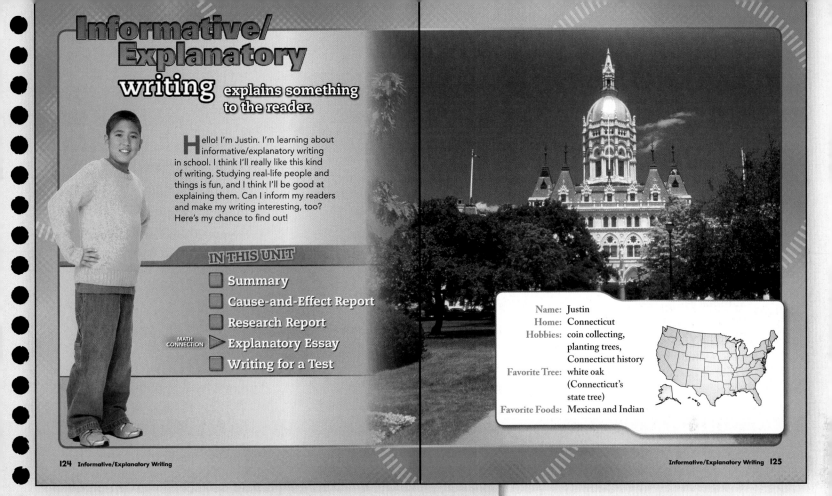

Informative/Explanatory writing explains something to the reader.

Hello! I'm Justin. I'm learning about informative/explanatory writing in school. I think I'll really like this kind of writing. Studying real-life people and things is fun, and I think I'll be good at explaining them. Can I inform my readers and make my writing interesting, too? Here's my chance to find out!

IN THIS UNIT

☐ Summary
☐ Cause-and-Effect Report
☐ Research Report
MATH CONNECTION ▷ Explanatory Essay
☐ Writing for a Test

Name: Justin
Home: Connecticut
Hobbies: coin collecting, planting trees, Connecticut history
Favorite Tree: white oak (Connecticut's state tree)
Favorite Foods: Mexican and Indian

Meet Your Writing Partner, Justin

The writing partner for this chapter is Justin, a boy from Connecticut. Have students locate Connecticut on a map. Then ask them to share what they know about the state. Next have students look at the picture of Justin and read about his favorite activities and interests. Explain to students that Justin will use what he knows to make decisions about his topics—a process that makes his writing authentic. Encourage students to use their own background knowledge, interests, and personalities as they write. Informative/explanatory writing explores many real-world topics, and your students will have a variety of interesting, unique, and authentic ideas to explain.

To differentiate instruction and maximize student achievement, use the Extensions Online activities available at **www.sfw.z-b.com.**

Created by Amy Humphreys, Ed.M., these engaging activities can be used to meet a wide range of learner needs. Each activity uses a combination of visual, written, oral, and kinesthetic elements, and deliberately leverages the power of collaboration and conversation so students learn to think like writers in fun and engaging ways. For more information on Differentiated Instruction, see page Z12.

Summary Planner

WEEK 1

Day 1
Introduce
a Summary

Student Objectives
- Review the elements of a summary.
- Consider purpose and audience.
- Learn the traits of informative/explanatory writing.

Student Activities
- Read and discuss **What's in a Summary?** (p. 126)
- Read and discuss **Why Write a Summary?** (p. 127)
- Read **Linking Informative/Explanatory Writing Traits to a Summary.** (p. 128)

Day 2
Analyze
Read a Summary

Student Objectives
- Read a model summary.

Student Activities
- Read **"A Touch of Genius."** (pp. 129, 130–131)

Day 3
Analyze
Introduce the Rubric

Student Objectives
- Learn to read a rubric.

Student Activities
- Review **"A Touch of Genius."** (p. 129)
- Read and discuss the **Summary Rubric.** (pp. 132–133)

WEEK 2

Day 1
Write
Prewrite: Ideas

Student Objectives
- Read and understand a prewriting strategy.

Student Activities
- Read and discuss **Prewrite: Focus on Ideas.** (pp. 138–140)
- Apply the prewriting strategy.

Day 2
Write
Prewrite: Organization

Student Objectives
- Make a Spider Map to organize and connect details.

Student Activities
- Read and discuss **Prewrite: Focus on Organization.** (p. 141)
- Apply the prewriting strategy to create a Spider Map.
- Participate in a peer conference.

Day 3
Write
Draft: Ideas

Student Objectives
- Use a Spider Map to begin writing.

Student Activities
- Read and discuss **Draft: Focus on Ideas.** (p. 142)
- Apply the drafting strategy by using a Spider Map to write a draft.

WEEK 3

Day 1
Write
Revise: Voice

Student Objectives
- Revise to use third-person point of view plus facts.

Student Activities
- Read and discuss **Revise: Focus on Voice.** (p. 145)
- Reflect on the model draft.
- Apply the revising strategy.
- Participate in a peer conference.

Day 2
Write
Revise: Word Choice

Student Objectives
- Revise to use succinct language.

Student Activities
- Read and discuss **Revise: Focus on Word Choice.** (p. 146)
- Reflect on the model draft.
- Apply the revising strategy.

Note: Optional Revising Lessons appear on the *Strategies for Writers* CD-ROM.

Day 3
Write
Edit: Conventions

Student Objectives
- Edit for correct subject-verb agreement and clear modifiers.

Student Activities
- Read and discuss **Edit: Focus on Conventions.** (p. 147)
- Reflect on the model draft.
- Apply the editing strategy.

Note: Teach the Conventions mini-lessons (pp. 148–149) if needed.

Day 4

Analyze
Ideas, Organization, and Voice

Student Objectives
- Read a model summary.
- Use the summary rubric.
- Use the model summary to study Ideas, Organization, and Voice.

Student Activities
- Review **"A Touch of Genius."** (p. 129)
- Read and discuss **Using the Rubric to Study the Model.** (pp. 134–135)

Day 5

Analyze
Word Choice, Sentence Fluency, and Conventions

Student Objectives
- Read a model summary.
- Use the summary rubric.
- Use the model summary to study Word Choice, Sentence Fluency, and Conventions.

Student Activities
- Review **"A Touch of Genius."** (p. 129)
- Read and discuss **Using the Rubric to Study the Model.** (pp. 136–137)

Day 4

Write
Draft

Student Objectives
- Complete a draft.

Student Activities
- Finish the draft. (p. 143)
- Participate in a peer conference.

Day 5

Write
Revise: Organization

Student Objectives
- Revise to include an interesting detail in the opening paragraph.

Student Activities
- Read and discuss **Revise: Focus on Organization.** (p. 144)
- Reflect on the model draft.
- Apply the revising strategy.

Day 4

Write
Publish: +Presentation

Student Objectives
- Discuss preparation for publishing and presentation.
- Use a final editing checklist to publish their work.

Student Activities
- Read and discuss **Publish: +Presentation.** (p. 150)
- Apply the publishing strategy.

Day 5

Write
Publish: +Presentation

Student Objectives
- Use a summary rubric.
- Share a published summary.

Student Activities
- Share their work.
- Use the rubric to reflect upon and evaluate the model and their own writing. (pp. 132–133, 151)

To complete the chapter in fewer days, combine the learning objectives and activities in a way that supports students as they write.

Resources at-a-Glance

Grammar, Usage & Mechanics

Differentiating Instruction

For additional Differentiating Instruction activities, see Strategies for Writers *Extensions Online at* **www.sfw.z-b.com.**

English Language Learners

Conferencing

Technology Tip

 Connection Letter
Reproducible letter (in English and Spanish) appears on the *Strategies for Writers* CD-ROM and at **www.sfw.z-b.com.**

Online Writing Center

Provides IWB resources, interactive games and practice activities, videos, eBooks, and a virtual file cabinet.

 Strategies for Writers Online

Go to **www.sfw.z-b.com** for free online resources for students and teachers.

Introduce
a Summary

Student Objectives

- Review the elements of a summary. (p. 126)
- Consider purpose and audience. (p. 127)
- Learn the traits of informative/explanatory writing. (p. 128)

What's a Summary?

Discuss with students the definition of a summary. Ask whether any students keep a journal or a blog. If they write reviews of books or movies, they probably include a summary as part of each review. Then explain that any time students summarize the main ideas of a longer piece of writing, they are using the summary genre.

What's in a Summary?

Read and discuss with students the four elements of a summary listed on page 126: length, organization, a clear beginning, and interest. Then discuss specific reasons that each element may be important to writing a summary.

Strategies for Writers Online
Go to **www.sfw.z-b.com** for additional online resources for students and teachers.

What's a **Summary?**

A summary is a short piece of writing that tells the main points of a longer piece. I think explaining the main ideas of another piece of writing in as few words as possible will be an interesting challenge. It reminds me of packing only what I need when I go on a trip!

What's in a **Summary?**

Length
The point of a summary is to condense information, and that's not always easy to do. I'll have to decide what's important enough to be included and what I should leave out.

Organization
I can't waste a word in my summary, so I'm going to organize things very carefully. I'll focus on just the main ideas and organize my points logically. I'll use only relevant details that support the main ideas.

A Clear Beginning
My readers need to know right away what I'm writing about. I'll start my summary with a clear and interesting topic sentence.

Interest
Sometimes nonfiction writing can sound a bit dull. To keep my audience reading, I'm going to bring out interesting points about my subject.

126 Informative/Explanatory Writing

Informative/Explanatory Text Exemplars (Summary)

"Geology." U*X*L Encyclopedia of Science. Edited by Rob Nagel. Gale Cengage Learning, 2007. CCSS
The U*X*L Encyclopedia of Science provides the most current information on a variety of subjects, including Earth, technology, and the environment. This article summarizes information about geology.

Johnson, Jinny. Animal Tracks and Signs: Track Over 400 Animals From Big Cats to Backyard Birds. National Geographic Children's Books, 2008. Animal Tracks and Signs is a collection of different tracks and signs animals leave behind. The book helps readers identify what to look for when tracking animals in the wild or in their own backyard, as well as other signs of animal behavior.

Why write a **Summary?**

I've been thinking about some good reasons to write a summary. Here are a few of my ideas. Can you think of any more?

> **Information**
> Everybody can't read everything! I can use a summary to inform other people about a piece of writing they haven't read.

> **Clarification**
> When there's a lot of information in a written piece, summarizing can help me be clear about what's important. I can also make sure I really understand the author's explanations and main points.

> **Research**
> Summarizing could be really useful when I'm doing research. When I'm starting a project, I read a lot of different reference materials before I focus on my topic. If I write a summary of each reference article, I can keep track of things.

Why write a Summary?

Read and discuss with students the reasons for writing a summary. Point out that all writing has a purpose and is aimed at a specific audience. These authentic purposes help authors shape their writing. Someone writing to inform may write a summary to explain a longer piece of writing. If a writer's purpose is to clarify, he or she may read a piece of writing and write a summary to gain a clear understanding of what is important in the longer piece. Other writers may want to write a summary to help them clearly focus on their topic when they are doing research. Encourage students to share their own reasons for writing a summary. Ask if they are writing to inform, to clarify, or to conduct research. Then have them discuss how their reason will affect the purpose and style of their writing.

Morrison, Taylor. *Wildfire.* **Houghton Mifflin Books for Children, 2006.** A fascinating overview of wildfires, their causes, and the techniques and equipment used to control them. The book also describes how firefighters work to stop wildfires, as well as some of the dangers they face.

Gifford, Clive. *1000 Years of Famous People.* **Kingfisher, 2002.** This book is a collection of the most famous, and infamous, figures of the past thousand years. Readers will learn about explorers, leaders, writers, explorers, among others, and the achievements and legacies they left behind.

CCSS Common Core State Standards

W.6.2: Write informative/explanatory texts to examine a topic and convey ideas, concepts, and information through the selection, organization, and analysis of relevant content. **SL.6.1:** Engage effectively in a range of collaborative discussions (one-on-one, in groups, and teacher-led) with diverse partners on *grade 6 topics, texts, and issues,* building on others' ideas and expressing their own clearly. **SL.6.1.a:** Come to discussions prepared, having read or studied required material; explicitly draw on that preparation by referring to evidence on the topic, text, or issue to probe and reflect on ideas under discussion.

Introduce
a Summary

Linking Informative/ Explanatory Writing Traits to a Summary

Explain to students that they will follow Justin as he models using the writing process and the traits together. As they follow Justin through the writing process, students will see how the Informative/Explanatory Writing Traits have been adapted and applied to writing a summary. They will see that a summary has many factors in common with other types of informative/explanatory writing. However, the particular audience and purpose of a summary determine how the traits are used.

Linking Informative/Explanatory Writing Traits to a **Summary**

In this chapter, you will write a brief account of an article you have read. This type of expository writing is called a summary. Justin will guide you through the stages of the writing process: Prewrite, Draft, Revise, Edit, and Publish. In each stage, Justin will show you important writing strategies that are linked to the Informative/Explanatory Writing Traits below.

Informative/Explanatory Writing Traits

Ideas	• a clear, focused topic • credible, engaging facts and details that support and develop the topic
Organization	• information that is organized logically into a strong introduction, body, and conclusion • transitions that clarify relationships between ideas
Voice	• a voice and tone that are appropriate for the purpose and audience
Word Choice	• language that is precise and concise • domain-specific vocabulary that is used correctly and explained as necessary
Sentence Fluency	• sentences that vary in length and flow smoothly
 **Conventions**	• no or few errors in grammar, usage, mechanics, and spelling

Before you write, read Keesha Kane's summary of the article "A Touch of Genius." Then use the summary rubric on pages 132–133 to decide how well she did. (You might want to look back at What's in a Summary? on page 126, too!)

128   Informative/Explanatory Writing

Informative/Explanatory Writing Traits in a Summary

 **Ideas** The writer builds the summary around main points that point to a clear, focused topic. Credible, engaging facts and details support and develop the topic.

 Organization The paragraphs in the summary are organized into a strong introduction that grabs the reader's attention, a body, and a conclusion. Details are organized logically and are connected in a thoughtful way.

 **Voice** The writer uses a knowledgeable and formal tone that connects with the audience.

"A Touch of Genius"

by Patricia Millman
Summary by Keesha Kane

Organization · Clear beginning · Short length

Michael Naranjo is a Native American sculptor in Santa Fe, New Mexico. He chose his career when he was a boy helping his mother make pottery in the pueblo. At age 23, however, Naranjo was wounded in the Vietnam War. He was blinded and left without the complete use of one hand.

Interesting point

Naranjo was unsure if he would still be able to sculpt. While recovering in the hospital, he molded several clay sculptures of animals. One was so good that it was photographed for the newspaper. That convinced him to pursue his dream.

Although he cannot see, he can remember images from his past. His mind carries the images to his fingertips.

Interesting point

Naranjo has won awards for his work and leads sculpture workshops. His sculptures are displayed in museums and public buildings around the world. Private collectors also seek his art.

Michael A. Naranjo

Summary 129

Word Choice The writer uses concise language and avoids wordiness.

Sentence Fluency The writer uses a variety of sentence lengths and structures to create smooth flow.

Conventions The writer carefully edits his or her work prior to publishing. Subjects and verbs agree, and there are no dangling or misplaced modifiers.

Analyze
the Model

Student Objectives

• Read a model summary. *(p. 129)*

Read the Model

Read Keesha Kane's summary "A Touch of Genius" aloud. Ask students to listen for a clear and focused topic. (Michael Naranjo is a Native American sculptor in Santa Fe, New Mexico.) Instruct students to notice the organization the writer uses and the short length of the summary. The model also points out how Keesha includes credible, engaging facts and details to support her purpose. Also ask students to think about and discuss how the voice affects how they connect with the writer. (Possible response: The voice is knowledgeable and formal. It shows that the writer knows the topic, and the reader should take the writer's ideas seriously.) Are their reactions different from their peers?

Elements of a Summary

Have students refer to What's in a Summary? on page 126 as you refer to the model. Discuss the notes written on the model to enhance students' understanding of the terms.

CCSS Common Core State Standards

R/Inf.6.1: Cite textual evidence to support analysis of what the text says explicitly as well as inferences drawn from the text. R/Inf.6.2: Determine a central idea of a text and how it is conveyed through particular details; provide a summary of the text distinct from personal opinions or judgments. SL.6.1.a: Come to discussions prepared, having read or studied required material; explicitly draw on the topic, text, or issue to probe and reflect on ideas under discussion.

A Touch of Genius

by Patricia Millman

Michael Naranjo is a Native American, a Vietnam War veteran, and "a sculptor who happens to be blind." Behind this statement lies a remarkable story.

Michael grew up in the Tewa Indian pueblo of Santa Clara, New Mexico. As a boy, he roamed the scenic foothills west of the pueblo community and explored the Rio Grande, a river to the south and east. His world was enriched by the beautiful sights and sounds of the desert country.

This artist sees with his hands.

Michael's love of sculpting was born at the pueblo, too. "My mother was a potter, and I would help her fix clay," he recalls. "She gathered her clay in a place in the hills that only she knew about. Every potter has their own source of clay, and when they find that clay, they're very secretive about it.

"My mother would bring in the clay and screen it to get out anything that didn't belong, and then she would soak it in tubs. After that, she'd put the clay into a square of canvas cloth, and she'd sprinkle a different white kind of clay on top. Then she would fold this square of canvas and press on it this way and that way, and when she unfolded the canvas I could see this little log of clay inside.

"Then I would take off my shoes and perform a little dance with the clay. I would sidestep on this log of clay. I could feel the moist clay on the side of my foot and between my toes. And when I reached the other end, I'd step off the square of canvas, and she'd fold it and push it this way and that way and refold it, and I would have this little log of clay again. And once again I would perform my little dance."

Michael's dance served a very important purpose. He was blending the white clay and the brown clay to make it stronger. With this strong clay, his mother could make pots that would last a long time.

"That's probably how I started sculpting. . . playing with clay," Michael says. "Not long after that, I wanted to make figures of animals. And as they became more detailed, they became sculptures. So even way back then, I knew that what I wanted to do was be an artist someday."

One More by **Michael A. Naranjo**

Seeing with His Hands

Michael's goal would not be reached easily. While serving with the Army in Vietnam, Michael was badly wounded in battle. He lost his sight and partial use of one hand. For the first time, Michael wondered if he could ever be a sculptor.

One day, while recovering in the hospital, Michael asked if he could have a small piece of clay. From it he made an inchworm.

The next sculpture Michael made, an Indian on a horse, was so good it was photographed by the newspapers. Lucky thing! Because when

Books for Professional Development

Strausser, Jeffrey. *Painless Writing.* **Hauppauge, NY. Barron's Educational Series, 2001.** This textbook supplement's approach is meant to appeal to students who find writing boring, too difficult, or both. The author gives practical advice that transforms essay writing into a satisfying experience for students. He offers tips on enlivening writing by adding vivid words and rhythm, smoothing out sentences, and silencing the dull passive voice.

Urquhart, Vickie, and Monett McIver. *Teaching Writing in the Content Areas.* **Alexandria, VA. ASCD, 2005.** This book shows how to quickly integrate writing assignments into content areas by using strategic, practical tools. Included in the book are 35 classroom strategies that will help teachers guide students through the steps of preparing written assignments (prewriting), getting their thoughts down (drafting), and refining their work (revising).

Strategies for Writers Online

Go to **www.sfw.z-b.com** for additional online resources for students and teachers.

Michael enjoys teaching sculpting workshops. "One step at a time and you can do it," he reminds his students.

Michael decided to make his next sculpture, he found that the hospital didn't have any more clay. So he reshaped the Indian on a horse into a bear with a fish in its mouth.

Today, Michael has lots of material to use to make his memories come to life. "I was able to see until I was twenty-three years old, so I have a very good idea of what most things look like," he said. "So I sit, and I think about it, and I get a picture in my mind. If you close your eyes and think of. . . well, if you have a cat or a dog, you can picture this pet. The same process happens with me.

"Once you have the material in your hand that you can mold and shape, then you can carry it over from your mind to your fingertips; and your mind tells your fingers, 'Make that bigger or smaller. . .' until this whole process slowly starts happening.

"Nowadays, when I make animals, I sit there and think about the days when I'd take a moment sitting on a cliff side and look down and see a deer down there or watch some turkeys walk through the forest. Or the time I followed a mountain stream and a deer stopped in this pool of water and looked at me with his huge brown eyes. It lasted just a few moments, but it's one of those moments that I draw on for inspiration."

Michael inspires others by leading sculpture workshops for children and adults, veterans and seniors, both sighted and visually impaired.

In 1999, Michael was named the Outstanding Disabled Veteran of the Year and received the LIFE Presidential Unsung Hero Award. His sculptures can be seen in museums and public buildings across the United States, in the Vatican, and in the White House.

A Special Fan

Many people like to collect Michael's work, but Michael fondly remembers one special young "collector."

"It was maybe twenty years ago at the Indian Market in Santa Fe. One day there was this little boy who came, and he was looking at my work and I was telling him about it. Next year, he came back and said, 'I was here last year. Do you remember me?' And I said, 'Yes.' He said, 'I want to buy that little buffalo.' And I said, 'OK.' I told him how much it was.

"As he paid for it, he said, 'I worked all last summer and this summer, and saved my money.' I had no words to describe the emotion I felt. I still can't describe what a moment like that feels like."

Does Michael have one piece of sculpture that is his very favorite? Could it be the buffalo from the Santa Fe Indian Market? Or the bear with a fish in its mouth?

"You know, it's the same as with children," Michael said. "If you have more than one, you love them all equally. That's how I feel about my sculptures."

Cole, Ardith Davis. *Better Answers: Written Performance That Looks Good and Sounds Smart.* Portland, ME. Stenhouse, 2002. This book offers step-by-step protocol for helping students focus on acquiring the basic literacy skills to meet state standards for writing. Each of the five progressive steps (Restate the Questions; Construct a Gist Answer; Use Details to Support Your Answer; Stay on the Topic; Use Proper Conventions) to teaching writing are laid out in individual chapters.

Gallagher, Kelly. *Teaching Adolescent Writers.* Portland, ME. Stenhouse, 2006. Infused with humor and illuminating anecdotes, Gallagher's book draws on his classroom experiences and work as co-director of a regional writing project to offer teachers practical ways to incorporate writing instruction into their day.

CCSS **Common Core State Standards**
R/Inf.6.2: Determine a central idea of a text and how it is conveyed through particular details; provide a summary of the text distinct from personal opinions or judgments.

Analyze the Model

Week 1 • Day 3

Student Objectives

- Learn to read a rubric.
  (pp. 132–133)

Use the Rubric

Explain the Rubric Explain that a rubric is a tool for planning, improving, and assessing a piece of writing. Tell students that a rubric helps a writer focus on key elements, or traits, in writing (**Ideas, Organization, Voice, Word Choice, Sentence Fluency, Conventions,** and **Presentation**).

Explain that column 6 describes a very good summary, one that has received the highest score in all categories. This is what students should strive for in their own writing.

Point out that a writer might learn that he or she usually does well with **Organization,** but not as well with **Word Choice.** Using the traits rubric can help writers improve their writing.

Discuss the Rubric Read the descriptors that go with each trait and explain the relationship between them. Remind students that they will use the rubric as they write their summary, and again as they revise and edit it.

Online Writing Center

Provides a variety of **interactive rubrics,** including 4-, 5-, and 6-point models.

Summary

Rubric

Use this 6-point rubric to plan and score a summary.

	6	**5**	**4**	
Ideas	Relevant facts and concrete details focus on the main points. There are no unnecessary details.	Facts and details focus on the main points. There are no unnecessary details.	Most facts and details focus on the main points. There are a few unnecessary details.	
Organization	Details are organized logically and are connected in a thoughtful way. The beginning introduces the topic and grabs the reader's attention.	Details are arranged in order. The beginning works well.	Some of the details are out of order or poorly connected. The beginning is unexciting but clear.	
Voice	The writer establishes and maintains a formal style.	The writer uses a formal style throughout most of the summary.	The writer uses a formal style, but there are a few moments where the tone is too casual or lacks confidence.	
Word Choice	The language is concise and clear. No unnecessary words are used.	Most words and phrases are clear and used correctly. One or two could be cut.	A few vague or unnecessary words are used, but most of the language is concise.	
Sentence Fluency	Sentences flow smoothly. There is striking variety in sentence lengths and structures.	Sentences flow smoothly. There is noticeable variety in lengths and structures. The writing is easy to read aloud.	There is some variety in sentence lengths and structures. The writing is not difficult to read.	
Conventions	Subjects and verbs agree. There are no dangling or misplaced modifiers. Conventions are used skillfully.	The writing contains a few minor errors with subject-verb agreement or modifiers.	The writing has some noticeable errors with subject-verb agreement and modifiers. They do not interfere with meaning.	
✚ Presentation	Paragraphs are indented.			

132 Informative/Explanatory Writing

CCSS Common Core State Standards

Summary

Strategies for Writers was designed to incorporate the Common Core State Standards throughout every unit. By presenting the standards in multiple applications, your students' exposure to them will be ensured.

The rubric and writing strategies for a summary reflect the standards for Informative/Explanatory writing. The traits of Ideas and Organization align with standards **W.6.2, W.6.2.a,** and **W.6.2.b,** which address introducing and developing a topic. Standard **W.6.2.c** also aligns with Organization by highlighting the use of transition words to connect details in a thoughtful, logical way. In addition, standard **W.6.2.d** aligns with the rubric and writing strategies for Word Choice by supporting concise, clear language. The rubric and writing

3	2	1	
The focus of the details is not always clear. Several unnecessary or distracting details are included.	The main points of the summary are not clear. Numerous unrelated details confuse the reader.	The main points of the summary are impossible to pick out. The details are an unrelated list.	**Ideas**
The order of details is hard to follow in places. The beginning needs work.	The writing is not organized. There is no clear beginning. The summary is a challenge to read.	The reader feels lost. The writing is a list of thoughts that often don't go together. The beginning is missing.	**Organization**
The writer uses a formal tone only part of the time. The voice comes and goes.	The writer uses a tone not suitable for the purpose. It is hard for the reader to take the summary seriously.	The voice is absent. The writer isn't connected to the topic. The reader doesn't understand the writer's purpose.	**Voice**
Vague and unnecessary words make the meaning unclear in spots.	Too many vague and unnecessary words make the summary hard to understand.	The writer uses too many words that are vague or unconnected to the main ideas. The summary is impossible to follow.	**Word Choice**
There is little variety in the sentences. The writing is sometimes easy to read aloud.	Many sentence problems create bumps for the reader. There are lots of choppy and run-on sentences.	The writing lacks complete sentences. It is hard to read.	**Sentence Fluency**
Errors with subject-verb agreement and modifiers are noticeable and occasionally interfere with the message.	The writing has many errors with subject-verb agreement and modifiers that make reading difficult.	Serious errors with subject-verb agreement and modifiers are repeated. The writing is very hard to read.	**Conventions**

See Appendix B for 4-, 5-, and 6-point informative/explanatory rubrics.

Summary 133

Apply the Rubric

Assign Groups Assign students to small groups and ask them to check the model for one trait. One person in each group should be responsible for recording one or two strong examples of the trait as described by the rubric. Ask students to score the trait accordingly. They should be able to support their scores. Note that although the model was written to score high in each trait, students should not assume each trait would receive a 6, the top score. Encourage students to discuss each trait thoroughly before assigning the score.

Reassemble Class Bring the class together and ask one person from each group to report the group's findings to the class. The point of this exercise is less to score the model than it is to learn to talk about the traits.

Additional Rubrics Appendix B includes 4-, 5-, and 6-point rubrics that can be used with any piece of argument writing. The rubrics are also available as blackline masters, beginning on page T545.

strategies for Voice align with standard **W.6.2.e**, establishing and maintaining a formal style.

The language standards for grade 6 students are addressed during editing and skills practice (**L.6.1–3**). In addition, there are multiple opportunities to address the speaking and listening standards during the writing process. Most importantly, this chapter will help students examine a topic and convey ideas and information to produce clear and coherent writing (**W.6.4**), improve writing (**W.6.5**), and use technologies to publish and present finished pieces (**W.6.6**). In addition, students will be given the opportunity to draw evidence from texts to support analysis (**W.6.9**) and write routinely over extended time frames (**W.6.10**).

CCSS **C**ommon **C**ore **S**tate **S**tandards
SL.6.1.b: Follow rules for collegial discussions, set specific goals and deadlines, and define individual roles as needed. **SL.6.1.c:** Pose and respond to specific questions with elaboration and detail by making comments that contribute to the topic, text, or issue under discussion. **SL.6.1.d:** Review the key ideas expressed and demonstrate understanding of multiple perspectives through reflection and paraphrasing.

Analyze
the Model

Week 1 • Day 4

Student Objectives

- Read a model summary. (pp. 129, 130–131)
- Use the summary rubric. (pp. 132–133)
- Use the model summary to study Ideas, Organization, and Voice. (pp. 134–135)

Study the Model

Assess the Model Have volunteers read aloud each section on pages 134–135. Ask them to review Justin's assessments of the model. Use questions such as the following to discuss the pages with students:

- Does the writer state the main topic and points of her summary clearly? (Possible response: Yes, Keesha states the main points in a clear and focused way.)

- Does she include any unnecessary details? (Possible responses: Keesha gives just enough credible and concrete facts and definitions to support the main points. She avoids a lot of unnecessary detail.)

 Strategies for Writers Online

Go to **www.sfw.z-b.com** for additional online resources for students and teachers.

Using the Rubric to Study the Model

Did you notice that the model on page 129 points out some key elements of a summary? As she wrote the summary of "A Touch of Genius," Keesha Kane used these elements to help her. She also used the 6-point rubric on pages 132–133 to plan, draft, revise, and edit the writing. A rubric is a great tool to evaluate writing during the writing process.

Now let's use the same rubric to score the model. To do this, we'll focus on each trait separately, starting with Ideas. We'll use the top descriptor for each trait (column 6) along with examples from the model, to help us understand how the traits work together. How would you score Keesha on each trait?

Ideas
- Relevant facts and concrete details focus on the main points.
- There are no unnecessary details.

The writer states the main points in a clear and focused way. She gives just enough relevant and concrete details to support the main points. For example, the paragraph below tells how successful the sculptor is, without a lot of unnecessary detail.

[from the writing model]

Naranjo has won awards for his work and leads sculpture workshops. His sculptures are displayed in museums and public buildings around the world. Private collectors also seek his art.

134 Informative/Explanatory Writing

English Language Learners

BEGINNING

The 5 W's Locate a photograph of the first moon landing. On the board write *what, who, when, why,* and *where.* Point to the picture and ask, *What is happening?* When a student gives an answer, repeat it, and write it on the board. Repeat for *who, when, where,* and *why.* Review the list. Ask, *What is happening? Who is there?* and so on. Demonstrate how to answer in a complete sentence. Students may use answers to questions like this to help them create a summary.

INTERMEDIATE

Topic and Summary Read a brief, level-appropriate nonfiction text to students. Ask them what the text was about. Tell them this is the *topic.* Ask students to give a few more details about the text. Tell them they have just created a *summary* of the text.

Organization

- Details are organized logically and are connected in a thoughtful way.
- The beginning introduces the topic and grabs the reader's attention.

In each paragraph, Keesha's details are well organized and all related to each other. In her opening paragraph, the first sentence gives clear, identifying information to pull the reader in. Then she includes important details about Naranjo's early life.

[from the writing model]

Michael Naranjo is a Native American sculptor in Santa Fe, New Mexico. He chose his career when he was a boy helping his mother make pottery in the pueblo. At age 23, however, Naranjo was wounded in the Vietnam War. He was blinded and left without the complete use of one hand.

Voice

- The writer establishes and maintains a formal style.

In a summary, it's important for the writer to establish a knowledgeable and formal tone. Keesha does just that, which helps me take her writing seriously and feel confident that she has written an accurate and thorough summary.

[from the writing model]

While recovering in the hospital, he molded several clay sculptures of animals. One was so good that it was photographed for the newspaper. That convinced him to pursue his dream.

Summary 135

- How does the writer organize her response? (Possible responses: In the opening paragraph, Keesha's first sentence gives clear, identifying information to pull the reader in. In each paragraph her details are logically organized and all related to each other.)

- Does the writer use a voice that is appropriate for the purpose and audience? (Possible response: Yes, Keesha uses a formal, knowledgeable voice to show that she is serious about her writing.)

ADVANCED

Identifying the Main Points Tell students about a special moment in history, for example, the first moon landing. Write on the board *what, who, when, why,* and *where.* Ask, *What happened in my story? Who was there?* and so on. Write students' answers in a Spider Map. Have partners tell each other about a fun vacation, or have them tell a funny adventure story. Have one student fill in the Spider Map for their partner's story.

ADVANCED HIGH

Using a Spider Map Ask each student to read an article from the school newspaper. After students have read their piece, have them include the main points of the article in a Spider Map. Then have them trade selections and Spider Maps with a partner. The partner should read the selection and review the graphic organizer for mistakes.

CCSS **Common Core State Standards**

W.6.9: Draw evidence from literary or informational texts to support analysis, reflection, and research. **SL.6.1.b:** Follow rules for collegial discussions, set specific goals and deadlines, and define individual roles as needed. **SL.6.1.c:** Pose and respond to specific questions with elaboration and detail by making comments that contribute to the topic, text, or issue under discussion. **SL.6.1.d:** Review the key ideas expressed and demonstrate understanding of multiple perspectives through reflection and paraphrasing.

Analyze
the Model

Week 1 • Day 5

Student Objectives

- Read a model summary. (pp.129, 130–131)
- Use the summary rubric. (pp. 132–133)
- Use the model summary to study Word Choice, Sentence Fluency, and Conventions. (pp. 136–137)

Continue Discussing the Traits

Use questions such as the following to discuss the traits analyzed on pages 136–137:

Does the writer

- use concise language to inform readers about the topic? Does she avoid wordiness? (Possible responses: Keesha uses concise and clear language to make her point. She chooses her words carefully and uses as few of them as possible.)

- vary sentence patterns to keep the response flowing along? (Possible responses: Yes, Keesha's sentences are varied in length and structure. She avoids short, choppy sentences. In some places, she combines ideas and uses longer sentences.)

- use correct subject and verb agreement? Does she avoid dangling or misplaced modifiers? (Possible responses: Yes, Keesha uses correct subject and verb agreement. There are no dangling or misplaced modifiers.)

Strategies for Writers Online

Go to **www.sfw.z-b.com** for additional online resources for students and teachers.

Word Choice
- The language is concise and clear.
- No unnecessary words are used.

Keesha knows that a summary needs to be as short as possible, so she makes sure her writing is not wordy. For the second sentence below, she might have written *He sits and thinks about the image in his mind. After he gets a picture of it, the image goes to his fingertips.* Instead she carefully chooses her words and uses as few of them as possible.

[from the writing model]

Although he cannot see, he can remember images from his past. His mind carries the images to his fingertips.

Sentence Fluency
- Sentences flow smoothly.
- There is striking variety in sentence lengths and structures.

Keesha did a great job using a variety of sentence lengths and structures. She avoids short, choppy sentences. In some places, she combines ideas and uses longer sentences. For example, Keesha could have written her last paragraph this way: *Naranjo has won awards for his work. He leads sculpture workshops. His sculptures are displayed in museums. They are also displayed in public buildings around the world. Private collectors also seek his art.* You can read below how she really wrote the paragraph.

[from the writing model]

Naranjo has won awards for his work and leads sculpture workshops. His sculptures are displayed in museums and public buildings around the world. Private collectors also seek his art.

136 Informative/Explanatory Writing

 **for 21st Century Literacies**

A key to twenty-first century literacy is knowing how to navigate the flood of information available online by using tools like RSS feeders. A site like Scoop.it can help students see the benefit in using an RSS aggregator and also "curating" an information site for others to use as a reference. Ask students to create a Scoop.it site that aggregates data across sources and serves as a resource when writing their summaries.

See **www.sfw.z-b.com** for further information about and links to these websites and tools.

Conventions

- Subjects and verbs agree.
- There are no dangling or misplaced modifiers.
- Conventions are used skillfully.

I checked Keesha's summary for mistakes, but I couldn't find any. She did a great job on spelling, punctuation, and capitalization. All verbs agree with their subjects, and there are no dangling modifiers. For example, look at the sentence below. *His mind* is a singular subject, so it needs the singular verb *carries*. She wrote it correctly.

> [from the writing model]
>
> His mind carries the images to his fingertips.

This sentence contains a perfectly placed modifier.

> [from the writing model]
>
> Although he cannot see, he can remember images from his past.

+Presentation Paragraphs are indented.

My Turn!

I'm going to write a summary using good writing strategies. I'll also use what I learned from the rubric and good writing strategies. Follow along and see how I do it.

Summary 137

Differentiating Instruction

ENRICHMENT

Summarize Stories or Movies Challenge students to choose a familiar story or movie to retell as a summary. Remind them to keep the summary short and to the point. They should remember to include relevant details and interesting points to give the summary a formal, knowledgeable style.

REINFORCEMENT

Evaluate a Summary Find short summaries of movies (for example, in a movie review section of a newspaper) or books (for example, in a library journal or on a book cover). Ask students to comment on the summaries. Do they tell enough information? Too much?

Presentation Explain to students that Presentation is just as important as the other traits. Appearance should be considered as students prepare their final copies. Neatness is always a priority, and text should be clearly handwritten in pen or typed, using only a few readable fonts. White space should be used to create neat margins. All paragraphs should be indented (using the tab key if typed), and the title and writer's name should be centered at the top of the first page. Page numbers and footers should be used to help organize the summary. Point out that these functions ensure that no pages get lost or put in the wrong order.

Think About the Traits Once students have discussed Keesha's model summary, ask them which traits they think are most important. Of course, all the traits are important in every piece of writing, but some traits stand out more in some genres than in others. Students might say that in a summary the trait of **Ideas** is important because if the information is irrelevant, the summary makes no sense. Others may think that **Word Choice** is more important because concise, clear language keeps the summary short and informative.

CCSS Common Core State Standards

R/Inf.6.2: Determine a central idea of a text and how it is conveyed through particular details; provide a summary of the text distinct from personal opinions or judgments. **R/Inf.6.4:** Determine the meaning of words and phrases as they are used in a text, including figurative, connotative, and technical meanings. **R/Inf.6.5:** Analyze how a particular sentence, paragraph, chapter, or section fits into the overall structure of a text and contributes to the development of the ideas. **SL.6.1.d:** Review the key ideas expressed and demonstrate understanding of multiple perspectives through reflection and paraphrasing.

Write
a Summary

Week 2 • Day 1

Student Objectives

• Read and understand a prewriting strategy. *(p. 138)*

Prewrite

Focus on Ideas

Collect Information Point out that Justin chose to summarize an article that combined his interest in trees, the history of his state, and coins. Help students select an article by working with your school librarian to supply a selection of appropriate magazine, newspaper, and/or journal articles for placement in your classroom. Allow class time for students to skim through the resources to look for articles of interest. Suggest that students first read through the article they are going to summarize and then take notes on the main points, as Justin plans to do.

Strategies for Writers Online
Go to **www.sfw.z-b.com** for additional online resources for students and teachers.

Prewrite   Focus on Ideas

The Rubric Says Relevant facts and concrete details focus on the main points.

Writing Strategy Read an article and take notes on the main points.

My teacher asked us to write a summary of an article. I chose the article below because it combines my interests in trees, the history of my state, and coins. As I read the article, I found the main points in it. On page 140, you can see the notes I took as I read.

The Tree That Saved History
by Jane Sutcliffe

An unusual funeral took place in Hartford, Connecticut, on August 21, 1856. The city's bells tolled in mourning, and a band played funeral hymns. It was an outpouring of grief fit for a hero—except that this hero was a tree, a white oak to be exact.

For nearly 169 years this special tree had been known simply as the Charter Oak in honor of the part it played in the history of colonial America.

The Charter Oak was an old and respected tree even before colonial times. Native Americans of the area held meetings under its branches. And when the tree's new leaves were as big as a mouse's ear, they knew that it was time to plant corn.

In time, the English came to the valley surrounding the big oak. They settled there and founded the colony of Connecticut. Every colony had to obtain a contract, called a charter, from the king of England. The charter helped to protect the colony's rights. The charter given to Connecticut by King Charles II in 1662 was the pride of the colony. It allowed the colonists to govern themselves by their own constitution. More than a century before the Declaration of Independence, the charter treated Connecticut almost as if it were an independent country.

138 Informative/Explanatory Writing

English Language Learners

BEGINNING
Unnecessary Details Ask students to tell what they use to brush their teeth. Ask, *Do you need a toothbrush?* After students answer, say, *Yes. A toothbrush is necessary.* Have students repeat the sentence. Then ask, *Is toothpaste necessary (for brushing your teeth)? Is a television necessary?* When students say *no*, tell them that a TV is unnecessary for brushing teeth. Say the word and have students repeat. Continue the procedure for another topic to reinforce students' understanding.

INTERMEDIATE
Avoid Unnecessary Words Review third-person personal pronouns. Give each student a short newspaper article. Have them underline compound or complex sentences. Discuss the varied sentence lengths within the article. Finally, have students rewrite it using pronouns in place of people's names.

Then, in 1685, King Charles died. The new English ruler, King James II, not only disapproved of Connecticut's charter but he also disliked having so many colonies. He thought it would be better to combine the colonies of the northeast into one big colony.

King James ordered Sir Edmund Andros, the governor of the Dominion of New England, to seize any documents recognizing the colonies' old rights. Most colonies felt they had no choice and turned over their charters. Only Connecticut delayed. Again and again, Andros demanded that Connecticut give up its charter to him. Again and again, the colonists politely but firmly refused. Finally, Andros had had enough. On All Hallow's Eve, 1687, Andros and more than sixty British soldiers marched into Hartford.

Connecticut Governor Robert Treat was waiting for Andros at the door of the meetinghouse, where leaders of the colony were assembled. Politely he escorted Andros inside. Andros wasted no time. He demanded that Connecticut obey the king and surrender its charter.

By now a crowd of townspeople had gathered outside. As they strained to hear every word, Governor Treat spoke passionately about the struggles of the people to build their colony, and about their love of freedom. Giving up the charter, he said, would be like giving up his life. Andros was unmoved. At dark, candles were lit so that the meeting could continue, but Andros had heard enough. He demanded to see the charter. The colonists could delay no longer. They brought out the charter and placed it on the table before him.

Suddenly all the candles in the room went out. In the darkness, a young patriot, Captain Joseph Wadsworth, snatched the charter and jumped out an open window. Carefully wrapping the document in his cloak, he placed it in the hollow of the great white oak. Had the brave captain simply seized the opportunity provided by the sudden darkness, or had it all been a clever plan? No one would ever know. By the

Captain Joseph Wadsworth carefully placed Connecticut's charter in the hollow of the great white oak.

time the candles were lit again, Andros was looking at nothing but innocent faces.

If Andros was furious at being outsmarted, he did not show it. With or without the charter, he said that the government of the colony was over. Fortunately, King James was soon overthrown. Andros was imprisoned and then sent back to England. The new rulers, King William III and Queen Mary II, agreed that since Connecticut had never surrendered its charter, the colony could take up its old freedoms again.

The Charter Oak became a beloved symbol of freedom throughout the land. After it was blown down in a storm on August 21, 1856, people requested keepsakes of its wood. There was plenty to go around—so much, in fact, that author Mark Twain said there was enough "to build a plank road from here (Hartford) to Great Salt Lake City."

Craftsmen fashioned pianos, chairs, and even a cradle of Charter Oak wood. One of the fanciest pieces was an elaborately carved chair that is still used in the Senate Chamber in the State Capitol Building in Hartford. It occupies a place of honor in memory of the Charter Oak, one of the most unusual heroes in our country's struggle for liberty.

The Charter Oak appears on the Connecticut quarter, issued in 1999 by the U.S. Mint. Connecticut became a state in 1788.

If possible, provide students with copies of articles that they can write on. Tell them to read the article through at least once to get the gist of it. Then have them reread the article with pen in hand and underline or highlight the key ideas. Students who are learning to mark text tend to mark everything, so suggest that they mark just one or two ideas per paragraph.

ADVANCED/ADVANCED HIGH

Strong Introductions Demonstrate attention-grabbing by doing something unexpected, such as singing a song. Say, *I just grabbed your attention.* Write *attention-grabbing introduction* on the board. Under the topic *Moon Landing,* write the following introductions: *The first moon landing was in July 1969. What was the name of the first man on the moon? "One small step for man, one giant leap for mankind."* Ask students to rank the introductions according to how interesting they are. Remind students to use simple phrases, questions, or single words to capture the attention of the audience.

Write several more topics on the board, and have students write a snappy introductory phrase or sentence for each one. Then read as a class, discuss the merits of each, and vote for the best introduction for each topic.

CCSS **Common Core State Standards**

W.6.2: Write informative/explanatory texts to examine a topic and convey ideas, concepts, and information through the selection, organization, and analysis of relevant content. **W.6.2.a:** Introduce a topic; organize ideas, concepts, and information, using strategies such as definition, classification, comparison/contrast, and cause/effect; include formatting (e.g., headings), graphics (e.g., charts, tables), and multimedia when useful to aiding comprehension. **R/Inf.6.2:** Determine a central idea of a text and how it is conveyed through particular details; provide a summary of the text distinct from personal opinions or judgments.

Record Information Point out that Justin understands that he is to record only the most important facts. These are the facts that students should have marked on their copies of the articles (see T139). Instruct students to write notes from their articles—the main topic and relevant, concrete details, excluding any irrelevant or overly detailed information. As students review their marked text, they will have a second chance to decide whether the information is worth going into the written notes.

There are tons of details that make learning about the Charter Oak interesting. My assignment, however, is to summarize the information in the article so only the most important facts stand out. I have to use as few words as possible, so using only relevant and concrete details is critical. Here are my notes from the article. Would you choose the same main points?

Notes on "The Tree That Saved History"

✔ Charter Oak grew in Hartford, CT. Important in CT's history. Funeral held for tree.

✔ English settlers who founded CT colony got charter (contract) from King Charles II to govern themselves. King Charles II died. New king (James II) wanted to take charter away.

✔ Edmund Andros (gov. of New England) tried to collect CT charter. Met with CT gov. and other leaders in Hartford. When candles went out, Captain Joseph Wadsworth grabbed charter and jumped through window. He hid the charter in a huge white oak.

✔ King James took away CT's freedom anyway. New king and queen said CT didn't give up charter so it got its freedom back.

✔ Tree became symbol of freedom: Wood made into fancy chair. Tree is on CT state quarter.

Apply

Choose an article about an interesting topic. Read the article and take notes on the main points.

140 Informative/Explanatory Writing

Online Writing Center

Provides **interactive graphic organizers** as well as a variety of graphic organizers in PDF format.

Prewrite

Focus on Organization

The Rubric Says Details are organized logically and are connected in a thoughtful way.

Writing Strategy Make a Spider Map from your notes.

Writer's Term

Spider Map
A **Spider Map** organizes information about a topic. The subject is written in the body, and a main point is written on each leg.

Now, to organize and connect my details in a logical way, I'll organize my notes into a Spider Map. Each leg of my spider will be a main point about the Charter Oak. You can see my Spider Map below.

Spider Map

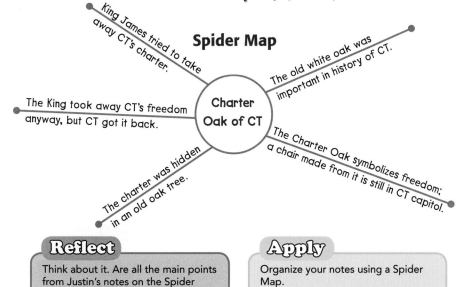

King James tried to take away CT's charter.

The old white oak was important in history of CT.

The King took away CT's freedom anyway, but CT got it back.

Charter Oak of CT

The charter was hidden in an old oak tree.

The Charter Oak symbolizes freedom; a chair made from it is still in CT capitol.

Reflect

Think about it. Are all the main points from Justin's notes on the Spider Map?

Apply

Organize your notes using a Spider Map.

Conferencing

PEER TO PEER When students have completed their Spider Maps, have pairs exchange papers. Ask students to review each other's maps and comment on whether the details give a complete picture of the main idea.

PEER GROUPS Separate students into small groups. Instruct them to discuss the importance of organizing their notes into a focused Spider Map. Have students read their Spider Maps aloud. Encourage other students to take turns offering one suggestion.

TEACHER-LED Conference with individual students about their Spider Maps. Prompt students with questions such as the following: *Do the main points give a complete picture of the topic? Are all the details important enough to include in a summary?*

Write
a Summary

Week 2 • Day 2

Student Objectives

• Make a Spider Map to organize and connect details. *(p. 141)*

Prewrite

Focus on Organization

Organize Details Read page 141. Explain that writers use a variety of organizers to get started writing. Justin used a Spider Map to organize and connect his ideas. Have students study the organizer to see how Justin organized his notes to support his topic. Have them notice that Justin put the topic in the middle of the organizer, or on the body of the spider. Each of the spider's legs gives a main point about Justin's topic, the Charter Oak.

Writer's Term _____

Spider Map A Spider Map makes it easy to select and organize an author's main points. It is a helpful visual tool that helps writers keep track of main ideas as they write a summary.

CCSS **C**ommon **C**ore **S**tate **S**tandards

W.6.2: Write informative/explanatory texts to examine a topic and convey ideas, concepts, and information through the selection, organization, and analysis of relevant content. **W.6.2.a:** Introduce a topic; organize ideas, concepts, and information, using strategies such as definition, classification, comparison/contrast, and cause/effect; include formatting (e.g., headings), graphics (e.g., charts, tables), and multimedia when useful to aiding comprehension. **W.6.2.b:** Develop the topic with relevant facts, definitions, concrete details, quotations, or other information and examples.

Write
a Summary

Week 2 • Day 3

Student Objectives

• Use a Spider Map to begin writing. *(p. 142)*

Draft

Focus on Ideas

Draft a Summary Review the *draft* step with students, making sure they realize that a draft is a rough form of a written document. Drafting lets students get ideas on paper without having to worry about mistakes.

Read page 142 aloud. Then ask students to read Justin's draft on page 143 independently. Students should agree that Justin used his organizer to include clear and concise details in his draft. Remind students that Justin knows that his summary should be about one third as long as the original article. This means that he needs to be sure to include only the most important ideas and details in this summary.

Point out that Justin repeatedly refers to the rubric as he writes. Encourage students to remember to use the rubric to guide their own writing.

Draft

Focus on Ideas

The Rubric Says	There are no unnecessary details.
Writing Strategy	Include only the most important ideas and details.

It's time to start writing! The rubric reminds me to use only necessary details. That means I need to be clear and concise. I'll start with the topic of my article. My teacher said that most summaries are about one-third as long as the original article. This guideline will help me keep my summary short.

As I write my draft, I will do my best with spelling, punctuation, capitalization, and grammar. I can correct any errors I make later.

[DRAFT]

The Charter Oak

The Charter Oak was important in the history of Connecticut. This tree has an interesting history.

→ [clear topic sentence]

142 Informative/Explanatory Writing

Differentiating Instruction

ENRICHMENT

Expand the Topic Justin wrote about the Charter Oak's importance in Connecticut's history. Many businesses there use the name in association with their products. Have students use the Internet to research Connecticut businesses using the name *Charter Oak*. Have them select a business (for example, college, credit union, healthcare plan) associated with the Charter Oak and write a short summary about the business.

REINFORCEMENT

Oral Summaries Some students have trouble limiting their writing to the main points. To practice brevity, ask them to orally summarize a familiar TV show, book, or movie in as few sentences as possible.

[DRAFT]

The Charter Oak

In colonal times, England's King Charles II granted charters to the American colonies that he ruled in those days before they became the United States. The charters from the king was contracts that gave the colonies the freedom to govern themselves instead of having Great Britain govern them. Connecticut had the privilege of receiving its charter in 1662. In 1685, 23 years later, after King Charles II died, King James II gave orders to go and take away the charters and join all the New England colonies into one. Edmund Andros, the govenor of New England, got all the charters except Connecticut's.   [main points]

Andros went to Hartford, Connecticut, to ask for the charter. He brought 60 British soldiers and met with the colony's governor, Robert Treat, on All Hallow's Eve. Other leaders of the colony was there, too. Before Andros could take the charter, however, the candles in the room blew out. A patriot named Captain Joseph Wadsworth grabbed the charter and leeped out the window. He wrapped the charter in his cloak and hid it in an old white oak tree.

Reflect

What do you think of the beginning of Justin's draft? Is this part of the draft clear and concise?

Apply

Write a draft using the main points from your Spider Map. Include only the most important ideas and details.

Summary 143

Conferencing

PEER TO PEER Have pairs of students exchange drafts. Ask students to think of two or three questions they would like to ask to clarify information. Are there too many details? Too few? Instruct students to ask questions and provide helpful comments regarding the overall organization of their summaries.

PEER GROUPS Organize students into small groups. Have them take turns reading sections of their summaries aloud. Other students provide helpful commentary to strengthen specific areas of the summary.

TEACHER-LED Conference with individual students to help students refine their summaries. Point out one or two details in each summary. Ask: *Would the summary make sense without this detail? Is any essential detail missing?*

Write
a Summary

Student Objectives

• Complete a draft. *(p. 143)*

Finish the Draft Students should continue to capture their ideas on paper. At this point, they should not be overly concerned with correctness. To help them focus on getting their thoughts down on paper, have students circle anything in their drafts that they might want to change later but not to worry about revising or editing their writing now.

It is important that students are given ample time to draft their summary. As conferencing is important throughout the writing process, be sure to plan time for peer-to-peer, peer group, or teacher-led conferences.

Point out that the proofreader's marks are provided as a reference on the draft. They will be helpful during the revising and editing stages of the writing process.

CCSS Common Core State Standards

W.6.5: With some guidance and support from peers and adults, develop and strengthen writing as needed by planning, revising, editing, rewriting, or trying a new approach. **SL.6.1:** Engage effectively in a range of collaborative discussions (one-on-one, in groups, and teacher-led) with diverse partners on *grade 6 topics, texts, and issues*, building on others' ideas and expressing their own clearly. **SL.6.1.b:** Follow rules for collegial discussions, set specific goals and deadlines, and define individual roles as needed. **SL.6.1.c:** Pose and respond to specific questions with elaboration and detail by making comments that contribute to the topic, text, or issue under discussion.

Write a Summary

Week 2 • Day 5

Student Objectives

- Revise to include an interesting detail in the opening paragraph. (p. 144)

Revise

Focus on

Grab the Reader's Attention
Read page 144. Discuss the importance of writing a beginning that introduces the topic and grabs the reader's attention. Have one volunteer read the draft excerpt without the revisions and another read the revised excerpt. Ask students to identify what Justin added. (*even had a funeral*) Point out how much more engaging the beginning is after Justin added this information. Discuss why students should include an interesting detail in the opening paragraph. (Possible response: Starting with an interesting detail grabs the reader's attention right away and draws the reader in.)

✎ Writer's Term _____

Details An interesting introduction grabs the reader's attention and draws the reader into the text. Memorable details hold and keep the reader's interest.

▶ Strategies for Writers Online

Go to **www.sfw.z-b.com** for additional online resources for students and teachers.

Revise   Focus on

The Rubric Says	The beginning introduces the topic and grabs the reader's attention.
Writing Strategy	Include an interesting detail in the opening paragraph.

✎ Writer's Term _____

Details
The **details** are the words used to describe a person, convince an audience, explain a process, or in some way support a main idea.

The rubric says the beginning of my summary should introduce the topic and grab my reader's attention. Well, I know my topic's clear in the first sentence, but maybe the beginning could be more engaging. I decided to use an interesting detail to draw the reader in. What do you think of my revision?

The Charter Oak   **[DRAFT]**

The Charter Oak was important in the history of Connecticut. This
~~even had a funeral~~ ◄
tree ~~has an interesting history.~~
          ⌃   [included interesting detail]

Apply
Check your summary to make sure the beginning clearly introduces the topic and grabs the reader's attention.

144 Informative/Explanatory Writing

English Language Learners

BEGINNING/INTERMEDIATE

Subject-Verb Agreement Write *A dog, A cat, A bird, A cow,* and *A mouse* on index cards. Write their plurals on five more cards. Have students shuffle and sort the words into plural and singular. Add ten more cards: *bark, barks, meow, meows, chirp, chirps, moo, moos, squeak,* and *squeaks.* Then have students match each verb to an appropriate singular or plural noun. Point out that the subject and verb must agree.

ADVANCED/ADVANCED HIGH

Relevant Facts Give students the main idea, such as *The first moon landing was a huge success,* and list several facts and non-facts, such as *Neil Armstrong was the first man to step on the moon, There were three astronauts on the mission, Their families watched the landing together,* and so on. Have students circle the facts that support the main idea. Say, *relevant,* and have students repeat.

Revise

Focus on Voice

The Rubric Says	The writer establishes and maintains a formal style.
Writing Strategy	Use third-person point of view plus facts.

When summarizing anything written by someone else, third-person point of view is most appropriate. Using third person helps me establish a formal style, which is necessary if I want my reader to take me seriously. Including facts about my topic strengthens my voice and gives my writing credibility.

When I reread my draft, I found a place where I forgot to use third person. I'll fix that now to maintain a formal style throughout my summary.

[DRAFT]

[maintained third person]

~~I learned that~~ King James II didn't get the charter, but he took away Connecticut's freedom anyway. ~~As you might expect,~~   Soon another English king and queen came into power.

Reflect

What do you think? How have Justin's revisions strengthened his writing?

Apply

Look for any first- or second-person point of view pronouns, and replace them with third-person pronouns.

Conferencing

PEER TO PEER Have pairs of students exchange drafts. After reading the draft, each student offers helpful feedback on places where the writer can change first- or second-person point of view to third-person point of view.

PEER GROUPS Separate students into small groups. Have them take turns reading sections of their drafts aloud. Group members suggest areas that need to change to third-person point of view.

TEACHER-LED Conference with individual students about their drafts. Ask questions to help students look at their drafts with a focused eye. For example: *Is your writer's voice consistent all the way through? Do you use the word I or you?*

Write
a Summary

Week 3 • Day 1

Student Objectives

- Revise to use third-person point of view plus facts. *(p. 145)*

Revise

Focus on Voice

Use Third-Person Point of View
Have students read page 145. Third-person point of view takes the writer out of the text, which is appropriate for a summary. Have one volunteer read the excerpt without the revisions and another volunteer read the revised excerpt. Point out how much stronger Justin's writing sounds after he uses the third-person point of view. Have students check their drafts for places where they can change first- or second-person point of view to third person.

CCSS **C**ommon **C**ore **S**tate **S**tandards

W.6.2.a: Introduce a topic; organize ideas, concepts, and information, using strategies such as definition, classification, comparison/contrast, and cause/effect; include formatting (e.g., headings), graphics (e.g., charts, tables), and multimedia when useful to aiding comprehension. **W.6.2.b:** Develop the topic with relevant facts, definitions, concrete details, quotations, or other information and examples **W.6.2.e:** Establish and maintain a formal style.

Write a Summary

Week 3 • Day 2

Student Objectives

- Revise to use succinct language. (p. 146)

Revise

Focus on Word Choice

Take Out Unnecessary Words
Read page 146 aloud. Remind students that the rubric says that the language in a summary should be concise and clear. The summary should be brief and to the point, rather than wordy. A summary is not the place for rambling or repetitive writing. Concise language is especially important in summaries since they should be short and to the point.

Review Justin's revisions and discuss how they improved his draft. Encourage students to read their summaries and look for places where they can take out unnecessary words and replace them with succinct, or precise, language.

Writer's Term_____

Succinct Language A good summary uses succinct language to make salient points; the writer avoids extra words and fillers that can distract or confuse the reader.

Revise
Focus on Word Choice

The Rubric Says	The language is concise and clear. No unnecessary words are used.
Writing Strategy	Choose words carefully and replace wordy phrases with succinct language.

Writer's Term_____

Succinct Language
Succinct language is brief and to the point; there are no wasted words.

A summary has to be concise and clear. There should be no extra words. I read my paper aloud to listen for wordy phrases and sentences, and I heard a lot of unnecessary words! To fix this problem, I replaced unnecessary words with language that is to the point, or succinct. What do you think?

[removed unnecessary words] **[DRAFT]**

In colonial times, England's King Charles II granted charters to the American colonies ~~that he ruled in those days before they became the United States.~~ The charters from the king was contracts that gave the colonies the freedom to govern themselves ~~instead of having Great Britain govern them.~~ Connecticut ~~had the privilege of receiving~~ gained its charter in 1662. In 1685, ~~23 years later,~~ after King Charles II died, King James II gave orders to ~~go and take away~~ seize the charters and join all the New England colonies into one.

[used succinct words]

Apply
Take out any wordy phrases in your summary and use succinct language instead.

146 Informative/Explanatory Writing

Optional Revising Lessons

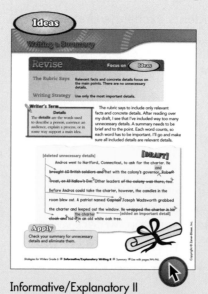

Informative/Explanatory 11

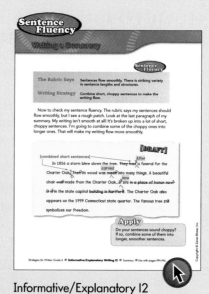

Informative/Explanatory 12

Go to ➤ *Strategies for Writers Grade 6 CD-ROM*

| The Rubric Says | Subjects and verbs agree. There are no dangling or misplaced modifiers. Conventions are used skillfully. |
| Writing Strategy | Be sure all subjects and verbs agree. Check that all modifiers are clear. |

✏ Writer's Term

Subject-Verb Agreement
Every sentence must have a subject and a verb. A **singular subject** requires a **singular verb**, and a **plural subject** requires a **plural verb**.

Now I need to fix any mistakes. I'll check my spelling, punctuation, and capitalization. The rubric also says to check subject-verb agreement and look for dangling or misplaced modifiers.

[DRAFT]

            colonial

In ~~colonial~~ times, England's King Charles II granted charters to the American colonies ~~that he ruled in those days before they became the~~   were

~~United States~~. The charters from the king ~~was~~ contracts that gave the colonies the freedom to govern themselves ~~instead of having Great~~   gained

~~Britain govern them~~. Connecticut ~~had the privilege of receiving~~ its

[corrected subject-verb agreement]

charter in 1662.

Reflect

How do the edits make the summary easier to read?

Apply   **Conventions**

Edit your draft for spelling, punctuation, and capitalization. Be sure to fix any problems with subject-verb agreement and modifiers.

For more practice fixing errors in subject-verb agreement and modifiers, use the exercises on the next two pages.

Summary 147

Related Grammar Practice

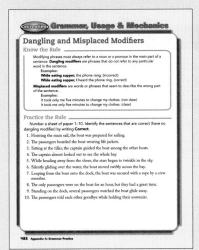

Student Edition page 488   Student Edition page 505

Go to ➡ **Appendix A: Grammar Practice**

Write
a Summary

Student Objectives

- Edit for correct subject-verb agreement and clear modifiers. (p. 147)

Edit

Focus on

Use Correct Subject-Verb Agreement Ask students to discuss the corrections in Justin's draft and then read their drafts, paying special attention to subject-verb agreement and modifiers. Use the mini-lessons on pages T148 and T149 for students having problems with subject and verb agreement and modifiers. Have students complete the exercises on pages 148 and 149.

✏ Writer's Term

Subject-Verb Agreement If a sentence has more than one subject joined by *and*, use a plural verb. If singular subjects are joined by *or* (or *nor*), use a singular verb. If a sentence has both singular and plural subjects joined by *or* (or *nor*), match the verb to the closest subject. Examples: Neither Justin nor his <u>cousins</u> *like* pizza. Neither his cousins nor <u>Justin</u> *likes* pizza.

CCSS Common Core State Standards

W.6.2.d: Use precise language and domain-specific vocabulary to inform about or explain the topic. **W.6.5:** With some guidance and support from peers and adults, develop and strengthen writing as needed by planning, revising, editing, rewriting, or trying a new approach. **L.6.1:** Demonstrate command of the conventions of standard English grammar and usage when writing or speaking.

Subject-Verb Agreement

Know the Rule

Every sentence must have a subject and a verb. A **singular subject** requires a **singular verb,** and a **plural subject** requires a **plural verb**.

In many sentences, a prepositional phrase comes between the subject and the verb. A prepositional phrase is a group of words that begins with a preposition and ends with an object. Do not mistake the object of the preposition for the subject of the sentence. The verb in every sentence must agree with its subject, not the object of the preposition (op).

            s   op   v

Incorrect: The charters from the king was contracts.

            s   op   v

Correct: The charters from the king were contracts.

        s   op   v

Incorrect: One of the patriots were named Joseph Wadsworth.

        s   op   v

Correct: One of the patriots was named Joseph Wadsworth.

Practice the Rule

Number a separate sheet of paper 1–10. Write the correct verb form for each sentence.

1. Connecticut (is/are/am) one of six New England states.
2. Maine (was/were) the last New England colony to become a state.
3. The U.S. Mint (has/have) issued a quarter for each state.
4. The first quarter for the New England states (was/were) for Connecticut.
5. Many people in this country (collect/collects) state quarters.
6. The distinctive design for each state (is/are) on the reverse side of the coin.
7. People often (buy/buys) bags of quarters from coin dealers.
8. A few places for keeping coins (is/are) folders, coin envelopes, and special plastic bags.
9. Rhode Island (is/are) the smallest New England state.
10. Rhode Island and Connecticut (share/shares) a border.

Mini-Lesson

Student Objectives

- Use correct subject-verb agreement. *(p. 148)*

Subject-Verb Agreement

Explain that every sentence must contain a subject and a verb and that singular verbs must be used with singular subjects, just as plural verbs must be used with plural subjects. Write this sentence on the board:

- *The puppy and the kitten from the shelter is very hungry.*

Point out the prepositional phrase. (from the shelter) Then ask students to identify the subjects of the sentence. (puppy, kitten) Ask them if the compound subject is singular or plural. (plural because the subjects are joined by *and*) Have students change the sentence so that the subject and verb agree. (*The puppy and the kitten from the shelter are very hungry.*)

Remind students that it is the writer's responsibility to use correct subject-verb agreement in their writing. Encourage students to consult writing resources as they write to make sure they achieve subject-verb agreement.

Online Writing Center

 Provides **interactive grammar games** and **practice activities** in student eBook.

Related Grammar Practice

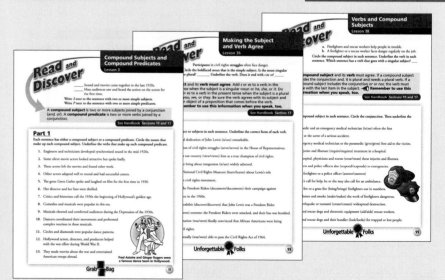

Pages 11, 95, 99

Go to ➡ **G.U.M. Student Practice Book**

Dangling and Misplaced Modifiers

Know the Rule

A **dangling modifier** is a phrase that does not clearly refer to any particular word in the sentence. When you begin a sentence with a verbal phrase, be sure the noun or pronoun that follows is correct. In the sentence below, who is freezing?

> **Example:** Freezing from the cold wind, a scarf can help you keep warm. (not clear)
> When you are freezing from the cold wind, a scarf can help you keep warm. (clear)

A **misplaced modifier** is a word that is in the wrong place and can cause confusion for the reader.

> **Example:** The stolen student's backpack was left on the playground. (incorrect)
> The student's stolen backpack was left on the playground. (correct)

Practice the Rule

Number a separate sheet of paper 1–8. Read each sentence and decide whether the modifying word or phrase clearly describes the intended noun or pronoun. If it does, write **yes**. If it does not, write **no**. Rewrite two of the unclear sentences correctly.

1. Stacked in a pile on the desk, Mr. Hamilton handed out our new textbooks. no
2. Mr. Hamilton told us to read chapter five, which is about the Pilgrims' voyage. yes
3. We read about how the Wampanoag grew squash and beans in our textbook. no
4. Only Mr. Hamilton said to answer questions 1, 3, and 4. no
5. Tika almost did all of her social studies homework. no
6. While I was reading a book in the library, the fire alarm went off. yes
7. Kent left the library just about ten minutes ago, so he should be here soon. yes
8. Keeping an eye on the clock, I found that time passed slowly. yes

Possible answers:
1. Mr. Hamilton handed out our new textbooks, which were stacked in a pile on the desk.
3. We read in our textbook about how the Wampanoag grew squash and beans.
4. Mr. Hamilton said to answer only questions 1, 3, and 4.
5. Tika did almost all of her social studies homework.

Summary 149

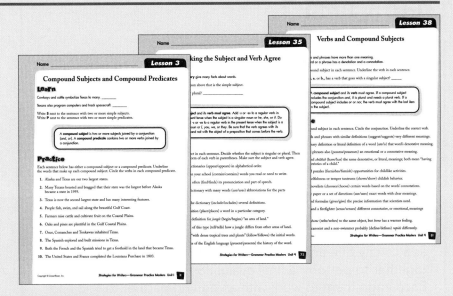

Pages 11, 75, 81

Go to ➡ *Grammar Practice Masters*

Mini-Lesson

Student Objectives

- Avoid using dangling and misplaced modifiers. *(p. 149)*

Dangling and Misplaced Modifiers

Point out the importance of using modifiers correctly. Discuss the difference between a dangling modifier and a misplaced modifier. Then write these sentences on the board:

- *Walking in the rain, an umbrella can keep you dry.* (dangling)
- *While watching the baseball game, it started to rain.* (dangling)
- *Only Mrs. Gonzales said to read the first three chapters of the book.* (misplaced)
- *I saw a deer on the way to school.* (misplaced)

Have volunteers read the sentences and provide corrections. Write the corrected sentences on the board. (Possible responses: When you are walking in the rain, an umbrella can keep you dry. While I was watching the baseball game, it started to rain. Mrs. Gonzales said to read only the first three chapters of the book. On the way to school, I saw a deer.)

CCSS Common Core State Standards

L.6.1.e: Recognize variations from standard English in their own and others' writing and speaking, and identify and use strategies to improve expression in conventional language. **L.6.3:** Use knowledge of language and its conventions when writing, speaking, reading, or listening.

Summary **T149**

Write
a Summary

Week 3 • Day 4

Student Objectives

- Discuss preparation for publishing and presentation. *(p. 150)*
- Use a final editing checklist to publish their work. *(p. 150)*

Publish +Presentation

Publishing Strategy Ask students if they like Justin's choice for sharing his summary by reading it to the class. Point out that Justin's choice is not the only option for publishing his work. Invite students to name other ways they could publish their own summaries. **(Possible responses: Include the summary in a collection of summaries, place it in the library as a resource for other students, submit it to a newspaper or another publication that publishes student work, or post it to a school website.)** Tell students that the summaries they have created provide readers with a breadth of knowledge about many different subjects in a short amount of time and space.

Have a student read Justin's checklist. Remind students that the checklist relates to the editing strategies they have been practicing. Have them use it or guide them to create a personalized checklist that will help students avoid errors they make frequently.

▶ Strategies for Writers Online

Go to **www.sfw.z-b.com** for additional online resources for students and teachers.

Publish +Presentation

Publishing Strategy	Read your summary to the class.
Presentation Strategy	Indent each paragraph.

There are different ways I could publish my summary. For example, I could include it in my scrapbook about Connecticut. First, though, my classmates and I are going to read our summaries aloud so we can all learn about the articles we've read. Before I read my summary aloud, I want to make sure it is neat and easy to read. Whether I handwrite or type my summary, indenting each paragraph will visually group related information. I'll also use this final checklist to check my summary one last time.

My Final Checklist

Did I—

✓ make sure all the subjects and verbs agree?

✓ correct any dangling or misplaced modifiers?

✓ make sure my paragraphs are indented?

✓ proofread carefully for spelling, grammar, and punctuation?

Apply

Make a checklist to help you check your summary. How did you do?

150 Informative/Explanatory Writing

Differentiating Instruction

ENRICHMENT

Summarize Again Have students think about a new project. Suggest that they choose another topic and draft a summary. Justin summarized an article that combined his interests in history, trees, and coins. He could expand his knowledge by choosing a topic related to art, such as summarizing an article about a famous painter. Have students consult other teachers for suggestions.

REINFORCEMENT

Edit With a Checklist Discuss the checklist with students. Add anything to the checklist that they may overlook, such as a catchy title and the author's name. Have them work together to perform a final evaluation of their final copy. Encourage them to work with an editing partner to find and correct errors.

"The Tree That Saved History" by Jane Sutcliffe

Summary by Justin

The Charter Oak was important in the history of Connecticut. This tree even had a funeral.

In colonial times, England's King Charles II granted charters to the American colonies. The charters from the king were contracts that gave the colonies the freedom to govern themselves. Connecticut gained its charter in 1662. In 1685, after King Charles II died, King James II gave orders to seize the charters and join all the New England colonies into one. Edmund Andros, the governor of New England, collected all the charters except Connecticut's.

Andros went to Hartford, Connecticut, to ask for the charter. He met with the colony's governor and other leaders. Before Andros could take the charter, however, the candles in the room blew out. A patriot named Joseph Wadsworth grabbed the charter and leaped out the window. He hid the charter in the hollow of an old white oak tree.

King James II didn't get the charter, but he took away Connecticut's freedom anyway. Soon another English king and queen came into power. They ruled that the colony could have its freedom back because it never surrendered its charter.

In 1856 a storm blew down the tree. After a funeral for the Charter Oak, its wood was carved into many things. A beautiful chair made from the Charter Oak now sits in the state capitol. The Charter Oak also appears on the 1999 Connecticut state quarter. The famous tree still symbolizes our freedom.

Reflect

Think about Justin's summary. Does the writing contain all the traits of a good summary? Check it against the rubric. Don't forget to use the rubric to check your own summary.

Summary **151**

Technology Tip — for 21st Century Literacies

Posting information online requires planning as to how that information can be retrieved or located by other users. One aspect to consider is how the information is "tagged" when posted. Tags work as keywords attached to information posted online. Tagging content accurately and intentionally helps make work "findable" and also helps execute smarter online searches. Encourage students to use Tag Galaxy or a similar search tool to determine appropriate tags for use with their digital content.

See **www.sfw.z-b.com** for further information about and links to these websites and tools.

Write
a Summary

Week 3 • Day 5

Student Objectives

- Use a summary rubric. (pp. 132–133)
- Share a published summary. (p. 151)

Presentation Strategy Remind students that if writing is clear and inviting, readers will be drawn in. If students use the computer, instruct them to make good design decisions. They should use neat margins and spacing and select a couple of clear fonts. Students should remember to indent every paragraph of their summary. If they are adding graphics, students should make sure the graphics complement and enhance the text.

Reflecting on a Summary

Have students refer to the rubric on pages 132–133 as they reread Justin's final copy. Then ask students to share their responses to this question:

- How did the writing strategies and rubric help during the writing process?

CCSS Common Core State Standards

W.6.4: Produce clear and coherent writing in which the development, organization, and style are appropriate to task, purpose, and audience. **W.6.6:** Use technology, including the Internet, to produce and publish writing as well as to interact and collaborate with others; demonstrate sufficient command of keyboarding skills to type a minimum of three pages in a single sitting. **W.6.10:** Write routinely over extended time frames (time for research, reflection, and revision) and shorter time frames (a single sitting or a day or two) for a range of discipline-specific tasks, purposes, and audiences.

Cause-and-Effect Report Planner

WEEK 1

Day 1	Day 2	Day 3
Introduce a Cause-and-Effect Report	**Analyze** Read a Cause-and-Effect Report	**Analyze** Introduce the Rubric

Day 1 — Introduce a Cause-and-Effect Report

Student Objectives
- Review the elements of a cause-and-effect report.
- Consider purpose and audience.
- Learn the traits of informative/explanatory writing.

Student Activities
- Read and discuss **What's in a Cause-and-Effect Report?** (p. 152)
- Read and discuss **Why Write a Cause-and-Effect Report?** (p. 153)
- Read **Linking Informative/Explanatory Writing Traits to a Cause-and-Effect Report.** (p. 154)

Day 2 — Analyze Read a Cause-and-Effect Report

Student Objectives
- Read a model cause-and-effect report.

Student Activities
- Read **"Understanding the Barrier Islands."** (p. 155)

Day 3 — Analyze Introduce the Rubric

Student Objectives
- Learn to read a rubric.

Student Activities
- Review **"Understanding the Barrier Islands."** (p. 155)
- Read and discuss the **Cause-and-Effect Report Rubric.** (pp. 156–157)

WEEK 2

Day 1	Day 2	Day 3
Write Prewrite: Ideas	**Write** Prewrite: Organization	**Write** Draft: Organization

Day 1 — Write Prewrite: Ideas

Student Objectives
- Read and understand a prewriting strategy.

Student Activities
- Read and discuss **Prewrite: Focus on Ideas.** (pp. 162–163)
- Apply the prewriting strategy.

Day 2 — Write Prewrite: Organization

Student Objectives
- Make a Cause-and-Effect Chain to organize the information.

Student Activities
- Read and discuss **Prewrite: Focus on Organization.** (pp. 164–165)
- Apply the prewriting strategy to create a Cause-and-Effect Chain.
- Participate in a peer conference.

Day 3 — Write Draft: Organization

Student Objectives
- Use a Cause-and-Effect Chain to begin writing.

Student Activities
- Read and discuss **Draft: Focus on Organization.** (p. 166)
- Apply the drafting strategy by using a Cause-and-Effect Chain to write a draft.

WEEK 3

Day 1	Day 2	Day 3
Write Revise: Word Choice	**Write** Revise: Sentence Fluency	**Write** Edit: Conventions

Day 1 — Write Revise: Word Choice

Student Objectives
- Revise to use and define specific words.

Student Activities
- Read and discuss **Revise: Focus on Word Choice.** (p. 169)
- Participate in a peer conference.

Day 2 — Write Revise: Sentence Fluency

Student Objectives
- Revise to rewrite long, confusing sentences.

Student Activities
- Read and discuss **Revise: Focus on Sentence Fluency.** (p. 170)

Note: Optional Revising Lessons appear on the *Strategies for Writers* CD-ROM.

Day 3 — Write Edit: Conventions

Student Objectives
- Edit to use correct forms of pronouns and irregular verbs.

Student Activities
- Read and discuss **Edit: Focus on Conventions.** (p. 171)

Note: Teach the Conventions mini-lessons (pp. 172–173) if needed.

Day 4	Day 5
Analyze Ideas, Organization, and Voice	**Analyze** Word Choice, Sentence Fluency, and Conventions
Student Objectives • Read a model cause-and-effect report. • Use the cause-and-effect report rubric. • Use the model cause-and-effect report to study Ideas, Organization, and Voice. **Student Activities** • Review **"Understanding the Barrier Islands."** (p. 155) • Read and discuss **Using the Rubric to Study the Model.** (pp. 158–159)	**Student Objectives** • Read a model cause-and-effect report. • Use the cause-and-effect report rubric. • Use the model cause-and-effect report to study Word Choice, Sentence Fluency, and Conventions. **Student Activities** • Review **"Understanding the Barrier Islands."** (p. 155) • Read and discuss **Using the Rubric to Study the Model.** (pp. 160–161)

Day 4	Day 5
Write Draft	**Write** Revise: Voice
Student Objectives • Complete a draft. **Student Activities** • Finish the draft. (p. 167) • Participate in a peer conference.	**Student Objectives** • Revise to speak directly to the reader. **Student Activities** • Read and discuss **Revise: Focus on Voice.** (p. 168) • Reflect on the model draft. • Apply the revising strategy.

Day 4	Day 5
Write Publish: +Presentation	**Write** Publish: +Presentation
Student Objectives • Discuss preparation for publishing and presentation. • Use a final editing checklist to publish their work. **Student Activities** • Read and discuss **Publish: +Presentation.** (p. 174) • Apply the publishing strategy.	**Student Objectives** • Use a cause-and-effect report rubric. • Share a published cause-and-effect report. **Student Activities** • Share their work. • Use the rubric to reflect upon and evaluate the model and their own writing. (pp. 156–157, 175)

To complete the chapter in fewer days, combine the learning objectives and activities in a way that supports students as they write.

Resources at-a-Glance

Grammar, Usage & Mechanics

Differentiating Instruction

For additional Differentiating Instruction activities, see Strategies for Writers *Extensions Online at* **www.sfw.z-b.com.**

English Language Learners

Conferencing

Technology Tip

 Connection Letter
Reproducible letter (in English and Spanish) appears on the *Strategies for Writers* CD-ROM and at **www.sfw.z-b.com.**

Online Writing Center

Provides IWB resources, interactive games and practice activities, videos, eBooks, and a virtual file cabinet.

 Strategies for Writers Online

Go to **www.sfw.z-b.com** for free online resources for students and teachers.

Introduce
a Cause-and-Effect Report

Student Objectives

- Review the elements of a cause-and-effect report. (*p. 152*)
- Consider purpose and audience. (*p. 153*)
- Learn the traits of informative/ explanatory writing. (*p. 154*)

What's a Cause-and-Effect Report?

Help students understand that a cause-and-effect report deals with reasons (causes) that lead to specific results (effects). Discuss with students reasons they might need to write a cause-and-effect report, such as to explain why something happens. Point out that any time they explain in writing how and why things occur, they are using the cause-and-effect report genre.

What's in a Cause-and-Effect Report?

Read and discuss with students the three elements of a cause-and-effect report listed on page 152: connections, interest, and research. Then discuss specific reasons that each element may be important to writing a cause-and-effect report.

 Strategies for Writers Online

Go to **www.sfw.z-b.com** for additional online resources for students and teachers.

What's a **Cause-and-Effect Report?**

A cause-and-effect report tells how a cause or causes produce certain effects. It might also describe certain effects and trace them back to their causes. This kind of writing really makes you think!

What's in a **Cause-and-Effect Report?**

Connections
Cause-and-effect writing is about showing connections. I really have to understand the cause-and-effect relationships and make them clear to my readers. So it's important to organize my report well and to include plenty of supporting details.

Interest
To capture my audience's attention from the start, I'll begin my report with a fascinating fact. Once I have them interested, I'll keep them reading with good reasoning and smooth writing.

Research
A cause-and-effect report isn't based on opinions. I'll have to do some research to find facts that support the cause-and-effect relationships. I'll use a variety of references to get the whole story on my topic. And I won't use just any source—I need reliable references I can trust!

152 Informative/Explanatory Writing

Informative/Explanatory Text Exemplars (Cause-and-Effect Report)

Brynie, Faith Hickman. *101 Questions Your Brain Has Asked About Itself But Couldn't Answer . . . Until Now.* Twenty-First Century Books, 2007. Using a question-and-answer format, this book answers questions about the brain and how it works, including the effects of drugs and diseases on the brain, memory, and senses. The author also explains what the most recent research has learned about the brain.

Moore, Kay. *If You Lived at the Time of the American Revolution.* Scholastic, 1998. *If You Lived at the Time of the American Revolution* describes the causes of the Revolutionary War. Using a question-and-answer format, the book describes conditions for people in the colonies during and immediately after the war.

Why write a
Cause-and-Effect Report?

I can think of a lot of reasons for writing a cause-and-effect report, and I've listed some of them below. What's my reason? I'm still thinking about that!

Reasoning Skills
To write a cause-and-effect report, I have to really think things through. Looking at causes and figuring out their effects, or looking at effects and examining their causes, makes me use my reasoning skills. I have to think logically and make sure all my points are valid. This is the kind of thinking I need in all my subjects—and in life!

Information
A cause-and-effect report is a good way to inform other people about our world—and about why things happen the way they do. I can help others learn about nature, current events, historical happenings, and many other things with this kind of writing.

Practice
I've had to write cause-and-effect reports in social studies, science, and English. I'm sure I'll be assigned more of this kind of writing in the future, so I can use the practice!

Jones, Charlotte Foltz. *Accidents May Happen: Fifty Inventions Discovered by Mistake.* Demco Media, 1998. This entertaining book describes how many of our everyday items, from telephones to microwaves, were created by accident. This interesting collection also includes funny cartoons and interesting facts.

Sandler, Martin. *America's Great Disasters.* HarperCollins Publishers, 2003. *America's Great Disasters* chronicles the causes behind some of the greatest disasters that occurred on American soil, such as the San Francisco earthquake of 1906. This book also describes the effects of these disastrous events, including new safety laws and building codes.

Why write a Cause-and-Effect Report?

Read and discuss with students the reasons for writing a cause-and-effect report. Point out that all writing has a purpose and is aimed at a specific audience. These authentic purposes help authors shape their writing. For example, someone writing to gain reasoning skills wants to analyze the way things relate to other things. This writer looks at causes to figure out effects, or looks at effects to examine the causes. Critical thinking is a valuable life skill. Another writer may write a cause-and-effect report to explain why things happen as they do. Another writer may choose to write cause-and-effect reports for practice in thinking more deeply about a cause-and-effect relationship. Good writers know that they will be called on to use this genre in the future. Practice is always a good thing! Encourage students to share their own reasons for writing a cause-and-effect report. Ask if they are writing to reason, inform, or practice. Then have them discuss how their reason will affect the purpose and style of their writing.

CCSS **C**ommon **C**ore **S**tate **S**tandards
W.6.2: Write informative/explanatory texts to examine a topic and convey ideas, concepts, and information through the selection, organization, and analysis of relevant content. **SL.6.1:** Engage effectively in a range of collaborative discussions (one-on-one, in groups, and teacher-led) with diverse partners on *grade 6 topics, texts, and issues,* building on others' ideas and expressing their own clearly. **SL.6.1.a:** Come to discussions prepared, having read or studied required material; explicitly draw on that preparation by referring to evidence on the topic, text, or issue to probe and reflect on ideas under discussion.

Introduce
a Cause-and-Effect Report

Linking Informative/ Explanatory Writing Traits to a Cause-and-Effect Report

Explain to students that they will follow Justin as he models using the writing process and the traits together. As they follow Justin through the writing process, students will see how the Informative/ Explanatory Writing Traits have been adapted and applied to writing a cause-and-effect report. They will see that a cause-and-effect report has many factors in common with other types of informative/ explanatory writing. However, the particular audience and purpose of a cause-and-effect report determine how the traits are used.

Linking Informative/Explanatory Writing Traits to a **Cause-and-Effect Report**

In this chapter, you will write a report about how one thing can cause another. This type of expository writing is called a cause-and-effect report. Justin will guide you through the stages of the writing process: Prewrite, Draft, Revise, Edit, and Publish. In each stage, Justin will show you important writing strategies that are linked to the Informative/ Explanatory Writing Traits below.

Informative/Explanatory Writing Traits

	• a clear, focused topic • credible, engaging facts and details that support and develop the topic
	• information that is organized logically into a strong introduction, body, and conclusion • transitions that clarify relationships between ideas
	• a voice and tone that are appropriate for the purpose and audience
	• language that is precise and concise • domain-specific vocabulary that is used correctly and explained as necessary
	• sentences that vary in length and flow smoothly
	• no or few errors in grammar, usage, mechanics, and spelling

Before you write, read Julia Tazzi's cause-and-effect report on the next page. After you read, use the cause-and-effect rubric on pages 156–157 to decide how well she did. (You might want to look back at What's in a Cause-and-Effect Report? on page 152, too!)

Informative/Explanatory Writing Traits in a Cause-and-Effect Report

 Ideas The writer builds the report around a clear, focused topic. Credible, engaging facts and details support and develop the topic.

 **Organization** The information in the report is logically organized into a clear cause-and-effect pattern. There is a strong introduction, body, and conclusion. Transitions clarify relationships among causes and ideas.

 **Voice** The writer uses a second-person voice that is appropriate for the purpose and audience. The voice enhances the writing and consistently connects with the reader.

Understanding the Barrier Islands
by Julia Tazzi

Interesting beginning ↷

Research

The barrier islands are called the "children of the sea." Born after the last ice age, they stretch along the Atlantic coast in long, narrow chains. Some of these chains extend for 100 miles or more. The islands have been around for nearly 18 centuries, but did you know they may not last forever?

What caused the islands to form? At the end of the ice age, the air warmed and the glaciers melted. The melting ice caused rivers and streams to rise. As they flooded over the beaches, they carried sand and sediment to shallow areas just off the Atlantic coast. Ridges formed there. Then waves deposited more sand on the ridges. The ridges slowly became islands. Ocean currents pushed the sand up and down the islands. That caused them to lengthen into narrow strips.

Cause

Effects

Connections

The barrier islands have broad beaches and dunes on the ocean side. They have mud flats and salt marshes on the mainland side. This low, sandy structure is vulnerable to erosion. However, plants in the dunes, flats, and marshes help stabilize the islands. The plants and the dunes themselves slow the wind. As the wind slows down, it is not strong enough to pick up sand and carry it away. Plant roots also hold the sand in place.

Natural erosion isn't the only danger to these islands. People who enjoy the beach love to vacation on the barrier islands. To build houses, hotels, and roads for them, developers flatten the dunes. As they fill in mud flats and marshes, they bury the plants growing there. As they change the islands, developers increase the erosion that occurs.

Since communities want to save their islands, they try to stop the erosion with "beach nourishment." This involves dumping many truckloads of sand on eroding beaches. However, this helps only for a while. The erosion starts up again because there are no dunes to break the wind or plants to hold the sand in place. The new sand is soon washed away. As a result, the islands continue to be in danger.

Research

Erosion has caused many changes in the islands. For example, the Cape Hatteras Lighthouse had to be moved. The beach had eroded, so in 1999, the lighthouse was moved about one-half mile inland.

We need to learn ways to deal with the relentless force of erosion so we can preserve these sandy national treasures.

Cause-and-Effect Report 155

Word Choice The writer uses language that is exact and concise. Domain-specific vocabulary is explained as necessary.

Sentence Fluency The writer helps the writing flow by using clear sentences that vary in length and structure.

Conventions The writer carefully edits his or her work prior to publishing. Compound and complex sentences are punctuated correctly, and commas are used correctly and effectively.

Analyze
the Model

Week 1 • Day 2

Student Objectives

- Read a model cause-and-effect report. *(p. 155)*

Read the Model

Read "Understanding the Barrier Islands" to the class. Ask students to listen for a clear and focused topic (barrier islands) supported by relevant facts from credible research. Ask them to notice how the report is organized. (a logical cause-and-effect pattern) Also ask students to think about and discuss how the author's use of the pronoun *you* in a second-person voice affects how they connected with the writer. Are their reactions different from their peers?

Elements of a Cause-and-Effect Report

Have students refer to What's in a Cause-and-Effect Report? on page 152 as you refer to the model. Discuss the notes on the model to enhance students' understanding of the terms.

CCSS Common Core State Standards

R/Inf.6.1: Cite textual evidence to support analysis of what the text says explicitly as well as inferences drawn from the text. **R/Inf.6.2:** Determine a central idea of a text and how it is conveyed through particular details; provide a summary of the text distinct from personal opinions or judgments. **SL.6.1.a:** Come to discussions prepared, having read or studied required material; explicitly draw on the topic, text, or issue to probe and reflect on ideas under discussion.

Analyze
the Model

Week 1 • Day 3

Student Objectives

- Learn to read a rubric.
  (*pp. 156–157*)

Use the Rubric

Explain the Rubric Explain that a rubric is a tool for planning, improving, and assessing a piece of writing. Tell students that a rubric helps a writer focus on key elements, or traits, in writing (**Ideas, Organization, Voice, Word Choice, Sentence Fluency, Conventions,** and **Presentation**).

Explain that column 6 describes a very good report, one that has received the highest score in all categories. This is what students should strive for in their own writing.

Discuss the Rubric Guide students in a discussion of the rubric. Read the descriptors that go with each trait and explain the relationship between them. Remind students that they will use the rubric as they write their cause-and-effect report, and again as they revise and edit it.

Online Writing Center

Provides a variety of **interactive rubrics,** including 4-, 5-, and 6-point models.

Rubric

Use this 6-point rubric to plan and score a cause-and-effect report.

	6	5	4	
Ideas	The topic is focused and supported by credible sources. Relevant facts support and explain causes and effects.	The topic is clear and supported. One or two facts are not related to the causes and effects.	The topic is clear, but parts are not well supported by credible sources. Most of the facts explain causes and effects.	
Organization	The report is organized in a clear cause-and-effect pattern. Transitions clarify relationships among causes and effects.	The writing is organized in a cause-and-effect pattern. Transitions work well.	The cause-and-effect organization of the writing works most of the time. Transitions are present.	
Voice	Second-person voice connects immediately and consistently with the reader. The voice enhances the writing.	Second-person voice is appealing to the reader. The writing stands out from other writing.	Second-person voice is used inconsistently. It engages the reader from time to time.	
Word Choice	Precise language and specific vocabulary are used and, where necessary, defined.	The writer's language is clear and precise. Most unfamiliar words are defined.	Most of the writing is clear. A few words or phrases are inaccurate or need to be defined.	
Sentence Fluency	All sentences are clearly written and logically structured. They flow smoothly.	Most sentences are clearly written and well structured. They are easy to read aloud.	Some sentences are poorly structured and hard to follow. They interrupt the flow of the writing.	
Conventions	Correct forms of pronouns and verbs are used. The writer's strong knowledge of conventions strengthens the writing.	Correct forms of pronouns and verbs are used. There are a few convention errors, but they are hard to find.	Some pronouns and verbs in the wrong form cause confusion. Noticeable errors do not interfere with reading.	

＋Presentation The cause-and-effect report is neat and legible.

CCSS Common Core State Standards
Cause-and-Effect Report

Strategies for Writers was designed to incorporate the Common Core State Standards throughout every unit. By presenting the standards in multiple applications, your students' exposure to them will be ensured.

The rubric and writing strategies for a cause-and-effect report reflect the writing standards for Informative/Explanatory writing. The traits of Ideas and Organization align with standards **W.6.2, W.6.2.a,** and **W.6.2.b,** which address introducing and developing a topic. Standard **W.6.2.c** also aligns with Organization by highlighting the use of transitions to clarify relationships among causes and effects. The rubric and writing strategies for Voice reflect standard **W.6.2.e** by highlighting a formal style that connects with the audience and enhances writing. The rubric and writing strategies for Word

3	2	1	
The topic is not clear but can be guessed. Several facts are not related to causes and effects.	The topic is unclear. Many facts are missing or unrelated to causes and effects.	The topic is impossible to determine. No causes or effects are mentioned.	**Ideas**
The organization of the writing is often hard to follow. Transitions may or may not be present.	The writing is disorganized. It is difficult to follow the writing. Transitions are missing.	The writing lacks any pattern. It is a list of ideas that doesn't always make sense.	**Organization**
Second-person voice is used once or twice, but it does not engage the reader.	The writer's voice is weak and does not appeal to the reader.	The writer's voice is missing. The writer doesn't seem interested in the topic.	**Voice**
The writing is often unclear but the main idea is understood. Some words need to be defined.	The writing is very unclear. Several words are misused or need to be defined.	The writer has a limited vocabulary. Words are vague or best guesses.	**Word Choice**
Several sentences are too long and confusing. The reader has to stop and reread.	Many poorly structured, confusing sentences make the report hard to understand.	Many incomplete sentences run together. The report is impossible to follow.	**Sentence Fluency**
Noticeable errors in the use of pronouns and verbs make the reader slow down.	Many errors in the use of pronouns and verbs make reading difficult.	Frequent errors in the use of pronouns and verbs sometimes make the text unreadable.	**Conventions**

See Appendix B for 4-, 5-, and 6-point informative/explanatory rubrics.

Apply the Rubric

Assign Groups Assign students to small groups and ask them to check the model for one trait. One person in each group should be responsible for recording one or two strong examples of the trait as described by the rubric. Ask students to score the trait accordingly for the model. They should be able to support their scores. Note that although the model was written to score high in each trait, students should not assume each trait would receive a 6, the top score. Encourage students to discuss each trait thoroughly before assigning a score.

Reassemble the Class Bring the class together and ask one person from each group to report the group's findings to the class. The point of this exercise is less to score the traits than it is to practice identifying and evaluating them within a piece of writing.

Additional Rubrics Appendix B includes 4-, 5-, and 6-point rubrics that can be used with any piece of informative/explanatory writing. The rubrics are also available as blackline masters, beginning on page T545.

Choice are based on standard **W.6.2.d,** which encourages the use of precise language.

The language standards for grade 6 students are addressed during editing and skills practice (**L.6.1, L.6.3, L.6.6**). In addition, there are multiple opportunities to address the speaking and listening standards during the writing process. Most importantly, this chapter will help students examine a topic and convey ideas and information to produce clear and coherent writing (**W.6.4**), improve writing (**W.6.5**), and use technologies to publish and present finished pieces (**W.6.6**). It will also give students the opportunity to conduct short research projects to answer questions (**W.6.7**), draw evidence from informational texts to support analysis (**W.6.8** and **W.6.9**), and write routinely over extended time frames (**W.6.10**).

CCSS **Common Core State Standards**

SL.6.1.b: Follow rules for collegial discussions, set specific goals and deadlines, and define individual roles as needed. **SL.6.1.c:** Pose and respond to specific questions with elaboration and detail by making comments that contribute to the topic, text, or issue under discussion. **SL.6.1.d:** Review the key ideas expressed and demonstrate understanding of multiple perspectives through reflection and paraphrasing.

Analyze
the Model

Week 1 • Day 4

Student Objectives

- Read a model cause-and-effect report. (*p. 155*)
- Use the cause-and-effect report rubric. (*pp. 156–157*)
- Use the model cause-and-effect report to study Ideas, Organization, and Voice. (*pp. 158–159*)

Study the Model

Assess the Model Have volunteers read aloud each section on pages 158 and 159. Use questions such as the following to discuss the pages with students:

- **Does Julia Tazzi have a focused topic?** (Possible responses: Yes, the writer stays on one topic throughout the essay.)

- **Do the facts explain and support the causes and effects?** (Yes, Julia uses relevant facts to explain the cause-and-effect relationships. She cites an interesting fact about the Cape Hatteras Lighthouse.)

▶ **Strategies for Writers Online**
Go to **www.sfw.z-b.com** for additional online resources for students and teachers.

Using the Rubric to Study the Model
Cause-and-Effect Report

Did you notice that the model on page 155 points out some key elements of a cause-and-effect report? As she wrote "Understanding the Barrier Islands," Julia Tazzi used these elements to help with her report. She also used the 6-point rubric on pages 156–157 to plan, draft, revise, and edit her writing. A rubric is a great tool for evaluating writing during the writing process.

Now let's use the same rubric to score the model. To do this, we'll focus on each trait separately, starting with Ideas. We'll use the top descriptor for each trait (column 6), along with examples from the model, to help us understand how the traits work together. How would you score Julia on each trait?

> **Ideas**
> - **The topic is focused and supported by credible sources.**
> - **Relevant facts support and explain causes and effects.**
>
> Julia stays with one topic throughout the essay and uses relevant facts to explain the cause-and-effect relationships. One fact that stood out for me was the need to move the Cape Hatteras Lighthouse. Erosion must have really washed away the beach around it! I bet the lighthouse was hard to move, too!
>
> *[from the writing model]*
>
> Erosion has caused many changes in the islands. For example, the Cape Hatteras Lighthouse had to be moved. The beach had eroded, so in 1999, the lighthouse was moved about one-half mile inland.

English Language Learners

BEGINNING
Cause and Effect Show a photo of a child who's been playing in mud. Say, *I am dirty*, write the sentence on the board, and have students repeat. Do the same for *I take a bath*. Write *cause* and *effect* next to the appropriate sentences on the board, read the words, and have students repeat. Explain that *cause* is why something happens and *effect* is what happens as a result. Repeat for other examples.

INTERMEDIATE
Cause and Effect Write *I am dirty, so I take a bath.* Underline the cause with one color and the effect with another. Explain that *cause* is an action and *effect* is what happens as a result. On strips of paper, give students causes such as *I didn't eat dinner, I told a funny joke,* and *Tiernan is hot.* Have students write an effect to complete the sentences.

Organization

- The report is organized in a clear cause-and-effect pattern.
- Transitions clarify relationships among causes and effects.

Julia uses a logical pattern for cause and effect, stating the causes first and then the effects. Transitions, such as *As they flooded over the beaches*, help me understand how the causes and effects are related.

[from the writing model]

At the end of the ice age, the air warmed and the glaciers melted. The melting ice caused rivers and streams to rise. As they flooded over the beaches, they carried sand and sediment to shallow areas just off the Atlantic coast.

Voice

- Second-person voice connects immediately and consistently with the reader.
- The voice enhances the writing.

Julia begins with fascinating information about the barrier islands. She ends her first paragraph with a question in second-person point of view. I felt like she was addressing me directly, which helped me feel involved with her topic.

[from the writing model]

The barrier islands are called the "children of the sea." Born after the last ice age, they stretch along the Atlantic coast in long, narrow chains. Some of these chains extend for 100 miles or more. The islands have been around for nearly 18 centuries, but did you know they may not last forever?

Cause-and-Effect Report 159

- How does Julia organize her report? (Julia uses a logical pattern for cause and effect, stating the causes first and then the effects. She uses transitions like *As they flooded over the beaches* to explain the relationships between the causes and effects.)

- Is the writer's voice appropriate for the purpose and audience? (Possible responses: Yes, Julia uses a second-person voice to enhance her writing. She connects immediately and consistently with the reader.)

ADVANCED

Cause and Effect Write the following sentences on the board: *After school is over, I have to do my chores. I was happy because I finished my chores.* Explain that although one action follows another, it doesn't necessarily make it a cause-and-effect sentence. Read the sentences and ask students to determine which one is a cause-and-effect sentence.

ADVANCED HIGH

Cause and Effect Complete the Advanced activity above. Then have students write three sentences on the board, two of which show cause and effect. Have partners determine which are the cause-and-effect sentences.

CCSS **Common Core State Standards**

W.6.9: Draw evidence from literary or informational texts to support analysis, reflection, and research. **SL.6.1.b:** Follow rules for collegial discussions, set specific goals and deadlines, and define individual roles as needed. **SL.6.1.c:** Pose and respond to specific questions with elaboration and detail by making comments that contribute to the topic, text, or issue under discussion. **SL.6.1.d:** Review the key ideas expressed and demonstrate understanding of multiple perspectives through reflection and paraphrasing.

Cause-and-Effect Report **T159**

Analyze
the Model

Week 1 • Day 5

Student Objectives

- Read a model cause-and-effect report. *(p. 155)*
- Use the cause-and-effect report rubric. *(pp. 156–157)*
- Use the model cause-and-effect report to study Word Choice, Sentence Fluency, and Conventions. *(pp. 160–161)*

Continue Discussing the Traits

Use questions such as the following to discuss the traits analyzed on pages 160 and 161:

- Does the writer correctly use and define precise language and specific vocabulary? (Possible responses: Julia makes sure to use words that best describe the barrier islands and what is happening to them. She defines words her readers might not be familiar with.)

- Does the model flow smoothly? What makes the report easy to follow? (Possible responses: Yes, the model flows very smoothly. Julia uses easy-to-understand sentences, not long, confusing ones. The shorter, clearer sentences are more interesting and much easier to read.)

- Does Julia use pronouns and verbs correctly? (Possible responses: Yes, she chooses the correct pronouns and uses the correct verb forms.)

Strategies for Writers Online

Go to **www.sfw.z-b.com** for additional online resources for students and teachers.

Word Choice
- Precise language and specific vocabulary are used and, where necessary, defined.

Julia makes sure she is precise in her word choice, using the vocabulary that best describes the barrier islands and what is happening to them. She even defines words her readers might not be familiar with, which helps me fully understand her report.

[from the writing model]

Since communities want to save their islands, they try to stop the erosion with "beach nourishment." This involves dumping many truckloads of sand on eroding beaches. However, this helps only for a while. The erosion starts up again because there are no dunes to break the wind or plants to hold the sand in place. The new sand is soon washed away. As a result, the islands continue to be in danger.

Sentence Fluency
- All sentences are clearly written and logically structured. They flow smoothly.

Julia uses easy-to-understand sentences, not long, confusing ones. If she had connected each sentence below with *and*, I would have quit reading before I got to the end. The shorter, clearer sentences are much easier to read, and they keep me interested.

[from the writing model]

The barrier islands have broad beaches and dunes on the ocean side. They have mud flats and salt marshes on the mainland side. This low, sandy structure is vulnerable to erosion.

160 Informative/Explanatory Writing

Technology Tip — for 21st Century Literacies

Information literacy is as much about finding content as it is about knowing the rules for acknowledging and attributing those sources in subsequent work. As many students may still operate from a perspective of "if it's online, it must be free to use," it is increasingly important to take time to discuss copyright law and fair use. Consider using the resources of the Temple University Media Education Lab to become familiar with current policies. Also, a key local resource is the library/media specialist at your school.

See **www.sfw.z-b.com** for further information about and links to these websites and tools.

Conventions

- Correct forms of pronouns and verbs are used.
- The writer's strong knowledge of conventions strengthens the writing.

The spelling, punctuation, and capitalization are all correct in this report. Notice how Julia chooses the correct pronouns—*who* and *them*—and uses the correct verb forms.

[from the writing model]

Natural erosion isn't the only danger to these islands. People who enjoy the beach love to vacation on the barrier islands.
To build houses, hotels, and roads for them, developers flatten the dunes.

✚Presentation The cause-and-effect report is neat and legible.

My Turn!

Now I'm going to write a cause-and-effect report! I'll use the rubric and good writing strategies to help me. Follow along and learn with me.

Cause-and-Effect Report **161**

Differentiating Instruction

ENRICHMENT

Expand the Rubric Explain that rubrics can be found in other venues, such as restaurants and supermarkets. Have students pretend they are restaurant critics dining at a new restaurant. Have them identify the traits that might be in a restaurant rubric. (Possible responses: food quality, cleanliness, service, menu, pricing) Then have them develop a rubric describing the traits that would enable a restaurant to get a six-star rating.

REINFORCEMENT

Qualities of Writing Ask students what makes a piece of writing good. Make a list of their ideas, such as an interesting topic, good choice of words, sentences that are easy to read, and so forth. Point out that these qualities can be categorized as the traits of writing (Ideas, Organization, Voice, Word Choice, Sentence Fluency, Conventions).

Presentation Explain that Presentation is just as important as the other traits. Appearance should be considered as students prepare their final copies. Neatness is always a priority, and text should be clearly handwritten in pen or typed, using only a few readable fonts. White space should be used to create neat margins of an appropriate width. All paragraphs should be indented (using the tab key if typed), and the title and writer's name should be centered at the top of the first page. Encourage students to remember the importance of these visual elements as they prepare the final draft of their reports.

Think About the Traits Once students have discussed Julia's model cause-and-effect report, ask them which traits they think are most important. All the traits are important in every piece of writing, but some traits stand out more in some genres than in others. Students might say that in a cause-and-effect report **Organization** is important because if the information is poorly organized, the report makes no sense. Others may think that **Word Choice** is more important because precise language informs the reader about the topic.

CCSS **Common Core State Standards**
R/Inf.6.4: Determine the meaning of words and phrases as they are used in a text, including figurative, connotative, and technical meanings. **SL.6.1.d:** Review the key ideas expressed and demonstrate understanding of multiple perspectives through reflection and paraphrasing.

Cause-and-Effect Report **T161**

Write
a Cause-and-Effect Report

Week 2 • Day 1

Student Objectives

- Read and understand a prewriting strategy. (p. 162)

Prewrite

Focus on Ideas

Collect Information Read page 162. Discuss how Justin chose his topic. (He got interested in irrigation when he visited relatives on their farm in Nevada.) Help students understand the importance of selecting websites carefully. If your school has a policy on Internet research, this is a good time to present it. Explain to students that it is always important to keep track of sources, even if the assignment doesn't require making a works consulted list.

✏️ Writer's Term

Credible Sources A credible source is factual, current, and unbiased. The author has good credentials and provides comprehensive information about the topic. Post a list of credible, reliable sources.

▶️ Strategies for Writers Online

Go to **www.sfw.z-b.com** for additional online resources for students and teachers.

Prewrite

Focus on Ideas

The Rubric Says The topic is focused and supported by credible sources.

Writing Strategy Use the Internet to find credible sources of information on the topic.

✏️ Writer's Term

Credible Source
A **credible source** is one that can be trusted to have accurate, unbiased, up-to-date information. School librarians can help you find credible sources if you need guidance.

When our teacher asked us to write a cause-and-effect report, I thought about what I wanted to do. Then I zeroed in on the topic of irrigation in Nevada. I got interested in that subject last year when I visited my cousins, who live in Nevada. It was fun to stay on their farm and learn about a completely different way of life!

I wanted to do some of my research on the Internet. My teacher told us that some websites might not be good. Some sites are too complicated for me to understand. Other sites are out of date. Our librarian says we can trust a website run by a government agency, most news organizations, an encyclopedia, or an educational organization (like a university or a museum).

I found two credible sources for my topic on the Internet.

162 Informative/Explanatory Writing

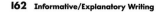

English Language Learners

BEGINNING

Cause-and-Effect Chain Show students a chain or a photo of one. Say *chain* and have students repeat. Write the following in a Cause-and-Effect Chain graphic organizer: *It was hot. We went swimming. We had fun.* If available, show photos of the sun and of children swimming. Ask, *Why did we have fun?* Students should understand that the reason for fun was the swimming and that the reason for swimming was that it was hot. Repeat with other examples.

INTERMEDIATE

Cause-and-Effect Chain Repeat the Beginning activity above. Give students strips of paper with a cause or one of several effects written on each strip. Have them organize the causes and effects into a Cause-and-Effect Chain graphic organizer. Review as a group.

Then I carefully took notes from my sources. I put the notes for each source on a separate sheet of paper. You can see some of my notes below. I found other sources, too, so I will have more pages of notes for my report.

I might not use all the facts in these notes. I will choose the ones that best explain the causes and effects in my report.

Notes From the US Geological Survey—Water Science for Schools: Irrigation Water Use

http://www.usgs.gov

1. About 60 percent of the world's fresh water is used for irrigation.
2. About 40 percent of the fresh water used in the United States is used to irrigate crops.
3. Farms could not feed the world without irrigation from rivers, lakes, reservoirs, and wells.
4. Of the water used for flood irrigation, one half is lost through evaporation or in transit (leaking pipes).

Notes From Colorado River Water Users Association: Nevada

http://www.crwua.org/ColoradoRiver/MemberStates/Nevada.aspx

1. Nevada gets less rainfall than any other state, an average of 9 inches a year.
2. Building Hoover Dam on the Colorado River helped Nevada with water supply and hydroelectric power.
3. Agriculture uses 75 percent of the water in Nevada.
4. Water conservation is common and necessary in Nevada.

Apply

Choose a topic that interests you and gather information about it from credible sources, including the Internet. Take notes on what you read.

ADVANCED

Credible Sources Have volunteers explain the terms *credible, accurate,* and *unbiased.* Check students' understanding that they mean "believable," "correct," and "without personal opinion," respectively. Remind them that only credible sources should be used when researching their writing. Review that online sites with the domains .gov, .edu, and .org are more widely regarded as credible sources.

ADVANCED HIGH

Using Sources Print several online articles for a given topic, such as *natural fertilizers.* Include articles from a variety of sources: .gov, .edu .org, .com, and .net. Discuss what makes an article reliable or unreliable. Point out that .gov, .edu, and .org are generally considered to be more reliable domains than .com or .net. Have students highlight the characteristics that make each source reliable or unreliable and share their findings with a partner.

Compile Information Have students read Justin's words and source notes on page 163. Explain that when surveying sources, students should study the information carefully to determine if it is relevant and reliable. What makes a source reliable? (Possible responses: current, factual, and unbiased information written by experts) Emphasize that source information can be organized in many ways. Justin numbered his notes and used a separate sheet of paper for each source. At the top of each page he included the title of the article and the website he consulted. This format helps keep his notes and sources organized.

Students will need to conduct research to collect information from their sources. Tell students that, like Justin, they will use a separate sheet of paper to take notes for each source. To sound knowledgeable, students should consult at least three reliable sources. Make sure students have access to both print and digital resources.

CCSS Common Core State Standards

W.6.2: Write informative/explanatory texts to examine a topic and convey ideas, concepts, and information through the selection, organization, and analysis of relevant content. **W.6.2.a:** Introduce a topic; organize ideas, concepts, and information, using strategies such as definition, classification, comparison/contrast, and cause/effect; include formatting (e.g., headings), graphics (e.g., charts, tables), and multimedia when useful to aiding comprehension. **W.6.7:** Conduct short research projects to answer a question, drawing on several sources and refocusing the inquiry when appropriate. **W.6.8:** Gather relevant information from multiple print and digital sources; assess the credibility of each source; and quote or paraphrase the data and conclusions of others while avoiding plagiarism and providing basic bibliographic information for sources.

Write
a Cause-and-Effect Report

Week 2 • Day 2

Student Objectives

• Make a Cause-and-Effect Chain to organize information. *(p. 164)*

Prewrite

Focus on

Organize Ideas A writer has several options when choosing how to organize causes and effects. Point out how Justin thinks through this process. He finally comes to the realization that a Cause-and-Effect Chain is the best graphic organizer for structuring the kind of paper he wants to write. Advise students to go through a similar process: Decide how the causes and effects are related and choose a visual way to represent them (possibly a Cause-and-Effect Chain).

✎ Writer's Term_____

Cause-and-Effect Chain A Cause-and-Effect Chain is a visual way of showing how a cause leads to an effect, which in turn becomes a cause and leads to another effect.

Online Writing Center

 Provides **interactive graphic organizers** as well as a variety of graphic organizers in PDF format.

Prewrite

Focus on **Organization**

The Rubric Says	The report is organized in a clear cause-and-effect pattern.
Writing Strategy	Make a Cause-and-Effect Chain to organize your notes.

As I looked over my notes, I noticed how some things cause other things. For example, Nevada gets little rain, so the farmers have to use irrigation.

The rubric reminds me to organize my report into a cause-and-effect pattern. This will help me show what causes what. I know that sometimes one cause has several effects, like when a storm blows down trees, causes rivers to overflow, and brings lightning.

Other times, several causes lead to the same effect. One example I can think of is when you pay attention in class, read the assigned chapters, and do your homework. What's the effect? You get good grades! (You also learn more, of course!)

A Cause-and-Effect Chain shows how events connect. The effect of one event can become the cause of the next event. The events link together in a chain.

You can see part of my chain on the next page.

✎ Writer's Term__

Cause-and-Effect Chain
A **Cause-and-Effect Chain** shows actions and their results. One effect can have several causes, and one cause can have several effects.

Cause-and-Effect Chain

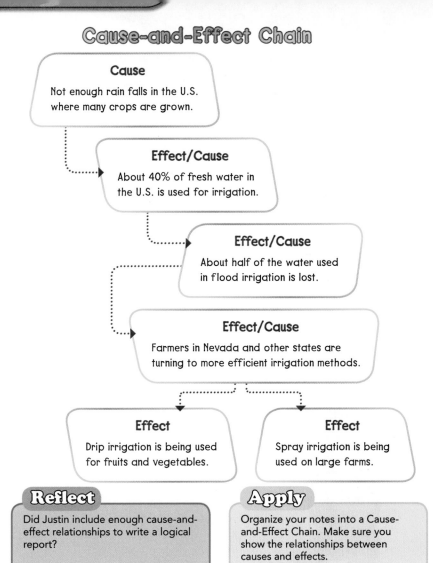

Cause
Not enough rain falls in the U.S. where many crops are grown.

Effect/Cause
About 40% of fresh water in the U.S. is used for irrigation.

Effect/Cause
About half of the water used in flood irrigation is lost.

Effect/Cause
Farmers in Nevada and other states are turning to more efficient irrigation methods.

Effect
Drip irrigation is being used for fruits and vegetables.

Effect
Spray irrigation is being used on large farms.

Reflect
Did Justin include enough cause-and-effect relationships to write a logical report?

Apply
Organize your notes into a Cause-and-Effect Chain. Make sure you show the relationships between causes and effects.

Have students study the organizer on page 165; then ask why a Cause-and-Effect Chain is an effective tool for writing a Cause-and-Effect Report. (It is easy to see how each cause connects to its corresponding effect.) Ask whether Justin has included enough causes and effects to write an informative report. Guide students in using their notes to make their own graphic organizer. Help students understand that the better organized their notes are, the easier it will be to place them in a graphic organizer and then write a report.

Conferencing

PEER TO PEER When students have completed their Cause-and-Effect Chains, have pairs exchange chains. Ask students to review each other's chains and comment on which areas might need more explanation.

PEER GROUPS Assign students to small groups. Instruct them to present their Cause-and-Effect Chains to the group. The group members listen and point out any information that is missing.

TEACHER-LED To demonstrate the importance of a focused Cause-and-Effect Chain, create your own chain on the board, leaving several areas blank. Discuss how the missing information might affect the writing of an effective cause-and-effect report.

CCSS **Common Core State Standards**

W.6.2: Write informative/explanatory texts to examine a topic and convey ideas, concepts, and information through the selection, organization, and analysis of relevant content. **W.6.2.a:** Introduce a topic; organize ideas, concepts, and information, using strategies such as definition, classification, comparison/contrast, and cause/effect; include formatting (e.g., headings), graphics (e.g., charts, tables), and multimedia when useful to aiding comprehension. **W.6.2.b:** Develop the topic with relevant facts, definitions, concrete details, quotations, or other information and examples. **W.6.7:** Conduct short research projects to answer a question, drawing on several sources and refocusing the inquiry when appropriate.

Write

a Cause-and-Effect Report

Week 2 • Day 3

Student Objectives

- Use a Cause-and-Effect Chain to begin writing. (p. 166)

Draft

Focus on Organization

Draft a Cause-and-Effect Report
Review the *draft* step, making sure students realize that they will first write a rough form of a written document. Drafting lets students get ideas down without having to worry about mistakes.

Point out how Justin uses a little-known fact to engage the reader and introduce the topic. Students should agree that Justin's writing is organized, using a clear cause-and-effect pattern. Tell students that Justin used his Cause-and-Effect Chain to draft his report. Have students review both the chain and the report, side by side. This will help them evaluate how well Justin followed his Cause-and-Effect Chain. Point out that Justin repeatedly refers to the rubric as he writes. Encourage students to remember to use the rubric and writing strategy as they draft their essay.

Online Writing Center

 Provides student eBooks with an **interactive writing pad** for drafting, revising, editing, and publishing.

Draft

Focus on **Organization**

The Rubric Says	The report is organized in a clear cause-and-effect pattern.
Writing Strategy	Introduce the topic and present causes and effects in a logical order.

Now it's time to start writing. I'll use my Cause-and-Effect Chain to show how each cause leads to an effect. I'll add facts and details along the way.

I'll also think of a way to begin that grabs the attention of my audience—my classmates, in this case. They may not have to irrigate crops, but natural resources like water are important to everyone. I'll start with an introduction that gets them thinking about how we use our water. Then I'll include interesting facts that will keep them reading.

I'll do my best with spelling, punctuation, and grammar now and check for mistakes when I edit my draft.

You can read the beginning of my draft on the next page.

166 Informative/Explanatory Writing

Differentiating Instruction

ENRICHMENT

Expand the Topic Students can expand their topics with further exploration. For example, Justin could investigate other forms of irrigation used by farmers in the western United States. He could ask himself questions such as *What challenges does each form of irrigation pose?* and *How have irrigation methods improved recently?* Have students write a short report on what they learn.

REINFORCEMENT

Talk Through the Writing For some students, expressing themselves orally is easier than writing. Ask students to describe what they would like to write about. Take a few notes as they talk so that you can offer them an outline to guide their writing.

Proofreading Marks

⊐ Indent	ℓ Take out something
≡ Make a capital	⊙ Add a period
/ Make a small letter	¶ New paragraph
∧ Add something	SP Spelling error

[DRAFT]

[interesting introduction] Almost 40 percent of the fresh water in the United States is used in a special way. It's not used for drinking or baths or swimming pools. It's used for irrigation! Many areas in the United States don't get enough rainfall to grow crops, so the land must be irrigated.

[cause] Most irrigation is in the western states. Water is scarce there. Nevada gets less rainfall than any other state. Farmers in nevada must depend on irrigation to grow their crops. [effect]

The oldest and cheapest type of irrigation is flood irrigation. However, about half of the water used in this type of irrigation evaporates or runs off the feelds. To keep water from running off there fields, farmers whom live in hilly areas make their feelds as level as possible. They also release water at intervals. This reduces runoff, too. In addition, some farmers capture the runoff in ponds. There it is stored for they to use again. [cause]

To conserve water, farmers across the West have experimented with irrigation. Many of they now use more efficient methods. [effect]

Reflect
What do you think? How has the Cause-and-Effect Chain helped Justin draft his report? Does the order in which he presents his facts make sense to you?

Apply
Write a draft of your report using your Cause-and-Effect Chain as a guide. Grab your reader's attention with an interesting fact right at the beginning.

Cause-and-Effect Report 167

Write
a Cause-and-Effect Report

Week 2 • Day 4

Student Objectives
• Complete a draft. *(p. 167)*

Finish the Draft It is important that students are given ample time to draft cause-and-effect reports. As conferencing is important throughout the writing process, be sure to plan time for peer-to-peer, peer group, or teacher-led conferences. Remind students that this is the time for getting their ideas down in a creative and engaging way. Assure them that they will have plenty of time to fix any mistakes later.

Conferencing

PEER TO PEER Students exchange and read drafts to determine if the report is organized in a clear cause-and-effect pattern. Have students think of several questions they would like to ask to clarify information. Have them write their questions on sticky notes and affix them to their partner's draft.

PEER GROUPS Students work in groups of four. Students pass their draft to the student on the right. That student writes one comment on a sticky note and passes the draft along to the right. The review ends when everyone has received his or her own draft back with three comments.

TEACHER-LED Conference with individual students. Use questions and comments to help them identify places in their writing that need work. For example: *I'm not sure I understand this part. Is there a detail you can add to explain this more clearly?*

CCSS Common Core State Standards

W.6.5: With some guidance and support from peers and adults, develop and strengthen writing as needed by planning, revising, editing, rewriting, or trying a new approach. SL.6.1: Engage effectively in a range of collaborative discussions (one-on-one, in groups, and teacher-led) with diverse partners on *grade 6 topics, texts, and issues,* building on others' ideas and expressing their own clearly. SL.6.1.b: Follow rules for collegial discussions, set specific goals and deadlines, and define individual roles as needed. SL.6.1.c: Pose and respond to specific questions with elaboration and detail by making comments that contribute to the topic, text, or issue under discussion.

Write
a Cause-and-Effect Report

Week 2 • Day 5

Student Objectives

• Revise to speak directly to the reader. *(p. 168)*

Revise

Focus on Voice

Use Second-Person Point of View Discuss the importance of engaging the reader's attention. Point out that the rubric says the best way to accomplish this is to use the word *you* to connect with the reader. When writers use the word *you*, they are using a second-person point of view. Although reports are primarily written in third person, using the second-person point of view allows writers to connect directly to the audience while still maintaining a formal style. Recommend to students that they use it only once or twice for effect.

Have one volunteer read the excerpt without the revisions and another volunteer read the revised excerpt. Point out how much more engaging and direct the writing sounds after Justin uses second-person point of view. Have students read their drafts. Remind them to look for places where they can ask a question or engage the reader more.

 Strategies for Writers Online
Go to **www.sfw.z-b.com** for additional online resources for students and teachers.

Revise   Focus on Voice

The Rubric Says	Second-person voice connects immediately and consistently with the reader. The voice enhances the writing.
Writing Strategy	Speak directly to the reader.

When you write a report, you want to pull the reader right in. The rubric reminds me that this is easy to do by addressing the reader directly with *you*—the second-person point of view. But I need to remember to write most of my report in third-person point of view to present the information that I researched. Look at the first paragraph where I added a second-person point of view. Does it sound like I'm talking directly to my reader now?

[DRAFT]

Do you know how [added second-person point of view]

~Almost 40 percent of the fresh water in the United States is used ~in a special way~. It's not used for drinking or baths or swimming pools. It's used for irrigation! Many areas in the United States don't get enough rainfall to grow crops, so the land must be irrigated.

Apply
Try adding second-person point of view to connect directly with your reader.

168   Informative/Explanatory Writing

English Language Learners

BEGINNING/INTERMEDIATE
Subject and Object Pronouns On the board, write *Eli uses a computer. Please give the computer to Eli.* Ask students if *Eli* is the subject or object of the first sentence. The second sentence? Erase *Eli* from each sentence. Write *he* and *him* and ask students which word replaces *Eli* in each sentence. Introduce the terms *subject pronoun* and *object pronoun* and have students repeat.

ADVANCED/ADVANCED HIGH
Cause-and-Effect Transition Words On the board, write *The corn and beans grew larger that year. The farmers used natural fertilizers on their crops.* Ask, *Which is the cause? The effect?* After students identify each, demonstrate different ways to express the cause-and-effect relationship using words such as *because, so,* or *as a result.* For example, *Because the farmers used natural fertilizers, crops of corn and beans grew larger.*

Revise
Focus on Word Choice

The Rubric Says Precise language and specific vocabulary are used and, where necessary, defined.

Writing Strategy Use specific words. Define them, if necessary.

When you write a report, you have to make sure all of your explanations are clear so the reader understands exactly what you are talking about. The rubric tells me that I should use precise language. Sometimes vocabulary is very specific to the topic and may be unfamiliar to the audience. If I have words like that, I should be sure to define them in my writing. Notice that I added a sentence to explain flood irrigation.

[DRAFT]

The oldest and cheapest type of irrigation is flood irrigation. In this method, water is allowed to flow along rows of plants. However, about half of the water used in this type of irrigation evaporates or runs off the feelds.

[defined specific language]

Reflect
How does using precise language strengthen Justin's writing? How does adding a definition improve the report?

Apply
Add more precise language to your report and define any new terms for the reader.

Cause-and-Effect Report **169**

Conferencing

PEER TO PEER Have pairs of students exchange drafts. After reading the draft, each student offers helpful feedback on different ways to strengthen Voice, Word Choice, and Sentence Fluency.

PEER GROUPS Have students form small groups. Have them take turns reading sections of their drafts aloud. Group members suggest areas where domain-specific vocabulary should be added and/or explained.

TEACHER-LED Conference with individual students about their drafts. Point out places where their draft could be improved, using the revising strategies on pages 168–170.

Student Objectives

• Revise to use and define specific words. *(p. 169)*

Revise

Focus on Word Choice

Define Specific Words Read the text on page 169. Discuss the importance of using and defining specific vocabulary. Justin knows that some vocabulary is very specific to the topic. Although he understands the words, he realizes that some may be unfamiliar to his audience. When he read his draft for **Word Choice,** he explained a term some readers may not know. Discuss why students should use and define specific language in their own cause-and-effect reports. (Possible response: Adding precise language and definitions helps readers understand exactly what the writer is trying to explain.) Have students read their drafts to make sure they use and define domain-specific vocabulary.

CCSS **C**ommon **C**ore **S**tate **S**tandards

W.6.2.d: Use precise language and domain-specific vocabulary to inform about or explain the topic. **W.6.2.e:** Establish and maintain a formal style. **L.6.5.b:** Use the relationship between particular words (e.g., cause/effect, part/whole, item/category) to better understand each of the words. **L.6.6:** Acquire and use accurately grade-appropriate general academic and domain-specific words and phrases; gather vocabulary knowledge when considering a word or phrase important to comprehension or expression.

Write
a Cause-and-Effect Report

Week 3 • Day 2

Student Objectives

- Revise to rewrite long, confusing sentences. *(p. 170)*

Revise

Focus on  Sentence Fluency

Rewrite Long, Confusing Sentences Have students read Justin's words on page 170 independently. Remind them that the rubric says all sentences should be clearly written and logically structured for a smooth flow. Explain that this is important in order to make the report clear and easy to read. One way to create a smooth flow is to rewrite long, confusing sentences.

Have one volunteer read the excerpt without the revisions and another volunteer read the revised excerpt. Point out how much clearer and easier to understand the writing sounds after Justin divided one long, confusing sentence into three shorter sentences. Have students check their drafts to look for long, confusing sentences. Instruct them to rewrite the sentences to make them clearer and easier to understand.

Online Writing Center

 Provides **interactive proofreading activities** for each genre.

Revise   Focus on **Sentence Fluency**

The Rubric Says — All sentences are clearly written and logically structured. They flow smoothly.

Writing Strategy — Rewrite long, confusing sentences.

I read my draft to my friend, Eric. He can always tell when something isn't quite clear. He pointed out the long, confusing sentence in this paragraph. So I divided it into three sentences! Now it's easier to read and understand, don't you think? Long sentences can confuse readers, so I'm glad I revised this section for clarity.

[DRAFT]

Many farmers, including those in Nevada, now uses drip irrigation for fruits and vegetables. The water runs through plastic pipes laid along crop rows or buried in the soil and holes in the pipes allow the water to drip directly into the soil and the water soaks into the ground instead of running off or evaporating.

[rewrote long sentence]

Apply

Do you have any long, confusing sentences in your report? If you do, rewrite them to make them clearer and easier to understand.

170 Informative/Explanatory Writing

Optional Revising Lessons

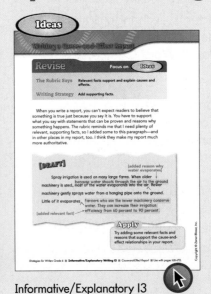

Informative/Explanatory 13

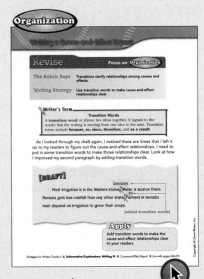

Informative/Explanatory 14

 Go to **Strategies for Writers Grade 6 CD-ROM**

Edit — Focus on **Conventions**

The Rubric Says	Correct forms of pronouns and verbs are used.
Writing Strategy	Make sure subject and object pronouns are used correctly and that irregular verbs are in the correct form.

Writer's Term

Subject and Object Pronouns
A **subject pronoun** takes the place of the subject in a sentence. An **object pronoun** replaces the object of a verb or a preposition.

This is the time to check spelling, capitalization, punctuation, and grammar. I'll also make sure I used irregular verbs and subject and object pronouns correctly. When to use *who* and *whom* can be confusing, so I'll look for those errors, too.

[DRAFT]

[changed to a subject pronoun]

or runs off the ~~fields~~. To keep water from running off ~~there~~ their fields,
who
farmers ~~whom~~ live in hilly areas make their ~~feelds~~ fields as level as

possible. They also release water at intervals. This reduces runoff, too. In addition, some farmers capture the runoff in ponds. There it
them
is stored for ~~they~~ to use again.

[changed to an object pronoun]

Reflect

Is Justin's report clear and interesting? Are the sentences easy to read and understand? Are the subject and object pronouns and irregular verbs correct?

Apply — **Conventions**

Edit your draft for spelling, punctuation, and capitalization errors. Correct any problems with subject and object pronouns and irregular verbs.

For more practice fixing subject and object pronouns and irregular verbs, use the exercises on the next two pages.

Cause-and-Effect Report 171

Related Grammar Practice

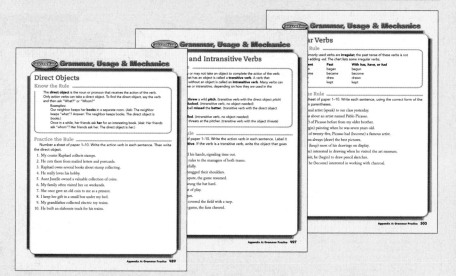

Student Edition pages 489, 497, 503

Go to ➡ **Appendix A: Grammar Practice**

Student Objectives

- Edit to use correct forms of pronouns and irregular verbs. *(p. 171)*

Edit

Focus on **Conventions**

Use Subject and Object Pronouns and Irregular Verbs Correctly Ask students to notice the corrections in Justin's draft. Have students read their drafts, paying special attention to subject and object pronouns and irregular verbs. Use the mini-lessons on pages T172 and T173 for students having problems with subject and object pronouns and irregular verbs. Have students complete the exercises on pages 172 and 173.

Writer's Term

Subject and Object Pronouns
Subject pronouns can replace or rename subjects in a sentence. Object pronouns can replace objects of verbs or prepositions. The nouns being replaced (antecedents) should be clear and unmistakable.

CCSS **Common Core State Standards**
L.6.1: Demonstrate command of the conventions of standard English grammar and usage when writing or speaking. **L.6.1.a:** Ensure that pronouns are in the proper case (subjective, objective, possessive). **L.6.2.b:** Spell correctly. **L.6.3.a:** Vary sentence patterns for meaning, reader/listener interest, and style.

Mini-Lesson

Student Objectives

• Use subject and object pronouns correctly. *(p. 172)*

Subject and Object Pronouns

Using pronouns correctly helps to avoid redundancy. Write the following on the board:

• *Leanne visited Nevada on her vacation. She took some great pictures of Hoover Dam.*

Ask students whether the word *she* in the sentence is a subject or an object pronoun. (subject pronoun because it replaces the subject, *Leanne*)

Then display this sentence:

• *Leanne's friends want her to post them online.*

Ask students whether the words *her* and *them* in this sentence are subject or object pronouns. (object pronouns because they replace objects of the verbs)

To help students use *who* and *whom*, display the following:

• *Leanne, _____ is an amateur photographer, takes pictures wherever she travels. It is photographers like Leanne for _____ the website was created.*

Ask students to supply the correct missing pronouns. (who; whom)

Online Writing Center

 Provides **interactive grammar games** and **practice activities** in student eBook.

Subject and Object Pronouns

Know the Rule

A **subject pronoun** takes the place of the subject in a sentence.
  Example: **Leanne** lives near Hoover Dam.
       She lives near Hoover Dam.

An **object pronoun** replaces the object of a verb or a preposition.
  Example: The dam helps **farmers** irrigate.
       The dam helps **them** irrigate.

Use *who* as a subject pronoun. Use *whom* as an object pronoun.
  Example: Herbert Hoover, **who** was president then, made a speech.
       He talked to farmers for **whom** the dam would make a huge difference. (*Who* is the subject of the verb *was*. *Whom* is the object of the preposition *for*.)

Practice the Rule

Number a separate piece of paper 1–10. Choose the correct pronoun for each sentence and write it on your paper. Add **S** if you chose a subject pronoun or **O** if you chose an object pronoun.

1. People (who/whom) live in the desert value water. S
2. (I/me) grew up in the Mojave Desert in Nevada. S
3. Hoover Dam was built near (us/we) in the early 1930s. O
4. For (who/whom) was Hoover Dam built? O
5. It was built for all of (we/us) in the Southwest. O
6. My family and (I/me) went to see Hoover Dam last year. S
7. The tour guide told (we/us) that the dam is a National Historic Landmark. O
8. The Colorado River runs through the turbines in the dam, and (they/them) can handle all that water. S
9. The people of Nevada benefit from the dam as it creates power for (them/they). O
10. (Whom/Who) knew moving water could be so powerful and helpful? S

172 Informative/Explanatory Writing

Related Grammar Practice

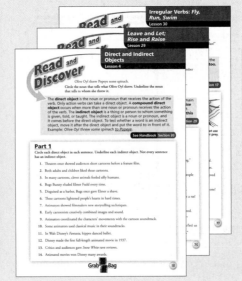
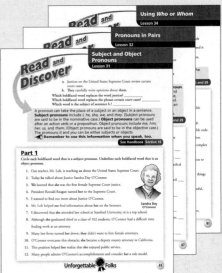

Pages 13, 75, 77, 85, 87, 91

Go to ➡ **G.U.M. Student Practice Book**

Irregular Verbs

Know the Rule

Many verbs are **irregular;** they do not add *-ed* in the past tense. Here are some irregular verbs:

Present	Past	With *has, had,* or *have*
eat	ate	eaten
hear	heard	heard
teach	taught	taught
read	read	read
write	wrote	written

Example: We **eat** the same pizza every Friday night.
We now have **eaten** mushroom pizza ten weeks in a row!

Practice the Rule

On a separate piece of paper, rewrite the following sentences using the correct form of the verb in parentheses.

1. Last year, Mr. Li (read) a lot of books about Earth's water supply. **read**
2. He had (hear) that the water supply is very limited in some places. **heard**
3. Water was on his mind because during last year's flood we only (drink) water after we had boiled it. **drank**
4. The author of Mr. Li's book (write) that of all the water on Earth, more than 97 percent is salt water. **wrote**
5. My science teacher (teach) us that salt water is poisonous if you drink too much of it. **taught**
6. I have (swim) in salt water, but I didn't know that humans can't survive by drinking it. **swum**
7. Since he read the book, Mr. Li has (write) some letters to the newspaper about the world's water supply. **written**
8. It's a topic he has (think) about a lot. **thought**
9. When we (eat) dinner at his house, he talked about it at great length. **ate**
10. I've (read) some books about the subject myself. **read**

Cause-and-Effect Report **173**

 **Conventions**

Mini-Lesson

Student Objectives

• Use irregular verbs correctly. (*p. 173*)

Irregular Verbs

Point out that all regular verbs consist of three parts: present, past, and past participle. Regular verbs have an *-ed* ending added to the root verb for both the simple past and past participle. Irregular verbs do not follow this pattern. To demonstrate, write these sentences on the board:

• *My sister Josefina read her speech for me yesterday.*

• *I set a stopwatch to make sure her speech was the right length.*

• *She has written some great speeches in her history class.*

• *She speaks well in front of an audience!*

Have volunteers identify each verb and its tense. (*read,* past; *set,* past; *was,* past; *has written,* past participle; *speaks,* present) Have students consult online resources to find irregular verbs, and post them in the writing center for quick reference.

CCSS **Common Core State Standards**
W.6.5: With some guidance and support from peers and adults, develop and strengthen writing as needed by planning, revising, editing, rewriting, or trying a new approach. **L.6.1.a:** Ensure that pronouns are in the proper case (subjective, objective, possessive). **L.6.2:** Demonstrate command of the conventions of standard English capitalization, punctuation, and spelling when writing.

Cause-and-Effect Report **T173**

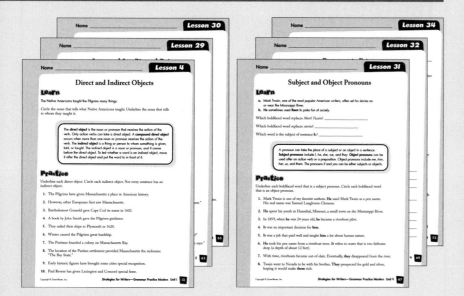

Pages 13, 63, 65, 67, 69, 73

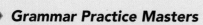 **Grammar Practice Masters**

Write a Cause-and-Effect Report

Week 3 • Day 4

Student Objectives

- Discuss preparation for publishing and presentation. *(p. 174)*
- Use a final editing checklist to evaluate their work. *(p. 174)*

Publish ⁺Presentation

Publishing Strategy Ask students if they like Justin's choice for sharing his Cause-and-Effect Report in a class binder. Ask how Justin could enhance his presentation. (Possible responses: Justin could add pictures or charts.) Point out that Justin's choice is not the only option for publishing his work. Discuss other ways students could publish their reports. Someone might choose to display the report in the school library, while another student may prefer to send it to a local newspaper.

Read Justin's checklist. Remind students that the checklist relates to the writing strategies they have been practicing. Have them make their own checklist and use it to perform a final evaluation before publishing their work.

Strategies for Writers Online
Go to **www.sfw.z-b.com** for additional online resources for students and teachers.

Publish ⁺Presentation

Publishing Strategy	Add your cause-and-effect report to the class binder.
Presentation Strategy	Neatly handwrite or type the report.

Now it's time to publish my cause-and-effect report! I could submit it to a science website. But I think I'll add my report to the science binder my class is putting together. Other people will read my report, so it has to be neatly handwritten, or, better yet, neatly word-processed. I'll keep in mind, too, that the margins have to be wide enough for the three-ring binder. Before I publish my work, I'll check it one more time using this final checklist.

My Final Checklist

Did I—

✓ make sure all the subject and object pronouns are correct?

✓ check that I used the correct forms of irregular verbs?

✓ make sure my report is neat and legible?

✓ make sure I used appropriate margins?

Apply

Make a checklist to check your own cause-and-effect report. Then make a final copy to publish.

174 Informative/Explanatory Writing

Differentiating Instruction

ENRICHMENT

Copyedit the Report Have pairs of students exchange papers to proofread each other's work. When partners have finished proofreading, have them swap papers again so that each student has his or her own report. Then have students discuss and defend their edits.

REINFORCEMENT

Edit Against a Final Checklist Meet with a small group of students to discuss the checklists. Have students work together to perform a final evaluation of their cause-and-effect reports. Encourage them to check spelling, grammar, and punctuation. Remind them to especially check that they have used irregular verbs and pronouns correctly. Students should also make sure that only a few clear fonts are used in the paper. Help students make their corrections.

Why Are Nevada's Crops Irrigated?

by Justin

Do you know how almost 40 percent of the fresh water in the United States is used? It's not used for drinking or baths or swimming pools. It's used for irrigation! Many areas in the United States don't get enough rainfall to grow crops. That land must be irrigated.

Most irrigation is in the Western states because water is scarce there. Nevada gets less rainfall than any other state, so farmers in Nevada must depend on irrigation to grow their crops. In Nevada, 67 percent of all cropland requires irrigation. In fact, the U.S. government's first irrigation project was in Nevada.

The oldest and cheapest type of irrigation is flood irrigation. In this method, water is allowed to flow along rows of plants. However, about half of the water used in this type of irrigation evaporates or runs off the fields. To keep water from running off their fields, farmers who live in hilly areas make their fields as level as possible. They also release water at intervals. This reduces runoff, too. In addition, some farmers capture the runoff in ponds. There it is stored for them to use again.

To conserve water, farmers across the West have experimented with other methods of irrigation. Many of them now use more efficient methods. Farmers who have to deal with the Nevada desert must be especially careful. Nevada potato farmers, in particular, need to irrigate their fields. Potatoes need seven times more water than crops like wheat!

Many farmers, including those in Nevada, now use drip irrigation for fruits and vegetables. The water runs through plastic pipes laid along crop rows or buried in the soil. Holes in the pipes allow the water to drip directly into the soil. The water soaks into the ground instead of running off or evaporating.

Spray irrigation is used on many large farms. When older machinery is used, most of the water evaporates into the air because water shoots through the air to the ground. Newer machinery gently sprays water from a hanging pipe onto the ground. Little of it evaporates. Farmers who use the newer machinery conserve water. They can increase their irrigation efficiency from 60 percent to 90 percent.

In Nevada, if you want to grow crops, you must irrigate!

Reflect

How does Justin's report look? Check the writing against the rubric. Be sure to use the rubric to check your own writing, too!

Cause-and-Effect Report **175**

Technology Tip — for 21st Century Literacies

Ask students to articulate and share a model think-aloud as they select sources for use in supporting their work. As much as credibility and validity are key, so is demonstrating confidence and self-direction when evaluating information to support one's writing. During the think aloud, expect that students maintain a critical stance but that they also show persistence despite those instances where a search comes up short. Model and share your own processes as lead-learner in the classroom.

See **www.sfw.z-b.com** for further information about and links to these websites and tools.

Write
a Cause-and-Effect Report

Week 3 • Day 5

Student Objectives

- Use a cause-and-effect report rubric. *(pp. 156–157)*
- Share a published cause-and-effect report. *(p. 175)*

Presentation Strategy Remind students that if writing is messy or illegible, readers may decide not to read it. If it is clear and inviting, readers will be drawn in. Instruct students to use the computer to make good design decisions. They should use neat margins and spacing and select a couple of clear fonts. Students should remember to indent every paragraph of their cause-and-effect report.

Reflecting on a Cause-and-Effect Report

Have students refer to the rubric on pages 156 and 157 as they reread Justin's final copy. Then have students reflect on the assignment as a whole and share their thoughts.

CCSS **C**ommon **C**ore **S**tate **S**tandards

W.6.4: Produce clear and coherent writing in which the development, organization, and style are appropriate to task, purpose, and audience. **W.6.6:** Use technology, including the Internet, to produce and publish writing as well as to interact and collaborate with others; demonstrate sufficient command of keyboarding skills to type a minimum of three pages in a single sitting. **W.6.10:** Write routinely over extended time frames (time for research, reflection, and revision) and shorter time frames (a single sitting or a day or two) for a range of discipline-specific tasks, purposes, and audiences.

Research Report Planner

WEEK 1

Day 1	Day 2	Day 3
Introduce a Research Report	**Analyze** Read a Research Report	**Analyze** Introduce the Rubric

Day 1 — Introduce a Research Report

Student Objectives
- Review the elements of a research report.
- Consider purpose and audience.
- Learn the traits of informative/explanatory writing.

Student Activities
- Read and discuss **What's in a Research Report?** (p. 176)
- Read and discuss **Why Write a Research Report?** (p. 177)
- Read **Linking Informative/Explanatory Writing Traits to a Research Report.** (p. 178)

Day 2 — Analyze Read a Research Report

Student Objectives
- Read a model research report.

Student Activities
- Read **"Digging Into Backyard Archaeology."** (pp. 179–181)

Day 3 — Analyze Introduce the Rubric

Student Objectives
- Learn to read a rubric.

Student Activities
- Review **"Digging Into Backyard Archaeology."** (pp. 179–181)
- Read and discuss the **Research Report Rubric.** (pp. 182–183)

WEEK 2

Day 1	Day 2	Day 3
Write Prewrite: Ideas	**Write** Prewrite: Organization	**Write** Draft: Voice

Day 1 — Write Prewrite: Ideas

Student Objectives
- Read and understand a prewriting strategy.

Student Activities
- Read and discuss **Prewrite: Focus on Ideas.** (pp. 188–189)
- Apply the prewriting strategy.

Day 2 — Write Prewrite: Organization

Student Objectives
- Make an Outline to organize notes.

Student Activities
- Read and discuss **Prewrite: Focus on Organization.** (pp. 190–191)
- Apply the prewriting strategy to create an Outline from note cards.
- Participate in a peer conference.

Day 3 — Write Draft: Voice

Student Objectives
- Use an Outline to begin writing.

Student Activities
- Read and discuss **Draft: Focus on Voice.** (p. 192)
- Apply the drafting strategy by using an Outline to write a draft.

WEEK 3

Day 1	Day 2	Day 3
Write Revise: Word Choice	**Write** Revise: Sentence Fluency	**Write** Edit: Conventions

Day 1 — Write Revise: Word Choice

Student Objectives
- Revise to define all domain-specific words.

Student Activities
- Read and discuss **Revise: Focus on Word Choice.** (p. 195)
- Participate in a peer conference.

Day 2 — Write Revise: Sentence Fluency

Student Objectives
- Revise to use sentences of different lengths and structures.

Student Activities
- Read and discuss **Revise: Focus on Sentence Fluency.** (p. 196)

Note: Optional Revising Lessons appear on the *Strategies for Writers* CD-ROM.

Day 3 — Write Edit: Conventions

Student Objectives
- Edit for correct capitalization of proper nouns and proper adjectives.

Student Activities
- Read and discuss **Edit: Focus on Conventions.** (p. 197)

Note: Teach the Conventions mini-lessons (pp. 198–199) if needed.

Day 4	Day 5
Analyze Ideas, Organization, and Voice	**Analyze** Word Choice, Sentence Fluency, and Conventions

Student Objectives

- Read a model research report.
- Use the research report rubric.
- Use the model research report to study Ideas, Organization, and Voice.

Student Activities

- Review **"Digging Into Backyard Archaeology."** (pp. 179–181)
- Read and discuss **Using the Rubric to Study the Model.** (pp. 184–185)

Student Objectives

- Read a model research report.
- Use the research report rubric.
- Use the model research report to study Word Choice, Sentence Fluency, and Conventions.

Student Activities

- Review **"Digging Into Backyard Archaeology."** (pp. 179–181)
- Read and discuss **Using the Rubric to Study the Model.** (pp. 186–187)

Day 4	Day 5
Write Draft	**Write** Revise: Ideas

Student Objectives

- Complete a draft.

Student Activities

- Finish the draft. (p. 193)
- Participate in a peer conference.

Student Objectives

- Revise to take out unrelated details or facts.

Student Activities

- Read and discuss **Revise: Focus on Ideas.** (p. 194)
- Reflect on the model draft.
- Apply the revising strategy.

Day 4	Day 5
Write Publish: +Presentation	**Write** Publish: +Presentation

Student Objectives

- Discuss preparation for publishing and presentation.
- Use a final editing checklist to publish their work.

Student Activities

- Read and discuss **Publish: +Presentation.** (p. 200)
- Apply the publishing strategy.

Student Objectives

- Use a research report rubric.
- Share a published research report.

Student Activities

- Share their work.
- Use the rubric to reflect upon and evaluate the model and their own writing. (pp. 182–183, 201–203)

To complete the chapter in fewer days, combine the learning objectives and activities in a way that supports students as they write.

Resources at-a-Glance

Grammar, Usage & Mechanics

Kinds of Nouns T198
Proper Nouns and Proper
   Adjectives T199
Grammar Practice T197–T199

Differentiating Instruction

Using the Rubric T187
Draft. .T192
Publish T200
For additional Differentiating Instruction activities, see Strategies for Writers *Extensions Online at* **www.sfw.z-b.com.**

English Language Learners

Using the Rubric T184–T185
Prewrite T188–T189
Revise. T194

Conferencing

Peer to Peer T191, T193, T195
Peer Groups. T191, T193, T195
Teacher-Led T191, T193, T195

Technology Tip

Using the Rubric T186
Publish. T201

 Connection Letter
Reproducible letter (in English and Spanish) appears on the *Strategies for Writers* CD-ROM and at **www.sfw.z-b.com.**

Online Writing Center

Provides IWB resources, interactive games and practice activities, videos, eBooks, and a virtual file cabinet.

 Strategies for Writers Online

Go to **www.sfw.z-b.com** for free online resources for students and teachers.

Introduce
a Research Report

Student Objectives

- Review the elements of a research report. *(p. 176)*
- Consider purpose and audience. *(p. 177)*
- Learn the traits of informative/explanatory writing. *(p. 178)*

What's a Research Report?

Help students understand that a research report gives writers the opportunity to share what they've discovered after asking questions, researching answers, and exploring a topic. Gathering facts from different sources is similar to piecing a puzzle together.

What's in a Research Report?

Read and discuss with students the four elements of a research report. Explain that these elements are common to other types of writing whose purpose is to inform or explain, such as an explanatory essay.

Strategies for Writers Online
Go to **www.sfw.z-b.com** for additional online resources for students and teachers.

What's a **Research Report?**

To write a research report, a writer gathers information from multiple reliable sources, organizes it, and explains the main points to readers. This kind of writing is a challenge, but I like the idea of gathering facts from different sources and putting them together like a puzzle!

What's in a **Research Report?**

Multiple and Varied Sources
Hey, there's a reason they call it a research report! I need to do plenty of research to really understand my topic. And I should mix up my sources instead of relying on just one type of information, such as encyclopedia articles.

Organization
With all the information I'll be gathering, organization will be very important. I have to focus on the topic and organize all the main points in a logical way. I'll need good supporting details and a strong conclusion to pull it all together.

Lively Writing
It's easy to slip into dull language when you're writing something factual. I'm going to watch out for that! I want to use a variety of interesting and strong sentences to keep my writing lively.

Fully Cited Sources
It's important that I fully cite the sources for my research report. After all, I'm presenting factual information. Using another person's words or information without giving credit is plagiarism, a serious offense.

176 Informative/Explanatory Writing

Informative/Explanatory Text Exemplars (Research Report)

Lord, Walter. *A Night to Remember.* **Henry Holt, 1955.** CCSS Using the information gained from interviews with survivors, Walter Lord describes the sinking of the *Titanic* in 1912. From its initial contact with the iceberg to the rescue of many of its passengers, *A Night to Remember* captures the details of this legendary disaster at sea.

Mackay, Donald A. *The Building of Manhattan.* **Dover Publications, 2010.** CCSS This book chronicles how the island of Manhattan grew from a small Dutch outpost to one of the largest and most significant cities in the world. Using hundreds of line drawings, Mackay describes the construction of Manhattan above and below ground, including subway lines and skyscrapers.

Why write a **Research Report?**

There are many good reasons to write a research report. I'm still thinking about why I want to do this kind of writing. Here are some possible reasons.

Information
A good research report contains tons of valuable information. Readers can learn a lot from this kind of report.

Mastery
I can learn a lot by reading an article or a chapter about a subject, but researching a topic myself is even better! Gathering facts and putting everything together helps me really absorb the information and make it my own.

Going Deeper
Sometimes I'm interested in a topic, but I don't really know much about it. Writing a research report can help me get deeper into a subject. I might find out new things about that particular topic. My research could help me understand a subject better or lead me to other fascinating topics.

Why write a Research Report?

Read and discuss with students the reasons for writing a Research Report. Point out that all writing has a purpose and is aimed at a specific audience. These authentic purposes help authors shape their writing. A writer who is writing to inform others will want to include a great deal of valuable information since readers learn from this kind of report. A person who enjoys gathering facts and putting them together for the sake of gaining information often masters a topic and gets others excited about it, too. Others may be curious about a topic and want to learn more about it. So, they dig deeper and find out new things about their topic. Encourage students to think about how their reasons will give purpose to their writing.

Macaulay, David. *Cathedral: The Story of Its Construction.* Houghton Mifflin, 1981. **CCSS**
Cathedral: The Story of Its Construction describes the planning and construction of a Gothic cathedral in the fictional French town of Chultreaux in the 13th century. Macaulay describes in intricate detail the tools used to build the cathedral, as well as providing fascinating facts about a cathedral's construction.

Murphy, Jim. *The Great Fire.* Scholastic, 1995. **CCSS**
The Great Fire explores the Great Chicago Fire that swept through much of Chicago in 1871, as seen through the eyes of survivors. The author uses photos and maps to show how the fire spread across the city.

CCSS **C**ommon **C**ore **S**tate **S**tandards

SL.6.1: Engage effective in a range of collaborative discussions (one-on-one, in groups, and teacher-led) with diverse partners on *grade 6 topics, texts, and issues*, building on others' ideas and expressing their own clearly. **SL.6.1.a:** Come to discussions prepared, having read or studied required material; explicitly draw on that preparation by referring to evidence on the topic, text, or issue to probe and reflect on ideas under discussion. **W.6.2:** Write informative/explanatory texts to examine a topic and convey ideas, concepts, and information through the selection, organization, and analysis of relevant content.

Introduce
a Research Report

Linking Informative/ Explanatory Writing Traits to a Research Report

Explain to students that they will follow Justin as he models using the writing process and the traits together. As they follow Justin through the writing process, students will see how the Informative/Explanatory Writing Traits have been adapted and applied to writing a research report. They will see that a research report has many factors in common with other types of informative/ explanatory writing. However, the particular audience and purpose of a research report determine how the traits are used.

Online Writing Center

Provides six **interactive anchor papers** for each mode of writing.

TI78 Informative/Explanatory Writing

Linking Informative/Explanatory Writing Traits to a **Research Report**

In this chapter, you will choose a topic to research thoroughly, and then explain what you have learned. This type of expository writing is called a research report. Justin will guide you through the stages of the writing process: Prewrite, Draft, Revise, Edit, and Publish. In each stage, Justin will show you important writing strategies that are linked to the Informative/ Explanatory Writing Traits below.

Informative/Explanatory Writing Traits

	• a clear, focused topic • credible, engaging facts and details that support and develop the topic
	• information that is organized logically into a strong introduction, body, and conclusion • transitions that clarify relationships between ideas
	• a voice and tone that are appropriate for the purpose and audience
	• language that is precise and concise • domain-specific vocabulary that is used correctly and explained as necessary
	• sentences that vary in length and flow smoothly
	• no or few errors in grammar, usage, mechanics, and spelling

Before you write, read Peter Nuan's research report on the next three pages. Then use the research report rubric on pages 182–183 to decide how well he did. (You might want to look back at What's in a Research Report? on page 176, too!)

Informative/Explanatory Writing Traits in a Research Report

 Ideas The writer builds the report around a clearly defined topic. Relevant facts and concrete details from reliable sources enhance the ideas for the reader.

 **Organization** The structure of the writing is perfect for the topic and enhances the reader's understanding. A thoughtful conclusion follows from the information presented.

 Voice To ensure that the reader is engaged throughout the research report, the writer uses an active voice.

Digging Into Backyard Archaeology

by Peter Nuan

Lively writing

    With a toothbrush, Jan Haas carefully removed dirt from a little lump in her hand. The object under the dirt glinted in the sunlight. Was it a piece of gold jewelry? She continued to brush off the soil hiding the object. The shape became clear. It was round and fairly flat. Then she saw a design. Soon it was clear that the object was a tarnished brass button.

    It had been buried six inches deep in Jan's backyard in Baltimore, Maryland. She dug it up near an old washhouse. The washhouse had been built in the mid-1700s. Later, Jan learned the button was from the Colonial period.

    As a backyard archaeologist, Jan was pleased with her find. Backyard archaeologists are amateurs. Like the professionals, they search for and study objects made by people long ago.

Organization—main point

    Across America, people like Jan Haas are digging up their backyards. They hope to find treasures. These treasures will probably not be gold or diamonds. More likely, they will be old buttons or chipped glass. They are still valuable, though. They tell about an area's history and culture. A dig in the backyards of Alexandria, Virginia, uncovered items from more than a century ago. They included marbles, medicine bottles, and pottery shards. Before the Civil War, free African American people lived in the area. "By studying these artifacts, we were able to trace the development of this neighborhood and the lifestyles of its inhabitants," said the city's archaeologist, Pamela J. Cressey, Ph.D.

    Archaeologists urge people who dig as a hobby to follow a few guidelines. If amateurs just start digging, they may destroy valuable old objects.

    First, property owners should research their site. Town records may provide facts about former owners. Many libraries and museums may have collections of news clippings and photos. Information about early Native American groups living in the region is usually available at history museums.

Organization—supporting details

Organization—main point

Research Report **179**

Student Objectives

• Read a model research report. *(pp. 179–181)*

Read the Model

Read "Digging Into Backyard Archaeology" to the class. Ask students to listen for a clear topic supported by concrete details and relevant facts. As you read, they should also notice the structure of the writing. Ask students to think about how the writer connects with the reader and shows enthusiasm for the topic. After reading, have students compare and discuss their responses to the model report.

Elements of a Research Report

Have students look back at What's in a Research Report? on page 176 as you refer to the model. Discuss the notes written on the model to enhance students' understanding. Also point out the works consulted section at the end of the report. Explain that good writers keep track of their sources and include them all in a list at the end of their report.

 **Word Choice** A good writer knows that it is important to use domain-specific content vocabulary to inform the reader about the topic.

 **Sentence Fluency** Sentences are lively and highly varied in length and structure. They move the reader along.

 **Conventions** A good writer carefully edits his or her work prior to publishing. The writer uses a variety of nouns correctly.

CCSS Common Core State Standards

R/Inf.6.1: Cite textual evidence to support analysis of what the text says explicitly as well as inferences drawn from the text. R/Inf.6.2: Determine a central idea of a text and how it is conveyed through particular details; provide a summary of the text distinct from personal opinions or judgments. SL.6.1.a: Come to discussions prepared, having read or studied required material; explicitly draw on that preparation by referring to evidence on the topic, text, or issue to probe and reflect on ideas under discussion.

Backyard archaeologists should then contact authorities and explain what they have learned about the site. The state archaeologist is a good person to contact. Other possible contacts are historical societies and college archaeology departments. An expert will often arrange a survey of the site.

Some backyard sites contain valuable objects. Unless such a site is in danger of being destroyed, archaeologists usually ask property owners not to dig there. They believe the past should be left untouched so it will be preserved for the future. If the site is in danger, the archaeologists may conduct a dig. They often ask the property owner to help.

Whatever diggers find at the site belongs to the property owners. Some backyard archaeologists donate the items to a historical society or museum. There, trained professionals can catalog and care for the items. Objects removed from the ground may dry out, rot, or get moldy. Professionals know how to preserve these objects. They can keep them safe for study and display.

Lively writing

Some backyard archaeologists get started by volunteering at a dig site. Several government agencies offer a chance to work in the field. For example, Passport in Time (PIT) is a volunteer program of the U.S. Forest Service. Its aim is to preserve landmarks and historical sites in national forests. PIT volunteers work with archaeologists on sites around the country. Linda Ruys volunteered at a PIT site in Idaho. She learned a lot about the people of the past—and made friends in the present! "The words 'kindred spirits' and 'family' were repeated often in a group that had just met," she said. She found joy in working with these people. "We understood our connectedness as human beings—a life lesson worth learning." **Organization—main point**

School programs are another place to learn the basics of archaeology. Sixth-grade students at Blake Middle School in Medfield, Massachusetts, learn through a hands-on experience. Each fall they work in teams on an old trash heap owned by a local family. They have found old nails, jars, and pieces of an old toy bank. **Organization—supporting details**

The students learn to use the correct tools and methods. They are shown how to mark the site into square plots. They learn how to properly dig with a trowel. They also practice sifting buckets of soil through screens. Any objects in the soil remain on the screen while the dirt falls through. Finally, they learn to record what they find and where they find it.

Books for Professional Development

Gilmore, Barry. *Plagiarism: Why It Happens and How to Prevent It.* Portsmouth, NH. Heinemann, 2008. With the digital revolution, the availability of online source material has further increased teachers' concerns about plagiarism in the classroom. Gilmore's book provides classroom-tested strategies for increasing students' understanding of plagiarism, setting expectations for academic honesty, learning prewriting and research techniques that encourage originality, and reducing or eliminating the incidence of plagiarism.

Fitzgibbon, Kathleen. *Teaching With Wikis, Blogs, Podcasts & More.* New York. Scholastic, 2010. For those who are new to the world of wikis, blogs, and other online tools, Fitzgibbon's book is a valuable resource that shows how using digital resources helps teachers and students alike thrive in today's classroom.

Strategies for Writers Online
Go to **www.sfw.z-b.com** for additional online resources for students and teachers.

Another place to learn about archaeology is a website called "Dr. Dig." This Web site is about archaeology in general, but the advice on the site can help backyard archaeologists, too. For example, Dr. Dig suggests using tools that fit the location and the job in order to avoid damaging artifacts. Dr. Dig once used a tongue depressor to excavate some flint! "As a general rule," says Dr. Dig, "small tools are used to uncover small artifacts, large-scale tools for large artifacts." He also cautions amateurs to contact their local utility companies before starting to dig. This will protect any buried wires on their property.

Archaeology requires patience and attention to detail. It requires caring about the past and the future. Many backyard archaeologists love their hobby for these reasons. Some professional archaeologists worry about what might be lost if the amateurs are not careful. However, amateurs can learn how to dig the right way by consulting experts and working as volunteers in the field. As Dr. Dig might say to backyard archaeologists, every tarnished button counts, so be careful!

Organization—strong conclusion

Works Consulted

"Archaeology." *Encyclopedia Britannica*. 2007 ed.

Ask Dr. Dig. DIG Magazine. 2006, accessed April 5, 2012, http://www.digonsite.com/drdig.

Atkin, Ross. "Kids dig history." *Christian Science Monitor*. 23 Nov. 1999: 22.

Haas, Jan. Personal interview. 12 Sept. 2001.

Kersting, Jane. "The PIT Experience: Life Lessons and So Much More." *Passport in Time*. 6 Dec. 2006, accessed April 6, 2012, http://www.passportintime.com.

Proeller, Marie. "Backyard Archaeology." *Country Living*. Aug. 1998: 40.

Multiple and varied sources, fully cited

Tompkins, Gail E. *Teaching Writing: Balancing Process and Product*. 4th ed. Upper Saddle River. Prentice Hall, 2003. This book contains information on teaching writing strategies for grades K–8, covering prewriting, drafting, revising, editing, and publishing through writing workshop, literature focus units, and thematic units. Numerous authentic children's writing samples are interspersed throughout the material.

Overmeyer, Mark. *What Student Writing Teaches Us: Formative Assessment in the Writing Workshop*. Portland, ME. Stenhouse, 2009. Assessing writing is not an easy endeavor. This book looks at the role of formative assessment within the context of writing workshop. Overmeyer provides various tools for analyzing elementary and middle school writing from the perspective of the teacher and the student.

CCSS Common Core State Standards

W.6.2.f: Provide a concluding statement or section that follows from the information or explanation presented. **W.6.8:** Gather relevant information from multiple print and digital sources; assess the credibility of each source; and quote or paraphrase the data and conclusions of others while avoiding plagiarism and providing basic bibliographic information for sources.

Analyze
the Model

Week 1 • Day 3

Student Objectives

• Learn to read a rubric.
  (pp. 182–183)

Use the Rubric

Explain the Rubric Explain that a rubric is a tool for planning, improving, and assessing a piece of writing. Tell students that a rubric helps a writer focus on key elements, or traits, in writing (**Ideas, Organization, Voice, Word Choice, Sentence Fluency, Conventions,** and **Presentation**).

Tell students that the columns on page 182 describe a paper that is quite good but perhaps needs some polishing. The columns on page 183 describe a paper that needs quite a lot of improvement.

Discuss the Rubric Guide students in a discussion of the rubric. Read the descriptors that go with each trait. Discuss the difference between columns to be sure students fully understand the point system. Explain that a rubric helps to inform and improve writing by giving writers a clear description of each trait. Remind students to keep the rubric in mind when they write their own research report and again as they revise and edit it.

Online Writing Center

Provides a variety of **interactive rubrics,** including 4-, 5-, and 6-point models.

Rubric

Use this 6-point rubric to plan and score a research report.

	6	5	4	
Ideas	The report focuses on one clearly defined, well-researched topic. Relevant facts and concrete details develop the topic thoroughly.	The report focuses on one topic. Most details and facts are relevant to the topic.	The report focuses on one topic, but it may be too narrow or broad. Some details are irrelevant or lacking.	
Organization	The structure of the writing is perfect for the topic and enhances the reader's understanding. A thoughtful conclusion follows from the information presented.	The structure of the writing works well. The conclusion follows logically from the information presented.	The structure of the writing is easy to follow. The conclusion works.	
Voice	Active voice connects to the reader. It is clear the writer cares about the topic.	The writer's knowledge of the topic engages the reader. Active voice is used throughout.	Active voice is used inconsistently at times. The writer occasionally sounds indifferent to the topic.	
Word Choice	Domain-specific content vocabulary informs the reader about the topic and is clearly defined.	Some domain-specific content vocabulary words are used and defined.	Domain-specific content vocabulary words are used, but several are not defined.	
Sentence Fluency	Sentences are lively and highly varied in length and structure. They move the reader along.	There is noticeable variety in sentence length and style. The writing is easy to read.	There is some variety in sentence length and style. The writing is easy to read.	
Conventions	The report uses a variety of nouns correctly. It is well edited and ready to publish.	A variety of nouns are used correctly. A few errors are present, but they are hard to spot.	Noticeable errors with nouns may distract the reader.	
+ Presentation	Media, such as illustrations and sound, are all well integrated into the report.			

CCSS Common Core State Standards

Research Report

Strategies for Writers was designed to incorporate the Common Core State Standards throughout every unit. By presenting the standards in multiple applications, your students' exposure to them will be ensured.

The rubric and writing strategies for the research report reflect the Informative/Explanatory writing standards. The traits of Ideas and Organization align with standards **W.6.2, W.6.2.a,** and **W.6.b,** which address choosing, introducing, and developing a topic. Standard **W.6.2.f** aligns with Organization by explaining that a concluding statement follows from the information presented. The trait of Word Choice aligns with standard **W.6.2.d,** which emphasizes precise language and domain-specific vocabulary. The trait of Voice reflects standard **W.6.2.e,** which establishes and maintains a formal style.

3	2	1	
The topic is not clearly stated and has to be guessed. Several details are irrelevant or poorly researched.	The topic is unclear and hard to guess. Most details are irrelevant or poorly researched.	The report is not focused on a topic. Facts and details read like an unconnected list.	**Ideas**
Parts of the report are hard to follow. The conclusion could be improved.	The reader often feels lost. The writing is out of order. The conclusion is missing or needs work.	The writing is extremely difficult to follow. The report lacks an opening or a conclusion.	**Organization**
The writer's voice fades in and out. Active voice is used inconsistently.	The writer's interest in the topic rarely comes through. Many sentences should be in the active voice.	It sounds like the writer doesn't care about the topic. Sentences are incorrect or in the passive voice.	**Voice**
A lack of domain-specific words makes it difficult for the reader to understand the topic. Many unfamiliar words are not defined.	Many words are unclear. Poorly defined terms make it hard for the reader to understand the report.	The writer's words are vague and confusing. The reader cannot understand the report.	**Word Choice**
Too many sentences are similar in length and structure. Some are fragments or run-on sentences.	Many sentences are poorly written and repetitious. Fragments, run-ons, and incomplete sentences are present.	The writing lacks complete sentences. Sentences run together and are hard to read.	**Sentence Fluency**
Several noticeable errors with nouns may affect the meaning.	Many errors with nouns interfere with the meaning. Reading takes effort.	The writer struggles with the correct use of nouns. The errors continually interfere with reading.	**Conventions**

See Appendix B for 4-, 5-, and 6-point informative/explanatory rubrics.

The language standards for grade 6 students are addressed during editing and skills practice (**L.6.1–4, L.6.6**). In addition, there are multiple opportunities to address the speaking and listening standards during the writing process. Specifically, students are encouraged to work collaboratively, review key ideas, and demonstrate understanding (**SL.6.1**). Most importantly, this chapter will help students examine a topic and convey information to produce clear and coherent writing (**W.6.4**), improve writing (**W.6.5**), and use technologies to publish and present finished pieces (**W.6.6**). It also provides the opportunity to conduct short research projects (**W.6.7**), gather relevant information from multiple sources (**W.6.8**), draw evidence from texts to support their research (**W.6.9**), and write routinely over extended time frames (**W.6.10**).

Apply the Rubric

Assign Groups Assign students to small groups and ask them to check the model for one trait. One person in each group should be responsible for recording one or two strong examples of the trait as described by the rubric. Ask students to score each trait accordingly for the model. They should be able to support their scores. Note that although the model was written to score high in each trait, students should not assume each trait would receive a 6, the top score. Encourage students to discuss each trait thoroughly before assigning each score.

Reassemble Class Bring the class together and ask one person from each group to report the group's findings to the class. The point of this exercise is less to score the model than it is to practice identifying and evaluating the traits within a piece of writing.

Additional Rubrics Appendix B includes 4-, 5-, and 6-point rubrics that can be used with any piece of informative/explanatory writing. The rubrics are also available as blackline masters, beginning on page T525.

CCSS Common Core State Standards

SL.6.1.b: Follow rules for collegial discussions, set specific goals and deadlines, and define individual roles as needed. **SL.6.1.c:** Pose and respond to specific questions with elaboration and detail by making comments that contribute to the topic, text, or issue under discussion. **SL.6.1.d:** Review the key ideas expressed and demonstrate understanding of multiple perspectives through reflection and paraphrasing.

Analyze
the Model

Student Objectives

- Read a model research report. (pp. 179–181)
- Use the research report rubric. (pp. 182–183)
- Use the model research report to study Ideas, Organization, and Voice. (pp. 184–185)

Study the Model

Assess the Model Have volunteers read aloud each section on pages 184 and 185. Use questions such as the following to discuss each section with students:

- Does Peter Nuan focus on one clearly defined, well-researched topic? (Possible response: Yes, Peter sticks to one very clear topic, amateur archeologists.)

- Are his facts relevant to the topic? (Possible response: Peter uses relevant, accurate facts and concrete details to develop his topic for the reader.)

 Strategies for Writers Online
Go to **www.sfw.z-b.com** for additional online resources for students and teachers.

Research Report

Using the Rubric to Study the Model

Did you notice that the model on pages 179–181 points out some key elements of a research report? As he wrote "Digging Into Backyard Archaeology," Peter Nuan used these elements to help him write a report. He also used the 6-point rubric on pages 182–183 to plan, draft, revise, and edit the writing. A rubric is a great tool for evaluating writing during the writing process.

Now let's use the same rubric to score the model. To do this, we'll focus on each trait separately, starting with Ideas. We'll use the top descriptor for each trait (column 6), along with examples from the model, to help us understand how the traits work together. How would you score Peter on each trait?

Ideas
- The report focuses on one clearly defined, well-researched topic.
- Relevant facts and concrete details develop the topic thoroughly.

Peter sticks to one very clear topic: amateur archeologists. The facts and details he includes are accurate and relevant to his topic. In these sentences, he gives some tips for amateur archaeologists.

[from the writing model]

First, property owners should research their site. Town records may provide facts about former owners. Many libraries and museums may have collections of news clippings and photos. Information about early Native American groups living in the region is usually available at history museums.

184 Informative/Explanatory Writing

English Language Learners

BEGINNING
Main Ideas and Details Write *Italian Food* in the middle of a Web graphic organizer. Ask students to give examples of the different Italian foods they know about. Then write their answers, such as *spaghetti*, *lasagna*, and *gnocchi*, in the next layer of circles. Explain that *Italian food* is the main idea, and the examples are details.

INTERMEDIATE
Outlines Complete the Beginning activity above. Use the information to create an outline for a report about Italian foods. Each of the specific types of food can be the main idea of a paragraph. Discuss the ingredients for each dish. These can be used as the details in the outline. After the outline is created, say, *outline*, and have students repeat the word.

Organization

- The structure of the writing is perfect for the topic and enhances the reader's understanding.
- A thoughtful conclusion follows from the information presented.

Peter organizes his writing perfectly. He opens with an attention-grabbing introduction, includes one or two paragraphs about each of his main points, and then neatly wraps up his report with a strong conclusion. Notice how his conclusion picks up the ideas of his report and wraps them up in an engaging way.

[from the writing model]

However, amateurs can learn how to dig the right way by consulting experts and working as volunteers in the field. As Dr. Dig might say to backyard archaeologists, every tarnished button counts, so be careful!

Voice

- Active voice connects to the reader.
- It is clear the writer cares about the topic.

Peter uses active voice to make the reader feel connected to the information. He could have said, "Patience and attention to detail are required for archaeology. Caring about the past and future are also required." Instead, he chose to make stronger statements in the active voice. You can see, too, that he cares about his topic and about amateur archaeologists learning to do it right.

[from the writing model]

Archaeology requires patience and attention to detail. It requires caring about the past and the future. Many backyard archaeologists love their hobby for these reasons. Some professional archaeologists worry about what might be lost if the amateurs are not careful. However, amateurs can learn how to dig the right way by consulting experts and working as volunteers in the field. As Dr. Dig might say to backyard archaeologists, every tarnished button counts, so be careful!

Research Report **185**

- How does Peter organize his report? (Possible responses: Peter uses a structure that is perfect for the topic and enhances the reader's understanding. He opens with a lively introduction and includes one or two paragraphs about each of his main points. A thoughtful conclusion follows from the information he presents.)

- Does Peter use a style and voice that are appropriate for the purpose and audience? (Possible responses: Peter uses an active voice to connect to the reader. It is clear that Peter cares about his topic.)

ADVANCED

Relevant Facts Students must decide if a fact is relevant to the main idea. Give students a main idea, such as *There are many different kinds of Italian foods.* Then list several facts and non-facts, such as *Northern Italians eat creamy sauces, while Southern Italians eat tomato sauces; I absolutely love lasagna; Gnocchi is usually made with potatoes,* and so on. Have students circle the facts that are relevant to the main idea.

ADVANCED HIGH

Credible Sources Have students use print and credible online resources to find several relevant facts that support their topic. Have students write their findings in outline form and use that information to write a paragraph.

CCSS Common Core State Standards

W.6.9: Draw evidence from literary or informational texts to support analysis, reflection, and research. **SL.6.1.b:** Follow rules for collegial discussions, set specific goals and deadlines, and define individual roles as needed. **SL.6.1.c:** Pose and respond to specific questions with elaboration and detail by making comments that contribute to the topic, text, or issue under discussion. **SL.6.1.d:** Review the key ideas expressed and demonstrate understanding of multiple perspectives through reflection and paraphrasing.

Analyze the Model

Student Objectives

- Read a model research report. (pp. 179–181)
- Use the research report rubric. (pp. 182–183)
- Use the model research report to study Word Choice, Sentence Fluency, and Conventions. (pp. 186–187)

Continue Discussing the Traits

Use questions such as the following to discuss the traits analyzed on pages 186 and 187:

- Did Peter correctly use and define domain-specific content vocabulary? (Possible responses: Yes, Peter knows that the language in a research report has to be accurate. Whenever he uses a domain-specific word, he gives a detailed explanation.)

- Does the model flow smoothly? What makes the report easy to follow? (Possible response: Peter creates good flow by mixing up the structure with sentences of different lengths and patterns. This helps make the report lively and easy to read.)

- Did Peter use nouns correctly? (Possible responses: Yes, Peter uses a variety of nouns correctly throughout his report. I noticed that he capitalizes all proper nouns, proper adjectives, abbreviations, and initials.)

Strategies for Writers Online

Go to **www.sfw.z-b.com** for additional online resources for students and teachers.

Word Choice

- Domain-specific content vocabulary informs the reader about the topic and is clearly defined.

For the report to offer clear explanations to the reader, the language has to be accurate and describe the details well. When Peter uses a domain-specific word, he gives a detailed explanation to make sure the reader knows what it means.

[from the writing model]

Several government agencies offer a chance to work in the field. For example, Passport in Time (PIT) is a volunteer program of the U.S. Forest Service. Its aim is to preserve landmarks and historical sites in national forests. PIT volunteers work with archaeologists on sites around the country.

Sentence Fluency

- Sentences are lively and highly varied in length and structure. They move the reader along.

Peter does a good job of making his sentences lively. Look at how he does it in the following paragraphs. He uses short sentences and long sentences. Some sentences start with dependent clauses; some do not. Peter mixes up the structure of his sentences, too, using different patterns throughout the report.

[from the writing model]

It had been buried six inches deep in Jan's backyard in Baltimore, Maryland. She dug it up near an old washhouse. The washhouse had been built in the mid-1700s. Later, Jan learned the button was from the Colonial period.

As a backyard archaeologist, Jan was pleased with her find. Backyard archaeologists are amateurs. Like the professionals, they search for and study objects made by people long ago.

186 Informative/Explanatory Writing

Technology Tip — for 21st Century Literacies

Ask students to use a tool like Tildee to create a how-to video depicting how they locate and use online information. Screen several videos and discuss as a class, identifying the areas of similarity and patterns that emerge. These can also serve as good materials to use during student conferences or to demonstrate growth over time.

See **www.sfw.z-b.com** for further information about and links to these websites and tools.

Conventions

- The report uses a variety of nouns correctly.
- It is well edited and ready to publish.

I couldn't find any mistakes in spelling, punctuation, or capitalization in Peter's report. He even wrote all the proper nouns and proper adjectives correctly!

[from the writing model]

A dig in the backyards of Alexandria, Virginia, uncovered items from more than a century ago. They included marbles, medicine bottles, and pottery shards. Before the Civil War, free African American people lived in the area. "By studying these artifacts, we were able to trace the development of this neighborhood and the lifestyles of its inhabitants," said the city's archaeologist, Pamela J. Cressey, Ph.D.

➕ Presentation Media, such as illustrations and sound, are all well integrated into the report.

 My Turn!

I'm going to write a research report on my own topic. With the help of the rubric and good writing strategies, I think I'll write a good one. Follow along and see how I do it!

Research Report **187**

Differentiating Instruction

ENRICHMENT
Use the Rubric to Score a Model The research report rubric could be used to evaluate a scientific article. Find one or more articles for students to evaluate. Have students work in pairs to evaluate an article on all six traits. Each pair must come to a consensus on the scores.

REINFORCEMENT
Active Versus Passive Voice Choose one sentence from the model to rewrite in the passive voice. For example, the first sentence could be rewritten: *With a toothbrush, the dirt was carefully removed by Jan Haas from the lump in her hand.* Use the two sentences to discuss the difference between active voice (the subject does the action) and the passive voice (the subject is acted upon).

Presentation Explain that Presentation is just as important as the other traits. Appearance should be considered as students prepare their final copies. Neatness is always a priority, and text should be clearly handwritten in pen or typed, using a few readable fonts. White space should be used to create neat margins of an appropriate width. All paragraphs should be indented (using the tab key if typed), and the title and writer's name should be centered at the top of the first page or on a separate title page. All media should be integrated into the report. Encourage students to remember to add these visual elements as they prepare the final copy.

Think About the Traits Once students have discussed the model research report, ask them which traits they think are most important. All the traits are important in every piece of writing, but some traits stand out more in some genres than in others. Students might say that in a research report **Organization** is very important because if the information is poorly organized, the report makes no sense. Others may think that **Word Choice** is more important because domain-specific vocabulary informs the reader.

CCSS Common Core State Standards
R/Inf.6.2: Determine a central idea of a text and how it is conveyed through particular details; provide a summary of the text distinct from personal opinions or judgments. R/Inf.6.4: Determine the meaning of words and phrases as they are used in a text, including figurative, connotative, and technical meanings. SL.6.1.d: Review the key ideas expressed and demonstrate understanding of multiple perspectives through reflection and paraphrasing.

Research Report **T187**

Write
a Research Report

Week 2 • Day 1

Student Objectives

• Read and understand a prewriting strategy. (pp. 188–189)

Prewrite

Focus on Ideas

Collect Information Read aloud page 188. Remind students that when they first met Justin, they learned about his interests and hobbies and discussed how these would influence topics he chose to write about. Justin chose to turn his love for Indian food into a topic for his report. Point out that Justin narrowed his topic when he realized it was too large to cover in his report. He realized that he needed to be more specific; otherwise, the report would be too broad and unfocused.

Tell students they will choose a topic and make source notes for their own research report. Ask students to think about their interests, hobbies, and other activities that might direct them toward a suitable writing topic. Tell students that after choosing topics, they will have to do research to gather information to share with their audience. Remind them that they will need to use the encyclopedia and at least two other sources to research the topic.

 Strategies for Writers Online
Go to **www.sfw.z-b.com** for additional online resources for students and teachers.

Prewrite   Focus on Ideas

The Rubric Says	The report focuses on one clearly defined, well-researched topic.
Writing Strategy	Use an encyclopedia and at least two other sources to research the topic.

As soon as I heard we were going to write research reports, I thought of India because I love Indian food! I figured there was a lot about India that would be interesting to my classmates. They will be my audience.

When I looked up the word *India* in an encyclopedia, I found a long list of topics. They included India's people, geography, climate, natural resources, religions, history, government—the list went on and on. I needed to narrow my topic!

I noticed there was a section about Indian food. Maybe I could focus on just that area. But then I realized that even Indian food was too broad a topic for my report. There are so many kinds!

I learned from the encyclopedia that people in different parts of India eat different dishes. I decided to narrow my topic to regional foods of India. I think my classmates will find that interesting. They love anything that has to do with food!

188 Informative/Explanatory Writing

English Language Learners

BEGINNING/INTERMEDIATE
Active vs. Passive Voice Show students a photo of a student playing a sport and another photo of a student who isn't doing anything. Point to the first picture and say, *He is active. He is doing something.* For the second picture, say, *He is passive. He isn't doing anything.* Introduce an active sentence, such as *He is painting a picture.* Ask students to tell the subject (*He*) and what the subject is doing (*painting a picture*). Repeat the process for the passive sentence *A picture is painted by him.* Point out that in the passive sentence, the subject (*A picture*) is not doing any action.

In addition to the encyclopedia, I checked two other reliable sources. As I read, I took notes on note cards. Each card had one piece of information and its source. Here are two of my note cards.

Regional Food in India—South India

source: Voros, Sharon. "Fare of the Country; The Vegetarian Snacks of South India." http://query.nytimes.com (April 19, 2012)

foods made from rice:

"Idlis, which resemble spongy dumplings, are always served in pairs. Dosas are crepelike pancakes served neatly rolled."

Regional Food in India—Introduction

source: Kanitkar, V. P. Indian Food and Drink. New York: The Bookwright Press, 1987.

Religion and climate are two things that determine food habits in each region.

Apply

Choose a topic and look it up in the encyclopedia. Narrow the topic. Then check two more reliable sources and start making note cards.

Research Report **189**

ADVANCED/ADVANCED HIGH

Active vs. Passive Voice Repeat the activity above. Have each student write four sentences, two passive and two active. Review as a class, and have students tell why each sentence is active or passive.

Compile Information Explain that when surveying sources, students should look carefully at the information. Will it maintain a narrow focus? Is it relevant and reliable? Justin checked three reliable sources. How do you know if a source is reliable? (Possible responses: It contains current factual information that can be verified in other sources. The authors are known to be experts in the subject.) Students will also use note cards to take notes. Justin's cards include a category heading, one piece of information, and clear source citations. Remind students that they will cite their sources in a works consulted section at the end of the report. Display or distribute the school's preferred format for citing sources.

✎ **Writer's Term** _____

Note Card A note card forces students to record information in a succinct way. The advantage of note cards is that they can be reorganized easily.

CCSS Common Core State Standards

W.6.2: Write informative/explanatory texts to examine a topic and convey ideas, concepts, and information through the selection, organization, and analysis of relevant content. **W.6.2.a:** Introduce a topic; organize ideas, concepts, and information, using strategies such as definition, classification, comparison/contrast, and cause/effect; include formatting (e.g., headings), graphics (e.g., charts, tables), and multimedia when useful to aiding comprehension. **W.6.7:** Conduct short research projects to answer a question, drawing on several sources and refocusing the inquiry when appropriate. **W.6.8:** Gather relevant information from multiple print and digital sources; assess the credibility of each source; and quote or paraphrase the data and conclusions of others while avoiding plagiarism and providing basic bibliographic information for sources.

Write
a Research Report

Week 2 • Day 2

Student Objectives

- Make an Outline to organize notes. *(pp. 190–191)*

Prewrite

Focus on Organization

Organize Ideas To organize his notes, Justin used an Outline, which is a good choice for a research report. The structure of the Outline allows the writer to organize main ideas and related details so that they are grouped together visually. Help students understand how an Outline categorizes by explaining that each Roman numeral section moves from a general statement to specific, supporting details. In this way, an Outline helps form the paragraphs in the body of a piece of writing.

✏ Writer's Term _____

Outline Justin's Outline uses full sentences. Some outlines use only phrases. The advantage to sentences is that they can be placed right into the draft.

▸ Online Writing Center

 Provides **interactive graphic organizers** as well as a variety of graphic organizers in PDF format.

Prewrite

Focus on Organization

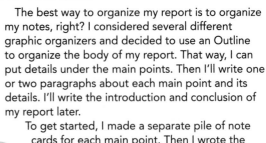

The Rubric Says	The structure of the writing is perfect for the topic and enhances the reader's understanding.
Writing Strategy	Make an outline to organize your notes.

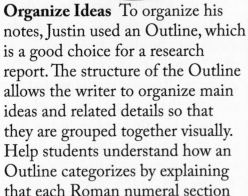

The best way to organize my report is to organize my notes, right? I considered several different graphic organizers and decided to use an Outline to organize the body of my report. That way, I can put details under the main points. Then I'll write one or two paragraphs about each main point and its details. I'll write the introduction and conclusion of my report later.

To get started, I made a separate pile of note cards for each main point. Then I wrote the Outline you see on the next page.

✏ Writer's Term _____

Outline

An **Outline** organizes notes by main points and supporting details. Each main point has a Roman numeral. The supporting details under each main point have capital letters. Any information listed under a supporting detail gets a number.

190 Informative/Explanatory Writing

Outline

Regional Food in India

I. Regional foods are determined by many things.
   A. One main influence is religion.
      1. Most people are vegetarian Hindus.
      2. Immigrants from other religions who eat meat influence the Hindu diet.
   B. India's many different climates also affect food production.
II. The North has a strong Muslim influence.
   A. Muslims live in the North.
      1. They eat lamb, chicken, beef, and fish.
      2. Many do not eat pork.
   B. Dates, nuts, and milk are used in sweets (desserts).
   C. Hindu bread and vegetarian dishes are also common.
III. Food in the South has a more traditional Hindu style.
   A. Rice is cooked in many ways.
   B. Two popular dishes are dosas and idlis.
   C. Vegetables served with rice include soupy dishes made from peas or beans.
IV. Coastal Indian food has many influences.
   A. Fish dishes are common and varied.
   B. They include carp with chilies, prawns with mustard seed, and fish curry.
   C. Some foods are made with coconut.

Reflect
How will the Outline help Justin write his research report?

Apply
Look through your note cards. Then organize your notes into an Outline.

Ask students to study the organizer on page 191. Then ask why an Outline is an effective tool when writing a research report. (Possible response: An Outline is an excellent tool for organizing a research report because it breaks down the topic in a very detailed, organized way.) Have a volunteer read aloud Justin's words on page 190. Note that he plans to rely on his Outline as he writes the body of his report. Remind students to refer to Justin's outline on page 191 as they use their note cards to draft their own.

Conferencing

PEER TO PEER Give pairs of students several questions to discuss about their research. For example: *Where did you find the best information? How did you choose your sources?*

PEER GROUPS Separate students into small groups. Instruct them to discuss the importance of organizing their note cards and share tips on keeping track of their sources to create a clear, well-organized outline.

TEACHER-LED To demonstrate the importance of a focused Outline, create an abbreviated one for a research topic you know well, leaving out important details or mixing up the order of main points. Discuss how the missing or misplaced information would affect the writing of an effective research report.

CCSS **C**ommon **C**ore **S**tate **S**tandards

W.6.2: Write informative/explanatory texts to examine a topic and convey ideas, concepts, and information through the selection, organization, and analysis of relevant content. **W.6.2.a:** Introduce a topic; organize ideas, concepts, and information, using strategies such as definition, classification, comparison/contrast, and cause/effect; include formatting (e.g., headings), graphics (e.g., charts, tables), and multimedia when useful to aiding comprehension. **W.6.2.b:** Develop the topic with relevant facts, definitions, concrete details, quotations, or other information and examples. **W.6.7:** Conduct short research projects to answer a question, drawing on several sources and refocusing the inquiry when appropriate.

Write
a Research Report

Week 2 • Day 3

Student Objectives

- Use an Outline to begin writing. (p. 192)

Draft

Focus on Voice

Draft a Research Report Remind students that drafting is a chance to get ideas on paper without worrying about revising and editing the writing.

Read page 192; then ask students to read Justin's draft on page 193 independently. After reading, discuss whether Justin's draft includes a strong introduction, body, and conclusion. How does using an active voice make his report come alive? (Possible responses: The subject is doing the action. The writing is direct and to the point.) Emphasize that Justin repeatedly refers to the rubric as he writes. Encourage students to use the rubric and writing strategy to guide their writing and their Outlines to organize their reports.

✏️ Writer's Term _____

Active Voice and Passive Voice
As always, the audience and purpose determine the writer's voice. Most of the time, active voice is appropriate. However, there are times when passive voice is a better choice.

Online Writing Center

 Provides student eBooks with an **interactive writing pad** for drafting, revising, editing, and publishing.

T192 Informative/Explanatory Writing

Draft

Focus on **Voice**

The Rubric Says Active voice connects to the reader. It is clear the writer cares about the topic.

Writing Strategy Use active voice.

✏️ Writer's Term _____

Active Voice and Passive Voice
A verb is in **active voice** if the subject of the sentence is doing the action. A verb is in **passive voice** if the subject is being acted upon.
Active Voice: **George ate his lunch.**
Passive Voice: **The lunch was eaten by George.**

Now I'll write one or two paragraphs for each point in my Outline. This will be the body of my report. I'll make sure there's plenty of good information to interest my audience.

I know this is a draft and I will be revising it. But I can start now to think about how I want my voice to sound. In a report, I want my information to sound strong, like I know what I'm talking about. Active voice will help me do that.

Later I'll add an engaging introduction and a strong conclusion. I'll also watch out for subject-verb agreement. Look at the start of my draft on the next page.

192 Informative/Explanatory Writing

Differentiating Instruction

ENRICHMENT
Expand the Research Challenge students to find out about another culture's food. Ask why certain foods, such as rice, fish, or even insects, are prevalent in areas around the globe. How do climate and location affect the diets of the people who live there? How has the culture evolved around that food? To get students started, recommend a reliable website, such as www.nationalgeographic.com.

REINFORCEMENT
Find the Voice Gather examples of writing by several different authors. Read aloud excerpts from each and guide students to notice the way each writer sounds. Ask questions to help students focus on what makes up the voice. Is it the word choice, the sentence structures, the ideas, or a little of each?

[DRAFT]

    The foods people eat in each region of India are determined by **[active voice]** many things. Religion is a major factor. In India, 80 percent of the population is hindu, and strict hindus are vegetarians and **do not** eat meat. Over the centuries, Immigrants whom practice other religions have come to India. Many of these people do eat meat. **They have** influenced the traditional hindu diet in some places.

    Another big thing is climate. The type of food production of a region is affected by the climate there. For example, rice is grown mostly in the tropical south and the rainy northeast (I heard that people's personalities can change during the long monsoon season), and wheat is an important crop in the dry northern plains.

[active voice]   The North has a strong muslim influence. Muslims eat lamb, chicken, beef, and fish but not pork. One favorite dish is lamb kebab. Lamb kebab is pieces of mildly spiced meat roasted on skewers. Another favorite is tandoori chicken, spiced chicken cooked in a clay oven. Dates, nuts, and milk are in many deserts called milk sweets. The milk **comes** from water buffalos. They are the main source of milk in India. Kheer is a milk sweet similar to rice pudding.

Reflect

Read the beginning of Justin's draft. Do the details hold the reader's interest? How does the active voice strengthen the writing?

Apply

Use your Outline to write a draft. Include concrete details and use active voice to keep your writing strong.

Research Report **193**

Write
a Research Report

Week 2 • Day 4

Student Objectives

• Complete a draft. *(p. 193)*

Finish the Draft It is important that students are given ample time to draft research reports, possibly several days. As conferencing is important throughout the writing process, be sure to plan time for periodic peer-to-peer, peer group, and teacher-led conferences. Remind students that this is the time for getting their ideas down in a knowledgeable and enthusiastic way. Assure them that they will have plenty of time to revise and edit their writing later.

Conferencing

PEER TO PEER During drafting, have pairs of students exchange drafts. Encourage them to provide helpful comments regarding the organization of the writing. (Does the writer open with an attention-grabbing introduction? Is the body of information organized so it's easy to follow?) Be sure the reviewing focus is not on mechanics at this time.

PEER GROUPS Have students form small groups and take turns reading sections of their research reports aloud. Have other students provide helpful commentary to strengthen the reports, using the research report rubric to guide their feedback.

TEACHER-LED Read aloud the draft excerpt on page 193. Ask volunteers to comment on examples of Voice in the excerpt. Encourage students to keep these comments in mind when writing their own drafts.

CCSS **C**ommon **C**ore **S**tate **S**tandards

W.6.5: With some guidance and support from peers and adults, develop and strengthen writing as needed by planning, revising, editing, rewriting, or trying a new approach. **SL.6.1:** Engage effectively in a range of collaborative discussions (one-on-one, in groups, and teacher-led) with diverse partners on *grade 6 topics, texts, and issues*, building on others' ideas and expressing their own clearly. **SL.6.1.b:** Follow rules for collegial discussions, set specific goals and deadlines, and define individual roles as needed. **SL.6.1.c:** Pose and respond to specific questions with elaboration and detail by making comments that contribute to the topic, text, or issue under discussion. **L.6.3.b:** Maintain consistency in style and tone.

Write
a Research Report

Week 2 • Day 5

Student Objectives

• Revise to take out unrelated details or facts. *(p. 194)*

Revise

Focus on Ideas

Take Out Unrelated Details Ask a volunteer to read Justin's words and the excerpt before the revision. Then discuss the importance of using only relevant, solid facts and details in a research report. Justin knows that his message will be compromised if he includes unnecessary information. He read the writing strategy and found a place in his draft where he had included information that was not necessary.

Ask a volunteer to read the excerpt with the revision. Have students talk about how removing the unrelated detail improves the writing. **(Possible response: The detail was unrelated to the topic and could have thrown readers off track.)** Direct students to read their drafts to make sure they include only relevant details and facts that develop their topic.

 Strategies for Writers Online
Go to **www.sfw.z-b.com** for additional online resources for students and teachers.

Revise   Focus on Ideas

The Rubric Says	Relevant facts and concrete details develop the topic thoroughly.
Writing Strategy	Take out unrelated details or facts.

I used my outline to write a draft of my report. As I wrote, I tried to keep my readers in mind and explain all my points clearly, using only relevant, solid details and facts that are related to what I am saying. I know that my message will be weakened if I include information that isn't necessary. I see in this section that I have some extra information. Does the paragraph sound better without it?

[DRAFT]

Another big thing is climate. The type of food production of a region is affected by the climate there. For example, rice is grown mostly in the tropical south and the rainy northeast (I heard that people's personalities can change during the long monsoon season), and wheat is an important crop in the dry northern plains.

[removed unrelated detail]

Apply

Are there any places where you included unnecessary information? Be sure to take out any details or facts that are not relevant to the topic.

194 Informative/Explanatory Writing

English Language Learners

BEGINNING/INTERMEDIATE

Plagiarize/Paraphrase Explain the term *plagiarize*. Ask, *Is it okay to copy someone else's writing?* Repeat for *paraphrase*. Read a language-level appropriate newspaper article. Cut up the article and give students different sections. Have students write a paraphrase of their portion of the article. Then have a volunteer read the paraphrased article to the class.

ADVANCED/ADVANCED HIGH

Paraphrasing Ask a volunteer to define the terms *plagiarize* and *paraphrase*. Clarify as necessary. Have two students read the same short newspaper article. Separately, have them rewrite the article in their own words. Have students compare paraphrases and decide which one was most appropriate. Discuss as a group.

Revise — Focus on Word Choice

The Rubric Says Domain-specific content vocabulary informs the reader about the topic and is clearly defined.

Writing Strategy Define all domain-specific words.

The rubric says to use and define domain-specific content vocabulary. *Domain-specific words* are words that relate to a specialized area of knowledge, such as cooking. I understand that some of my readers may not be familiar with the food-related terms I include. If I don't properly explain the terms, my readers won't fully understand my report. Look how I added a definition of *dahl*. Does it help you better understand what dahl is?

[DRAFT]

Two popular South Indian foods are made from rice. Dosas are thin rice-flour pancakes. Idlis are steamed rice dumplings. Vegetables served with rice include dahl , which is a soupy dish made from split peas or beans.

[defined domain-specific word]

Reflect
How does Justin's revision help you connect to his writing?

Apply
Define any terms that you think readers may not understand.

Research Report **195**

Conferencing

PEER TO PEER Have pairs of students exchange drafts. Have each reviewer offer helpful feedback with different ways to strengthen Ideas, Word Choice, and Sentence Fluency, using the rubric and revising lessons to guide their response.

PEER GROUPS Have students form small groups and take turns reading sections of their drafts aloud. Have group members identify topic-related words that need definitions.

TEACHER-LED Conference with individual students about their drafts. Use comments and questions to focus each student's attention on areas of revision. For example: *This part is not clear to me. What else can you tell me about this point? What other word can you use here?*

Write
a Research Report

Week 3 • Day 1

Student Objectives

- Revise to define all domain-specific words. *(p. 195)*

Revise

Focus on Word Choice

Define Domain-Specific Words
Have a volunteer read Justin's words about **Word Choice**. Emphasize that the rubric says to use and define domain-specific content vocabulary. Justin realizes that some readers may be unfamiliar with some terms related to Indian food. He knows that he needs to define these domain-specific words to help readers understand his report.

Have one volunteer read the excerpt with the revisions and another volunteer read the revised excerpt. Discuss why students should explain words related to their topics. (Possible responses: Defining content vocabulary clarifies the writer's ideas and shows respect for the reader. Definitions assure that the reader understands the report.) Direct students to read their drafts to make sure they have explained all words related to their topic.

CCSS Common Core State Standards
W.6.2.d: Use precise language and domain-specific vocabulary to inform about or explain the topic.
R/Inf.6.4: Determine the meaning of words and phrases as they are used in a text, including figurative, connotative, and technical meanings. **L.6.6:** Acquire and use accurately grade-appropriate general academic and domain-specific words and phrases; gather vocabulary knowledge when considering a word or phrase important to comprehension or expression.

Research Report **T195**

Write
a Research Report

Week 3 • Day 2

Student Objectives

• Revise to use sentences of different lengths and structures. (p. 196)

Revise

Focus on Sentence Fluency

Write Lively Sentences Have students read Justin's words and note the changes he made to his draft. Explain that when sharing information from sources, it is easy to pack too much information into too few sentences. Caution students that long, wordy sentences can make the writing hard to understand and test the reader's patience.

Remind students of ways to vary sentences; for example, start with a phrase or a clause, use different structures (e.g., compound, complex, compound-complex), use different types (e.g., declarative, interrogative), combine short sentences to make long ones, or break apart long sentences to make short ones.

Have students check their drafts for sentence variety. Explain that they may have to revise some sentences multiple times in order to achieve the right mix of sentences.

Online Writing Center

Provides **interactive proofreading activities** for each genre.

Revise

The Rubric Says	Sentences are lively and highly varied in length and structure. They move the reader along.
Writing Strategy	Use sentences of different lengths and structures.

Focus on **Sentence Fluency**

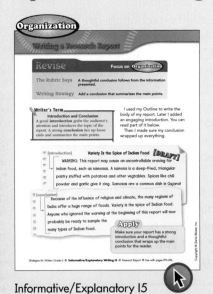

According to the rubric, I should use lively sentences that vary in length and structure. When I reread this section of my report, I realized I wasn't doing that at all. Many of my sentences are the same length, and they follow the same pattern. Look at how I rewrote this part of my report to spice up the sentences!

[DRAFT]

[changed sentences for variety]

Coastal indian food has many influences. ~~People on the coast of~~
Naturally, people there ~~live near rivers and the bay of Bengal~~
~~indid~~ eat a lot of fish. The residents of west Bengal ~~eat fish from the~~
enjoy   Another favorite Bengali recipe is
~~rivers, too~~. They ~~like~~ carp cooked with chilies. ~~They also like~~ prawns,

which are large shrimp, spiced with mustard seeds.
[changed sentences for variety]

Apply

Do a lot of your sentences sound alike? Are too many of them a similar length? Vary your sentences, and make your writing more lively!

196 Informative/Explanatory Writing

Optional Revising Lessons

Organization

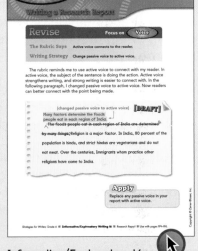

Informative/Explanatory 15

Voice

Informative/Explanatory 16

Go to ⇨ **Strategies for Writers Grade 6 CD-ROM**

Edit — Focus on Conventions

The Rubric Says	The report uses a variety of nouns correctly. It is well edited and ready to publish.
Writing Strategy	Make sure proper nouns and proper adjectives are capitalized correctly.

✏️ **Writer's Term**

Proper Nouns and Proper Adjectives
Proper nouns name a specific person, place, thing, or idea. **Proper adjectives** are formed from proper nouns.

Now I'll check my spelling, grammar, and punctuation. I'll make sure I capitalized and punctuated proper nouns and proper adjectives correctly.

[capitalized proper noun]   [capitalized proper adjective]   **[DRAFT]**

Food in the south has a more traditional hindu style. Rice is prepared in many ways. VoPo Kanitkar, author of <u>Indian Food and Drink</u>, says "Rice grains simply boiled may appear to us to be a poor meal, but different processes like grinding, pounding, steaming, and frying transform rice and other cereals into tasty dishes."

[capitalized proper initials]

Reflect

Do Justin's sentence revisions make his writing more enjoyable to read? Has he corrected every error?

Apply — Conventions

Edit your draft for grammar, spelling, punctuation, and capitalization. Be sure to check proper nouns and proper adjectives.

For more practice capitalizing and punctuating proper nouns and adjectives, use the exercises on the next two pages.

Research Report 197

Related Grammar Practice

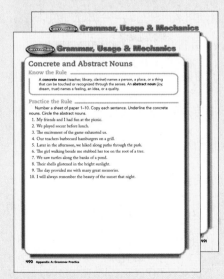

Student Edition pages 490, 491

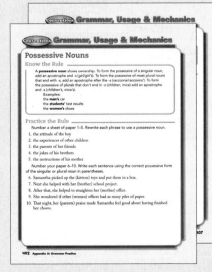

Student Edition pages 492, 507

Go to ➡️ **Appendix A: Grammar Practice**

Student Objectives

- Edit for correct capitalization of proper nouns and proper adjectives. (p. 197)

Edit

Focus on  Conventions

Capitalize Proper Nouns and Proper Adjectives Point out that in research report writing, formal names and sources need to be reported accurately. Read the information in the Writer's Term box and remind students to check their reports for capitalization of proper nouns and proper adjectives. Use the mini-lessons on pages 198 and 199 for students having problems with capitalization and punctuation of proper nouns and adjectives. Have students complete the exercises on pages 198 and 199 in their books.

✏️ **Writer's Term**

Proper Nouns and Proper Adjectives It is important to capitalize and punctuate proper nouns and proper adjectives correctly. Errors can confuse the reader, misrepresent credible sources, and cast doubts on the quality of the writer's research.

CCSS **Common Core State Standards**
W.6.5: With some guidance and support from peers and adults, develop and strengthen writing as needed by planning, revising, editing, rewriting, or trying a new approach **L.6.1:** Demonstrate command of the conventions of standard English grammar and usage when writing or speaking. **L.6.3.a:** Vary sentence patterns for meaning, reader/listener interest, and style.

Conventions

Mini-Lesson

Student Objectives

• Use different kinds of nouns correctly. *(p. 198)*

Kinds of Nouns

Read the information in Know the Rule. Then write the following sentences on the board:

• *Yesterday I went to a great museum.*

• *It is called the National Museum of the American Indian.*

• *This is the first national museum dedicated expressly to Native Americans.*

• *The museum's artifacts were assembled by George Gustav Heye.*

Ask students to identify the different kinds of nouns in each sentence.

(*museum*-common-singular)

(*National Museum of the American Indian*-proper-singular)

(*museum*-common-singular; *Native Americans*-proper-plural)

(*museum's*-common-possessive; *artifacts*-common-plural; *George Gustav Heye*-proper-singular)

Point out that in each of these cases, the proper noun is capitalized.

Online Writing Center

 Provides **interactive grammar games** and **practice activities** in student eBook.

T198 Informative/Explanatory Writing

Kinds of Nouns

Know the Rule

A **noun** names a person, a place, a thing, or an idea.
Common Noun: names any person, place, thing, or idea (*sister, museum, dream*)
Proper Noun: names a specific person, place, thing, or idea (*Antoine, Chicago, Presidents' Day*)
Singular Noun: names one person, place, thing, or idea (*bus, library, mouse*)
Plural Noun: names more than one (*buses, libraries, mice*)
Possessive Noun: shows ownership (*bus's, buses', mice's*)

Practice the Rule

Number a separate sheet of paper 1–10. Write the noun(s) in each sentence. Write the type of each noun as well. The number after each sentence tells you how many nouns to look for.

1. Italian cuisine is very popular. (1) common
2. Many meals take little time to prepare. (2) plural, common
3. My aunt's husband is Italian. (2) possessive, common
4. Uncle Tony is from Lombardy. (2) proper, proper
5. This region is also known for its cheeses. (2) common, plural
6. White truffles grow in Tuscany. (2) plural, proper
7. Parts of the coast are known for seafood. (3) plural, common, common
8. Of the three pasta dishes, I prefer my uncle's. (2) plural, possessive
9. Water buffalo's milk is common in some regions. (3) possessive, common, plural
10. The food of Sicily includes many fruits and vegetables. (4) common, proper, plural, plural

---

Related Grammar Practice

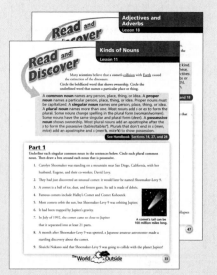

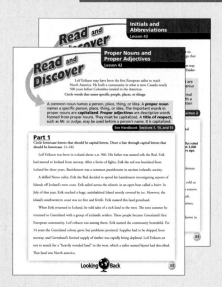

Pages 33, 47, 113, 115

Go to ➡️ **G.U.M. Student Practice Book**

Proper Nouns and Proper Adjectives

Know the Rule

1. Capitalize **proper nouns**.
   Example: My family immigrated to the **United States** from **India**.

2. Capitalize **proper adjectives**.
   Example: Have you ever tasted **Indian** food?

3. Capitalize **titles of respect** before a person's name.
   Example: **Mr.** Raj Chopra gave a presentation to our class.

4. Capitalize **proper abbreviations** (words in addresses, such as *street* and *avenue*, days, months, and parts of business names in informal notes). End the abbreviation with a period.
   Example: Sakthi's address is 247 Fourteenth **St.**

5. Capitalize an **initial** when it replaces the name of a person or place. Follow the initial with a period.
   Example: Our new neighbor's name is **P. R.** Phalke.

Practice the Rule

Number a sheet of paper 1–8. Write the proper nouns and proper adjectives correctly.

1. The indian film industry is over 100 years old.   **Indian**
2. The French Lumière brothers showed six short silent films at a bombay hotel in 1886.   **Bombay**
3. Shortly afterwards, Hiralal Sen and H S. Bhatavdekar started making films.   **H.**
4. india's first talkie, *Alam Ara*, was released in march 1931.   **India's, March**
5. Imperial Film Co was the producer of that film.   **Co.**
6. Years later, mr. S. k. Patil saw the commercial value in many of India's films.   **Mr., K.**
7. In 1995, director Satyajit Ray, from the region of bengal, made the film *pather Panchali*.   **Bengal, Pather**
8. The hollywood influence on Indian cinema is apparent in the musical *Bombay* from 1995.   **Hollywood**

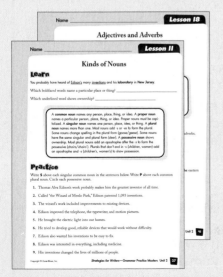
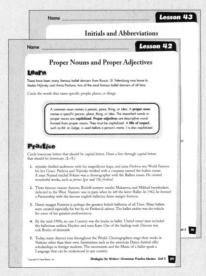

Pages 27, 41, 89, 91

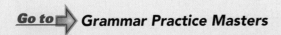

Go to ➡ **Grammar Practice Masters**

Mini-Lesson

Student Objectives

• Use proper nouns and proper adjectives correctly. *(p. 199)*

Proper Nouns and Proper Adjectives

Have students identify the proper nouns, proper adjectives, titles of respect, proper abbreviations, and initials in the Know the Rule examples. (United States, India, Indian, Mr., St., P. R.)

Before assigning the practice, point out that a proper adjective is formed from a proper noun. Write the first two example sentences on the board:

• *My family immigrated to the United States from India.*

Ask students to identify the proper nouns. (United States and India name countries.)

• *Have you ever tasted Indian food?*

Ask students to identify the proper adjective. (Indian describes food.)

Remind students to capitalize proper nouns, proper adjectives, titles of respect, abbreviations, and initials in their research reports. Refer students to their sources to double-check proper nouns and adjectives they use in their reports.

CCSS Common Core State Standards

L.6.1.e: Recognize variations from standard English in their own and others' writing and speaking, and identify and use strategies to improve expression in conventional language. **L.6.2:** Demonstrate command of the conventions of standard English capitalization, punctuation, and spelling when writing. **L.6.4.c:** Consult reference materials (e.g., dictionaries, glossaries, thesauruses), both print and digital to find the pronunciation of a word or determine or clarify its precise meaning or its part of speech.

Write
a Research Report

Week 3 • Day 4

Student Objectives

- Discuss preparation for publishing and presentation. *(p. 200)*
- Use a final editing checklist to publish their work. *(p. 200)*

Publish +Presentation

Publishing Strategy Ask students if they like Justin's choice for sharing his report as part of a multimedia presentation. Then have students talk about ways Justin could enhance his report. (Possible responses: add visuals, animation, and sound elements) Also discuss the elements of an oral presentation: practicing the presentation, speaking loudly and clearly, maintaining eye contact, and knowing the equipment and materials well.

To prepare their final copies, have students use the final checklist on page 200, as Justin did, or make one of their own. Remind students to include a works consulted list at the end of their reports, as Justin did. Refer them to the models on pages 181 and 203 for examples of citations. Or, distribute the citation format required by your school.

Strategies for Writers Online
Go to **www.sfw.z-b.com** for additional online resources for students and teachers.

Publish +Presentation

Publishing Strategy	Include my written report as part of a multimedia presentation to the class.
Presentation Strategy	Choose video, photos, and sound to enhance the report.

Publishing with multimedia doesn't mean you have to use a computer, although I plan to. It just means that you present information in more than one way. For example, you could use pictures, video, and sound.

I need to choose additional resources that support my report and that don't contradict any information or make it confusing. If I use too many resources, my audience will not know where to look! Because my report will be on cards, I should be able to read them while I am presenting other media. But first I want to check over my report one more time. I'll use this final checklist to help me make sure my report is ready for publication.

My Final Checklist

Did I—

✔ make sure all the proper nouns and proper adjectives are capitalized?

✔ use all the different kinds of nouns correctly?

✔ choose media that support and enhance my report?

✔ proofread my report for grammar, spelling, and punctuation?

Apply

Check your research report against your own checklist. Then make a final copy to publish.

200 Informative/Explanatory Writing

Differentiating Instruction

ENRICHMENT
Use Four Pairs of Eyes Have students work together and edit their reports for specific conventions, using the proofreading marks on page 193. Students can begin by checking only spelling and end punctuation. Then have them switch partners to edit for correct capitalization of proper nouns and adjectives. Have writers consult print and digital sources to verify the edits before making corrections.

REINFORCEMENT
Proofread Carefully Have students work together to perform a final check of the reports. Demonstrate how to use the proofreading features on a word processor. Remind students to check their sources to make sure that all proper nouns and adjectives are used correctly. Assist them as needed in making their final corrections.

Variety Is the Spice of Indian Food

by Justin

WARNING: This report may cause an uncontrollable craving for Indian food, such as samosas. A samosa is a deep-fried, triangular pastry stuffed with potatoes and other vegetables. Spices, such as chili powder and garlic, give it zing. Samosas are a common dish in Gujarat, one of India's many regions. People eat different types of foods in different regions of India.

Many factors determine the foods people eat in each region of India. Religion is a major factor. In India, 80 percent of the population is Hindu, and strict Hindus are vegetarians and do not eat meat. Over the centuries, immigrants who practice other religions have come to India. Many of these people do eat meat. They have influenced the traditional Hindu diet in some places.

Another major factor is climate. The climate of a region affects the food production there. For example, people grow rice mostly in the tropical South and the rainy Northeast. Wheat is an important crop in the dry northern plains.

Technology Tip for 21st Century Literacies

Writing a research report requires students to organize resources and information for reference when writing. Ask students to create a virtual notebook with a tool such as LiveBinders, which houses their online sources, allows for note taking, and creates a familiar structure of a paper bound binder. LiveBinders can also be shared or compiled collaboratively, allowing for a significant range in how to scaffold or open this task. Discuss the ways in which these virtual binders compare to the more traditional pen and paper strategies they might have used in the past.

See **www.sfw.z-b.com** for further information about and links to these websites and tools.

Write
a Research Report

Week 3 • Day 5

Student Objectives

- Use a research report rubric. (pp. 182–183)
- Share a published research report. (pp. 201–203)

Presentation Strategy Remind students of the importance of neatness when creating a final, polished copy of their work. The presentation of a piece of writing has a great impact on how or whether the reader gets the message. Messy or illegible work will turn readers away, while a neat and interesting format will be inviting. Remind students of the numerous word-processing options available on computers. Computers make it easy to set neat margins, indent paragraphs, and choose clear fonts.

Assist students in selecting clear visuals that enhance the text. Point out that visuals should be inserted as close as possible to the information they illustrate or added at the end of the report. Instruct students in creating and using templates to help them make good design decisions.

CCSS Common Core State Standards
SL.6.5: Include multimedia components (e.g., graphics, images, music, sound) and visual displays in presentations to clarify information.

Reflecting on a Research Report

Instruct students to refer to the rubric on pages 182 and 183 and review Justin's changes. As they review the final copy, ask them what they think of Justin's changes. Students should agree that Justin's revisions and edits strengthened his research report. Have students use the rubric to score the model. Be sure students can support their scores with examples from Justin's writing.

Finally, have students reflect on the assignment as a whole. Ask:

- What was your favorite part of this assignment?

- What part was challenging?

- What did you do better on this assignment than on the last writing assignment?

- What will you do the same or differently in your next research report?

Allow time for students to respond and share their thoughts.

 Strategies for Writers Online

Go to **www.sfw.z-b.com** for additional online resources for students and teachers.

The North has a strong Muslim influence. Muslims eat lamb, chicken, beef, and fish, but not pork. One favorite dish is lamb kebab. Lamb kebab is pieces of mildly spiced meat roasted on skewers. Another favorite is tandoori chicken, spiced chicken cooked in a clay oven. Dates, nuts, and milk are in many desserts called milk sweets. The milk comes from water buffalo. They are the main source of milk in India. Kheer is a milk sweet similar to rice pudding.

Bread and vegetarian dishes from the Hindu tradition are also common in the North. Most breads don't have any yeast, so they don't rise. Parathas are flat cakes of wheat dough baked on a hot stone and then pan-fried. Purees are flat circles of wheat dough deep-fried in oil until they puff up like balloons. A dish of spiced rice and vegetables called pullao is also popular. In the North, the pullao vegetables are usually cauliflower and peas.

Food in the South has a more traditional Hindu style. Rice is prepared in many ways. V. P. Kanitkar, author of *Indian Food and Drink*, says, "Rice grains simply boiled may appear to us to be a poor meal, but different processes like grinding, pounding, steaming, and frying transform rice and other cereals into tasty dishes."

Two popular South Indian foods are made from rice. Dosas are thin rice-flour pancakes. Idlis are steamed rice dumplings. Vegetables served with rice include dahl, which is a soupy dish made from split peas or beans.

202 Informative/Explanatory Writing

Coastal Indian food has many influences. Naturally, people there eat a lot of fish. The residents of West Bengal live near rivers and the Bay of Bengal. They enjoy carp cooked with chilies. Another favorite Bengali recipe is prawns, which are large shrimp, spiced with mustard seeds.

Goa has a strong Portuguese influence. Its fish curries are well known. A curry is a general term for a dish cooked with crushed spices and turmeric. Turmeric is an herb that adds a yellow color. Coconuts are plentiful in Kerala. Coconut milk is used in fish, rice, and vegetable curries.

Because of the influence of religion and climate, the many regions of India offer a huge range of foods. Variety is the spice of Indian food. Anyone who ignored the warning at the beginning of this report will now probably be ready to sample the many types of Indian food.

Works Consulted

"India." *The World Book Encyclopedia.* 2007 ed.
Kanitkar, V. P. *Indian Food and Drink.* New York: The Bookwright Press, 1987.
Voros, Sharon. "Fare of the Country; The Vegetarian Snacks of South India." http://query.nytimes.com (April 19, 2012)

Reflect

Check Justin's report. Does the writing show all the traits of a good research report? Check it against the rubric. Don't forget to use the rubric to check your own research report.

Note: There are many computer programs that make it easy to insert photographs or computer-generated graphics into text, resulting in professional, polished presentations. Encourage students to explore different possibilities before they make their decision. Provide guidance and models as needed.

CCSS **C**ommon **C**ore **S**tate **S**tandards

W.6.4: Produce clear and coherent writing in which the development, organization, and style are appropriate to task, purpose, and audience. **W.6.6:** Use technology, including the Internet, to produce and publish writing as well as to interact and collaborate with others; demonstrate sufficient command of keyboarding skills to type a minimum of three pages in a single sitting. **W.6.10:** Write routinely over extended time frames (time for research, reflection, and revision) and shorter time frames (a single sitting or a day or two) for a range of discipline-specific tasks, purposes, and audiences.

Explanatory Essay Planner

WEEK 1

Day 1
Introduce
an Explanatory Essay

Student Objectives
- Review the elements of an explanatory essay.
- Consider purpose and audience.
- Learn the traits of informative/explanatory writing.

Student Activities
- Read and discuss **What's in an Explanatory Essay?** (p. 204)
- Read and discuss **Why Write an Explanatory Essay?** (p. 205)
- Read **Linking Informative/Explanatory Writing Traits to an Explanatory Essay.** (p. 206)

Day 2
Analyze
Read an Explanatory Essay

Student Objectives
- Read a model explanatory essay.

Student Activities
- Read **"Parallel or Perpendicular?"** (p. 207)

Day 3
Analyze
Introduce the Rubric

Student Objectives
- Learn to read a rubric.

Student Activities
- Review **"Parallel or Perpendicular?"** (p. 207)
- Read and discuss the **Explanatory Essay rubric.** (pp. 208–209)

WEEK 2

Day 1
Write
Prewrite: Ideas

Student Objectives
- Read and understand a prewriting strategy.

Student Activities
- Read and discuss **Prewrite: Focus on Ideas.** (p. 214)
- Apply the prewriting strategy.

Day 2
Write
Prewrite: Organization

Student Objectives
- Make a Fact Web to organize the notes.

Student Activities
- Read and discuss **Prewrite: Focus on Organization.** (p. 215)
- Apply the prewriting strategy to create a Fact Web.
- Participate in a peer conference.

Day 3
Write
Draft: Word Choice

Student Objectives
- Use a Fact Web to begin writing.

Student Activities
- Read and discuss **Draft: Focus on Word Choice.** (p. 216)
- Apply the drafting strategy by using a Fact Web to write a draft.

WEEK 3

Day 1
Write
Revise: Organization

Student Objectives
- Revise to use transition words or phrases to connect sentences and paragraphs.

Student Activities
- Read and discuss **Revise: Focus on Organization.** (p. 219)
- Participate in a peer conference.

Day 2
Write
Revise: Sentence Fluency

Student Objectives
- Revise to add prepositional phrases to sentences.

Student Activities
- Read and discuss **Revise: Focus on Sentence Fluency.** (p. 220)

Note: Optional Revising Lessons appear on the *Strategies for Writers* CD-ROM.

Day 3
Write
Edit: Conventions

Student Objectives
- Edit to make sure all prepositions are correct.

Student Activities
- Read and discuss **Edit: Focus on Conventions.** (p. 221)

Note: Teach the Conventions mini-lessons (pp. 222–223) if needed.

Day 4

Analyze
Ideas, Organization, and Voice

Student Objectives
- Read a model explanatory essay.
- Use the explanatory essay rubric.
- Use the model explanatory essay to study Ideas, Organization, and Voice.

Student Activities
- Review **"Parallel or Perpendicular?"** (p. 207)
- Read and discuss **Using the Rubric to Study the Model.** (pp. 210–211)

Day 5

Analyze
Word Choice, Sentence Fluency, and Conventions

Student Objectives
- Read a model explanatory essay.
- Use the explanatory essay rubric.
- Use the model explanatory essay to study Word Choice, Sentence Fluency, and Conventions.

Student Activities
- Review **"Parallel or Perpendicular?"** (p. 207)
- Read and discuss **Using the Rubric to Study the Model.** (pp. 212–213)

Day 4

Write
Draft

Student Objectives
- Complete a draft.

Student Activities
- Finish the draft. (p. 217)
- Participate in a peer conference.

Day 5

Write
Revise: Ideas

Student Objectives
- Revise to replace unnecessary or weak details with strong facts and details.

Student Activities
- Read and discuss **Revise: Focus on Ideas.** (p. 218)
- Reflect on the model draft.
- Apply the revising strategy.

Day 4

Write
Publish: +Presentation

Student Objectives
- Discuss preparation for publishing and presentation.
- Use a final editing checklist to publish their work.

Student Activities
- Read and discuss **Publish: +Presentation.** (p. 224)
- Apply the publishing strategy.

Day 5

Write
Publish: +Presentation

Student Objectives
- Use an explanatory essay rubric.
- Share a published explanatory essay.

Student Activities
- Share their work.
- Use the rubric to reflect upon and evaluate the model and their own writing. (pp. 208–209, 225–227)

To complete the chapter in fewer days, combine the learning objectives and activities in a way that supports students as they write.

Grammar, Usage & Mechanics

Differentiating Instruction

For additional Differentiating Instruction activities, see Strategies for Writers *Extensions Online at* **www.sfw.z-b.com.**

English Language Learners

Conferencing

Technology Tip

 Connection Letter
Reproducible letter (in English and Spanish) appears on the *Strategies for Writers* CD-ROM and at **www.sfw.z-b.com**.

Online Writing Center

Provides IWB resources, interactive games and practice activities, videos, eBooks, and a virtual file cabinet.

Strategies for Writers Online

Go to **www.sfw.z-b.com** for free online resources for students and teachers.

Introduce
an Explanatory Essay

Week 1 • Day 1

Student Objectives

- Review the elements of an explanatory essay. *(p. 204)*
- Consider purpose and audience. *(p. 205)*
- Learn the traits of informative/explanatory writing. *(p. 206)*

What's an Explanatory Essay?

Help students understand that an explanatory essay explains or describes something in detail. It presents clear information and analyzes a topic for the reader. Discuss with students reasons they might need to write an explanatory essay. Point out that anytime they explain or describe something in detail in writing, they are using the explanatory essay genre.

What's in an Explanatory Essay?

Read and discuss with students the four elements of an explanatory essay. Then discuss specific reasons that each element is important to writing an explanatory essay. Point out that, above all, an explanatory essay should explain a concept or an idea in a way that makes a clear, strong impression on the reader.

 Strategies for Writers Online
Go to **www.sfw.z-b.com** for additional online resources for students and teachers.

What's an Explanatory Essay?

An explanatory essay explains or describes something. It might tell the reader where an idea came from, or why something is the way it is. This kind of writing is informative and helps the reader better understand the topic.

What's in an Explanatory Essay?

Introduction
The introduction is where I clearly state what my essay is about in the form of a well-written thesis statement. This is also where I need to grab my readers' attention and prepare them for the rest of my essay.

Body
The body consists of several well-sequenced paragraphs where I actually explain the subject. This is where I'll put all supporting details, examples, and facts to help my reader understand the topic.

Conclusion
This is the last section of my essay. Here's where I neatly wrap up my subject in a way that my reader will remember. My conclusion should be brief and to the point.

Precise Language
It's important that I use the most accurate words possible when explaining my topic. The more precise my language, the better my reader will understand the idea.

$2x + 4 = 2$

100%

3 4 5

204 Informative/Explanatory Writing

Informative/Explanatory Text Exemplars (Explanatory Essay)

Petroski, Henry. *"The Evolution of the Grocery Bag."* American Scholar. 72.4 (Autumn 2003). CCSS In this article, Petroski describes how the grocery bag changed the supermarket checkout lane. This simple product allowed baggers to pack groceries quickly, and allowed customers to take their groceries home with ease.

Peterson, Ivars, and Nancy Henderson. *Math Trek: Adventures in the Math Zone.* Jossey-Bass, 2000. CCSS *Math Trek: Adventures in the Math Zone* explores various aspects of math, such as knots and secret codes, and connects them to real life. Students can also complete math activities to learn about math.

Why write an **Explanatory Essay?**

There are many reasons to write an explanatory essay, and below I've mentioned a few. Why am I writing one? I need to explain a math concept to my teacher.

Understanding
To write a good explanatory essay, I have to really understand the topic. Maybe my purpose is to prove how well I grasp the subject. Maybe I'll be writing about something that will require me to do a little research. Either way, in the end, my understanding of the topic will be deeper than when I started.

Information
Another great reason for writing an explanatory essay is to share knowledge with the reader. Everyone wants to understand the world around them. If I have information about a specific idea or topic, sharing what I know is a fun and logical step to take.

Explanation
So many small ideas can be used to understand larger concepts in our world. When I explain my topic, I can help both myself and my reader see the relationship between my subject and the larger world.

Why write an Explanatory Essay?

Discuss with students the reasons to write an explanatory essay. Point out that all writing has a purpose and a specific audience. Having authentic purposes helps writers shape their writing. For example, someone may write an explanatory essay to deepen and expand his or her own understanding of a topic. Another writer whose purpose is to inform may write an explanation to share knowledge with the reader. Still another may write expressly for the purpose of demonstrating to readers how the topic relates to the larger world. Encourage students to share their own reasons for writing. Also ask them to discuss how their reasons will focus the tone and style of their writing.

Katz, John. *Geeks: How Two Lost Boys Rode the Internet Out of Idaho.* **Broadway Books, 2001.** `CCSS`
Geeks is the true story about Jesse and Eric, two outsiders living in Idaho who have a love for technology. The two friends use the Internet to leave Idaho and shape a new future for themselves in a new community they could belong to in Chicago.

Greenberg, Jan, and Sandra Jordan. *Vincent Van Gogh: Portrait of an Artist.* **Random House, 2001.** `CCSS` Vincent van Gogh was a passionate artist who pioneered new painting techniques and style. Although he never received fame or praise in his lifetime, today he is remembered as a brilliant and original artist.

`CCSS` **C**ommon **C**ore **S**tate **S**tandards

SL.6.1: Engage effectively in a range of collaborative discussions (one-on-one, in groups, and teacher-led) with diverse partners on *grade 6 topics, texts, and issues,* building on others' ideas and expressing their own clearly. **SL.6.1.a:** Come to discussions prepared, having read or studied required material; explicitly draw on that preparation by referring to evidence on the topic, text, or issue to probe and reflect on ideas under discussion. **W.6.2:** Write informative/explanatory texts to examine a topic and convey ideas, concepts, and information through the selection, organization, and analysis of relevant content.

Introduce
an Explanatory Essay

Linking Informative/ Explanatory Writing Traits to an Explanatory Essay

Explain to students that they will follow Justin as he models using the writing process and the traits together. As they follow Justin through the writing process, students will see how the Informative/ Explanatory Writing Traits have been adapted and applied to writing an explanatory essay. They will see that an explanatory essay has many factors in common with other types of informative/explanatory writing. However, the particular audience and purpose of an explanatory essay determine how the traits are used.

Linking Informative/Explanatory Writing Traits to an **Explanatory Essay**

In this chapter, you will provide a written explanation about an idea or a topic. This type of writing is called an explanatory essay. Justin will guide you through the stages of the writing process: Prewrite, Draft, Revise, Edit, and Publish. In each stage, Justin will show you important writing strategies that are linked to the Informative/Explanatory Writing Traits below.

Informative/Explanatory Writing Traits

- a clear, focused topic
- credible, engaging facts and details that support and develop the topic

- information that is organized logically into a strong introduction, body, and conclusion
- transitions that clarify relationships between ideas

- a voice and tone that are appropriate for the purpose and audience

- language that is precise and concise
- domain-specific vocabulary that is used correctly and explained as necessary

- sentences that vary in length and flow smoothly

- no or few errors in grammar, usage, mechanics, and spelling

Before you write, read Zoya Petrovich's explanatory essay on the next page. Then use the explanatory essay rubric on pages 208–209 to decide how well she did. (You might want to look back at What's in an Explanatory Essay? on page 204, too!)

Informative/Explanatory Writing Traits in an Explanatory Essay

Ideas The writer builds the essay around a clear, focused thesis. Credible facts, definitions, and details develop the topic.

Organization The essay is logically organized with an introduction, an informative body, and a conclusion that supports the information presented. Appropriate transitions connect ideas and clarify relationships.

Voice The writer uses a voice that is appropriate for the purpose and audience. Using a formal style is the best way to achieve this in an explanatory essay.

Online Writing Center

 Provides six **interactive anchor papers** for each mode of writing.

Parallel or Perpendicular?

by Zoya Petrovich

Introduction

I've always had a hard time remembering just what *parallel* and *perpendicular* mean. Both words start with the letter *p*. Both refer to concepts regarding lines and shapes that I've studied in math class. It was easy to confuse the two. But then I took the ideas of parallel and perpendicular and applied them to real-life examples, and I have not struggled since.

Precise language

The definition of *parallel* seems easy enough to understand. Parallel lines can extend in both directions forever, but never intersect. However, when I have had to identify parallel lines in two- or three-dimensional shapes, I struggled with applying the definition to the example. That's when I decided that if I could find examples of parallel lines in the concrete world around me, the definition would be so much easier to fully comprehend. I began to look for parallel lines everywhere I went. Let me say that once you start looking, they really are everywhere!

For example, railroad tracks are parallel. They extend mile after mile, and yet the two rails never cross each other. Most buildings have parallel edges, too. Skyscrapers may reach dizzying heights, but the vertical lines at each corner of the building still never intersect. Even the most common objects in our world, such as a television set, have parallel lines.

Body

Then I decided to search the world around me for examples of *perpendicular*. Perpendicular lines meet or intersect at a right angle. A right angle measures 90 degrees. Again, I understood the idea but would sometimes have a hard time applying that understanding in homework assignments or on quizzes.

One of the most common examples of perpendicular lines is street intersections. The next time you are waiting at a red light, take a moment and look at the street that runs to the left and right. That street is perpendicular to the street you are on. There are also many perpendicular lines in our homes. Walls and floors are perpendicular to each other, as are walls and most ceilings.

Conclusion

As you can see, these mathematical concepts do not have to be things we only think about. Parallel and perpendicular lines are everywhere and play critical roles in the physical world. Once that everyday connection was made, I never had to ask the question, "Is this parallel or perpendicular?" again.

Explanatory Essay **207**

Word Choice The writer uses precise language. Domain-specific vocabulary is used and defined correctly.

Sentence Fluency The writer creates good flow by using a variety of sentence beginnings and structures.

Conventions The writer carefully edits his or her work. Prepositions and prepositional phrases are used correctly.

Analyze
the Model

Week 1 • Day 2

Student Objectives

- Read a model explanatory essay. (p. 207)

Read the Model

Read aloud "Parallel or Perpendicular?" Ask students to listen for a clearly stated thesis and concrete details that support and develop the thesis. Direct them to note the essay's organization. (Possible response: The essay has an introduction, informative body paragraphs that explain the examples, and a conclusion that follows from the explanation.) Also point out that a formal style makes the explanation sound more knowledgeable and serious.

Elements of an Explanatory Essay

Have students refer to What's in an Explanatory Essay? on page 204 as you refer to the model. Discuss the notes written on the model to enhance students' understanding of the terms.

CCSS **C**ommon **C**ore **S**tate **S**tandards

R/Inf.6.1: Cite textual evidence to support analysis of what the text says explicitly as well as inferences drawn from the text. **R/Inf.6.2:** Determine a central idea of a text and how it is conveyed through particular details; provide a summary of the text distinct from personal opinions or judgments. **SL.6.1.a:** Come to discussions prepared, having read or studied required material; explicitly draw on that preparation by referring to evidence on the topic, text, or issue to probe and reflect on ideas under discussion.

Analyze
the Model

Week 1 • Day 3

Student Objectives

• Learn to read a rubric.
  (pp. 208–209)

Use the Rubric

Explain the Rubric Explain that a rubric is a tool for planning, improving, and assessing a piece of writing. Tell students that a rubric helps a writer focus on key elements, or traits, in writing (**Ideas, Organization, Voice, Word Choice, Sentence Fluency, Conventions,** and **Presentation**).

Tell students that the columns on page 208 describe a paper that is quite good but perhaps needs some polishing. The columns on page 209 describe a paper that needs quite a lot of improvement.

Discuss the Rubric Guide students in a discussion of the rubric. Read the descriptors that go with each trait and explain the relationship between them. Remind students that they will use the rubric as they write their own essay, and again as they revise and edit it.

Online Writing Center

Provides a variety of **interactive rubrics,** including 4-, 5-, and 6-point models.

Rubric

Use this 6-point rubric to plan and score an explanatory essay.

	6	**5**	**4**	
Ideas	The thesis is clearly stated. Relevant facts and concrete details support and develop the thesis.	The thesis is clearly stated. One or two more details would help to develop the thesis.	The thesis is stated. The facts are mostly relevant, and the details are mostly concrete.	
Organization	The introduction presents the topic, strong body paragraphs explain the examples, and a conclusion follows from the explanation. Appropriate transitions clarify relationships among ideas.	The essay has an introduction, a body, and a conclusion. One or two transitions are needed.	The essay has an introduction, a body, and a conclusion. More or better transitions are needed to clarify ideas.	
Voice	The writer establishes and maintains a formal style. The tone is ideal for the audience.	The writer uses a formal style most of the time. The tone is mostly appropriate for audience.	The writer uses a formal style inconsistently. The tone is somewhat appropriate.	
Word Choice	Domain-specific content vocabulary is used correctly and defined as appropriate.	Domain-specific content vocabulary words are used. One or two definitions or explanations could be clearer.	Domain-specific content vocabulary words are used. Definitions or explanations are needed or are unclear.	
Sentence Fluency	The writer varies sentence beginnings and structures. The sentences are interesting and enjoyable to read.	The writer varies most of the sentence structures. Several in a row share the same length.	The writer varies some of the sentence structures. Several in a row share the same beginning.	
Conventions	The writing has been carefully edited. Prepositions and prepositional phrases are used correctly.	Minor errors are present but do not interfere with meaning. Prepositions and phrases are used correctly.	A few errors cause confusion. One or two prepositional phrases may be misplaced.	
✚ Presentation	The format helps readers access the information.			

208 Informative/Explanatory Writing

CCSS Common Core State Standards

Explanatory Essay

Strategies for Writers was designed to incorporate the Common Core State Standards throughout every unit. By presenting the standards in multiple applications, your students' exposure to them will be ensured.

The rubric and writing strategies for the explanatory essay reflect the standards for Informative/Explanatory writing. The traits of Ideas and Organization align with standards **W.6.2, W.6.2.a,** and **W.6.2.b,** which address introducing and developing a topic. Standard **W.6.2.c** also aligns with Organization by highlighting the use of transitions to connect details in a thoughtful, logical way. The rubric and writing strategies for Voice reflect standard **W.6.2.e,** establishing and maintaining a formal style. The rubric and writing strategies

3	2	1	
A thesis is stated but needs clarification. A few details are not relevant, and some details are not specific.	A thesis is not stated. Details and facts are unrelated or unimportant.	A thesis is not stated. Details are randomly listed.	**Ideas**
The introduction or conclusion is weak or missing. Transitions clarifying ideas may be confusing or missing.	The paragraphs are not in order. Transitions are used incorrectly or not used.	The writing is not organized into paragraphs. Transitions are not used.	**Organization**
The writer's style is too casual in places. The tone is inconsistent.	The writer's style is too casual and does not connect with the audience. An appropriate tone is not established.	The voice is very weak or absent. The reader cannot determine who is writing, or why.	**Voice**
A few domain-specific content vocabulary words are used. Definitions are not provided.	Domain-specific content vocabulary words are not used. Many words are ordinary or overused.	Domain-specific content vocabulary words are not used. Many words are used incorrectly.	**Word Choice**
Most sentences share the same structure. The writing becomes dull and predictable in spots.	Most sentences share the same structure. Many sentences are short and choppy.	Too many sentences are incomplete, run on, or incorrect.	**Sentence Fluency**
Many errors are repeated and cause confusion. Prepositions may be confused. (Ex. uses *by* for *to*)	Serious errors interfere with meaning. Prepositions may be confused; phrases may be unclear.	The writing has not been edited.	**Conventions**

See Appendix B for 4-, 5-, and 6-point informative/explanatory rubrics.

Apply the Rubric

Evaluate an Explanatory Essay
Explanatory essays are very common. Find an example in an informational resource, a textbook, or a magazine. Share a sample of an essay with the class. Ask students to use the rubric to score the essay on each of the traits. Be sure that students can offer examples from the essay to support the scores.

Once the class has reached a consensus on the scores, ask these follow-up questions:

- Which trait is strongest in the essay? Why do you think so?

- Does the essay fit the audience and the purpose? How?

Additional Rubrics Appendix B includes 4-, 5-, and 6-point rubrics that can be used with any piece of informative/explanatory writing. The rubrics are also available as blackline masters, beginning on page T525.

for Word Choice are based on standard **W.6.2.d,** which encourages concise, clear language.

The language standards for grade 6 students are addressed during editing and skills practice (**L.6.1–3**). In addition, there are multiple opportunities to address the speaking and listening standards during the writing process. Most importantly, this chapter will help students examine a topic and convey ideas and information clearly to produce clear and coherent writing (**W.6.4**), improve writing (**W.6.5**), and use technologies to publish and present finished pieces (**W.6.6**). It also provides the opportunity to conduct short research projects to answer a question (**W.6.7**), draw evidence from informational texts to support research (**W.6.9**), and write routinely over extended time frames (**W.6.10**).

CCSS **Common Core State Standards**
SL.6.1.b: Follow rules for collegial discussions, set specific goals and deadlines, and define individual roles as needed. **SL.6.1.c:** Pose and respond to specific questions with elaboration and detail by making comments that contribute to the topic, text, or issue under discussion. **SL.6.1.d:** Review the key ideas expressed and demonstrate understanding of multiple perspectives through reflection and paraphrasing.

Analyze
the Model

Student Objectives

- Read a model explanatory essay. (p. 207)
- Use the explanatory essay rubric. (pp. 208–209)
- Use the model explanatory essay to study Ideas, Organization, and Voice. (pp. 210–211)

Study the Model

Assess the Model Have volunteers read aloud each section on pages 210–211. Use questions such as the following to discuss the sections with students:

- Does Zoya Petrovich have a thesis statement that tells the reader what to expect? (Possible responses: Yes, the writer lets the reader know exactly what the essay is about right away. Her thesis is clear and easy to understand.)

- Does she further explain the topic? (Possible response: Yes, the writer uses many solid, supporting details to explain her ideas.)

 Strategies for Writers Online
Go to **www.sfw.z-b.com** for additional online resources for students and teachers.

Explanatory Essay
Using the Rubric to Study the Model

Did you notice that the model on page 207 points out some key elements of an explanatory essay? As she wrote "Parallel or Perpendicular?" Zoya Petrovich used these elements to help her describe two math concepts. She also used the 6-point rubric on pages 208–209 to plan, draft, revise, and edit the writing. A rubric is a great tool to evaluate writing during the writing process.

Now let's use the same rubric to score the model. To do this, we'll focus on each trait separately, starting with Ideas. We'll use the top descriptor for each trait (column 6), along with examples from the model, to help us understand how the traits work together. How would you score Zoya on each trait?

Ideas

- The thesis is clearly stated.
- Relevant facts and concrete details support and develop the thesis.

Zoya lets me know exactly what her essay is about right away. I like that. Her thesis statement is clear and easy to understand. She also includes lots of solid supporting details to explain her ideas.

[from the writing model]

> For example, railroad tracks are parallel. They extend mile after mile, and yet the two rails never cross each other. Most buildings have parallel edges, too. Skyscrapers may reach dizzying heights, but the vertical lines at each corner of the building still never intersect.

210 Informative/Explanatory Writing

English Language Learners

BEGINNING

Topic Write the following sentence on the board: *Isaac Newton was a famous mathematician.* Ask, *What is this sentence about?* Tell students that *Isaac Newton* is the topic of the sentence. Say, *topic,* write it on the board, and have students repeat. Repeat the activity and have students determine the topics of several other sentences.

INTERMEDIATE

Specific vs. Broad On the board, write *mathematicians, Newton's laws of motion,* and *Isaac Newton.* Discuss the meanings of any words students don't know. Draw a pyramid on the board. Ask students, *What is the biggest topic?* When students answer, *mathematicians,* write it at the bottom of the pyramid and erase it from the original list. Then ask, *Now what?* Introduce the terms *broad* and *specific.*

Organization
- The introduction presents the topic, strong body paragraphs explain the examples, and a conclusion follows from the explanation.
- Appropriate transitions clarify relationships among ideas.

Zoya grabs my attention right away with her interesting and honest introduction. I have also struggled with these concepts, and I wanted to learn how she helped herself. Several body paragraphs and transitions make her ideas easy to follow. She wraps it all up with a neat and strong conclusion, too. I also like how she used transitions such as *But then* to link ideas.

[from the writing model]

I've always had a hard time remembering just what *parallel* and *perpendicular* mean. Both words start with the letter *p*. Both refer to concepts regarding lines and shapes that I've studied in math class. It was easy to confuse the two. But then I took the ideas of parallel and perpendicular and applied them to real-life examples, and I have not struggled since.

Voice
- The writer establishes and maintains a formal style.
- The tone is ideal for the audience.

Reading Zoya's essay feels effortless because she really knows how to connect with the reader—me! She uses words and phrases I understand, as well as a tone that's formal but friendly. She even includes imagery that's easy for me to visualize, such as city streets and the inside of my home.

[from the writing model]

One of the most common examples of perpendicular lines is street intersections. The next time you are waiting at a red light, take a moment and look at the street that runs to the left and right. That street is perpendicular to the street you are on.

Explanatory Essay **211**

- How does Zoya organize her essay? (Possible responses: The essay begins with a strong and interesting introduction that draws readers in and gets them excited about the topic. The body includes important and specific details about the topic, and the conclusion follows from the explanation. Zoya uses transitions to connect ideas. The essay is easy to follow.)

- Does the voice suit the writer's purpose and audience? (Possible responses: Zoya establishes and maintains a formal style. Reading her essay is enjoyable because she connects with the reader. She uses a friendly, informative tone.)

ADVANCED

Identifying a Thesis Statement Give students a copy of an explanatory essay. Ask, *What is this essay about?* Have them identify the topic of the essay in the introductory paragraph. Say, *This is a thesis statement.* Write the phrase and have students repeat it. Point out that the explanation often answers a question about the topic. Have students identify the theses of several other essays.

ADVANCED HIGH

Writing a Thesis Statement Repeat the Advanced activity above. Then cut apart the thesis statements from the other sentences in the introductory paragraphs. Mix them up, and have partners work together to match the correct thesis statements with the correct details. Finally, offer essay topics and have students practice writing a strong thesis statement for each.

CCSS Common Core State Standards

W.6.9: Draw evidence from literary or informational texts to support analysis, reflection, and research.
SL.6.1.c: Pose and respond to specific questions with elaboration and detail by making comments that contribute to the topic, text, or issue under discussion.
SL.6.1.d: Review the key ideas expressed and demonstrate understanding of multiple perspectives through reflection and paraphrasing.

Analyze the Model

Week 1 • Day 5

Student Objectives

- Read a model explanatory essay. (p. 207)
- Use the explanatory essay rubric. (pp. 208–209)
- Use the model explanatory essay to study Word Choice, Sentence Fluency, and Conventions. (pp. 212–213)

Continue Discussing the Traits

Use questions such as the following to discuss the traits analyzed on pages 212–213:

Does the writer

- define domain-specific content vocabulary correctly? (Possible responses: Yes, when the writer introduces a new word related to her topic, she takes the time to define it. It's clear that she wants her reader to understand her topic.)

- write sentences that flow smoothly? What makes the essay easy to follow? (Possible responses: The variety of sentences creates a smooth flow throughout the essay. It's easy to follow and fun to read.)

- use correct spelling, grammar, and punctuation? Does she use prepositions and prepositional phrases correctly? (Possible response: There are no spelling, punctuation, or capitalization errors. I also noticed that prepositions and prepositional phrases are used correctly.)

Strategies for Writers Online

Go to **www.sfw.z-b.com** for additional online resources for students and teachers.

Word Choice
- Domain-specific content vocabulary is used correctly and defined as appropriate.

Whenever Zoya uses a vocabulary word related to her topic, she takes the time to define it. I appreciate that. It's clear that she really wants her reader to understand her ideas as thoroughly as possible.

> **[from the writing model]**
>
> Then I decided to search the world around me for examples of *perpendicular*. Perpendicular lines meet or intersect at a right angle. A right angle measures 90 degrees.

Sentence Fluency
- The writer varies sentence beginnings and structures.
- The sentences are interesting and enjoyable to read.

Zoya uses a variety of sentences throughout her essay. She also keeps things interesting by using all kinds of sentence beginnings. Reading the same sentence structures over and over is boring and tiring. I'm glad Zoya avoided that trap.

> **[from the writing model]**
>
> The definition of *parallel* seems easy enough to understand. Parallel lines can extend in both directions forever, but never intersect. However, when I have had to identify parallel lines in two- or three-dimensional shapes, I struggled with applying the definition to the example.

Technology Tip for 21st Century Literacies

When working with computation and data, WolframAlpha, a computational search engine, is a valuable resource for student researchers and writers. Search engines link to a database of websites, whereas this tool links to and computes actual data. As a class, use WolframAlpha to explore some of the questions or topics raised in students' explanatory essays. How do the results enhance or complicate their thinking or writing? What does an answer to a search look like within WolframAlpha as opposed to a conventional search engine?

See **www.sfw.z-b.com** for further information about and links to these websites and tools.

Conventions
- The writing has been carefully edited.
- Prepositions and prepositional phrases are used correctly.

Zoya worked hard at editing and it shows. I can't find a single spelling, grammar, or punctuation error! She even uses all prepositions and prepositional phrases correctly. I want to be just as careful when I edit my own essay.

[from the writing model]

Again, I understood the idea but would sometimes have a hard time applying that understanding in homework assignments or on quizzes.

✛Presentation The format helps readers access the information.

My Turn!
Now it's my turn to write an explanatory essay. I'll use the rubric and good writing strategies to help me. Read on to see how I do it.

Explanatory Essay 213

Differentiating Instruction

ENRICHMENT
Analyze Organization Every paragraph in an essay should serve a purpose. Ask students to examine the paragraphs in Zoya's model and summarize each one. What purpose does each serve? Could any paragraph be omitted? Should Zoya have included any more paragraphs?

REINFORCEMENT
Analyze Sentence Fluency Assign one student or one pair of students to analyze the sentences in one paragraph of Zoya's model. Have them comment on the length, structure, and style of the sentences. Emphasize that each writer crafts a different combination of sentences in whatever way fits the audience and purpose.

Presentation Explain to students that Presentation is just as important as the other traits. Appearance should be considered as students prepare their final copies. Neatness is always a priority, and text should be clearly handwritten in pen or typed, using a clear, readable font. White space should be used to create neat margins. All paragraphs should be indented (using the tab key if typed), and the title and writer's name should be centered at the top of the first page or on a separate page. Slides and other visual aids should complement the text and be easy to read from a distance. Encourage students to remember the importance of these formatting elements as they prepare the final drafts of their essays.

Think About the Traits Once students have discussed the model essay, point out that all the traits are important in every piece of writing, but some traits stand out more in some genres than in others. For example, **Organization** is very important because if an essay is poorly organized, it will be difficult to follow the writer's ideas. **Voice** is equally important in conveying the writer's ideas and engaging the reader.

CCSS Common Core State Standards

R/Inf.6.4: Determine the meaning of words and phrases as they are used in a text, including figurative, connotative, and technical meanings. **R/Inf.6.5:** Analyze how a particular sentence, paragraph, chapter, or section fits into the overall structure of a text and contributes to the development of the ideas. **SL.6.1.d:** Review the key ideas expressed and demonstrate understanding of multiple perspectives through reflection and paraphrasing.

Explanatory Essay T213

Write an Explanatory Essay

Week 2 • Day 1

Student Objectives

- Read and understand a prewriting strategy. (p. 214)

Prewrite

Focus on Ideas

Collect Information Explain that students, like Justin, will write an explanatory essay. Once students have a topic (assigned or self-selected), they should begin assembling some notes. They should consult math resources, including textbooks, to find accurate information to supplement what they already know.

Instruct students to use note cards to take notes and keep track of sources. Point out that students should keep track of sources, even if the assignment does not require a works consulted section. Display a copy of the proper format for citing sources.

Note that writing an explanatory essay is a way for students to demonstrate their content-area knowledge. Consider working with students' math teacher(s) to select appropriate topics. Decide also whether all students should write on a single topic or whether they should select individual topics.

Online Writing Center

 Provides **interactive graphic organizers** as well as a variety of graphic organizers in PDF format.

Prewrite — Focus on Ideas

The Rubric Says	The thesis is clearly stated.
Writing Strategy	Choose and narrow a topic that can be explained in an essay. Take notes.

My math teacher just gave me an interesting assignment. She wants me to write an essay explaining some of the most common 3-dimensional shapes. My essay will show her how well I understand the topic and help any classmates who read it understand the subject better, too. Writing an explanatory essay for math sounds like fun. Time to get started!

First I'll take some notes. I want to get all the details down on paper before I start writing. That way I can organize all the facts, and I won't forget any important details. Once I have my facts in order, I can start writing my draft.

Notes on 3-Dimensional Shapes

✔ 3-D shapes have length, width, and depth
✔ 3-D shapes in real world can hold stuff, like liquid
✔ spheres—like a ball or an orange, similar to a circle
✔ cones—an ice cream cone—top opening is round
✔ cubes—like a box, sides (faces) are all square
✔ pyramids—base is either a triangle or square, think Egypt!

Apply

Takes notes on your subject. Include all the important facts and information.

English Language Learners

BEGINNING/INTERMEDIATE

Organizing an Explanatory Essay Post a simple essay on an overhead transparency or interactive whiteboard. Say, *essay,* and have students repeat. Point out the introduction, body, and conclusion. Say each word and have students repeat. Ask volunteers to circle the topic, supporting examples, and concluding idea.

ADVANCED/ADVANCED HIGH

Domain-Specific Vocabulary Ask, *What is vocabulary?* Students should know that *vocabulary* is words. Often the words are related. On the board, draw a Network Tree or a Web graphic organizer. Write *vocabulary* in the center circle. On the next layer, write *Science, Math, Social Studies, English.* Write a few different science topics around the *Science* circle, and say, *This is specific vocabulary.* Continue adding details to one science topic.

Prewrite
Focus on Organization

The Rubric Says	The introduction presents the topic, strong body paragraphs explain the examples, and a conclusion follows from the explanation.
Writing Strategy	Make a Fact Web to organize my notes.

Writer's Term____

Fact Web
Use a **Fact Web** to organize several categories and facts about a given topic. Write the main topic in the center circle. Write your categories in circles around the main topic circle. Then write your facts in the circles around each category.

I decided that creating a Fact Web for three-dimensional shapes was the best way to organize my notes. When I go to write my draft, I can then use each category circle for a new paragraph. This will really help me write strong body paragraphs and keep all my information in order. Check out my Fact Web below. What do you think?

Fact Web

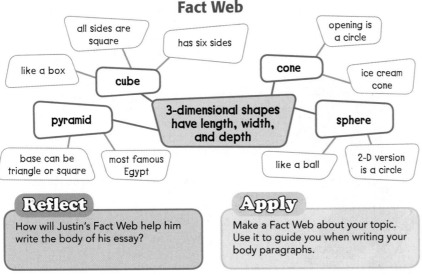

- all sides are square
- has six sides
- like a box
- **cube**
- opening is a circle
- **cone**
- ice cream cone
- **pyramid**
- **3-dimensional shapes have length, width, and depth**
- **sphere**
- base can be triangle or square
- most famous Egypt
- like a ball
- 2-D version is a circle

Reflect
How will Justin's Fact Web help him write the body of his essay?

Apply
Make a Fact Web about your topic. Use it to guide you when writing your body paragraphs.

Explanatory Essay **215**

Conferencing

PEER TO PEER Have students exchange their Fact Webs and ask questions as they read their partners' Webs: *Is the main topic clear? Do the categories give additional information about the main topic? Do supporting details help me understand the main points?* Have reviewers write helpful comments on sticky notes and affix them on the Webs.

PEER GROUPS Have students form small groups and discuss tips for organizing notes on a Fact Web. Then have students take turns sharing their Webs. Encourage group members to take turns offering one suggestion to improve each Web.

TEACHER-LED Conference with individual students about their prewriting work. Before they speak with you, encourage students to think of questions to ask about using their notes to create their Webs.

Write
an Explanatory Essay

Student Objectives

- Make a Fact Web to organize the notes. (p. 215)

Prewrite

Focus on  **Organization**

Organize Ideas Discuss how Justin placed his main topic in the center, his categories in smaller circles surrounding the main topic, and his facts in still smaller circles around each category. Show how this process keeps information in order by starting with the broadest piece (main topic), moving to smaller pieces (categories), and ending with the most detailed pieces (facts).

Writer's Term____

Fact Web In addition to organizing information, a Fact Web makes it easy to notice if information is missing or miscategorized.

CCSS Common Core State Standards
W.6.2: Write informative/explanatory texts to examine a topic and convey ideas, concepts, and information through the selection, organization, and analysis of relevant content. **W.6.2.a:** Introduce a topic; organize ideas, concepts, and information, using strategies such as definition, classification, comparison/contrast, and cause/effect; include formatting (e.g., headings), graphics (e.g., charts, tables), and multimedia when useful to aiding comprehension. **W.6.2.b:** Develop the topic with relevant facts, definitions, concrete details, quotations, or other information and examples. **W.6.7:** Conduct short research projects to answer a question, drawing on several sources and refocusing the inquiry when appropriate.

Write
an Explanatory Essay

Week 2 • Day 3

Student Objectives

• Use a Fact Web to begin writing. (p. 216)

Draft

Focus on  Word Choice

Draft an Explanatory Essay
Review the word *draft*, making sure students realize a draft is a rough form of a written document. Drafting lets students get ideas on paper without worrying about making changes or correcting errors. Make sure students use their Fact Web to guide their writing.

Read page 216 together. Then have students read Justin's draft on page 217 independently. After reading, point out that Justin's draft includes words that are specific to his topic. Discuss why he explained or defined these words in his draft. (Possible responses: The rubric says to use and define domain-specific vocabulary. Justin does not assume the reader knows the content vocabulary words, so he defines them.) Point out that Justin refers to the rubric as he writes. Encourage students to use the rubric to guide their own writing.

Online Writing Center

 Provides student eBooks with an **interactive writing pad** for drafting, revising, editing, and publishing.

Draft — Focus on Word Choice

The Rubric Says	Domain-specific content vocabulary is used correctly and defined as appropriate.
Writing Strategy	Make sure unfamiliar words are defined.

Now that my Fact Web is done, writing my draft will be easier. All the information I need is organized, so I just need to get started.

The rubric says I should use domain-specific content vocabulary words. I'll make sure I use words specific to the 3-dimensional shapes I'm describing. The more accurate my language, the better my reader will understand the topic.

The rubric also says I should define any words my reader might not understand. That makes sense. I want my reader to learn more about 3-dimensional shapes. It won't help if I use unfamiliar words without defining them. I want to show I really know what I'm talking about. I might even look up a few terms in a reference source, like a dictionary, but I'll be sure to use my own words when I write.

Time to get started! I won't worry too much about spelling and grammar at first. I can go back later to fix any mistakes. Right now the most important goal is to get my ideas written down. Check out the beginning of my draft on the next page. What do you think?

216 Informative/Explanatory Writing

Differentiating Instruction

ENRICHMENT

Add Visuals Have students discuss what types of graphics (drawings, charts, tables) they may use to enhance their essays. Do they plan to create diagrams themselves? If not, where can they find this type of information? Encourage students to research places where they can find visual information for their essays.

REINFORCEMENT

Plan Visuals Have students mark one part of their Fact Webs where a visual could help to explain the information. Discuss what kind of visual students should plan (e.g., a graph, a diagram, a photo). Explain that the visual should be planned and drafted in the same way that the text is.

[DRAFT]

Everyday 3-Dimensional Shapes Explained

by Justin

We all live in a 3-dimensional world, but most of us probably never think about it that way. Two-dimensional shapes have only length and width. Shapes like circles, squares, and triangles are great on paper, but they are flat and cannot hold substances, such as liquids, solids, or gases. In fact, our world, our entire universe, could not exist in only two dimensions. However, 3-dimensional shapes have not only length and width, but they also have depth. This third dimension makes all the difference and is a crucial—absolutely necessary—element of life as we know it. Circles become spheres, squares transform into cubes, and triangles can morph into either cones or pyramids. It's cool! Check it out!

[used and defined domain-specific words]

Spheres are everywhere! In fact, the universe is full of spheres. Planets, moons, stars, even our own sun, all are spheres. The easiest way to envision a sphere is to imagine a ball. That ball has a length and width, but it also has depth. It can hold a substance, like the water in a water balloon.

Reflect

How did Justin do? Does he include and define enough domain-specific content words to help his reader better understand the essay?

Apply

Use your Fact Web as a guide and write a draft of your essay. Use and define domain-specific words to explain your subject.

Explanatory Essay **217**

Conferencing

PEER TO PEER Have students exchange drafts to determine if the writer has organized the essay into clear parts and defined words related to the topic. Have reviewers write their comments and suggestions on sticky notes and affix them to their partner's draft.

PEER GROUPS Have students form groups of four. Have students pass their drafts to the right. Have the receiving student write one comment on a sticky note and pass the draft along to the right. The review ends when everyone has received his or her own draft back with three comments.

TEACHER-LED Conference with pairs of students. Have them read each other's drafts. Coach them in giving and receiving constructive criticism, using the rubric to guide their feedback.

Write
an Explanatory Essay

Week 2 • Day 4

Student Objectives
• Complete a draft. (p. 217)

Finish the Draft Remind students what it means to write a draft (getting ideas down on paper). They should be concerned with the accuracy of the information, but the expression of the information can be refined later. To help them focus on getting their thoughts down on paper, have students circle anything in their draft they might want to change later but not to worry about revising or editing their writing now.

It is important that students have ample time to draft their essays. As conferencing is important throughout the writing process, be sure to plan time for peer-to-peer, peer group, or teacher-led conferences. Remind students that this is the time for getting their ideas down in a creative and engaging way. Assure them that they will have plenty of time to fix any mistakes later.

Note: Proofreading marks are provided as a reference on page 217. They will be useful during revising and editing.

CCSS **C**ommon **C**ore **S**tate **S**tandards

W.6.2.d: Use precise language and domain-specific vocabulary to inform about or explain the topic. **W.6.5:** With some guidance and support from peers and adults, develop and strengthen writing as needed by planning, revising, editing, rewriting, or trying a new approach. **SL.6.1.b:** Follow rules for collegial discussions, set specific goals and deadlines, and define individual roles as needed. **SL.6.1.c:** Pose and respond to specific questions with elaboration and detail by making comments that contribute to the topic, text, or issue under discussion.

Explanatory Essay **T217**

Write
an Explanatory Essay

Week 2 • Day 5

Student Objectives

• Revise to replace unnecessary or weak details with strong facts and details. (p. 218)

Revise

Focus on Ideas

Replace Weak Details Have students read Justin's words and the Writer's Term box on page 218. Discuss the importance of including only concrete, relevant details about the topic. Vague or unrelated information detracts from the essay and interferes with meaning.

Have one volunteer read the draft excerpt without the revisions and another volunteer read the revised excerpt. Ask students what Justin replaced in his essay. (Possible response: He replaced weak details with strong facts.) Have students read their drafts. Remind them to make sure that they use only relevant facts and concrete details to support and develop their topic.

✏️ Writer's Term

Concrete Details Concrete details are facts and specific examples that can be verified and/or replicated. They are important when explaining a math concept.

▶️ Strategies for Writers Online

Go to **www.sfw.z-b.com** for additional online resources for students and teachers.

Revise

Focus on **Ideas**

The Rubric Says	Relevant facts and concrete details support and develop the thesis.
Writing Strategy	Replace unnecessary or weak details with strong facts and details.

✏️ Writer's Term

Concrete Details
A **concrete detail** is a specific detail that can be verified by more than one reliable source. Examples of reliable sources are textbooks, reliable websites, magazine and newspaper articles, or an encyclopedia.

Now that my draft is done, I can start revising. The rubric says I should include relevant facts and concrete details about my topic. All details must be related to my subject, or my reader will become confused. Also, the details I include should be concrete, not vague. Vague details don't really provide much information and will weaken my writing. As I read my draft, I found a weak detail that needed revision. I'll go and fix that now.

[DRAFT]

A square consists of four sides, each with the same
→ exactly six congruent   put together in such a way ←
measurement. A cube is ~~a bunch of~~ squares that∧ they ←

form a box.∧   Congruent means having the same shape and size.

——————— [replaced weak details with strong facts]

Apply

To strengthen your essay, replace weak, vague details with strong, concrete details.

218 Informative/Explanatory Writing

English Language Learners

BEGINNING/INTERMEDIATE

Concrete Details Write each of the following words on an index card: *sphere, Earth, oval, racetrack, octagon, stop sign*. Mix up the cards and have students match each shape with a specific example. Tell students that *Earth, stop sign,* and *racetrack* are concrete examples of the shapes. Say, *concrete*, and have students repeat.

ADVANCED/ADVANCED HIGH

Using Precise Words Identify a few vague words that students wrote in their drafts, for example, *get* or *think*. Challenge partners to come up with more precise words, for example, *acquire* or *imagine*. Then have students revise their drafts to replace vague words with more precise ones.

Revise

Focus on Organization

The Rubric Says	Appropriate transitions clarify relationships among ideas.
Writing Strategy	Use transition words or phrases to connect sentences and paragraphs.

Revising is easy when I tackle one aspect of my writing at a time. The rubric says that using transitions will clarify how my ideas are related. I can use transitions like *however*, *but*, and *in addition* to show how several points made about one idea are related. Also, repeating certain words can show how sentences are connected. I read over my draft, looking for places where transitions would help clarify an idea. My paragraph on cones could really use some clarification. I'll take care of that now.

[DRAFT]   [used transitions to connect ideas]

First,
Cones are interesting 3-dimensional shapes. Imagine an ice

When you look straight
down at a cone,   Then again,
cream cone. You'll notice that the top, or opening, is a circle. When

you view a cone from the side, you'll see a triangle. A cone is kind of

like a triangle that has been wrapped around so two edges meet.

Reflect

What do you think? How do Justin's revisions clarify and strengthen this paragraph?

Apply

Use transitions or repeat certain key words to show how sentences or ideas are related.

Explanatory Essay **219**

Conferencing

PEER TO PEER Have pairs of students exchange drafts. After reading the drafts, students should offer each other helpful feedback on different ways to strengthen Ideas, Organization, and Sentence Fluency, using the rubric and revising lessons to inform their response.

PEER GROUPS Have students form small groups and take turns reading sections of their drafts aloud. Have each group member ask one question about each draft to prompt a revision.

TEACHER-LED Conference with individual students about their drafts. Help students use the rubric and revising strategies to assess and improve their writing.

Write
an Explanatory Essay

Week 3 • Day 1

Student Objectives

• Revise to use transition words or phrases to connect sentences and paragraphs. *(p. 219)*

Revise

Focus on Organization

Add Transitions Explain the importance of using transitions to clarify relationships among ideas and concepts. Justin knows that transitions guide the reader from one idea to the next and from one paragraph to the next. He realized that in this instance he could also repeat certain key words to show how sentences are connected.

Have one volunteer read the draft excerpt without the revisions and another volunteer read the revised excerpt. Students should agree that Justin's revisions clarify and connect the ideas, making them easier to follow.

Encourage students to select helpful transitions to connect and clarify ideas in their essay. Refer them to the list of transitions on page 524.

CCSS **C**ommon **C**ore **S**tate **S**tandards

W.6.2.a: Introduce a topic; organize ideas, concepts, and information, using strategies such as definition, classification, comparison/contrast, and cause/effect; include formatting (e.g., headings), graphics (e.g., charts, tables), and multimedia when useful to aiding comprehension. **W.6.2.b:** Develop the topic with relevant facts, definitions, concrete details, quotations, or other information and examples **W.6.2.c:** Use appropriate transitions to clarify the relationships among ideas and concepts.

Explanatory Essay **T219**

Write
an Explanatory Essay

Week 3 • Day 2

Student Objectives

• Revise to add prepositional phrases to sentences. *(p. 220)*

Revise

Focus on  Sentence Fluency

Add Prepositional Phrases to Sentences Remind students that the rubric says that sentences should be interesting and enjoyable to read. In reading his draft, Justin realizes that he began several sentences in a row the same way. This interrupted the flow and possibly the meaning.

Prepositional phrases can usually go in more than one place in a sentence. Encourage students to experiment moving them around to see where they best belong in a sentence. However, placing them at the beginning is one way to achieve variety in the way sentences begin.

Encourage students to read their drafts to look for places where too many sentences in a row share the same pattern. Have students vary sentence beginnings and structures for interest and flow.

Online Writing Center

Provides **interactive proofreading activities** for each genre.

Revise Focus on Sentence Fluency

The Rubric Says	The writer varies sentence beginnings and structures. The sentences are interesting and enjoyable to read.
Writing Strategy	Add prepositional phrases to sentences.

Now the rubric says to vary sentence beginnings to add variety. I know that prepositional phrases add more information in a sentence, but they can also be used to change how sentences begin. When several sentences in a row start the same way, the writing seems stiff and uninteresting. I'll use some introductory prepositional phrases to mix things up, while at the same time adding more information to the sentences.

[DRAFT]

Triangles also appear in another 3-dimensional shape: the
Throughout this year, I've learned about ←
pyramid. ~~There are~~ two kinds of pyramids. One has a square base
In math class, we also discussed
and four triangular faces, which all meet in a point at the top.
that
Another version has a triangle for a base and three more
[used prepositional phrases for variety]
triangles for the sides.

Apply

Use introductory prepositional phrases to add information and variety, and keep your writing interesting.

Optional Revising Lessons

Word Choice

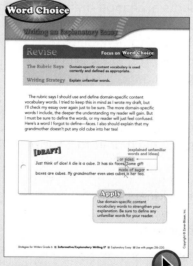

Informative/Explanatory 17

Voice

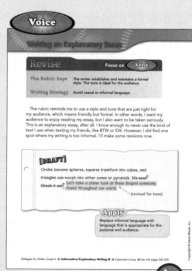

Informative/Explanatory 18

Go to ▷ Strategies for Writers Grade 6 CD-ROM

Edit

Focus on Conventions

The Rubric Says	The writing has been carefully edited. Prepositions and prepositional phrases are used correctly.
Writing Strategy	Make sure all prepositions are correct.

Writer's Term

Prepositional Phrases

A **prepositional phrase** begins with a preposition (**about, around, from, on**) and ends with the object of the preposition. It is placed near the noun or verb it describes. Use prepositional phrases to add information to a sentence, but make sure you use the right preposition.

The rubric reminds me to make sure I've used each prepositional phrase correctly. Prepositional phrases are a great way to provide the reader with more information. But if a preposition is used incorrectly, the reader will just be confused.

[DRAFT]

as you can see, these common 3-dimensional shapes are everywhere. It's important to remember how rare it is to find perfect mathematical examples of these shapes at our everyday world.
in ← [used correct preposition]

Reflect

How will Justin's edits make his essay easier to read? How does the fixed prepositional phrase clarify his idea?

Apply — Conventions

Edit your draft for spelling, punctuation, and capitalization errors. Be sure that all of your prepositions are used correctly.

For more practice using prepositions and prepositional phrases, do the activities on the next two pages.

Explanatory Essay 221

Related Grammar Practice

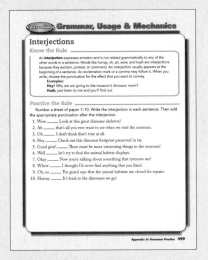

Student Edition page 499

Go to ▷ Appendix A: Grammar Practice

Student Objectives

- Edit to make sure all prepositions are correct. *(p. 221)*

Edit

Focus on Conventions

Use Prepositions Correctly Have students read Justin's words and the information in the Writer's Term box before they begin editing their essays. Ask students to notice how Justin corrected a preposition to clarify his ideas.

Have students edit their essays. If possible, have them put their writing aside for a day or two and re-edit the piece with fresh eyes.

Use the mini-lessons on pages T222 and T223 for students who are confused by prepositions. Have students complete the exercises on pages 222 and 223.

Writer's Term

Prepositional Phrase Used appropriately, prepositional phrases add details and depth, expand sentences, and improve the flow of ideas.

CCSS Common Core State Standards

W.6.5: With some guidance and support from peers and adults, develop and strengthen writing as needed by planning, revising, editing, rewriting, or trying a new approach. **L.6.1:** Demonstrate command of the conventions of standard English grammar and usage when writing or speaking. **L.6.3.a:** Vary sentence patterns for meaning, reader/listener interest, and style.

Conventions

Mini-Lesson

Student Objectives

- Use prepositional phrases correctly. *(p. 222)*

Prepositional Phrases

Explain that a prepositional phrase is placed near the noun or verb it describes. Also point out that a prepositional phrase can appear at the beginning, middle, or end of a sentence. However, sometimes they can be misplaced. (*The birds flew near the lake over the trees.*)

Adding prepositional phrases to sentences is one way to create variety and add valuable information. To demonstrate, write these examples on the board and prompt students to come up with prepositional phrases based on where, when, how, and why questions:

- *Mom abruptly stopped the car.* (Possible response: at the top of the hill)

- *Ten turkeys marched.* (Possible response: on the eve of Thanksgiving)

- *My whole family stared.* (Possible response: in amazement)

Also have them identify the object of the preposition in each phrase. (Possible responses: top, hill, eve, Thanksgiving, amazement)

Online Writing Center

Provides **interactive grammar games** and **practice activities** in student eBook.

Prepositional Phrases

Know the Rule

A **prepositional phrase** can tell *how, what kind, when, how much,* or *where.* A prepositional phrase begins with a **preposition** such as *about, around, at, by, from, in, into, of, on, over, to,* or *with.* It ends with a noun or pronoun that is the **object of the preposition**. The words between the preposition and its object are part of the prepositional phrase. A prepositional phrase can appear at the beginning, middle, or end of a sentence.

Example: The best bakery (in) the city is right next door.

Practice the Rule

Number a piece of paper 1–10. Copy each of the prepositional phrases in the following sentences. Then circle each preposition.

1. Preparing (for) a math test is important.
2. First, be sure to sleep well the night (before) the exam.
3. (Without) a healthy breakfast, you won't have the energy you need.
4. Look (at) your notes one more time when you get (to) school.
5. Keep your work area tidy—don't let clutter gather (on) your desk.
6. Don't let any worries or doubts (about) your math abilities trouble you.
7. (Between) problems, mentally encourage yourself—you're doing great!
8. Try not to work (over) the allotted time.
9. Place the pages (of) the exam (into) a neat stack and turn them in.
10. Remember—doing well starts (with) a positive attitude.

Related Grammar Practice

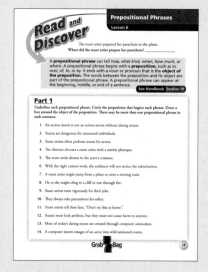

Page 17

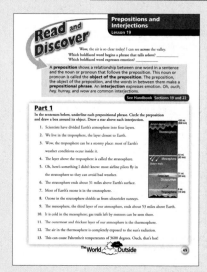

Page 49

Go to ➡ **G.U.M. Student Practice Book**

Prepositional Phrases

Know the Rule

A **prepositional phrase** can be used to add information to a sentence. Be sure to use the correct preposition so as not to confuse the reader.

Practice the Rule

Number a piece of paper 1–10. Copy the following sentences, choosing the correct preposition for each.

1. Write the percent sign (before/after) the number.
2. Parallel lines can extend forever (in/on) both directions, but they never intersect.
3. A circle's diameter extends (across/below) its center.
4. All octagons consist (in/of) eight sides.
5. If two lines intersect (at/around) a 90-degree angle, they are perpendicular to each other.
6. (Before/Between) reducing a fraction, you must first determine the greatest common factor for both the numerator and the denominator.
7. When you multiply a number by ½, you'll get the same answer as if you divided the number (on/by) 2.
8. When we subtract the *subtrahend* (into/from) the *minuend*, we are left with the *difference*.
9. When discussing circles, it's important to remember that all radii extend (toward/beyond) the center and meet at the circle's central point.
10. All angles fall (upon/into) one of three major categories—acute, right, or obtuse.

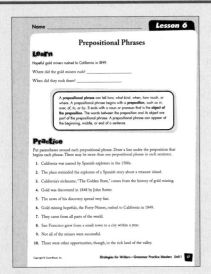

Page 17

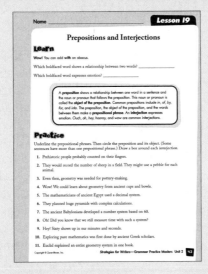

Page 43

Go to ➡ Grammar Practice Masters

Conventions

Mini-Lesson

Student Objectives

• Use prepositions correctly. *(p. 223)*

Prepositional Phrases

Remind students that a prepositional phrase begins with a preposition and ends with the object of the preposition, a noun or pronoun. Explain that it is the writer's responsibility to use prepositions correctly so as not to confuse the reader. Then write the following practice sentences on the board:

• *Jorge rushed (in/into) the cafeteria and grabbed a small tray.*

• *He stacked a salad, a sandwich, pretzels, juice, and an apple (in/on) it.*

• *As he turned (away/toward) his seat, the apple flew (of/off) his tray!*

• *It hit the floor (with/width) a thud and rolled straight (at/ate) the principal!*

Ask volunteers to read the sentences and choose the correct prepositions. *(into, on, toward, off, with, at)* Then have students identify the objects of the prepositions. *(cafeteria, it, seat, tray, thud, principal)*

CCSS **C**ommon **C**ore **S**tate **S**tandards

L.6.2: Demonstrate command of the conventions of standard English capitalization, punctuation, and spelling when writing. **L.6.3.a:** Vary sentence patterns for meaning, reader/listener interest, and style. **L.6.4.d:** Verify the preliminary determination of the meaning of a word or phrase (e.g., by checking the inferred meaning in context or in a dictionary).

Write
an Explanatory Essay

Week 3 • Day 4

Student Objectives

- Discuss preparation for publishing and presentation. *(p. 224)*
- Use a final editing checklist to publish their work. *(p. 224)*

Publish +Presentation

Publishing Strategy Ask students if they like Justin's choice for sharing his essay. Invite them to name other ways to publish an explanatory essay. Perhaps some will suggest a presentation at a school assembly, while others might want to include the essay as part of a display in the math lab.

Point out to students that they can enhance their presentation by using special text features to create a clear format that guides readers through the text. Talk about the things that make a good presentation: speaking loudly and clearly, maintaining eye contact with the audience, and knowing the materials and equipment.

Have a volunteer read Justin's checklist. Remind students that the checklist relates to the editing strategies they have been practicing. Have them use it or guide them to make individualized checklists based on errors they make frequently.

Strategies for Writers Online

Go to **www.sfw.z-b.com** for additional online resources for students and teachers.

Publish +Presentation

Publishing Strategy	Present the essay as a slide show.
Presentation Strategy	Display information clearly.

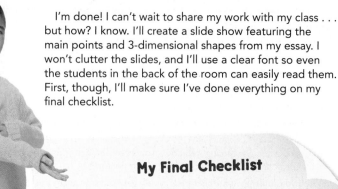

I'm done! I can't wait to share my work with my class . . . but how? I know. I'll create a slide show featuring the main points and 3-dimensional shapes from my essay. I won't clutter the slides, and I'll use a clear font so even the students in the back of the room can easily read them. First, though, I'll make sure I've done everything on my final checklist.

My Final Checklist

Did I—

✓ use the correct prepositions?

✓ use prepositional phrases accurately in my writing?

✓ create informative slides, using an easy-to-read font?

✓ include only the main points on my slides?

✓ use appropriate and topic-related visuals on my slides?

Apply

Make a checklist to check your own explanatory essay. Then make a final copy to publish.

224 Informative/Explanatory Writing

Differentiating Instruction

ENRICHMENT

Publish Like a Pro Have students explore multimedia options for publishing their essays. When options have been selected, encourage students to build in time for giving and receiving editorial and technical assistance.

REINFORCEMENT

Edit With a Partner Have pairs of students work together to edit their drafts for one specific thing at a time. Ask them to begin by trading essays and proofreading only for end punctuation or spelling. Next, edit for correct use of prepositional phrases. Have pairs return the essays and discuss the edits before finalizing them.

Everyday 3-Dimensional Shapes Explained

by Justin

We all live in a 3-dimensional world, but most of us probably never think about it that way. Two-dimensional shapes have only length and width. Shapes like circles, squares, and triangles are great on paper, but they are flat and cannot hold substances, such as liquids, solids, or gases. In fact, our world, our entire universe, could not exist in only two dimensions. However, 3-dimensional shapes have not only length and width, but they also have depth. This third dimension makes all the difference and is a crucial—absolutely necessary—element of life as we know it. Circles become spheres, squares transform into cubes, and triangles can morph into either cones or pyramids. Let's take a closer look at these shapes commonly found throughout our world.

Spheres are everywhere! In fact, the universe is full of spheres. Planets, moons, stars, even our own sun, all are spheres. The easiest way to envision a sphere is to imagine a ball. That ball has a length and width, but it also has depth. It can hold a substance, like the water in a water balloon. A multitude of fruits and vegetables are sphere-like. For instance, oranges, tomatoes, grapes, apples, and pomegranates are all delicious examples of sphere-like foods.

Technology Tip for 21st Century Literacies

Students can use Diigo to express their thoughts on the validity of a webpage directly on that page. Criteria include examining the information about the author(s), the domain ending (i.e., .edu or .com), the pages that link to the site, and so on. Diigo allows for highlighting on a page as well as inserting virtual post-it notes on which students can write their own content/notes/ideas/questions or begin a threaded discussion. Housing this annotation within Diigo allows students to archive their work, thereby capturing the discussion to return to later.

See **www.sfw.z-b.com** for further information about and links to these websites and tools.

Write
an Explanatory Essay

Week 3 • Day 5

Student Objectives

- Use an explanatory essay rubric. (pp. 208–209)
- Share a published explanatory essay. (pp. 225–227)

Presentation Strategy Remind students that if their work is messy or illegible, readers may decide not to read it. If it is clear and inviting, readers will be drawn in. Instruct students to use the computer to make good design decisions. They should use neat margins and spacing and select a clear, readable font. Students should remember to create uncluttered visuals that complement the text. Advise them to give their essays clear, appropriate titles and add their names. They should also be sure to save their work each time they make changes.

CCSS Common Core State Standards
SL.6.5: Include multimedia components (e.g., graphics, images, music, sound) and visual displays in presentations to clarify information.

Reflecting on an Explanatory Essay

Have students refer to the rubric on pages 208–209 as they reread Justin's essay on pages 225–227. What score would Justin earn for each trait? Next have students use the rubric to evaluate their essay.

Finally, have students reflect on the assignment as a whole. Ask:

- What is the strongest part of your essay? What makes it so strong?
- What will you do the same or differently next time?

Allow time for students to respond and share their thoughts.

Strategies for Writers Online
Go to **www.sfw.z-b.com** for additional online resources for students and teachers.

T226 Informative/Explanatory Writing

To understand cubes, you need to first understand the 2-dimensional square. A square consists of four sides, each with the same measurement. A cube is exactly six congruent squares put together in such a way that they form a box. Congruent means having the same shape and size. Just think of dice! A die is a cube. It has six faces, or sides. Some gift boxes are cubes. My grandmother even uses cubes made of sugar in her tea.

Cones are interesting 3-dimensional shapes. First, imagine an ice cream cone. When you look straight down at a cone, you'll notice that the top, or opening, is a circle. Then again, when you view a cone from the side, you'll see a triangle. A cone is kind of like a triangle that has been wrapped around so two edges meet. Other common examples of cones are party hats, megaphones, and Victorian Christmas candy cones.

Triangles also appear in another 3-dimensional shape: the pyramid. Throughout this year, I've learned about two kinds of pyramids. One has a square base and four triangular faces, which all meet in a point at the top. In math class, we also discussed another version that has a triangle for a base and three more triangles for the sides. Perhaps the most identifiable pyramids in the world are the Egyptian pyramids in Giza. Other everyday examples are some church steeples and the food pyramid.

226 Informative/Explanatory Writing

As you can see, these common 3-dimensional shapes are everywhere. It's important to remember how rare it is to find perfect mathematical examples of these shapes in our everyday world. A church steeple is not a perfect pyramid, for example, but the general shape is there. Take a moment and look around. You just might be surprised at how many of these shapes you will find.

3-Dimensional Shapes

- 3-dimensional objects have length, width, and depth.
- 3-dimensional objects can hold substances.
- Our universe and world are full of common 3-dimensional shapes such as the sphere, cube, cone, and pyramid.

A sphere is basically a ball.

Reflect

How did Justin do? Check his writing against the rubric. Be sure to check your own writing against the rubric, too!

CCSS **C**ommon **C**ore **S**tate **S**tandards

W.6.4: Produce clear and coherent writing in which the development, organization, and style are appropriate to task, purpose, and audience. **W.6.6:** Use technology, including the Internet, to produce and publish writing as well as to interact and collaborate with others; demonstrate sufficient command of keyboarding skills to type a minimum of three pages in a single sitting. **W.6.10:** Write routinely over extended time frames (time for research, reflection, and revision) and shorter time frames (a single sitting or a day or two) for a range of discipline-specific tasks, purposes, and audiences.

Informative/Explanatory Test Planner

WEEK 1

Day 1
Introduce
Informative/Explanatory Test Writing

Student Objectives
- Learn the components of the writing prompt.

Student Activities
- Read and discuss **Read the Writing Prompt.** *(pp. 228–229)*

Day 2
Analyze
Introduce the Scoring Guide

Student Objectives
- Recognize the relationship of the scoring guide to the rubric and the six traits of writing.
- Read a model writing test response.

Student Activities
- Read **Writing Traits in the Scoring Guide.** *(p. 230)*
- Read the writing prompt response model. *(p. 231)*

Day 3
Analyze
Apply the Scoring Guide

Student Objectives
- Apply the scoring guide to the writing prompt response model.

Student Activities
- Read and discuss **Using the Scoring Guide to Study the Model.** *(pp. 232–233)*

WEEK 2

Day 1
Write
Prewrite: Ideas

Student Objectives
- Read and understand a writing prompt for informative/explanatory writing.
- Apply the six traits of writing to the writing prompt.

Student Activities
- Read and discuss **Prewrite: Focus on Ideas.** *(pp. 236–237)*

Day 2
Write
Prewrite: Ideas

Student Objectives
- Learn how to respond to the task in the writing prompt.

Student Activities
- Read and discuss **Prewrite: Focus on Ideas.** *(p. 238)*
- Apply the prewriting strategy to take notes.

Day 3
Write
Prewrite: Organization

Student Objectives
- Learn how to choose a graphic organizer for the writing prompt.

Student Activities
- Read and discuss **Prewrite: Focus on Organization.** *(p. 239)*
- Apply the prewriting strategy to create a Spider Map.

WEEK 3

Day 1
Write
Revise: Organization

Student Objectives
- Revise to use transition words to clarify connecting ideas.

Student Activities
- Read and discuss **Revise: Focus on Organization.** *(p. 244)*

Day 2
Write
Revise: Voice

Student Objectives
- Revise to use active voice and first-person point of view.

Student Activities
- Read and discuss **Revise: Focus on Voice.** *(p. 245)*

Day 3
Write
Revise: Word Choice

Student Objectives
- Revise to use specific words.

Student Activities
- Read and discuss **Revise: Focus on Word Choice.** *(p. 246)*

Note: Optional Revising Lessons appear on the *Strategies for Writers* CD-ROM.

Day 4

Analyze
Apply the Scoring Guide

Student Objectives
- Continue to apply the scoring guide to a model test response.

Student Activities
- Read and discuss **Using the Scoring Guide to Study the Model.** *(p. 234)*

Day 5

Analyze
Time Management

Student Objectives
- Learn how to plan time during a writing test.

Student Activities
- Read and discuss **Planning My Time.** *(p. 235)*

Day 4

Write
Prewrite: Organization

Student Objectives
- Learn how to check the graphic organizer against the scoring guide.

Student Activities
- Read and discuss **Prewrite: Focus on Organization.** *(pp. 240–241)*

Day 5

Write
Draft: Ideas

Student Objectives
- Use a Spider Map to draft an informative/explanatory writing test, making sure to state the topic clearly.

Student Activities
- Read and discuss **Draft: Focus on Ideas.** *(pp. 242–243)*
- Draft an informative/explanatory writing test.

Day 4

Write
Edit: Conventions

Student Objectives
- Edit the writing test for proper grammar, spelling, capitalization, and punctuation.

Student Activities
- Read and discuss **Edit: Focus on Conventions.** *(pp. 247–248)*

Day 5

Review
Test Tips

Student Objectives
- Review tips for writing for a test.

Student Activities
- Read and discuss **Test Tips.** *(p. 249)*

To complete the chapter in fewer days, combine the learning objectives and activities in a way that supports students as they write.

Resources at-a-Glance

Differentiating Instruction

For additional Differentiating Instruction activities, see Strategies for Writers Extensions Online *at* **www.sfw.z-b.com.**

English Language Learners

Connection Letter
Reproducible letter (in English and Spanish) appears on the *Strategies for Writers* CD-ROM and at **www.sfw.z-b.com.**

Online Essay Grader and Writing Tutor
Powered by Vantage Learning's MY Access!®, includes writing prompts and ongoing feedback for students as they write. Available for Grades 5–8.

Online Writing Center
Provides IWB resources, interactive games and practice activities, videos, eBooks, and a virtual file cabinet.

 Strategies for Writers Online
Go to **www.sfw.z-b.com** for free online resources for students and teachers.

Introduce
an Informative/Explanatory Test

Week 1 • Day 1

Student Objectives

• Learn the components of the writing prompt. *(pp. 228–229)*

Read the Writing Prompt

Informative/Explanatory Test Writing When students write on demand for a test, they will receive a writing prompt and a certain amount of time to write. The strategies students have learned will help them do a good job. Direct their attention to the three parts of the writing prompt on page 228:

Setup The setup does just what its name says: It gets writers ready to do a good job. The setup helps writers think about the writing topic in general before they choose an appropriate topic.

Task The task tells students not only what to write about, but also what kind of writing to do: narrative, descriptive, informative/explanatory, or argument. Tell students that the best-written test will not receive a strong grade if it misses the topic or uses a form of writing other than the assigned form.

Strategies for Writers Online
Go to **www.sfw.z-b.com** for additional online resources for students and teachers.

Informative/ Explanatory test writing

Read the Writing Prompt

Every writing test starts with a writing prompt. Most writing prompts have three parts:

Setup This part of the writing prompt gives you the background information you need to get ready to write.

Task This part of the writing prompt tells you exactly what you are supposed to write: an explanation of a problem in your school or community with ideas on how to fix it.

Scoring Guide This section tells how your writing will be scored. To do well on the test, you should make sure your writing does everything on the list.

Remember the rubrics you used earlier in this unit? When you take a writing test, you don't always have all of the information that's on a rubric. But the scoring guide is a lot like a rubric. It lists everything you need to think about to write a good paper. Like the rubrics you've used in this unit, many scoring guides are based upon these important traits of writing:

Ideas   Organization   Voice
Word Choice   Sentence Fluency   Conventions

228 Informative/Explanatory Writing

Online Essay Grader and Writing Tutor

Powered by Vantage Learning's MY Access!®, this tool gives students

• immediate, ongoing, sentence-by-sentence feedback.

• helpful suggestions to improve their draft.

• a holistic score and a trait-specific score on their final draft.

• unlimited response submissions to the prompts.

Think about a problem in your school or community that should be fixed.

Explain what the problem is, why it needs to be corrected, and how you would go about fixing it.

Be sure your writing

- has a topic that is clear and includes relevant, credible details that appeal to your audience.

- is well organized and uses transitions to clarify relationships among ideas.

- uses active voice and first-person point of view to engage your readers.

- uses specific words to explain the topic.

- has a variety of sentence patterns.

- contains correct grammar, punctuation, capitalization, and spelling.

Scoring Guide The scoring guide helps students plan and evaluate their writing. Help students understand how a scoring guide is similar to a writing rubric by asking these questions:

- Which trait corresponds to the first bullet? (Ideas)

- Which trait corresponds to the fourth bullet? (Word Choice)

- Which trait corresponds to the last bullet? (Conventions)

CCSS Common Core State Standards

W.6.2: Write informative/explanatory texts to examine a topic and convey ideas, concepts, and information through the selection, organization, and analysis of relevant content. **W.6.5:** With some guidance and support from peers and adults, develop and strengthen writing as needed by planning, revising, editing, rewriting, or trying a new approach. **W.6.9:** Draw evidence from literary or informational texts to support analysis, reflection, and research **SL.6.1:** Engage effectively in a range of collaborative discussions (one-on-one, in groups, and teacher-led) with diverse partners on *grade 6 topics, texts, and issues*, building on others' ideas and expressing their own clearly

Analyze
the Model

Student Objectives

- Recognize the relationship of the scoring guide to the rubric and the six traits of writing. *(p. 230)*
- Read a model writing test response. *(p. 231)*

Writing Traits in the Scoring Guide

Use Scoring Guide as a Rubric Remind students that the scoring guide, like the rubrics they have used, are based on the traits of informative/explanatory writing. Use the first item in the scoring guide as an example: *Be sure your topic is clear and includes relevant, credible details that appeal to your audience.* Ask which trait this item corresponds with. (Ideas) Continue down the list and discuss each item in the scoring guide and corresponding writing traits. Explain that **Conventions** are the same for all genres of writing.

Tell students that they will sometimes receive writing prompts that do not include guidance for each of the six categories in the rubric by name. However, students can rely on their writing experiences to remember the traits of informative/explanatory writing as shown on page 231.

Online Writing Center

Provides six **interactive anchor papers** for each mode of writing.

Writing Traits
in the Scoring Guide

The scoring guide in the prompt on page 229 has been made into this chart. Does it remind you of the rubrics you've used? Not all prompts include all of the writing traits, but this one does. Use them to do your best writing. Remember to work neatly and put your name on each page.

- Be sure your topic is clear and includes relevant, credible details that appeal to your audience.

- Be sure your writing is well organized and uses transitions to clarify relationships among ideas.

- Be sure to use active voice and first-person point of view to engage your readers.

- Be sure your writing uses specific words to explain the topic.

- Be sure your writing has a variety of sentence patterns.

- Be sure your writing contains correct grammar, punctuation, capitalization, and spelling.

Look at Bonnie Campbell's essay on the next page. Did she follow the scoring guide?

230 Informative/Explanatory Writing

English Language Learners

BEGINNING
The Writing Process Review the steps in the writing process using simple words. Use the following words to substitute for *prewrite, draft, revise, edit,* and *publish: about/plan, write, change, fix,* and *show.* Remind students to follow all of these steps during a writing test.

INTERMEDIATE
Organizing an Explanatory Essay Have partners review how to organize an explanatory essay. What information belongs in the introductory paragraph? In the body? In the last paragraph? Have them discuss which type of graphic organizer would be most helpful.

A Place for Us
by Bonnie Campbell

A big problem in our community is that many middle school students have nowhere to go after school. I would like to explain my solution to this problem.

There are many kids in our town who would like to spend time together after school. I'm not talking about kids who play sports. I'm concerned about a whole group of other kids like me who have nothing to do after school. Our parents don't like us to get together at our homes when no adults are there, so where can we go?

There is no place for us to hang out without getting in trouble. If we go to the diner for a snack, we can't stay there very long. The servers complain that we don't spend enough money to take up the tables. If we go to the library, people complain that we are too noisy. If we get together outside the shops downtown, sometimes adults tell us to move. They say we're blocking the sidewalk.

Now that I've explained the problem, I'd like to explain my solution to it. There is an empty store on Main Street. If we could make this a drop-in center, it would keep students off the street. We could play table tennis and air hockey. There could also be quiet areas for kids to do their homework. In addition, it would be great if we had a little kitchen or some machines with snacks. I also know kids would like it if we could listen to music there and maybe watch some videos.

This way, kids would not have to go home to empty houses or apartments after school. They would not be on the street. Kids with no place else to go would not be bored and would stay out of trouble. There could be one or two adults at the center to make sure everyone behaves. We kids could even help out. We could keep the place clean and do other jobs like making snacks. We could help pay for the center by having fundraisers, such as car washes or bake sales.

With a special place for kids to go after school, everybody wins! Kids stay busy and have fun, and parents don't have to worry about them.

Informative/Explanatory Test Writing 231

Read the Model

Read aloud "A Place for Us" as students follow along in their books. Tell students to keep the requirements of the scoring guide in mind as they follow along. After reading the model, have students break into small groups to discuss how each element of the scoring guide relates to the model.

ADVANCED
Organizing Details Suggest students use a Spider Map graphic organizer during an informative/explanatory writing test. Give partners a brief informative text to read. Have them complete a Spider Map to identify the topic and the important details in the text. Then have them trade texts and graphic organizers with another pair who will verify that the correct details were included on the Spider Map.

ADVANCED HIGH
Active vs. Passive Voice Ask a volunteer to explain the terms *active* and *passive*. If necessary, tell students that if a person is *active*, he or she is doing something. If a person is *passive*, he or she lets things happen. Illustrate with photos. Have partners write two active and two passive sentences. Then review all sentences as a group to identify which are active and which are passive.

CCSS **Common Core State Standards**

SL.6.1: Engage effectively in a range of collaborative discussions (one-on-one, in groups, and teacher-led) with diverse partners on *grade 6 topics, texts, and issues,* building on others' ideas and expressing their own clearly. **SL.6.1.a:** Come to discussions prepared, having read or studied required material; explicitly draw on that preparation by referring to evidence on the topic, text, or issue to probe and reflect on ideas under discussion. **R/Inf.6.1:** Cite textual evidence to support analysis of what the text says explicitly as well as inferences drawn from the text.

Analyze
the Model

Week 1 • Day 3

Student Objectives

- Apply the scoring guide to the writing prompt response model. (pp. 232–233)

Using the Scoring Guide to Study the Model

Review the Scoring Guide Remind students that the scoring guide is the tool that an evaluator—a teacher or another trained professional—will use to score the writing test. Students are given the scoring guide so they will know the criteria for judging their writing. They should use the scoring guide as they write to make sure they meet all requirements.

Use the Scoring Guide Have students use the Writing Traits in the Scoring Guide on page 230 to evaluate Bonnie Campbell's model writing test. The chart is based on the scoring guide in the writing prompt.

Find More Examples Explain that pages 232–234 show how the model on page 231 meets all six writing traits. Have students read pages 232–233 and look for additional examples of **Ideas, Organization, Voice,** and **Word Choice** in the model. Ask students if they agree with Justin's assessment of Bonnie's essay for each of the traits in the scoring guide.

 Strategies for Writers Online
Go to **www.sfw.z-b.com** for additional online resources for students and teachers.

Using the Scoring Guide to Study the Model

Let's use the scoring guide to check Bonnie's writing test, "A Place for Us." How well does her explanation meet each of the six writing traits?

 Ideas
- The topic is clear.
- The writing includes relevant, credible details that appeal to the audience.

Bonnie's first paragraph announces the topic: the middle school kids need a place to hang out. She then begins to give relevant, credible details that sound authoritative and reach out to the reader in a friendly way.

> A big problem in our community is that many middle school students have nowhere to go after school.

> There are many kids in our town who would like to spend time together after school.... I'm concerned about a whole group of other kids like me who have nothing to do after school. Our parents don't like us to get together at our homes when no adults are there, so where can we go?

 **Organization**
- The writing is well organized.
- The writing uses transitions to clarify relationships among ideas.

In the body, Bonnie explains the problem, offers a solution, and explains the solution. Transitions help move the reader easily from one idea to the next. This example contains a smooth transition from describing the problem to introducing the next topic: the solution.

> If we get together outside the shops downtown, sometimes adults tell us to move. They say we're blocking the sidewalk.

> Now that I've explained the problem, I'd like to explain my solution to it.

232 Informative/Explanatory Writing

Differentiating Instruction

ENRICHMENT

Announce the Topic To demonstrate the importance of presenting a clear topic, select a short essay from your files. Make copies for students to read that do not include the essay's introduction. After reading, ask students what is missing from the essay. (Possible responses: the introduction; The writer's topic is not clear.) Then challenge them to use the information from the body and conclusion of the altered essay to create an introduction. Have students share and compare their introductions.

Voice

- The writing uses active voice and first-person point of view to engage the reader.

Bonnie uses first person—*we* and *I*—to make the reader feel part of the discussion. She also uses active voice to keep her writing engaging. Instead of using dull sentences such as *The adults could be helped by us*, or *The place could be cleaned by kids*, she writes active sentences like these.

> We kids could even help out. We could keep the place clean and do other jobs like making snacks. We could help pay for the center by having fundraisers, such as car washes or bake sales.

Word Choice

- The writing uses specific words to explain the topic.

Specific and precise words help make the writer's meaning clear. Bonnie uses words like *snacks*, *fundraisers*, and *car washes* so the reader knows exactly what she is suggesting.

> We kids could help out. We could keep the place clean and do other jobs like making snacks. We could help pay for the center by having fundraisers, such as car washes or bake sales.

Think About the Traits Once students have thoroughly discussed Bonnie Campbell's essay, ask them which traits they think are most important in an essay. Of course, all the traits are important in every piece of writing, but some of the traits stand out more in some types of writing than in others. For example, students might say that the trait of **Organization** is very important because if an essay is not well organized, the evaluator may not be able to follow the writer's ideas. Others may say that **Word Choice** is very important because the test writing needs to be precise and succinct.

REINFORCEMENT

Use Transitions Read the fourth paragraph of the model essay on page 231 without the transition words (*Now that, If, also, In addition, also*). Then discuss the role of transitions in this paragraph. Ask students to consider how they connect the ideas and how they help the reader follow the writer's main points and examples. Assist students in listing transition words they have used in their writing. Post the list and invite students to add words from time to time.

CCSS Common Core State Standards

SL.6.1: Engage effectively in a range of collaborative discussions (one-on-one, in groups, and teacher-led) with diverse partners on *grade 6 topics, texts, and issues*, building on others' ideas and expressing their own clearly. **SL.6.1.a:** Come to discussions prepared, having read or studied required material; explicitly draw on that preparation by referring to evidence on the topic, text, or issue to probe and reflect on ideas under discussion. **SL.6.1.b:** Follow rules for collegial discussions, set specific goals and deadlines, and define individual roles as needed. **SL.6.1.c:** Pose and respond to specific questions with elaboration and detail by making comments that contribute to the topic, text, or issue under discussion.

Analyze
the Model

Student Objectives

• Continue to apply the scoring guide to a model test response. (p. 234)

Analyze the Model Help students focus on **Sentence Fluency** by telling them that the scoring guide reminds them that their writing should use a variety of sentence patterns to create a smooth flow. Point out that Bonnie begins by stating there is no place for students to hang out. Then she follows up with several "if" clauses to further explain her original statement. The clauses connect one sentence to the next, which makes the writing flow. Remind students that varying sentence beginnings will make their writing more interesting and keep the reader's attention.

Focus on **Conventions** by reminding students that they should use correct grammar, punctuation, and spelling in their writing test. Tell them to use the editing strategies they have learned and to check their spelling, punctuation, and capitalization before turning in the test.

 Strategies for Writers Online
Go to **www.sfw.z-b.com** for additional online resources for students and teachers.

Using the Scoring Guide to Study the Model

 **Sentence Fluency**
• The writing has a variety of sentence patterns.

Bonnie uses a variety of sentence patterns. She begins by stating that there's no place to go, and then she follows up with several *if* clauses that further explain her original statement. The clauses connect one sentence to the next, which makes the writing flow.

> There is no place for us to hang out without getting in trouble. If we go to the diner for a snack, we can't stay there very long. The servers complain that we don't spend enough money to take up the tables. If we go to the library, people complain that we are too noisy. If we get together outside the shops downtown, sometimes adults tell us to move. They say we're blocking the sidewalk.

 **Conventions**
• The writing contains correct grammar, punctuation, capitalization, and spelling.

As far as I can tell, Bonnie didn't make any mistakes in capitalization, punctuation, spelling, or grammar. But don't forget to check for mistakes in your own work. For example, if you know you often misspell words, you should pay close attention to spelling. Editing for grammar and mechanics at every step of the writing process will help you to avoid errors on your final test!

Planning My Time

Before giving us a writing test prompt, my teacher tells us how much time we'll have to complete the test. Since I'm already familiar with the writing process, I can think about how much total time I need and then divide it up into the different parts of the writing process. If the test takes an hour, here's how I can organize my time. Planning your time will help you, too!

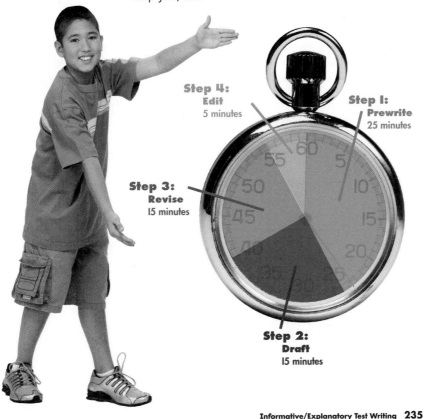

Step 4:
Edit
5 minutes

Step 1:
Prewrite
25 minutes

Step 3:
Revise
15 minutes

Step 2:
Draft
15 minutes

Informative/Explanatory Test Writing **235**

Differentiating Instruction

REINFORCEMENT

Practice Time Many students have grown up with digital rather than analog clocks. Practice dividing the writing time (60 minutes) using a digital clock. Give students a starting time of 9:00, for example. Have them plan their time by minutes: 9:00–9:25 Prewrite; 9:25–9:40 Draft; 9:40–9:55 Revise; 9:55–10:00 Edit. You may want to repeat the exercise with another start time. Remind students that these times are estimates. Students may use several minutes less or more for a step of the process as long as they stay pretty close to their time plan and leave time at the end for editing.

Analyze
Time Management

Week 1 • Day 5

Student Objectives

- Learn how to plan time during a writing test. *(p. 235)*

Planning My Time

Time Management Explain that when students write for a test, they must complete all the steps of the writing process quickly. Students may be surprised that Justin has allotted so much time—25 minutes out of 60—to prewriting. Ask why this is necessary. (Possible response: Without a plan, students may write a draft that does not respond to the task. Then they will not have time to write another draft.)

Remind students that revising is part of the task. Drafting and revising together take more time—30 minutes—than prewriting; five minutes remain to edit. Tell students that when they have a shorter or longer time in which to write a test, they can use a similar time plan: about the same amount of time for prewriting and for drafting/revising, with a shorter time left for editing.

CCSS **C**ommon **C**ore **S**tate **S**tandards

W.6.10: Write routinely over extended time frames (time for research, reflection, and revision) and shorter time frames (a single sitting or a day or two) for a range of discipline-specific tasks, purposes, and audiences.
SL.6.1.c: Pose and respond to specific questions with elaboration and detail by making comments that contribute to the topic, text, or issue under discussion.
SL.6.1.d: Review the key ideas expressed and demonstrate understanding of multiple perspectives through reflection and paraphrasing.

Write
an Informative/ Explanatory Test

Week 2 • Day 1

Student Objectives

- Read a writing prompt for informative/explanatory writing. *(p. 236)*
- Apply the six traits of writing to the writing prompt. *(p. 237)*

Prewrite

Focus on Ideas

Study the Writing Prompt Before reading Justin's thoughts, ask students to predict what he will do first. (Possible response: Label the three parts of the writing prompt—Setup, Task, Scoring Guide.) Have students study the writing prompt carefully to make sure they can identify its parts.

Discuss why Justin took time to circle the three parts of the writing prompt. (Possible response: It will be easy for Justin to glance at the prompt to remember what to do.)

Strategies for Writers Online
Go to **www.sfw.z-b.com** for additional online resources for students and teachers.

Prewrite

Focus on **Ideas**

Writing Strategy Study the writing prompt to find out what to do.

Once I have my writing prompt, I study it and make sure I know exactly what I'm supposed to do. Usually a writing prompt has three parts, but the parts aren't always labeled. You should find and label the setup, task, and scoring guide on your writing prompt, just like I did on mine below. Then you can circle key words in the setup and the task that tell what kind of writing you need to do and who your audience will be. I circled my topic in blue. I also circled what kind of writing I'll be doing (an explanation) in orange. The writing prompt doesn't say who the reader is, so I'll write for my teacher.

My Writing Test Prompt

Setup — Suppose you have an opportunity to travel on a space shuttle.

Task — Write an essay explaining why you would or would not want to go on a space shuttle.

Be sure your writing

Scoring Guide

- has a topic that is clear and includes relevant, credible details that appeal to your audience.
- is well organized and uses transitions to clarify relationships among ideas.
- uses active voice and first-person point of view to engage your readers.
- uses specific words to explain the topic.
- has a variety of sentence patterns.
- contains correct grammar, punctuation, capitalization, and spelling.

236 Informative/Explanatory Writing

English Language Learners

BEGINNING

Writing Prompt Give students a copy of the informative/ explanatory test writing prompt. Have them look at each word in the prompt and circle the words they do not know. Then teach the most important words, such as *opportunity, space shuttle, essay, credible.* You might have a higher-level ELL work with a lower-level ELL to review the meanings of these words.

INTERMEDIATE

Writing Prompt Have students read the informative/ explanatory test writing prompt and write down words they do not know. Review how to ask for help, such as *What does* credible *mean? Does* credible *mean "believable"?* Have students practice asking and answering with two other students. Finally, ask them to write their answers; for example, *If a source is credible, then it is believable.*

Think about how the scoring guide relates to the writing traits you've studied in the rubrics. All of the traits might not be included in every scoring guide, but you need to remember them all to write a good essay!

Ideas
- Be sure your topic is clear and includes relevant, credible details that appeal to your audience.

I want my reader to know right away what my topic is, believe the details I give, and feel drawn into the writing.

Organization
- Be sure your writing is well organized and uses transitions to clarify relationships among ideas.

My reader will have an easier time following my explanation if I use transition words to identify how ideas connect.

Voice
- Be sure to use active voice and first-person point of view to engage your readers.

Strong, active-voice verbs and the first-person pronouns *I* and *we* will help keep my reader engaged.

Word Choice
- Be sure your writing uses specific words to explain the topic

My reader will understand the information better if I use specific words to express what I mean.

Sentence Fluency
- Be sure your writing has a variety of sentence patterns.

I can add liveliness to my writing by using different kinds of sentences. This will keep my reader interested and help make my writing flow.

Conventions
- Be sure your writing contains correct grammar, punctuation, capitalization, and spelling.

I should always remember to check my grammar and mechanics any time I write!

Informative/Explanatory Test Writing 237

Then walk students through page 237. Read and discuss how Justin thinks through each bulleted item to help him plan his essay.

ADVANCED

Writing Prompt Make a few copies of the informative/explanatory test writing prompt. Cut apart the sentences in the scoring guide. Have partners work together to assign each sentence to one of the rubric writing traits—Ideas, Organization, Voice, Word Choice, Sentence Fluency, and Conventions.

ADVANCED HIGH

Writing Prompt Have students read the informative/explanatory test writing prompt and write down no more than three words in each part of the prompt that they think are most important. Then have them compare with a partner and discuss the differences.

CCSS Common Core State Standards

SL.6.1: Engage effectively in a range of collaborative discussions (one-on-one, in groups, and teacher-led) with diverse partners on *grade 6 topics, texts, and issues*, building on others' ideas and expressing their own clearly. **SL.6.1.c:** Pose and respond to specific questions with elaboration and detail by making comments that contribute to the topic, text, or issue under discussion. **SL.6.1.d:** Review the key ideas expressed and demonstrate understanding of multiple perspectives through reflection and paraphrasing.

Write an Informative/ Explanatory Test

Week 2 • Day 2

Student Objectives

• Learn how to respond to the task in the writing prompt. *(p. 238)*

Prewrite

Focus on Ideas

Respond to the Task After reading Justin's thoughts on the task, point out that in a timed situation, a writer has to decide on an appropriate topic quickly. Justin first figured out how to respond to the task; then he selected a topic and made some notes. They provide a good starting point for organizing his essay.

Ask students why graphic organizers are important in writing, even when writing for a test. (Possible response: They help writers clarify, expand, and organize ideas before drafting.) Note that using a graphic organizer can actually help students save time because it will ensure their essays are organized before they begin their drafts. Tell students to look at page 239 to see the organizer Justin chose.

T238 Informative/Explanatory Writing

Prewrite   Focus on Ideas

Writing Strategy   Respond to the task.

I've learned that good writers always gather information before they begin writing. When you write to take a test, you can gather information from the writing prompt. Let's take another look at the task, since this is the part of the writing prompt that explains what I'm supposed to write. Remember, you won't have much time when writing for a test! That's why it's really important to think about how you'll respond before you begin to write.

I see that first I have to decide whether I want to take a ride on a space shuttle. I think blasting off into space would be fun, but now I have to explain why. I think jotting down some notes will help, but I have to do it quickly because the clock is ticking!

Task —— [Write an essay explaining why you would or would not want to go on a space shuttle.

Notes

✔ I'd do well in space, and I'm not afraid to go.

✔ I would like the feeling.

✔ It would be fun.

Apply

Make sure you think about how you'll respond to the task in your writing prompt before you write. Then you can jot down some notes to help you gather information.

238   Informative/Explanatory Writing

Differentiating Instruction

ENRICHMENT

Write a Prompt To help students better understand the parts of a writing prompt, ask them to refer to the one on page 229 and use it as a model to write a different test prompt. For example, suggest a short cause-and-effect report or an informative essay. Remind them that they should use the writing traits to develop the scoring guide. Have students exchange their prompts and suggest ways to improve them.

Prewrite

Focus on **Organization**

Writing Strategy Choose a graphic organizer.

I don't have much time, so I'll begin organizing my ideas. First, I'll choose a useful graphic organizer. I'm writing an explanation, so a Spider Map will help me remember the important ideas I want to include. The map will help me keep track of main ideas and details. Some of the information comes right out of the setup and the task.

I've decided I would like to fly on a space shuttle. I'll write that in the center circle of my Spider Map. Next, I'll identify the reasons why and write the main ones on each leg.

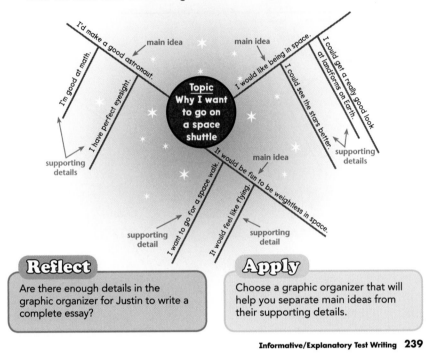

Reflect

Are there enough details in the graphic organizer for Justin to write a complete essay?

Apply

Choose a graphic organizer that will help you separate main ideas from their supporting details.

Informative/Explanatory Test Writing 239

REINFORCEMENT

Understand Graphic Organizers To help students understand how ideas are organized in a graphic organizer, ask them to complete a Spider Map with the information in the writing prompt response model, "A Place for Us," on page 231. Draw a Spider Map on the board and write *topic* in the center. Note that students should find the topic of the essay in the first paragraph. Work with students to complete the organizer.

Write
an Informative/ Explanatory Test

Week 2 • Day 3

Student Objectives

• Learn how to choose a graphic organizer for the writing prompt. *(p. 239)*

Prewrite

Focus on **Organization**

Choose a Graphic Organizer

During a writing test students might not be assigned an organizer. They must think about how they have used graphic organizers in the past and decide which one will be most useful. Point out that Justin used a Spider Map to organize his notes and separate main ideas from supporting details.

Have students read Justin's Spider Map. What part of the map should Justin include in his introduction? (information from the center, or *body*, of the spider) What might each of the paragraphs in the body of the essay include? (information from each of the *legs*) Discuss whether Justin has enough details to write a complete essay. Have students choose a graphic organizer that will help them organize ideas for their test.

CCSS **C**ommon **C**ore **S**tate **S**tandards

W.6.2: Write informative/explanatory texts to examine a topic and convey ideas, concepts, and information through the selection, organization, and analysis of relevant content. **W.6.2.a:** Introduce a topic; organize ideas, concepts, and information, using strategies such as definition, classification, comparison/contrast, and cause/effect; include formatting (e.g., headings), graphics (e.g., charts, tables), and multimedia when useful to aiding comprehension. **W.6.2.b:** Develop the topic with relevant facts, definitions, concrete details, quotations, or other information and examples.

Informative/Explanatory Test Writing T239

Write
an Informative/ Explanatory Test

Week 2 • Day 4

Student Objectives

• Learn how to check the graphic organizer against the scoring guide. (*pp. 240–241*)

Prewrite

Focus on Organization

Check the Graphic Organizer

Demonstrate how Justin has used each writing trait to make sure that his prewriting (gathering and organizing information) has stayed on track. Point out that each step in his Spider Map gives information about the main topic, *Why I want to go on a space shuttle.* Why should Justin take additional time to check his Spider Map before he starts writing a draft? (Possible responses: He wants to be sure he hasn't missed anything. It's easier to catch and change things now than after his paper is already written.)

Emphasize the importance of paying attention to the scoring guide throughout test writing. Note that on page 241 Justin again refers to the scoring guide. Explain that during the prewriting step of the test writing process, students should add or change information in their graphic organizers to meet the criteria on the scoring guide.

 Strategies for Writers Online
Go to **www.sfw.z-b.com** for additional online resources for students and teachers.

Prewrite   Focus on **Organization**

Writing Strategy   Check the graphic organizer against the scoring guide.

In a test, you don't always get much time to revise. That makes prewriting more important than ever! So before I write, I'll check my Spider Map against the scoring guide in the writing prompt.

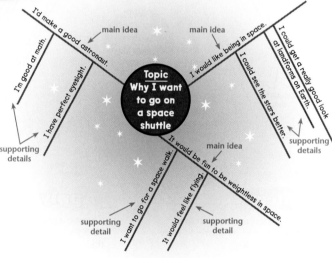

Spider Map labels: main idea — I'd make a good astronaut. (supporting details: I'm good at math. I have perfect eyesight.); main idea — I would like being in space. (I could see the stars better. I could get a really good look at landforms on Earth. — supporting details); Topic: Why I want to go on a space shuttle; main idea — It would be fun to be weightless in space. (supporting detail: I want to go for a space walk. It would feel like flying. It would be fun to be weightless in space. — supporting detail)

Ideas
- Be sure your topic is clear and includes relevant, credible details that appeal to your audience.

The Spider Map clearly states my topic and includes details that are relevant and credible. I'll use those in my writing.

Organization
- Be sure your writing is well organized and uses transitions to clarify relationships among ideas.

My Spider Map doesn't show connecting sentences yet, but as I write, I'll use transition words to connect my ideas.

Voice
- Be sure to use active voice and first-person point of view to engage your readers.

Since my topic is why I want to go on a space shuttle, it should be easy to use the first-person pronoun *I*. I'll also use active voice to keep the discussion engaging.

Word Choice
- Be sure your writing uses specific words to explain the topic.

My Spider Map already includes some specific words, such as *eyesight*, *space walk*, and *landforms*, that I will talk about.

Sentence Fluency
- Be sure your writing has a variety of sentence patterns.

I'll need to remember to do this when I start writing!

Conventions
- Be sure your writing contains correct grammar, punctuation, capitalization, and spelling.

I'll check for proper grammar and mechanics when I edit my draft.

Reflect

The Spider Map doesn't include every point in the scoring guide, but it covers most of them. Is anything else missing?

Apply

Before you start to write, reread the scoring guide in the writing prompt to be sure you know what to do.

Prepare to Draft Point out to students that Justin cannot check his work against all six writing traits yet. He will have to draft, for example, before he can check to see if he used a variety of sentence patterns to help his writing flow smoothly. Since this is the case, ask students why Justin stops to check his work against the scoring guide at this point. (Possible responses: Justin does not want to start writing if he is not responding to the task. He does not have much time to draft, so he must be sure he is on the right track before he starts drafting.) Explain to students that by going over the writing traits again, Justin is also reminding himself of what to keep in mind as he drafts.

CCSS Common Core State Standards

W.6.2: Write informative/explanatory texts to examine a topic and convey ideas, concepts and information through the selection, organization, and analysis of relevant content. **W.6.2.a:** Introduce a topic; organize ideas, concepts, and information, using strategies such as definition, classification, comparison/contrast, and cause/effect; include formatting (e.g., headings), graphics (e.g., charts, tables), and multimedia when useful to aiding comprehension. **W.6.2.b:** Develop the topic with relevant facts, definitions, concrete details, quotations, or other information and examples.

Write
an Informative/Explanatory Test

Week 2 • Day 5

Student Objectives

- Use a Spider Map to draft an informative/explanatory writing test, making sure to state the topic clearly. *(p. 242)*

Draft

Focus on Ideas

Tips for Test Writing Remind students to write on every other line of their paper. This makes it easier to reread their drafts and make changes and corrections. Despite the time constraints, encourage students to work neatly. Not only will neat writing help the essay grader, it will help students during revising and editing.

State the Topic Clearly Read Justin's words on page 242. Emphasize the importance of using a graphic organizer as a guide during drafting. Tell students to set their organizers on their desks and refer to them frequently. Because Justin identified his topic in his Spider Map, he knows what he needs to include in his opening paragraph. Ask students to read the first sentence from Justin's draft. Students should agree that he identified the topic in there.

Online Writing Center

Provides student eBooks with an **interactive writing pad** for drafting, revising, editing, and publishing.

Draft
Focus on **Ideas**

Writing Strategy State the topic clearly.

I can use the information in my Spider Map to start drafting. As I look back at the scoring guide, I can see that it's important to identify my topic early in the paper. I think I'll use my opening sentence to do this. This way my reader will know right away what I am writing about. In later paragraphs, I'll add relevant, interesting details.

[DRAFT]

The Sky's the Limit!
by Justin

[clear topic]

If I ever had an opportunity to go on the Space Shuttle, I would jump at the chance. Actually, maybe I should say I would fly at the chance! There are several reasons why I think this would be the experience of a lifetime.

First of all, being an astronaut would be fun. I like all of the rides at amusement parks, even the ones where you turn upside down. I'm also good in math, and I have perfect eyesight, so those are two more things in my favor.

I would be fascinated by the whole experience of being in space. I love looking at the stars from here on Earth. I can only imagine how

242 Informative/Explanatory Writing

English Language Learners

BEGINNING
First-Person Pronouns Review usage of the first-person pronouns *I, me,* and *my.* Give several simple examples, such as *I am an artist. Painting makes me happy. My name is Diana.* Write other examples on the board, but do not include the pronouns. Have students fill in the appropriate pronouns.

INTERMEDIATE
Proofreading After students have written and revised their writing tests, have them trade papers and proofread each other's paper. Ask them to circle any words whose spelling looks incorrect and then look them up in a dictionary. Remind students to use their knowledge of spelling patterns, search in ABC order, compare the dictionary spelling, and correct misspellings.

[relevant, credible details]

much better stargazing would be up in the sky. The other astronauts and me could look down at Earth when we got tired of stargazing. I've read that you can see Rivers, Mountains, and other landforms from space.

    I think that moving around without gravity wood be fun. My greatest dream is to be free in space. Walking in space would be just about the best thing I can imagine. Some people might be afraid of floating into space forever I don't think that would be a problem. The people who designed the space shuttle and all of it's equipment is very careful about everything they do.

    I know that not many people would enjoy eating and drinking food from tubes especially while being cooped up with other people in such a small space. Those things wouldn't bother me, though. Instead, being in space would make me really appreciate what I have here on earth.

Reflect

Think about the draft. Is the topic in a good place, and is it stated clearly?

Apply

The topic should be identified in the introduction so that the reader will know right away what the writing is about. Then add believable details that are appealing to the reader.

Informative/Explanatory Test Writing **243**

Students should ask themselves these questions:

- Does my first paragraph state the topic clearly?
- Do the body paragraphs contain relevant, credible details that appeal to readers?
- Is the writing well organized?

If students answer no to any of these questions, they should take another look at their organizers and decide where they need to include additional information.

Finally, review the proofreading marks with students. Tell them that these marks will be helpful as they revise and edit their drafts.

ADVANCED

Using Powerful Verbs After students have written their first drafts, have them circle all the verbs they used in the first paragraph. Then have them trade with a partner who will read the paragraph and change each of the circled verbs to a more specific one, if possible. Then have the partners discuss why they made each change. Monitor that students' changes were appropriate. Repeat for adjectives or adverbs.

ADVANCED HIGH

Peer Review After students have drafted their explanatory essays, have them trade with another student. Partners should review each other's draft and look for specific details. Students should point out weak voice and suggest more specific words their partners could use. As you monitor, identify two or three examples of weak words or sentences, and discuss ways to strengthen them as a class.

CCSS **C**ommon **C**ore **S**tate **S**tandards

W.6.2: Write informative/explanatory texts to examine a topic and convey ideas, concepts, and information through the selection, organization, and analysis of relevant content. **W.6.2.a:** Introduce a topic; organize ideas, concepts, and information, using strategies such as definition, classification, comparison/contrast, and cause/effect; include formatting (e.g., headings), graphics (e.g., charts, tables), and multimedia when useful to aiding comprehension. **W.6.2.b:** Develop the topic with relevant facts, definitions, concrete details, quotations, or other information and examples.

Informative/Explanatory Test Writing **T243**

Write
an Informative/ Explanatory Test

Week 3 • Day 1

Student Objectives

• Revise to use transition words to clarify connecting ideas. (*p. 244*)

Revise

Focus on  Organization

Time Management Point out that students have about fifteen minutes to revise their drafts, and that there are three revision tasks. (If you are using the Optional Revising Lessons, you will need to plan accordingly. See page T246.) Students might wish to subdivide their planned revising time into segments and tackle one strategy at a time.

Add Transition Words Read page 244. Remind students that an effective essay introduces the topic clearly, includes credible details, and is well organized. Using transitions helps clarify and connect ideas.

Have students read Justin's draft. Did the revisions improve his writing? (Possible response: Yes, Justin added transition words such as *Second, so, What's more,* and *In fact* to clarify relationships among ideas and make his writing clearer.) Then have them check to see where they might need to add transitions to better connect their ideas.

Strategies for Writers Online
Go to **www.sfw.z-b.com** for additional online resources for students and teachers.

T244   Informative/Explanatory Writing

Revise
Focus on Organization

Writing Strategy   Use transition words to clarify connecting ideas.

I'll read my paper again and see if any parts could be clearer. The scoring guide says that I should use transition words to clarify how ideas are related. I see some places where I can add transition words that will make my writing clearer.

[DRAFT]

[added transition words]

Second,
I would be fascinated by the whole experience of being in space.
, so
I love looking at the stars from here on Earth. I can only imagine how
                                              What's more,
much better stargazing would be up in the sky. The other astronauts
and me could look down at Earth when we got tired of stargazing.
In fact,
I've read that you can see Rivers, Mountains, and other landforms
from space.

Apply
Make sure your writing is clear. Use transition words to clarify relationships among ideas.

244   Informative/Explanatory Writing

Differentiating Instruction

ENRICHMENT

Transition This Challenge students to write a brief story that uses as many transition words from page 524 as possible. As students share their stories, discuss with them when transitions are helpful and whether there is such a thing as having too many transition words.

Writing Strategy Use active voice and first-person point of view.

I know I'm really interested in my topic—it's very exciting to me! But I need to connect with my readers and get them interested in what I have to say as well. Active voice will help with that. Since this is my personal experience, I'll use first-person point of view to draw readers in. Look where I found two more places to use first person and active voice.

[DRAFT] [added first person]

I think I would make a good astronaut.

First of all, being an astronaut would be fun. I like all of the rides at amusement parks, even the ones where you turn upside down. I'm also good in math, and I have perfect eyesight, so those are two more things in my favor.

Second,   fascinates me

I would be fascinated by the whole experience of being in space.

Reflect

What do you think of the revisions? Do first person and active voice help you connect with what Justin is saying?

Apply

Find places to use first-person point of view and active voice to engage your reader.

Informative/Explanatory Test Writing 245

REINFORCEMENT

Hunt for Transitions Distribute copies of text that contains transition words, such as recipes, instructions, or other informative texts. Have students work in pairs to highlight transition words and phrases that they find in the texts. Have each pair share their findings with the class. Discuss how and when transitions are useful.

Write
an Informative/ Explanatory Test

Week 3 • Day 2

Student Objectives

- Revise to use active voice and first-person point of view. (p. 245)

Revise

Focus on **Voice**

Review Voice Have students read one paragraph at a time, checking to make sure they have used an appropriate voice. Since Justin's essay is about a personal experience, he uses a first-person point of view to engage readers. He knows that using the pronoun *I* will show his excitement. Justin also connects with readers by using an active voice. He chooses strong verbs that jump right in on the action.

Remind students to make their revisions as neatly as possible. Advise them to use a caret to add words. This shows additional information without leaving a messy, hard-to-read draft behind.

CCSS **Common Core State Standards**

W.6.2.a: Introduce a topic; organize ideas, concepts, and information, using strategies such as definition, classification, comparison/contrast, and cause/effect; include formatting (e.g., headings), graphics (e.g., charts, tables), and multimedia when useful to aiding comprehension. **W.6.2.b:** Develop the topic with relevant facts, definitions, concrete details, quotations, or other information and examples. **W.6.2.c:** Use appropriate transitions to clarify the relationships among ideas and concepts. **W.6.2.e:** Establish and maintain a formal style. **L.6.3.b:** Maintain consistency in style and tone.

Write
an Informative/ Explanatory Test

Week 3 • Day 3

Student Objectives

• Revise to use specific words. (p. 246)

Revise

Focus on  Word Choice

Replace Vague Words With Specific Words Have students read the page independently. After, remind students that the scoring guide says they should use specific words to explain the topic. Justin knows that choosing precise words makes his meaning clear and helps readers understand his ideas. Guide students to notice that Justin found a place in his essay where he needed to replace vague words with specific words. Discuss Justin's revisions. Students should agree that they improve this part of his essay. Stress that using specific words strengthens writing and helps create a clear picture in the reader's mind.

Students may have time left in the revising period. Encourage students to use every minute they have to improve their essays, even if they want to finish early.

Online Writing Center

 Provides **interactive proofreading activities** for each genre.

Revise

Focus on **Word Choice**

Writing Strategy Use specific words.

The scoring guide says I should use specific words to explain my topic. Choosing just the right words makes my meaning clear and helps the reader quickly grasp what I'm trying to say. I'll check for vague words that I can replace with specific words to make my writing clearer. I think I found one or two in this section.

[DRAFT]   [replaced vague words with specific words]

just like flying

I think that moving around without gravity wood be fun. My greatest

go for a space walk

dream is to be free in space. Walking in space would be just about the

best thing I can imagine.

Apply

Vague words make your writing sound weak and harder to understand. Replace those words with more specific words to create a sharp picture in the reader's mind.

246 Informative/Explanatory Writing

Optional Revising Lessons

Informative/Explanatory 19

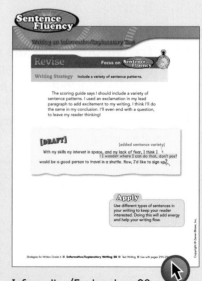

Informative/Explanatory 20

Go to **Strategies for Writers Grade 6 CD-ROM**

Edit

Focus on **Conventions**

Writing Strategy Check the grammar, punctuation, capitalization, and spelling.

Now there's just one last step! The scoring guide says to use correct grammar and mechanics. I always leave plenty of time to check for errors in these important areas.

[FINAL DRAFT]

The Sky's the Limit!

by Justin

If I ever had an opportunity to go on the Space Shuttle, I would jump at the chance. Actually, maybe I should say I would fly at the chance! There are several reasons why I think this would be the experience of a lifetime.

I think I would make a good astronaut.
First of all, ~~being an astronaut would be fun.~~ I like all of the rides at
, so all of the motion wouldn't bother me
amusement parks, even the ones where you turn upside down. I'm also
good in math, and I have perfect eyesight, so those are two more
Plus, I like working on a team with other people,
things in my favor. and I have a knack for helping others get along.
Second,
the whole experience of being in space fascinates me. I love
so
looking at the stars from here on Earth. I can only imagine how

Apply

Check your grammar, punctuation, capitalization, and spelling every time you write for a test.

Informative/Explanatory Test Writing 247

Write
an Informative/ Explanatory Test

Student Objectives

• Edit the writing test for proper grammar, spelling, capitalization, and punctuation. *(p. 247)*

Edit

Focus on Conventions

Edit the Test Explain that while an essay written for a test will rarely be perfect, students should find and correct as many errors as they can. Test graders know that students are writing quickly and watching the clock; graders know that a few errors may slip through. However, graders also look for evidence that students took time to edit. When they see misspelled words crossed out and correctly spelled words inserted instead, for example, graders know that students are paying attention.

Review the proofreading marks on page 243. Point out the insertions in Justin's draft. Remind students that they should not plan for time to recopy their drafts—every minute of writing time should be put to good use, making the essay stronger, not to produce a perfectly neat final copy.

CCSS Common Core State Standards
W.6.2.d: Use precise language and domain-specific vocabulary to inform about or explain the topic. **L.6.2:** Demonstrate command of the conventions of standard English capitalization, punctuation, and spelling when writing. **L.6.2.a:** Use punctuation (commas, parentheses, dashes) to set off nonrestrictive/ parenthetical elements. **L.6.2.b:** Spell correctly. **L.6.3:** Use knowledge of language and its conventions when writing, speaking, reading, or listening.

Review
Test Tips

Week 3 • Day 5

Student Objectives

- Review tips for writing for a test. (p. 249)

Test Tips

Reviewing Test Writing Explain that not all writing test prompts will be as clear as the one in this chapter. However, students can still find and label the three important sections. Students can even generate a scoring guide if they must. Write this prompt on the board:

Think about a country that you have studied in social studies and now have the opportunity to visit. Tell why you would or would not want to travel there. Be sure to include a clear topic and relevant, credible details. Remember to revise and edit.

Ask:

- What is the setup? (Think about a country you have studied in social studies that you have the opportunity to visit.)

Circle and label the setup. Ask students how they might expand it to get a better sense of the background for this prompt. (Possible response: I might make a list of all the countries that I have learned about in social studies.)

Strategies for Writers Online

Go to **www.sfw.z-b.com** for additional online resources for students and teachers.

[FINAL DRAFT]

What's more,
much better stargazing would be up in the sky. The other astronauts
and me could look down at Earth when we got tired of stargazing.
In fact,
I've read that you can see Rivers, Mountains, and other landforms
from space.

would   just like flying
I think that moving around without gravity wood be fun. My greatest
, however,   go for a space walk
dream is to be free in space. Walking in space would be just about
the best thing I can imagine. Some people might be afraid of floating
, but
into space forever I don't think that would be a problem. The people
are
who designed the space shuttle and all of it's equipment is very careful
about everything they do.

I know that not many people would enjoy eating and drinking food
from tubes especially while being cooped up with other people in such
a small space. Those things wouldn't bother me, though. Instead, being
in space would make me really appreciate what I have here on earth.

With my skills my interest in space, and my lack of fear, I think I
! I wonder where I can do that, don't you?
would be a good person to travel in a shuttle. Now, I'd like to sign up.

Reflect

Is the writing missing anything? Check it against the scoring guide. Remember to use your writing prompt's scoring guide to check your writing any time you take a test!

We're finished! That wasn't so bad! Remember these important tips when you write for a test.

TEST TiPS

1. **Study the writing prompt before you start to write.** Most writing prompts have three parts: the setup, the task, and the scoring guide. The parts probably won't be labeled. You'll have to figure them out for yourself!

2. **Make sure you understand the task before you start to write.**
   - Read all three parts of the writing prompt carefully.
   - Circle key words in the task part of the writing prompt that tell what kind of writing you need to do. The task might also identify your audience.
   - Make sure you know how you'll be graded.
   - Say the assignment in your own words to yourself.

3. **Keep an eye on the clock.** Decide how much time you will spend on each part of the writing process and try to stick to your schedule. Don't spend so much time prewriting that you don't have enough time left to write.

4. **Reread your writing. Compare it to the scoring guide at least twice.** Remember the rubrics you have used all year? A scoring guide on a writing test is like a rubric. It can help you keep what's important in mind.

5. **Plan, plan, plan!** You don't get much time to revise during a test, so planning is more important than ever.

6. **Write neatly.** Remember: If the people who score your test can't read your writing, it doesn't matter how good your essay is!

Informative/Explanatory Test Writing 249

Next, ask:

- What is the task? (Explain how I feel about this country and determine if I would want to travel there.)

Circle and label the task. Ask what it requires. (The task asks students to write an explanatory essay.) Finally, ask students what they can do to make up a scoring guide since the writing prompt has only the general instructions to revise and edit.

(Possible responses: Present a clear topic and credible, relevant details; organize the essay well and use transitions to clarify relationships among ideas; use an active voice and first-person point of view to engage readers; use specific words to explain the topic; write a variety of interesting sentences; and edit for correct grammar, spelling, punctuation, and capitalization.)

As students provide these responses, write them on the board in bulleted form. Show students that they have just figured out a useful scoring guide from their own experience. Students will see that even a brief writing prompt can give them the tools and guidance they need to write a successful test response.

CCSS Common Core State Standards

W.6.5: With some guidance and support from peers and adults, develop and strengthen writing as needed by planning, revising, editing, rewriting, or trying a new approach. **W.6.10:** Write routinely over extended time frames (time for research, reflection, and revision) and shorter time frames (a single sitting or a day or two) for a range of discipline-specific tasks, purpose, and audiences. **SL.6.1.d:** Review the key ideas expressed and demonstrate understanding of multiple perspectives through reflection and paraphrasing.

Argument writing

Response to Literature Pages T252A–T277

This genre opens the door to argument writing by encouraging students to choose two similar books and express an informed opinion about them.

Prewrite Find two similar books. Take notes in a response journal.
Make a Venn Diagram from the notes and the response journal.

Draft Write a clear thesis statement and include relevant supporting evidence.

Revise Link ideas with transitions, such as *same, similarly, however, yet,* and *on one hand.*
Use a formal style throughout.
Avoid loaded words that cause a strong negative reaction.

Edit Check that all dependent clauses are part of complex sentences and are punctuated correctly.

Publish Publish book review in the school newspaper.

Argument Essay Pages T278A–T299

Students will further develop their argument writing skills as they explore how to build a convincing argument in an essay.

Prewrite Choose an issue and find information to support the opinion.
Use a Network Tree to organize the ideas.

Draft Write well-organized paragraphs.

Revise Use second-person point of view, as appropriate.
Replace loaded words with neutral words.
Choose punctuation for effect.

Edit Recognize and correct inappropriate shifts in pronoun number and person.

Publish Post the essay on a class bulletin board.

Business Letter Pages T300A–T321

In the context of functional writing, students will extend their argument writing skills as they learn and apply strategies for writing a business letter to a manager of a business.

Prewrite Pick something that needs to change. List reasons for the change.
Use an Order-of-Importance Organizer to organize the reasons.

Draft Use formal language.

Revise Add details to support the opinion.
Replace vague nouns and verbs.
Make sure each sentence reflects the purpose of the letter.

Edit Check the use of homophones.

Publish Mail the business letter.

Unit Overview

SCIENCE
CONNECTION

Speech
Pages T322A–T343

Students will demonstrate knowledge of a scientist and extend their argument writing skills as they learn and apply strategies for writing a speech. They will learn how to include a call to action, use supporting evidence, and maintain a convincing tone to motivate an audience.

Prewrite	Decide on a position and do some research. Use an Argument Map to plan the speech.
Draft	Define unfamiliar words.
Revise	Use credible sources. Use effective transitions to show how ideas are connected. Use phrases and clauses to vary sentences.
Edit	Check forms of *be* and change passive voice to active.
Publish	Give the speech to the class.

Argument Test Writing
Pages T344A–T365

Students learn and practice how to read an argument test prompt and how to plan their time while taking a writing test. They also learn and practice writing strategies for successful test writing in the mode of argument writing.

Prewrite	Study the writing prompt to find out what to do. Respond to the task. Choose a graphic organizer. Check the graphic organizer against the scoring guide.
Draft	State the position clearly. Support the position with relevant evidence.
Revise	Use helpful transitions to guide the reader. Establish and maintain a formal style. Choose words and phrases that convey ideas precisely.
Edit	Check the grammar, punctuation, capitalization, and spelling.

Online Writing Center
Interactive Whiteboard Ready

Complete Digital Writing Instruction!

- My Writing Pad
- Interactive Rubrics
- Anchor Papers
- Graphic Organizers

- Content Area Writing Prompts
- Grammar Games
- Proofreading Activities
- Instructional Videos

- Virtual File Cabinet
- eBooks
- Assessments

For information, go to
www.sfw.z-b.com

Also available: **Online Essay Grader and Writing Tutor,** powered by Vantage Learning's MY Access®.

21st Century Literacies
Technology, Digital Media & Writing

by **Julie Coiro, Ph.D.,** University of Rhode Island & **Sara Kajder, Ph.D.,** University of Pittsburgh

 **INQUIRE** First Locate, Then Evaluate

Locating Resources: Reading Within Websites

Model for students the following strategy to help them learn to stop, think, and anticipate where important information about a website's content might be found.

1. Read the title of the page and the title of the website in the margin at the top of the window.

2. To get a big picture of the information within the site, scan menu choices by holding your mouse over the navigational or topical menus that often appear along the sides of the frame or across the top of the window, but don't click yet.

3. Make predictions about where each of the major links may lead and anticipate a link's path through multiple levels of a website.

4. Explore interactive features of dynamic images (animated images or images that change as a viewer holds the mouse over them), pop-up menus, and scroll bars that may reveal additional levels of information.

5. Identify the creator of the website and when it was last updated. You can often find this information by clicking on a button labeled "About This Site." Consider what this information indicates about the site.

6. Notice and try out any electronic supports the site has, such as an organizational site map or internal search engine.

7. Make a judgment about whether to explore the site further. If the site looks worthwhile, decide which areas of the site to explore first.

After several demonstrations, have students practice these strategies in their own online reading.

Critical Evaluation: Evaluating Author's Perspective

One aspect of reading critically involves the ability to detect the author's perspective. Information on the Internet is much more widely available from people who have strong political, economic, or religious stances that profoundly influence the nature of the information they present to others.

One strategy for helping students understand the concepts of bias and perspective involves helping them to distinguish among facts, opinions, and point of view. A classroom discussion about persuasive writing techniques can provide an excellent context within which to introduce these ideas. Your students are bound to have different opinions about various topics, so you might wish to highlight these differences by selecting a topic that some students really like and others really don't. Ask students to write three sentences that give an opinion and attempt to persuade others to agree with it. Encourage students to share their sentences with the class while others try to guess whether they're facts or opinions. Categorize the sentences that reflect one point of view (e.g., *I like broccoli*) versus another (e.g., *I don't like broccoli*) and explain that both are valid but come from different perspectives. Thus, the ideas are biased toward one perspective or another. Explain that a more complete explanation of this topic would include sentences that represent both perspectives.

Point out to students that many websites are written from only one perspective. This is important to know so that students do not base their whole thinking about an issue on one person's point of view. If they feel they are not getting "the whole story" from one website, they should look at another website that offers a different perspective.

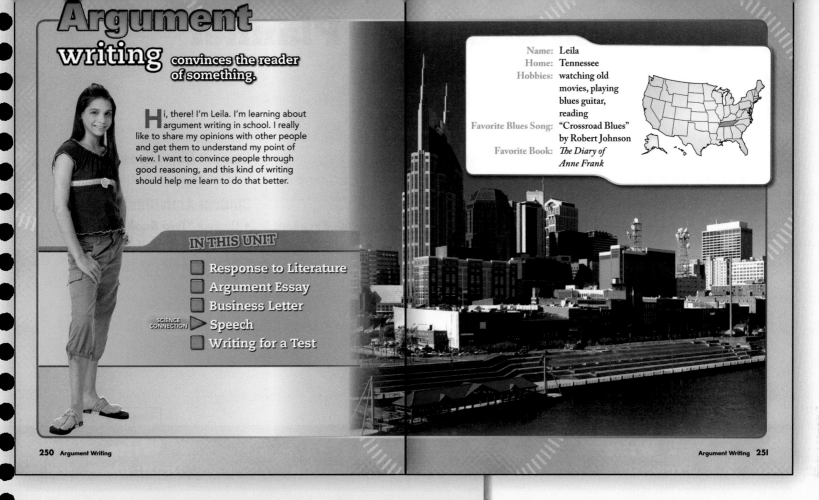

Argument writing convinces the reader of something.

Hi, there! I'm Leila. I'm learning about argument writing in school. I really like to share my opinions with other people and get them to understand my point of view. I want to convince people through good reasoning, and this kind of writing should help me learn to do that better.

Name:	Leila
Home:	Tennessee
Hobbies:	watching old movies, playing blues guitar, reading
Favorite Blues Song:	"Crossroad Blues" by Robert Johnson
Favorite Book:	*The Diary of Anne Frank*

IN THIS UNIT

- ☐ Response to Literature
- ☐ Argument Essay
- ☐ Business Letter
- SCIENCE CONNECTION ▷ Speech
- ☐ Writing for a Test

To differentiate instruction and maximize student achievement, use the Extensions Online activities available at **www.sfw.z-b.com.**

Created by Amy Humphreys, Ed.M., these engaging activities can be used to meet a wide range of learner needs. Each activity uses a combination of visual, written, oral, and kinesthetic elements, and deliberately leverages the power of collaboration and conversation so students learn to think like writers in fun and engaging ways. For more information on Differentiated Instruction, see page Z12.

Meet Your Writing Partner, Leila

The writing partner for this chapter is Leila, a girl from Tennessee. You may wish to explore with students how Leila's background, hobbies, interests, and personality connect with her choices of writing topics. Explain to students that Leila will use what she knows to make decisions about her topics—a process that makes her writing authentic. Encourage students to follow Leila's lead by using their own background knowledge, interests, and voice as they write. In this unit, your students will explore several genres and use the Argument Writing Traits, along with proven writing strategies, to express and support opinions on diverse topics.

Response to Literature Planner

WEEK 1

Day 1
Introduce
a Response to Literature

Student Objectives
- Review the elements of a response to literature.
- Consider purpose and audience.
- Learn the traits of argument writing.

Student Activities
- Read and discuss **What's in a Response to Literature?** *(p. 252)*
- Read and discuss **Why Write a Response to Literature?** *(p. 253)*
- Read **Linking Argument Writing Traits to a Response to Literature.** *(p. 254)*

Day 2
Analyze
Read a Response to Literature

Student Objectives
- Read a model response to literature.

Student Activities
- Read **"Two Books by One Excellent Author."** *(p. 255)*

Day 3
Analyze
Introduce the Rubric

Student Objectives
- Learn to read a rubric.

Student Activities
- Review **"Two Books by One Excellent Author."** *(p. 255)*
- Read and discuss the **Response to Literature Rubric.** *(pp. 256–257)*

WEEK 2

Day 1
Write
Prewrite: Ideas

Student Objectives
- Find two similar books. Take notes in a response journal.

Student Activities
- Read and discuss **Prewrite: Focus on Ideas.** *(pp. 262–263)*
- Apply the prewriting strategy.

Day 2
Write
Prewrite: Organization

Student Objectives
- Make a Venn Diagram from the notes and response journal.

Student Activities
- Read and discuss **Prewrite: Focus on Organization.** *(pp. 264–265)*
- Apply the prewriting strategy.
- Participate in a peer conference.

Day 3
Write
Draft: Ideas

Student Objectives
- Write a clear thesis statement and include relevant supporting evidence.

Student Activities
- Read and discuss **Draft: Focus on Ideas.** *(p. 266)*
- Apply the drafting strategy.

WEEK 3

Day 1
Write
Revise: Voice

Student Objectives
- Revise to use a formal style.

Student Activities
- Read and discuss: **Revise: Focus on Voice.** *(p. 269)*
- Participate in a peer conference.

Day 2
Write
Revise: Word Choice

Student Objectives
- Revise to avoid loaded words.

Student Activities
- Read and discuss: **Revise: Focus on Word Choice.** *(p. 270)*

Note: Optional Revising Lessons appear on the *Strategies for Writers* CD-ROM.

Day 3
Write
Edit: Conventions

Student Objectives
- Check that all dependent clauses are part of complex sentences and are punctuated correctly.

Student Activities
- Read and discuss **Edit: Focus on Conventions.** *(p. 271)*

Note: Teach the Conventions mini-lessons *(pp. 272–273)* if needed.

Day 4

Analyze
Ideas, Organization, and Voice

Student Objectives
- Read a model response to literature.
- Use the response to literature rubric.
- Use the model response to literature to study Ideas, Organization, and Voice.

Student Activities
- Review **"Two Books by One Excellent Author."** (p. 255)
- Review the rubric. (pp. 256–257)
- Read and discuss **Using the Rubric to Study the Model.** (pp. 258–259)

Day 4

Write
Draft

Student Objectives
- Complete a draft.

Student Activities
- Finish writing the draft. (p. 267)
- Participate in a peer conference.

Day 4

Write
Publish: +Presentation

Student Objectives
- Present a response to literature in class.
- Use a final editing checklist to publish a response to literature.

Student Activities
- Read and discuss **Publish: +Presentation.** (p. 274)
- Apply the publishing strategy.

Day 5

Analyze
Word Choice, Sentence Fluency, and Conventions

Student Objectives
- Read a model response to literature.
- Use the response to literature rubric.
- Use the model response to literature to study Word Choice, Sentence Fluency, and Conventions.

Student Activities
- Review **"Two Books by One Excellent Author."** (p. 255)
- Review the rubric. (pp. 256–257)
- Read and discuss **Using the Rubric to Study the Model.** (pp. 260–261)

Day 5

Write
Revise: Organization

Student Objectives
- Revise to use transitions effectively.

Student Activities
- Read and discuss **Revise: Focus on Organization.** (p. 268)
- Reflect on the model draft.
- Apply the revising strategy.

Day 5

Write
Publish: +Presentation

Student Objectives
- Use a response to literature rubric.
- Share a published response to literature.

Student Activities
- Share their work.
- Use the rubric to reflect upon and evaluate the model and their own writing. (pp. 256–257; 275–277)

To complete the chapter in fewer days, combine the learning objectives and activities in a way that supports students as they write.

Resources at-a-Glance

Grammar, Usage & Mechanics

Complex Sentences T272
Commas After Introductory
    Clauses. T273
Grammar Practice T271–T273

Differentiating Instruction

Using the Rubric T261
Draft. T266
Publish T274

For additional Differentiating Instruction activities, see Strategies for Writers *Extensions Online at* **www.sfw.z-b.com.**

English Language Learners

Using the Rubric T258–T259
Prewrite T262–T263
Revise T268

Conferencing

Peer to Peer T265, T267, T269
Peer Groups T265, T267, T269
Teacher-Led T265, T267, T269

Technology Tip

Using the Rubric T260
Publish T275

 Connection Letter
Reproducible letter (in English and Spanish) appears on the *Strategies for Writers* CD-ROM and at **www.sfw.z-b.com.**

Online Writing Center

Provides IWB resources, interactive games and practice activities, videos, eBooks, and a virtual file cabinet.

 Strategies for Writers Online

Go to **www.sfw.z-b.com** for free online resources for students and teachers.

Response to Literature **252B**

Introduce
a Response to Literature

Week 1 • Day 1

Student Objectives

- Review the elements of a response to literature. (p. 252)
- Consider purpose and audience. (p. 253)
- Learn the traits of argument writing. (p. 254)

What's a Response to Literature?

Encourage students to share why people talk about books. (Possible responses: to convince others to read or not read the book; to reflect on a work that has inspired or motivated them; to share their excitement or disappointment in a book) Explain that a response to literature is argument writing because the writer expresses an opinion about a book and tries to convince others that the opinion is valid and supported.

What's in a Response to Literature?

Read and discuss the elements of a response to literature with the students. Discuss how each of the elements is important in a well-written response to literature.

 Strategies for Writers Online
Go to **www.sfw.z-b.com** for additional online resources for students and teachers.

What's a **Response to Literature?**

A response to literature is a way to express my opinions and ideas about what I have read. I am going to write a book review, in which my opinion will be supported with facts and details from the book. In a book review, I can convince other people to read a book I like.

What's in a **Response to Literature?**

Thesis Statement
This expresses the writer's opinion. I'll make my thesis statement very clear, and I'll put it right in the first paragraph so my audience knows where I stand.

Organization
One effective way to organize a response to literature is to use a compare-and-contrast pattern. I'm going to do that in my review. That will make my comparisons very clear to my readers.

Supporting Evidence
If I want to convince my readers of my opinion, I have to have some evidence supporting my point of view. Quoting directly from the book can help support my opinions, and so can adding facts about what happens in the book.

Clear Writing
Since I'll have to leave a lot of the details out of my response, I need to be careful that things don't get confusing. All my sentences must be complete and clear, smooth and interesting.

252 Argument Writing

Argument Text Exemplars
(Response to Literature)

Meltzer, Milton. *Edgar Allan Poe: A Biography.* Twenty-First Century Books, 2003. This biography examines the life of Edgar Allen Poe, an American writer best known for his poetry, short stories, and mysteries. The book delves into Poe's struggles with family and his own personal demons, and how they influenced his work.

Meigs, Cornelia. *Invincible Louisa: The Story of the Author of Little Women.* Little, Brown Books for Young Readers, 1995. Louisa May Alcott is best known as the author of such classics as *Little Women*. This fascinating biography chronicles Alcott's life from her childhood in Pennsylvania and Boston to her success as a writer.

Why write a Response to Literature?

I've never written a book review before, but I can think of all sorts of reasons to write one. I've listed some of my ideas below—and I'm still thinking!

Encouragement
A book review can encourage other people to read. After reading a review, they may decide to read the same book, another book by the same author, or a book on a similar topic or theme.

Personal Reflection
Sometimes I get in a big rush because I can't wait to finish one book and start another! Writing a book review can help me stop and really think about what I've read and what it means to me.

Sharing My Opinion
My friends and family know this is one of my favorite things to do! Writing a book review gives me the chance to express my opinions about something I really love—books!

Responding to Literature
When you respond to literature, you analyze it by looking at the parts of the work, their relationship to each other, and their relationship to the whole. This is an important kind of thinking that I'll need in other subjects and in real life. Responding to literature takes analytical thinking, so this will be good practice.

Rosen, Michael. *Dickens: His Work and His World.* **Candlewick, 2008.** *Dickens: His Work and His World* chronicles the author Charles Dickens's childhood, focusing on the people Dickens met and places he visited and how they each influenced his writing. This biography also examines the author's best-known works, including *A Christmas Carol* and *David Copperfield*.

Cleary, Beverly. *A Girl from Yamhill.* **HarperCollins, 1996.** *A Girl from Yamhill* is a memoir by Newbery Medalist, Beverly Clearly. This fascinating memoir chronicles her life from childhood to the publication of her first book, *Henry Huggins*.

Why write a Response to Literature?

Read and discuss with students the reasons for writing a response to literature as listed here. Explain that expressing an opinion on books they have read is one reason for writing a response to literature. Invite students to read and reflect on Leila's reasons. Point out that authentic reasons help to shape writing and determine audience. Encourage students to think about their own reasons for writing a response to literature. Add that their purpose will also affect the tone and style of writing.

CCSS **Common Core State Standards**
SL.6.1: Engage effectively in a range of collaborative discussions (one-on-one, in groups, and teacher-led) with diverse partners on *grade 6 topics, texts, and issues,* building on each other's ideas and expressing their own clearly. **SL.6.1.a:** Come to discussions prepared, having read or studied required material; explicitly draw on that preparation by referring to evidence on the topic, text, or issue to probe and reflect on ideas under discussion.

Introduce
a Response to Literature

Linking Argument Writing Traits to a Response to Literature

Explain to students that they will follow Leila as she models using the writing process and the traits together. As they follow Leila through the writing process, students will see how the Argument Writing Traits have been adapted and applied to writing a response to literature. They will see that a response to literature, because it expresses an opinion, has many factors in common with other types of argument writing. However, the particular audience and purpose of a response to literature determine how the traits are used.

Linking Argument Writing Traits to a **Response to Literature**

In this chapter, you will write an opinion about a book you have read. This type of argument writing is called a book review. Leila will guide you through the stages of the writing process: Prewrite, Draft, Revise, Edit, and Publish. In each stage, Leila will show you important writing strategies that are linked to the Argument Writing Traits below.

Argument Writing Traits

Ideas	• clearly stated claims, often balanced by alternate or opposing claims • supporting evidence from accurate and credible sources
 **Organization**	• a strong introduction that presents the writer's position • reasons and evidence that are organized logically • a conclusion that restates the thesis and possibly provides a call to action • transitions that clarify the relationships between ideas
Voice	• a voice that supports the writer's purpose
Word Choice	• language that is compelling
Sentence Fluency	• sentences that vary in length and begin in different ways
Conventions	• no or few errors in grammar, usage, mechanics, and spelling

Before you write, read Juan Cepeda's book review on the next page. Then use the response to literature rubric on pages 256–257 to decide how well he did. (You might want to look back at What's in a Response to Literature? on page 252, too!)

Argument Writing Traits in a Response to Literature

 Ideas A well-written book review clearly states the writer's opinion and includes relevant supporting evidence from the source.

 **Organization** The writer uses a clear compare-and-contrast pattern to organize the information. Helpful transitions guide the reader through the review.

 **Voice** The writer establishes and maintains a formal style.

Two Books by One Excellent Author

by Juan Cepeda

Virginia Hamilton has written a wide range of stories. *The House of Dies Drear*, for example, is a spellbinding mystery. In contrast, *Cousins* is an emotional story of love and betrayal. Although different, both books are ideal for middle graders. *Thesis statement*

Organization—comparing characters

These readers can easily identify with the young main characters in these two books. While these characters are both independent, they love their families. In *The House of Dies Drear*, Thomas Small attempts to unravel the dark secrets of his new house by himself. Thomas wants to prove that he is brave and smart, like his father. He also wants to protect his family from dangers in the house. In *Cousins*, on the other hand, young Cammy loves being her mother's "baby." Like Thomas, though, she also enjoys freedom. She wants to visit her grandmother whenever she pleases. Unlike Thomas, Cammy rarely sees her father. Instead, she looks up to her big brother. Sometimes she feels "like she would burst with love" for him. *Clear writing*

Supporting evidence

Organization—comparing settings

The settings of both books combine the familiar and the unfamiliar. Thomas's new home is a mysterious old house. The huge mansion had been a stop on the Underground Railroad. It has a homey kitchen, but it also has secret passages. The house looms over the story, creating a dark mood. In contrast, the pleasant little town in *Cousins* creates a sunny mood. As in *The House of Dies Drear*, however, that setting can turn threatening. In *Cousins*, a river swallows one of Cammy's cousins.

Organization—comparing themes

Each book addresses the theme of dealing with changes. Many middle-grade readers can identify with this theme, as they are also dealing with changes. Thomas has to overcome his fears about moving to a new place. Similarly, Cammy copes with her grief over the death of her cousin.

Virginia Hamilton tells stories that middle graders can understand and enjoy. Read *The House of Dies Drear*, *Cousins*, or any of Hamilton's other novels. You will see how the characters, settings, and themes make her stories so appealing. *Clear writing*

 **Word Choice** The writer's words are precise and convincing. Neutral language presents the writer's claim fairly.

 **Sentence Fluency** Sentence patterns are varied and interesting. The review flows smoothly and is enjoyable to read.

 **Conventions** The writer has edited carefully. Dependent clauses are used correctly.

Analyze
the Model

Week 1 • Day 2

Student Objectives

- Read a model response to literature. (p. 255)

Read the Model

Direct students' attention to the notes written on the model, making sure they can identify the writer's thesis statement and supporting evidence. Also point out that the writer uses a compare-and-contrast pattern to organize the response for the reader. What is the effect? (Possible responses: The writer presents his thesis statement in the introduction. The text is well organized, and the ideas are easy to follow. Supporting evidence is relevant and helps to convince the audience of the writer's viewpoint.)

Elements of a Response to Literature

After reading "Two Books by One Excellent Author," have students return to What's in a Response to Literature? on page 252. Discuss the elements within the model.

CCSS **C**ommon **C**ore **S**tate **S**tandards

R/Inf.6.1: Cite textual evidence to support analysis of what the text says explicitly as well as inferences drawn from the text. **R/Inf.6.6:** Determine an author's point of view or purpose in a text and explain how it is conveyed in the text. **SL.6.1.b:** Follow rules for collegial discussions, set specific goals and deadlines, and define individual roles as needed.

Analyze
the Model

Week 1 • Day 3

Student Objectives

- Learn to read a rubric. (pp. 256–257)

Use the Rubric

Explain the Rubric Explain that a writing rubric is a tool for planning, improving, and assessing a piece of writing. A rubric helps a writer focus on key elements, or traits, in writing (**Ideas, Organization, Voice, Word Choice, Sentence Fluency, Conventions,** and **Presentation**).

Explain the 6-point system. Point out that the columns on page 256 represent a good response to literature that might need some polishing while the columns on page 257 represent writing that needs considerable improvement.

Discuss the Rubric Guide students in a discussion of the rubric. Read the descriptors that go with each trait, and take a moment to explain the relationship between them. Discuss the differences between columns to be sure students fully understand the point system. Remind students to keep the rubric in mind as they write their own response to literature and again as they revise and edit it.

Online Writing Center

Provides a variety of **interactive rubrics,** including 4-, 5-, and 6-point models.

Rubric

Use this 6-point rubric to plan and score a response to literature.

	6	5	4
Ideas	A clear thesis statement states the writer's opinion. Comparisons are well supported with relevant facts and quotations from reliable sources.	The thesis statement includes the writer's opinion. Relevant facts and quotations support the thesis.	The thesis statement is present but may be unclear. The writer may focus the review on only one book. Facts or quotations are used.
Organization	A clear compare-contrast pattern organizes the information. Transition words effectively clarify similarities and differences.	A compare-contrast pattern is used well. Transitions clarify ideas.	A compare-contrast pattern is used and is fairly easy to follow. Transitions are often helpful.
Voice	The writer establishes and consistently maintains a formal style.	The writer establishes a formal style and maintains it most of the time.	The writer establishes a formal style but does not maintain it consistently.
Word Choice	Neutral language presents the writer's opinion fairly. Precise words clarify and enhance opinions.	The writer uses neutral language well. Precise words clarify and enhance comparisons.	The writer uses neutral language. Most comparisons are clear and easy to understand.
Sentence Fluency	Great variety in sentence patterns and lengths makes the writing flow smoothly.	Variety in sentence patterns and lengths makes the writing flow smoothly.	Some variety in sentence patterns and lengths makes the writing easy to read.
Conventions	The writing has been thoroughly edited. Complex sentences are punctuated correctly.	A few hard-to-find errors are present. Most complex sentences are punctuated correctly.	Some errors are present but don't take away from the meaning. Some complex sentences are punctuated correctly.

+ Presentation White space organizes the text for easy reading.

256 Argument Writing

CCSS Common Core State Standards

Response to Literature

The Common Core State Standards (CCSS) are woven throughout the instruction in *Strategies for Writers*. Writing in the Argument mode can engage the standards for all forms of Argument writing. The rubric and writing strategies for Ideas reflect writing standard **W.6.1,** to write arguments to support claims with clear reasons and relevant evidence, and standards **W.6.1.a** and **W.6.1.b,** to introduce and support a claim. The rubric and writing strategies for Organization are also drawn from standards **W.6.1.a** and **W.6.1.b,** to organize the ideas logically, and standard **W.6.1.e,** to provide an effective conclusion. The rubric and writing strategies for Voice and Word Choice reflect standard **W.6.1.c,** to use language to create cohesion and clarify relationships among ideas, and standard **W.6.1.d,** to establish and maintain a formal style.

3	2	1	
The thesis statement takes work to discover. Facts and quotations are limited and may be irrelevant or unreliable. The reader is left with questions.	The topic is not clear. The writer's opinion is not shared. Vague information lacks relevant facts or quotations.	The writing is not clear and contains no thesis statement. It lacks information.	**Ideas**
The writing is not organized in a compare-contrast pattern. Sometimes transitions are missing or do not make the ideas clear.	The writing is hard to follow, and transitions are unclear or missing.	Transitions are missing, and the reader feels lost. The writing lacks any organization.	**Organization**
The style wavers between formal and informal throughout the writing.	The style is mainly informal, with occasional moments of formality.	The writing has no clear voice and is too casual throughout.	**Voice**
The writer uses some biased words. Some comparisons are hard to follow because vague words are used.	Much of the writer's language is biased or too general. Comparisons are hard to understand.	Words simply fill the page. The reader feels lost.	**Word Choice**
Some sentences are choppy. Sentence beginnings and lengths are often the same.	Sentences are either too short or too long. Sentences are incomplete, run-on, or choppy.	The writing is difficult to read. Sentences are incomplete or incorrect.	**Sentence Fluency**
Errors in complex sentences are noticeable and may take away from the meaning.	Writing contains frequent errors in complex sentences that take away from the meaning.	The writing is not edited. Many serious errors in complex sentences make the reading hard or impossible to read.	**Conventions**

See Appendix B for 4-, 5-, and 6-point argument rubrics.

Apply the Rubric

Assign Groups Assign students to small groups and ask them to check the model for one trait. One person in each group should be responsible for recording one or two strong examples of the trait as described by the rubric. Ask students to score the trait accordingly for the model. They should be able to support their scores. Note that although the model was written to score high in each trait, students should not assume each trait would receive a 6, the top score. Encourage students to discuss each trait thoroughly before assigning a score.

Reassemble Class Bring the class together and ask one person from each group to report the group's findings to the class. The point of this exercise is less to score the model than it is to practice identifying and evaluating the traits within a piece of writing.

Additional Rubrics Appendix B includes 4-, 5-, and 6-point rubrics that can be used with any piece of argument writing. The rubrics are also available as blackline masters, beginning on page T525.

The language standards for grade 6 students are addressed during editing and skills practice (**L.6.1–L.6.6**). In addition, there are multiple opportunities to address the speaking and listening standards during the writing process. Specifically, students are encouraged to work collaboratively, review key ideas, and demonstrate understanding (**SL.6.1**). Most importantly, this chapter will help students produce coherent writing (**W.6.4**), improve their writing with the help of peers and adults (**W.6.5**), use technologies to polish and publish their finished pieces (**W.6.6**), draw evidence from texts to use in their writing (**W.6.9**), and use writing to respond and reflect (**W.6.10**).

CCSS **C**ommon **C**ore **S**tate **S**tandards
W.6.9: Draw evidence from literary or informational texts to support analysis, reflection, and research.
SL.6.1.c: Pose and respond to specific questions with elaboration and detail by making comments that contribute to the topic, text, or issue under discussion.
SL.6.1.d: Review the key ideas expressed and demonstrate understanding of multiple perspectives through reflection and paraphrasing.

Analyze
the Model

Week 1 • Day 4

Student Objectives

- Read a model response to literature. *(p. 255)*
- Use the response to literature rubric. *(pp. 256–257)*
- Use the model response to literature to study Ideas, Organization, and Voice. *(pp. 258–259)*

Study the Model

Assess the Model Point out that these pages show how the model includes the traits of **Ideas, Organization,** and **Voice.** Read each section with students. Encourage them to try to find other examples of each trait in the writing model. Use questions such as the following to discuss the pages with students:

- Does the writer express a thesis statement? (Yes, Juan Cepeda states his opinion in the introduction.)

- Does Juan support his opinion? (Possible response: The writer uses relevant examples and direct quotations from the books to convince the reader.)

Strategies for Writers Online
Go to **www.sfw.z-b.com** for additional online resources for students and teachers.

Using the Rubric to Study the Model

Response to Literature

Did you notice that the model on page 255 points out some key elements of a response to literature? As he wrote "Two Books by One Excellent Author," Juan Cepeda used these elements to help him write his opinion. He also used the 6-point rubric on pages 256–257 to plan, draft, revise, and edit the writing. A rubric is a great tool for evaluating writing during the writing process.

Now let's use the same rubric to score the model. To do this, we'll focus on each trait separately, starting with Ideas. We'll use the top descriptor for each trait (column 6), along with examples from the model, to help us understand how the traits work together. How would you score Juan on each trait?

Ideas

- A clear thesis statement states the writer's opinion.
- Comparisons are well supported with relevant facts and quotations from reliable sources.

Juan gives his opinion in the first paragraph. He points out that Virginia Hamilton has written many books and names two of them. Then he clearly states that middle graders should read these two books.

[from the writing model]

Virginia Hamilton has written a wide range of stories. *The House of Dies Drear*, for example, is a spellbinding mystery. In contrast, *Cousins* is an emotional story of love and betrayal. Although different, both books are ideal for middle graders.

258 Argument Writing

English Language Learners

BEGINNING

Review Read a very simple fiction story to students; for example, Snow White. Ask, *Did you like the story?* Help students answer in complete sentences. Then ask *yes/no* questions, such as *Was Snow White a kind girl? Did you like the witch?* As students' ability allows, introduce open-ended questions, such as *Why didn't you like the witch?*

INTERMEDIATE

Summary and Theme Read the same fiction story to students. Have partners list the characters and the important plot points. As a class, discuss the theme of the story. Write a few themes for the story on the board, and have students discuss which one best describes the author's message. For Snow White, you might use *Be kind and good things will happen; Rich princes make good husbands; It's easy to go from rags to riches.*

Organization

- A clear compare-contrast pattern organizes the information.
- Transition words effectively clarify similarities and differences.

Juan writes a paragraph each on the characters, settings, and themes of the books. Juan first states a way both books appeal to readers. Then he demonstrates how each book does that. Notice the transition word *Similarly* that tells readers the author is making a comparison.

[from the writing model]

Each book addresses the theme of dealing with changes. Many middle-grade readers can identify with this theme, as they are also dealing with changes. Thomas has to overcome his fears about moving to a new place. Similarly, Cammy copes with her grief over the death of her cousin.

Voice

- The writer establishes and consistently maintains a formal style.

Juan's writing style is appropriate for a book review; he keeps his language formal. That doesn't mean he sounds stuffy or dull. It does mean he avoids casual, slangy language. Juan's formal, direct style encourages the reader to take him seriously.

[from the writing model]

Virginia Hamilton tells stories that middle graders can understand and enjoy. Read *The House of Dies Drear, Cousins,* or any of Hamilton's other novels. You will see how the characters, settings, and themes make her stories so appealing.

Response to Literature **259**

- How does the writer organize the response? (Possible response: The writer states his purpose for writing in the introduction, uses a compare-and-contrast pattern to hold interest, and restates his opinion in the conclusion.)

- What does the writer's voice sound like? (Possible responses: The writer speaks knowledgeably and sounds like an expert on both books. It's obvious that Juan wants to share his opinion with the audience.)

ADVANCED

Taking Notes Read a language- and grade-level-appropriate story. Have students take notes about the parts of the story, including plot details. Tell them to rewrite the story in their own words. Then have a volunteer read the summarized story to the class. Teach the terms *taking notes* and *summary* to students. Say each word or phrase, write it on the board, and have students repeat.

ADVANCED HIGH

Stating Opinions Have students practice giving clear opinions. Offer a topic, such as *reading novels,* and have students talk about whether they enjoy reading novels. Ask them to list their reasons for liking or not liking to read. Have them use this information to write a three- or four-sentence introduction that clearly states their opinion. Have them trade papers and check for strong statements of opinion.

CCSS **C**ommon **C**ore **S**tate **S**tandards
W.6.9: Draw evidence from literary or informational texts to support analysis, reflection, and research.
SL.6.1.c: Pose and respond to specific questions with elaboration and detail by making comments that contribute to the topic, text, or issue under discussion.
SL.6.1.d: Review the key ideas expressed and demonstrate understanding of multiple perspectives through reflection and paraphrasing.

Analyze
the Model

Week 1 • Day 5

Student Objectives

- Read a model response to literature. (*p. 255*)
- Use the response to literature rubric. (*pp. 256–257*)
- Use the model response to literature to study Word Choice, Sentence Fluency, and Conventions. (*pp. 260–261*)

Continue the Discussion Use questions such as the following to discuss the traits analyzed on pages 260 and 261:

- What do you think of the writer's language? (Possible response: The writer's language is appropriate and convincing. I also notice that he does not use biased or overly emotional language to get his ideas across to the reader.)

- How would you describe Juan's sentences? (Possible responses: Juan's sentences are interesting and energetic. They move along at a good pace and keep the audience engaged in the ideas.)

- Was the model edited? (Possible responses: It's obvious that the response to literature was carefully edited. Nothing distracts or confuses the reader. All introductory clauses are punctuated correctly, too.)

 **Strategies for Writers Online**
Go to **www.sfw.z-b.com** for additional online resources for students and teachers.

Word Choice

- Neutral language presents the writer's opinion fairly.
- Precise words clarify and enhance opinions.

Juan is careful to be fair in presenting his opinions. He doesn't use biased or negative words. In the example below, he uses precise words like *mysterious*, *looms*, *pleasant* and *little* to contrast the dark mood in one book with the sunny mood in the other book. Words like these gave me a very clear picture of how the two books are different.

[from the writing model]

Thomas's new home is a mysterious old house. The huge mansion had been a stop on the Underground Railroad. It has a homey kitchen, but it also has secret passages. The house looms over the story, creating a dark mood. In contrast, the pleasant little town in *Cousins* creates a sunny mood.

Sentence Fluency

- Great variety in sentence patterns and lengths makes the writing flow smoothly.

Juan uses a variety of sentences throughout his review to keep things flowing smoothly, but I especially like this paragraph. The sentences are well written and clear, and none of them follow the same pattern. There's even a command in there!

[from the writing model]

Virginia Hamilton tells stories that middle graders can understand and enjoy. Read *The House of Dies Drear*, *Cousins*, or any of Hamilton's other novels. You will see how the characters, settings, and themes make her stories so appealing.

260 Argument Writing

 **for 21st Century Literacies**

Invite students to maintain a response journal to their reading using an online, sharable website such as Google Documents. Using Google Docs allows the writer to share his or her writing with anyone invited to the text, and it also allows readers to respond to the ideas or simply to follow along. Adding this level of audience helps students add purpose as it invites discourse and challenges them to capture insight and not just musings. Using this space also allows students to open their work to readers beyond the classroom walls.

See **www.sfw.z-b.com** for further information about and links to these websites and tools.

Conventions
- The writing has been thoroughly edited.
- Complex sentences are punctuated correctly.

Juan seems to have edited his book review well—I didn't find any mistakes. He was even careful to correctly put a comma after the introductory clause in this complex sentence.

[from the writing model]

While these characters are both independent, they love their families.

+Presentation White space organizes the text for easy reading.

Now it's my turn to write! How can I apply good writing strategies in my own response to literature? Just watch! I'm going to use what I learned from the rubric and some good writing strategies.

Differentiating Instruction

ENRICHMENT

Review Two Have students locate several compare-and-contrast book reviews in publications geared for middle-school readers or find reviews on the Internet. (The American Library Association website, **www.ala.org,** provides links to many age-appropriate books and reviews.) Ask students to note effective features of the reviews.

REINFORCEMENT

Bookmarks Students might find sticky notes easier to use than a response journal. The notes can be used to mark information that they want to remember. A brief phrase or sentence on the sticky note will help students remember why the pages are important.

Presentation Explain to students that Presentation is just as important as the other traits. Appearance needs to be considered when students prepare a final copy. Neatness is always a priority, and text should be typed, using only a few readable fonts. Good margins and good spacing make the response to literature easy to read.

Think About the Traits After students have thoroughly discussed the model, ask them which traits they think are the most important. Remind them that all of the traits are important in every piece of writing; however, some traits play a more important role in specific types of writing. For example, some students may feel that **Organization** is very important to compare and contrast two books effectively. Some students may argue that **Voice** is important because the writer needs to convince the audience. Still others may feel that **Word Choice** is important because the writer's language should neither distract nor offend the audience.

CCSS **C**ommon **C**ore **S**tate **S**tandards
R/Inf.6.6: Determine an author's point of view or purpose in a text and explain how it is conveyed in the text. **SL.6.1.d:** Review the key ideas expressed and demonstrate understanding of multiple perspectives through reflection and paraphrasing.

Write
a Response to Literature

Week 2 • Day 1

Student Objectives

• Find two similar books. Take notes in a response journal. (p. 262)

Prewrite

Focus on Ideas

Find Similar Books Read Leila's words together. Discuss her reasons for choosing the books. Point out that students might decide to compare a fiction and a nonfiction book on the same topic, two books by the same author, two books with the same illustrator, two books with similar main characters, two books set in the same period, and so on.

Then ask students to compare and contrast Leila's notes (page 262) and response journal (page 263). (Possible responses: Her notes are brief but full of information. Her response journal is more conversational and includes her opinions and quotations.)

Online Writing Center

Provides **interactive graphic organizers** as well as a variety of graphic organizers in PDF format.

Prewrite

Focus on **Ideas**

The Rubric Says	A clear thesis statement states the writer's opinion. Comparisons are well supported with relevant facts and quotations from reliable sources.
Writing Strategy	Find two similar books. Take notes in a response journal.

Recently I read *Number the Stars* by Lois Lowry. I chose it because it was about my Jewish heritage. I'll use it for my next writing assignment: a book review that compares two books. The review on page 255 compares two books by the same author. I decided to compare two fiction books on the same topic. *Good Night, Maman* is a fiction book like *Number the Stars*, but it's by a different author, Norma Fox Mazer. I need to take good notes so the thesis statement and supporting evidence I write later are clear and complete. I wrote these notes from memory about *Number the Stars* before I read *Good Night, Maman*.

My Notes on <u>Number the Stars</u>

✔ World War II: Nazi soldiers all over Copenhagen, Denmark

✔ 1943: Nazis begin arresting Jews. Jewish Rosens leave their daughter Ellen with her friend Annemarie Johansen and her family. Johansens pretend Ellen is their daughter.

✔ Annemarie and her mom take Ellen to Uncle Henrik's house at the coast. Ellen's parents come there. They have a fake funeral so Jews can gather at the house disguised as mourners. Nazis investigate; girls are terrified, but brave.

✔ Annemarie's parents, Uncle Henrik, and others help Jews hide on fishing boats to escape to Sweden.

✔ Annemarie meets Nazis in woods; she is frightened, but brave. Rosens get to Sweden safely.

262 Argument Writing

English Language Learners

BEGINNING

Same and Different Show a photo of a cat and a dog and ask, *Does a cat have four legs?* When students answer *yes*, model the sentence *A cat has four legs.* Point to the dog and ask, *Does a dog have four legs?* Model the sentence *A dog has four legs.* Point to the legs in both pictures and model the sentence *This is the same.* Repeat for *different* using a different attribute.

INTERMEDIATE

Compare and Contrast Show a photo of a cat and a dog and say, *Let's compare. What is the same?* Students might notice that both are animals, have four legs, have whiskers, and so on. Model answers in complete sentences and have students repeat. List answers in a Venn diagram on the board. Say, *When we compare, we tell how things are the same.* Repeat the activity for contrast.

Instead of taking notes as I read my second book, I'm keeping a response journal. That way, I can write down my thoughts as I read the book. This book is also about a Jewish girl and her family hiding from the Nazis during World War II. I included my own reactions and lots of quotations (with the page numbers where I found them). See what I've written so far?

✏️ **Writer's Term**_____

Response Journal

A **response journal** is a notebook or other place where someone jots down his or her impressions about an experience, such as reading a book.

My Response Journal for <u>Good Night, Maman</u>
(page 1)

I couldn't stay quiet for a year like Karin Levi did in that attic closet. I guess she just had to.

Maman is strict but sweet. You can see why Karin loves her so much. Marc acts so mature. He's trying to be the man since his dad was shot.

It must have been terrible to run from your home, begging for food, with no place to live. Karin said, "It had been weeks since I'd slept on a real bed, in a real room." (p. 31) She said, "We were free and unfree. We were in our own beloved land, but it was not ours." (p. 36)

It was so sad when Karin kissed Maman goodbye. Karin was worried Maman wouldn't find them after she got better. "How was she going to do that? Find us where?" Karin said. (p. 58)

I thought everyone who helped the Jews was nice to them, but Madame Zetain wasn't. The farmer and Maria Theresa were. Maria Theresa even told them about a ship that could take them to America.

Apply

Choose a book you've already read and liked, and make notes on it. Then keep a response journal as you read a second book that you plan to compare with it.

Response to Literature **263**

Have students look at Leila's notes on page 262 as they study her response journal entries. Point out that in order to write a good review, students must have read their books and have them on hand for easy reference.

To assist students in getting the most from the prewriting lessons, tell them they will follow Leila's lead to

- choose two books to compare.
- decide on their purpose for writing.
- state and support their opinion.
- find supporting evidence, including quotations.
- create an organizer to plan their response.

✏️ **Writer's Term**_____

Response Journal A response journal is a tool to help students keep track of their experiences. Writing down ideas while they are still fresh helps writers remember important details.

ADVANCED

Similarities and Differences Show two similar (but slightly different) photos, or use a spot-the-differences activity from a children's magazine. Have partners make a list of the similarities and differences between the pictures. Have students say sentences that compare or contrast the pictures. For example, *The people are working in the first photo. In the second photo they are eating lunch.*

ADVANCED HIGH

Transition Words Teach students several transition words or phrases that can be used to show compare and contrast, such as *different, but, however, in contrast,* and *same.* Then repeat the Advanced ELL activity above. Ask students to use a transition word or phrase to connect the two sentences, as in *The people are working in the first photo, but in the second photo they are eating lunch.*

Write
a Response to Literature

Week 2 • Day 2

Student Objectives

- Make a Venn Diagram from the notes and response journal. (p. 264)

Prewrite

Focus on  Organization

Make a Venn Diagram Leila used a Venn Diagram to organize her notes, along with her personal observations and reflections. Ask how a Venn Diagram can be an effective tool when writing a book review. (Possible response: A Venn Diagram helps organize ideas about two books that are related in important ways. By listing major similarities and differences in the books, the writer can support the main points of comparison.)

✏️ **Writer's Term** _____

Venn Diagram In their content-area classes, students may be asked to compare historical events, scientific discoveries, or mathematical constructs. A Venn Diagram can facilitate discussions, generate new research questions, stimulate discovery, and reveal valuable connections.

 Online Writing Center

Provides student eBooks with an **interactive writing pad** for drafting, revising, editing, and publishing.

Prewrite
Focus on Organization

The Rubric Says	A clear compare-contrast pattern organizes the information.
Writing Strategy	Make a Venn Diagram from the notes and response journal.

The rubric stresses the importance of organizing my book review. I'll review my notes and my response journal and organize the important points into a Venn Diagram. This diagram will help me keep track of the ways that the books are similar and different.

✏️ **Writer's Term** _____

Venn Diagram
A **Venn Diagram** is two overlapping circles that show how two things are similar and different. Ways the things are similar are described in the overlapping section. Ways they are different are described in the outside part of each circle.

One of the first things I notice is that *Number the Stars* is set in Denmark, but *Good Night, Maman* is set in France and other countries. That's one way the two books are different. I'll put that information in each outside circle.

However, both books take place during World War II. That's one way they are the same. I'll write that in the overlapping part of the circles. I already have a good start on my Venn Diagram!

264 Argument Writing

Here is my completed Venn Diagram. Besides the settings, I compared the characters, the main events, and the themes. I decided that the theme is the same in both books: Hope and bravery help the children survive.

VENN DIAGRAM
Comparing My Books

Number the Stars
- set in Denmark
- Annemarie and Ellen are warm and fed.
- Rosens are together and safe.
- Rosens escape to Sweden.

Both Books
- 10-year-old girls
- set in WWII
- Nazis are searching for Jews.
- People help Jews escape.
- Hope and bravery help the children survive.

Good Night, Maman
- set in France, Italy, USA
- Karin and Marc are homeless and hungry.
- Levi family splits up; mother dies later.
- Karin and Marc escape to USA.

Reflect
How does Leila's Venn Diagram look? Does it make the major similarities and differences clear?

Apply
Organize your ideas by using a Venn Diagram.

Response to Literature 265

Identify Leila's main points of comparison. (setting, characters, main events, theme) Have students use their notes and reflections to create their organizer. Tell students to limit their main points to three or four important ones. Have them underline their main points on the organizer. Remind students that they will use it to write their draft.

Point out that students may not always have equivalent information to list in each portion of the circles, such as *set in Denmark; set in France, Italy, USA;* and *set in WWII.* In this case, have students use something besides the setting for comparison.

Conferencing

PEER TO PEER Have writers share their main points of comparison. Have partners identify these on their Venn Diagrams and make sure they are supported.

PEER GROUPS Have students work in small groups and take turns sharing their organizers. Have group members take turns offering one comment or suggestion to make it more helpful, based on the prewriting lessons.

TEACHER-LED Schedule conferences with individual students. Before they speak with you, tell students to underline the main points on their Venn Diagram and add supporting evidence for each.

CCSS **Common Core State Standards**

R/Inf.6.7: Integrate information presented in different media or formats (e.g., visually, quantitatively) as well as in words to develop a coherent understanding of a topic or issue. **R/Inf.6.9:** Compare and contrast one author's presentation of events with that of another (e.g., a memoir written by and a biography on the same person). **W.6.1:** Write arguments to support claims with clear reasons and relevant evidence. **W.6.9:** Draw evidence from literary or informational texts to support analysis, reflection, and research.

Write
a Response to Literature

Week 2 • Day 3

Student Objectives

- Write a clear thesis statement and include relevant supporting evidence. *(p. 266)*

Draft

Focus on Ideas

Draft a Response Point out that Leila begins her review by summarizing the main points in one of the books, *Number the Stars*. Then she summarizes the main points in *Good Night, Maman*, comparing and contrasting them with the points she covered in *Number the Stars*.

Explain to students that one good way to convince readers to agree with your opinion is to support it with examples and quotations from the source. Remind students to include examples and/or quotations to support their comparisons.

 Writer's Term _____

Thesis Statement In argument writing, a well-written thesis statement expresses the writer's opinion of the topic. An engaging thesis statement includes an insight or observation that grabs the reader's attention right from the start.

Strategies for Writers Online

Go to **www.sfw.z-b.com** for additional online resources for students and teachers.

Draft

Focus on (Ideas)

The Rubric Says   A clear thesis statement states the writer's opinion.

Writing Strategy   Write a clear thesis statement and include relevant supporting evidence.

The rubric reminds me that my thesis statement should be very clear. It should prepare the reader for what's coming in my book review, so I need to put it in my first paragraph.

After looking at my notes and response journal, I think I like *Good Night, Maman* better than *Number the Stars*. That will be my thesis statement!

Next I'll summarize the plot of each book. I'll support my thesis with relevant facts and quotations from both stories and show why I think *Good Night, Maman* is better in some ways. The first part of my draft is on the next page.

> **Writer's Term** _____
>
> **Thesis Statement**
> A **thesis statement** is the opinion the writer is attempting to prove. The writer tries to convince readers to accept or believe his or her opinion or thesis statement.

266   Argument Writing

Differentiating Instruction

ENRICHMENT

Link Ideas Have students return to the compare-and-contrast book reviews they evaluated earlier (see page 261). Have them locate and underline transitions that the writer uses to compare. Then have them locate and circle transition words that the writer uses to contrast. Have students create a two-column chart and list the transitions. Post it as a reference in the writing center.

REINFORCEMENT

State Your Thesis Some students may find it easier to state their thesis orally than in writing. Prompt them with questions such as *What was the book about? What did you think about the book? Why?* Have students talk through their ideas before trying to craft their responses to literature on paper.

Proofreading Marks

⊐ Indent	ℓ Take out something
☰ Make a capital	⊙ Add a period
/ Make a small letter	¶ New paragraph
∧ Add something	SP Spelling error

[DRAFT]

Bravery and Hope
by Leila

<u>Number the Stars</u>, by Lois Lowry, and <u>Good Night, Maman</u>, by Norma Fox Mazer, tell about brave young girls during World War II. I prefer <u>Good Night, Maman</u>. It shows better than <u>Number the Stars</u> that children needed both hope and bravery to get through terrible experiences during the war.   **[thesis statement]**

In <u>Number the Stars</u>, Annemarie Johansen and Ellen Rosen are friends. They are 10 years old and live in Copenhagen, Denmark. It is 1943, and the Nazis have started arresting Jews in Copenhagen. The Rosens are Jewish.   **[relevant facts]**

Ellen stays with Annemarie and pretends to be her sister. Although scared, Annemarie and Ellen face the Nazis when they come to the Johansens' apartment.

Reflect
What do you think? Is Leila's thesis statement clear? How do the facts support her thesis?

Apply
Write a draft using your Venn Diagram. Write a clear thesis statement and use relevant facts and quotations to support it.

Conferencing

PEER TO PEER Have partners exchange and read their drafts. Tell students to think of two or three questions they would like to ask to clarify information. Have them write their questions on sticky notes and affix them to the appropriate places on their partner's draft.

PEER GROUPS Have students work in groups of four. Tell students to pass their draft to the student on the right to read. Using the rubric on pages 256–257 to guide their response, each student should write one comment or suggestion on a sticky note. Students then affix their note to the draft and pass the draft along to the right. The review ends when everyone has received his or her own draft back with three helpful comments.

TEACHER-LED Schedule conferences with pairs of students. Have students read each other's draft and coach them in giving constructive criticism using the rubric as a guide.

Write
a Response to Literature

Student Objectives
• Complete a draft. *(p. 267)*

Continue Drafting Have a volunteer read Leila's draft. Ask whether they think Leila has written a clear thesis statement. Remind students what it means to write a draft (get ideas down on paper) and that they should not be overly concerned with correctness at this point. Point out that the proofreader's marks are provided as a reference on the draft. To help them focus on getting their thoughts down on paper, have students circle anything in their drafts they might want to change later but tell them not to worry about revising or editing their writing now.

CCSS Common Core State Standards

W.6.1.a: Introduce claim(s) and organize the reasons and evidence clearly. **W.6.1.b:** Support claim(s) with clear reasons and relevant evidence, using credible sources and demonstrating an understanding of the topic or text. **W.6.5:** With some guidance and support from peers and adults, develop and strengthen writing as needed by planning, revising, editing, rewriting, or trying a new approach.

Write
a Response to Literature

Week 2 • Day 5

Student Objectives

- Revise to use transitions effectively. *(p. 268)*

Revise

Focus on

Use Effective Transitions Explain that Leila wants her audience to follow her comparisons. As she read her draft, she found a place where she could add transition words to clarify her ideas. Point out to students that weak comparisons can confuse the reader.

Have students read their drafts, looking for places where transitions can connect and clarify their comparisons. If needed, provide transition words to compare (*another way, one way, finally*) and contrast (*even though, however, on the other hand*). Refer students to the list of transitions on page 524.

Writer's Term____

Transition Words Helpful, appropriate transition words illuminate similarities and differences in comparisons. Writers use transitions to connect their ideas and guide the reader.

Strategies for Writers Online

Go to **www.sfw.z-b.com** for additional online resources for students and teachers.

T268 Argument Writing

Revise

Focus on **Organization**

The Rubric Says	Transition words effectively clarify similarities and differences.
Writing Strategy	Link ideas with transitions, such as *same, similarly, however, yet,* and *on one hand.*

The rubric points out that transition words can help make comparisons clearer. Useful transition words for comparing and contrasting include *in the same way, similarly, likewise, like, as, also, on the other hand, in contrast, unlike, although, more/less, yet,* and *but.* I added a few transition words to this paragraph. Read what I wrote to see if it's clearer.

Writer's Term____

Transition Words
Transition words show how ideas are linked to one another. In argument writing, transition words can help tell the reader that two ideas are similar or different.

[DRAFT]

[added transition words]

Danish people help the Jews in Number the Stars. *Similarly,* French and Italian people help them in Good Night, Maman. In Number the Stars, Ellen is separated from her parents for only a few days. *In contrast,* Karin and Marc are separated from Maman for months.

Apply
Add transition words to clarify the similarities and differences in your review.

268 Argument Writing

English Language Learners

BEGINNING/INTERMEDIATE

Using Precise Words Write a generic word, such as *bad,* on the board. Use the Web graphic organizer to brainstorm other words that have the same meaning as *bad* or that have stronger meanings. For example, you could write *bad, no good, awful, terrible,* and *dreadful.* Tell students to use this idea when choosing words for their responses.

ADVANCED/ADVANCED HIGH

Loaded Words Ask students to imagine each word in the following pairs: *house/shack, car/jalopy, food/slop, animal/beast.* Ask them how the second word in each pair compares to the first. Tell them that words like *shack* and *beast* are loaded words and cause the reader to imagine something less appealing than is real. Loaded words can also create a more appealing idea. Challenge students to come up with other examples.

Revise

Focus on **Voice**

The Rubric Says	The writer establishes and consistently maintains a formal style.
Writing Strategy	Use a formal style throughout.

The rubric points out that I need to keep my style formal throughout my review. After all, I want my readers to take me and my opinions seriously. I can't let my voice fade and become too casual halfway through my writing. I also need to show that I've read the books carefully and that I know my topic. I see a place in this paragraph where I can make my voice sound more appropriate.

[DRAFT]

[used more formal language]

The separation becomes

~~I realized the separation was~~ wider when Karen and Marc board a
→ taking
ship ~~that takes lots of~~ Jewish refugees to the United States. Annemarie
has only
and Ellen can depend on their parents for help, but Karin ~~doesn't have~~

~~anybody but~~ Marc.

Reflect

How did Leila make the style of her writing more formal?

Apply

Read over your draft. Make sure you maintain a formal style throughout your paper. Revise for voice where necessary.

Response to Literature 269

Conferencing

PEER TO PEER During revising, have partners exchange drafts. After reading, ask each student to offer feedback on how to strengthen the review. If needed, have students consult the model, the rubric, and the lessons for revising Organization, Voice, and Word Choice.

PEER GROUPS Have students form small revising groups. Then have each student read aloud parts in his or her draft that might need improving. Ask each group member to offer one suggestion on how to strengthen it. Have writers consult the revising lessons in their book to inform their revision.

TEACHER-LED Schedule conferences to read each student's draft. Point out strengths and weaknesses. Talk about ways to improve the draft. If a student seems stalled or discouraged, revisit steps in the process to make improvements and keep going.

Write
a Response to Literature

Week 3 • Day 1

Student Objectives

- Revise to use a formal style. (p. 269)

Revise

Focus on **Voice**

Use a Formal Style Have students read the introduction to this page. Then ask a volunteer to read aloud Leila's draft without the highlighted changes; have another volunteer read aloud the revised version. Then direct students' attention to the question in the Reflect box. Students should agree that Leila's changes improved the overall tone and style of the passage.

Also point out that when writing about literature, writers use present-tense verbs (*The separation becomes; Karen and Marc board; Annemarie and Ellen can depend; Karin has*). This style convention also helps maintain a formal, traditional style.

CCSS **Common Core State Standards**

W.6.1.c: Use words, phrases, and clauses to clarify the relationships among claim(s) and reasons. **W.6.1.d:** Establish and maintain a formal style. **W.6.5:** With some guidance and support from peers and adults, develop and strengthen writing as needed by planning, revising, editing, rewriting, or trying a new approach. **L.6.3.b:** Maintain consistency in style and tone. **L.6.5.c:** Distinguish among the connotations (associations) of words with similar denotations (definitions) (e.g., *stingy, scrimping, economical, unwasteful, thrifty*).

Write
a Response to Literature

Week 3 • Day 2

Student Objectives

- Revise to avoid loaded words. (p. 270)

Revise

Focus on Word Choice

Use Precise, Neutral Language

Have students read the introduction to this lesson. Then ask a volunteer to read aloud the draft excerpt without the changes; ask another volunteer to read it with the revisions. Discuss the changes. Students should agree that using precise words and replacing casual expressions have improved the passage.

Discuss the terms *denotation* (a word's definition or meaning) and *connotation* (a word's association, suggestion, tone, or inference). Sometimes the connotation of a word can cause readers to be offended by the choice of language. Remind students to use neutral language to express and support their opinions.

Also point out that authors and editors consult word resources whenever they write. Dictionaries and thesauruses are a writer's best friends when it comes to improving **Word Choice**.

Online Writing Center

Provides **interactive proofreading activities** for each genre.

Revise — Focus on Word Choice

The Rubric Says	Neutral language presents the writer's opinion fairly. Precise words clarify and enhance opinions.
Writing Strategy	Avoid loaded words that cause a strong negative reaction.

The rubric cautions me about using language that is loaded—words that show my bias. Language like this won't convince my readers and can actually push them away. In addition, using vague or too-general words can confuse readers. I need to share my opinions by using neutral words and precise language.

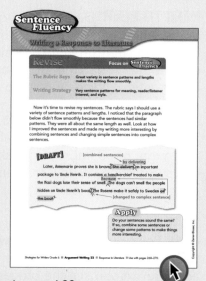

[DRAFT]   [used precise language]

Both of these books are about 10-year-old Jewish girls coping with ~~→ occupied by the~~ life in countries ~~where there are~~ Nazis. While I enjoyed reading both of them, ~~I thought the ending of *Number the Stars* was kind of dumb.~~

I liked *Good Night, Maman* a little better because I thought the ending ~~more realistic ←~~ was ~~so much cooler.~~ [used neutral, more precise language]

Apply

Is your language neutral so it presents your opinion fairly? Are your words precise? Look for loaded words that might cause a negative reaction and vague words that could confuse your readers.

270 Argument Writing

Optional Revising Lessons

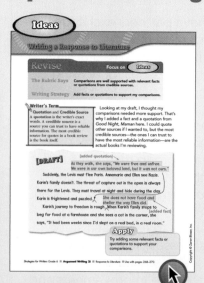

Argument 21

Argument 22

 Go to **Strategies for Writers Grade 6 CD-ROM**

Edit

Focus on Conventions

The Rubric Says	The writing has been thoroughly edited. Complex sentences are punctuated correctly.
Writing Strategy	Check that all dependent clauses are part of complex sentences and are punctuated correctly.

✏️ **Writer's Term_____**

Complex Sentence and Dependent Clause
A **complex sentence** contains an independent clause and a **dependent clause**. An independent clause has a subject and a verb. It is also a simple sentence. A dependent clause has a subject and a verb but does not make sense by itself. It is a sentence fragment.

Now it's time to check my draft for mistakes in spelling, capitalization, and punctuation. I also need to check my use of dependent clauses. By themselves, they are sentence fragments. I'll make sure they are part of complex sentences and punctuated correctly.

[DRAFT] [made dependent clause part of a complex sentence]

"It had been years since I'd had friends my own age. I hardly even remembered how to act like a friend, but I pretended I did." Karin , Karin does well says. Although it's not easy being in a new country. Perhaps Ellen does

well in Sweden, too, but <u>Number the Stars</u> does not discus that.

Reflect

It takes hard work to select the best words and to make sure all the sentences are complete. How have Leila's revisions and edits strengthened her book review?

Apply Conventions

Edit your draft for spelling, punctuation, and capitalization. Be sure that any dependent clauses are contained within complex sentences.

For more practice with complex sentences and dependent clauses, use the exercises on the next two pages.

Response to Literature 271

Related Grammar Practice _____

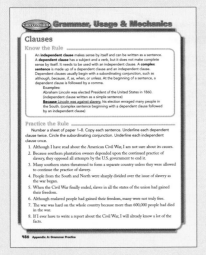

Student Edition page 486

Go to ➡️ **Appendix A: Grammar Practice**

Write
a Response to Literature

Week 3 • Day 3

Student Objectives

- Check that all dependent clauses are part of complex sentences and are punctuated correctly. *(p. 271)*

Edit

Focus on Conventions

Use Dependent Clauses Correctly Have students use the information on page 271 to check that dependent clauses are part of complex sentences and punctuated correctly in their own drafts. Use the mini-lessons on pages 272 and 273 for students who need additional practice with punctuating complex sentences.

✏️ **Writer's Term_____**

Complex Sentence and Dependent Clause A comma follows a dependent clause when it begins a sentence. Subordinating conjunctions or relative pronouns are often used to begin a dependent clause.

CCSS Common Core State Standards
L.6.1: Demonstrate command of the conventions of standard English grammar and usage when writing or speaking. **L.6.1.e:** Recognize variations from standard English in their own and others' writing and speaking, and identify and use strategies to improve expression in conventional language. **L.6.2.b:** Spell correctly. **L.6.4.c:** Consult reference materials (e.g., dictionaries, glossaries, thesauruses), both print and digital, to find the pronunciation of a word or determine or clarify its precise meaning or its part of speech.

Response to Literature **T271**

Conventions

Mini-Lesson

Student Objectives

- Write complex sentences correctly. *(p. 272)*

Complex Sentences

Explain to students that complex sentences contain at least one independent clause and one dependent clause. The independent clause has a subject and a verb; it can stand on its own. A dependent clause has a subject and a verb but cannot stand on its own; it is a fragment. Write this example on the board:

- *When she shared that part of the story, I began to laugh.*

Explain to the students that the introductory clause begins with a subordinating conjunction. Ask students to identify it. (When) Ask them to identify the dependent clause in the sentence. (When she shared that part of the story)

Before assigning the practice, write a second example on the board:

- *The book is about a boy who spends a summer on a dude ranch.*

Some complex sentences contain a clause that begins with a relative pronoun, such as *which, who,* or *that.* Ask them to identify the relative pronoun (who) and the dependent clause. (who spends a summer on a dude ranch)

Online Writing Center

Provides **interactive grammar games** and **practice activities** in student eBook.

Conventions Grammar, Usage & Mechanics

Complex Sentences

Know the Rule

A **complex sentence** contains an independent clause and a dependent clause. An **independent clause** has a subject and a verb. It is also a simple sentence. A **dependent clause** has a subject and a verb but does not make sense by itself. It is one kind of **sentence fragment**. Dependent clauses begin with **subordinating conjunctions** such as *although, because, if, as, before,* or *when.*

> **Example:**
> **(independent clause)**
> You will make wise decisions.
> **(dependent clause)**
> If you think carefully.
> **(dependent clause + independent clause = complex sentence)**
> If you think carefully, you will make wise decisions.

Practice the Rule

Number a separate sheet of paper from 1–8. Read each group of words and write **CX** if it is a complex sentence or **F** (fragment) if it is a dependent clause.

1. Although Lois Lowry has written many books, *Number the Stars* was her first to win the Newbery Award. **CX**
2. When Lowry learned about the World War II rescue of Jews in Denmark. **F**
3. After the Nazis began to threaten the Danish Jews, the Danish Resistance smuggled nearly 7,000 Jews to safety. **CX**
4. If you were a Jew in Denmark during the early 1940s. **F**
5. A resistance is a secret organization because it works against a government. **CX**
6. Although most European Jews had to wear a yellow star on their clothing during World War II. **F**
7. Because Norma Fox Mazer wanted to write both fiction and history, she wrote the historical novel *Good Night, Maman.* **CX**
8. When Mazer prepared to write her book. **F**

Related Grammar Practice

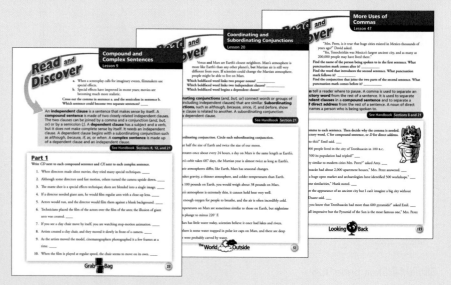

Pages 23, 51, 123

Go to ➡ **G.U.M. Student Practice Book**

Commas After Introductory Clauses

Know the Rule

When a complex sentence begins with a dependent clause, a **comma** separates it from the rest of the sentence.

> **Example:**
> After you finish your homework, we can go out to eat. (Sentence begins with a dependent clause.)
> We can go out to eat after you finish your homework. (Sentence begins with an independent clause.)

Practice the Rule

Number a separate sheet of paper from 1–10. Rewrite and correctly punctuate the sentences that require a comma. Write **Correct** if the sentence does not need a comma.

1. Before the bell rang, our teacher assigned our book review.
2. Because Jenna likes animals, she looked for a book about animals to read and review.
3. After I talked to my teacher, I decided on a book about the Underground Railroad.
4. I started to read the book before I went to bed. Correct
5. Dan didn't read his book in time because he started it too late. Correct
6. While we read our books, the teacher asked us to make notes in our response journals about the story.
7. When we give our opinions, we use neutral language and a formal tone.
8. Although Pietro finished his book review, he is proofreading it again.
9. If Lisette reads her book review aloud, the whole class will listen.
10. I think my book review is excellent because I worked hard on it. Correct

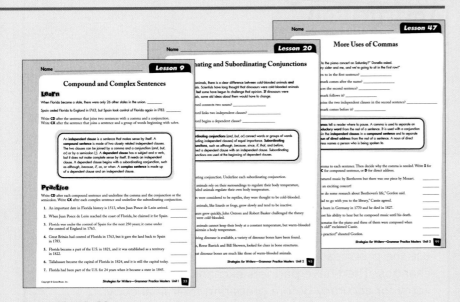

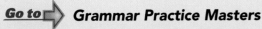

Go to ➡ Grammar Practice Masters

Mini-Lesson

Student Objectives

• Use commas after introductory clauses. *(p. 273)*

Commas After Introductory Clauses

Read the information and example in Know the Rule. Then review the previous example:

> • *When she shared that part of the story, I began to laugh.*

Explain that a comma is used to join the introductory dependent clause to the independent clause. In this example, the sentence is punctuated correctly. When the dependent clause follows the independent clause, no comma is necessary.

For students in need of additional practice, assign the activity. Be sure to go over their editing in class.

CCSS Common Core State Standards

L.6.2.a: Use punctuation (commas, parentheses, dashes) to set off nonrestrictive/parenthetical elements. **L.6.3:** Use knowledge of language and its conventions when writing, speaking, reading, or listening. **W.6.5:** With some guidance and support from peers and adults, develop and strengthen writing as needed by planning, revising, editing, rewriting, or trying a new approach.

Write
a Response to Literature

Student Objectives

- Present a response to literature in class. *(p. 274)*
- Use a final editing checklist to publish a response to literature. *(p. 274)*

Publish +Presentation

Publishing Strategy Discuss other publishing options, such as entering a book review contest, starting a book review club, or presenting the review to an audience. Ask students to brainstorm publishing ideas, and encourage them to pursue one or two options.

Read aloud Leila's final checklist. Have students use it or one you provide to check their own book review. Once they have completed their final copy, have students submit their book review to their school newspaper, magazine, or journal for publication.

As students put the finishing touches on their writing, remind them to use available technologies and incorporate good design and formatting features.

Strategies for Writers Online
Go to **www.sfw.z-b.com** for additional online resources for students and teachers.

Publish +Presentation

Publishing Strategy	Publish the review in the school newspaper.
Presentation Strategy	Use white space to organize the information.

I like to share my opinions about what I read. A lot of people can read my review in the school newspaper! As I prepare my review, I need to include enough white space to make it easy to read and understand. I'll check to make sure my title is centered, the margins are wide enough, my paragraphs are indented, and the line spacing is appropriate. If I prepare my final copy on the computer, this will be easy to do. Then I'll check my review over one last time using this checklist to help me.

My Final Checklist

Did I—

✔ make sure all the dependent clauses are connected to independent clauses?

✔ use commas after dependent clauses at the beginnings of sentences?

✔ use white space to help organize my information and make it easy to read?

✔ proofread for spelling, capitalization, grammar, and punctuation?

Apply

Make a final checklist to check your book review. Then make a final copy to publish.

274 Argument Writing

Differentiating Instruction

ENRICHMENT
Present Encourage students to create invitations for faculty, family members, and friends who would be interested in hearing the book reviews. Students may also want to create programs for the event and include a list of presenters and titles of their books.

REINFORCEMENT
Proofread Have pairs of students exchange drafts and edit strategically. For example, have each pair begin by proofreading only for punctuation or spelling. Then have them look for easily confused words. Remind editors to use the proofreading marks on page 267 to mark their changes. Then have partners exchange edited reviews and verify for accuracy before preparing their final copy.

BOOK REVIEW CORNER

Bravery and Hope
by Leila

Number the Stars by Lois Lowry and *Good Night, Maman* by Norma Fox Mazer tell about brave young girls during World War II. I prefer *Good Night, Maman.* It shows better than *Number the Stars* that children needed both hope and bravery to get through terrible experiences during the war.

In *Number the Stars,* Annemarie Johansen and Ellen Rosen are friends. They are 10 years old and live in Copenhagen, Denmark. It is 1943, and the Nazis have started arresting Jews in Copenhagen. The Rosens are Jewish.

Ellen stays with Annemarie and pretends to be her sister. Although scared, Annemarie and Ellen face the Nazis when they come to the Johansens' apartment.

The Johansens then take Ellen to Uncle Henrik's house by the sea. There Ellen is reunited with her parents. Annemarie realizes her family and friends are in danger, but she is unsure that she is brave enough to help them. Uncle Henrik says, "I think you are like your mama, and your papa, and like me. Frightened, but determined, and if the time came to be brave, I am quite sure you would be very, very brave."

Later, Annemarie proves she is brave by delivering an important package to Uncle Henrik. It contains a handkerchief treated to make the Nazi dogs lose their sense of smell. Because the dogs can't smell the people hidden on Uncle Henrik's boat, the Rosens make it safely to Sweden.

The main character in *Good Night, Maman* is also a 10-year-old girl. Karin Levi lives in Paris, France, with her mother (Maman) and her brother, Marc. The Nazis have also occupied this country and have been searching for Jewish people like the Levis. They have shot Karin's father already. Her family must hide in a

Technology Tip — for 21st Century Literacies

Classroom walls don't need to exist when that class has access to an Internet-connected computer. Using Skype, iChat, or other communication tools, invite students to speak with the authors whose texts they read—or other experts who could add a needed perspective or challenge students' developing thinking. Allow choices to be driven by students' questions and needs, and model the process used in contacting and facilitating the dialogue. We're all learning how to be connected learners with a toolset that allows us to look into any context with any person at any time. Work together to learn together.

See **www.sfw.z-b.com** for further information about and links to these websites and tools.

Write
a Response to Literature

Week 3 • Day 5

Student Objectives

- Use a response to literature rubric. *(pp. 256–257)*
- Share a published response to literature. *(pp. 275–277)*

Presentation Strategy Explain to students how important neatness is when creating a final copy of their work. Messy or illegible work detracts from the message, while a neat and interesting format shows the writer cares about the message. Remind students to use formatting features as they type their responses to literature. It's easy to set neat margins, use the tab key to indent paragraphs, double-space the text, select one or two clear fonts, insert visuals, and choose complementary design elements. Also remind students to use the header and footer functions to label their pages.

CCSS Common Core State Standards

W.6.5: With some guidance and support from peers and adults, develop and strengthen writing as needed by planning, revising, editing, rewriting, or trying a new approach. **W.6.6:** Use technology, including the Internet, to produce and publish writing as well as to interact and collaborate with others; demonstrate sufficient command of keyboarding skills to type a minimum of three pages in a single sitting. **W.6.10:** Write routinely over extended time frames (time for research, reflection, and revision) and shorter time frames (a single sitting or a day or two) for a range of discipline-specific tasks, purposes, and audiences.

Reflecting on a Response to Literature

Instruct students to refer to the rubric on pages 256–257 as they read Leila's final copy on pages 275–277. As they read, remind them that Leila's revisions and edits have shaped her final copy. After students have finished reading, ask them to discuss how the revisions and edits strengthened her writing.

Then have students use the rubric to score Leila's review. Take a poll to see how close the scores are. Be sure students can support their scores with examples from Leila's review.

Now have students think back on this assignment as a whole. You might ask questions such as these to prompt students' thinking:

- What did you like about writing a response to literature?

- What is one thing that you learned about using the writing process? The traits?

- What might you do the same or differently the next time?

Ask students to jot down their responses in a personal writer's journal or share them with a partner.

Strategies for Writers Online
Go to **www.sfw.z-b.com** for additional online resources for students and teachers.

---

tiny attic closet for a year. This is worse than anything Annemarie or Ellen goes through, but Karin stays hopeful.

Suddenly the Levis must flee Paris. Annemarie and Ellen see Nazis. Karin's family doesn't. On the other hand, the threat of capture out in the open is always there for the Levis. They must travel at night and hide during the day. Karin is frightened and puzzled. As they walk, she says, "We were free and unfree. We were in our own beloved land, but it was not ours."

Karin's journey to freedom is rough. She does not have food and shelter the way Ellen did. When Karin's family stops to beg for food at a farmhouse and she sees a cot in the corner, she says, "It had been weeks since I'd slept on a real bed, in a real room."

Danish people help the Jews in *Number the Stars.* Similarly, French and Italian people help them in *Good Night, Maman.* In *Number the Stars,* Ellen is separated from her parents for only a few days. In contrast, Karin and Marc are separated from Maman for months.

The separation becomes wider when Karin and Marc board a ship taking Jewish refugees to the United States. Annemarie and Ellen can depend on their parents for help, but Karin has only Marc. She begins writing letters to Maman. The letters show how brave and strong she is. In her first letter, she writes, "I never wanted to go so far away from you. I didn't want to get on this boat. But Marc said we wouldn't be safe anywhere in Europe until the war was over, and that you would absolutely want us to do this."

In the United States, Karin and Marc stay in a refugee camp and learn American ways. Karin still writes to Maman, but she also is determined to make new friends. "It had been years since I'd had friends my own age. I hardly even remembered how to act like a friend, but I pretended I did," Karin says. Although it's not easy being in a new country, Karin does well. Perhaps

---

Books for Professional Development

Cole, Ardith Davis. *Better Answers: Written Performance That Looks Good and Sounds Smart.* **Portland, ME. Stenhouse, 2002.** This book offers step-by-step protocol for helping students focus on acquiring the basic literacy skills to meet state standards for writing. Each of the five progressive steps to teaching writing are laid out in individual chapters.

Urquhart, Vicki, and Monette McIver. *Teaching Writing in the Content Areas.* **Alexandria, VA. ASCD, 2005.** This book shows how to quickly integrate writing assignments into content areas by using strategic, practical tools. Included in the book are 35 classroom strategies that will help teachers guide students through the steps of preparing written assignments (prewriting), getting their thoughts down (drafting), and refining their work (revising).

Ellen does well in Sweden, too, but *Number the Stars* does not discuss that.

Finally Karin learns the truth: her mother is dead. Marc has known about it for a few months. He helps Karin handle her grief.

When the war ends, Annemarie waits for Ellen to come back to Copenhagen. Karin plans to live in California with her aunt. Although Karin has no parents, she has bravery and hope. Karin says, "I thought about everything I had learned about people—some bad, some good. And I had learned that you can't look back for too long. You just have to keep going."

Both of these books are about 10-year-old Jewish girls coping with life in countries occupied by the Nazis. While I enjoyed reading both of them, I liked *Good Night, Maman* a little better because I thought the ending was more realistic. Many Jewish families were separated forever by that war, and *Good Night, Maman* showed that clearly.

Reflect

What do you think? Does Leila's paper have all the traits of a good book review? Check it against the rubric. Then use the rubric to check your own book review.

Gallagher, Kelly. *Teaching Adolescent Writers.* **Portland, ME. Stenhouse, 2006.** Infused with humor and illuminating anecdotes, Gallagher's book draws on his classroom experiences and work as codirector of a regional writing project to offer teachers practical ways to incorporate writing instruction into their day.

Strausser, Jeffrey. *Painless Writing.* **Hauppauge, NY. Barron's Educational Series, 2001.** This book is especially for classroom use with middle school and high school students who find writing boring, too difficult, or both. The author is an experienced educator who gives practical advice that transforms essay writing into a satisfying experience for students. He offers tips on enlivening writing by adding vivid words and rhythm, smoothing out sentences, and silencing the dull passive voice.

CCSS **Common Core State Standards**

W.6.6: Use technology, including the Internet, to produce and publish writing as well as to interact and collaborate with others; demonstrate sufficient command of keyboarding skills to type a minimum of three pages in a single sitting.

Argument Essay Planner

WEEK 1

Day 1
Introduce
an Argument Essay

Student Objectives
- Review the elements of an argument essay.
- Consider purpose and audience.
- Learn the traits of argument writing.

Student Activities
- Read and discuss **What's in an Argument Essay?** (p. 278)
- Read and discuss **Why Write an Argument Essay?** (p. 279)
- Read **Linking Argument Writing Traits to an Argument Essay.** (p. 280)

Day 2
Analyze
Read an Argument Essay

Student Objectives
- Read a model argument essay.

Student Activities
- Read **"The Right Angle on the Triangle."** (p. 281)

Day 3
Analyze
Introduce the Rubric

Student Objectives
- Learn to read a rubric.

Student Activities
- Review **"The Right Angle on the Triangle."** (p. 281)
- Read and discuss the **Argument Essay Rubric.** (pp. 282–283)

WEEK 2

Day 1
Write
Prewrite: Ideas

Student Objectives
- Choose an issue and find information to support the opinion.

Student Activities
- Read and discuss **Prewrite: Focus on Ideas.** (p. 288)
- Apply the prewriting strategy.

Day 2
Write
Prewrite: Organization

Student Objectives
- Use a Network Tree to organize the ideas.

Student Activities
- Read and discuss **Prewrite: Focus on Organization.** (p. 289)
- Apply the prewriting strategy.
- Participate in a peer conference.

Day 3
Write
Draft: Organization

Student Objectives
- Write well-organized paragraphs.

Student Activities
- Read and discuss **Draft: Focus on Organization.** (p. 290)
- Apply the drafting strategy.

WEEK 3

Day 1
Write
Revise: Word Choice

Student Objectives
- Replace loaded words with neutral words.

Student Activities
- Read and discuss: **Revise: Focus on Word Choice.** (p. 293)
- Participate in a peer conference.

Day 2
Write
Revise: Sentence Fluency

Student Objectives
- Revise to choose punctuation for effect.

Student Activities
- Read and discuss: **Revise: Focus on Sentence Fluency.** (p. 294)

Note: Optional Revising Lessons appear on the *Strategies for Writers* CD-ROM.

Day 3
Write
Edit: Conventions

Student Objectives
- Recognize and correct inappropriate shifts in pronoun number and person.

Student Activities
- Read and discuss **Edit: Focus on Conventions.** (p. 295)

Note: Teach the Conventions mini-lessons (pp. 296–297) if needed.

Day 4

Analyze
Ideas, Organization, and Voice

Student Objectives
- Read a model argument essay.
- Use the argument essay rubric.
- Use the model argument essay to study Ideas, Organization, and Voice.

Student Activities
- Review **"The Right Angle on the Triangle."** *(p. 281)*
- Review the rubric. *(pp. 282–283)*
- Read and discuss **Using the Rubric to Study the Model.** *(pp. 284–285)*

Day 5

Analyze
Word Choice, Sentence Fluency, and Conventions

Student Objectives
- Read a model argument essay.
- Use the argument essay rubric.
- Use the model argument essay to study Word Choice, Sentence Fluency, and Conventions.

Student Activities
- Review **"The Right Angle on the Triangle."** *(p. 281)*
- Review the rubric. *(pp. 282–283)*
- Read and discuss **Using the Rubric to Study the Model.** *(pp. 286–287)*

Day 4

Write
Draft

Student Objectives
- Complete a draft.

Student Activities
- Finish writing the draft. *(p. 291)*
- Participate in a peer conference.

Day 5

Write
Revise: Voice

Student Objectives
- Revise to use second-person point of view, as appropriate.

Student Activities
- Read and discuss **Revise: Focus on Voice.** *(p. 292)*
- Reflect on the model draft.
- Apply the revising strategy.

Day 4

Write
Publish: +Presentation

Student Objectives
- Discuss preparation for publishing and presentation.
- Use a final editing checklist.

Student Activities
- Read and discuss **Publish: +Presentation.** *(p. 298)*
- Apply the publishing strategy.

Day 5

Write
Publish: +Presentation

Student Objectives
- Use an argument essay rubric.
- Share a published argument essay.

Student Activities
- Share their work.
- Use the rubric to reflect upon and evaluate the model and their own writing. *(pp. 282–283; 299)*

To complete the chapter in fewer days, combine the learning objectives and activities in a way that supports students as they write.

Resources at-a-Glance

Grammar, Usage & Mechanics

Differentiating Instruction

For additional Differentiating Instruction activities, see Strategies for Writers *Extensions Online at* **www.sfw.z-b.com.**

English Language Learners

Conferencing

Technology Tip

School Home Connection Letter
Reproducible letter (in English and Spanish) appears on the *Strategies for Writers* CD-ROM and at **www.sfw.z-b.com.**

Online Writing Center

Provides IWB resources, interactive games and practice activities, videos, eBooks, and a virtual file cabinet.

 Strategies for Writers Online

Go to **www.sfw.z-b.com** for free online resources for students and teachers.

Introduce
an Argument Essay

Week 1 • Day 1

Student Objectives

- Review the elements of an argument essay. *(p. 278)*
- Consider purpose and audience. *(p. 279)*
- Learn the traits of argument writing. *(p. 280)*

What's an Argument Essay?

Ask how students could present their opinions about an issue to the school or community. (Possible responses: write an article for the school or local newspaper; talk about it on school or community cable TV)

Explain that whether students are speaking or writing, when their purpose is to convince others that their opinion is valid, they will use the elements of argument. The written form is an argument essay.

What's in an Argument Essay?

Read and discuss the elements of an argument essay. Explain that some of these elements can also be found in other forms of writing, such as an editorial or a speech. Discuss how each element is important in a well-written essay.

 Strategies for Writers Online
Go to **www.sfw.z-b.com** for additional online resources for students and teachers.

What's an **Argument Essay?**

An argument essay expresses a writer's opinion on a topic. It tries to convince readers to agree with the writer and maybe even act in a certain way. For example, an argument essay might try to convince readers to conserve energy in specific ways.

I think I'll like writing an argument essay. I get to act like a lawyer and present a case for my opinion!

What's in an **Argument Essay?**

Clear Opinion
I need to decide exactly what I think of the issue I'm writing about. Then I have to make that opinion clear to my readers. That means stating the opinion convincingly so my audience knows just where I stand.

Good Reasoning
Readers aren't going to be convinced that my opinion is right just because I say so. I need to write a well-organized essay with plenty of supportive, relevant facts and good, logical reasons for my opinions.

Neutral Language
When you're expressing an opinion on something you care about, it's easy to get emotional. But negative language or emotionally loaded words just turn readers off. I'll use neutral language in my essay so my audience will be willing to consider my opinion.

Question-and-Answer Pattern
Facts are important in this kind of writing, but I don't want my essay to be boring! I'm going to use a question-and-answer pattern to keep things interesting.

278 Argument Writing

Argument Text Exemplars (Argument Essay)

Shuster, Kate. *Can Earth Support Our Growing Population?* Heinemann-Raintree, 2008. This is one of eight books in the *What Do You Think?* series. Author Kate Shuster explores both sides of the argument over whether or not Earth can support our growing population. She presents the readers with facts and figures, allowing them to think critically and choose/defend their own position.

Freedman, Russell. *Kids at Work: Lewis Hine and the Crusade Against Child Labor.* Sandpiper, 1998. Lewis Hine was an investigative reporter for the National Child Labor Committee. He took photographs of underprivileged child workers that provided evidence that the United States needed laws against child labor.

Why write an Argument Essay?

I enjoy convincing people of an opinion I think is right, but there are other reasons to write an argument essay. I've listed a few suggestions here to give you some ideas.

Changing Lives

Maybe that sounds a bit dramatic, but I really think an argument essay can do this! A good essay can change someone's point of view—and even encourage him or her to do something differently.

Reasoning Skills

You really have to think things through to write an argument essay. So this kind of writing gives me some good practice in reasoning skills, such as organizing my thoughts, backing up a point, and following a logical train of thought.

Informing

Even if an argument essay doesn't change a reader's opinion, it gives him or her more information on the topic. He or she might learn something completely new—or develop a deeper understanding of the issue.

Keeping Calm

Writing an argument essay helps make a disagreement about an issue less emotional and personal. This kind of writing turns things into a debate instead of a fight!

Why write an Argument Essay?

Read and discuss the reasons for writing an argument essay. Remind students that all writing has a purpose and that the tone and focus of their writing will be shaped by their reasons for writing. Point out that one reason for writing an argument essay—Reasoning Skills—involves practicing a life-long skill. A well-written essay can also affect others by changing lives and by informing them of something of which they were unaware. Have students think about these and other reasons to write an argument essay. Explain that their purpose for writing will determine their audience and affect the tone of a piece.

Hopkins, Andy. *Animals in Danger.* **Oxford University Press, 2008.** In this book, Andy Hopkins discusses the many ways that humans pose a danger to animals. Some of the key points include the destruction of animal habitats, pollution, and poaching, all of which have placed approximately 7,000 species of animals in danger.

Myers, R.E. *Writing a Persuasive Essay, Grades 5–8+.* **Mark Twain, 2006.** *Writing a Persuasive Essay, Grades 5–8+* provides students with a comprehensive guide detailing how to write a persuasive essay. Students will learn the important steps to writing an essay, from choosing a subject and supporting an argument to revising and finalizing.

CCSS **C**ommon **C**ore **S**tate **S**tandards

SL.6.1: Engage effectively in a range of collaborative discussions (one-on-one, in groups, and teacher-led) with diverse partners on *grade 6 topics, texts, and issues,* building on others' ideas and expressing their own clearly. **SL.6.1.a:** Come to discussions prepared, having read or studied required material; explicitly draw on that preparation by referring to evidence on the topic, text, or issue to probe and reflect on ideas under discussion.

Introduce
an Argument Essay

Linking Argument Writing Traits to an Argument Essay

Explain to students that they will follow Leila as she models using the writing process and the traits together. As they follow Leila through the writing process, students will see how the Argument Writing Traits have been adapted and applied to writing an argument essay. They will see that an argument essay, because it expresses an opinion, has many factors in common with other types of argument writing. However, the particular audience and purpose of an argument essay determine how the traits are used.

Linking Argument Writing Traits to an Argument Essay

In this chapter, you will write an essay that expresses your opinion about a topic. This type of argument writing is called an argument essay. Leila will guide you through the stages of the writing process: Prewrite, Draft, Revise, Edit, and Publish. In each stage, Leila will show you important writing strategies that are linked to the Argument Writing Traits below.

Argument Writing Traits

 Ideas
- clearly stated claims, often balanced by alternate or opposing claims
- supporting evidence from accurate and credible sources

 **Organization**
- a strong introduction that presents the writer's position
- reasons and evidence that are organized logically
- a conclusion that restates the thesis and possibly provides a call to action
- transitions that clarify the relationships between ideas

 Voice
- a voice that supports the writer's purpose

 Word Choice
- language that is compelling

 Sentence Fluency
- sentences that vary in length and begin in different ways

 Conventions
- no or few errors in grammar, usage, mechanics, and spelling

Before you write, read Arina Zubatova's argument essay on the next page. Then use the argument essay rubric on pages 282–283 to decide how well she did. (You might want to look back at What's in an Argument Essay? on page 278, too!)

Argument Writing Traits in an Argument Essay

 **Ideas** The writer expresses a clear position. The writer also acknowledges and refutes opposing viewpoints, using strong, supporting evidence to convince the reader that the writer's position is informed and valid.

 Organization The essay is well organized and easy to follow. Helpful transitions guide the reader. A compelling concluding section leaves a strong impression on the reader.

 **Voice** The writer reaches out to the reader and sounds informed, earnest, and convincing. The formal style is appropriate and helps the reader take the writer's ideas seriously.

The Right Angle on the Triangle
by Arina Zubatova

Question →

When you think about the Bermuda Triangle, what comes to your mind? Do you picture mysterious forces, time warps, and the underwater city of Atlantis? That is how some people explain the disappearances of boats and planes in the Bermuda Triangle. However, the dangers there are natural, not supernatural.

← Answer

↳ Clear opinion

The corners of the Bermuda Triangle are Bermuda, Puerto Rico, and Fort Lauderdale, Florida. About 100 boats and planes have disappeared in this region. About 1,000 people have died there in the past century. However, that is only ten people a year, not a high number for such a large area. If this region were especially dangerous, insurance companies would charge higher rates for crafts that pass through it. They do not.

Logical reasoning

Question →

Why did those 100 boats and planes disappear in the Triangle? The causes were natural, not supernatural. In the tropics, sudden storms—even giant waterspouts—can destroy ships and aircraft. The Gulf Stream, a strong ocean current, can pull amateur sailors far off course. In addition, the region has trenches thousands of feet deep. In fact, the deepest trench in the Atlantic Ocean is in the Bermuda Triangle. Remains of boats and planes may be buried in these trenches.

Answer →

↳ Neutral language

Despite these facts, many accidents in the Bermuda Triangle have been described as mysterious. The 1945 disappearance of five Navy bombers off the coast of Florida was one of them. The planes disappeared during a training flight for rookies. The flight was led by an experienced pilot. However, radio transcripts show that his compass was not working. It caused him to lead the group out to sea instead of toward Florida. Then a storm blew in. The planes vanished, and no wreckage was ever found.

What happened to those Navy bombers? The planes probably ended up far out in the Atlantic. There they ran out of gas and fell into the sea. Sharks took the pilots. A trench swallowed the wreckage. In spite of this logical explanation, this and many other disappearances have been blamed on mysterious forces in the Triangle.

↳ Neutral language

People like a good story. Still, we must not ignore the facts about the Bermuda Triangle. The dangers are real, not supernatural. ← Clear opinion

Argument Essay 281

Word Choice The writer's words are precise and convincing. Neutral language presents the writer's claim fairly.

Sentence Fluency Sentences are varied and interesting. The essay flows smoothly and is enjoyable to read.

Conventions The writer has edited carefully. All pronouns are used correctly.

Analyze
the Model

Week 1 • Day 2

Student Objectives

- Read a model argument essay. *(p. 281)*

Read the Model

Direct students' attention to the model. Point out that the writer uses a question-and-answer pattern to organize the response for the reader. What is the effect? (Possible responses: The writer expresses a clear opinion about historical evidence. The essay is well organized, and the ideas are easy to follow. Facts and examples are relevant and help support the writer's viewpoint.)

Elements of an Argument Essay

After reading "The Right Angle on the Triangle," have students return to What's in an Argument Essay? on page 278. Discuss how the elements appear in the model. (An introduction engages the reader and presents the writer's position, the body paragraphs are organized in a question-and-answer pattern and include supporting evidence, and the concluding section restates the writer's opinion, leaving a strong impression on the reader.)

CCSS **C**ommon **C**ore **S**tate **S**tandards
R/Inf.6.1: Cite textual evidence to support analysis of what the text says explicitly as well as inferences drawn from the text. **R/Inf.6.6:** Determine an author's point of view or purpose in a text and explain how it is conveyed in the text. **SL.6.1.b:** Follow rules for collegial discussions, set specific goals and deadlines, and define individual roles as needed.

Analyze
the Model

Week 1 • Day 3

Student Objectives

- Learn to read a rubric. (pp. 282–283)

Use the Rubric

Explain the Rubric Explain that a writing rubric is a tool for planning, improving, and assessing a piece of writing. A rubric helps a writer focus on key elements, or traits, in writing (**Ideas, Organization, Voice, Word Choice, Sentence Fluency, Conventions,** and **Presentation**).

Explain the 6-point system. Point out that the columns on page 282 represent a good argument essay that might need some polishing while the columns on page 283 represent writing that needs considerable improvement.

Discuss the Rubric Guide students in a discussion of the rubric. Read the descriptors that go with each trait, and take a moment to explain the relationship between them. Discuss the differences between columns to be sure students fully understand the point system. Remind students to keep the rubric in mind as they write their own argument essay and again as they revise and edit it.

Online Writing Center

Provides a variety of **interactive rubrics,** including 4-, 5-, and 6-point models.

Rubric

Use this 6-point rubric to plan and score an argument essay.

	6	5	4
Ideas	The topic is clearly presented. Clear reasons and relevant facts support the opinion and show an understanding of the topic.	The topic is stated. Reasons and facts support the opinion and show some understanding of the topic.	The topic can be identified. Several reasons and facts are included, but some may not be relevant.
Organization	The essay is organized into an introduction, body, and conclusion that work together to promote the argument.	The essay has a clear introduction, body, and conclusion. All parts relate clearly to the argument.	The essay has an introduction, body, and conclusion, but parts may be unclear or do not support the argument.
Voice	The writer establishes and consistently maintains a direct, formal style.	The writer's style is direct and formal most of the time.	Occasionally the writer's voice becomes vague or too informal, but overall the style is appropriate.
Word Choice	Neutral words create a balanced and fair tone. The writer avoids loaded or negative words.	The writer's words are fair. The writer avoids loaded or negative words.	Some words are loaded or negative in tone. The reader may question the writer's opinion.
Sentence Fluency	Varied sentences hold the reader's interest. Thoughtful questions move the reader along.	Most sentences use varied patterns. Questions move the reader along.	Some variety in sentence patterns is present. The writing could use another question or two.
Conventions	The writing has been thoughtfully edited. Pronouns are correct, and their antecedents are clear.	The writing is edited well. Just a few errors are present. Most pronouns are correct and antecedents are clear.	A few noticeable errors in pronoun use and unclear antecedents don't confuse the reader.

✛ Presentation The essay is neatly prepared and legible.

282 Argument Writing

CCSS Common Core State Standards

Argument Essay

The Common Core State Standards (CCSS) are woven throughout the instruction in *Strategies for Writers.* Writing in the Argument mode can engage the standards for all forms of Argument writing. The rubric and writing strategies for Ideas reflect writing standard **W.6.1,** to write arguments to support claims with clear reasons and relevant evidence, and standards **W.6.1.a** and **W.6.1.b,** to introduce and support a claim. The rubric and writing strategies for Organization are also drawn from standards **W.6.1.a** and **W.6.1.b,** to organize the ideas logically, and standard **W.6.1.e,** to provide an effective conclusion. The traits of Voice and Word Choice reflect standard **W.6.1.c,** to use language to create cohesion

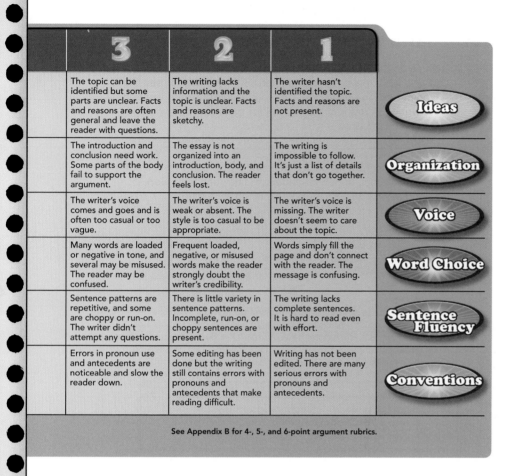

	3	2	1	
	The topic can be identified but some parts are unclear. Facts and reasons are often general and leave the reader with questions.	The writing lacks information and the topic is unclear. Facts and reasons are sketchy.	The writer hasn't identified the topic. Facts and reasons are not present.	Ideas
	The introduction and conclusion need work. Some parts of the body fail to support the argument.	The essay is not organized into an introduction, body, and conclusion. The reader feels lost.	The writing is impossible to follow. It's just a list of details that don't go together.	Organization
	The writer's voice comes and goes and is often too casual or too vague.	The writer's voice is weak or absent. The style is too casual to be appropriate.	The writer's voice is missing. The writer doesn't seem to care about the topic.	Voice
	Many words are loaded or negative in tone, and several may be misused. The reader may be confused.	Frequent loaded, negative, or misused words make the reader strongly doubt the writer's credibility.	Words simply fill the page and don't connect with the reader. The message is confusing.	Word Choice
	Sentence patterns are repetitive, and some are choppy or run-on. The writer didn't attempt any questions.	There is little variety in sentence patterns. Incomplete, run-on, or choppy sentences are present.	The writing lacks complete sentences. It is hard to read even with effort.	Sentence Fluency
	Errors in pronoun use and antecedents are noticeable and slow the reader down.	Some editing has been done but the writing still contains errors with pronouns and antecedents that make reading difficult.	Writing has not been edited. There are many serious errors with pronouns and antecedents.	Conventions

See Appendix B for 4-, 5-, and 6-point argument rubrics.

Apply the Rubric

Assign Groups Assign students to small groups and ask them to check the model for one trait. One person in each group should be responsible for recording one or two strong examples of the trait as described by the rubric. Ask students to score the trait accordingly for the model. They should be able to support their scores. Note that although the model was written to score high in each trait, students should not assume each trait would receive a 6, the top score. Encourage students to discuss each trait thoroughly before assigning a score.

Reassemble Class Bring the class together and ask one person from each group to report the group's findings to the class. The point of this exercise is less to score the model than it is to practice identifying and evaluating the traits within a piece of writing.

Additional Rubrics Appendix B includes 4-, 5-, and 6-point rubrics that can be used with any piece of argument writing. The rubrics are also available as blackline masters, beginning on page T525.

and clarify relationships among ideas, and standard **W.6.1.d**, to establish and maintain a formal style.

The language standards for grade 6 students are addressed during editing and skills practice (**L.6.1–L.6.6**). In addition, there are multiple opportunities to address the speaking and listening standards during the writing process. Specifically, students are encouraged to work collaboratively, review key ideas, and demonstrate understanding (**SL.6.1.a–d**). Most importantly, this chapter will help students produce coherent writing (**W.6.4**), improve their writing with the help of peers and adults (**W.6.5**), draw evidence from reliable sources (**W.6.9**), and use writing to respond and reflect (**W.6.10**).

CCSS Common Core State Standards

W.6.9: Draw evidence from literary or informational texts to support analysis, reflection, and research.
SL.6.1.c: Pose and respond to specific questions with elaboration and detail by making comments that contribute to the topic, text, or issue under discussion.
SL.6.1.d: Review the key ideas expressed and demonstrate understanding of multiple perspectives through reflection and paraphrasing.

Analyze
the Model

Student Objectives

- Read a model argument essay. *(p. 281)*
- Use the argument essay rubric. *(pp. 282–283)*
- Use the model argument essay to study Ideas, Organization, and Voice. *(pp. 284–285)*

Study the Model

Assess the Model Point out that these pages show how the model includes the traits of **Ideas, Organization,** and **Voice.** Read each section with students. Encourage them to try to find other examples of each trait in the writing model. Use questions such as the following to discuss the pages with students.

- Does the writer express an opinion on a topic? (Possible response: Yes, Arina states her opinion about the Bermuda Triangle in the introduction.)

- Does the writer support the opinion? (Possible response: The writer uses relevant facts and examples to convince the reader.)

▶ **Strategies for Writers Online**
Go to **www.sfw.z-b.com** for additional online resources for students and teachers.

Argument Essay
Using the Rubric to Study the Model

Did you notice that the model on page 281 points out some key elements of an argument essay? As she wrote "The Right Angle on the Triangle," Arina Zubatova used these elements to help her express her opinion persuasively. She also used the 6-point rubric on pages 282–283 to plan, draft, revise, and edit the writing. A rubric is a great tool for evaluating writing during the writing process.

Now let's use the same rubric to score the model. To do this, we'll focus on each trait separately, starting with Ideas. We'll use the top descriptor for each trait (column 6), along with examples from the model, to help us understand how the traits work together. How would you score Arina on each trait?

Ideas
- **The topic is clearly presented.**
- **Clear reasons and relevant facts support the opinion and show an understanding of the topic.**

Arina clearly states her topic in the first paragraph. Then she carefully lays out her reasons and facts to support her opinion. For example, she lists the natural hazards within the Bermuda Triangle that can endanger ships and planes alike. I must admit, her facts are pretty convincing, and it's clear Arina knows what she's talking about!

[from the writing model]

In the tropics, sudden storms—even giant waterspouts—can destroy ships and aircraft. The Gulf Stream, a strong ocean current, can pull amateur sailors far off course.

284 Argument Writing

English Language Learners

BEGINNING
Facts and Opinions Read a simple nonfiction text about snakes. Write *Snakes are animals.* Ask, *Is this always true?* Then say, *Facts are always true.* Say, *facts* and have students repeat. Show pictures from the book to encourage students to give more simple facts about snakes. Repeat the process for opinions, such as *Some snakes are beautiful.* Then read each sentence and have students repeat.

INTERMEDIATE
Fact and Opinion Review the meanings of *fact* and *opinion.* Draw a Network Tree on the board with *Bullying* as the topic. Ask students to make statements about bullying and then have other students tell whether each statement is fact or opinion. Write answers on the Network Tree.

Organization

- The essay is organized into an introduction, body, and conclusion that work together to promote the argument.

The introduction clearly states Arina's topic: strange disappearances in the Bermuda Triangle. The body presents her supporting facts, and the conclusion neatly sums up her opinion. Notice how clearly she presents her facts in the body.

> [from the writing model]
>
> The corners of the Bermuda Triangle are Bermuda, Puerto Rico, and Fort Lauderdale, Florida. About 100 boats and planes have disappeared in this region. About 1,000 people have died there in the past century. However, that is only ten people a year, not a high number for such a large area.

Voice

- The writer establishes and consistently maintains a direct, formal style.

Arina establishes a direct style right away by addressing the reader as *you* in the introduction. This helps her make a solid connection with the reader while maintaining a formal, serious style.

> [from the writing model]
>
> When you think about the Bermuda Triangle, what comes to your mind? Do you picture mysterious forces, time warps, and the underwater city of Atlantis? That is how some people explain the disappearances of boats and planes in the Bermuda Triangle. However, the dangers there are natural, not supernatural.

Argument Essay 285

- How is the response organized? (Possible response: The writer states her purpose for writing in the introduction, uses a question-and-answer pattern to engage the reader in the argument, and restates her opinion in the conclusion.)

- How would you describe the writer's voice? (Possible responses: The writer speaks knowledgeably and sounds like an expert on the topic. It's obvious that she wants to convince the audience that her viewpoint is correct.)

ADVANCED

Opinion and Reasons Read an editorial in the school newspaper. On the board write the author's opinion. Have partners highlight the reasons the author gives for that opinion. In small groups have students share the reasons they found. Have students write a short paragraph about bullying, giving their opinion and reasons for their opinion.

ADVANCED HIGH

Logical Reasoning Ask a volunteer to define *logical*. Simply put, something that is logical makes sense. To illustrate, ask, *Is it logical to put your socks on after you put your shoes on? Is it logical for leaves to be green? Is it logical if I say that 2 × 2 = 4?* Tell students that *logical reasoning* is an argument that has an organized and clear presentation.

CCSS **C**ommon **C**ore **S**tate **S**tandards

W.6.9: Draw evidence from literary or informational texts to support analysis, reflection, and research.
SL.6.1.c: Pose and respond to specific questions with elaboration and detail by making comments that contribute to the topic, text, or issue under discussion.
SL.6.1.d: Review the key ideas expressed and demonstrate understanding of multiple perspectives through reflection and paraphrasing.

Analyze
the Model

Week 1 • Day 5

Student Objectives

- Read a model argument essay. (p. 281)
- Use the argument essay rubric. (pp. 282–283)
- Use the model argument essay to study Word Choice, Sentence Fluency, and Conventions. (pp. 286–287)

Continue the Discussion Use questions such as the following to discuss the traits analyzed on pages 286 and 287:

- How would you describe the language? (Possible response: The writer's language is appropriate and convincing. I also notice that she does not use biased or overly emotional language to get her ideas across to the reader.)

- What are Arina's sentences like? (Possible responses: Arina's sentences are interesting and energetic. They move along at a good pace and keep the audience engaged in the ideas.)

- Was the essay edited? (Possible response: It's obvious that Arina edited her essay carefully. All pronouns are used correctly, too.)

 **Word Choice**
- Neutral words create a balanced and fair tone.
- The writer avoids loaded or negative words.

Arina might have used loaded, negative words, like *fool*, to show that she is amazed that some people believe there are mysterious forces in the Bermuda Triangle. However, she doesn't say, "Some fools will believe anything." Instead, her language is balanced and fair, like this:

[from the writing model]

People like a good story. Still, we must not ignore the facts about the Bermuda Triangle. The dangers are real, not supernatural.

 **Sentence Fluency**
- Varied sentences hold the reader's interest.
- Thoughtful questions move the reader along.

To help keep the reader interested, Arina varies her sentence patterns. For example, she includes a few questions to keep the reader moving through the essay. Here, she really got my attention by using a question and then answering it with details.

[from the writing model]

What happened to those Navy bombers? The planes probably ended up far out in the Atlantic. There they ran out of gas and fell into the sea. Sharks took the pilots. A trench swallowed the wreckage.

Technology Tip for 21st Century Literacies

Use MixedInk or another real-time collaborative writing tool to challenge students to work together as they write their argument essays. Collaborate to revise to a stronger, more articulated draft. For example, have one student take the alternate point of view and raise needed counterpoints as students read, or collaborate to find support to substantiate the points offered. This could be expanded further by engaging with collaborators who are not present within the classroom, which requires more setup and monitoring but heightens the relevance and motivation for learners.

See **www.sfw.z-b.com** for further information about and links to these websites and tools.

Strategies for Writers Online
Go to **www.sfw.z-b.com** for additional online resources for students and teachers.

Conventions

- The writing has been thoughtfully edited.
- Pronouns are correct, and their antecedents are clear.

I didn't find a single mistake in spelling, punctuation, or capitalization. The writer was also careful with pronouns. Can you tell what the pronoun *it* refers to in the first sentence below? It refers to *region*, right? *It* and *region* are both singular, so they agree. In the second sentence, it's clear that *They* refers to *companies*. These words are both plural, so they agree.

[from the writing model]

If this region were especially dangerous, insurance companies would charge higher rates for crafts that pass through it. They do not.

✛Presentation   The essay is neatly prepared and legible.

My Turn!

Now it's my turn to write an argument essay. I'll use what I learned from the rubric and good writing strategies. Follow along with me to see how I do it.

Argument Essay   **287**

Differentiating Instruction

ENRICHMENT

Speak Up Have students find information on issues that interest and concern them. Then challenge them to use the information as springboards for giving short speeches or starting a blog site in which they present the problem, recommend solutions, and call the audience to action.

REINFORCEMENT

Solve a Problem Together Have pairs of students select a problem that they care about and propose workable solutions. Then ask them to work with partners to find facts to support their recommendations. Have them keep the information to use when they collect their notes for their essays.

Presentation Explain to students that Presentation is just as important as the other traits. Appearance should be considered when students prepare their final copies. Neatness is always a priority, and text should be typed, using only a few readable fonts. An interesting title, good margins, and good spacing make the argument essay inviting and easy to read.

Think About the Traits After students have thoroughly discussed the model, ask them which traits they think are the most important. Remind them that all of the traits are important in every piece of writing; however, some traits play a more important role in specific types of writing. For example, some students may feel that the trait of **Ideas** is very important to present a position and refute opposing claims effectively. Some students may argue that **Voice** is important because the writer needs to convince the audience. Still others may feel that **Word Choice** is important because the writer's language should neither distract nor offend the audience.

CCSS Common Core State Standards

R/Inf.6.6: Determine an author's point of view or purpose in a text and explain how it is conveyed in the text. **R/Inf.6.8:** Trace and evaluate the argument and specific claims in a text, distinguishing claims that are supported by reasons and evidence from claims that are not. **SL.6.1.d:** Review the key ideas expressed and demonstrate understanding of multiple perspectives through reflection and paraphrasing.

Write
an Argument Essay

Week 2 • Day 1

Student Objectives

• Choose an issue and find information to support the opinion. (p. 288)

Prewrite

Focus on ⬭Ideas⬭

Select and Research a Topic Read Leila's words together and discuss her reasons for choosing this topic. Then ask students to comment on her notes. (Possible response: Her notes are brief but include many facts to support her opinion that people should not stereotype people on the basis of where they live.) Point out that Leila conducted research by reading about her topic and gathering the most current information.

Instruct students to select a topic about which they have strong feelings, as Leila did. A bit of passion should result in better writing.

Online Writing Center

 Provides **interactive graphic organizers** as well as a variety of graphic organizers in PDF format.

Prewrite   Focus on ⬭Ideas⬭

The Rubric Says The topic is clearly presented. Clear reasons and relevant facts support the opinion and show an understanding of the topic.

Writing Strategy Choose an issue and find information to support the opinion.

I live in Tennessee, but California is the main location of one of my hobbies—old movies. My favorite aunt lives in California, too, and I visit her whenever I can.

Some people think that all Californians care only about how they look and what the latest fads are. That upsets me.

When our teacher asked us to write an argument essay, I decided to try to convince my classmates not to stereotype people based on where they live. I read some articles about California and took these notes.

Notes on Californians

CA's population grew 50 percent between 1970 and 1990.

CA has more immigrants from other countries than any other state.

Californians come in all shapes and sizes.

One in four Californians is Hispanic.

In 1990 census, nearly 5 million Californians had German ancestors; 3.5 million were from Irish families.

1990 census: more than half of the people living in CA were not born there.

Migrants come from all over the nation, especially the South and Northeast.

Apply
Choose an issue about which you have an opinion. Do some research and find facts to support your opinion.

288 Argument Writing

English Language Learners

BEGINNING/INTERMEDIATE
Second-Person Write _____ *are eating at Rosie's*. Fill in the blank with *We,* say the sentence, and have students repeat. Ask if the sentence is first, second, or third person. Replace *We* with *They* and repeat the process. Finally, replace *They* with *You.* Tell students that when *you* is the subject, the sentence is written in second person. Say *second person* and have students say it. Repeat for other examples until the concept is clear to students.

ADVANCED/ADVANCED HIGH
Loaded Words Review the idea of loaded words. Write the following sentences on the board: *Selena is arrogant. Selena seems proud of herself.* Ask students which word in each sentence gives a positive or negative idea of Selena. Give other examples of loaded words and have partners make changes to create less emotional images.

The Rubric Says The essay is organized into an introduction, body, and conclusion that work together to promote the argument.

Writing Strategy Use a Network Tree to organize the ideas.

✏️ **Writer's Term____**

Network Tree
A **Network Tree** organizes information about a topic. The topic or opinion goes at the top, with main ideas or reasons on the next level. The bottom level contains facts to support the main ideas or reasons.

A Network Tree can help me get my ideas in order. I'll put my opinion at the top, the reasons for my opinion under that, and supportive facts underneath each reason. The Network Tree will help me state my topic in the introduction and organize my facts for the body of my essay.

Network Tree

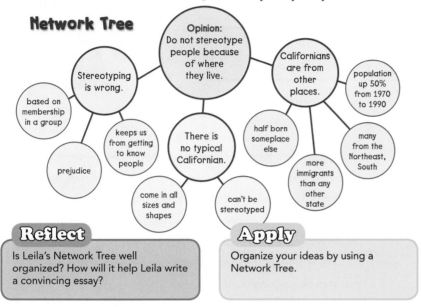

Reflect

Is Leila's Network Tree well organized? How will it help Leila write a convincing essay?

Apply

Organize your ideas by using a Network Tree.

Argument Essay 289

Student Objectives

• Use a Network Tree to organize the ideas. (p. 289)

Prewrite

Focus on

Make a Network Tree Read page 289. Then direct attention to Leila's organizer. Have students look back at her notes. Discuss how she organizes them on the Network Tree.

Point out that Leila first states her opinion in the largest oval. (Do not stereotype people because of where they live.) Next Leila lists her three main points or reasons. (Stereotyping is wrong; Californians are from other places; There is no typical Californian.) Then she lists supporting information for each reason in the smallest ovals.

✏️ **Writer's Term____**

Network Tree The Network Tree is a visual representation of a writer's main ideas and supporting details. It's helpful to see the levels of organization as main ideas are defined and supported by relevant facts and examples.

CCSS Common Core State Standards
W.6.1: Write arguments to support claims with clear reasons and relevant evidence. **W.6.9:** Draw evidence from literary or informational texts to support analysis, reflection, and research. **R/Inf.6.5:** Analyze how a particular sentence, paragraph, chapter, or section fits into the overall structure of a text and contributes to the development of the ideas. **R/Inf.6.7:** Integrate information presented in different media or formats (e.g., visually, quantitatively) as well as in words to develop a coherent understanding of a topic or issue.

Conferencing

PEER TO PEER Have partners exchange organizers and make sure the opinions are well supported. Partners should write down their comments and suggestions and share their responses with each other.

PEER GROUPS Have students work in small groups for the purpose of sharing their organizers. Have group members take turns offering one comment or suggestion to improve them, based on the prewriting lessons.

TEACHER-LED Schedule conferences with individual students. Before they speak with you, tell students to go over their organizers and verify their supporting evidence.

Write
an Argument Essay

Student Objectives

• Write well-organized paragraphs. (p. 290)

Draft

Focus on Organization

Draft an Argument Explain that the way to convince readers that your opinion is correct is to support it with verifiable facts and examples. Ask students why they think facts are important in argument writing. **(Possible response: The writer's opinion is not enough. It must be supported by current information to convince the audience.)** Remind students to include reliable facts and examples to support their position.

✎ Writer's Term

Opinion In argument writing, the writer expresses an informed opinion supported by compelling facts and examples. The writer selects supporting details that will convince the audience to agree with the writer.

Online Writing Center

Provides student eBooks with an **interactive writing pad** for drafting, revising, editing, and publishing.

Writing an Argument Essay

Draft   Focus on Organization

The Rubric Says	The essay is organized into an introduction, body, and conclusion that work together to promote the argument.
Writing Strategy	Write well-organized paragraphs.

Now I'm ready to write my draft. Well-organized paragraphs will promote my argument. I'll use my Network Tree as a guide. The information in the middle-sized circles will be the main ideas in my body paragraphs. The small circles contain the details for the paragraphs. I know I can fix any mistakes later, so for now I'll just focus on getting my ideas down on paper. Here's a part of my draft.

✎ Writer's Term

Opinion
An **opinion** is a belief, often strong, that cannot be proven to be true.

[DRAFT]

Don't Stereotype by State!

by Leila

Some people think all Californiains pay way too much attention to how they look. Others believe they all follow the latest fads, no matter how temporary. When we lump people together like this. In this **[opinion/thesis]** case, we are forming an opinion about them based on where they live. That's wrong! The people who live in California are as different from one another as the people who live in every other state. We must stop stereotyping them! **[fact]**

290 Argument Writing

Differentiating Instruction

ENRICHMENT

Network Together Discuss how a Network Tree is useful for organizing ideas. Have students work together to create Network Trees from online editorials or letters to the editor. Have students use the organizers to analyze the writers' arguments.

REINFORCEMENT

Reason Well To help students understand the importance of neutral language, write this opinion on the board: *Those who came up with the stupid idea of a longer school day need help.* Why would this statement make supporters of a longer school day less likely to agree? **(Possible responses: It may offend them and make them less likely to change their minds.)** Remind students to refrain from negative language, as doing so may cause the audience to dismiss their viewpoint.

[DRAFT]

[reason]

Stereotyping is wrong. It's a kind of prejudice. Some ignorant people use stereotypes to jump to decisions. They decide whether they like people because of the group they belong to. They don't bother to get to know him. It's like being prejudiced against people because of the shabby clothes they wear or the strange language she speaks. You could miss meeting good friends if you make decisions based on stereotypes.

[fact]

It's really a dumb mistake to stereotype Californians. In the 1990 census, California had more than 29 million residents. More than half of Californians were born someplace else, and he moved there. Between 1970 and 1990, the population of california grew by 50 percent. Many of these new residents came from the northeastern and southern states. California also has more imigrants from other countries than any other state. They can't really be grouped together because they are not the same.

Reflect

Is Leila's thesis or opinion clearly stated in the introduction? Are the reasons and the supporting facts clear?

Apply

Write a draft using your Network Tree to help you. Remember to state your opinion at the beginning, support it in the body, and sum it up in the conclusion.

Argument Essay 291

Write
an Argument Essay

Week 2 • Day 4

Student Objectives

• Complete a draft. *(p. 291)*

Continue Drafting Have students read Leila's draft. Ask whether they think Leila has stated a clear opinion. Remind students what it means to draft an essay (get ideas down on paper). Remind them that they should not be overly concerned with errors at this point.

Tell students to state their opinion in the introduction. It is important that students are given ample time for drafting. As conferencing is important throughout the writing process, be sure to plan time for peer-to-peer, peer group, or teacher-led conferences. Remind students that this is the time for getting their ideas down in a creative and engaging way. Assure them that they will have plenty of time later to revise and edit.

Conferencing

PEER TO PEER Have partners exchange and read drafts. Tell students to think of several questions they would like to ask to clarify information. Have them write their questions on sticky notes and affix them to their partners' drafts.

PEER GROUPS Have students work in groups of four. Tell students to pass their draft to the student on the right. Using the rubric on pages 282–283 as a guide, each student writes one comment or suggestion on a sticky note, affixes the note to the draft, and passes the draft to the right. The review ends when everyone has received his or her own draft back with three comments.

TEACHER-LED Schedule conferences with pairs of students. Have students read each other's draft. Prompt their revisions by asking questions.

CCSS Common Core State Standards

W.6.1.a: Introduce claim(s) and organize the reasons and evidence clearly. **W.6.1.b:** Support claim(s) with clear reasons and relevant evidence, using credible sources and demonstrating an understanding of the topic or text. **W.6.5:** With some guidance and support from peers and adults, develop and strengthen writing as needed by planning, revising, editing, rewriting, or trying a new approach.

Write
an Argument Essay

Week 2 • Day 5

Student Objectives

- Revise to use second-person point of view, as appropriate. (p. 292)

Revise

Focus on Voice

Address the Audience Read Leila's words and the draft excerpt. Then discuss the importance of addressing the audience directly. (Possible response: In argument writing, the writer's goal is to get the audience to agree with his or her position.) Point out that Leila revised her draft to ask questions that engage her audience.

Explain that the rubric says to use a formal style throughout the essay. Using the second-person point of view where it is appropriate involves the audience in the writer's argument. Point out that Leila forms the questions in a positive way, gets readers thinking about her position, and invites them to consider her viewpoint.

 Strategies for Writers Online
Go to **www.sfw.z-b.com** for additional online resources for students and teachers.

Revise

Focus on Voice

The Rubric Says	The writer establishes and consistently maintains a direct, formal style.
Writing Strategy	Use second-person point of view, as appropriate.

I need to convince my reader that I believe passionately in my opinion. I know that second-person point of view will help me sound like I am speaking directly to the reader. If I do this immediately in my essay, my reader will be involved right away. Then I'll continue addressing my readers in a formal style, so that they'll take my views seriously.

[DRAFT]

———— [used second person] ————

Do you

~~Some people~~ think all Californians pay way too much attention

? Do you

to how they look? Others believe they all follow the latest fads, no

matter how temporary?

Apply
Try adding second-person point of view to speak directly to the reader.

English Language Learners

BEGINNING/INTERMEDIATE

Pronouns Write the subject and object pronouns. Write two related sentences, such as *Harry watched a movie. Harry liked the movie.* Underline in the second sentence *Harry* and *the movie.* Ask, *Which pronoun could replace* Harry? Repeat for *the movie.* Write *He liked it* and have students read both sentences. Repeat with other examples. Point out that pronouns must agree in number and gender with the nouns they replace.

ADVANCED/ADVANCED HIGH

Pronouns and Antecedents Review the activity above. Point to *He liked it* and ask, *Who is "He"*? When students say *Harry,* tell them that *Harry* is the antecedent for the pronoun *He.* Ask, *What is the antecedent for* it? Write *antecedent,* say it, and have students repeat the word. Underline *ante-* in *antecedent* and ask if anyone knows what the prefix means. If needed, tell them it means "coming before."

Revise

Focus on  Word Choice

The Rubric Says	Neutral words create a balanced and fair tone. The writer avoids loaded or negative words.
Writing Strategy	Replace loaded words with neutral words.

 Writer's Term___

Loaded Word

A **loaded word** has an emotional meaning. It can be a positive meaning or a negative one. For example, **shack** is a negatively loaded word for **house**. **Mansion** is a positively loaded word. Loaded words can influence a reader's thinking unfairly.

I feel strongly about my opinion, and I want to make it clear. Yet when I read my argument essay to myself, I realized that I might be using loaded words to sway readers unfairly. I replaced those words with more objective words. Now my essay seems more reasonable than emotional. You can see how it helped in this paragraph.

[DRAFT]

Stereotyping is wrong. It's a kind of prejudice. Some ~~ignorant~~
make
people use stereotypes to ~~jump to~~ decisions. They decide whether
they like people because of the group they belong to. They don't
[replaced
loaded ——→ take the time
words] ~~bother~~ to get to know him. It's like being prejudiced against people
kind of
because of the ~~shabby~~ clothes they wear or the ~~strange~~ language
she speaks.

[deleted loaded words]

Reflect

Did changing the loaded words make Leila's essay seem more objective?

Apply

Replace any loaded words with neutral words.

Argument Essay **293**

Conferencing

PEER TO PEER During revising, have partners exchange drafts. After reading, ask each student to offer feedback on how to strengthen the essay. If needed, have students consult the model, the rubric, and the lessons for revising Voice, Word Choice, and Sentence Fluency.

PEER GROUPS Have students form small revising groups. Each student should read aloud a section of his or her essay that needs improvement. Ask each group member to offer one suggestion. Have writers consult the revising lessons (pages 292–294) to inform their revisions.

TEACHER-LED Schedule conferences to read each student's draft. Talk about ways to improve the draft. If a student seems stalled, revisit steps in the process to make improvements and keep going.

Write
an Argument Essay

Week 3 • Day 1

Student Objectives

• Replace loaded words with neutral words. *(p. 293)*

Revise

Focus on Word Choice

Avoid Loaded Words Have a volunteer read Leila's thoughts about **Word Choice.** Then read the definition in the Writer's Term box. Ask how avoiding overly emotional language keeps writing clear and fair. (Possible responses: Loaded words use emotions, rather than logic, to convince an audience. Using loaded words often backfires by distracting or offending readers. Writers should use facts, not emotions, to argue fairly.)

Ask students to review their drafts to be sure there are no loaded words. Have them replace any they find with neutral words.

Writer's Term___

Loaded Word Words become "loaded" because of the connotations they carry. If readers associate a negative meaning with a word, they may dismiss the argument.

CCSS **Common Core State Standards**
W.6.1.c: Use words, phrases, and clauses to clarify the relationships among claim(s) and reasons.
W.6.1.d: Establish and maintain a formal style.
W.6.5: With some guidance and support from peers and adults, develop and strengthen writing as needed by planning, revising, editing, rewriting, or trying a new approach. **L.6.3.b:** Maintain consistency in style and tone. **L.6.5.c:** Distinguish among the connotations (associations) of words with similar denotations (definitions) (e.g., *stingy, scrimping, economical, unwaste-ful, thrifty*).

Argument Essay **T293**

Write
an Argument Essay

Week 3 • Day 2

Student Objectives

• Revise to choose punctuation for effect. *(p. 294)*

Revise

Focus on

Use Punctuation for Effect Ask a volunteer to read the introduction. Then ask a volunteer to read the draft excerpt before the revisions. Note that Leila read her draft and once again referred to the rubric to find out if she had missed anything in her essay. Because she had not varied her sentences enough, she revised to add thoughtful questions.

Have a volunteer read the draft excerpt with the changes. Point out that Leila's question-and-answer sentence patterns help make her case and add interest. They also keep the reader involved in the ideas and improve the flow. Encourage students to read their drafts and find places where they can use a question-and-answer pattern to engage the reader.

Online Writing Center

 Provides **interactive proofreading activities** for each genre.

Revise Focus on Sentence Fluency

The Rubric Says Varied sentences hold the reader's interest. Thoughtful questions move the reader along.

Writing Strategy Choose punctuation for effect.

The rubric says that if I vary the types of sentences in my writing, I create more interest for my reader. Most of my sentences are statements, but I can include exclamations to show my passion about the topic and thoughtful questions to keep the reader moving along. You can see where I changed some statements to an exclamation and questions to make the writing more interesting.

[DRAFT] How could you group all these people together? How could you say they are all the same?

Between 1970 and 1990, the poplulation of california grew by 50 percent. Many of these new residents came from the northeastern and southern states. California also has more imigrants from other countries than any other state. ~~They can't really be grouped together because they are not the same.~~

[varied punctuation for effect] [added thoughtful questions]

Apply

Look over your writing and insert a question or two to engage the reader. Vary punctuation when appropriate for effect, too.

294 Argument Writing

Optional Revising Lessons

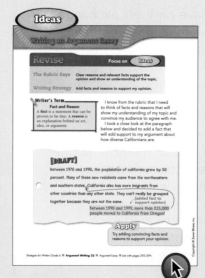

Argument 23

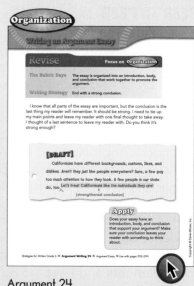

Argument 24

Go to *Strategies for Writers Grade 6 CD-ROM*

Edit

Focus on **Conventions**

The Rubric Says	The writing has been thoughtfully edited. Pronouns are correct, and their antecedents are clear.
Writing Strategy	Recognize and correct inappropriate shifts in pronoun number and person.

✎ **Writer's Term**_____

Pronoun and Antecedent
A **pronoun** is a word that takes the place of a noun. An **antecedent** is the noun or phrase that the pronoun refers to.

Now I have to fix my mistakes in spelling, grammar, and punctuation. I also need to make sure that my pronouns and antecedents match and that each pronoun has a clear antecedent. If I'm not careful with my pronouns, my audience will wonder whom or what I'm talking about.

Here's some of my draft, so you can see the kinds of errors I corrected.

[DRAFT]

[corrected pronoun]

census, California had more than 29 million residents. More than half
                                                          they
of Californians were born someplace else, and ~~he~~ moved there.
                        population
Between 1970 and 1990, the ~~popluation~~ of california grew by 50
                          .
percent‸Many of these new residents came from the northeastern
                                                    m
and southern states. California also has more im‸igrants from

Reflect

Did adding questions make the writing more interesting? Are all the pronouns and antecedents clear? How have Leila's revisions and edits strengthened her essay?

Apply **Conventions**

Edit your draft for spelling, punctuation, and capitalization. Be sure that all pronouns have clear antecedents that match.

For more practice with antecedents and relative pronouns, use the exercises on the next two pages.

Argument Essay 295

Related Grammar Practice_____

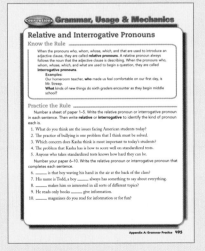

Student Edition page 495

Go to ⇨ **Appendix A: Grammar Practice**

Student Objectives

• Recognize and correct inappropriate shifts in pronoun number and person. *(p. 295)*

Edit

Focus on

Use Pronouns Correctly Direct students' attention to the pronoun correction in the draft excerpt. What is the antecedent? (Californians) Because it is plural, the pronoun also needs to be plural. (they) Go over the other corrections. Have students read and edit their own drafts.

If students are typing their essays, remind them to use the editing features on the computer. Use the mini-lessons on pages 296 and 297 for students who need practice in using pronouns correctly.

✎ **Writer's Term**_____

Pronoun and Antecedent A pronoun and antecedent must agree in number, person, and gender. A common mistake is to use a singular subject followed by a plural pronoun (e.g., *The cat licked their whiskers.*).

CCSS **Common Core State Standards**
L.6.1: Demonstrate command of the conventions of standard English grammar and usage when writing or speaking. **L.6.1.d:** Recognize and correct vague pronouns (i.e., ones with unclear or ambiguous antecedents). **L.6.2:** Demonstrate command of the conventions of standard English capitalization, punctuation, and spelling when writing. **L.6.4.c:** Consult reference materials (e.g., dictionaries, glossaries, thesauruses), both print and digital, to find the pronunciation of a word or determine or clarify its precise meaning or its part of speech.

Argument Essay **T295**

Conventions

Mini-Lesson

Student Objectives

- Use pronouns and antecedents correctly. *(p. 296)*

Pronouns and Antecedents

Explain that a pronoun and antecedent should agree in number. Write the following example on the board:

- *When the <u>students</u> heard the bell ring, (he/she/they) hurried to class.*

Ask students to select the correct pronoun for this sentence. (they)

Explain that a pronoun and antecedent should agree in gender. Write the following example on the board:

- *If the <u>company</u> makes a profit this year, (it/they) will build stores in three more states.*

Ask students to select the correct pronoun for this sentence. (it) Point out that the neuter pronoun agrees with *company*, which is neither male nor female.

Write the following on the board:

- *<u>James</u> and his friend <u>Isaiah</u> will try out for the team. As a child, he played soccer.*

Ask students to make the meaning clear in the second sentence.
(Possible responses: As a child, James played soccer. As a child, Isaiah played soccer.)

Online Writing Center

 Provides **interactive grammar games** and **practice activities** in student eBook.

Pronouns and Antecedents

Know the Rule

A **pronoun** must agree with its **antecedent** in two ways:
- The pronoun is singular if its antecedent is singular. The pronoun is plural if its antecedent is plural.
- The pronoun is female if its antecedent is female—or male if its antecedent is male.
  Example: Stereotyping might lead a girl to choose **her** friends based on the clothes **they** wear. (*Her* is singular and female, so it agrees with its singular antecedent, *girl*. *They* is plural and agrees with its plural antecedent, *friends*.)

When you use a pronoun, make sure its antecedent is clear.
  Example: Mark's friend is named Jamal. **He** lives down the street. (It is unclear whether *He* refers to *Mark* or *Jamal*.)
  Mark's friend Jamal lives down the street. (Sometimes the best way to correct an unclear antecedent is not to use a pronoun at all!)

Practice the Rule

Number a sheet of paper 1–8. Identify the antecedent for the underlined pronoun in each sentence.

1. (Stereotyping) is a part of our culture. <u>It</u> is something we should try to change.
2. Stereotyping occurs when (people) are grouped together. Perhaps <u>they</u> are grouped because they all play football or chess.
3. We make poor judgments when we stereotype (individuals). We do not respect <u>them</u>.
4. (Stereotypes) can be positive or negative, but <u>they</u> are almost always unfair.
5. Victims of (stereotyping) often do not know what to do about <u>it</u>.
6. When we don't see (people) as individuals, it is easy to stereotype <u>them</u>.
7. We may feel good about ourselves if we belong to a (group) that people value and other people do not belong to <u>it</u>.
8. In literature and drama, (stereotypes) are common. <u>They</u> are often referred to as stock characters.

Related Grammar Practice

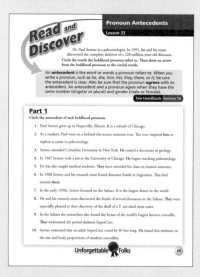

Page 89

Go to ⇨ *G.U.M. Student Practice Book*

Relative Pronouns

Know the Rule

When the pronouns *who*, *whom*, *whose*, *which*, and *that* are used to introduce an adjective clause, they are called **relative pronouns**. A relative pronoun always follows the noun described by the adjective clause it begins.
Example: I have several cousins **who** live in California.

Practice the Rule

Number a sheet of paper 1–10. Write the pronoun that correctly completes the sentence. Choose from the pronouns *who*, *whom*, *whose*, *which*, and *that*.

1. Many places _____ have stereotypes are viewed unfairly. **that**
2. New Yorkers _____ enjoy nature can go to Central Park to take a break from the urban environment. **who**
3. New York workers, _____ people stereotype as moving too fast, are just like workers everywhere. **whom**
4. Bad drivers _____ live in Massachusetts are stereotypes of that state. **who**
5. Massachusetts, _____ was a common destination for immigrants from Europe, took in many Irish immigrants. **which**
6. Southerners, _____ love of country music is well known, may also like classical or pop music. **whose**
7. Not all people _____ live in Florida spend most of their time on the beach. **who**
8. States _____ have the most open space have stereotypes of cowboys and ranchers. **that**
9. Football, _____ people all over the country watch, isn't necessarily more popular in one region than another. **which**
10. The farmers in Nebraska, _____ many people stereotype as having immense farms, work both large and small farms. **whom**

Argument Essay **297**

Student Objectives

• Use relative pronouns correctly. *(p. 297)*

Relative Pronouns

Read the information and example in Know the Rule. Explain that relative pronouns serve two functions: They replace nouns and connect clauses in a complex sentence.

Then direct students' attention to the example sentence. Point out that *who* refers to *cousins* and begins the adjective clause in the sentence.

Adjective clauses are useful for building informative and varied sentences, which strengthens both **Ideas** and **Sentence Fluency**.

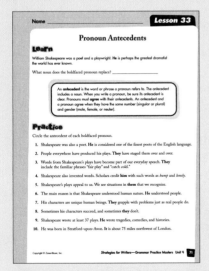

Page 71

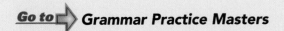

Go to **Grammar Practice Masters**

CCSS Common Core State Standards

W.6.5: With some guidance and support from peers and adults, develop and strengthen writing as needed by planning, revising, editing, rewriting, or trying a new approach. **L.6.1.d:** Recognize and correct vague pronouns (i.e., ones with unclear or ambiguous antecedents). **L.6.3:** Use knowledge of language and its conventions when writing, speaking, reading, or listening.

Argument Essay **T297**

Write
an Argument Essay

Week 3 • Day 4

Student Objectives

- Discuss preparation for publishing and presentation. *(p. 298)*
- Use a final editing checklist. *(p. 298)*

Publish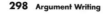

Publishing Strategy Have students discuss other publishing options, such as reading the essay in class or turning it into a speech. Read Leila's final checklist. Have students use it or one that you provide to check their own essays. Consider adding to the checklist items that appear frequently in students' writing. Once students have completed their final copies, post them on the class bulletin board.

Strategies for Writers Online

Go to **www.sfw.z-b.com** for additional online resources for students and teachers.

T298 Argument Writing

Publish +Presentation

Publishing Strategy	Post the essay on a class bulletin board.
Presentation Strategy	The essay is neatly prepared and legible.

Now it's time to publish my argument essay! I think I'll post it on the class bulletin board so all my classmates can read it. Before that, I want to make sure my writing is neat and legible. If my classmates can't even read my work they'll never be convinced by it! I'll either use my very best handwriting or choose a couple of readable fonts on the computer—not fancy or italic fonts. Then I'll read over my essay one more time, using the items on this final checklist.

My Final Checklist

Did I—

✔ make sure all my pronouns and antecedents agree?

✔ use relative pronouns correctly?

✔ make sure the essay looks neat and is legible?

✔ check to make sure my name is on the paper?

Apply

Make a final checklist and use it to check your argument essay. Then make a final copy to publish.

298 Argument Writing

Differentiating Instruction

ENRICHMENT

Add Helpful Visuals Encourage students to add graphics to their essays. Helpful diagrams, charts, and tables can summarize data effectively for the reader.

REINFORCEMENT

Proofread Have pairs of students exchange drafts and edit strategically. For example, have each pair begin by proofreading only for punctuation or spelling. Then have them check pronouns and antecedents. Remind editors to use the proofreading marks on page 291 to mark their changes. Then have partners exchange and explain their edits before preparing their final copies.

Don't Stereotype by State!

by Leila

Do you think all Californians pay too much attention to how they look? Do you believe they all follow the latest fads, no matter how temporary? When we group people together like this, we are stereotyping them. In this case, we are forming an opinion about them based on where they live. That's wrong! The people who live in California are as different from one another as the people who live in every other state. We must stop stereotyping Californians!

Stereotyping is wrong. It's a kind of prejudice. Some people use stereotypes to make decisions. They decide whether they like people because of the group those people belong to. They don't take the time to get to know them. It's like being prejudiced against people because of the kind of clothes they wear or the language they speak. You could miss meeting good friends if you make decisions based on stereotypes.

It's really unwise to stereotype Californians. More than half of Californians were born someplace else. Then they moved to California. Between 1970 and 1990, the population of California grew by 50 percent! Many of these new residents came from the northeastern and southern states. Between 1990 and 1999, more than 233,000 people moved to California from Oregon! California also has more immigrants from other countries than any other state. How could you group all these people together? How could you say they are all the same?

There is no typical Californian. One in four Californians is Hispanic. In the 1990 census, nearly 5 million Californians said they had German ancestors. Another 3.5 million Californians had Irish ancestors.

Californians have different backgrounds, customs, likes, and dislikes. Aren't they just like people everywhere? Sure, a few pay too much attention to how they look. A few people in our state do, too. Let's treat Californians like the individuals they are!

Reflect

What do you think? Are all the traits of a good argument essay in the writing? Check it against the rubric. Then check your own argument essay against the rubric.

Argument Essay **299**

See **www.sfw.z-b.com** for further information about and links to these websites and tools.

Technology Tip for 21st Century Literacies

While a typical tweet can share something as simple as the details of what someone had for lunch, the work of capturing a thought or statement within 140 characters requires precision and focus. Ask students to create a summary of their argument that is no more than 140 characters. How does the summary capture what is written in the essay? Which summary statements capture the interest of other students? Another option is to challenge students to write a tweet that summarizes the argument of another student's paper. Ask them to use those tweets to revise their work.

Write
an Argument Essay

Student Objectives

- Use an argument essay rubric. *(pp. 282–283)*
- Share a published argument essay. *(p. 299)*

Presentation Strategy Explain the importance of neatness. Remind students that messy or illegible work detracts from the message, while a neat and interesting format shows that the writer cares. Remind students to use formatting features as they type their essays. It's easy to set neat margins, indent paragraphs, double-space the text, select one or two clear fonts, insert visuals, and choose appropriate design elements.

Reflecting on an Argument Essay

Have students refer to the rubric on pages 282–283 as they read Leila's final copy on page 299. Discuss how the revisions and edits strengthened her writing.

Now have students think back on the assignment. Ask:

- What is the strongest part of your argument essay? What makes it strong?

CCSS Common Core State Standards

W.6.1: Write arguments to support claims with clear reasons and relevant evidence. **W.6.5:** With some guidance and support from peers and adults, develop and strengthen writing as needed by planning, revising, editing, rewriting, or trying a new approach. **W.6.10:** Write routinely over extended time frames (time for research, reflection, and revision) and shorter time frames (a single sitting or a day or two) for a range of discipline-specific tasks, purposes, and audiences.

Business Letter Planner

WEEK 1

Day 1
Introduce
a Business Letter

Student Objectives
- Review the elements of a business letter.
- Consider purpose and audience.
- Learn the traits of argument writing.

Student Activities
- Read and discuss **What's in a Business Letter?** (p. 300)
- Read and discuss **Why Write a Business Letter?** (p. 301)
- Read **Linking Argument Writing Traits to a Business Letter.** (p. 302)

Day 2
Analyze
Read a Business Letter

Student Objectives
- Read a model business letter.

Student Activities
- Read the model letter. (p. 303)

Day 3
Analyze
Introduce the Rubric

Student Objectives
- Learn to read a rubric.

Student Activities
- Review the model letter. (p. 303)
- Read and discuss the Business Letter Rubric. (pp. 304–305)

WEEK 2

Day 1
Write
Prewrite: Ideas

Student Objectives
- Pick something to change. List reasons for the change.

Student Activities
- Read and discuss **Prewrite: Focus on Ideas.** (p. 310)
- Apply the prewriting strategy.

Day 2
Write
Prewrite: Organization

Student Objectives
- Use an Order-of-Importance Organizer to organize the reasons.

Student Activities
- Read and discuss **Prewrite: Focus on Organization.** (p. 311)
- Apply the prewriting strategy.
- Participate in a peer conference.

Day 3
Write
Draft: Voice

Student Objectives
- Use formal language.

Student Activities
- Read and discuss **Draft: Focus on Voice.** (p. 312)
- Apply the drafting strategy.

WEEK 3

Day 1
Write
Revise: Word Choice

Student Objectives
- Revise to replace vague nouns and verbs.

Student Activities
- Read and discuss: **Revise: Focus on Word Choice.** (p. 315)
- Reflect on the model draft.
- Participate in a peer conference.

Day 2
Write
Revise: Sentence Fluency

Student Objectives
- Revise to make sure each sentence reflects the purpose of the letter.

Student Activities
- Read and discuss: **Revise: Focus on Sentence Fluency.** (p. 316)

Note: Optional Revising Lessons appear on the *Strategies for Writers* CD-ROM.

Day 3
Write
Edit: Conventions

Student Objectives
- Check the use of homophones.

Student Activities
- Read and discuss **Edit: Focus on Conventions.** (p. 317)
- Reflect on the model draft.

Note: Teach the Conventions mini-lessons (pp. 318–319) if needed.

Analyze
Ideas, Organization, and Voice

Student Objectives
- Read a model business letter.
- Use the business letter rubric.
- Use the model business letter to study Ideas, Organization, and Voice.

Student Activities
- Review the model letter. *(p. 303)*
- Review the rubric. *(pp. 304–305)*
- Read and discuss **Using the Rubric to Study the Model.** *(pp. 306–307)*

Analyze
Word Choice, Sentence Fluency, and Conventions

Student Objectives
- Read a model business letter.
- Use the business letter rubric.
- Use the model business letter to study Word Choice, Sentence Fluency, and Conventions.

Student Activities
- Review the model letter. *(p. 303)*
- Review the rubric. *(pp. 304–305)*
- Read and discuss **Using the Rubric to Study the Model.** *(pp. 308–309)*

Write
Draft

Student Objectives
- Complete a draft.

Student Activities
- Finish writing the draft. *(p. 313)*
- Participate in a peer conference.

Write
Revise: Ideas

Student Objectives
- Revise to add details to support the opinion.

Student Activities
- Read and discuss **Revise: Focus on Ideas.** *(p. 314)*
- Reflect on the model draft.
- Apply the revising strategy.

Write
Publish: +Presentation

Student Objectives
- Discuss preparation for publishing and presentation.
- Use a final editing checklist.

Student Activities
- Read and discuss **Publish: +Presentation.** *(p. 320)*
- Apply the publishing strategy.

Write
Publish: +Presentation

Student Objectives
- Use a business letter rubric.
- Share a published letter.

Student Activities
- Share their work.
- Use the rubric to reflect upon and evaluate the model and their own writing. *(pp. 304–305; 321)*

To complete the chapter in fewer days, combine the learning objectives and activities in a way that supports students as they write.

Resources at-a-Glance

Grammar, Usage & Mechanics
Homophones T318
More Homophones T319
Grammar Practice T317–T319

Differentiating Instruction
Using the Rubric T309
Draft T312
Publish T320
For additional Differentiating Instruction activities, see Strategies for Writers *Extensions Online at* **www.sfw.z-b.com.**

English Language Learners
Using the Rubric T306–T307
Prewrite T310
Revise T314

Conferencing
Peer to Peer T311, T313, T315
Peer Groups T311, T313, T315
Teacher-Led T311, T313, T315

Technology Tip
Using the Rubric T308
Publish T321

 Connection Letter
Reproducible letter (in English and Spanish) appears on the *Strategies for Writers* CD-ROM and at **www.sfw.z-b.com.**

Online Writing Center
Provides IWB resources, interactive games and practice activities, videos, eBooks, and a virtual file cabinet.

 Strategies for Writers Online
Go to **www.sfw.z-b.com** for free online resources for students and teachers.

Introduce
a Business Letter

Student Objectives

- Review the elements of a business letter. *(p. 300)*
- Consider purpose and audience. *(p. 301)*
- Learn the traits of argument writing. *(p. 302)*

What's a Business Letter?

Explain that every day, thousands and thousands of business letters that are written for a variety of purposes change hands. Ask students to imagine why some of these business letters are sent. (Possible responses: to request a job or customer service, to express an opinion, to clarify or add information) Tell students that any time they write a letter to an individual or an organization for the purpose of requesting some action on the part of the recipient, they are writing a business letter.

What's in a Business Letter?

Explain that the elements of a business letter are also common to other forms of argument writing. Discuss why the format of a business letter matters. (Possible response: Each part provides essential information.)

 Strategies for Writers Online
Go to **www.sfw.z-b.com** for additional online resources for students and teachers.

What's a Business Letter?

You can write a business letter to express an opinion and to convince readers to consider that opinion. This isn't just a note for fun—it's a professional communication. I like the idea of writing something meaningful that I can mail to a real person!

What's in a Business Letter?

Organization
A business letter isn't very long, so my writing needs to be organized and efficient! I'll make my opinion clear at the start, and I'll stay focused on my topic and list my reasons in a logical order.

Correct Form
An effective business letter has a six-part format: the heading, inside address, salutation (or greeting), body, closing, and signature. I want to stick to the proper form so my readers will see that I care enough to do things the right way.

Formal Style
If I want my audience to consider my opinion, I have to be businesslike. A business letter is not the place for personal comments. The way I sound and the sentences I write should be consistently formal and direct.

Supporting Details
Just expressing my opinion won't be enough to convince readers. I need to show I have reasoned my way to that opinion. That's why I'll be including relevant details that clearly support my point of view.

Argument Text Exemplars (Business Letter)

Shelley Harwayne. *Messages to Ground Zero.* Heinemann, 2002. *Messages to Ground Zero* is a collection of letters, poems, and artwork by children from New York City and all across the country in response to the terrorist attack on September 11, 2001. The book is a document of the children's thoughts and emotions.

Roop, Peter, and Connie Roop. *Grace's Letter to Lincoln.* Hyperion Books, 1998. In *Grace's Letter to Lincoln,* based on a true story, eleven-year-old Grace writes a letter to Abraham Lincoln suggesting that he grow a beard in order to win the presidential election of 1960. In addition to responding to her letter, President Lincoln actually visits Grace's hometown once elected.

Why write a **Business Letter?**

I haven't yet decided the reason for my business letter, but I have a lot of ideas about why someone might do this kind of writing. I've listed some of my ideas below.

Expressing an Opinion
I have a lot of opinions about a lot of things! A business letter gives me a good way to share those opinions with the appropriate people.

Information
Sometimes a company may not know about a problem. If I write a business letter, I can inform the company about the trouble and explain how at least one customer feels about it.

Business Skills
This kind of writing is part of many jobs. In my career, I'll probably need to know how to use the six-part format correctly and how to write in a professional way. This assignment should be good practice for that!

Encouraging Change
Sometimes more than one person will write a business letter about the same issue. If company presidents, politicians, and other decision-makers receive a lot of these letters, they might be convinced to change things. Sometimes even just one powerfully written letter can have a positive impact!

Parks, Rosa. *Dear Mrs. Parks: A Dialogue With Today's Youth.* **Lee & Low Books, 1997.** Rosa Parks refused to give up her seat on a Montgomery bus and helped spark the civil rights movement. In this book, Parks answers letters from children and gives advice and opinions on a wide range of topics.

De Young, C. Coco. *A Letter to Mrs. Roosevelt.* **Yearling, 2000.** Due to hard economic times during the Great Depression, eleven-year-old Margo Bandini's family is in danger of losing their home. Margo decides to write a letter to Mrs. Roosevelt asking for help, and her home is saved as a result of the New Deal relief program.

Why write a Business Letter?

Read and discuss the reasons for writing a business letter listed here. Be sure students understand that the writer's purpose for writing must be focused and clear. For example, someone expressing an opinion will make sure to use relevant, important details to support his or her position. Someone writing to inform will include accurate facts and examples to convince the reader. Someone writing to encourage change may address opposing claims to strengthen the writer's recommendation.

Encourage students to think about their own reasons for writing letters in the past. Ask how their reasons affected the tone and focus of their writing. Conclude the discussion by explaining to students that they are going to analyze a business letter model and practice strategies for writing their own. Let them know that the goal is to send the letter to its recipient.

CCSS **Common Core State Standards**
SL.6.1: Engage effectively in a range of collaborative discussions (one-on-one, in groups, and teacher-led) with diverse partners on grade 6 topics, texts, and issues, building on others' ideas and expressing their own clearly. **SL.6.1.a:** Come to discussions prepared, having read or studied required material; explicitly draw on that preparation by referring to evidence on the topic, text, or issue to probe and reflect on ideas under discussion.

Introduce
a Business Letter

Linking Argument Writing Traits to a Business Letter

Explain to students that they will follow Leila as she models using the writing process and the traits together. As they follow Leila through the writing process, students will see how the Argument Writing Traits have been adapted and applied to writing a business letter. They will see that a business letter, which can be used to express an opinion, has many factors in common with other types of argument writing. However, the particular audience and purpose of a business letter determine how the traits are used.

Online Writing Center

 Provides six **interactive anchor papers** for each mode of writing.

T302 Argument Writing

Linking Argument Writing Traits to a **Business Letter**

In this chapter, you will write a letter expressing your opinion to the owner or manager of a business you use. This type of argument writing is called a business letter. Leila will guide you through the stages of the writing process: Prewrite, Draft, Revise, Edit, and Publish. In each stage, Leila will show you important writing strategies that are linked to the Argument Writing Traits below.

Argument Writing Traits

Trait	Description
Ideas	• clearly stated claims, often balanced by alternate or opposing claims • supporting evidence from accurate and credible sources
Organization	• a strong introduction that presents the writer's position • reasons and evidence that are organized logically • a conclusion that restates the thesis and possibly provides a call to action • transitions that clarify the relationships between ideas
Voice	• a voice that supports the writer's purpose
Word Choice	• language that is compelling
 **Sentence Fluency**	• sentences that vary in length and begin in different ways
Conventions	• no or few errors in grammar, usage, mechanics, and spelling

Before you write, read Jean Silverstone's business letter on the next page. Then use the business letter rubric on pages 304–305 to decide how well she did. (You might want to look back at What's in a Business Letter? on page 300, too!)

Argument Writing Traits in a Business Letter

 Ideas The letter clearly states the writer's purpose and includes supporting details that convince the reader. Opposing claims are acknowledged and addressed.

 **Organization** The letter includes a strong introduction that presents the writer's purpose for writing. Reasons (main ideas) and evidence (supporting details) are organized logically. Logical transition words help the reader follow the writer's ideas. The conclusion calls the reader to action.

 **Voice** The writer uses a convincing voice and formal style that supports the writer's purpose and connects with the reader.

Tiny Tikes Daycare Center
333 Willow Park Road
Lexington, KY 40509
May 4, 2012

Heading

Customer Service Manager
Real Cereal, Inc.
2128 N. Jarvis St.
Trenton, NJ 08620

Inside address

Dear Customer Service Manager: *Salutation*

Businesslike tone

I own a daycare center that serves breakfast cereal to children in the morning. I am usually pleased with Real Cereal products. However, the "new and improved" Oaty Boats is not satisfactory. I refuse to continue to buy Oaty Boats until Real Cereal addresses its problems. *Clear opinion*

The boats now have little taste, and they sink instead of floating. Furthermore, the food dye in the new boats turns the milk in the bowl greenish brown.

Supporting details

In addition, I do not like a recent commercial that shows Oaty Boats as destroyers in a battle. What does your ad tell children about the uses of a boat? It tells them only that a boat is used to fight.

Body

There are sailboats, tugboats, and freighters in Oaty Boats, too. It would be more positive and educational to show children a range of boats and a range of uses. You're as responsible for molding their young minds as I am. I would like to see more thoughtful advertising from Real Cereal. Remember, it takes a community to raise a child. Please change the cereal back to its original flavor and natural color. Also, think more carefully about how you use boats in your advertising. Until Oaty Boats is returned to its original form, I will no longer purchase it for the children in my daycare center. *Clear opinion*

Sincerely, *Closing*

Jean Silverstone *Signature*

Jean Silverstone, Director

Business Letter 303

Word Choice The writer's language is appropriate and convincing. Word choice creates meaning and cohesion among the writer's opinion, reasons, and supporting details.

Sentence Fluency Sentences vary in length and begin in different ways. The writer's ideas flow smoothly and hold the reader's attention.

Conventions The writer has proofread carefully to make sure there are no errors in grammar, usage, mechanics, and spelling to distract the reader.

Analyze
the Model

Student Objectives

• Read a model business letter. (p. 303)

Read the Model

Read the model business letter to the class. Ask students to listen for the director's opinion and supporting details. Then ask them to notice how the details are organized. Also ask students to think about and discuss how a formal, businesslike tone suits the writer's purpose and audience (the recipient of the letter).

Elements of a Business Letter

Have students look at What's in a Business Letter? on page 300 as they review the model business letter. Discuss the model to enhance students' understanding of the terms. Point out that they will also use the model to analyze the traits of a good business letter.

CCSS **Common Core State Standards**
R/Inf.6.1: Cite textual evidence to support analysis of what the text says explicitly as well as inferences drawn from the text. **R/Inf.6.6:** Determine an author's point of view or purpose in a text and explain how it is conveyed in the text. **SL.6.1.b:** Follow rules for collegial discussions, set specific goals and deadlines, and define individual roles as needed.

Analyze
the Model

Week 1 • Day 3

Student Objectives

- Learn to read a rubric. *(pp. 304–305)*

Use the Rubric

Explain the Rubric Explain that a writing rubric is a tool for planning, improving, and assessing a piece of writing. A rubric helps a writer focus on key elements, or traits, in writing (**Ideas, Organization, Voice, Word Choice, Sentence Fluency, Conventions,** and **Presentation**).

Explain the 6-point system. Point out that the columns on page 304 represent a good business letter that might need some polishing while the columns on page 305 represent writing that needs considerable improvement.

Discuss the Rubric Guide students in a discussion of the rubric. Read the descriptors that go with each trait, and take a moment to explain the relationship between them. Discuss the differences between columns to be sure students fully understand the point system. Remind students to keep the rubric in mind as they write their own business letter and again as they revise and edit it.

Online Writing Center

 Provides a variety of **interactive rubrics,** including 4-, 5-, and 6-point models.

T304 Argument Writing

Business Letter

Rubric

Use this 6-point rubric to plan and score a business letter.

	6	5	4	
Ideas	The purpose is clearly stated. Clear reasons and relevant, important evidence support the writer's opinion.	The purpose is clearly stated. The details are clear and most are supported with relevant evidence.	The reader can tell what the purpose of the writing is. Some details are unclear or poorly supported.	
Organization	Reasons and supporting evidence are organized in order of importance. The purpose is strongly restated in the conclusion.	Most of the reasons and evidence are organized in order of importance. The purpose is restated in the conclusion.	Some reasons and evidence may be out of order, but the reader is not confused. The purpose is stated in the conclusion but may not be clear.	
Voice	The writer's tone is respectful and business-like and fits the purpose well. The writer speaks directly to the reader.	The writer speaks to the reader. The tone fits the purpose and the audience.	The tone is acceptable for the audience and purpose. The writer sometimes speaks directly to the reader.	
Word Choice	Specific nouns and strong verbs make the writing lively and informative.	The writing is clear and informative. Specific nouns and verbs help with the meaning.	The writing is usually clear, but some verbs are weak or overused. Some nouns are too general.	
Sentence Fluency	Sentences are well written, smooth, and easy to read. They reflect the purpose of the letter.	Sentences are well written and reflect the writer's purpose.	There is some variety in sentences. The writing is easy to read silently, but harder to read aloud.	
Conventions	The writing has been thoughtfully edited. Homophones are used correctly.	A few errors can be found if you look for them. Most homophones are used correctly.	Errors with homophones or other conventions are present but don't confuse the reader.	

✛Presentation The business letter is in the proper format.

304 Argument Writing

CCSS Common Core State Standards

Business Letter

The Common Core State Standards (CCSS) are woven throughout the instruction in *Strategies for Writers*. Writing in the Argument mode can engage the standards for all forms of Argument writing. The rubric and writing strategies for Ideas reflect writing standard **W.6.1,** to write arguments to support claims with clear reasons and relevant evidence, and standards **W.6.1.a** and **W.6.1.b,** to introduce and support a claim. The rubric and writing strategies for Organization are also drawn from standards **W.6.1.a** and **W.6.1.b,** to organize the ideas logically, and standard **W.6.1.e,** to provide an effective conclusion. The traits of Voice and Word Choice reflect standard **W.6.1.c,** to use language to create cohesion and clarify relationships among ideas, and standard **W.6.1.d,** to establish and maintain a formal style.

Trait	3	2	1
Ideas	Some parts of the writing are unclear. Details are often general.	The purpose of the writing is unclear. The details are sketchy and leave the reader with questions.	The purpose in writing the letter is not stated. Details are confusing.
Organization	Some reasons and evidence are not in order. The reader may be confused. The purpose is not restated in the conclusion.	The organization is not clear. The conclusion is missing or lacks any focus.	The writing is just a list of random details that don't fit together. The reader can't follow the writing.
Voice	The voice is hesitant or distant. The writer does not connect with the reader.	The voice is very weak or absent. The reader does not know the writer's purpose.	The writer's voice is absent. It does not connect with the reader at all.
Word Choice	Several words are weak, too general, or over-used. The words do not convince the reader.	Many words and phrases are misused or vague. It is hard to picture what the writer means.	The words are vague and confusing. The meaning is not clear.
Sentence Fluency	Sentence beginnings and lengths are alike. There are some choppy sentences, and the writing takes practice to read aloud.	There is no variety in sentence beginnings. Sentences are choppy and hard to read aloud.	Sentences are incomplete. It is hard to tell where sentences begin and end. The writing is hard to read, even silently.
Conventions	Some errors with homophones or other conventions slow down reading.	The writing has many errors with homophones and other conventions that get in the way of the message.	The writing is filled with many different kinds of mistakes. Reading is difficult even with effort.

See Appendix B for 4-, 5-, and 6-point argument rubrics.

Apply the Rubric

Evaluate a Letter Many business letters are sent through the mail to convince consumers to sign up for a product or service. Choose a letter on an appropriate topic to share with the class. Ask students to use the rubric to score the letter on each of the traits. Be sure that they can offer examples from the letter to support the score.

Once the class has reached a consensus on the scores, ask these follow-up questions:

- Which trait is strongest in the letter? Why do you think so?
- Does the letter fit the audience and the purpose? How?

Additional Rubrics Appendix B includes 4-, 5-, and 6-point rubrics that can be used with any piece of argument writing. The rubrics are also available as blackline masters, beginning on page T525.

The language standards for grade 6 students are addressed during editing and skills practice (**L.6.1–L.6.6**). In addition, there are multiple opportunities to address the speaking and listening standards during the writing process. Specifically, students are encouraged to work collaboratively, review key ideas, and demonstrate understanding (**SL.6.1.a–d**). Most importantly, this chapter will help students produce coherent writing (**W.6.4**), improve their writing with the help of peers and adults (**W.6.5**), use technologies to polish and publish their finished pieces (**W.6.6**), draw evidence from texts to use in their writing (**W.6.9**), and use writing to respond and reflect (**W.6.10**).

CCSS Common Core State Standards

W.6.9: Draw evidence from literary or informational texts to support analysis, reflection, and research.
SL.6.1.c: Pose and respond to specific questions with elaboration and detail by making comments that contribute to the topic, text, or issue under discussion.
SL.6.1.d: Review the key ideas expressed and demonstrate understanding of multiple perspectives through reflection and paraphrasing.

Analyze
the Model

Week 1 • Day 4

Student Objectives

- Read a model business letter. *(p. 303)*
- Use the business letter rubric. *(pp. 304–305)*
- Use the model business letter to study Ideas, Organization, and Voice. *(pp. 306–307)*

Study the Model

Assess the Model Have volunteers read aloud each section on pages 306–307. Discuss as a class whether students agree or disagree with Leila's assessments of the model. Use questions such as the following to discuss the pages with students.

- Does the writer state a clear purpose for writing? (Possible responses: Yes, Jean Silverstone states her writing purpose in the introduction. She is writing to Real Cereal, Inc. because she is not satisfied with one of its products.)

- Does the writer include reasons and supporting details? (Possible response: Yes, the writer gives evidence to support her opinion.)

Strategies for Writers Online

Go to **www.sfw.z-b.com** for additional online resources for students and teachers.

T306 Argument Writing

Using the Rubric to Study the Model

Business Letter

Did you notice that the model on page 303 points out some key elements of a business letter? As she wrote it, Jean Silverstone used these elements to help her write her letter. She also used the 6-point rubric on pages 304–305 to plan, draft, revise, and edit the writing. A rubric is a great tool for evaluating writing during the writing process.

Now let's use the same rubric to score the model. To do this, we'll focus on each trait separately, starting with Ideas. We'll use the top descriptor for each trait (column 6), along with examples from the model, to help us understand how the traits work together. How would you score Jean on each trait?

Ideas
- The purpose is clearly stated.
- Clear reasons and relevant, important evidence support the writer's opinion.

Jean's purpose of complaining about the cereal is very clear in the first paragraph. In addition, she does a good job of supporting her opinion. She uses enough details to prove her point, but she doesn't distract her reader with details that aren't important. In this paragraph, she gives some relevant details about why the cereal is unsatisfactory.

[from the writing model]

The boats now have little taste, and they sink instead of floating. Furthermore, the food dye in the new boats turns the milk in the bowl greenish brown.

306 Argument Writing

English Language Learners

BEGINNING
Parts of a Letter Post a business letter. Circle the following parts of the letter: Heading, Inside Address, Salutation, Body, Closing, and Signature. Say each word and have students repeat. Then check students' understanding by pointing to each part and having the group say its name. Then do individual concept checking.

INTERMEDIATE
Parts of a Letter Review the parts of a business letter and the placement of each element. Also point out that paragraphs are not indented in a business letter. Brainstorm possible greetings, such as *Dear Mr. Perry* or *Dear Sir or Madam*, and possible closings, such as *Yours truly* or *Sincerely*.

Organization

- Reasons and supporting evidence are organized in order of importance.
- The purpose is strongly restated in the conclusion.

Jean is very clear about what she doesn't like about the new Oaty Boats, and she states her complaints in order of importance. I like the way she lists her reasons in this paragraph.

[from the writing model]

> The boats now have little taste, and they sink instead of floating. Furthermore, the food dye in the new boats turns the milk in the bowl greenish brown.

In her conclusion, Jean repeats her purpose in different words.

[from the writing model]

> Until Oaty Boats is returned to its original form, I will no longer purchase it for the children in my daycare center.

Voice

- The writer's tone is respectful and businesslike and fits the purpose well.
- The writer speaks directly to the reader.

Jean uses a businesslike tone to express her thoughts in a direct way. For example, she is angry about the commercial, but she doesn't use angry words. Instead, she uses a tone that is polite and formal.

[from the writing model]

> There are sailboats, tugboats, and freighters in Oaty Boats, too. It would be more positive and educational to show children a range of boats and a range of uses.

Business Letter 307

- How are the ideas organized? (Possible response: By order of importance; the writer presents her most important reason first. This way the reader gets her main point right away.)

- What does the conclusion do? (Possible responses: The conclusion follows from the writer's argument. The writer emphasizes her position again.)

- How would you describe the writer's voice? (Possible response: The writer sounds convincing and uses a businesslike style throughout the letter. It's clear that she wants the customer service manager to take her reason for writing seriously.)

ADVANCED

Audience and Purpose Ask students who the audience is for a business letter. Most likely it will be someone they do not know. Then ask, *Why would you write a business letter?* Allow students time to brainstorm ideas. Remind them that this business letter will be addressed to a manager of a business.

ADVANCED HIGH

Audience and Purpose Have partners discuss activity clubs or events that are currently happening at the school. Ask them to choose one topic that interests both of them and make notes about it. What local business would also be interested in the club or event? Tell them that the business could be the *audience* of their letter. Their *purpose* would be to discuss the important issue. Have students share their audience and purpose ideas with the group.

CCSS Common Core State Standards
W.6.9: Draw evidence from literary or informational texts to support analysis, reflection, and research. **R/Inf.6.4:** Determine the meaning of words and phrases as they are used in a text, including figurative, connotative, and technical meanings. **SL.6.1.c:** Pose and respond to specific questions with elaboration and detail by making comments that contribute to the topic, text, or issue under discussion. **SL.6.1.d:** Review the key ideas expressed and demonstrate understanding of multiple perspectives through reflection and paraphrasing.

Analyze
the Model

Week 1 • Day 5

Student Objectives

- Read a model business letter. *(p. 303)*
- Use the business letter rubric. *(pp. 304–305)*
- Use the model business letter to study Word Choice, Sentence Fluency, and Conventions. *(pp. 308–309)*

Continue the Discussion Use questions such as the following to discuss the traits analyzed on pages 308–309:

- How would you describe the writer's choice of words? (Possible responses: The writer's words are purposeful and convincing. She uses precise words to make her meaning clear.)

- What kinds of sentences does the writer use? (Possible responses: The writer uses a variety of well-written, interesting sentences. The letter is easy to follow.)

- Has the letter been edited? (Possible response: It is obvious that the letter was carefully edited. I noticed that all homophones are used correctly, too.)

Strategies for Writers Online
Go to **www.sfw.z-b.com** for additional online resources for students and teachers.

T308 Argument Writing

 **Word Choice**
- Specific nouns and strong verbs make the writing lively and informative.

Jean wants to convince the customer service manager that she is not pleased with the product. Specific nouns, like *sailboats* and *tugboats*, and strong verbs, such as *molding*, help make the writing lively. If she had simply written "There are other kinds of boats" or "You're as responsible for helping to form their young minds," her writing would have been weaker and less gripping.

[from the writing model]

There are sailboats, tugboats, and freighters in Oaty Boats, too. It would be more positive and educational to show children a range of boats and a range of uses. You're as responsible for molding their young minds as I am.

Sentence Fluency
- Sentences are well written, smooth, and easy to read. They reflect the purpose of the letter.

Jean doesn't waste the time of the busy customer service manager at the cereal company. She makes sure that each and every sentence of her letter relates to the business at hand. For example, in the section of the letter shown below, the writer could have started talking about how difficult it is to be responsible for young children, but that would not have reflected the purpose of her letter. Take a look.

[from the writing model]

You're as responsible for molding their young minds as I am. I would like to see more thoughtful advertising from Real Cereal. Remember, it takes a community to raise a child.

308 Argument Writing

Technology Tip for 21st Century Literacies

Add a layer of purpose to writing a business letter by asking students to write with the intent of accomplishing a real task or advocating for a real group or person. As a class or as individuals, use a tool like Scrumblr (an online, collaborative whiteboard) to brainstorm content and ideas for audience, or even to list what they know makes a business letter particularly effective or persuasive.

See **www.sfw.z-b.com** for further information about and links to these websites and tools.

Conventions

- The writing has been thoughtfully edited.
- Homophones are used correctly.

I went back and checked the letter to see if there were any mistakes, but I couldn't find any. Spelling, punctuation, and capitalization are all correct. The writer also used homophones correctly. When she had to choose among words such as *to/too/two* and *your/you're*, she chose the right word every time.

[from the writing model]

There are sailboats, tugboats, and freighters in Oaty Boats, too.

+Presentation The business letter is in the proper format.

I'm going to write a business letter about a change I'd like a business to make. Follow along and see how I use the rubric and good writing strategies to do it!

Differentiating Instruction

ENRICHMENT

Score Models Have students find short business letters in collections or online, or select several from samples you provide. Have them work in pairs to score the letters using the rubric on pages 304–305. Make sure they include Presentation. Ask groups to share and defend their scores for each trait.

REINFORCEMENT

Identify Homophones Challenge students to list words in the letter that have homophones that are pronounced the same but have different meanings from those used in the letter. (**Possible responses: to/two/too, your/you're, buy/by, dye/die, do/due, would/wood, see/sea**) Point out that computer spell checkers will not catch these words when they are misused.

Presentation Explain that Presentation should be considered as students prepare a final copy of their letters. Neatness is always a priority; text should be clearly handwritten in pen or typed, using only a few readable fonts. White space should be used to create neat margins and to format text in each part of the letter. Paragraphs should be block style (flush left).

Think About the Traits Ask students which traits they think are most important in a letter. Remind them that all of the traits are important in every piece of writing; however, some traits matter more in specific types of writing. For example, some students may feel that the traits of **Ideas** and **Organization** are equally important because if the ideas are confusing and hard to follow, the recipient may not take the writer seriously. Others may argue that **Voice** and **Word Choice** work together because sounding respectful and using appropriate language help strengthen the writer's message. Explain that all the traits work together to help the writer reach his or her goal: getting the reader to agree and respond.

CCSS Common Core State Standards

W.6.9: Draw evidence from literary or informational texts to support analysis, reflection, and research.
SL.6.1.c: Pose and respond to specific questions with elaboration and detail by making comments that contribute to the topic, text, or issue under discussion.
SL.6.1.d: Review the key ideas expressed and demonstrate understanding of multiple perspectives through reflection and paraphrasing.

Write
a Business Letter

Week 2 • Day 1

Student Objectives

- Pick something to change. List reasons for the change. *(p. 310)*

Prewrite

Focus on Ideas

Think of a Topic Point out that Leila was specific about what she liked about the radio program.

Brainstorm a list of topics about which students have strong opinions, using the business letter model on page 303 and the writing partner's topic on this page as jumping-off points. After creating a list of potential topics, have students circle their favorites.

To help students determine their audience, have them ask and answer this question: *To whom should I write about the change I want?* Have each student write down the name and address of a person or department head at the business or organization. Discuss students' choices with them before they proceed. Then encourage students to think about the facts and examples they will use to support their positions.

Online Writing Center

Provides **interactive graphic organizers** as well as a variety of graphic organizers in PDF format.

Prewrite
Focus on Ideas

The Rubric Says The purpose is clearly stated.

Writing Strategy Pick something you would like a business to change. List reasons for the change.

I love music, especially the blues. One of our local radio stations, KTNT, used to have a great blues show called "Down to the Blues." A few weeks ago, they decided to cancel it! When my teacher said we were going to write a business letter, I decided to write to KTNT to ask the station to put "Down to the Blues" back on the air. Here are my reasons.

Reasons To Bring Back "Down to the Blues"

- It was the only radio program in the area that educated listeners about the blues.
- The program played songs by classic blues artists like Robert Johnson, Blind Lemon Jefferson, and Ma Rainey. It also played songs by modern blues artists like B. B. King, Luther Allison, and Koko Taylor. It was a good show for fans of both styles of the blues.
- I was learning a lot about the blues from the show. One night a week, it had a guest musician. I learned all about the guest artists and their music. Once a month, a blues guitarist taught listeners a new blues song.
- My dog, Muddy, loves to howl the blues, and he misses the show, too! He's named after Muddy Waters.
- The show was on from 7 to 9 P.M. on two weeknights, so kids could listen to it after finishing their homework and before going to bed.

Apply

Think of a change you would like a business to make. Jot down some notes about why the change is a good idea.

310 Argument Writing

English Language Learners

BEGINNING/INTERMEDIATE

Formal vs. Informal Use the greetings *How are you?* and *What's up?* to introduce the terms *formal* and *informal*. Ask, *Which would you say to your best friend? Your teacher?* Repeat for other words and phrases, such as *That is very good news!/That's awesome!, No way/I don't think so,* and so on.

ADVANCED/ADVANCED HIGH

Using a Formal Tone Remind students that the audience for their letter will be a manager of a business. Because of this, it should have a formal tone. Write several informal sentences on the board. Have partners change the sentences to a more formal tone. For example, the sentence *It would be super if you could send money for the fundraiser* could be changed to *Would you agree to donate a few items to be sold at our craft fair?*

Prewrite
Focus on Organization

The Rubric Says	Reasons and supporting evidence are organized in order of importance.
Writing Strategy	Use an Order-of-Importance Organizer to organize the reasons.

According to the rubric, I should organize the reasons in my letter by order of importance. I'll start with the most important and end with the least important.

I'll use an Order-of-Importance Organizer. The upside-down triangle shows my points from most to least important.

Writer's Term_____

Order-of-Importance Organizer
An **Order-of-Importance Organizer** shows the main points in order of importance. The points can be ordered from most to least important or from least to most important.

Order-of-Importance Organizer

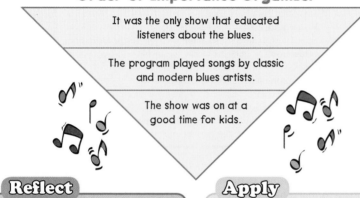

It was the only show that educated listeners about the blues.

The program played songs by classic and modern blues artists.

The show was on at a good time for kids.

Reflect
Will the Order-of-Importance Organizer give Leila's letter a useful structure?

Apply
Organize your ideas by using an Order-of-Importance Organizer.

Business Letter 3II

Conferencing

PEER TO PEER Have writers share their main points. Have partners identify these on the organizers and determine if they are listed in the best order.

PEER GROUPS Have students work in small groups and take turns sharing organizers. Have group members take turns offering one suggestion to make the organizer more helpful.

TEACHER-LED Schedule conferences with individual students. Before they speak with you, tell students to use their notes to complete their organizers.

Write
a Business Letter

Student Objectives

- Use an Order-of-Importance Organizer to organize the reasons. (p. 311)

Prewrite

Focus on Organization

Make an Order-of-Importance Organizer Explain that writers use different types of organizers to structure their ideas. Leila used an Order-of-Importance Organizer to help her organize the details she had gathered in her notes. Have students study the organizer on this page. Then ask how an Order-of-Importance Organizer can be an effective tool when writing a business letter. (Possible responses: It helps writers organize their ideas. The reasons are the writer's main points and will be presented in the body paragraphs.)

Writer's Term_____

Order-of-Importance Organizer
The shape of an Order-of-Importance Organizer reminds writers to arrange their reasons logically. In a business letter, it is a good strategy to present the most important reason first in order to build a strong argument.

CCSS **C**ommon **C**ore **S**tate **S**tandards
W.6.1: Write arguments to support claims with clear reasons and relevant evidence. **W.6.5:** With some guidance and support from peers and adults, develop and strengthen writing as needed by planning, revising, editing, rewriting, or trying a new approach. **R/Inf.6.7:** Integrate information presented in different media or formats (e.g., visually, quantitatively) as well as in words to develop a coherent understanding of a topic or issue.

Business Letter T3II

Write
a Business Letter

Week 2 • Day 3

Student Objectives

• Use formal language. *(p. 312)*

Draft

Focus on Voice

Draft a Business Letter Discuss Leila's ideas and the information in the Writer's Term box. Be sure each student has chosen an audience. Remind students that their purpose will determine their audience. Explain that often writers don't know the person to whom they are writing. To make a good impression, writers should use formal language—a respectful and businesslike tone.

Remind students to use their notes and organizers to present their claim and support their reasons. Also remind students that they should not be overly concerned with correctness at this point.

✎ Writer's Term_____

The Six Parts of a Business Letter
Have students use model business letters to identify the six parts of a business letter. Recommend print and online writing resources for titles, abbreviations, and forms of address. Many word processing programs include business letter templates.

Online Writing Center

Provides student eBooks with an **interactive writing pad** for drafting, revising, editing, and publishing.

T312 Argument Writing

Draft
Focus on Voice

The Rubric Says	The writer's tone is respectful and businesslike and fits the purpose well.
Writing Strategy	Use formal language.

If my letter is going to get results, I have to send it to someone who might be able to make the change I want. I think the KTNT station manager will be my audience.

The rubric says to use a businesslike tone, and using the proper format is part of that. Business letters have six parts and are commonly in block style.

✎ Writer's Term_____

The Six Parts of a Business Letter
• The **heading** is about an inch from the top and on the left-hand side of the page. It has the sender's complete address and the date.
• The **inside address** is below the heading. It has the reader's complete address. The reader's title is below his or her name.
• The **salutation** (greeting) is below the inside address, followed by a colon.
• The **body** of the letter is below the salutation.
• The **closing** is below the body. It begins with *Yours truly* or *Sincerely* and ends with a comma.
• Type full name below the closing. Leave enough space for the **signature** between the closing and your typed name.

As I write my letter using this form, I'll use language that sounds like I'm talking to my reader, but with an appropriate formal tone. I want to sound businesslike and respectful so my reader will pay attention to what I have to say. Part of my letter is on the next page.

312 Argument Writing

Differentiating Instruction

ENRICHMENT
Restate the Purpose Ask students to examine sample business letters. Ask them to select those in which the writer restates the purpose for writing the letter in the concluding section. Have them share the letters with the class, noting how the writers stressed their purpose and re-emphasized their position.

REINFORCEMENT
Use a Template To help students with business letter formatting, create a template that shows the information for each part of the letter. Post the template or distribute copies for students to use as a reference.

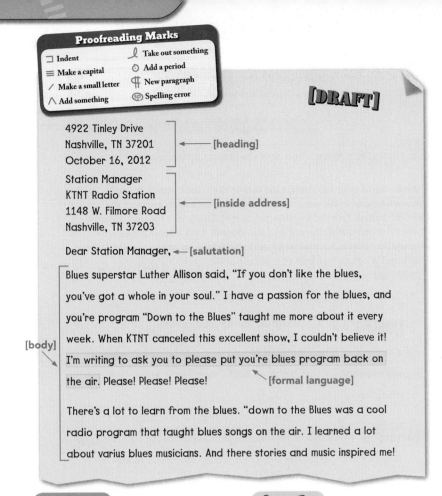

Proofreading Marks

⌐ Indent   ℓ Take out something
≡ Make a capital   ⊙ Add a period
/ Make a small letter   ¶ New paragraph
∧ Add something   ⑤ℙ Spelling error

[DRAFT]

4922 Tinley Drive
Nashville, TN 37201   ←— [heading]
October 16, 2012

Station Manager
KTNT Radio Station
1148 W. Filmore Road   ←— [inside address]
Nashville, TN 37203

Dear Station Manager, ←— [salutation]

[body]

Blues superstar Luther Allison said, "If you don't like the blues, you've got a whole in your soul." I have a passion for the blues, and you're program "Down to the Blues" taught me more about it every week. When KTNT canceled this excellent show, I couldn't believe it! I'm writing to ask you to please put you're blues program back on the air. Please! Please! Please!   ←— [formal language]

There's a lot to learn from the blues. "down to the Blues was a cool radio program that taught blues songs on the air. I learned a lot about varius blues musicians. And there stories and music inspired me!

Reflect

Did Leila use the correct business letter format? How does she make her voice sound respectful and businesslike?

Apply

Write a draft using your Order-of-Importance Organizer as a guide. Be sure to use a formal tone and format!

Business Letter 313

Conferencing

PEER TO PEER Have partners exchange and read drafts. Tell students to think of two or three questions to ask to clarify information. Have them write their questions on sticky notes and affix them to their partner's drafts.

PEER GROUPS Have students work in groups of four. Tell them to pass their drafts to the student on the right. Using the rubric on pages 304–305, have each student write one suggestion on a sticky note. Students should affix the note to the draft and pass the draft to the right. The review ends when everyone has received his or her own draft back with three comments.

TEACHER-LED Schedule conferences with pairs of students. Have students read each other's draft and coach them in giving and receiving constructive criticism.

Write
a Business Letter

Student Objectives

• Complete a draft. (p. 313)

Draft a Business Letter

Finish the Draft Remind students to use their notes and Order-of-Importance Organizers to write their drafts. Emphasize that supporting details should be accurate and complete. Have students refer to the model letter on page 303 and Leila's draft on page 313 to format their letters. Also point out the proofreader's marks provided as a reference on page 313, which will be useful when students revise and edit.

It is important that students are given ample time to draft their letters. As conferencing is important throughout the writing process, be sure to plan time for peer-to-peer, peer group, or teacher-led conferences. Remind students that this is the time for getting their ideas down in a creative and engaging way. Assure them that they will have plenty of time to improve their writing in the revising step of the process.

CCSS **C**ommon **C**ore **S**tate **S**tandards

W.6.1.a: Introduce claim(s) and organize the reasons and evidence clearly. **W.6.1.b:** Support claim(s) with clear reasons and relevant evidence, using credible sources and demonstrating an understanding of the topic or text. **W.6.5:** With some guidance and support from peers and adults, develop and strengthen writing as needed by planning, revising, editing, rewriting, or trying a new approach.

Write
a Business Letter

Student Objectives

- Revise to add details to support the opinion. (p. 314)

Revise

Focus on Ideas

Add Details Have a volunteer read Leila's words on page 314. Ask students why they feel Leila decided to take out the line about the show playing different songs by different artists. (Possible response: It was rather vague and irrelevant; most music stations do the same thing.) Ask them why they feel the revision improves this part of her letter. (Possible response: It adds specific information about the show and supports her argument.)

As students read their drafts for the trait of **Ideas**, instruct them to look for places where they can add relevant details to make their arguments stronger. Also have them remove any details that are weak, repetitive, or irrelevant.

Strategies for Writers Online
Go to **www.sfw.z-b.com** for additional online resources for students and teachers.

Writing a Business Letter

Revise   Focus on Ideas

The Rubric Says	Clear reasons and relevant, important evidence support the writer's opinion.
Writing Strategy	Add details to support the opinion.

After I read over my draft, I looked at the rubric again. It says I should include clear reasons and relevant details to support my opinion. I think I stated my reasons quite plainly, but I found a part of my letter that didn't have enough details. So I added a piece of information that's both relevant and important to my argument. Also, I took out a detail that wasn't relevant at all.

[DRAFT]

songs by classic blues artists and modern blues artists, too ← [added detail]

I really liked it that the show played ~~different songs by different blues artists.~~ They made "Down to the Blues" entertaining four any blues fan.

The timing of the program was perfect for me and other kids, to. The 7 P.M. time slot was late enough that I could finish my homework before the program started, but it didnt keep me up to late. ~~I have to get up at six o'clock in the morning.~~
← [took out irrelevant detail]

Apply
Try adding some relevant details to support your opinions. Take out any details that aren't relevant.

314   Argument Writing

English Language Learners

BEGINNING/INTERMEDIATE
Homophones Use photos or demonstrations to convey the meanings of several homophone pairs. For example, write the words *threw/through, right/write, meet/meat*. Point to each pair and have students repeat the words. Ask, *Do they sound the same?* Tell students that the words are *homophones*. Have students repeat the word. Check students' understanding by presenting several more pairs.

ADVANCED/ADVANCED HIGH
Homophones Write the following sentence on the board: *The principle could not except they're excuse for being late.* Tell students that the underlined words are part of a homophone pair and are possibly used incorrectly in the sentence. Demonstrate using a dictionary to check homophone spellings. Check the definition of each homophone and select the spelling for the word with the appropriate definition.

Revise

Focus on  Word Choice

The Rubric Says	Specific nouns and strong verbs make the writing lively and informative.
Writing Strategy	Replace vague nouns and verbs.

When I checked the rubric, I realized that not all my nouns and verbs are strong enough. If they are vague and weak, it will be harder to get my opinion across. Look at where I revised a noun and a verb. Do you agree that my message is stronger now?

[added specific words]

blues fans   enjoy

I really miss "Down to the Blues." All kinds of ~~people like~~ the program

and learn so much from listening, especially us kids!

Reflect

Do the stronger, more specific nouns and verbs make the writing more interesting to read?

Apply

Make your writing more lively by replacing vague nouns and verbs with specific and strong ones.

Business Letter 315

Conferencing

PEER TO PEER During revising, have partners exchange drafts. After reading, ask each student to offer feedback on how to strengthen the letter. If needed, have students consult the model, the rubric, and the lessons for revising Ideas, Word Choice, and Sentence Fluency.

PEER GROUPS Have students form small revising groups. Have each student read aloud a section of his or her letter that might need improving. Ask each group member to offer one suggestion on how to strengthen it.

TEACHER-LED Schedule conferences to read each student's draft. Point out strengths and weaknesses. Ask questions to prompt students' revisions: *How can you make your opinion clearer? What details will strengthen your opinion? Is this the best word to use?*

Write
a Business Letter

Student Objectives

• Revise to replace vague nouns and verbs. *(p. 315)*

Revise

Focus on Word Choice

Use Specific Words Have students read this page independently. Then discuss how replacing weak words with strong words improves the writer's meaning. Explain that during drafting, ordinary nouns and verbs are often used so the writer can proceed with getting ideas down on paper. During revising, precise words can replace the placeholders.

Be sure to recommend print and online word resources for students to consult as they revise. An up-to-date dictionary and a thesaurus are good tools as they revise for the trait of **Word Choice**. Remind students to make sure they have used homophones correctly also.

CCSS Common Core State Standards

W.6.1.b: Support claim(s) with clear reasons and relevant evidence, using credible sources and demonstrating an understanding of the topic or text. W.6.1.c: Use words, phrases, and clauses to clarify the relationships among claim(s) and reasons. W.6.5: With some guidance and support from peers and adults, develop and strengthen writing as needed by planning, revising, editing, rewriting, or trying a new approach. L.6.4.c: Consult reference materials (e.g., dictionaries, glossaries, thesauruses), both print and digital, to find the pronunciation of a word or determine or clarify its precise meaning or its part of speech.

Write
a Business Letter

Week 3 • Day 2

Student Objectives

• Revise to make sure each sentence reflects the purpose of the letter. (p. 316)

Revise

Focus on  Sentence Fluency

Convey Purpose Ask a student to read Leila's words on this page. Then read the sentences that she changed. Especially ask students why they think she deleted *Please! Please! Please!* (Possible response: Pleading weakens the writer's position because it sounds whiny or immature.)

Have students read through their drafts and identify any phrases or sentences that do not reflect the purpose of their letters, in particular those that are demanding or pleading. It is a helpful strategy to have students read their letters to a revising partner. As they revise, remind them to avoid using exclamation points and all caps for emphasis in the text of a business letter because it looks very unprofessional.

Online Writing Center

Provides **interactive proofreading activities** for each genre.

Revise

Focus on Sentence Fluency

The Rubric Says Sentences are well written, smooth, and easy to read. They reflect the purpose of the letter.

Writing Strategy Make sure each sentence reflects the purpose of the letter.

Now to check my sentence fluency. The rubric says that each sentence of my letter should reflect why I'm writing, but I see some sentences that don't. I need to clearly state my feelings about my favorite radio show being canceled. And that last sentence interrupts the smooth flow of my sentences without adding anything to my argument.

[DRAFT]

[changed sentence to better reflect purpose]

Blues superstar Luther Allison said, "If you don't like the blues, you've got a whole in your soul." I have a passion for the blues, and you're program "Down to the Blues" taught me more about it every week. When KTNT canceled this excellent show, ~~I couldn't believe it.~~ I was very disappointed.

I'm writing to ask you to please put you're blues program back on the air. ~~Please! Please! Please!~~ [deleted sentence that didn't reflect purpose]

Apply

Does every sentence in your letter reflect your purpose for writing? Take out or rewrite any sentences that don't.

316 Argument Writing

Optional Revising Lessons

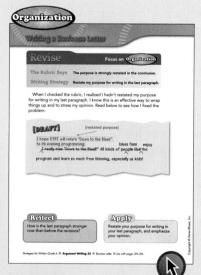

Argument 25

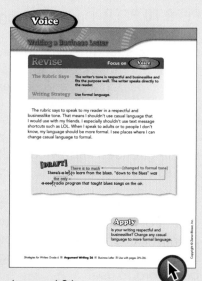

Argument 26

Go to **Strategies for Writers Grade 6 CD-ROM**

Edit — Focus on  Conventions

The Rubric Says The writing has been thoughtfully edited. Homophones are used correctly.

Writing Strategy Check the use of homophones.

Writer's Term

Homophones
Homophones are words that are pronounced the same but have different spellings and meanings.

Now I need to check my spelling, punctuation, and capitalization. The rubric also says to be sure I've used homophones correctly. Sometimes I get confused with homophones because those words sound alike but are spelled differently. I'll really have to check carefully!

[DRAFT]

There is so much
~~There's a lot~~ to learn from the blues. "down to the Blues" was

a cool radio program that taught blues songs on the air. I learned a
                                    various   their
lot about ~~varius~~ blues musicians. And ~~there~~ stories and music

inspired me!   [corrected homophone]

Reflect

Are all the homophones correct now? The spell checker on the computer won't catch homophone mistakes, so they need to be checked carefully.

Apply — Conventions

Edit your draft for spelling, punctuation, and capitalization. Be sure to check that any homophones are correct.

For more practice with homophones, use the exercises on the next two pages.

Business Letter 317

Related Grammar Practice

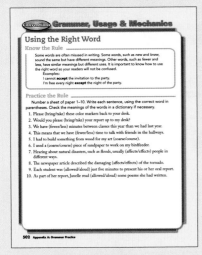

Student Edition page 502

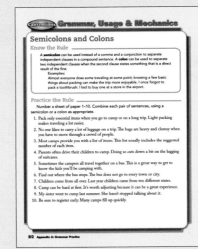

Student Edition page 512

Go to ➡ **Appendix A: Grammar Practice**

Write
a Business Letter

Student Objectives

• Check the use of homophones. *(p. 317)*

Edit

Focus on Conventions

Edit for Accuracy Ask students to name some easily confused words. (Possible responses: *by/bye, its/it's, there/their/they're, to/too/two, whose/who's, wood/would, your/you're*) Ask students how they remember which word to use. (Possible response: Memorize the meanings and spellings of sound-alike words.)

Have students read their business letters to be sure there are no mistakes. If students are typing their letters, remind them that the spell checker will not identify misused homophones. Use the mini-lessons on pages 318 and 319 for students who need practice using homophones correctly.

Writer's Term

Homophones In writing, spelling matters. If the misspelled word is a homophone, the error may reveal that the writer does not know what the word means.

CCSS Common Core State Standards

L.6.1: Demonstrate command of the conventions of standard English grammar and usage when writing or speaking. **L.6.2.b:** Spell correctly. **L.6.4:** Determine or clarify the meaning of unknown and multiple-meaning words and phrases based on grade 6 reading and content, choosing flexibly from a range of strategies.

Business Letter T317

Conventions

Mini-Lesson

Student Objectives

- Use homophones correctly. (p. 318)

Homophones

Remind students that homophones are words that are pronounced the same but have different spellings and meanings. Students should become familiar with common homophones and their correct uses. Before assigning the practice, write the following sentence on the board: *I sea you moved the couch over their.*

Ask students to correct the misspelled homophones in the sentence. (*sea to see, their to there*)

Explain to students that using contractions can form commonly misused homophones, such as *it's, you're, there's, they're,* and *who's.* Ask students to identify the words that form these contractions. (it is/has, you are, there is, they are, who is/has) To help improve their editing skills, recommend that students get into the habit of reading contractions as two words to be sure they are used correctly.

Online Writing Center

Provides **interactive grammar games** and **practice activities** in student eBook.

Conventions **Grammar, Usage & Mechanics**

Homophones

Know the Rule

Homophones are words that are pronounced the same but have different spellings and meanings.

Here are some examples of homophones and their meanings. Make sure you are using the correct word.

its—possessive pronoun meaning "belonging to it"
it's—contraction of *it is* or *it has*

there—adverb meaning "in that place"
their—possessive pronoun meaning "belonging to them"
they're—contraction of *they are*

your—possessive pronoun meaning "belonging to you"
you're—contraction of *you are*

whose—possessive pronoun meaning "belonging to someone"
who's—contraction of *who is* or *who has*

Practice the Rule

Number your paper 1–10. Write the correct word to complete each sentence.

1. Three chords and a simple pattern give the blues (its/it's) unique form.
2. (It's/Its) one of the oldest forms of American music.
3. (There/Their/They're) are several views about the origins of the blues.
4. The songs are called the blues because (there/their/they're) often sad.
5. At first, only people in the South sang or listened (two/to/too) the blues.
6. By the 1920s, people in the North were enjoying the blues, (two/to/too).
7. Today, (your/you're) likely to hear blues mixed with other styles of music.
8. If you could play blues-style piano, (would/wood) you?
9. There are many famous musicians (who's/whose) first love in music was the blues.
10. What's (your/you're) favorite blues song?

Related Grammar Practice

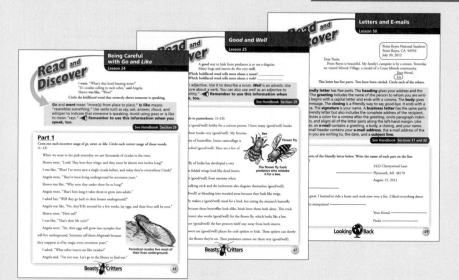

Pages 65, 67, 129

Go to ➡ **G.U.M. Student Practice Book**

More Homophones

Know the Rule

know—verb meaning "to have information about something in your mind"
no—adverb that indicates the negative

theirs—adjective meaning "belonging to them"
there's—contraction of *there is*

too—adverb meaning "more, in addition, also"
two—adjective meaning the number 2
to—preposition meaning "in order to be in a certain place"

vary—verb meaning "to be different from each other"
very—adverb used for emphasis

weak—adjective meaning "not strong"
week—noun meaning "the seven days from Sunday through Saturday"

whether—conjunction that indicates a choice
weather—noun that refers to the temperature and other conditions, like rain, snow, wind, sun, clouds

Practice the Rule

Number a sheet of paper 1–10. Write the correct word to complete each sentence.

1. (Theirs/There's) nothing more joyful than moving to the beat of music you love.
2. Do you (no/know) a lot about the folk music of Ireland?
3. Most people like at least (to/two/too) kinds of music.
4. (Whether/Weather) you like rock or blues, pop or rap, classical or reggae, you can find a music festival that features your favorite music.
5. Next (week/weak) there is a concert I want to go to.
6. My cousins were here for the weekend, and these CDs are (there's/theirs).
7. Country music is (vary/very) popular in the South.
8. Since my brother came back from New Orleans, he likes (to/two/too) listen to jazz.
9. Jin likes to (vary/very) the kind of music she downloads.
10. On any given day, she might listen (to/two/too) country or dance music.

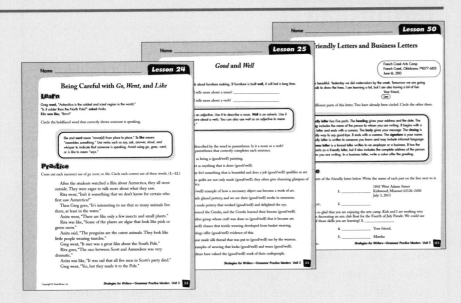

Pages 53, 55, 105

Go to Grammar Practice Masters

Mini-Lesson

Student Objectives

• Use homophones correctly. (p. 319)

More Homophones

Have students read the information in Know the Rule. Ask them to suggest other homophones that have been used incorrectly in their writing. (Sample responses: altogether/all together, ant/aunt, board/bored, brake/break, by/bye/buy, desert/dessert, for/four, loose/lose, peace/piece, principal/principle, scene/seen, right/write) List their examples on the board. Suggest others that you have noticed in your students' writing. Discuss how using homophones incorrectly can cause unintended humor or confusion.

Ask students to share tips for associating the variations in spellings with the correct meanings. Invite them to look up the most problematic of words in print and online resources.

CCSS Common Core State Standards
L.6.2: Demonstrate command of the conventions of standard English capitalization, punctuation, and spelling when writing. **L.6.4:** Determine or clarify the meaning of unknown and multiple-meaning words and phrases based on grade 6 reading and content, choosing flexibly from a range of strategies.

Write
a Business Letter

Week 3 • Day 4

Student Objectives

- Discuss preparation for publishing and presentation. (p. 320)
- Use a final editing checklist. (p. 320)

Publish ⁺Presentation

Publishing Strategy Explain to students that Leila's decision to mail her letter shows commitment to expressing her opinion. Review the publishing strategy with students. Point out that before Leila mails her letter to her reader, she takes another look at her checklist to be sure she hasn't missed anything. Have students read Leila's finished letter on page 321, using her checklist to assess the letter. Did she include all of the items on her checklist?

Encourage students to use the checklist or one you provide to make their final copies. To prepare the envelope for mailing, be sure students follow the preferred United States Postal Service style of using all caps and no punctuation in addresses. Students can go online to **www.usps.com** for advice about properly addressing an envelope.

Strategies for Writers Online
Go to **www.sfw.z-b.com** for additional online resources for students and teachers.

Publish ⁺Presentation

Publishing Strategy	Mail the business letter.
Presentation Strategy	Include all the parts of a business letter.

Now that I've finished my business letter, I can't wait to mail it to the station manager! Before I do that, I'm going to make sure my letter is in proper business letter format. The six parts of a business letter are listed on page 312. I'll refer to that list to make sure I've included all the parts and written them correctly. Then I'll check over my letter one last time, using the items in the final checklist below. Finally I'll carefully handwrite or type a copy on the computer and mail it.

My Final Checklist

Did I—

✔ make sure all the homophones are correct?

✔ use correct business letter format?

✔ check for all six parts of a business letter?

✔ make sure my grammar, punctuation, and spelling are correct?

Apply
Make a final checklist to check your business letter. Then make a final copy to publish.

320 Argument Writing

Differentiating Instruction

ENRICHMENT
Business E-Mail Explain that an e-mail written for business purposes should follow many of the same guidelines as business letters. Encourage students to write an e-mail to a business person, perhaps to request information to use in a science or social studies report.

REINFORCEMENT
Proofread Carefully Have pairs of students exchange drafts and edit strategically. For example, have each pair begin by proofreading only for punctuation or spelling. Then have them look for easily confused words. Remind editors to use the proofreading marks on page 313 to mark their changes. Then have partners exchange edited letters and verify for accuracy before preparing and printing out their final copy.

4922 Tinley Drive
Nashville, TN 37201
October 16, 2012

Station Manager
KTNT Radio Station
1148 W. Filmore Road
Nashville, TN 37203

Dear Station Manager:

Blues superstar Luther Allison said, "If you don't like the blues, you've got a hole in your soul." I have a passion for the blues, and your program "Down to the Blues" taught me more about it every week. When KTNT canceled this excellent show, I was very disappointed. I'm writing to ask you to please put your blues program back on the air.

There is so much to learn about the blues. "Down to the Blues" was the only radio program that taught blues songs on the air. I learned a lot about various blues musicians. And their stories and music inspired me!

I really liked it that the show played songs by classic blues artists and modern blues artists, too. The good mix made "Down to the Blues" entertaining for any blues fan.

The timing of the program was perfect for me and other kids, too. The 7 P.M. time slot was late enough that I could finish my homework before the program started, but it didn't keep me up too late.

I hope KTNT will return "Down to the Blues" to its evening programming. All kinds of blues fans enjoy the program and learn so much from listening, especially us kids!

Yours truly,

Leila Hirsch

Leila Hirsch

Reflect

What did you think? Does Leila's letter have all the traits of a good business letter that makes an argument? Check it against the rubric. Then use the rubric to check your own business letter.

Business Letter **321**

Technology Tip for 21st Century Literacies

Student writers often benefit from reading their work aloud. Introduce an element of play (or of security as in the use of an avatar or pseudonym for more reluctant students) by asking students to create an audio text of their work using Blabberize. Allow time to view these, and consider how reading the text aloud helps writers revise and strengthen their work. Given the playfulness of the tool, also consider how the character/avatar pairing impacts meaning.

See **www.sfw.z-b.com** for further information about and links to these websites and tools.

Write a Business Letter

Student Objectives

- Use a business letter rubric. (pp. 304–305)
- Share a published business letter. (p. 321)

Presentation Strategy Review the importance of neatness. Remind students to set neat margins; use block style; and select one clear, businesslike font such as Arial or Times New Roman so the recipient has no trouble reading the letter.

Encourage students to consult online resources, such as dictionaries and thesauruses. Point out common mistakes, such as the spelling of the closings *Yours truly* and *Sincerely*. Remind students to sign their letter with their full names.

Reflecting on a Business Letter

Have students refer to the rubric on pages 304–305 as they read Leila's final copy on page 321. Then have students think back on this assignment. Ask:

- What did you learn about writing a business letter?

CCSS Common Core State Standards

W.6.4: Produce clear and coherent writing in which the development, organization, and style are appropriate to task, purpose, and audience. **W.6.5:** With some guidance and support from peers and adults, develop and strengthen writing as needed by planning, revising, editing, rewriting, or trying a new approach. **W.6.10:** Write routinely over extended time frames (time for research, reflection, and revision) and shorter time frames (a single sitting or a day or two) for a range of discipline-specific tasks, purposes, and audiences.

Business Letter **T321**

Speech Planner

WEEK 1

Day 1
Introduce a Speech

Student Objectives
- Review the elements of a speech.
- Consider purpose and audience.
- Learn the traits of argument writing.

Student Activities
- Read and discuss **What's in a Speech?** (p. 322)
- Read and discuss **Why Write a Speech?** (p. 323)
- Read **Linking Argument Writing Traits to a Speech.** (p. 324)

Day 2
Analyze Read a Speech

Student Objectives
- Read a model speech.

Student Activities
- Read **"The Mother of Modern Physics."** (p. 325)

Day 3
Analyze Introduce the Rubric

Student Objectives
- Learn to read a rubric.

Student Activities
- Review **"The Mother of Modern Physics."** (p. 325)
- Read and discuss the **Speech Rubric.** (pp. 326–327)

WEEK 2

Day 1
Write Prewrite: Ideas

Student Objectives
- Decide on a position and do some research.

Student Activities
- Read and discuss **Prewrite: Focus on Ideas.** (p. 332)
- Apply the prewriting strategy.

Day 2
Write Prewrite: Organization

Student Objectives
- Use an Argument Map to plan a speech.

Student Activities
- Read and discuss **Prewrite: Focus on Organization.** (p. 333)
- Apply the prewriting strategy.
- Participate in a peer conference.

Day 3
Write Draft: Word Choice

Student Objectives
- Define unfamiliar words.

Student Activities
- Read and discuss **Draft: Focus on Word Choice.** (p. 334)
- Apply the drafting strategy.

WEEK 3

Day 1
Write Revise: Organization

Student Objectives
- Use effective transitions to show how ideas are connected.

Student Activities
- Read and discuss: **Revise: Focus on Organization.** (p. 337)
- Reflect on the model draft.
- Participate in a peer conference.

Day 2
Write Revise: Sentence Fluency

Student Objectives
- Use phrases and clauses to vary sentences.

Student Activities
- Read and discuss: **Revise: Focus on Sentence Fluency.** (p. 338)

Note: Optional Revising Lessons appear on the *Strategies for Writers* CD-ROM.

Day 3
Write Edit: Conventions

Student Objectives
- Check forms of *be* and change passive voice to active.

Student Activities
- Read and discuss **Edit: Focus on Conventions.** (p. 339)
- Reflect on the model draft.

Note: Teach the Conventions mini-lessons (pp. 340–341) if needed.

Student Objectives
- Read a model speech.
- Use the speech rubric.
- Use the model speech to study Ideas, Organization, and Voice.

Student Activities
- Review **"The Mother of Modern Physics."** (p. 325)
- Review the rubric. (pp. 326–327)
- Read and discuss **Using the Rubric to Study the Model.** (pp. 328–329)

Student Objectives
- Read a model speech.
- Use the speech rubric.
- Use the model speech to study Word Choice, Sentence Fluency, and Conventions.

Student Activities
- Review **"The Mother of Modern Physics."** (p. 325)
- Review the rubric. (pp. 326–327)
- Read and discuss **Using the Rubric to Study the Model.** (pp. 330–331)

Student Objectives
- Complete a draft.

Student Activities
- Finish writing the draft. (p. 335)
- Participate in a peer conference.

Student Objectives
- Use credible sources.

Student Activities
- Read and discuss **Revise: Focus on Ideas.** (p. 336)
- Reflect on the model draft.
- Apply the revising strategy.

Student Objectives
- Discuss preparation for publishing and presentation.
- Use a final editing checklist.

Student Activities
- Read and discuss **Publish: +Presentation.** (p. 342)
- Apply the publishing strategy.

Student Objectives
- Use a speech rubric.
- Share a published speech.

Student Activities
- Share their work.
- Use the rubric to reflect upon and evaluate the model and their own writing. (pp. 326–327; 343)

To complete the chapter in fewer days, combine the learning objectives and activities in a way that supports students as they write.

Resources at-a-Glance

Grammar, Usage & Mechanics

Differentiating Instruction

For additional Differentiating Instruction activities, see Strategies for Writers *Extensions Online at* **www.sfw.z-b.com.**

English Language Learners

Conferencing

Technology Tip

School Home Connection Letter
Reproducible letter (in English and Spanish) appears on the *Strategies for Writers* CD-ROM and at **www.sfw.z-b.com.**

Online Writing Center

Provides IWB resources, interactive games and practice activities, videos, eBooks, and a virtual file cabinet.

 Strategies for Writers Online

Go to **www.sfw.z-b.com** for free online resources for students and teachers.

Introduce
a Speech

Student Objectives

- Review the elements of a speech. *(p. 322)*
- Consider purpose and audience. *(p. 323)*
- Learn the traits of argument writing. *(p. 324)*

What's a Speech?

Discuss with students the definition of a speech. Ask students to recall speeches they have read or heard. Discuss how a speech is different from an essay. (Speeches are written to be presented to an audience.) Then ask students if they have ever written and given an argument speech. Invite them to share their experiences.

What's in a Speech?

Read and discuss with students the elements of a speech on page 322. Explain that these elements are common to other forms of argument writing, such as book reviews, essays, and business letters. Be sure to stress how to avoid plagiarism: The original source must be given credit for the idea. Then discuss how the elements work together in a speech.

Strategies for Writers Online
Go to **www.sfw.z-b.com** for additional online resources for students and teachers.

What's a **Speech?**

A speech is a spoken expression of a writer's opinion. In an argument speech, a presenter speaks to convince an audience of listeners to believe in and support a message or cause. Writing a speech will be fun. What better way to have your actual voice be heard?

What's in a **Speech?**

Claim
The main idea of my speech is the claim that I will be making. It must be something that can be argued, or something that has at least two sides to it, so I can build an argument that will convince people to be on my side!

Supporting Evidence
I'll need details and facts that support my main idea, or claim, to make my view believable. I'll use information and facts from credible and trusted sources so that my points are valid.

Plagiarism
Plagiarism is using someone else's words and ideas without giving them credit. It is a serious offense. I'll provide a full reference for the source of the facts and details I use in my speech. I'll also put ideas into my own words.

322 Argument Writing

Argument Text Exemplars (Speech)

Churchill, Winston. "Blood, Toil, Tears and Sweat: Address to Parliament on May 13th, 1940." *Lend Me Your Ears: Great Speeches in History*, 3rd ed. W.W. Norton, 2004. **CCSS** Winston Churchill, the Prime Minister of England, gave this speech to the House of Commons in 1940. His goal was to boost the morale of the British people during the war against Nazi Germany.

Hossell, Karen Price. *John F. Kennedy's Inaugural Speech.* **Heinemann-Raintree, 2005.** "Ask not what your country can do for you, but what you can do for your country." These words, spoken by President John F. Kennedy at his inauguration, are part of one of the most inspirational speeches in United States history. This book examines John F. Kennedy's speech, as well as the events that led up to it.

Why write a **Speech?**

I've never given a speech before, but it sounds like a good way to express my opinions. Here are some more reasons to write an argument speech.

Argument
A good speech can convince others to agree with your opinion. This kind of writing can give readers (or listeners) the information they need to make up their minds—or change their minds—about an issue.

Information
Because an argument speech is on a topic about which the writer feels strongly, the writer really wants you to agree with his or her side. So a good speech is filled with important facts and details. An audience can learn a lot from a speech.

Understanding
To give a speech, you have to become an expert on the topic. To become an expert, you need to find out as much as you can about the subject matter. Giving a speech is like being a teacher, in a way, because you are making others aware of something. You know you understand something when you can teach it to others.

Why write a Speech?

Read and discuss with students the reasons for writing a speech as listed here. Point out that all writing has a purpose and a specific audience. Encourage students to discuss how having authentic purposes helps writers shape their writing. For example, someone writing to convince others might include examples and anecdotes that support the writer's opinion or position on an important issue. Someone writing to inform would probably include up-to-date factual data from reliable sources to convince the audience. A person writing for understanding might build on prior knowledge to connect ideas and information in new ways. Encourage students to think about their own reasons for writing a speech. Add that their purpose also will affect the tone and style of writing.

Lincoln, Abraham. *The Gettysburg Address.* Sandpiper, 1998. On November 19, 1863, President Abraham Lincoln delivered a short speech at the dedication of the Soldier's National Cemetery in Gettysburg, Pennsylvania. It became one of the most famous speeches in American history.

Brezina, Corona. *Sojourner Truth's "Ain't I a Woman?" Speech: A Primary Source Investigation.* Rosen Publishing Group, 2004. Sojourner Truth was an abolitionist and women's right activist. In *Sojourner Truth's "Ain't I a Woman?" Speech: A Primary Source Investigation*, the author describes the events surrounding Truth's speech that she delivered in 1851 at the Ohio Women's Rights Convention in Akron, Ohio.

CCSS Common Core State Standards

SL.6.1: Engage effectively in a range of collaborative discussions (one-on-one, in groups, and teacher-led) with diverse partners on grade 6 topics, texts, and issues, building on others' ideas and expressing their own clearly. **SL.6.1.a:** Come to discussions prepared, having read or studied required material; explicitly draw on that preparation by referring to evidence on the topic, text, or issue to probe and reflect on ideas under discussion.

Introduce
a Speech

Linking Argument Writing Traits to a Speech

Explain to students that they will follow Leila as she models using the writing process and the traits together. As they follow Leila through the writing process, students will see how the Argument Writing Traits have been adapted and applied to writing a speech. They will see that a speech, because it can express an opinion, has many factors in common with other types of argument writing. However, the particular audience and purpose of a speech determine how the traits are used.

Linking Argument Writing Traits to a **Speech**

In this chapter, you will write about something you believe in strongly and then try to convince listeners to agree with your argument. This type of argument writing is called a speech. Leila will guide you through the stages of the writing process: Prewrite, Draft, Revise, Edit, and Publish. In each stage, Leila will show you important writing strategies that are linked to the Argument Writing Traits below.

Argument Writing Traits

Ideas	• clearly stated claims, often balanced by alternate or opposing claims • supporting evidence from accurate and credible sources
Organization	• a strong introduction that presents the writer's position • reasons and evidence that are organized logically • a conclusion that restates the thesis and possibly provides a call to action • transitions that clarify the relationships between ideas
Voice	• a voice that supports the writer's purpose
Word Choice	• language that is compelling
Sentence Fluency	• sentences that vary in length and begin in different ways
Conventions	• no or few errors in grammar, usage, mechanics, and spelling

Before you write, read Linnea Moore's speech on the next page. Then use the speech rubric on pages 326–327 to decide how well she did. (You might want to look back at What's in a Speech? on page 322, too!)

Argument Writing Traits in a Speech

 Ideas The speech clearly states a claim and includes supporting evidence.

 **Organization** The speech includes a strong introduction that presents the writer's opinion. Reasons (main ideas) and evidence (supporting details) are organized logically in the middle part. Appropriate transition words clarify and connect ideas to help the audience follow the writer's argument. The conclusion restates the writer's opinion.

 Voice The writer uses a convincing voice that supports the writer's purpose and engages the audience.

The Mother of Modern Physics
by Linnea Moore

She won two Nobel Prizes, coined the term *radioactivity*, and discovered the elements radium and polonium. She believed in working for the betterment of humanity. **Claim** Her name is Marie Curie, and she is the most influential woman in the history of science.

Marie Curie (born Maria Sklodowska) was born in Poland in 1867. Marie was a curious child with a gift for learning. She excelled in high school, graduating ahead of schedule and at the head of her class.

Marie had hopes for a higher education. She was interested in mathematics, physics, and chemistry, but because she was female, she could not go to a university at home. To overcome this discrimination, Marie and her sister promised to put each other through school where women were welcome. Marie helped put her sister through medical school in Paris, France. Then her sister, as promised, returned the favor, and off Marie went to the University of Paris, the Sorbonne.

Supporting evidence

At the University, Marie immersed herself in the studies she loved. She earned Master's degrees in physics and mathematics. She also married Pierre Curie. Together, they studied what Marie called radioactivity, or how certain substances spontaneously react, and they discovered the elements radium and polonium. For their discovery, which would lead to aiding cancer treatments, the Curies won the Nobel Prize in physics in 1903. That same year, Marie became the first woman in France to earn her doctorate degree in physics.

Marie did not stop at one Nobel Prize. She went on to earn another in chemistry in 1911 for her work with radium. She was the first person in history to win two such prizes. Marie also became the first female professor at the Sorbonne. With all of her fame, Marie remained committed to science and humanity. She said, "You cannot hope to build a better world without improving the individuals." To show her humanitarianism, she decided to help World War I casualties. By using x-rays, she assisted doctors in locating bullets and shrapnel to aid treatment.

Marie Curie's contributions to society are numerous, and her love of learning and desire to discover are unmatched. As a woman, she forged ahead, breaking down barriers. Marie Curie's achievements are unsurpassed by any other scientist in history.

used quotes to avoid plagiarism

Speech 325

Word Choice The writer's words are purposeful and convincing. Specific words related to the topic are defined for the audience.

Sentence Fluency Sentence variety makes the speech enjoyable and easy to follow. The writer's ideas flow smoothly and hold the audience's attention.

Conventions The writer has edited carefully. Verbs are used correctly.

Analyze
the Model

Week 1 • Day 2

Student Objectives

• Read a model speech. *(p. 325)*

Read the Model

Read the model speech with emphasis and good pacing. Direct students' attention to the notes written on the model, making sure they can identify the writer's claim and supporting evidence. Be sure to ask how Linnea avoids plagiarism in her speech. (She puts Marie Curie's words in quotation marks.)

Elements of a Speech

Have students look at What's in a Speech? on page 322. Discuss how the text is organized. (An introduction presents the writer's main idea and grabs the listener's attention; the body includes factual, verifiable information that supports the writer's claim; and the conclusion restates the writer's opinion.) Also invite students to discuss formatting considerations (using a word processor, leaving white space, indenting paragraphs, editing carefully, etc.). Discuss how these features assist the reader.

CCSS Common Core State Standards

R/Inf.6.1: Cite textual evidence to support analysis of what the text says explicitly as well as inferences drawn from the text. **R/Inf.6.6:** Determine an author's point of view or purpose in a text and explain how it is conveyed in the text. **SL.6.1.b:** Follow rules for collegial discussions, set specific goals and deadlines, and define individual roles as needed. **SL.6.3:** Delineate a speaker's argument and specific claims, distinguishing claims that are supported by reasons and evidence from claims that are not.

Analyze the Model

Student Objectives

- Learn to read a rubric. (pp. 326–327)

Use the Rubric

Explain the Rubric Explain that a writing rubric is a tool for planning, improving, and assessing a piece of writing. A rubric helps a writer focus on key elements, or traits, in writing (**Ideas, Organization, Voice, Word Choice, Sentence Fluency, Conventions,** and **Presentation**).

Explain the 6-point system. Point out that the columns on page 326 represent a good speech that might need some polishing while the columns on page 327 represent writing that needs considerable improvement.

Discuss the Rubric Guide students in a discussion of the rubric. Read the descriptors that go with each trait, and take a moment to explain the relationship between them. Discuss the differences between columns to be sure students fully understand the point system. Remind students to keep the rubric in mind as they write their own speech and again as they revise and edit it.

Online Writing Center

Provides a variety of **interactive rubrics,** including 4-, 5-, and 6-point models.

Speech

Rubric

Use this 6-point rubric to plan and score a speech.

	6	5	4	
Ideas	The writer's claim is clear and compelling. Supporting evidence is accurate. Credible sources are cited.	The writer's claim is clear. Most supporting evidence is accurate and taken from credible sources.	The writer's claim is stated. Some evidence is lacking. Some sources are not credible or incorrectly cited.	
Organization	The introduction, body, and conclusion are strong and compelling. Appropriate transitions clarify relationships among ideas.	The introduction, body, and conclusion are strong. Transitions show how ideas are related.	The introduction, body, and conclusion are fairly strong. Only one or two transitions are used.	
Voice	The voice is lively and direct. Active voice provides energy.	The voice is lively and direct most of the time. Active voice is used.	The voice could sound more lively and direct in parts. Active voice is used.	
Word Choice	Domain-specific content words are used correctly and defined clearly.	Domain-specific content words are used correctly. One or two words need definitions.	Most domain-specific content words are used correctly. The definitions could be clearer.	
Sentence Fluency	A variety of sentence patterns makes the text flow smoothly.	A variety of sentence patterns is used.	Some variety of sentence patterns is present. The flow is interrupted in a few places.	
Conventions	The writing has been carefully edited. All forms of verbs are used correctly and effectively.	Minor errors are present but do not interfere with meaning. Forms of *be* are used correctly.	A few errors cause confusion. Forms of *be* are used correctly.	
+Presentation	Visuals support and enhance the meaning of the text.			

326 Argument Writing

CCSS Common Core State Standards

Speech

The Common Core State Standards (CCSS) are woven throughout the instruction in *Strategies for Writers*. Writing in the Argument mode can engage the standards for all forms of Argument writing. The rubric and writing strategies for Ideas reflect writing standard **W.6.1,** to write arguments to support claims with clear reasons and relevant evidence, and standards **W.6.1.a** and **W.6.1.b,** to introduce and support a claim, and to address opposing claims. The rubric and writing strategies for Organization are also drawn from standards **W.6.1.a** and **W.6.1.b,** to organize and connect the ideas logically, and standard **W.6.1.e,** to provide an effective concluding section. The traits of Voice and Word Choice reflect standard **W.6.1.c,** to use words to create cohesion and

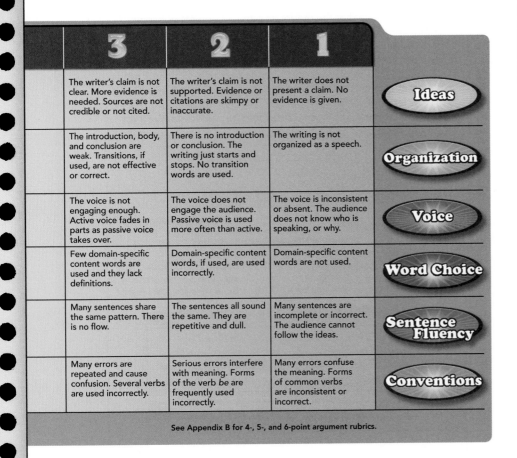

3	2	1	
The writer's claim is not clear. More evidence is needed. Sources are not credible or not cited.	The writer's claim is not supported. Evidence or citations are skimpy or inaccurate.	The writer does not present a claim. No evidence is given.	**Ideas**
The introduction, body, and conclusion are weak. Transitions, if used, are not effective or correct.	There is no introduction or conclusion. The writing just starts and stops. No transition words are used.	The writing is not organized as a speech.	**Organization**
The voice is not engaging enough. Active voice fades in parts as passive voice takes over.	The voice does not engage the audience. Passive voice is used more often than active.	The voice is inconsistent or absent. The audience does not know who is speaking, or why.	**Voice**
Few domain-specific content words are used and they lack definitions.	Domain-specific content words, if used, are used incorrectly.	Domain-specific content words are not used.	**Word Choice**
Many sentences share the same pattern. There is no flow.	The sentences all sound the same. They are repetitive and dull.	Many sentences are incomplete or incorrect. The audience cannot follow the ideas.	**Sentence Fluency**
Many errors are repeated and cause confusion. Several verbs are used incorrectly.	Serious errors interfere with meaning. Forms of the verb *be* are frequently used incorrectly.	Many errors confuse the meaning. Forms of common verbs are inconsistent or incorrect.	**Conventions**

See Appendix B for 4-, 5-, and 6-point argument rubrics.

Apply the Rubric

Assign Groups Assign students to small groups and ask them to check the model for one trait. One person in each group should be responsible for recording one or two strong examples of the trait as described by the rubric. Ask students to score the trait accordingly for the model. They should be able to support their scores. Note that although the model was written to score high in each trait, students should not assume each trait would receive a 6, the top score. Encourage students to discuss each trait thoroughly before assigning each score.

Reassemble Class Bring the class together and ask one person from each group to report their findings to the class. The point of this exercise is less to score the model than it is to practice identifying and evaluating the traits within a piece of writing.

Additional Rubrics Appendix B includes 4-, 5-, and 6-point rubrics that can be used with any piece of argument writing. The rubrics are also available as blackline masters, beginning on page T525.

clarify relationships among ideas, and standard **W.6.1.d,** to establish and maintain a formal style.

The language standards for grade 6 students are addressed during editing and skills practice (**L.6.1–L.6.6**). In addition, there are multiple opportunities to address the speaking and listening standards during the writing process. Specifically, students are encouraged to work collaboratively, review key ideas, and demonstrate understanding (**SL.6.1.a–d**). Most importantly, this chapter will help students produce coherent writing (**W.6.4**), improve their writing with the help of peers and adults (**W.6.5**), use technologies (**W.6.6**) and multimedia components (**SL.6.5**) to polish and present their finished pieces, draw evidence from texts to use in their writing (**W.6.8** and **W.6.9**), and use writing to respond and reflect (**W.6.10**).

CCSS **Common Core State Standards**

W.6.9: Draw evidence from literary or informational texts to support analysis, reflection, and research.
SL.6.1.c: Pose and respond to specific questions with elaboration and detail by making comments that contribute to the topic, text, or issue under discussion.
SL.6.1.d: Review the key ideas expressed and demonstrate understanding of multiple perspectives through reflection and paraphrasing.

Analyze
the Model

Week 1 • Day 4

Student Objectives

- Read a model speech. *(p. 325)*
- Use the speech rubric. *(pp. 326–327)*
- Use the model speech to study Ideas, Organization, and Voice. *(pp. 328–329)*

Study the Model

Assess the Model Discuss as a class whether students agree or disagree with Leila's assessments of the model for **Ideas, Organization, and Voice.** Use questions such as the following to discuss the pages with students.

- Does the writer express her opinion clearly and convincingly? (Possible response: Yes, Linnea states her opinion—Marie Curie is the most influential woman in science—and supports it with facts, such as winning two Nobel Prizes and discovering the elements radium and polonium.)

- Does the writer use credible sources? (Possible response: It's obvious that Linnea consulted reliable sources of information about her topic. She also uses the words of Marie Curie to support her message.)

Strategies for Writers Online
Go to **www.sfw.z-b.com** for additional online resources for students and teachers.

T328 Argument Writing

Using the Speech Rubric to Study the Model

Did you notice that the model on page 325 points out some key elements of a speech? As she wrote "The Mother of Modern Physics," Linnea Moore used these elements to help express her opinion through a speech. She also used the 6-point rubric on pages 326–327 to plan, draft, revise, and edit the writing. A rubric is a great tool for evaluating writing during the writing process.

Now let's use the same rubric to score the model. To do this, we'll focus on each trait separately, starting with Ideas. We'll use the top descriptor for each trait (column 6), along with examples from the model, to help us understand how the traits work together. How would you score Linnea on each trait?

Ideas
- The writer's claim is clear and compelling.
- Supporting evidence is accurate.
- Credible sources are cited.

Linnea opens her speech with a clear and convincing claim. She also supports her claim with accurate facts about Marie Curie. For her quote she cites the most credible source about Marie Curie—the scientist herself.

> [from the writing model]
>
> She won two Nobel Prizes, coined the term *radioactivity*, and discovered the elements radium and polonium. She believed in working for the betterment of humanity. Her name is Marie Curie, and she is the most influential woman in the history of science.

> [from the writing model]
>
> With all of her fame, Marie remained committed to science and humanity. She said, "You cannot hope to build a better world without improving the individuals."

328 Argument Writing

English Language Learners

BEGINNING
Claim Illustrate what a *claim* is by asking students to choose their favorite type of vacation, going to the beach or camping. Show a photo of each and ask, *Which do you like better?* Record students' answers on the board and review them by saying, *José's claim is that he likes camping better.* Repeat for other students. Review using the verb form in sentences, too, such as *José claims to like camping better.* After you say each sentence, have students repeat.

INTERMEDIATE
Evidence Demonstrate finding clues to a mystery. Explain that *evidence* is proof or details that support an opinion or idea. Say, *evidence* and have students repeat. Use simple brainteasers or mystery stories and have students identify the evidence in each. Have students give evidence in support of a topic, such as *Galileo made many discoveries about stars.*

Organization

- The introduction, body, and conclusion are strong and compelling.
- Appropriate transitions clarify relationships among ideas.

This writer grabs my attention right from the first paragraph. I am interested to find out who this "she" is, who has so many great achievements. Then the body describes Marie's achievements in greater detail, and the conclusion strongly restates the claim, tying everything together.

Transitional phrases such as *At the University* link ideas and helped me follow the story of Marie's life.

> [from the writing model]
>
> Marie helped put her sister through medical school in Paris, France. Then her sister, as promised, returned the favor, and off Marie went to the University of Paris, the Sorbonne.
>
> At the University, Marie immersed herself in the studies she loved. She earned Master's degrees in physics and mathematics.

Voice

- The voice is lively and direct.
- Active voice provides energy.

Linnea uses direct, energetic language to talk about Marie's achievements. Notice the strong, direct statement at the start of the excerpt below. Similarly, Linnea avoids boring phrases such as "she was named to be a professor." Instead she uses active voice to state, "Marie also became the first female professor at the Sorbonne."

> [from the writing model]
>
> Marie did not stop at one Nobel Prize. She went on to earn another in chemistry in 1911 for her work with radium. She was the first person in history to win two such prizes. Marie also became the first female professor at the Sorbonne.

Speech **329**

- **How is the speech organized?** (Possible response: The writer states her opinion and purpose in the introduction, supports her opinion with logical reasons and evidence, and wraps things up by restating her opinion in the conclusion.)

- **What transitions does Linnea use? Are they effective?** (Possible responses: Yes, Linnea connects her ideas with phrases, such as *Then her sister, For their discovery, That same year*, and *With all of her fame*. As a result, the speech is easy to follow.)

- **How would you describe Linnea's voice?** (Possible responses: Linnea's writing voice is enthusiastic and convincing from start to finish. It's clear that she wants her listeners to agree with her.)

ADVANCED

Claim, Reasons, and Supporting Evidence Have partners discuss how they feel about a topic, such as space exploration. Allow them to research the topic. They should come up with an argument, or *claim*, regarding the topic. Ask, *Why do you think your claim is correct?* Tell students that these are their *reasons*. Have them write the claim and reasons in an Argument Map. Using the information they researched, they should add several pieces of *supporting evidence* for each reason. Review the meanings of the terms, write them, and have students repeat.

ADVANCED HIGH

Argument Map Complete the Advanced activity above. Have students cut out the statements and switch with another pair who should correctly identify each statement as the claim, a reason, or a piece of supporting evidence.

CCSS **Common Core State Standards**

W.6.9: Draw evidence from literary or informational texts to support analysis, reflection, and research.
SL.6.1.c: Pose and respond to specific questions with elaboration and detail by making comments that contribute to the topic, text, or issue under discussion.
SL.6.1.d: Review the key ideas expressed and demonstrate understanding of multiple perspectives through reflection and paraphrasing.

Analyze
the Model

Week 1 • Day 5

Student Objectives

- Read a model speech. *(p. 325)*
- Use the speech rubric. *(pp. 326–327)*
- Use the model speech to study Word Choice, Sentence Fluency, and Conventions. *(pp. 330–331)*

Continue the Discussion Use questions such as the following to discuss the traits analyzed on pages 330 and 331:

- What do you think of the writer's choice of words? (Possible response: The writer's language is appropriate and convincing. I also notice that she does not use biased or overly emotional language to get her point across.)

- What kinds of sentences does Linnea use? (Possible responses: The sentences are interesting and well written. They move along at a good pace and keep the audience engaged in the ideas.)

- Has the model been edited? (Possible responses: It's obvious that the speech was carefully edited. Nothing distracts or confuses the reader. All verbs are used correctly, too.)

Word Choice

- Domain-specific content words are used correctly and defined clearly.

Linnea clearly defines *radioactivity*, a term closely related to the topic of this speech.

[from the writing model]

Together, they studied what Marie called radioactivity, or how certain substances spontaneously react, and they discovered the elements radium and polonium.

Sentence Fluency

- A variety of sentence patterns makes the text flow smoothly.

Linnea uses a variety of sentence patterns to make the text flow smoothly. She uses simple sentences, as well as compound, complex, and compound complex sentences. Can you identify them all? The varied sentence structure gives her speech a nice flow. Read the following paragraph aloud to hear for yourself.

[from the writing model]

Marie had hopes for a higher education. She was interested in mathematics, physics, and chemistry, but because she was female, she could not go to a university at home. To overcome this discrimination, Marie and her sister promised to put each other through school where women were welcome. Marie helped put her sister through medical school in Paris, France. Then her sister, as promised, returned the favor, and off Marie went to the University of Paris, the Sorbonne.

330 Argument Writing

Technology Tip
for 21st Century Literacies

Part of considering audience is also considering how to leverage what others know. Encourage students to generate and share polls using tools like Poll Everywhere or Survey Monkey through which they query their audience either prior to or during their speeches. Valuing an audience as participants is a 21st century literacy. Querying the audience prior to a speech also allows the speaker to shape the content to the group's interests and needs.

See **www.sfw.z-b.com** for further information about and links to these websites and tools.

Strategies for Writers Online
Go to **www.sfw.z-b.com** for additional online resources for students and teachers.

Conventions

- The writing has been carefully edited.
- All forms of verbs are used correctly and effectively.

The writing has been carefully edited because I didn't find a single mistake. Also, all forms of verbs are used correctly. In the first sentence below, do you see how the verb *be* takes its singular form (*was*) to agree with the singular subject (*Marie*)? In the next sentence, the plural form (*were*) agrees with the plural subject (*women*).

[from the writing model]

Marie was a curious child with a gift for learning.

To overcome this discrimination, Marie and her sister promised to put each other through school where women were welcome.

✛ Presentation Visuals support and enhance the meaning of the text.

Now it's my turn to write an argument speech. I'll use the rubric and good writing strategies to help me. Read on to see how I do it.

Speech **331**

Differentiating Instruction

ENRICHMENT

Use the Internet Challenge students to find reliable websites on famous people or science topics they care about. Then have them create a list of the best websites for everyone's use. Set aside time for students to present their list in class. Encourage them to explain why each website made the final list.

REINFORCEMENT

Understand the Elements Some students may benefit from seeing additional samples of argument speeches. Find your favorites to share with students. Have them work in pairs to identify the writer's opinion. They should also take note of the evidence that supports the writer's claim and whether the writer has used credible sources.

Presentation Explain to students that Presentation is just as important as the other traits. The format needs to be considered when students prepare their final copies. Neatness is always a priority, and text should be typed, using only a few readable fonts. Good margins and good spacing make the speech easy to read.

Think About the Traits After students have thoroughly discussed the model, ask them which traits they think are the most important. Remind them that all of the traits are important in every piece of writing; however, some traits play a more important role in specific types of writing. For example, some students may feel that **Organization** is very important to present ideas effectively. Some students may argue that **Voice** is important because the writer needs to convince the audience. Still others may feel that **Word Choice** is important because the writer's language should neither distract nor offend the audience.

CCSS **C**ommon **C**ore **S**tate **S**tandards

R/Inf.6.6: Determine an author's point of view or purpose in a text and explain how it is conveyed in the text. **SL.6.1.d:** Review the key ideas expressed and demonstrate understanding of multiple perspectives through reflection and paraphrasing.

Write a Speech

Week 2 • Day 1

Student Objectives

• Decide on a position and do some research. *(p. 332)*

Prewrite

Focus on Ideas

Choose a Topic Read this page and invite students to share their opinions on issues that matter to them. List these on the board and discuss how people express opinions on many topics. Point out that in argument writing, however, expressing an opinion is not enough to convince others to agree. Emphasize that evidence from credible sources must support an opinion in order to convince the audience. Point out that speechwriters often help educate people about important topics and provide starting points for further research.

Tell students they will each follow Leila's lead to

- choose a topic.
- find evidence to support the position.
- keep track of sources.
- create an Argument Map to plan the speech.

Online Writing Center

Provides **interactive graphic organizers** as well as a variety of graphic organizers in PDF format.

Prewrite

Focus on **Ideas**

The Rubric Says	The writer's claim is clear and compelling. Supporting evidence is accurate. Credible sources are cited.
Writing Strategy	Decide on a position and do some research.

I'm excited about writing an argument speech because I like to have my voice heard. Linnea's speech got me thinking about important women in science, so I thought it would be interesting to learn more about the first African American woman in space, Dr. Mae Jemison. I'll need to find lots of good facts and details about her to make my writing clear and convincing, and I'll have my teacher approve my sources. As I do my research, I'll be sure to keep track of the source information, so I can give credit accordingly.

Notes on Mae Jemison

Source	Note
• Jemison, Mae. *Where the Wind Goes: Moments from My Life.* New York: Scholastic Press: 2001.	• Mae Jemison worked as a medical officer in the Peace Corps.
• Dejoie, Joyce, and Elizabeth Truelove. "Dr. Mae Jemison." http://starchild.gsfc.nasa.gov/docs/StarChild/whos_who_level2/jemison.html.	• Mae Jemison went into space in September of 1992 as a mission specialist.

Apply

Choose a topic and find some sources on it that you can trust to be accurate. Do some research and take some notes of your own.

332 Argument Writing

English Language Learners

BEGINNING/INTERMEDIATE

Unfamiliar Words Ask a student to define *familiar*. Ask other students to give examples of things that are familiar. Repeat for *unfamiliar*. If students use a word that is unfamiliar in their writing, they should explain the word more fully. Point out that an extra sentence can be added to give more information about the unfamiliar word or idea.

ADVANCED/ADVANCED HIGH

Plagiarize/Paraphrase Explain the term *plagiarize*. Ask, *Is it okay to copy someone else's writing?* Repeat for *paraphrase*. Read a language-level appropriate newspaper article. Cut up the article and give students different sections. Have students write a paraphrase of their portion of the article. Then have a volunteer read the paraphrased article to the class.

Prewrite

Focus on **Organization**

The Rubric Says	The introduction, body, and conclusion are strong and compelling.
Writing Strategy	Use an Argument Map to plan the speech.

Writer's Term

Argument Map
An **Argument Map** organizes reasons and supporting evidence that support a claim.

An Argument Map can help me organize my thoughts. I'll put my claim at the left and connect my reasons to that. Then I'll connect supporting evidence to my reasons.

Argument Map

Claim:
Mae Jemison is the most driven and accomplished woman in astronautic history.

Reason:
She doesn't let anything hold her back.

Supporting Evidence: She graduated high school at age 16.

Supporting Evidence: She applied to NASA a second time to be admitted.

Supporting Evidence: She lived out her dreams regardless of her gender and ethnicity.

Reason:
She holds multiple degrees.

Supporting Evidence: She has Bachelor's degrees in chemical engineering and African and Afro-American Studies, and a Doctorate degree in medicine.

Reason:
She has many varied experiences.

Supporting Evidence: She has worked as a medical officer and teacher in the Peace Corps.

Supporting Evidence: She has worked in a Cambodian refugee camp and had her own practice in L.A.

Supporting Evidence: After becoming a doctor, she became an astronaut.

Reflect
How will the Argument Map help Leila organize her writing?

Apply
Organize your notes for your speech in an Argument Map.

Speech **333**

Conferencing

PEER TO PEER After each student has selected a topic, have partners share their work to this point. After reviewing their prewriting notes and organizers, partners should then consult on making necessary changes to complete their Argument Maps.

PEER GROUPS Have students work in groups of three or four. Have each student read his or her Argument Map aloud. Ask the other students in the group to take turns offering one suggestion to make it more helpful.

TEACHER-LED Schedule conferences with individual students. Before they speak with you, have students list their sources and add factual evidence to their Argument Maps.

Write
a Speech

Student Objectives

• Use an Argument Map to plan a speech. (p. 333)

Prewrite

Focus on **Organization**

Make an Argument Map Leila used an Argument Map to help her expand on her notes. Give students time to study the parts of the organizer. Review Leila's notes on page 332 and her Argument Map on page 333. Ask how the organizer differs from the notes. (Possible response: The notes list facts and their sources. The Map lists Leila's reasons for her claim and supporting details for each reason.)

Writer's Term

Argument Map Point out that the Argument Map begins with a compelling claim, which is the writer's opinion. The writer's reasons for the claim need to be supported by evidence from credible sources.

CCSS **Common Core State Standards**
W.6.1: Write arguments to support claims with clear reasons and relevant evidence. **W.6.8:** Gather relevant information from multiple print and digital sources; assess the credibility of each source; and quote or paraphrase the data and conclusions of others while avoiding plagiarism and providing basic bibliographic information for sources. **W.6.9:** Draw evidence from literary or informational texts to support analysis, reflection, and research. **SL.6.1:** Engage effectively in a range of collaborative discussions (one-on-one, in groups, and teacher-led) with diverse partners on *grade 6 topics, texts, and issues,* building on others' ideas and expressing their own clearly.

Speech **T333**

Write
a Speech

Week 2 • Day 3

Student Objectives

• Define unfamiliar words. *(p. 334)*

Draft

Focus on Word Choice

Draft a Speech After reading Leila's thoughts on this page, have students discuss how to sound knowledgeable, like an expert on the topic. Be sure students understand that words related to a topic serve to authenticate and enhance a speech. Point out that Leila's plan to use and define words related to her topic will establish her as an expert on her topic and inform the audience. Most importantly, remind students that it is the writer's responsibility to use and define domain-specific content words correctly.

Remind students what it means to draft a speech. (using their Argument Map to get ideas down on paper) They should not be overly concerned with correctness at this point.

Online Writing Center

Provides student eBooks with an **interactive writing pad** for drafting, revising, editing, and publishing.

Draft

Focus on **Word Choice**

The Rubric Says	Domain-specific content words are used correctly and defined clearly.
Writing Strategy	Define unfamiliar words.

As I write my draft, I'll use my Argument Map to get all of the important details down and to make sure I state my claim. I want to be accurate in my writing, so I'll use the correct domain-specific content words to describe my topic. Domain-specific content words are words that apply to a certain field, such as medicine or space exploration. If I use a word I don't think my readers will know, I'll be sure to explain its meaning. I may need to check the definitions in a dictionary or other resource. If I do, I will be sure to rewrite the definition in my own words.

Sometimes it's hard to avoid making mistakes in grammar, punctuation, and spelling when I'm getting my ideas on paper. That's OK. I know I can fix my mistakes later when I edit my writing. Part of my draft is on the next page.

334 Argument Writing

Differentiating Instruction

ENRICHMENT

Speech! Speech! Invite students to use the model speech and Leila's topic as springboards for writing and presenting short speeches (2–3 minutes) on role models of their choice. Be sure students verify evidence and practice their speeches before presentation.

REINFORCEMENT

Stake Your Claim Some students may need to recheck their planning notes to make sure they begin their draft strongly and engage the audience. Go over each student's claim to make sure it is clear and compelling. Remind students to include it near the beginning of their speech.

[DRAFT]

Mae Jemison
by Leila

On September 12, 1992, the Shuttle *Endeavor* hurtled off the launch pad, carrying the first African American woman into space. Mae Jemison had years of education and experience behind her. This space mission would add yet another achievement to her list of successes. She did not let her ethnicity, or cultural makeup, or the fact she was a woman hold her back. Mae Jemison is the most driven and accomplished woman in astronautic (having to do with astronauts) history.   **[claim]**

Born in Decatur, Alabama, in 1956 and raised in Chicago, Illinois, Mae Jemison became interested in science at an early age. A gifted student, she finished high school at age 16, won a scholarship, and attended college, where she earned Bachelor's degrees in chemical engineering and African and Afro-American Studies. She went on to earn a Doctorate of Medicine.   **[domain-specific content word]**

Reflect

How does Leila make her writing clear? What details help you agree with her claim?

Apply

Using your Argument Map as a guide, write a draft. Don't forget to clearly state your claim.

Write
a Speech

Student Objectives

• Complete a draft. *(p. 335)*

Continue Drafting Have a volunteer read Leila's draft. Students should agree that Leila has written a clear claim and defined content words correctly. Also recommend to students that they consult both print and digital word resources as they write their drafts.

Point out that the proofreading marks are provided as a reference for when students revise and edit their drafts. To help them focus on getting their thoughts down on paper, have students circle anything in their drafts they might want to change later but tell them not to worry about revising or editing their writing now.

Conferencing

PEER TO PEER Have partners exchange drafts and think of several questions they would like to ask to clarify information. Have them write their questions on sticky notes and affix them to their partners' drafts.

PEER GROUPS Have students work in groups of four. Students pass their drafts to the student on the right. Using the rubric on pages 326–327, each student writes one suggestion on a sticky note. Students affix their note to the draft and pass the draft to the right. The review ends when everyone receives his or her draft back with three helpful comments.

TEACHER-LED Schedule conferences with pairs of students. Have students read each other's drafts and coach them in giving and receiving constructive criticism.

CCSS Common Core State Standards

W.6.1.a: Introduce claim(s) and organize the reasons and evidence clearly. **W.6.1.b:** Support claim(s) with clear reasons and relevant evidence, using credible sources and demonstrating an understanding of the topic or text. **W.6.5:** With some guidance and support from peers and adults, develop and strengthen writing as needed by planning, revising, editing, rewriting, or trying a new approach.

Write
a Speech

Week 2 • Day 5

Student Objectives

- Use credible sources. (p. 336)

Revise

Focus on Ideas

Use Credible Websites Read Leila's thoughts and the information in the Writer's Term box with students. Then talk about using the Internet safely. If your library has a policy on using the Internet, share it with students. Remind them that a credible website means the information contained therein is accurate. Also point out that the facts they include in their speech should be current and verifiable. One way to verify information is to check for accuracy across several sources. Students should keep track of their sources in order to authenticate their findings.

Writer's Term _____

Credible Websites Consult the American Library Association (ALA) Great Web Sites for Kids at **www.ala.org/greatsites**. It provides a comprehensive list of credible websites on many topics. Use the site's key to find age-appropriate materials.

 Strategies for Writers Online

Go to **www.sfw.z-b.com** for additional online resources for students and teachers.

T336 Argument Writing

Revise
Focus on **Ideas**

The Rubric Says	Supporting evidence is accurate. Credible sources are cited.
Writing Strategy	Use credible sources.

Writer's Term _____
Credible Websites
Credible means "believable" or "trusted." Websites should always be evaluated to make sure they are credible and reliable.

I know from the rubric that the evidence I use has to be accurate. I'll get this kind of information from sources I can trust. Because websites vary in their reliability, or how much you can trust their information, my teacher has given me a checklist to evaluate sites. I'll look at who runs the website, whether there are advertisements (and, if so, who advertises), and whether the links are good and work. I'll also be sure to double-check my facts and details across several sources to make sure each source provides the same information about a certain fact. That way I'll know that the facts I use in my speech are true.

[DRAFT]   [checked facts in more than one source]

Born in Decatur, Alabama, in 1956 and raised in Chicago, Illinois, Mae Jemison became interested in science at an early age. A gifted student, she finished high school at age 16, won a scholarship, and attended college, where she earned Bachelor's degrees in chemical engineering and African and Afro-American Studies. She went on to earn a Doctorate of Medicine.

Apply

Check your sources to make sure they are reliable. Check your facts across multiple sources to see if the sources agree on similar facts.

336 Argument Writing

English Language Learners

BEGINNING/INTERMEDIATE

Transition Words Tell students that *transition* means "movement from one place or thing to another." In writing, transition words help us move between ideas. Write these sentences: *Many astronauts are scientists. Some astronauts are doctors. All astronauts are well trained. Most missions are successful.* Suggest they combine the sentences and show comparison or contrast using transition words such as *and, both, too, in addition, however, but,* and *in contrast.*

ADVANCED/ADVANCED HIGH

Credible Sources Explain that some websites are better than others because the information can be trusted. In other words, it is *credible*. Write *.org, .edu, .com, .net,* and *.gov* on the board. Circle *.org, .edu,* and *.gov*. Tell students that sites from these domains are usually more credible than others.

Revise

Focus on Organization

The Rubric Says	Appropriate transitions clarify relationships among ideas.
Writing Strategy	Use effective transitions to show how ideas are connected.

✏️ **Writer's Term**_____

Transitions

Transitions help readers move smoothly through a piece of writing. They show how ideas are connected. Transitions such as **first, next,** and **last** show sequence. Transitions such as **not only . . . but also** and **as a result** show how ideas relate.

Because my main audience will be listening to my speech, I want to make sure my ideas flow smoothly. My audience won't be able to go back and reread if they miss a connection! Using appropriate transitions will help me show how my ideas are related.

[DRAFT]

Not only has
∧Mae Jemison practiced medicine in the United States, in Los
, but she also has   In addition,
Angeles. ~~She also~~ practiced in a Cambodian refugee camp. ∧She

served as a medical officer in the Peace Corps in West Africa.

[inserted transitions to show relationships]

Reflect

How do transitions help Leila's speech?

Apply

Insert appropriate transitions to show your readers how your ideas relate to each other.

Speech 337

Conferencing

PEER TO PEER Have partners exchange drafts. After reading, ask each student to offer feedback on how to strengthen the speech. If needed, have students consult the model, the rubric, and the lessons for revising Ideas, Organization, and Sentence Fluency.

PEER GROUPS Have students form small groups. Have each student read aloud a section of his or her speech that might need improving. Ask each group member to offer one suggestion on how to strengthen it.

TEACHER-LED Schedule conferences to read each student's draft. Point out strengths and weaknesses. Talk about ways to improve the draft.

Write
a Speech

Student Objectives

- Use effective transitions to show how ideas are connected. (*p. 337*)

Revise

Focus on Organization

Use Transitions Have students read this page independently. Then write the words *not only, but also* on the board. Stress that these transitions (correlative conjunctions) are used in tandem when the writer wants to connect two related ideas, as Leila has done in the draft excerpt.

Then have students consider the Reflect question. They should agree that transitions connect and clarify ideas for the reader. Refer students to the list of transitions on page 524.

✏️ **Writer's Term**_____

Transitions Some transitions show time and location. Others are used to make a point (*in fact, for this reason*), compare/contrast (*similarly, although*), add information (*another, for example*), and summarize (*in the end, therefore*).

CCSS **Common Core State Standards**

W.6.1.b: Support claim(s) with clear reasons and relevant evidence, using credible sources and demonstrating an understanding of the topic or text. **W.6.1.c:** Use words, phrases, and clauses to clarify the relationships among claim(s) and reasons. **W.6.5:** With some guidance and support from peers and adults, develop and strengthen writing as needed by planning, revising, editing, rewriting, or trying a new approach. **L.6.4.c:** Consult reference materials (e.g., dictionaries, glossaries, thesauruses) both print and digital, to find the pronunciation of a word or determine or clarify its precise meaning or its part of speech.

Write a Speech

Week 3 • Day 2

Student Objectives

- Use phrases and clauses to vary sentences. *(p. 338)*

Revise

Focus on

Vary Sentence Beginnings Point out Leila's changes in the excerpt. Remind students that repeating sentence patterns can be boring for the audience. Have students return to the model on page 325 and look at the sentence patterns. Remind them that one of the reasons the speech is effective and enjoyable to read is sentence variety.

Have students read their drafts to find places where they can connect ideas and improve the flow. Recommend to students that they read aloud their speeches before making changes.

Writer's Term _____

Clauses and Phrases To vary sentence patterns, begin sentences with subordinating clauses and phrases. Subordinating conjunctions include common transition words, such as *after, as long as, since, unless,* and *while.*

Online Writing Center

Provides **interactive proofreading activities** for each genre.

Writing a Speech

Revise
Focus on **Sentence Fluency**

The Rubric Says	A variety of sentence patterns makes the text flow smoothly.
Writing Strategy	Use phrases and clauses to vary sentences.

Writer's Term _____

Clauses and Phrases
A **clause** is a group of words that has a subject and verb. A **phrase** is a group of words that has no subject or verb separate from those in the main part of the sentence.

As you know, my speech has to flow smoothly when I read it to an audience of listeners. Inserting some clauses and phases will vary the sentence patterns to make for easy listening. Added clauses and phrases will also be a way to include more information about my opinion. Here's some of my draft with a clause and a phrase that I added. Read it aloud to hear how the writing becomes less choppy and how the added text adds helpful information.

[DRAFT]

In addition,
She served as medical officer in the Peace Corps in
    where she also did some teaching
West Africa.
    [added clause]
    After pursuing engineering and medicine,
    It were time to look to space. She applied to NASA's training program. Her first application did not go through, so she applied again and was accepted.

[inserted phrase]

Apply
Use clauses and phrases to vary your sentences, add information, and make for easy listening.

338 Argument Writing

Optional Revising Lessons _____

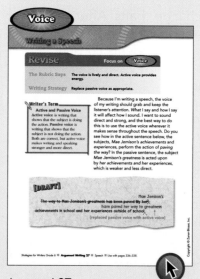

Argument 27

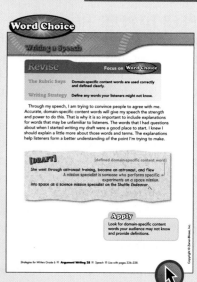

Argument 28

Go to ➡ **Strategies for Writers Grade 6 CD-ROM**

Edit
Focus on Conventions

The Rubric Says	The writing has been carefully edited. All forms of verbs are used correctly and effectively.
Writing Strategy	Check forms of *be* and change passive voice to active.

Writer's Term_____

Active and Passive Voice
A sentence in which the subject performs an action is in **active voice**. A sentence in which the subject is acted upon by something else is said to be in **passive voice**.

Now is the time for me to make sure that spelling, grammar, capitalization, and punctuation are all correct. I will check forms of the verb *be*, making sure the forms agree with their subjects. I will also change any instances of passive voice to active voice for a more direct and lively speech.

[DRAFT]

After pursuing engineering and medicine,
It were time to look to space. She applied to NASA's training
∧   ∧ was   [corrected form of verb *be*]
program. Her first application did not go through, so she applied
                    NASA accepted her
again and was accepted.
                    ∧   [changed passive voice to active voice]

Reflect

How does editing help Leila's speech? Do these edits make her writing more engaging?

Apply — Conventions

Edit your draft for spelling, grammar, capitalization, and punctuation.
Check for correct use of the verb *be*, and make sure you've avoided using passive sentences.
For more practice with the verb *be* and active voice, use the exercises on the next two pages.

Speech 339

Related Grammar Practice _____

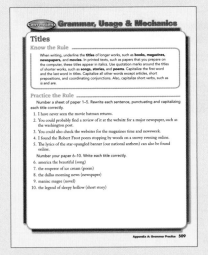

Student Edition page 509

Go to ➡ **Appendix A: Grammar Practice**

Student Objectives

• Check forms of *be* and change passive voice to active. *(p. 339)*

Edit

Focus on

Use Active Voice Remind students that accurate spelling, grammar, punctuation, and capitalization make a positive impression on the reader. Read and discuss page 339. Have students edit their writing for active voice.

If students are typing their speeches, remind them to use the editing features on the computer. Use the mini-lessons on pages T340 and T341 for students who need practice using forms of *be* and active voice.

Writer's Term_____

Active and Passive Voice Active voice announces the subject as the "doer" in the sentence. Passive voice relies on a helping verb plus a past-tense verb to create distance between the "doer" and the action.

CCSS Common Core State Standards
L.6.1: Demonstrate command of the conventions of standard English grammar and usage when writing or speaking. **L.6.3.a:** Vary sentence patterns for meaning, reader/listener interest, and style.

Conventions — Mini-Lesson

Student Objectives

- Use forms of *be* correctly. (p. 340)

Forms of *Be*

Have students read the information in Know the Rule. Ask students to explain the basic purpose of linking verbs. (to connect the subject to a word or words in the predicate that tell about the subject) To illustrate, write the following sentence on the board:

- *My friends are music enthusiasts.*

Ask students to identify the subject in the sentence. (friends) Then ask students to identify the *be* verb in the sentence. (are) Ask which words describe the friends. (music enthusiasts)

Before assigning the practice, remind students to use *am* after the pronoun *I*.

Online Writing Center

Provides **interactive grammar games** and **practice activities** in student eBook.

Forms of *Be*

Know the Rule

Am, is, was, are, and **were** are forms of the verb **be.** They often serve as linking verbs, connecting the subject of a sentence to a word or words in the predicate that tell about the subject.

First Person Singular	Second Person Singular and Plural	Third Person Singular
am	are, were	is, was

Practice the Rule

Number a sheet of paper from 1–10. Choose a verb from the list above to complete each sentence.

1. Right now, we _____ studying space exploration at school. are
2. I _____ excited to learn more about outer space this week. am
3. Some students _____ starting to think up space project ideas. are
4. Starting at a young age, Mae Jemison _____ motivated to become an astronaut. was
5. As she went through school, she _____ always drawn to the sciences. was
6. Her family _____ a great support to her and encouraged her love of science. was
7. They _____ always there to cheer her on with each new challenge. were
8. Mae _____ the first African American woman to enter space. was
9. Becoming an astronaut _____ a commendable achievement. is
10. I _____ hopeful that one day I will be an astronaut. am

Related Grammar Practice

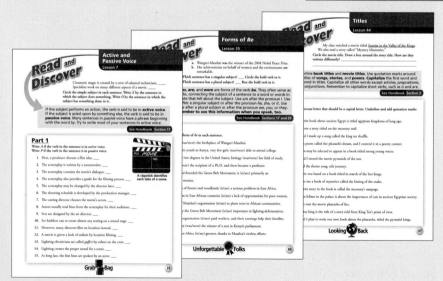

Pages 19, 93, 117

Go to → **G.U.M. Student Practice Book**

Active and Passive Voice

Know the Rule

If the subject performs an action, the verb is said to be in **active voice**. If the subject is acted upon by something else, the verb is said to be in **passive voice**. Many sentences in passive voice have a phrase beginning with the word *by*. Both are correct. However, active voice makes writing more interesting for the reader.

Practice the Rule

Number a sheet of paper 1–10. Write **passive** for each sentence that is in passive voice. Write **active** for each sentence that is in active voice.

1. School was taken seriously by Mae Jemison. passive
2. She had a variety of interests and excelled at each. active
3. It is important to follow your dreams. active
4. Dr. Jemison was accepted into NASA's astronaut training program. passive
5. Final tests on the space unit were passed out to us. passive
6. Many people find the requirements to be an astronaut difficult to meet. active
7. We were taken to the spacesuit fitting room. passive
8. Envelopes were handed out, revealing who would be the next science mission specialist. passive
9. She intends to fly to the moon. active
10. Mistakes were made that delayed the launch of the spacecraft. passive

Speech **341**

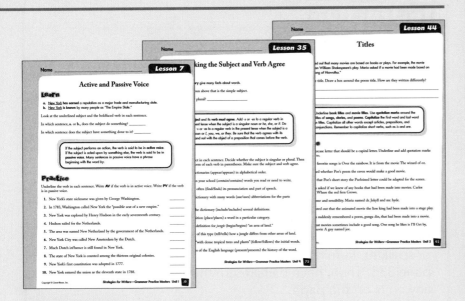

Pages 19, 75, 93

Go to ⟹ *Grammar Practice Masters*

Student Objectives

• Use active and passive voice correctly. *(p. 341)*

Active and Passive Voice

Read and discuss the information in Know the Rule. Remind students that using active voice reaches out to the listener/reader. Before assigning the practice, write the following pair of sentences on the board:

• *I know more about Marie Curie after reading the model speech.*

• *More about Marie Curie is known by me after reading the model speech.*

Have a volunteer read the sentences aloud. Students should agree that the information in the first sentence is clearer than in the second. Explain that often the passive voice uses more words to state the same information in a roundabout, sometimes awkward way. However, there are times when passive voice is appropriate.

Have students complete the practice, and go over their answers together. To extend the mini-lesson, assist students in rewriting all the sentences using active voice.

CCSS **Common Core State Standards**

W.6.5: With some guidance and support from peers and adults, develop and strengthen writing as needed by planning, revising, editing, rewriting, or trying a new approach. **L.6.3:** Use knowledge of language and its conventions when writing, speaking, reading, or listening. **L.6.3.b:** Maintain consistency in style and tone.

Speech **T341**

Write
a Speech

Student Objectives

- Discuss preparation for publishing and presentation. (p. 342)
- Use a final editing checklist. (p. 342)

Publish ✛Presentation

Publishing Strategy Discuss other publishing options, such as entering a speech contest or presenting to a school group. Also talk about the importance of practicing a speech. Ask students what they will need to do ahead of time. (Possible responses: type the speech, memorize the introduction and conclusion, practice good eye contact, use pacing and voice effectively) Discuss the responsibilities of the audience. (being attentive, respectful, quiet) Have students use the final checklist or one you provide to prepare a final copy of their speeches.

▶ Strategies for Writers Online
Go to **www.sfw.z-b.com** for additional online resources for students and teachers.

Writing a Speech

Publish ✛Presentation

Publishing Strategy	Give the speech to the class.
Presentation Strategy	Choose visuals that support the claim.

Now I am ready to publish my speech. One way to publish a piece of writing is to read it aloud to an audience, and that is just what a speech is meant for! To add to my speech, I will use visuals that support my claim. I could project images from a computer, but I have decided to make a poster with photos of Mae Jemison.

My pictures show Mae's many achievements: graduating from Cornell Medical College, working in the Peace Corps, Mae's NASA head shot, and floating in zero gravity on her monumental space flight. Before I give my final speech, I'll read it one more time, going through this final checklist.

My Final Checklist

Did I—

- ✔ make sure all verb forms are used correctly, especially the verb *be*?
- ✔ replace passive voice with active voice, as appropriate?
- ✔ check all spelling, grammar, punctuation, and capitalization?
- ✔ create presentation visuals that support my claim?

Apply
Make a final checklist and use it to finalize your speech. Then get ready to give your speech!

Differentiating Instruction

ENRICHMENT
Plan a Presentation Encourage students to create invitations to faculty, family members, and friends who would be interested in hearing the speeches. Students may also want to design programs for the event and include a list of the speakers and speech titles. Remind students to edit for accuracy before making copies.

REINFORCEMENT
Proofread Like a Pro Have pairs of students exchange drafts and edit strategically. For example, have each pair begin by proofreading only for active voice, or punctuation, or spelling. Remind editors to use the proofreading marks on page 335. Then, have pairs return the speeches and verify any edits on the page.

Mae Jemison

by Leila

On September 12, 1992, the Shuttle *Endeavor* hurtled off the launch pad, carrying the first African American woman into space. Mae Jemison had years of education and experience behind her. This space mission would add yet another achievement to her list of successes. She did not let her ethnicity, or cultural makeup, or the fact she was a woman hold her back. Mae Jemison is the most driven and accomplished woman in astronautic (having to do with astronauts) history.

Born in Decatur, Alabama, in 1956 and raised in Chicago, Illinois, Mae Jemison became interested in science at an early age. A gifted student, she finished high school at age 16, won a scholarship, and attended college, where she earned Bachelor's degrees in chemical engineering and African and Afro-American Studies. She went on to earn a Doctorate of Medicine.

Not only has Mae Jemison practiced medicine in the United States, in Los Angeles, but she also has practiced in a Cambodian refugee camp. In addition, she served as a medical officer in the Peace Corps in West Africa, where she also did some teaching.

After pursuing engineering and medicine, it was time to look to space. She applied to NASA's training program. Her first application did not go through, so she applied again and NASA accepted her. She went through astronaut training, became an astronaut, and flew into space as a science mission specialist on the Shuttle *Endeavor*. A mission specialist is someone who performs specific experiments on a space mission.

Mae Jemison's achievements in school and her experiences outside of school have paved her way to greatness. Her accomplishments have set her apart from all other astronauts of her time.

Works Consulted:

Dejoie, Joyce, and Elizabeth Truelove. "Dr. Mae Jemison." http://starchild.gsfc .nasa.gov/docs/StarChild/whos_who_level2/jemison.html.

Jemison, Mae. *Where the Wind Goes: Moments from My Life.* New York: Scholastic Press: 2001.

"Mae Jemison." http://www.notablebiographies.com/Ho-Jo/Jemison-Mae.html.

Reflect

How well do you think Leila did as she brought her speech through the writing process?

Speech 343

Technology Tip — for 21st Century Literacies

Publishing students' work doesn't have to be limited to printing a hard copy or pressing "post and publish." Consider creating a free password-protected video stream from the classroom using a tool such as Ustream. Broadcast student speeches, poetry slams, presentations, and so on to an audience with whom you share the URL and password. Purposefully expanding the audience expands the possibility that students can use these speeches to teach or to do something. Further, the audience provides feedback through a real-time chat, which extends the options for assessment and learning.

See **www.sfw.z-b.com** for further information about and links to these websites and tools.

Write a Speech

Week 3 • Day 5

Student Objectives

- Use a speech rubric. *(pp. 326–327)*
- Share a published speech. *(p. 343)*

Presentation Strategy Students should remember to use good formatting. Explain that a neat, legible copy will help them practice their presentations. If the speeches will be recorded, schedule enough time for students to prepare their final speeches, including visuals, and to practice giving their speeches several times.

Invite students to add visual elements to enhance their presentation. Remind students that visuals should be neat and large enough for the audience to see or incorporated into a slide presentation.

Reflecting on a Speech

Have students refer to the rubric on pages 326–327 as they read Leila's final copy on page 343. Remind them that Leila's revisions and edits have shaped her final copy.

CCSS Common Core State Standards

W.6.4: Produce clear and coherent writing in which the development, organization, and style are appropriate to task, purpose, and audience. **W.6.6:** Use technology, including the Internet, to produce and publish writing as well as to interact and collaborate with others; demonstrate sufficient command of keyboarding skills to type a minimum of three pages in a single sitting. **W.6.10:** Write routinely over extended time frames (time for research, reflection, and revision) and shorter time frames (a single sitting or a day or two) for a range of discipline-specific tasks, purposes, and audiences. **SL.6.5:** Include multimedia components (e.g., graphics, images, music, sound) and visual displays in presentations to clarify information.

Argument Test Planner

WEEK 1

Day 1
Introduce
Argument Test Writing

Student Objectives
- Learn the parts of a writing prompt.

Student Activities
- Discuss the components of the writing prompt. (pp. 344–345)

Day 2
Analyze
Introduce the Scoring Guide

Student Objectives
- Relate a scoring guide to a traits rubric.
- Read a writing prompt response model.

Student Activities
- Read and discuss **Writing Traits in the Scoring Guide.** (p. 346)
- Read the writing prompt response model. (p. 347)

Day 3
Analyze
Apply the Scoring Guide

Student Objectives
- Apply the scoring guide to the writing prompt response model.

Student Activities
- Read and discuss **Using the Scoring Guide to Study the Model.** (pp. 348–349)

WEEK 2

Day 1
Write
Prewrite: Ideas

Student Objectives
- Study a writing prompt to know what to do.
- Apply the six traits of writing to the writing prompt.

Student Activities
- Read and discuss **Prewrite: Focus on Ideas.** (pp. 352–353)
- Apply the prewriting strategy.

Day 2
Write
Prewrite: Ideas

Student Objectives
- Respond to the task.

Student Activities
- Read and discuss **Prewrite: Focus on Ideas.** (p. 354)
- Apply the prewriting strategy.

Day 3
Write
Prewrite: Organization

Student Objectives
- Choose a graphic organizer.

Student Activities
- Read and discuss **Prewrite: Focus on Organization.** (p. 355)
- Apply the prewriting strategy.

WEEK 3

Day 1
Write
Revise: Organization

Student Objectives
- Use transitions to organize the writing.

Student Activities
- Read and discuss **Revise: Focus on Organization.** (p. 360)

Day 2
Write
Revise: Voice

Student Objectives
- Avoid language that is too casual.

Student Activities
- Read and discuss **Revise: Focus on Voice.** (p. 361)

Day 3
Write
Revise: Word Choice

Student Objectives
- Choose words and phrases to convey ideas precisely.

Student Activities
- Read and discuss **Revise: Focus on Word Choice.** (p. 362)

Note: Optional Revising Lessons appear on the *Strategies for Writers* CD-ROM.

Analyze
Apply the Scoring Guide

Student Objectives

- Continue to apply the scoring guide to the writing prompt response model.

Student Activities

- Read and discuss **Using the Scoring Guide to Study the Model.** *(p. 350)*

Analyze
Time Management

Student Objectives

- Learn how to plan time during a writing test.

Student Activities

- Read and discuss **Planning My Time.** *(p. 351)*

Write
Prewrite: Organization

Student Objectives

- Check the graphic organizer against the scoring guide.

Student Activities

- Read and discuss **Prewrite: Focus on Organization.** *(pp. 356–357)*

Write
Draft: Ideas

Student Objectives

- State the position clearly.
- Include reasons and supporting details.

Student Activities

- Read and discuss **Draft: Focus on Ideas.** *(p. 358–359)*
- Draft an argument writing test.

Write
Edit: Conventions

Student Objectives

- Check the grammar, spelling, capitalization, and punctuation.

Student Activities

- Read and discuss **Edit: Focus on Conventions.** *(pp. 363–364)*
- Apply the editing strategy.

Review
Test Tips

Student Objectives

- Review tips for writing for a test.

Student Activities

- Read and review the **Test Tips.** *(p. 365)*

To complete the chapter in fewer days, combine the learning objectives and activities in a way that supports students as they write.

Resources at-a-Glance

Differentiating Instruction

Using the Scoring
   Guide T348–T350
Planning T351
Prewrite T354–T355
Revise T360–T361
Edit T363

For additional Differentiating Instruction activities, see Strategies for Writers *Extensions Online at* **www.sfw.z-b.com.**

English Language Learners

Using the Scoring
   Guide T346–T347
Prewrite T352–T353
Draft T358–T359

School Home Connection Letter

Reproducible letter (in English and Spanish) appears on the *Strategies for Writers* CD-ROM and at **www.sfw.z-b.com.**

Online Essay Grader and Writing Tutor

Powered by Vantage Learning's MY Access!®, includes writing prompts and ongoing feedback for students as they write. Available for Grades 5–8.

Online Writing Center

Provides IWB resources, interactive games and practice activities, videos, eBooks, and a virtual file cabinet.

 Strategies for Writers Online

Go to **www.sfw.z-b.com** for free online resources for students and teachers.

Introduce
Argument Test Writing

Week 1 • Day 1

Student Objectives

- Learn the parts of a writing prompt. *(pp. 344–345)*

Read the Writing Prompt

Argument Test Writing Tell students that they are going to apply what they have learned about argument writing to writing an argument test. Note that when they write for a test, they will be given a specific writing prompt and a certain amount of time in which to write. Then their writing will be evaluated, as with any test. Assure students that they do not need to be anxious about writing a test, because the skills they have already practiced will help them do a good job.

Make sure students understand that the scoring guide contains traits similar to those they have seen in the rubrics throughout this unit. Note that just as a rubric includes the qualities of a good paper, the scoring guide includes the qualities of a good writing test.

Read the writing prompt model. Tell students that their writing will not receive a strong grade if it misses the topic or uses a form of writing other than the assigned form.

Strategies for Writers Online
Go to **www.sfw.z-b.com** for additional online resources for students and teachers.

Argument
test writing

Read the Writing Prompt

When you take a writing test, you'll be given a writing prompt. Most writing prompts have three parts:

Setup This part of the writing prompt gives you the background information you need to get ready to write.

Task This part of the writing prompt tells you exactly what you are supposed to write: an argument essay.

Scoring Guide This section tells how your writing will be scored. To do well on the test, you should make sure your writing does everything on the list.

> **R**emember the rubrics you have been using? When you take a writing test, you don't always have all of the information that's on a rubric. However, the scoring guide is a lot like a rubric. It lists everything you need to think about to write a good paper. Like the rubrics you've used in this unit, many scoring guides are based upon the six important traits of writing:

Ideas   Organization   Voice

Word Choice   Sentence Fluency   Conventions

Online Essay Grader and Writing Tutor

Powered by Vantage Learning's MY Access!®, this tool gives students

- immediate, ongoing, sentence-by-sentence feedback.
- helpful suggestions to improve their draft.
- a holistic score and a trait-specific score on their final draft.
- unlimited response submissions to the prompts.

Writing MODEL Prompt

Your community is trying to decide between adding a skateboard park in the empty lot adjacent to the city park or putting in more picnic tables. Some of the members of the community feel a skateboard park would be too dangerous, but others say there are plenty of picnic tables and a skateboard park would provide a safer alternative for all the kids in the community who like to skateboard.

Write an argument essay for members of your community stating your support for either the skateboard park or the new picnic tables.

Be sure your writing

- clearly identifies your position and contains supporting facts and reasons.

- is well organized and contains an introduction, body, and conclusion.

- establishes and maintains a formal style.

- uses precise language.

- has varied sentence structures.

- contains correct grammar, punctuation, capitalization, and spelling.

Stress the importance of following the instructions in the task for a writing test. Then write the following terms on the board and review:

Setup The setup does just what its name says: It gets writers ready to do a good job. The setup gets writers to think about the writing in general before they choose a topic.

Task The task tells students not only what to write about, but also what kind of writing to do: narrative, descriptive, informative/ explanatory, or argument.

Scoring Guide The scoring guide helps students plan and evaluate their writing. Help students understand how the scoring guide is similar to the rubrics they have used by asking these questions:

- Which bullet focuses on ideas? (first)

- Which bullet focuses on organizing the ideas? (second)

- Which bullet focuses on voice? (third)

- Which bullet focuses on choosing the right words? (fourth)

- Which bullet focuses on sentence fluency? (fifth)

- Which bullet focuses on perfecting the conventions of writing? (sixth)

CCSS Common Core State Standards

W.6.5: With some guidance and support from peers and adults, develop and strengthen writing as needed by planning, revising, editing, rewriting, or trying a new approach. **W.6.9:** Draw evidence from literary or informational texts to support analysis, reflection, and research. **SL.6.1:** Engage effectively in a range of collaborative discussions (one-on-one, in groups, and teacher-led) with diverse partners on grade 6 topics, texts, and issues, building on others' ideas and expressing their own clearly.

Analyze
the Scoring Guide

Student Objectives

- Relate a scoring guide to a traits rubric. *(p. 346)*
- Read a writing prompt response model. *(p. 347)*

Writing Traits in the Scoring Guide

Scoring Guide as a Rubric Use the first item in the scoring guide as an example: *Be sure your writing clearly identifies your position and contains supporting facts and reasons.* Ask which trait this item corresponds to. (Ideas) Ask if this description would apply to a personal narrative, a descriptive essay, or a factual report. (no, because it says to state and support a position) Discuss each of the items in the scoring guide and corresponding writing traits. Explain that Conventions are the same for all writing.

Point out that students will sometimes receive writing prompts that do not include guidance for each of the six categories in the rubric by name. However, students can rely on their writing experiences to remember the traits of good argument writing, as listed on page 346.

Online Writing Center

Provides six **interactive anchor papers** for each mode of writing.

T346 Argument Writing

Writing Traits in the Scoring Guide

The scoring guide in the prompt on page 345 has been made into this chart. Does it remind you of the rubrics you've used? Not all prompts include all of the writing traits, but this one does. Use them to do your best writing. Remember to work neatly and put your name on each page.

 **Ideas**
- Be sure your writing clearly identifies your position and contains supporting facts and reasons.

 **Organization**
- Be sure your writing is well organized and contains an introduction, body, and conclusion.

 **Voice**
- Be sure your writing establishes and maintains a formal style.

 **Word Choice**
- Be sure your writing uses precise language.

 **Sentence Fluency**
- Be sure your writing has varied sentence structures.

 **Conventions**
- Be sure your writing contains correct grammar, punctuation, capitalization, and spelling.

Look at Sam Patel's essay on the next page. Did he follow the scoring guide?

346 Argument Writing

English Language Learners

BEGINNING/INTERMEDIATE

The Writing Process Review the steps in the writing process using simple words. Use the following words to substitute for *prewrite, draft, revise, edit,* and *publish: about/plan, write, change, fix,* and *show.* Remind students to follow all of these steps during a writing test.

INTERMEDIATE

Organizing an Argument Essay Have partners review how to organize an argument essay. What information belongs in the introductory paragraph? In the body? In the last paragraph? Have students discuss which type of graphic organizer would be most helpful.

A Safe Place to Skate

by Sam Patel

By proposing a skateboard park to be built next to the city park, it's clear that members of our community realize that the large number of skateboarders who live here need a safe and accessible place to practice their sport. Although there are many people opposed to the skateboard park, I'd like to explain to you why I think this is a good idea.

First of all, our community's parks are there to provide enjoyment for the community and to promote the safety and welfare of the residents, and that should include skateboarders, too. Already, the park contains places to enjoy baseball, soccer, football, basketball, and tennis. But these days, skateboarding is just as popular. There is even a skateboard club in the community. These skateboarders need a place to go, yet there is not a place within our entire community that welcomes them.

Next, without a place that they can go to skateboard, many skateboarders use the street, which is not a safe alternative. I see many skateboarders riding along the streets and using curbs and stairways to practice their jumps. They also use plywood and other materials to build their own ramps, which do not look very safe at all. A skateboard park, though, would provide jumps that have been built with skateboarders' safety in mind. The many skateboarders who live in the community would not have to ride in the street and potentially get hit by cars.

Finally, although there are people in our town who want to add more benches, our park already contains enough benches and picnic tables. On the days that I have been to the park, including weekends, weekdays, and during the summer (when it is usually busiest) there have always been open benches and tables. It is clear to me that at this time we do not need additional benches.

Let's remember what our parks are here for, and let's put in something that will keep our skateboarders safe and address the needs of the many people enjoying this popular sport.

Read the Model

Understand the Prompt Remind students to keep the scoring guide in mind as they read the model essay, "A Safe Place to Skate." Read the title aloud. Then ask students if they have an idea what this essay will support. (the writer's position on having a safe place to skate) As they read the essay, tell students to look for the writer's argument and the evidence that supports it. After reading, ask a volunteer to read again the model writing prompt on page 345. Discuss how the writer responded to the prompt. Students should agree that the writer does state and support her position with convincing evidence.

ADVANCED
Organizing Supporting Arguments To help with organization during an argument writing test, suggest students use an Argument Map graphic organizer or an Outline. Give partners a topic, and have them complete a graphic organizer to record their opinions and reasons.

ADVANCED HIGH
Kinds of Sentences Tell students they can make their writing more interesting by varying the types of sentences they write. Write the following sentences on the board: *Share your opinions with your fellow students! Would you like to write an editorial for the school paper? Writing for the school paper can be a fun activity.* Ask students which sentence sounds more dramatic. Write a few plain sentences on the board, and have students suggest ways to make them more dramatic by using questions, exclamations, or commands.

CCSS Common Core State Standards
R/Inf.6.1: Cite textual evidence to support analysis of what the text says explicitly as well as inferences drawn from the text. **R/Inf.6.6:** Determine an author's point of view or purpose in a text and explain how it is conveyed in the text. **SL.6.1.a:** Come to discussions prepared, having read or studied required material; explicitly draw on that preparation by referring to evidence on the topic, text, or issue to probe and reflect on ideas under discussion.

Analyze
the Model

Student Objectives

- Apply the scoring guide to the writing prompt response model. *(pp. 348–349)*

Using the Scoring Guide to Study the Model

Review the Scoring Guide Write *Scoring Guide* on the board. Ask why the list of items on page 345 is called a scoring guide. (Possible response: It will be used to evaluate, or score, the essay.) Point out that a rubric and a scoring guide serve the same purposes.

Ask:

- Who uses the scoring guide? (evaluator and writer)

- When and why does the evaluator use the scoring guide? (when the test is finished; to evaluate and score the test)

- When and why would the writer use the scoring guide? (as he or she writes; to make sure to include the items to be scored)

Use the Scoring Guide Have students use the Writing Traits in the Scoring Guide chart on page 346 to evaluate the model essay on page 347.

 Strategies for Writers Online
Go to **www.sfw.z-b.com** for additional online resources for students and teachers.

Using the Scoring Guide to Study the Model

Now let's use the scoring guide to check Sam's writing test, "A Safe Place to Skate." Let's see how well his essay meets each of the six writing traits.

 **Ideas**
- The writing clearly identifies your position and contains supporting facts and reasons.

There is no doubt in the reader's mind that Sam is in favor of a skateboard park. In the first paragraph, he states this position clearly. He also offers a supporting reason that adults in the community agree with.

> By proposing a skateboard park to be built next to the city park, it's clear that members of our community realize that the large number of skateboarders who live here need a safe and accessible place to practice their sport. . . . I'd like to explain to you why I think this is a good idea.

Organization
- The writing is well organized and contains an introduction, body, and conclusion.

Sam's essay is well organized. He includes an introductory paragraph, three paragraphs to support his opinion, and a conclusion paragraph to wrap things up. Here is Sam's conclusion.

> Let's remember what our parks are here for, and let's put in something that will keep our skateboarders safe and address the needs of the many people enjoying this popular sport.

Differentiating Instruction

ENRICHMENT

Write a Rubric To further understand how the writing traits in the scoring guide relate to a writing rubric, have students create a 6-point rubric based on the writing traits for this writing test and provide descriptors in each column for each of the traits. Share the rubric with the class to guide their writing.

Voice

• The writer establishes and maintains a formal style.

Sam's audience is adults who make decisions about public spaces. He speaks directly to them in a respectful and formal tone. His purpose is to convince them that a skateboard park is needed, and he stays focused on that with supporting reasons.

> I see many skateboarders riding along the streets and using curbs and stairways to practice their jumps. They also use plywood and other materials to build their own ramps, which do not look very safe at all. A skateboard park, though, would provide jumps that have been built with skateboarders' safety in mind.

Word Choice

• The writing uses precise language.

Sam uses precise words to make a strong impression on the reader. Here he specifies which sports are already accommodated in the parks. He also uses the specific words *entire* and *welcomes* rather than using a more general phrase such as "there isn't a place for them to go."

> Already, the park contains places to enjoy baseball, soccer, football, basketball, and tennis. But these days, skateboarding is just as popular. There is even a skateboard club in the community. These skateboarders need a place to go, yet there is not a place within our entire community that welcomes them.

Argument Test Writing 349

Find More Examples Explain that pages 348–349 will show how the model meets the writing traits for **Ideas, Organization, Voice,** and **Word Choice.** Have students look for additional examples of each trait in the model.

Think About the Traits Once students have discussed the model argument essay, have them form discussion groups to consider which traits they think are most important. Of course, all the traits are important in every piece of writing, but in any piece of writing, some traits stand out more than other traits. Students might say, for example, that the trait of **Organization** is very important because the supporting evidence must be presented logically. Still others may say that **Word Choice** is important because compelling language helps to convince the reader. Have the groups decide on two or three traits and share their reasons for selecting them.

REINFORCEMENT

Use the Traits Review the function of the scoring guide. Have students review the rubric in the Argument Essay chapter on page 282. Point out the similarities and differences between that rubric and the scoring guide on page 346. Make sure students understand that although a scoring guide does not include criteria for various levels of accomplishment, it does provide guidance in the six key areas: Ideas, Organization, Voice, Word Choice, Sentence Fluency, and Conventions. Explain that just as traits in a rubric are used to assess writing, criteria in a scoring guide are used to assess test writing. Remind students to consult the scoring guide when they write for a test.

CCSS Common Core State Standards

R/Inf.6.8: Trace and evaluate the argument and specific claims in a text, distinguishing claims that are supported by reasons and evidence from claims that are not. **SL.6.1.b:** Follow rules for collegial discussions, set specific goals and deadlines, and define individual roles as needed. **SL.6.1.c:** Pose and respond to specific questions with elaboration and detail by making comments that contribute to the topic, text, or issue under discussion.

Analyze
the Model

Week 1 • Day 4

Student Objectives

- Continue to apply the scoring guide to the writing prompt response model. (p. 350)

Analyze the Model Have students read Leila's comments and example for **Sentence Fluency**. Ask students to find other sentences in the model that flow well. Explain that using a variety of sentences is a good strategy for creating interest and keeping an essay moving along.

Then have students read and consider the information and example for **Conventions**. Remind students that using conventions correctly is the writer's responsibility. Point out that even the most compelling ideas will be lost on readers if errors make the writing hard to understand. Ask students to think about how difficult it is to "read through errors." Then point out that in test writing, the writer does not have a second chance to correct mistakes. Emphasize that editing is done in the last five minutes of test writing. Therefore, students should remember to check their test for the kinds of errors they tend to make and correct them first.

Strategies for Writers Online
Go to **www.sfw.z-b.com** for additional online resources for students and teachers.

Using the Scoring Guide to Study the Model

- The writing has varied sentence structures.

In the paragraph below, Sam's sentences are varied. He includes introductory phrases, transition words, and a compound sentence. This variety helps keep the reader's interest.

First of all, our community's parks are there to provide enjoyment for the community and to promote the safety and welfare of the residents, and that should include skateboarders, too. Already, the park contains places to enjoy baseball, soccer, football, basketball, and tennis. But these days, skateboarding is just as popular. There is even a skateboard club in the community. These skateboarders need a place to go, yet there is not a place within our entire community that welcomes them.

- The essay contains correct grammar, punctuation, capitalization, and spelling.

I think Sam did a great job with his grammar and mechanics. From what I can see, he did not make any serious mistakes in capitalization, punctuation, sentence structure, or spelling. Look at the section below. See any mistakes? Neither did I.

By proposing a skateboard park to be built next to the city park, it's clear that members of our community realize that the large number of skateboarders who live here need a safe and accessible place to practice their sport. Although there are many people opposed to the skateboard park, I'd like to explain to you why I think this is a good idea.

Differentiating Instruction

ENRICHMENT

Set the Clock First ask students to explain the stopwatch visual on page 351. (Possible responses: Leila will have one hour to write the test. For this reason, the watch shows 60 minutes. The color sections tell Leila how much time she should spend on each task.) Challenge students to create two colorized versions: one to represent a shorter testing period and one to represent a longer one. Post their work in class and use the clocks for various timed writing projects.

Planning My Time

Before giving us a writing test prompt, my teacher tells us how much time we'll have to complete the test. Since I'm already familiar with the writing process, I can think about how much total time I need and then divide it up into the different parts of the writing process. If the test takes an hour, here's how I can organize my time. Planning your time will help you, too!

Step 4:
Edit
5 minutes

Step 1:
Prewrite
25 minutes

Step 3:
Revise
15 minutes

Step 2:
Draft
15 minutes

REINFORCEMENT

Start the Clock To prepare students for writing on demand, divide class work for a variety of activities. Using the clock on page 351 as a model, write a time schedule on the board. Have students practice using it so that they grow accustomed to dividing their time and completing their tasks. Talk about how observing time limits during test writing will help them succeed.

Analyze
Time Management

Week 1 • Day 5

Student Objectives

• Learn how to plan time during a writing test. *(p. 351)*

Planning My Time

Time Management Explain to students that when they write for a test, they must complete all the steps of the writing process quickly. Students may be surprised that Leila has allotted so much of the writing time—25 minutes out of 60—to prewriting. Ask students why this much time is necessary. (Without time for planning, they may begin to write a draft that does not respond to the task.) Point out that drafting and revising together take a little longer—30 minutes—than prewriting, leaving five minutes at the end for editing.

CCSS **C**ommon **C**ore **S**tate **S**tandards

W.6.10: Write routinely over extended time frames (time for research, reflection, and revision) and shorter time frames (a single sitting or a day or two) for a range of discipline-specific tasks, purposes, and audiences.
SL.6.1.c: Pose and respond to specific questions with elaboration and detail by making comments that contribute to the topic, text, or issue under discussion.
SL.6.1.d: Review the key ideas expressed and demonstrate understanding of multiple perspectives through reflection and paraphrasing.

Write
an Argument Test

Week 2 • Day 1

Student Objectives

- Study a writing prompt to know what to do. (*p. 352*)
- Apply the six traits of writing to the writing prompt. (*p. 353*)

Prewrite

Focus on Ideas

Study the Writing Prompt Walk students through Leila's thoughts on page 353, encouraging them to add their own responses. For example, how will they support their position? (Possible response: Be sure to include supporting evidence.) What belongs in the body paragraphs? (Possible response: logically ordered reasons backed up by facts and examples)

Discuss the Traits Help students build confidence in using the traits to guide and inform their writing. Divide students into small groups and assign each group a trait. Have the groups discuss why the traits are important. Encourage students to share reflections on their own argument writing experiences.

▶ Strategies for Writers Online

Go to **www.sfw.z-b.com** for additional online resources for students and teachers.

Prewrite
Focus on **Ideas**

Writing Strategy Study the writing prompt to find out what to do.

When you take a writing test, study the writing prompt so you know just what you need to do. The writing prompt usually has three parts. Although the parts may not be labeled, you should be able to find them and label them on your own. Take a look at how I marked my writing prompt. First I found the setup, task, and scoring guide in the writing prompt. Then I circled key words in the setup and the task that tell what kind of writing I need to do. I circled the setup in purple and the task in red.

My Writing Test Prompt

Setup —
Your school is trying to decide on a (cover image and saying for this year's school yearbook.) They want an image that will be visually appealing and a saying that will represent the school well.

Task —
Come up with an idea for the cover of your school's yearbook and (write an argument essay to convince the other students to agree with your choice.)

Scoring Guide —
Be sure your writing
- clearly identifies your position and contains supporting facts and reasons.
- is well organized and contains an introduction, body, and conclusion.
- establishes and maintains a formal style.
- uses precise language.
- has varied sentence structures.
- contains correct grammar, punctuation, capitalization, and spelling.

352 Argument Writing

English Language Learners

BEGINNING/INTERMEDIATE

Writing Prompt Give students a copy of the standard argument test writing prompt. Have them look at each word in the prompt and circle the words they do not know. Then teach the most important words, such as *argument essay*, *position*, *supporting facts*, *formal style*, or *conclusion*. Have higher-level ELLs work with lower-level ELLs to review meanings.

INTERMEDIATE

Writing Prompt Have students read the argument writing prompt and write down words they do not know. Review how to ask for help, such as, *What does* position *mean? Does* position *mean "my side in an argument"*? Have them practice asking and answering with two other students. Finally, ask students to write their answers; for example, *A position is the main idea of an argument.* Review as a class.

Think about how the scoring guide relates to the six writing traits you've studied in the rubrics. All of the traits might not be included in every scoring guide, but you need to remember them all to write a good argument test.

Ideas
- Be sure your writing clearly identifies your position and contains supporting facts and reasons.

I'll state my position clearly in the first paragraph. Then I'll include relevant supporting facts and reasons in each paragraph.

Organization
- Be sure your writing is well organized and contains an introduction, body, and conclusion.

I'll begin my essay with an introductory paragraph. Then I'll write the body and finish with a concluding statement that sums up my argument.

Voice
- Be sure your writing establishes and maintains a formal style.

As I write, I'll stay focused on my purpose and be convincing. I'll keep my language formal and respectful to my audience.

Word Choice
- Be sure your writing uses precise language.

Precise language that sticks to my topic will help me sound like I know what I'm talking about—and help convince my reader of my opinion.

Sentence Fluency
- Be sure your writing has varied sentence structures.

I don't want my reader to lose interest, so I'll be sure to use a variety of sentence types, including questions and exclamations.

Conventions
- Be sure your writing contains correct grammar, punctuation, capitalization, and spelling.

I'll read my essay once I have completed it to find and fix any spelling and grammar mistakes.

ADVANCED

Writing Prompt Make a few copies of the argument writing prompt. Cut apart the sentences in the scoring guide. Have partners work together to assign the sentences to one of the rubric writing traits—Ideas, Organization, Voice, Word Choice, Sentence Fluency, and Conventions.

ADVANCED HIGH

Writing Prompt Have students read the argument writing prompt and write down no more than three words in each part of the prompt that they think are most important. Then have them compare with a partner and discuss the differences.

CCSS Common Core State Standards
R/Inf.6.1: Cite textual evidence to support analysis of what the text says explicitly as well as inferences drawn from the text. SL.6.1.c: Pose and respond to specific questions with elaboration and detail by making comments that contribute to the topic, text, or issue under discussion. SL.6.1.d: Review the key ideas expressed and demonstrate understanding of multiple perspectives through reflection and paraphrasing.

Write
an Argument Test

Week 2• Day 2

Student Objectives

• Respond to the task. *(p. 354)*

Prewrite

Focus on Ideas

Prepare to Write Ask students to recall what they learned about preparing to write on a topic. Point out that on a writing test, the process is similar but condensed. Students should consider their task carefully in order to manage their time wisely.

Point out that Leila reviewed the writing task in order to make her planning notes. Thinking through a response is the key to planning a written response.

 Strategies for Writers Online

Go to **www.sfw.z-b.com** for additional online resources for students and teachers.

Prewrite   Focus on Ideas

Writing Strategy   Respond to the task.

When you write for a test, it's important to prepare before you begin writing. I'm going to gather some information and jot down notes before I start writing. The writing prompt is a good place to start gathering information. First, look at the task to find out what you are supposed to write. Think about how you'll respond to the task before you start writing. Even though you don't have a lot of time when you are writing for a test, prewriting can actually save you time by helping you get your ideas organized up front.

Since the task says to write an argument essay about my choice for this year's yearbook, I'll start jotting down some ideas.

Task — Come up with an idea for the cover of your school's yearbook and write an argument essay to convince the other students to agree with your choice.

Notes

✓ We did a lot of great things this year.

✓ Test scores were higher.

✓ Higher. . . what about something to do with that?

Apply
Jotting down notes about a topic can help you hone in on exactly what you are going to write.

354 Argument Writing

Differentiating Instruction

ENRICHMENT

State It Clearly To demonstrate the importance of stating one's position in the introduction, provide a sample argument essay, and read it to the class. Delete the introduction from the essay so that students hear only the body and conclusion. You may wish to make photocopies of the essay, with the lead paragraph deleted, so that students can refer to it more easily. Ask students to use the information from the body and conclusion of the essay to create an opening sentence and lead paragraph that state the writer's position. Ask for volunteers to share and compare the introductions.

Prewrite
Focus on Organization

Writing Strategy Choose a graphic organizer.

Now that I have decided what to write about (thanks to my notes!), I am going to arrange my ideas. A graphic organizer will help me organize my ideas. Since I am writing an argument essay, I think a Network Tree will be the best organizer to help me remember and organize all the details and ideas I want to include.

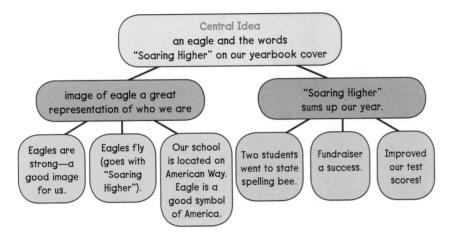

Reflect
Are there enough good reasons in Leila's Network Tree to convince readers?

Apply
A graphic organizer helps you arrange all the information you need to include in your essay.

Argument Test Writing 355

REINFORCEMENT

Use an Organizer Remind students that graphic organizers can help them structure their essay. Ask volunteers to name the graphic organizers that they used throughout the unit. (Venn Diagram, Network Tree, Order-of-Importance Organizer, Argument Map) Then ask students how they might decide which graphic organizer to use on a test. (Possible response: by thinking about which organizer they used for this genre) Remind students to look for clues in the writing prompt to help them choose a useful graphic organizer.

Write
an Argument Test

Week 2 • Day 3

Student Objectives

• Choose a graphic organizer. (p. 355)

Prewrite

Focus on Organization

Organize Information Have students review the writing task, being sure that students identify their purpose (write an argument essay) and audience. (classmates) Explain that Leila is using a Network Tree organizer to help her list and support her reasons.

First have students articulate a central idea and list their reasons (at least two). Tell them to follow Leila's organization and include three supporting details for each one. Encourage students to fill in the organizer completely. Remind students to use the prewriting time wisely because they will use their organizer to write their essay.

CCSS **C**ommon **C**ore **S**tate **S**tandards
W.6.1: Write arguments to support claims with clear reasons and relevant evidence. **W.6.1.a:** Introduce claim(s) and organize the reasons and evidence clearly. **W.6.1.b:** Support claim(s) with clear reasons and relevant evidence, using credible sources and demonstrating an understanding of the topic or text.

Argument Test Writing T355

Write
an Argument Test

Week 2 • Day 4

Student Objectives

- Check the graphic organizer against the scoring guide. *(pp. 356–357)*

Prewrite

Focus on **Organization**

Check the Graphic Organizer
Have students review Leila's Network Tree. Initiate discussion by pointing out that Leila wrote her central idea first. Then she gave two reasons and supports them with three strong details. Be sure students are clear about the information in each part of the organizer.

Ask students if Leila is ready to begin her draft. (Possible response: Leila needs to check her graphic organizer against the scoring guide first.) Emphasize the importance of paying attention to the scoring guide throughout test writing. Point out that Leila reviews each point in the scoring guide to be sure she has addressed them all. Explain that during this step of the test writing process, students should add or change information in their organizer to meet the criteria.

Online Writing Center

Provides **interactive graphic organizers** as well as a variety of graphic organizers in PDF format.

Prewrite
Focus on **Organization**

Writing Strategy   Check the graphic organizer against the scoring guide.

Since you won't get a lot of time to revise during a test, prewriting is super important. Before I dive in and start writing my essay, I'll take another look at my Network Tree and compare it to the scoring guide from my writing prompt.

> **Central Idea**
> an eagle and the words "Soaring Higher" on our yearbook cover
>
> - **image of eagle a great representation of who we are**
>   - Eagles are strong—a good image for us.
>   - Eagles fly (goes with "Soaring Higher").
>   - Our school is located on American Way. Eagle is a good symbol of America.
> - **"Soaring Higher" sums up our year.**
>   - Two students went to state spelling bee.
>   - Fundraiser a success.
>   - Improved our test scores!

Ideas
- Be sure your writing clearly identifies your position and contains supporting facts and reasons.

My position is clearly stated in the Central Idea space. I've also written down some good supporting explanations for why "Soaring Higher" and an eagle would make a great yearbook cover.

Organization
- Be sure your writing is well organized and contains an introduction, body, and conclusion.

My introductory paragraph will state my Central Idea. Then I'll use information from the rest of the Network Tree for the body. My conclusion will be a summary.

Voice
- Be sure your writing establishes and maintains a formal style.

I'll use appropriate formal language right from the beginning, and I'll be careful not to let casual words creep in as I write.

Word Choice
- Be sure your writing uses precise language.

I'll be sure to use precise, specific words to make my points. I'll avoid vague or general language that might bore or confuse my readers.

Sentence Fluency
- Be sure your writing has varied sentence structures.

I'm going to keep my reader interested by using different types of sentences.

Conventions
- Be sure your writing contains correct grammar, punctuation, capitalization, and spelling.

I don't want to leave any mistakes in my paper, so I will be sure to check my work carefully.

Reflect

There is good information in Leila's Network Tree. Now it all needs to be worked into a great essay!

Apply

Check your graphic organizer against the scoring guide.

Have a volunteer read Leila's thoughts on each trait and discuss her reasoning. Students should agree that Leila has used the prewriting time wisely and organized her ideas well. Before moving on, point out that although her notes and organizer address the scoring guide, Leila needs to remember to use the writing traits throughout the process.

CCSS Common Core State Standards

W.6.1: Write arguments to support claims with clear reasons and relevant evidence. **W.6.4:** Produce clear and coherent writing in which the development, organization, and style are appropriate to task, purpose, and audience. **W.6.5:** With some guidance and support from peers and adults, develop and strengthen writing as needed by planning, revising, editing, rewriting, or trying a new approach.

Write
an Argument Test

Week 2 • Day 5

Student Objectives

- State the position clearly. (pp. 358–359)

Draft

Focus on

Prepare to Draft Read the introduction on this page. Then focus on the writing strategy. Tell students that Leila used it to write her central idea.

Then emphasize the importance of using a graphic organizer to write a draft. Read and discuss Leila's draft on pages 358–359. Ask students to notice that Leila states her position in the lead sentence. As they read the draft, have students go back to Leila's graphic organizer to see where she included the information in the draft.

Online Writing Center

 Provides student eBooks with an **interactive writing pad** for drafting, revising, editing, and publishing.

T358 Argument Writing

Draft   Focus on [Ideas]

Writing Strategy   State the position clearly.

My position is that this year the school yearbook should feature an eagle along with the words "Soaring Higher." I'll state that in my opening sentence. Then I can use the rest of the essay to tell the readers why.

[DRAFT]   Let's Soar This Year!

by Leila   [my position]

If you want to feature a picture and words that really express our school on the cover of this years yearbook, then theres no better choice than using an eagle along with the words "Soaring Higher" to represent us. Here is while I feel so strongly about it.

First, the image of the eagle is a great representation of who we are. The school is located on American Way. Eagles are really cool animals, and having an animal on the cover with such a good, strong image will be uplifting for the students and teachers and will let everyone no that we are just awesome! Btw, the eagle is also an animal that flys, which would go nicely with the saying I am proposing we use, "Soaring Higher"

358 Argument Writing

English Language Learners

BEGINNING/INTERMEDIATE

Stating Opinions Using the task from the argument writing prompt, ask partners to come up with an idea for an image for the yearbook cover. Help them create a simple sentence to clearly state their reasons for choosing that image. For example, *I think we should have an eagle on the yearbook cover. It is our mascot.*

INTERMEDIATE

Replace Vague Words Identify a few vague words that students wrote in their drafts, for example, *do* or *think*. Challenge partners to come up with more precise words, for example, *perform* or *imagine.* Then have students revise their drafts and replace vague words.

Why "Soaring Higher" on the cover. This year we have truly been doing just that. Our overall test scores have improved. This gave us one of the top rankings in the area. We had not one, but two students go to the state spelling bee to represent our school. Last year we did not send any students. In addition, we did so well for our annual fundraiser that we were able to get a new Gym Floor. This will benfit the school for year's to come. If anyone has soared high this year, I would say it was us!

There is a final reason why I think this would be a good image and saying for our yearbook. And that is because you want your yearbook to be good. When you see an image of a bold and strong eagle next to the words "Soaring Higher," you will be happy.

So when you decide on what goes on this year's yearbook, think strength, think soring, and chose an eagle and the words "Soaring Higher." It will be a cover image the students won't soon forget.

Reflect

How good a job did Leila do with writing a convincing essay?

Apply

Your draft is your first attempt at getting all your ideas down on paper. Be thorough, but remember that you will have the opportunity to go back and do edits.

Argument Test Writing 359

Also point out that although there are mistakes present, Leila remembered to leave space to make corrections during the editing stage. Review the proofreading marks on this page. Tell students that these marks will be helpful as they revise and edit their drafts.

As they begin to draft, remind students to use their organizer to guide their writing. Also remind them to write neatly, even in the drafting stage, because the test evaluator should be able to read everything they have written, including their changes.

ADVANCED

Writing Arguments Have students use the Argument Map or Outline they created to write a paragraph or two. Monitor as they write to make sure they are beginning by stating their position. The rest of the essay should include strong sentences that support the writer's reasons for the position.

ADVANCED HIGH

Peer Review After students have drafted their argument essays, have them trade with another student. Partners should review the draft and look for specific details. Students should point out weak voice and suggest more specific words their partners could use. As you monitor, identify two or three examples of weak words or sentences, and discuss ways to strengthen them as a class.

CCSS Common Core State Standards

W.6.1: Write arguments to support claims with clear reasons and relevant evidence. **W.6.5:** With some guidance and support from peers and adults, develop and strengthen writing as needed by planning, revising, editing, rewriting, or trying a new approach. **R/Inf.6.6:** Determine an author's point of view or purpose in a text and explain how it is conveyed in the text.

Write
an Argument Test

Week 3 • Day 1

Student Objectives

- Use transitions to organize the writing. *(p. 360)*

Revise

Focus on

Time Management Point out to students that they will have about fifteen minutes to revise their drafts and that there are three revision tasks in this chapter. (If you are using the Optional Revising Lessons, you will need to plan accordingly. See page T362.) Students might wish to subdivide their planned revising time into three five-minute segments and tackle one strategy at a time.

Use Helpful Transitions Ask students how Leila's revision helps the reader. (Possible responses: The transition word connects Leila's ideas. It helps organize this part of the essay and makes it easier to follow.)

Also tell students as they revise for **Organization** to make sure they state the claim clearly in the introduction and restate it in the conclusion. If they have followed their organizers, their reasons should follow in good order.

 Strategies for Writers Online
Go to **www.sfw.z-b.com** for additional online resources for students and teachers.

Revise

Focus on Organization

Writing Strategy   Use transitions to organize the writing.

Now is the time to read my essay and be sure that my reasons are organized clearly. I know that transition words are like signposts that guide the reader. Since I am listing several reasons, I can use transitions to signal to the reader when I am moving from one reason to the next. I already used *First* and *final reason*. Here is a place in the middle where I can add another transition.

[DRAFT]   [added transition]

Next, why should we put
~~Why~~ "Soaring Higher" on the cover? This year we have truly been doing just that. Our overall test scores have improved. This gave us one of the top rankings in the area.

Apply
Good writers give the reader a clear guide to follow, using transitions to organize the writing.

Differentiating Instruction

ENRICHMENT

Time to Revise Enthusiastic writers in timed situations may think their draft is fine "as is." Suggest some proven strategies they can practice, such as reading their writing strategically to check for each writing trait. Remind them to refer to the rubric they created or to the one they used earlier in the unit (see page 282) to inform their revisions.

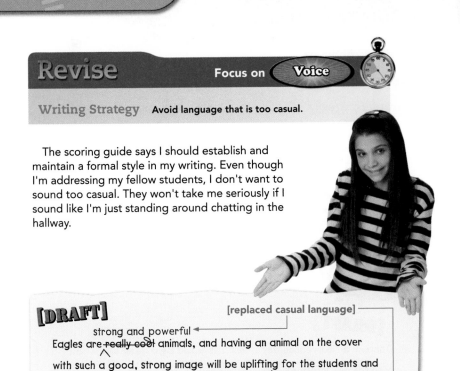

Revise

Focus on Voice

Writing Strategy Avoid language that is too casual.

The scoring guide says I should establish and maintain a formal style in my writing. Even though I'm addressing my fellow students, I don't want to sound too casual. They won't take me seriously if I sound like I'm just standing around chatting in the hallway.

[DRAFT]   [replaced casual language]

~~strong and powerful~~
Eagles are ~~really cool~~ animals, and having an animal on the cover

with such a good, strong image will be uplifting for the students and
                                               strong
teachers and will let everyone no that we are ~~just awesome~~! ~~Btw~~ the

eagle is also an animal that flys, which would go nicely with the saying

I am proposing we use, "Soaring Higher"

Reflect

Is the language appropriately formal now that it's been revised?

Apply

Use formal and direct language throughout your essay.

REINFORCEMENT

Keep a Word List To help students build a writer's vocabulary, have them keep a word list as they read others' writing and improve their own. Encourage them to consult word resources to learn the spelling, pronunciation, part of speech, and meaning of new words.

Write
an Argument Test

Week 3 • Day 2

Student Objectives

• Revise to avoid language that is too casual. *(p. 361)*

Revise

Focus on Voice

Use a Formal Style Read the writing strategy, and then have students read the rest of the page independently. Then ask:

• How does the writer improve Voice in this part? (Leila replaced language that sounded too casual for an essay.)

As students revise their work, remind them to make their changes as neatly as possible in the lines above or below their original writing, as Leila did. Assure them that the test evaluator welcomes changes that are clear and easy to read.

CCSS **Common Core State Standards**
W.6.1.c: Use words, phrases, and clauses to clarify the relationships among claim(s) and reasons. **W.6.1.d:** Establish and maintain a formal style. **L.6.3.b:** Maintain consistency in style and tone. **L.6.4.c:** Consult reference materials (e.g., dictionaries, glossaries, thesauruses), both print and digital, to find the pronunciation of a word or determine or clarify its precise meaning or its part of speech.

Write
an Argument Test

Week 3 • Day 3

Student Objectives

• Choose words and phrases to convey ideas precisely. (p. 362)

Revise

Focus on  Word Choice

Use Strong, Precise Words Ask a volunteer to read Leila's words aloud. Direct students' attention to the draft excerpt. Point out that the original draft did contain weak words and phrases. (*good image, good,* and *will be happy*) Read aloud the revised version. Students should agree that Leila's revisions make the writing stronger and the meaning clearer.

Explain that using placeholder words such as *good* while they draft is perfectly fine. During revising, however, weak and overused words should be replaced by words and phrases that convey ideas more precisely.

For students who have time left in the revising period, invite them to revise for **Ideas** and **Sentence Fluency,** using the scoring guide and the Optional Revising Lessons. Encourage students to use every minute remaining to improve and edit their writing, even if they want to finish early.

Online Writing Center

 Provides **interactive proofreading activities** for each genre.

Revise
Focus on Word Choice

Writing Strategy Choose words and phrases to convey ideas precisely.

Now is my chance to reread my essay and be sure that I have included only strong, precise words. After all, if I use weak words, my essay just won't fly! When I went back and read it again, I noticed that my final reason for wanting to use an eagle and "Soaring Higher" isn't that strong. Look at how I strengthened my sentences by using precise words!

[DRAFT]

There is a final reason why I think this would be a ~~good~~ **powerful** image and saying for our yearbook. And that is because you want your yearbook to be ~~good~~ **memorable**. When you see an image of a bold and strong eagle next to the words "Soaring Higher," you will ~~be happy~~ **feel a thrill**.

[used precise words]

Apply

Good writers use strong and precise words to sound more convincing.

362   Argument Writing

Optional Revising Lessons

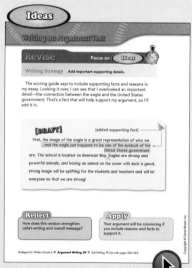

Argument 29

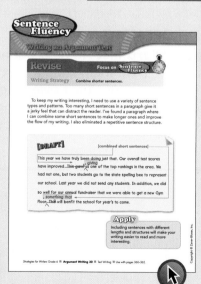

Argument 30

Go to ▷ *Strategies for Writers Grade 6 CD-ROM*

Edit — Focus on Conventions

Writing Strategy   Check my grammar, punctuation, capitalization, and spelling.

Always check your paper one last time. The scoring guide says to use correct grammar, punctuation, capitalization, and spelling. I always leave plenty of time to check for errors in these important areas.

[FINAL DRAFT]

Let's Soar This Year!
by Leila

If you want to feature a picture and words that really express our school on the cover of this years yearbook, then theres no better choice than using an eagle along with the words "Soaring Higher" to represent us. Here is ~~while~~ why I feel so strongly about it.

First, the image of the eagle is a great representation of who we , and the eagle just happens to be one of the strong and powerful symbols of the United States government. are. The school is located on American Way. Eagles are ~~really cool~~ animals, and having an animal on the cover with such a good, strong image will be uplifting for the students and teachers and will let everyone ~~no~~ know that we are ~~just awesome~~ strong! ~~Btw,~~ the eagle is also an animal flies that ~~flys~~ which would go nicely with the saying I am proposing we use, "Soaring Higher."

Apply
Even though you have read and reread your essay, you want to look at it carefully at this point to find and correct any mistakes.

Argument Test Writing **363**

Differentiating Instruction

ENRICHMENT
Edit Strategically Enthusiastic writers who often finish early may fall into the habit of simply waiting for the testing period to end. Suggest some proven strategies they can practice, such as using proofreading marks to make their changes clear and reading from bottom to top to check spelling.

REINFORCEMENT
Edit Purposefully To reduce students' anxiety about running out of time, direct students to look only for the kinds of errors they commonly make. Strategic editing will help them focus on the things they can change and make the most out of the final minutes.

Write
an Argument Test

Student Objectives
- Check the grammar, spelling, capitalization, and punctuation. *(pp. 363–364)*

Edit

Focus on Conventions

Edit the Test Explain that an essay written for a test will rarely be perfect. Test evaluators look for evidence that students care enough about their writing to edit. For example, when they see misspelled words crossed out and correctly spelled, they see that students are conscientiously editing.

Go over Leila's draft/final copy with students. Point out the proofreader's marks she used. Remind students that they should not plan for time to recopy their drafts. (Often students' planning and drafting work is required as part of the test.) The writer's goal is to make all changes legible, not to produce a perfectly neat final copy.

Remind them to check first for easy-to-miss errors, such as using pronouns correctly. Encourage students to use proofreading marks shown on page 359 as they edit their writing. Finally, remind them that it is the writer's responsibility to use and spell words correctly.

CCSS Common Core State Standards
L.6.1.a: Ensure that pronouns are in the proper case (subjective, objective, possessive). **L.6.1.c:** Recognize and correct inappropriate shifts in pronoun number and person. **L.6.1.d:** Recognize and correct vague pronouns (i.e., ones with unclear or ambiguous antecedents). **L.6.2:** Demonstrate command of the conventions of standard English capitalization, punctuation, and spelling when writing. **L.6.2.b:** Spell correctly.

Argument Test Writing   T363

Review
Test Tips

Week 3 • Day 5

Student Objectives

- Review tips for writing for a test. (p. 365)

Test Tips

Review Test Tips Explain to students that not all writing test prompts will be as clearly divided into parts as the writing prompt they used in this chapter. However, students can still find and label the three important parts of any writing prompt. They can even generate a scoring guide if they must. Write this prompt on the board:

- *Think about changing something in school. Present and support your idea with good reasons. Be sure to revise and edit your response.*

Now ask:

- What is the setup? (Think about changing something in your school.)

Circle and label the setup, and point out that it is rather brief. Ask students how they might expand on it to get a better sense of the background for this writing prompt. (Possible response: I might list some specific things that I would like to see improved.) Help students brainstorm ideas by providing examples, such as a longer lunch hour, or more free time, or a science field trip, and list them on the board.

 Strategies for Writers Online

Go to **www.sfw.z-b.com** for additional online resources for students and teachers.

[FINAL DRAFT]

Next, why should we put

Why "Soaring Higher" on the cover? This year we have truly been

doing just that. Our overall test scores have improved. ~~This gave~~ us *giving*

one of the top rankings in the area. We had not one, but two students

go to the state spelling bee to represent our school. Last year we

did not send any students. In addition, we did so well for our annual

fundraiser that we were able to get a new ~~G~~ym ~~f~~loor. ~~This~~ will benfit *, something that*

the school for year's to come. If anyone has soared high this year, I

would say it was us!

There is a final reason why I think this would be a ~~good~~ image and *powerful*

saying for our yearbook. And that is because you want your yearbook

to be ~~good~~. When you see an image of a bold and strong eagle next *memorable*

to the words "Soaring Higher," you will ~~be happy~~. *feel a thrill*

So when you decide on what goes on this year's yearbook, think

strength, think ~~soring~~, and chose an eagle and the words "Soaring *soaring*

Higher." It will be a cover image the students won't soon forget.

Reflect

Has Leila missed anything? Make sure you use your last few minutes to check your writing for grammar, punctuation, or spelling errors.

364 Argument Writing

The test is complete! When you follow the right steps, it's not that difficult at all. Here are some helpful tips to remember when you write for a test.

TEST TIPS

1. **Study the writing prompt before you start to write.** Most writing prompts have three parts: the setup, the task, and the scoring guide. The parts probably won't be labeled. You'll have to figure them out for yourself!

2. **Make sure you understand the task before you start to write.**
   - Read all three parts of the writing prompt carefully.
   - Circle key words in the task part of the writing prompt that tell what kind of writing you need to do. The task might also identify your audience.
   - Make sure you know how you'll be graded.
   - Say the assignment in your own words to yourself.

3. **Keep an eye on the clock.** Decide how much time you will spend on each part of the writing process and try to stick to your schedule. Don't spend so much time prewriting that you don't have enough time left to write.

4. **Reread your writing. Compare it to the scoring guide at least twice.** Remember the rubrics you have used all year? A scoring guide on a writing test is like a rubric. It can help you keep what's important in mind.

5. **Plan, plan, plan!** You don't get much time to revise during a test, so planning is more important than ever.

6. **Write neatly.** Remember: If the people who score your test can't read your writing, it doesn't matter how good your essay is!

Argument Test Writing 365

Next ask:

- **What is the task?** (Possible response: I need to choose one idea from my list, provide strong reasons, and support my reasons with facts that can be verified.)

Circle and label the task. Ask students how they can tell what kind of writing the task requires. (Possible response: The task says to present and support my idea. That's stating and backing up a position with evidence.)

Ask what students can do to make up a scoring guide, since the writing prompt provides only general instructions to "revise and edit." (Possible response: Ideas: State position clearly. Provide supporting evidence. Organization: Use an organizer like a Network Tree to arrange ideas. Voice: Use a formal style and sound convincing. Word Choice: Use clear, precise words. Sentence Fluency: Write interesting sentences. Conventions: Take time to correct errors.)

Write students' responses on the board. Tell students they have just made a useful scoring guide from their own writing experience.

CCSS **Common Core State Standards**
W.6.5: With some guidance and support from peers and adults, develop and strengthen writing as needed by planning, revising, editing, rewriting, or trying a new approach. **W.6.7:** Conduct short research projects to answer a question, drawing on several sources and refocusing the inquiry when appropriate. **W.6.10:** Write routinely over extended time frames (time for research, reflection, and revision) and shorter time frames (a single sitting or a day or two) for a range of discipline-specific tasks, purposes, and audiences.

Descriptive writing

Descriptive Essay

Pages T368A–T391

Writing a descriptive essay lets students hone their observational skills and create precise, evocative descriptions.

Prewrite Choose a picture and make notes about its sensory details.
Use a Spider Map to organize the notes.

Draft Use vivid imagery to help the reader visualize the picture.

Revise Make sure all the detail sentences relate to the topic sentence in every paragraph.
Choose punctuation for effect.
Replace vague words with precise ones.

Edit Check for correct use of appositives, predicate nouns, and predicate adjectives.

Publish Read the essay to classmates. Have them draw pictures based on the essay.

Observation Report

Pages T392A–T415

Students will describe a step-by-step process, using first-person point of view and clear descriptions to make the process understandable for readers.

Prewrite Observe and take notes.
Make a Sequence Chain of the steps in the experiment.

Draft Introduce the experiment in the introduction and use numbered steps to show the order.

Revise Maintain consistency in style and tone.
Choose words and phrases to convey ideas precisely.
Blend questions and exclamations into the report.

Edit Be sure apostrophes are used correctly in possessive nouns and contractions.

Publish Display the report on Family Night.

Descriptive Article

Pages T416A–T437

Just like professional writers, students will focus on audience appeal using fresh, descriptive language to write an article for a newspaper, magazine, or another publication.

Prewrite Jot down some notes that appeal to the senses.
Use a Five-Senses Chart to organize the notes.

Draft Use first-person point of view.

Revise Add sensory details.
Replace clichés with interesting phrases.
Repeat a sentence pattern to emphasize a point.

Edit Recognize and correct inappropriate shifts in verb tense.

Publish Publish the article in a family scrapbook.

Unit Overview

LITERATURE CONNECTION

Poem

Pages T438A–T459

Students will demonstrate their knowledge of nature by writing a poem about it.

Prewrite	Choose a topic. Make a list of descriptive details. Use a Web to plan the poem.
Draft	Use precise words and figurative language.
Revise	Choose details that bring the topic to life. Make sure each line or stanza conveys one clear idea. Place line breaks where they make sense.
Edit	Check the use and form of comparative and superlative adjectives and adverbs.
Publish	Choose video and audio that enhance the poem.

Descriptive Test Writing

Pages T460A–T481

Students will learn and practice how to analyze a descriptive test prompt and how to plan their time in order to complete the writing process. They will also use traits-based strategies for successful test writing.

Prewrite	Study the writing prompt to find out what to do. Respond to the task. Choose a graphic organizer. Check the graphic organizer against the scoring guide.
Draft	Include relevant sensory details.
Revise	Organize the information into paragraphs. Use a casual tone. Use lively and interesting language.
Edit	Check the grammar, punctuation, capitalization, and spelling.

Online Writing Center

Interactive Whiteboard Ready

Complete Digital Writing Instruction!

- My Writing Pad
- Interactive Rubrics
- Anchor Papers
- Graphic Organizers

- Content Area Writing Prompts
- Grammar Games
- Proofreading Activities
- Instructional Videos

- Virtual File Cabinet
- eBooks
- Assessments

For information, go to www.sfw.z-b.com

Also available: **Online Essay Grader and Writing Tutor,** powered by Vantage Learning's MY Access®.

21ˢᵗ Century Literacies
Technology, Digital Media & Writing

by **Julie Coiro, Ph.D.,** University of Rhode Island & **Sara Kajder, Ph.D.,** University of Pittsburgh

 INSPIRE **Websites to Spark Ideas**

Observational Reports about Social Studies

As part of this descriptive writing unit, you might wish to spend a few minutes of class time highlighting some of the online collections from which your students can learn how to summarize a current event in social studies or try out a science experiment at home and then formally write up their procedures and observations. By sharing the following collections with students and parents in an email newsletter or a classroom webpage, they can easily access these websites from home or print them out at the public library. This is an excellent opportunity for families to get involved and extend what their children are learning about in school.

Summarizing and Reporting On Important News Events

- **PBS NewsHour Extra (http://www.pbs.org/ newshour/extra/)** hosts hour-long daily newscasts about key events of interest to middle and high school students. **Student Reporting Lab Videos (http://www.pbs.org/newshour/extra/speakout/ srlabs/climatechange1.html)** connect high school students with local news professionals who help students investigate, synthesize and report on important topics just like real journalists. Many models of student-created videos serve to inspire young writers wanting to capture the essence of an important event in writing. The *Student Voices* section of the website provides space for students to publish their unique perspectives on issues and news events.

Writing Up Observations of Science Experiments

- **PBS Science Activities (http://www.pbskids.org/ zoom/activities/sci/)** includes experiments especially designed for children to explore concepts, such as chemistry, engineering, the five senses, forces, life science, patterns, sound, structures, and water.

- **Energy Quest Science Projects (http://www. energyquest.ca.gov/projects/index.html)** offers fun experiments to guide an exploration of simplified concepts related to chemical energy, geothermal energy, and nuclear energy.

- **Exploratorium Science Snacks (http://www. exploratorium.edu/snacks/snack_questions.html)** are miniature versions of some of the most popular exhibits at the Exploratorium Museum of Science, Art, and Human Perception in San Francisco, California. Each features ideas about what to do and notice after setting up the experiment.

- **Steve Spangler's Easy Science Experiment Projects (http://stevespanglerscience.com/experiments/)** feature a list of top ten science experiments as well as a range of others in categories such as rocks and minerals, air, electricity, weather, color, magnetism, and many more. Don't miss the videos too at http:// www.stevespanglerscience.com/video/. Steve Spangler, the website's creator, hosts a science television series and directs the Hands-On Science Institute in Denver, Colorado.

- **Science Experiments at Home (http://members. ozemail.com.au/~macinnis/scifun/miniexp.htm)** is an interesting collection of short experiments and explanations of what's happening that are sure to prompt writing ideas.

Descriptive writing describes something to the reader.

Hi! I'm Denise. I'm learning about descriptive writing in school. I like this kind of writing because it's so real. When you read a good description, you feel as if you're actually experiencing something right at that moment. I want to learn how to write like that!

IN THIS UNIT

- Descriptive Essay
- Observation Report
- Descriptive Article
- LITERATURE CONNECTION ▷ Poem
- Writing for a Test

Name: Denise
Home: Minnesota
Hobbies: modeling, cooking, and photography

To differentiate instruction and maximize student achievement, use the Extensions Online activities available at **www.sfw.z-b.com.**

Created by Amy Humphreys, Ed.M., these engaging activities can be used to meet a wide range of learner needs. Each activity uses a combination of visual, written, oral, and kinesthetic elements, and deliberately leverages the power of collaboration and conversation so students learn to think like writers in fun and engaging ways. For more information on Differentiated Instruction, see page Z12.

Meet Your Writing Partner, Denise

Denise, a girl from Minnesota, is the writing partner for this chapter. Point out Denise's hobbies and remind students that Denise will rely on her interests, background, and hobbies to come up with story ideas and make her writing more real. Explain to students that when they know about or are interested in the subject on which they are writing, their writing will likely be more genuine. Descriptive writing should bring details and information to life for the reader—and when students can make a connection with their subjects, it will be reflected positively in their writing.

Descriptive Essay Planner

WEEK 1

Day 1
Introduce
a Descriptive Essay

Student Objectives
- Review the elements of a descriptive essay.
- Consider purpose and audience.
- Learn the traits of descriptive writing.

Student Activities
- Read and discuss **What's in a Descriptive Essay?** (p. 368)
- Read and discuss **Why Write a Descriptive Essay?** (p. 369)
- Read **Linking Descriptive Writing Traits to a Descriptive Essay.** (p. 370)

Day 2
Analyze
Read a Descriptive Essay

Student Objectives
- Read a model descriptive essay.

Student Activities
- Read **"A Striking Image."** (p. 371)

Day 3
Analyze
Introduce the Rubric

Student Objectives
- Learn to read a rubric.

Student Activities
- Review **"A Striking Image."** (p. 371)
- Read and discuss the **Descriptive Essay Rubric.** (pp. 372–373)

WEEK 2

Day 1
Write
Prewrite: Ideas

Student Objectives
- Read and understand a prewriting strategy.

Student Activities
- Read and discuss **Prewrite: Focus on Ideas.** (pp. 378–379)
- Apply the prewriting strategy.

Day 2
Write
Prewrite: Organization

Student Objectives
- Use a Spider Map to organize the notes.

Student Activities
- Read and discuss **Prewrite: Focus on Organization.** (pp. 380–381)
- Reflect on the model Spider Map.
- Apply the prewriting strategy to create a Spider Map.
- Participate in a peer conference.

Day 3
Write
Draft: Ideas

Student Objectives
- Begin writing, using vivid sensory details.

Student Activities
- Read and discuss **Draft: Focus on Ideas.** (p. 382)
- Apply the drafting strategy by using a Spider Map to write a draft.

WEEK 3

Day 1
Write
Revise: Voice

Student Objectives
- Revise to use punctuation for effect.

Student Activities
- Read and discuss **Revise: Focus on Voice.** (p. 385)
- Reflect on a model draft.
- Apply the revising stategy.
- Participate in a peer conference.

Day 2
Write
Revise: Word Choice

Student Objectives
- Revise to replace vague words with precise ones.

Student Activities
- Read and discuss **Revise: Focus on Word Choice.** (p. 386)

Note: Optional Revising Lessons appear on the *Strategies for Writers* CD-ROM.

Day 3
Write
Edit: Conventions

Student Objectives
- Edit for correct use of appositives, predicate nouns, and predicate adjectives.

Student Activities
- Read and discuss **Edit: Focus on Conventions.** (p. 387)

Note: Teach the Conventions mini-lessons (pp. 388–389) if needed.

Day 4	Day 5
Analyze Ideas, Organization, and Voice	**Analyze** Word Choice, Sentence Fluency, and Conventions

Student Objectives
- Read a model descriptive essay.
- Use the descriptive essay rubric.
- Use the model descriptive essay to study Ideas, Organization, and Voice.

Student Activities
- Review **"A Striking Image."** *(p. 371)*
- Review the rubric. *(pp. 372–373)*
- Read and discuss **Using the Rubric to Study the Model.** *(pp. 374–375)*

Student Objectives
- Read a model descriptive essay.
- Use the descriptive essay rubric.
- Use the model descriptive essay to study Word Choice, Sentence Fluency, and Conventions.

Student Activities
- Review **"A Striking Image."** *(p. 371)*
- Review the rubric. *(pp. 372–373)*
- Read and discuss **Using the Rubric to Study the Model.** *(pp. 376–377)*

Day 4	Day 5
Write Draft	**Write** Revise: Organization

Student Objectives
- Complete a draft.

Student Activities
- Finish the draft. *(p. 383)*
- Participate in a peer conference.

Student Objectives
- Revise to make sure all detail sentences relate to the paragraph's topic sentence.

Student Activities
- Read and discuss **Revise: Focus on Organization.** *(p. 384)*
- Reflect on a model draft.
- Apply the revising strategy.

Day 4	Day 5
Write Publish: +Presentation	**Write** Publish: +Presentation

Student Objectives
- Discuss preparation for publishing and presentation.
- Use a final editing checklist to publish their work.

Student Activities
- Read and discuss **Publish: +Presentation.** *(p. 390)*
- Apply the publishing strategy.

Student Objectives
- Use a descriptive essay rubric.
- Share a published descriptive essay.

Student Activities
- Share their work.
- Use the rubric to reflect upon and evaluate the model and their own writing. *(pp. 372–373, 391)*

To complete the chapter in fewer days, combine the learning objectives and activities in a way that supports students as they write.

Resources at-a-Glance

Grammar, Usage & Mechanics
Appositives T388
Predicate Nouns and
    Adjectives T389
Grammar Practice T387–T389

Differentiating Instruction
Using the Rubric T377
Draft. .T382
Publish T390
For additional Differentiating Instruction activities, see Strategies for Writers Extensions Online at **www.sfw.z-b.com.**

English Language Learners
Using the Rubric T374–T375
Prewrite T378–T379
Revise. T384

Conferencing
Peer to Peer T381, T383, T385
Peer Groups. T381, T383, T385
Teacher-Led T381, T383, T385

Technology Tip
Using the Rubric T376
Publish. T391

 Connection Letter
Reproducible letter (in English and Spanish) appears on the *Strategies for Writers* CD-ROM and at **www.sfw.z-b.com.**

Online Writing Center
Provides IWB resources, interactive games and practice activities, videos, eBooks, and a virtual file cabinet.

 Strategies for Writers Online
Go to **www.sfw.z-b.com** for free online resources for students and teachers.

Introduce
a Descriptive Essay

Week 1 • Day 1

Student Objectives

- Review the elements of a descriptive essay. *(p. 368)*
- Consider purpose and audience. *(p. 369)*
- Learn the traits of descriptive writing. *(p. 370)*

What's a Descriptive Essay?

Ask a student to describe a favorite place or thing. Prompt him or her to provide details that will help the rest of the class get a vivid picture of this place or thing. Explain that when they write their own descriptive essays, they will be providing similar types of details to create a clear, detailed picture.

What's in a Descriptive Essay?

Explain that vivid imagery and lively language help give the reader a clear, detailed, and interesting picture of the topic. Point out that in a descriptive essay, it's not enough to write *He was wearing a hat.* Instead, the essay should give a precise description, such as *He was wearing a purple and gold baseball cap pulled low over his forehead, leaving his eyes barely visible.*

 Strategies for Writers Online

Go to **www.sfw.z-b.com** for additional online resources for students and teachers.

What's a Descriptive Essay?

A descriptive essay gives a clear, detailed picture of a person, a place, a thing, or an event. You have to be really observant to do this kind of writing. And you have to communicate what you've observed to your readers.

What's in a Descriptive Essay?

Vivid Imagery
A descriptive essay doesn't just give readers an idea of what something or someone is like—it makes the subject come alive! Powerful images in the essay help the audience clearly visualize the subject.

Precise Language
A descriptive essay needs precise language. Instead of vague, overused words, I'll use specific, interesting ones. Good metaphors will really strengthen my ideas.

Point of View
A descriptive essay can be written in either third person or first person. I'll have to decide which point of view fits my subject the best. Sometimes an essay is more powerful when I don't place myself inside it. At other times, I can breathe more life into a subject by making it personal. This will be a tough decision!

Organization
It's easy to ramble when you're writing a description. I'm going to organize my essay into paragraphs with topic sentences and supporting detail sentences. Each paragraph will tell about one main idea.

368 Descriptive Writing

Descriptive Text Exemplars (Descriptive Essay)

Knight, Tim. *Fantastic Feeders.* **Heinemann Library Paperbacks, 2005.** *Fantastic Feeders* describes the fascinating behavior and habitats of unusual plants and animals. Learn how different animals and plants adapt to survive, hunt, and escape being hunted.

Cooper, Floyd. *Jump! From the Life of Michael Jordan.* **Philomel, 2004.** *Jump! From the Life of Michael Jordan* chronicles the life of famous athlete Michael Jordan. Cooper's powerful illustrations and easy-to-read text describe Jordan's childhood, rise to fame, and accomplishments as a professional basketball player.

Why write a Descriptive Essay?

I've been thinking about why I want to write a descriptive essay. I've listed a few ideas below. Do you have some ideas of your own?

Observation Skills
Writing a descriptive essay can really help me improve my powers of observation. After all, to be able to describe something, you first have to observe it carefully!

Appreciation
Often I just glance at something and move on. Writing a description can make me stop and really reflect on what I'm seeing and appreciate what's interesting or beautiful or strange about it.

Sharing an Experience
If I do a really good job describing something, my readers will feel as if they experienced it, too. That's a great way to share my life with other people!

Language Skills
I have to choose my words carefully and use strong, effective language to write a good essay. I think descriptive writing is going to be a good experience for me.

Landau, Elaine. *Apples.* **Children's Press, 2000.** Landau describes the various types of apples in this factual text. Readers are also informed of the historical context, cultivation process, and many uses of apples.

Climo, Shirley. *City! Washington, D.C.* **Macmillan Publishing Company, 1991.** *City! Washington, D.C.* includes history, buildings and monuments, and maps of our nation's capital city. Climo also presents information on our present government as well as additional facts about Washington, D.C.

Why write a Descriptive Essay?

As students practice their own writing, it is helpful to remind them that all writing has a purpose and that learning the different genres of writing will help them become better writers. These authentic purposes also help shape their writing. Read and discuss with students the reasons for writing a descriptive essay. Ask students what reasons might move them to write a descriptive essay. Have students read a short descriptive essay and discuss what purposes the writer had in mind. Encourage students to think about their reasons for writing a descriptive essay and how these reasons will affect the tone and focus of their writing.

CCSS **C**ommon **C**ore **S**tate **S**tandards

SL.6.1: Engage effectively in a range of collaborative discussions (one-on-one, in groups, and teacher-led) with diverse partners on *grade 6 topics, texts, and issues*, building on others' ideas and expressing their own clearly. **SL.6.1.a:** Come to discussions prepared, having read or studied required material; explicitly draw on that preparation by referring to evidence on the topic, text, or issue to probe and reflect on ideas under discussion. **SL.6.2:** Interpret information presented in diverse media and formats (e.g., visually, quantitatively, orally) and explain how it contributes to a topic, text, or issue under study.

Introduce
a Descriptive Essay

Linking Descriptive Writing Traits to a Descriptive Essay

Explain to students that they will follow Denise as she models using the writing process and the traits together. As they follow Denise through the writing process, students will see how the Descriptive Writing Traits have been adapted and applied to writing a descriptive essay. They will see that a descriptive essay has many factors in common with other types of descriptive writing. However, the particular audience and purpose of a descriptive essay determine how the traits are used.

Linking Descriptive Writing Traits to a Descriptive Essay

In this chapter, you will describe a person, a place, a thing, or an event. This type of descriptive writing is called a descriptive essay. Denise will guide you through the stages of the writing process: Prewrite, Draft, Revise, Edit, and Publish. In each stage, Denise will show you important writing strategies that are linked to the Descriptive Writing Traits below.

Descriptive Writing Traits

 Ideas • a clear topic that is supported and enhanced by specific sensory details

 Organization • well-organized paragraphs that follow the order of the description, whether by time, location, or another order

 Voice • a voice and tone that are appropriate for the purpose and audience

 Word Choice • precise, descriptive words, possibly with figurative language, that create an accurate picture for the reader

 Sentence Fluency • sentences that vary in length and type to add flow to the writing

 **Conventions** • no or few errors in grammar, usage, mechanics, and spelling

Before you write, read Anna Yuishmal's descriptive essay on the next page. Then use the descriptive essay rubric on pages 372–373 to decide how well she did. (You might want to look back at What's in a Descriptive Essay? on page 368, too!)

Descriptive Writing Traits in a Descriptive Essay

 Ideas The writer maintains focus on the topic throughout the essay. Sensory details develop the topic and create vivid images for the reader.

 **Organization** Each paragraph is complete, with a solid topic sentence and supporting details that relate clearly to it. The topic is clearly introduced at the beginning of the essay.

 **Voice** The tone of the essay is friendly and engaging. It draws readers in and helps them feel connected to the writer.

Online Writing Center

 Provides six **interactive anchor papers** for each mode of writing.

A STRIKING IMAGE

by Anna Yuishmal

Vivid imagery

Point of view—first person

I was leisurely thumbing through a book about weather recently when I was suddenly struck by lightning—in a photograph. Filling the page was a lightning storm, a monstrous fire in the sky. Against an inky black sky, mounds of angry clouds piled on top of each other. A charred, smoky-gray mass smoldered near the bottom of the photo. A raging orange cloud exploded like lava. Looming above was a brilliant yellow cloudburst, singed red at its edges. The lightning bolts were a tangle of glowing white wires that sliced the night into jagged pieces.

Lightning is a split-second show, a glimpse of nature's awesome energy. Zing! Steely fingers reach out to snatch a piece of the sky. Poof! They are gone. The photographer captured the brief moment. As the lightning flashed, the shutter snapped.

Precise language

The image reminded me of what comes after a lightning strike. The metallic odor of burnt oxygen, or ozone, follows the flash. Then comes thunder, a distant rolling rumble or a sudden echoing boom. To me, thunder is the delicious dessert after the lightning.

As I closed the book, I could still feel the high-voltage force of the fleeting event caught in the photo. A shiver like a lightning bolt ran down my spine and stayed there.

Organization—topic sentence

Organization—supporting details

Descriptive Essay 371

Word Choice Precise, descriptive language creates vivid images for readers and helps them visualize the writer's observations.

Sentence Fluency A variety of sentence types and structures gives the writing energy and flow. The writer makes effective use of repeated sentence structures to emphasize a point.

Conventions The essay is carefully edited prior to publishing. There are no mistakes in grammar, usage, mechanics, and spelling to confuse the reader or obscure the author's purpose.

Analyze
the Model

Week 1 • Day 2

Student Objectives

- Read a model descriptive essay. *(p. 371)*

Read the Model

Have students read the descriptive essay on page 371. Before they read, remind students to look for the writing traits outlined on page 370.

Elements of a Descriptive Essay

Use the notes on the model to discuss how Anna Yuishmal has written an effective descriptive essay. Ask:

- How does Anna's use of first-person point of view engage the reader? (Anna invites the reader directly to share her experience.)

- What words would you use to describe the images Anna uses? (Possible responses: dramatic, colorful)

Ask volunteers to give examples of phrases that include precise language. Discuss why precise language makes a stronger impression. You may wish to have students refer to What's in a Descriptive Essay? on page 368 for review.

CCSS **C**ommon **C**ore **S**tate **S**tandards
R/Lit.6.1: Cite textual evidence to support analysis of what the text says explicitly as well as inferences drawn from the text. **R/Lit.6.4:** Determine the meaning of words and phrases as they are used in a text, including figurative and connotative meanings; analyze the impact of a specific word choice on meaning and tone.

Analyze
the Model

Week 1 • Day 3

Student Objectives

- Learn to read a rubric. (pp. 372–373)

Use the Rubric

Explain the Rubric Explain that a rubric is a tool that helps you plan, improve, and evaluate a piece of writing. A rubric also helps a writer focus on key elements, or traits, in writing (**Ideas, Organization, Voice, Word Choice, Sentence Fluency, Conventions,** and **Presentation**).

The 6-point rubric on pages 372 and 373 is based on the Descriptive Writing Traits that students read on page 370. Explain that the column under the numeral 6 describes a very good descriptive essay, one that has received the highest score in all categories. This is what students should strive for in their own writing.

Discuss the Rubric Guide the students in a discussion of the rubric. Read the descriptors that go with each trait. Note how the descriptors vary as you move from column to column. Remind students to keep the rubric in mind when they write their own descriptive essays.

Online Writing Center

Provides a variety of **interactive rubrics,** including 4-, 5-, and 6-point models.

Rubric

Use this 6-point rubric to plan and score a descriptive essay.

	6	5	4
Ideas	The topic is clear and focused. Vivid sensory details create a picture for the reader.	The topic is clear and focused. Strong sensory details create a picture for the reader.	The topic is often clear and focused. Solid sensory details are used.
Organization	The description is organized so that the topic is introduced at the beginning and the details are organized into logical paragraphs.	The topic is introduced at the beginning. Most details are organized into logical paragraphs.	The topic is mentioned at the beginning. The paragraphs are easy to follow, but some details are not logically organized.
Voice	The voice connects directly with the reader in a friendly way.	The writer's voice connects with the reader throughout most of the essay.	The writer's voice is sincere but sometimes fails to connect with the reader.
Word Choice	Precise words and phrases help the reader form a visual image.	Most words and phrases are precise and help the reader visualize the topic.	In a few places, the words are too general and do not create an image for the reader.
Sentence Fluency	The writer effectively uses repeated sentence structures to highlight related ideas.	The writer uses repeated sentence structures for related ideas with some effectiveness.	The writer attempts repeated sentence structures for related ideas but is not always effective.
Conventions	Appositives, predicate nouns, and predicate adjectives are used correctly and add style to the writing.	There are one or two minor errors with predicate nouns, predicate adjectives, and appositives.	Some appositives are not punctuated correctly. One or two predicate nouns or adjectives are used incorrectly.

+Presentation White space organizes the text for easy reading.

CCSS Common Core State Standards

Descriptive Essay

Writing in the Descriptive mode can engage the Common Core State Standards for both Narrative and Informative/Explanatory writing. The rubric and strategies for Ideas are drawn from informative/explanatory standards **W.6.2.a** and **W.6.2.b,** which focus on choosing a clear topic and developing and supporting it with solid, relevant details, and Narrative standard **W.6.3.d,** with its emphasis on descriptive and sensory details. The rubric and writing strategies for Organization are grounded in informative/explanatory standard **W.6.2.a** and narrative standard **W.6.3.a,** both of which focus on introducing the topic and organizing the writing logically. The rubric and writing strategies for

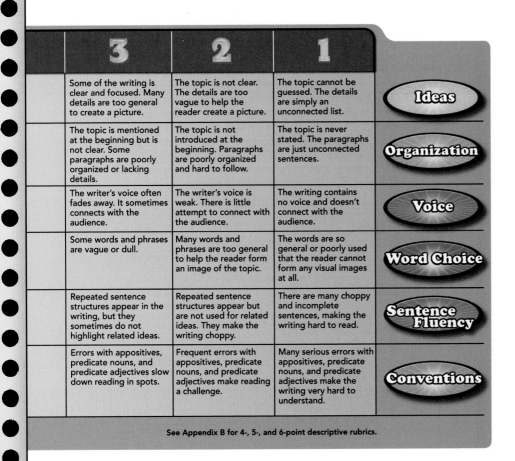

3	2	1	
Some of the writing is clear and focused. Many details are too general to create a picture.	The topic is not clear. The details are too vague to help the reader create a picture.	The topic cannot be guessed. The details are simply an unconnected list.	**Ideas**
The topic is mentioned at the beginning but is not clear. Some paragraphs are poorly organized or lacking details.	The topic is not introduced at the beginning. Paragraphs are poorly organized and hard to follow.	The topic is never stated. The paragraphs are just unconnected sentences.	**Organization**
The writer's voice often fades away. It sometimes connects with the audience.	The writer's voice is weak. There is little attempt to connect with the audience.	The writing contains no voice and doesn't connect with the audience.	**Voice**
Some words and phrases are vague or dull.	Many words and phrases are too general to help the reader form an image of the topic.	The words are so general or poorly used that the reader cannot form any visual images at all.	**Word Choice**
Repeated sentence structures appear in the writing, but they sometimes do not highlight related ideas.	Repeated sentence structures appear but are not used for related ideas. They make the writing choppy.	There are many choppy and incomplete sentences, making the writing hard to read.	**Sentence Fluency**
Errors with appositives, predicate nouns, and predicate adjectives slow down reading in spots.	Frequent errors with appositives, predicate nouns, and predicate adjectives make reading a challenge.	Many serious errors with appositives, predicate nouns, and predicate adjectives make the writing very hard to understand.	**Conventions**

See Appendix B for 4-, 5-, and 6-point descriptive rubrics.

Apply the Rubric

Assign Groups Assign small groups of students to check the model for one trait. One person in each group should be responsible for recording one or two strong examples of the trait as described by the rubric.

Reassemble the Class Bring the class together and ask one person from each group to report the group's findings to the class. The point of this exercise is less to score the model than it is to practice identifying and evaluating the traits within a piece of writing.

Additional Rubrics Appendix B includes 4-, 5-, and 6-point rubrics that can be used with any piece of descriptive writing. The rubrics are also available as blackline masters in the back of this Teacher Edition, beginning on page T525.

Voice reflect language standard **L.6.3.b,** which calls for the writer to maintain a consistent style and tone. The rubric and writing strategies for Word Choice take their focus on precise language from both informative/explanatory standard **W.6.2.d** and narrative standard **W.6.3.d**. The language standards **L.6.1** and **L.6.2,** which focus on command of the conventions of grammar, usage, capitalization, spelling, and punctuation, are evident in Conventions. Woven throughout the unit are writing standards **W.6.4–W.6.6** and **W.6.10,** which focus on writing appropriately for the task, the purpose, and the audience; using technology; and writing routinely over extended time frames.

CCSS Common Core State Standards

SL.6.1: Engage effectively in a range of collaborative discussions (one-on-one, in groups, and teacher-led) with diverse partners on *grade 6 topics, texts, and issues,* building on others' ideas and expressing their own clearly. **SL.6.1.a:** Come to discussions prepared, having read or studied required material; explicitly draw on that preparation by referring to evidence on the topic, text, or issue to probe and reflect on ideas under discussion. **SL.6.1.b:** Follow rules for collegial discussions, set specific goals and deadlines, and define individual roles as needed.

Analyze
the Model

Week 1 • Day 4

Student Objectives

- Read a model descriptive essay. (p. 371)
- Use the descriptive essay rubric. (pp. 372–373)
- Use the model descriptive essay to study Ideas, Organization, and Voice. (pp. 374–375)

Study the Model

Assess the Model Once students have read pages 374 and 375, ask them whether they agree or disagree with Denise's assessment of the model on each point. For example, do students feel that Anna organized her paragraphs effectively? Use questions such as the following to discuss the model and the traits with students.

- What details appeal to the senses of smell and touch? (Possible responses: the smell of ozone, a shiver down the spine)

 Strategies for Writers Online

Go to **www.sfw.z-b.com** for additional online resources for students and teachers.

Descriptive Essay
Using the Rubric to Study the Model

Did you notice that the model on page 371 points out some key elements of a descriptive essay? As she wrote "A Striking Image," Anna Yuishmal used these elements to help her describe an event. She also used the 6-point rubric on pages 372–373 to plan, draft, revise, and edit the writing. A rubric is a great tool for evaluating writing during the writing process.

Now let's use the same rubric to score the model. To do this, we'll focus on each trait separately, starting with Ideas. We'll use the top descriptor for each trait (column 6), along with examples from the model, to help us understand how the traits work together. How would you score Anna on each trait?

 **Ideas**

- The topic is clear and focused.
- Vivid sensory details create a picture for the reader.

Anna sticks with one topic in her essay—the photo of the lightning storm. She uses vivid and realistic details that make the reader see and hear the lightning storm as if it were really happening. Look at these sensory details.

[from the writing model]

Filling the page was a lightning storm, a monstrous fire in the sky. Against an inky black sky, mounds of angry clouds piled on top of each other. A charred, smoky-gray mass smoldered near the bottom of the photo.

374 Descriptive Writing

English Language Learners

BEGINNING

Descriptive Essay Write *describe*. Ask, *What does this word mean?* Students should know that it means "to tell details about something." Write *descriptive essay*. Say, *You are going to write and describe something.*

INTERMEDIATE

Imagery Use a photograph to teach the word *image*. Write it and have students repeat. Tell students to close their eyes and think about the beach. Ask, *Do you see the white sand and ocean?* Tell them that they are *imagining*. Write *imagine* and have students repeat. In writing, *imagery* is creating pictures with words. Write the word and have students repeat. Underline *imag* in each word to highlight that the words are from the same root.

Organization

- The description is organized so that the topic is introduced at the beginning and the details are organized into logical paragraphs.

Anna starts her essay with a clear and interesting statement about her topic. Then the essay flows from one well-organized paragraph to the next. Each paragraph has a clear topic sentence, which helps organize the information. See how a supporting detail expands on the topic sentence in this paragraph.

[from the writing model]

Lightning is a split-second show, a glimpse of nature's awesome energy. Zing! Steely fingers reach out to snatch a piece of the sky.

Voice

- The voice connects directly with the reader in a friendly way.

This essay uses a tone of voice that the reader can easily relate to. Anna talks about what the photo reminded her of. She also shares her feelings about thunder in a way that sounds friendly, like she is talking directly to us.

[from the writing model]

The image reminded me of what comes after a lightning strike. The metallic odor of burnt oxygen, or ozone, follows the flash. Then comes thunder, a distant rolling rumble or sudden echoing boom. To me, thunder is the delicious dessert after the lightning.

Descriptive Essay 375

- In the first paragraph, how do the details support the topic sentence? Does every sentence belong in this paragraph? (Possible responses: They describe the photograph and explain why it caught the writer's eye. Yes.)

- How does the friendly voice affect your experience as a reader of this essay? (Possible response: First-person point of view makes me feel connected to the writer and gives me a sense that I'm sharing her experience.)

ADVANCED

Main Ideas and Details Write the following paragraph on the board: *Our family loves to travel. It doesn't matter where we go, we just like to be together. We love camping in the brisk, fall weather or basking in the sun on a tropical island.* Ask students to tell the most important information in the paragraph. Underline the first sentence and write *main idea* under it. Tell students that the other sentences give more information about the main idea. They are the supporting details.

ADVANCED HIGH

Imagery Write the word *imagery* and ask for volunteers to guess its meaning. If needed, write *image* and *imagine,* too. Once students understand that *imagery* is creating pictures with words, have them brainstorm some ways they can include imagery in their writing. Discuss descriptive details, figurative language, and powerful verbs.

CCSS Common Core State Standards

R/Inf.6.2: Determine a central idea of a text and how it is conveyed through particular details; provide a summary of the text distinct from personal opinions or judgments. **R/Inf.6.5:** Analyze how a particular sentence, paragraph, chapter, or section fits into the overall structure of a text and contributes to the development of the ideas. **R/Inf.6.6:** Determine an author's point of view or purpose in a text and explain how it is conveyed in the text. **SL.6.1.b:** Follow rules for collegial discussions, set specific goals and deadlines, and define individual roles as needed. **SL.6.1.d:** Review the key ideas expressed and demonstrate understanding of multiple perspectives through reflection and paraphrasing.

Descriptive Essay T375

Analyze
the Model

Week 1 • Day 5

Student Objectives

- Read a model descriptive essay. (*p. 371*)
- Use the descriptive essay rubric. (*pp. 372–373*)
- Use the model descriptive essay to study Word Choice, Sentence Fluency, and Conventions. (*pp. 376–377*)

Continue Discussing the Traits

Use questions such as the following to discuss the traits analyzed on pages 376 and 377:

- What's another example of precise language that paints a vivid picture of the lightning storm? (Possible responses: *The metallic odor of burnt oxygen, or ozone, follows the flash. Then comes thunder, a distant rolling rumble or a sudden echoing boom.*)

- How do the interjections make an impression on you as a reader? (Possible responses: They add to the drama of the moment described by emphasizing the excitement. They create a staccato effect that mimics the flash of lightning.)

- How do you know Anna carefully edited her writing? (Possible response: I couldn't find any spelling or grammar mistakes.)

Strategies for Writers Online

Go to **www.sfw.z-b.com** for additional online resources for students and teachers.

T376 Descriptive Writing

- Precise words and phrases help the reader form a visual image.

Talk about great word choice! Anna used exciting words and created lively images of the lightning storm in the photograph. The reader almost doesn't need to see the photograph because Anna's descriptions are so dynamic and precise. Look at these powerful sentences about the colors in the sky.

[from the writing model]

A raging orange cloud exploded like lava. Looming above was a brilliant yellow cloudburst, singed red at its edges. The lightning bolts were a tangle of glowing white wires that sliced the night into jagged pieces.

- The writer effectively uses repeated sentence structures to highlight related ideas.

Sometimes writers use the same sentence structure in a short space to convey connected ideas. This can add power and depth to the writing. Notice how Anna repeats the dramatic sentence structure she uses to describe lightning's speed and power.

[from the writing model]

Zing! Steely fingers reach out to snatch a piece of the sky. Poof! They are gone.

376 Descriptive Writing

Technology Tip for 21st Century Literacies

Writing for global communities requires astute attention to detail, especially as perspectives are deeply influenced by the contexts in which we reside. Use images as a text from which to begin this work, as composing an image requires that attention to detail, but reading images also allows for access into differing points of view. GeoPanda is a useful site for kickstarting thinking around images as it captures geo-tagged images posted in real-time to Flickr and other image sites. Watch the feed, discuss with students, and consider how point of view is communicated in an image.

See **www.sfw.z-b.com** for further information about and links to these websites and tools.

Conventions

- Appositives, predicate nouns, and predicate adjectives are used correctly and add style to the writing.

I checked over Anna's essay, and I didn't find any mistakes. She even used appositives correctly. In the sentence below, *ozone* is an appositive that provides more information about the burnt oxygen. Anna sets the appositive off with commas.

[from the writing model]

The metallic odor of burnt oxygen, or ozone, follows the flash.

Looming above was a brilliant yellow cloudburst . . .

Lightning is a split-second show . . .

Presentation White space organizes the text for easy reading.

My Turn!

Now I'm ready to write my own descriptive essay. I already have some ideas. Read along and see how I do it. I'm going to use what I learned from the rubric and good writing strategies.

Differentiating Instruction

ENRICHMENT

Collect Precise Language Have students look through books and magazines to find a sample descriptive essay or paragraph. Ask them to highlight precise, descriptive words and phrases; elements that show a friendly, engaging voice; and sentence patterns used effectively for emphasis. Ask volunteers to read aloud the paragraphs or essays they chose and have the class decide whether they think the writing examples are effective.

REINFORCEMENT

Reinforce Topic Sentence and Supporting Details Give students examples of descriptive essays or short essays and have them practice identifying the topic sentence and supporting details of each paragraph. Then give students an object to describe. Have them create a topic sentence and list details that support it.

Presentation Remind students that they need to pay attention to space around the text as well as the text itself. White space provided by adequate margins and space between paragraphs makes writing easier to read. In contrast, a crowded page can distract and frustrate readers. Encourage students to use a word-processing program to write their descriptive essays so that they can make good use of tabs and other features to create white space.

Think About the Traits Now ask students which traits they think are most important in a descriptive essay. Explain that all traits are important in every piece of writing, but some stand out more in some genres than in others. Some students may feel that the trait of **Ideas** is very important because the purpose of a descriptive essay is to paint a verbal picture of a topic. Others may think that **Word Choice** is important because precise, descriptive words and phrases are needed to create a picture.

CCSS Common Core State Standards

SL.6.1.b: Follow rules for collegial discussions, set specific goals and deadlines, and define individual roles as needed. **SL.6.1.c:** Pose and respond to specific questions with elaboration and detail by making comments that contribute to the topic, text, or issue under discussion. **SL.6.1.d:** Review the key ideas expressed and demonstrate understanding of multiple perspectives through reflection and paraphrasing.

Write
a Descriptive Essay

Week 2 • Day 1

Student Objectives

• Read and understand a prewriting strategy. (pp. 378–379)

Prewrite

Focus on Ideas

Gather Information Remind students that one of Denise's hobbies is photography. Note that for her descriptive essay, she has chosen to write about a particular photo she found striking. Then she wrote down notes that provided descriptions of sensory details in the photo.

Provide illustrated books and magazines for students to look through or have them browse websites with age-appropriate content on topics that interest them. Before students start looking, briefly discuss the criteria they should use in choosing an image. Will students be looking for an image that is visually striking, funny, cute, sad, or surprising? Refer students to the purposes for writing listed on page 369. How might their purpose for writing affect their choice of images? Suggest that an image on a topic that interests students will be easier to describe and more enjoyable to write about.

 Strategies for Writers Online

Go to **www.sfw.z-b.com** for additional online resources for students and teachers.

Prewrite Focus on Ideas

The Rubric Says   The topic is clear and focused.

Writing Strategy   Choose a picture and make notes about its sensory details.

While I was looking for a subject for my descriptive essay assignment, I found this photograph of a cat and a fish. It was in a magazine ad, and I couldn't stop looking at it.

English Language Learners

BEGINNING

The Five Senses Demonstrate the meanings of *sight, sound, touch, taste,* and *smell,* and make sure students understand that each sense corresponds to a certain part of the body. Say a word, such as *salty, bumpy,* or *blue,* and have students point to the body part that we use to perceive the idea of the word. Then model a sentence for students to repeat, such as *The sky is blue.*

INTERMEDIATE

Sensory Details Prepare a set of index cards with words associated with a business such as a pizza shop, for example, *pepperoni, chewy, hot, phone ringing,* and so on. Draw a Spider Map with the label *Pizza Shop* with the five senses as the "legs" on the map. As you introduce a word on the index cards, ask students to tell which category the word belongs with on the Spider Map.

I took these notes on the sensory details in the photograph so I could use them in my essay. I had to use my imagination to capture the sight, sound, and feel of things in the picture. I didn't take any notes on smells or tastes, though. I don't think there are any—unless the cat catches the fish!

My Notes on the Picture of the Cat and Fish

✔ **see:** cat looking into fishbowl; looks like cat's face is inside bowl; cat's ears—small pink shark fins; eyes—big baby-blue and black marbles in pink ovals; nose—pale pink; whiskers—white; goldfish—on cat's nose, plump, shiny yellow with bright orange at front, black ink dot for eye, 2 tiny bubbles from open mouth; bowl—open on top, curved edges, water line below cat's ears, white gravel

✔ **feel:** cat's nose—velvety; ears—fluffy inside; whiskers—sharp; fish's tail—gauzy, delicate

✔ **hear:** cat saying, "Mmmm!"; fish saying, "Uh-oh!"

Choose an interesting subject to describe, and take notes about as many sensory details as possible.

Tell students to focus on one sense at a time as they take notes about their pictures. Point out that Denise used her imagination for the senses other than sight. For the hearing details, she put herself into the positions of the cat and the fish and imagined what they might be thinking at the time the photo was taken. Suggest that students imagine themselves in the image they have chosen. Ask volunteers for other ideas on how to think of sensory details.

ADVANCED

Topic Sentence Explain that a topic is what a paragraph or an entire essay is about. Write a topic sentence on the board. Give students strips of paper with sentences that may or may not go with this topic sentence. Students read the sentence to the class and tell whether it should be included in the paragraph. Using the correct sentences, write a paragraph on the board that goes with the topic sentence.

ADVANCED HIGH

Using Exact Words After students have written their first drafts, have them circle all the adjectives and verbs they used in the first paragraph. Then have them trade with a partner who will read the paragraph and change each of the circled words to a more descriptive one. Tell the partners to discuss why they made each change. Monitor that students' changes were appropriate.

CCSS Common Core State Standards

W.6.2.a: Introduce a topic; organize ideas, concepts, and information, using strategies such as definition, classification, comparison/contrast, and cause/effect; include formatting (e.g., headings), graphics (e.g., charts, tables), and multimedia when useful to aiding comprehension. **W.6.2.b:** Develop the topic with relevant facts, definitions, concrete details, quotations, or other information and examples. **W.6.3.d:** Use precise words and phrases, relevant descriptive details, and sensory language to convey experiences and events.

Write
a Descriptive Essay

Week 2 • Day 2

Student Objectives

- Use a Spider Map to organize the notes. *(pp. 380–381)*

Prewrite

Focus on Organization

Make a Spider Map Have students read Denise's words on page 380 and study the Spider Map on page 381. Point out that each leg of the spider includes one category of sensory details. This will help ensure that Denise does not focus too much on one aspect of the photo and neglect details about the other aspects. Note, too, that she provides details about the feel and sound of the photo—or what she thinks the elements of the photos might feel like or sound like.

Prewrite

Focus on **Organization**

The Rubric Says	The description is organized so that the topic is introduced at the beginning and the details are organized into logical paragraphs.
Writing Strategy	Use a Spider Map to organize the notes.

The rubric stresses that the details of my essay should be organized logically into paragraphs. Since I am describing a picture, I will organize my writing around the senses. I'll start by organizing my notes that way, but I see that most of my details are in the "see" category. I need to break my notes into more categories.

A Spider Map will help me organize my notes better. I can make each leg a different category of details, like what I can see of the cat in the photograph, what I can see of the fish, and so on.

When I get my notes organized into several categories, I will be able to write my essay in logically organized paragraphs. I'll also make sure I introduce my topic clearly right at the start.

✏️ Writer's Term

Spider Map
A **Spider Map** organizes information about a topic. The topic is written in the center circle. Each "leg" is one category of details.

380 Descriptive Writing

Online Writing Center

Provides **interactive graphic organizers** as well as a variety of graphic organizers in PDF format.

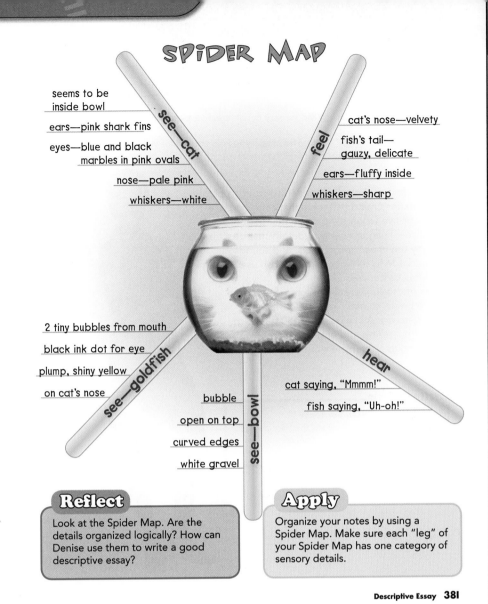

SPIDER MAP

see—cat
- seems to be inside bowl
- ears—pink shark fins
- eyes—blue and black marbles in pink ovals
- nose—pale pink
- whiskers—white

feel
- cat's nose—velvety
- fish's tail—gauzy, delicate
- ears—fluffy inside
- whiskers—sharp

see—goldfish
- 2 tiny bubbles from mouth
- black ink dot for eye
- plump, shiny yellow
- on cat's nose

see—bowl
- bubble
- open on top
- curved edges
- white gravel

hear
- cat saying, "Mmmm!"
- fish saying, "Uh-oh!"

Reflect
Look at the Spider Map. Are the details organized logically? How can Denise use them to write a good descriptive essay?

Apply
Organize your notes by using a Spider Map. Make sure each "leg" of your Spider Map has one category of sensory details.

Emphasize to students that their Spider Maps may have more or fewer legs than Denise's and that they may use more or fewer senses than she does. Then instruct students to create Spider Maps based on the notes they took.

✏ Writer's Term
Spider Map A Spider Map is an excellent tool for organizing writing into paragraphs. Each leg contains the topic of a paragraph and lists supporting details.

Conferencing

PEER TO PEER Have partners exchange Spider Maps and show each other the images they chose. Tell students to ask one question about a detail in their partner's map to elicit more information. Each student can decide whether to include the answer to the question in his or her Spider Map.

PEER GROUPS Have groups of three or four students pass their Spider Maps and the images they chose around the group. Each student asks the group for feedback on an issue they had trouble with while writing his or her map.

TEACHER-LED Work with individual students to improve their Spider Maps. Ask questions to elicit details that might appeal to senses students have not explored.

CCSS Common Core State Standards

W.6.2.a: Introduce a topic; organize ideas, concepts, and information, using strategies such as definition, classification, comparison/contrast, and cause/effect; include formatting (e.g., headings), graphics (e.g., charts, tables), and multimedia when useful to aiding comprehension. **W.6.2.b:** Develop the topic with relevant facts, definitions, concrete details, quotations, or other information and examples. **W.6.3.d:** Use precise words and phrases, relevant descriptive details, and sensory language to convey experiences and events.

Write
a Descriptive Essay

Week 2 • Day 3

Student Objectives

- Begin writing, using vivid sensory details. *(p. 382)*

Draft

Focus on Ideas

Begin a Draft Remind students that a draft is a temporary or rough form of a piece of writing. A draft will be changed and corrected several times before it is finished. That's why it's important to get information on paper and not worry too much about such things as mistakes in spelling and grammar.

Point out that Denise refers to the rubric and the Spider Map as she writes. That's how she can be sure her writing conveys vivid sensory images to the reader. Encourage students to get in the habit of using the rubric and the graphic organizer to help guide their own writing.

Online Writing Center

 Provides student eBooks with an **interactive writing pad** for drafting, revising, editing, and publishing.

Draft
Focus on **Ideas**

The Rubric Says	Vivid sensory details create a picture for the reader.
Writing Strategy	Use vivid imagery to help the reader visualize the picture.

According to the rubric, I need to create a picture in my reader's mind. After all, that's the purpose of descriptive writing—to make the reader "see" what I see. I can use sensory details that describe the way the image looks, feels, and sounds. My Spider Map has lots of notes I can use in my detail sentences.

This photograph really got a reaction from me, so I want to make my reader have the same reaction. As I write the draft, I'll do my best with spelling and grammar and check for any mistakes later. Here's the beginning of my essay.

> ✏️ **Writer's Term**___
>
> **Detail Sentence**
> A **detail sentence** supports the paragraph's main idea. The detail sentences in a paragraph should all relate to the main idea.

382 Descriptive Writing

Differentiating Instruction

ENRICHMENT

Expand Imagery Challenge students to use submerged metaphors, which are implied comparisons such as *She dove into her work.* Students may want to try extended metaphors, which involve several sentences. For example, several sentences might compare a busy playground with a circus.

REINFORCEMENT

Practice With Detail Sentences Supply students with a paragraph that includes a topic sentence, detail sentences that relate to the topic sentence, and one detail sentence that does not relate to the topic sentence. Ask students to identify the topic sentence and then the detail sentence that does not relate. Have students suggest a sentence that could replace the unrelated one. Repeat the exercise with one or two additional paragraphs.

[DRAFT]

Beware, Little Fishy!

Sometimes people feel like they're in a fishbowl and someone is looking at them. Well, I found a photograph about that idea. A white cat is looking at a goldfish in a bowl. The water changes what you see. It looks like the cat's face is inside the bowl, and the cat's face looks huge.

[detail sentences]

The cat's staring eyes, big blue marbles with black centers, are set in pink ovals. Its ears are like pink shark fins, with tufts of white fluff inside. The ears are above the water line, so they aren't changed. They are much smaller than the eyes and closer together. White whiskers sprout from the cat's furry cheeks. Its nose is pale pink.

Reflect
Think about the draft. Which sensory details help you picture what the photograph looks like?

Apply
Write a draft using interesting details from your Spider Map. Make sure you use vivid images to write your detail sentences.

Descriptive Essay 383

Conferencing

PEER TO PEER Have students exchange drafts with a partner. Each student underlines in pencil the sensory detail he or she likes best in the draft and circles a detail that is hard to understand or that could be made clearer.

PEER GROUPS Have students work in groups of three taking turns reading their drafts aloud to the group. Group members are to pick out the sensory detail they like best in the reader's draft, and then ask one question to clarify something they don't understand.

TEACHER-LED Work with pairs of students. Have each student read his or her draft aloud. Facilitate a discussion between students about what information they could add to make their drafts more complete.

Write
a Descriptive Essay

Week 2 • Day 4

Student Objectives
• Complete a draft. *(p. 383)*

Finish the Draft Have students read the draft excerpt on page 383. Discuss with the class how the highlighted detail sentences relate to the topic of the paragraph. Talk about the sensory details in the paragraph. To which sense do they appeal? (sight) What images do students find striking and engaging? (Possible response: the comparison of the cat's ears to shark fins)

Take a moment to review the proofreading marks at the top of the page. Explain to students that they will be using these marks when they revise and edit their writing.

✎ Writer's Term _____
Detail Sentence In descriptive and expository writing, detail sentences commonly give more information about the subject of the topic sentence. The information should be relevant and engaging to the reader. Writers should try to include details that the reader does not expect or already know.

CCSS Common Core State Standards
W.6.2.a: Introduce a topic; organize ideas, concepts, and information, using strategies such as definition, classification, comparison/contrast, and cause/effect; include formatting (e.g., headings), graphics (e.g., charts, tables), and multimedia when useful to aiding comprehension. **W.6.2.b:** Develop the topic with relevant facts, definitions, concrete details, quotations, or other information and examples. **W.6.3.d:** Use precise words and phrases, relevant descriptive details, and sensory language to convey experiences and events.

Write
a Descriptive Essay

Week 2 • Day 5

Student Objectives

- Revise to make sure all detail sentences relate to the paragraph's topic sentence. (p. 384)

Revise

Focus on Organization

Relate Details to Topic Sentences
Have students read the page. Then ask the class why the topic sentence often comes at the beginning of the paragraph. (Possible response: To tell the reader right away what the paragraph is about)

Point out the draft excerpt. Discuss with students whether the topic sentence Denise added makes sense for the paragraph. Ask students to point out details in the sentence that support the idea that the cat's face is "scary but sweet." (Possible responses: ears like shark fins—scary; tufts of white fur—sweet; staring eyes— scary; normal-looking ears—sweet)

Writer's Term

Topic Sentence Placing the topic sentence at the end of the paragraph can be an effective way of drawing the reader in. The writer builds reader interest by giving a series of details and then wraps them up neatly with a topic sentence that ties them together.

 Strategies for Writers Online
Go to **www.sfw.z-b.com** for additional online resources for students and teachers.

Writing a Descriptive Essay

Revise
Focus on **Organization**

The Rubric Says The description is organized so that the topic is introduced at the beginning and the details are organized into logical paragraphs.

Writing Strategy Make sure all the detail sentences relate to the topic sentence in every paragraph.

I've introduced my topic in the first paragraph. Now I want to make sure all my paragraphs are logically organized and easy to follow. I'll check that each one has a clear topic sentence and only details that relate to the topic. This paragraph has great details, but it needs a topic sentence to hold it together.

Writer's Term
Topic Sentence
The **topic sentence** states the main idea of a paragraph. It is often the first sentence in the paragraph.

[DRAFT]

[added topic sentence]
The cat's face is scary but sweet.

Its
~~The cat's~~ staring eyes, big blue marbles with black centers, are set in pink ovals. Its ears are like pink shark fins, with tufts of white fluff inside. The ears are above the water line, so they aren't changed. They are much smaller than the eyes and closer together.

Apply
Make sure all your paragraphs have topic sentences supported by detail sentences.

384 Descriptive Writing

English Language Learners

BEGINNING/INTERMEDIATE

Forming Questions Writing questions is sometimes difficult for ELLs. Remind them that the question word (*Who, What, When,* and so on) is usually the first word in the question. To practice, write declarative sentences on index cards. For example, *I am studying algebra.* Have students write the question form on the other side of the card. Repeat several times. Use the same procedure to practice forming *yes/no* questions.

ADVANCED/ADVANCED HIGH

Using Appositives On the board, write *The Sherpa helped the climbers reach the summit.* Ask students if they know what a *Sherpa* is. Revise the sentence to *The Sherpa, or mountain guide, helped the climbers reach the summit.* Tell students that the new information helps the reader understand the vocabulary and is called an appositive. Have students write an appositive for *summit.*

Revise

Focus on **Voice**

The Rubric Says The voice connects directly with the reader in a friendly way.

Writing Strategy Choose punctuation for effect.

The rubric says to connect with my reader and sound friendly. I can make the paragraph below friendlier by using second person *you*. That will help connect my reader with what I'm describing. I can also use questions and exclamation marks to share my surprise and enthusiasm.

[DRAFT]

[connected with reader by using second person]

~~Sometimes people feel like they're in a fishbowl and someone is~~
Do you ever feel like you're in a fishbowl and someone is looking at you?
~~looking at them?~~ Well, I found a photograph about that idea. A white
cat is looking at a goldfish in a bowl. The water changes what you
see. It looks like the cat's face is inside the bowl, and the cat's face
looks huge.!

[added exclamation]

Reflect
Does the writing sound more friendly? Why do you think so?

Apply
Add *you* to make it sound as if you are talking to the reader.

Descriptive Essay **385**

Conferencing

PEER TO PEER Have partners read their drafts aloud to a partner. The partner listens for the tone and offers suggestions for making it more friendly and direct.

PEER GROUPS Have students pass their essays around the group. Each group member underlines in pencil a word he or she thinks is vague and could be replaced with a more precise one.

TEACHER-LED Meet with individual students. Read each student's descriptive essay aloud and have the student listen for the tone in the essay. Discuss whether the tone is appropriate and consistent. If necessary, help the student think of ideas for making the tone more engaging for the reader.

Write
a Descriptive Essay

Week 3 • Day 1

Student Objectives

• Revise to use punctuation for effect. *(p. 385)*

Revise

Focus on **Voice**

Use Questions and Exclamations
Have students read the page and discuss how Denise's revisions change the tone of the draft excerpt. Do students agree that the voice sounds friendlier and more direct?

Help students practice turning statements into questions or exclamations and observing the differences in tone. Write sentences such as the following on the board:

• *I was so distracted I walked into a tree.*

• *We saw the eggs hatching in the nest.*

Have students experiment with turning these sentences into questions and exclamations. Prompt them with examples such as these: *Have you ever been so distracted you just walked right into something? I was so distracted I walked into a tree! Ouch!* Discuss how the changes in punctuation and sentence type change the voice and tone.

CCSS **C**ommon **C**ore **S**tate **S**tandards
W.6.2.a: Introduce a topic; organize ideas, concepts, and information, using strategies such as definition, classification, comparison/contrast, and cause/effect; include formatting (e.g., headings), graphics (e.g., charts, tables), and multimedia when useful to aiding comprehension. **W.6.2.b:** Develop the topic with relevant facts, definitions, concrete details, quotations, or other information and examples. **L.6.3.b:** Maintain consistency in style and tone.

Descriptive Essay **T385**

Write
a Descriptive Essay

Week 3 • Day 2

Student Objectives

- Revise to replace vague words with precise ones. *(p. 386)*

Revise

Focus on  **Word Choice**

Eliminate Vague Words Ask students why Denise changed the sentence to say *someone is watching you* instead of *someone is looking at you.* (Possible response: *Someone is watching you* sounds more threatening or creepy, which helps set the tone.)

Explain that students should be mindful not only of the precise meaning of a word but also of its connotation, or the associated feeling or emotion attributed to a word. The word *watching* implies intent, which is what gives it the connotation of being more purposeful or possibly threatening.

On the board, write *happy*, *people*, and *good*. Have students suggest words that could replace them. (Possible responses: *delighted, pleased, thrilled; fans, participants, diners; delicious, exciting, skillful*) Alert students to look for vague words as they review their drafts and to replace them with words that have the meaning (denotation) and the connotation to suit the purpose.

Online Writing Center

Provides **interactive proofreading activities** for each genre.

Revise

Focus on  **Word Choice**

The Rubric Says	Precise words and phrases help the reader form a visual image.
Writing Strategy	Replace vague words with precise ones.

The rubric says I should use precise words, but I see some places where I don't do that. I'm going to take out some vague words and replace them with precise words that will convey a clearer visual image. This will help my reader picture what I am describing.

[DRAFT]

~~Sometimes people feel like they're in a fishbowl and someone is~~ *watching* Do you ever feel like you're in a fishbowl and someone is ~~looking at you?~~ *peering intently* ~~looking at them.~~ Well, I found a photograph about that idea. A white cat is ~~looking~~ at a goldfish in a bowl. The water ~~changes~~ *distorts* what you see. It looks like the cat's face is inside the bowl, and the cat's face looks huge ! **[replaced vague words]**

Apply

Replace any vague words with more precise and interesting words.

386 Descriptive Writing

Optional Revising Lessons

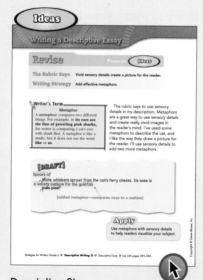

Descriptive 31

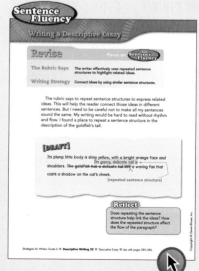

Descriptive 32

 Strategies for Writers Grade 6 CD-ROM

Edit
Focus on Conventions

The Rubric Says	Appositives, predicate nouns, and predicate adjectives are used correctly and add style to the writing.
Writing Strategy	Check for the correct use of appositives, predicate nouns, and predicate adjectives.

✏ Writer's Term____
Appositives
An **appositive** is a word or phrase that follows a noun and helps to identify or describe the noun.

Wow! I'm almost finished! Now I need to make sure my sentence structures are correct. Good structure makes sentences easy to follow. But if I make mistakes, such as forgetting to put commas around appositives, my readers will be confused.

[DRAFT]   [added commas to fix error in appositive]

When you look at the picture, you can imagine what the cat and the fish are thinking and saying. The cat, a silent and sly hunter, is thinking about the ~~juicy~~ (juicy) orange goldfish. The cat murmurs, "Mmmm!" and the fish replies, "Uh-oh!" Two tiny bubbles float up.

Reflect
What do you think? How have Denise's revisions strengthened her essay? Go back and look over her draft. Can you find any errors she's missed?

Apply   *Conventions*
Edit your draft for spelling, punctuation, appositives, and predicate nouns and adjectives.

For more practice with appositives and predicate nouns and adjectives, use the exercises on the next two pages.

Descriptive Essay **387**

Related Grammar Practice____

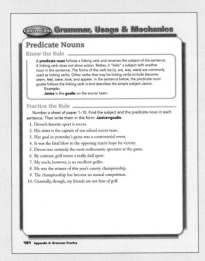

Student Edition page 484

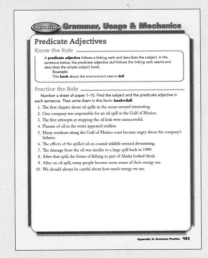

Student Edition page 485

Go to ➡ Appendix A: Grammar Practice

Write
a Descriptive Essay

Student Objectives
- Edit for correct use of appositives, predicate nouns, and predicate adjectives. (p. 387)

Edit

Focus on *Conventions*

Check Appositives, Predicate Nouns, and Predicate Adjectives
Have students read the page and discuss the revisions.

If students have trouble with appositives or predicate nouns and adjectives, teach the mini-lessons on pages T388 and T389. Then have students complete the exercises on pages 388 and 389.

✏ Writer's Term____

Appositive When appositives are *restrictive*, i.e., necessary for understanding the sentence, they are not set off with commas. In the sentence *My friend David is coming with us*, the word *David* is a restrictive appositive.

CCSS Common Core State Standards
W.6.2.d: Use precise language and domain-specific vocabulary to inform about or explain the topic. **W.6.3.d:** Use precise words and phrases, relevant descriptive details, and sensory language to convey experiences and events. **L.6.1:** Demonstrate command of the conventions of standard English grammar and usage when writing or speaking. **L.6.2:** Demonstrate command of the conventions of standard English capitalization, punctuation, and spelling when writing. **L.6.2.a:** Use punctuation (commas, parentheses, dashes) to set off nonrestrictive/parenthetical elements. **L.6.2.b:** Spell correctly. **L.6.5.c:** Distinguish among the connotations (associations) of words with similar denotations (definitions) (e.g., *stingy, scrimping, economical, unwasteful, thrifty*).

Conventions

Mini-Lesson

Student Objectives

- Learn to use appositives correctly. (p. 388)

Appositives

Explain to students that appositives are words or phrases that explain or identify a noun. An appositive often follows the noun it modifies, but it can precede the noun.

Write the following on the board: *Jack and Sam, the twins who lived next door, were known for being helpful.*

Ask students to identify the appositive in the sentence. (the twins who lived next door)

Explain to students that appositives are usually separated from the rest of the sentence by commas. Write the following on the board: *They took care of Sage our neighbor's Labrador retriever while the neighbor was away.* Ask a volunteer to write commas where necessary in the sentence. (They took care of Sage, our neighbor's Labrador retriever, while the neighbor was away.) If needed, write additional sentences on the board for students for more practice.

Online Writing Center

 Provides **interactive grammar games** and **practice activities** in student eBook.

Appositives

Know the Rule

An **appositive** is a word or phrase that follows a noun or pronoun and helps identify or describe it. Appositives are usually separated from the rest of the sentence by commas.

Example: Dolly, **my cat**, came to our house as a stray.
My neighbor's dogs, **two boxers**, bark at night.

Practice the Rule

Number your paper 1–10. For the first group of sentences below, write the noun and the appositive that follows.

1. Here are some tips, or guidelines, for getting good photographs of your pets.
2. The first tip, the most important one, is to study your pet.
3. Find your pet's favorite spot, the place where it likes to spend most of its time.
4. For example, Bubba, my shaggy sheepdog, likes to hang out on the braided rug in the den.
5. Observe your pet's typical behavior, what he or she does every day.

In this group of sentences, notice the underlined nouns or pronouns. Write an appositive that you could use for each underlined word. **Possible answers shown**

6. Our neighbor, _____, likes to take pictures of his dog. **Mr. Bergman**
7. His best picture, _____, won a prize last year. **one of his dog in snow**
8. Our neighbor's daughter, _____, takes the dog for walks. **Rachel**
9. They usually head for their favorite spot, _____. **Hillside Park**
10. Our neighbor has many pictures of the two of them, _____, at the park. **Rachel and himself**

Related Grammar Practice

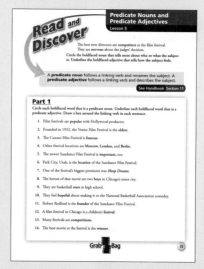

Page 15

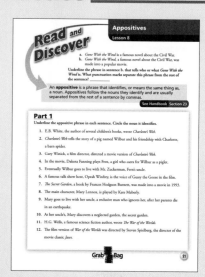

Page 21

 G.U.M. Student Practice Book

Predicate Nouns and Adjectives

Know the Rule

A **predicate noun** follows a linking verb and renames the subject.
Example: The cat's tail is a **snake** that can't keep still.
A **predicate adjective** follows a linking verb and describes the subject.
Example: Our dog is **chubby**!

Practice the Rule

Copy the following sentences. Underline the linking verbs. Draw two lines under the predicate nouns and circle the predicate adjectives.

1. Tabby cats are usually good pets.
2. My tabby is small with bright green eyes.
3. When I brush her, she is so relaxed that she almost falls asleep.
4. Our neighbor's dog, a St. Bernard, is a beast!
5. He seems gentle, but he really scares my cat.
6. My tabby feels threatened every time the dog barks.
7. My other cat is a mischievous kitten.
8. His claws and teeth are sharp, and he scratches and bites a lot.
9. The thing he likes least is the cat carrier.
10. When I put him in it, he looks so sad!

Descriptive Essay 389

Mini-Lesson

Student Objectives

- Learn to recognize predicate nouns and adjectives. *(p. 389)*

Predicate Nouns and Adjectives

Predicate nouns and adjectives describe the subject of a sentence. Like appositives, they give more information to the reader. Write the following sentences on the board:

- *Mr. Rodriguez is a tall man.*
- *He is polite to all the people in the neighborhood.*
- *His son Kiko is my best friend.*
- *Kiko is funny—he always makes me laugh!*

Have volunteers come to the board and point to the predicate nouns (*man, friend*) and the predicate adjectives. (*polite, funny*) If students are having trouble identifying predicate nouns and adjectives, provide more sentences for practice.

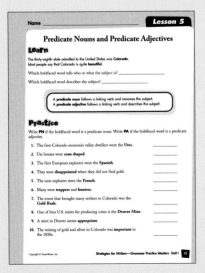

Page 15

Page 21

Go to ▶ *Grammar Practice Masters*

CCSS **Common Core State Standards**
L.6.1: Demonstrate command of the conventions of standard English grammar and usage when writing or speaking. **L.6.2:** Demonstrate command of the conventions of standard English capitalization, punctuation, and spelling when writing.

Write
a Descriptive Essay

Week 3 • Day 4

Student Objectives

- Discuss preparation for publishing and presentation. *(p. 390)*
- Use a final editing checklist to publish their work. *(p. 390)*

Publish +Presentation

Publishing Strategy Ask students if they like Denise's choice for sharing her descriptive essay. Explain that one of the definitions of *publish* is "to make publicly known." So even though Denise is not reprinting her essay, she is still publishing it by making it known to the class by reading it aloud.

Have each student make a checklist and perform a final evaluation of his or her descriptive essay before publishing it. Suggest that students tailor their checklists to cover errors that they make frequently. Encourage them to share copies of their essays with friends and relatives who might be interested in reading about what they wrote.

Strategies for Writers Online
Go to **www.sfw.z-b.com** for additional online resources for students and teachers.

Publish +Presentation

Publishing Strategy	Read your essay to your classmates. Ask them to draw their own pictures based on the essay.
Presentation Strategy	Adjust margins, line spacing, and paragraph indents for easy reading.

Our class likes to do art projects and discuss them. Reading my essay to my classmates would be a good publishing option. To make reading aloud easier, I need to check for good margins all around. Using generous line spacing and indenting paragraphs will also make the text clear on the page. Before I read my essay, I want to check it over one more time. I'll use the final checklist below.

My Final Checklist

Did I—

✔ check for correct use of appositives, including a comma before and after?

✔ use predicate nouns and predicate adjectives correctly?

✔ create margins, use line spacing, and indent my paragraphs for easy reading?

✔ proofread carefully for spelling, punctuation, and grammar?

Apply

Make a checklist to check your descriptive essay. Then make a final copy to publish.

390 Descriptive Writing

Differentiating Instruction

ENRICHMENT

Give a Dramatic Reading Discuss with students elements of dramatic reading, such as expression and clarity. Give them time to practice reading their essays aloud with appropriate—but not over-the-top—expression for the class.

REINFORCEMENT

Practice Word Processing Give students additional time to prepare their essays for publication. Have them work with a technology assistant or a more computer-literate student to create a neat paper by setting tabs, establishing margins, and selecting a line spacing option.

Beware, Little Fishy!

by Denise

Do you ever feel like you're in a fishbowl and someone is watching you? Well, I found a photograph about that idea. A white cat is peering intently at a goldfish in a bowl. The water distorts what you see. So it looks like the cat's face is inside the bowl, and it's huge!

The cat's face is scary but sweet. Its staring eyes, big blue marbles with black centers, are set in pink ovals. Its ears are like pink shark fins, with tufts of white fluff inside. The ears are above the water line, so they aren't changed. They are much smaller than the eyes and set closer together. Spears of white whiskers sprout from the cat's furry cheeks. Its nose is a velvety cushion for the goldfish.

Shimmering in the center of the glass bubble, the goldfish is particularly appealing. Its plump little body is shiny yellow, with a bright orange face and shoulders. Its gauzy, delicate tail is a waving fan that casts a shadow on the cat's cheek.

When you look at the picture, you can imagine what the cat and the fish are thinking and saying. The cat, a silent and sly hunter, is thinking about the juicy orange goldfish. The cat murmurs, "Mmmm!" and the fish replies, "Uh-oh!" Two tiny bubbles float up.

Normally carefree, the goldfish seems to sense the possible danger. Its eye, an inky black dot, glances backward nervously. The curving sides of the bowl frame the tense situation. Beware, little fishy! You may feel safe behind your glass wall, but remember this: The bowl is open on top!

Reflect

Look at Denise's essay. Does it use all the traits of a good descriptive essay? Check it against the rubric. Then use the rubric to check your own descriptive essay.

Technology Tip for 21st Century Literacies

Ask students to create or locate a digital image that either inspired their descriptive writing or grew out of it. Using Pixlr or another photo editing tool, ask students to annotate the image with key details that emerge in their written text. Or, as a peer-based activity, ask students to exchange images and annotate the key details they see when viewing only the image. The student writer can consider the draft based on the details or annotations received from their peer. How can details from an image influence a written text?

See **www.sfw.z-b.com** for further information about and links to these websites and tools.

Write a Descriptive Essay

Week 3 • Day 5

Student Objectives

- Use a descriptive essay rubric. *(pp. 372–373)*
- Share a published descriptive essay. *(p. 391)*

Presentation Strategy Remind students that even though they will be publishing their essays by reading them aloud, the essays should still be neatly written or typed and set off with adequate white space. Clean presentation will make it easier for students to read their essays aloud, and it will make a better impression on anyone who reads it.

Reflecting on a Descriptive Essay

Have students turn to a partner and share their responses to one or more of these questions:

- What is the best part of your descriptive essay? What makes it so good?
- What advice would you give to someone about to write a descriptive essay?

Then have volunteers share their responses with the class.

CCSS Common Core State Standards
W.6.4: Produce clear and coherent writing in which the development, organization, and style are appropriate to task, purpose, and audience. W.6.5: With some guidance and support from peers and adults, develop and strengthen writing as needed by planning, revising, editing, rewriting, or trying a new approach. W.6.6: Use technology, including the Internet, to produce and publish writing as well as to interact and collaborate with others; demonstrate sufficient command of keyboarding skills to type a minimum of three pages in a single sitting.

Observation Report Planner

WEEK 1

Day 1
Introduce
an Observation Report

Student Objectives
- Review the elements of an observation report.
- Consider purpose and audience.
- Learn the traits of descriptive writing.

Student Activities
- Read and discuss **What's in an Observation Report?** (p. 392)
- Read and discuss **Why Write an Observation Report?** (p. 393)
- Read **Linking Descriptive Writing Traits to an Observation Report.** (p. 394)

Day 2
Analyze
Read an Observation Report

Student Objectives
- Read a model observation report.

Student Activities
- Read **"Growing Paintbrush Mold."** (p. 395)

Day 3
Analyze
Introduce the Rubric

Student Objectives
- Learn to read a rubric.

Student Activities
- Review **"Growing Paintbrush Mold."** (p. 395)
- Read and discuss the **Observation Report Rubric.** (pp. 396–397)

WEEK 2

Day 1
Write
Prewrite: Ideas

Student Objectives
- Read and understand a prewriting strategy.

Student Activities
- Read and discuss **Prewrite: Focus on Ideas.** (p. 402)
- Apply the prewriting strategy.

Day 2
Write
Prewrite: Organization

Student Objectives
- Use a Sequence Chain to organize the steps of the experiment.

Student Activities
- Read and discuss **Prewrite: Focus on Organization.** (p. 403)
- Reflect on the model Sequence Chain.
- Apply the prewriting strategy to create a Sequence Chain.
- Participate in a peer conference.

Day 3
Write
Draft: Organization

Student Objectives
- Begin writing the steps in a logical order.

Student Activities
- Read and discuss **Draft: Focus on Organization.** (p. 404)
- Apply the drafting strategy by using a Sequence Chain to write a draft.

WEEK 3

Day 1
Write
Revise: Word Choice

Student Objectives
- Revise to use precise words and phrases.

Student Activities
- Read and discuss **Revise: Focus on Word Choice.** (p. 407)
- Reflect on a model draft.
- Apply the revising strategy.
- Participate in a peer conference.

Day 2
Write
Revise: Sentence Fluency

Student Objectives
- Revise to include questions and exclamations.

Student Activities
- Read and discuss **Revise: Focus on Sentence Fluency.** (p. 408)

Note: Optional Revising Lessons appear on the *Strategies for Writers* CD-ROM.

Day 3
Write
Edit: Conventions

Student Objectives
- Edit for correct use of apostrophes in possessive nouns and contractions.

Student Activities
- Read and discuss **Edit: Focus on Conventions.** (p. 409)

Note: Teach the Conventions mini-lessons (pp. 410–411) if needed.

Day 4	Day 5

Analyze
Ideas, Organization, and Voice

Student Objectives
- Read a model observation report.
- Use the observation report rubric.
- Use the model observation report to study Ideas, Organization, and Voice.

Student Activities
- Review **"Growing Paintbrush Mold."** (p. 395)
- Review the rubric. (pp. 396–397)
- Read and discuss **Using the Rubric to Study the Model.** (pp. 398–399)

Analyze
Word Choice, Sentence Fluency, and Conventions

Student Objectives
- Read a model observation report.
- Use the observation report rubric.
- Use the model observation report to study Word Choice, Sentence Fluency, and Conventions.

Student Activities
- Review **"Growing Paintbrush Mold."** (p. 395)
- Review the rubric. (pp. 396–397)
- Read and discuss **Using the Rubric to Study the Model.** (pp. 400–401)

Day 4	Day 5

Write
Draft

Student Objectives
- Complete a draft.

Student Activities
- Finish the draft. (p. 405)
- Participate in a peer conference.

Write
Revise: Voice

Student Objectives
- Revise to maintain consistency in style and tone.

Student Activities
- Read and discuss **Revise: Focus on Voice.** (p. 406)
- Reflect on a model draft.
- Apply the revising strategy.

Day 4	Day 5

Write
Publish: +Presentation

Student Objectives
- Discuss preparation for publishing and presentation.
- Use a final editing checklist to publish their work.

Student Activities
- Read and discuss **Publish: +Presentation.** (p. 412)
- Apply the publishing strategy.

Write
Publish: +Presentation

Student Objectives
- Use an observation report rubric.
- Share a published observation report.

Student Activities
- Share their work.
- Use the rubric to reflect upon and evaluate the model and their own writing. (pp. 396–397, 413–415)

To complete the chapter in fewer days, combine the learning objectives and activities in a way that supports students as they write.

Resources at-a-Glance

 Connection Letter
Reproducible letter (in English and Spanish) appears on the *Strategies for Writers* CD-ROM and at **www.sfw.z-b.com.**

Online Writing Center

Provides IWB resources, interactive games and practice activities, videos, eBooks, and a virtual file cabinet.

 Strategies for Writers Online

Go to **www.sfw.z-b.com** for free online resources for students and teachers.

Introduce
an Observation Report

Student Objectives

- Review the elements of an observation report. *(p. 392)*
- Consider purpose and audience. *(p. 393)*
- Learn the traits of descriptive writing. *(p. 394)*

What's an Observation Report?

Ask students to describe science experiments they have conducted. How did they record the results? What parts of an experiment should be recorded? (Possible responses: setup, materials and equipment, the steps of the experiment, what happened, conclusions) Explain that a written description of a science experiment is an observation report.

What's in an Observation Report?

Read and discuss the elements of an observation report. Note that first-person point of view is necessary, since the writer is writing what he or she observed. Ask students why they think organization is important in an observation report. (Possible response: It's important to describe the steps as they happen so the reader can understand the process.)

 Strategies for Writers Online
Go to **www.sfw.z-b.com** for additional online resources for students and teachers.

What's an Observation Report?

An observation report describes in detail an object, a person, an event, or a process. I think I'll enjoy this kind of writing because I like to watch what goes on around me, like my uncle fixing cars. A step-by-step process will be a lot of fun to describe.

What's in an Observation Report?

Point of View
An observation report has a first-person point of view. This makes sense, doesn't it? The writer is involved with the subject of the report and tells what he or she did and observed.

Details
This kind of report should include plenty of vivid details. I want to appeal to all the senses as I write so my readers can imagine every step I'm describing.

Organization
Organization is very important! I'm planning to give my report a short introduction to help readers focus on what's happening. After that, I'll describe the steps in the process, followed by some observations and a clear conclusion.

Clarity
I want to make the process I'm describing as clear as possible to my audience. Using headings and adding a visual aid such as a diagram or a chart can help. I'll also use transition words to make the sequence of events easy to follow.

392 Descriptive Writing

Descriptive Text Exemplars (Observation Report)

Spangler, Steve. *Naked Eggs and Flying Potatoes: Unforgettable Experiments That Make Science Fun.* **Greenleaf Book Group Press, 2010.** This book is a collection of hands-on science experiments that use everyday materials to create entertaining activities. Readers can also read "Take It Further" sections that provide would-be scientists with ideas for further experiments.

Young, Karen Romano. *Science Fair Winners: Experiments to Do on Your Family.* **National Geographic Children's Books, 2010.** *Science Fair Winners: Experiments to Do on Your Family* is a fun collection of experiments focused on genetics and psychology. Students will learn everything from the goal of each project to how the science relates to everyday life.

Why write an Observation Report?

There are tons of reasons for writing an observation report. I listed some here, since I'm still thinking about why I want to write. Do you have some ideas of your own?

Information
This kind of writing contains all kinds of information! Observation reports can educate readers about many different subjects, instruct them in procedures, or help them understand important concepts.

Observation Skills
They're called observation reports for a good reason! To do this kind of writing, you have to observe something well. Writing an observation report really hones your observation skills.

Note-Taking
I'll have to take notes in all kinds of subjects throughout my education. Doing an observation report will give me good practice in this important skill.

Scientific Method
Writing an observation report about an experiment involves following basic scientific methods. I'll have to make a prediction, set up a procedure to test it, evaluate my results, and come to a conclusion.

Why write an Observation Report?

As students practice their own writing, it is helpful to remind them that all writing has a purpose and that learning the different genres of writing will help them become better writers. These authentic purposes also help shape their writing.

Read and discuss with students the reasons for writing an observation report. Ask students why they think taking notes is helpful when writing an observation report. (Possible response: because detailed notes will help the writer remember exactly what happened during the experiment and explain it clearly to the reader) After reviewing the reasons to write an observation report, ask students what they feel the tone of an observation report should be—informal and breezy or matter-of-fact? (matter-of-fact) Why? (Possible response: The purpose of the report is to give information about the experiment, not to entertain.)

Harris, Elizabeth Snoke. *Save the Earth Science Experiments: Science Fair Projects for Eco-Kids.* **Lark Books, 2009.** *Save the Earth Science Experiments: Science Fair Projects for Eco-Kids* provides students with plenty of fun science projects that focus on the environment. Budding scientists will perform experiments that teach how to harness energy from windmills, make recycled paper, create alternative fuels, and many more!

Henderson, Joyce. *So You Have to Do a Science Fair Project.* **Jossey-Bass, 2002.** This book provides students with everything they will need to put together a successful science fair project. Students will learn about the basics of the scientific method, how to perform thorough research, how to create a successful experiment, and how to organize their data.

CCSS Common Core State Standards
SL.6.1.a: Come to discussions prepared, having read or studied required material; explicitly draw on that preparation by referring to evidence on the topic, text, or issue to probe and reflect on ideas under discussion. **SL.6.2:** Interpret information presented in diverse media and formats (e.g., visually, quantitatively, orally) and explain how it contributes to a topic, text, or issue under study.

Introduce
an Observation Report

Linking Descriptive Writing Traits to an Observation Report

Explain to students that they will follow Denise as she models using the writing process and the traits together. As they follow Denise through the writing process, students will see how the Descriptive Writing Traits have been adapted and applied to writing an observation report. They will see that an observation report has many factors in common with other types of descriptive writing. However, the particular audience and purpose of an observation report determine how the traits are used.

Linking Descriptive Writing Traits to an Observation Report

In this chapter, you will describe your observations. This type of descriptive writing is called an observation report. Denise will guide you through the stages of the writing process: Prewrite, Draft, Revise, Edit, and Publish. In each stage, Denise will show you important writing strategies that are linked to the Descriptive Writing Traits below.

Descriptive Writing Traits

 Ideas
- a clear topic that is supported and enhanced by specific sensory details

 Organization
- well-organized paragraphs that follow the order of the description, whether by time, location, or another order

 Voice
- a voice and tone that are appropriate for the purpose and audience

 Word Choice
- precise, descriptive words, possibly with figurative language, that create an accurate picture for the reader

 Sentence Fluency
- sentences that vary in length and type to add flow to the writing

 **Conventions**
- no or few errors in grammar, usage, mechanics, and spelling

Before you write, read Mark Volk's observation report on the next page. Then use the observation report rubric on pages 396–397 to decide how well he did. (You might want to look back at What's in an Observation Report? on page 392, too!)

Descriptive Writing Traits in an Observation Report

 **Ideas** The writer maintains focus on the topic throughout the report. Written details, as well as charts or diagrams, give readers a complete picture of the experiment and its results.

 Organization The steps are presented in a logical order and linked with transitions that help readers follow the process used in the experiment.

 **Voice** The writer consistently uses first-person point of view to explain the procedures, results, and conclusions. The voice connects with the audience.

Growing Paintbrush Mold
by Mark Volk

First-person point of view

Penicillium notatum is a green mold that grows on cheese, bread, and fruit. This disgusting mold is the source of penicillin, an antibiotic! I already knew that mold grows better in a moist environment. How would temperature affect this mold's growth? My prediction was that the mold would grow better in a warm, moist environment than in a cold, moist environment.

PROCEDURE ← Heading

Step 1: First, I rubbed two lemons on the floor to roughen up their skin. Then I left them on the kitchen table overnight. This way, penicillin mold spores, which are in soil and air, would be more likely to stick to the fruit.

Step 2: The next day, I put one of the lemons and one moist cotton ball in a paper bag and closed the bag. I put the bag in the refrigerator. Then I repeated this process with the other lemon and put that paper bag in a warm corner of the kitchen.

Step 3: For the next two weeks, I checked the lemons every day, took notes in my observation log, and made several color sketches.

Step 4: At the end of the two weeks, one lemon was covered with green mold. I scraped a little of this mold into a drop of water on a microscope slide and looked at it. I didn't get too close to the mold or breathe in any of it. Then I sketched the slide for my observation log.

Organization →

OBSERVATIONS

During the whole experiment, the lemon in the refrigerator didn't change much. By the end of the experiment, it was a little drier but still firm and bright yellow. However, on the third day the lemon in the warm corner began to show spots of green powder. By the end of the two weeks, it had turned into a spongy, aqua-colored fuzz ball. It also had a strong smell because it had started to rot. ← Vivid details

What did the mold look like under the microscope? It resembled a cluster of stems with feathery ends—something like a paintbrush. That makes sense because penicillin is named for the Latin word *penicillus*, which means "brush."

↳ Visual aid for clarity

CONCLUSION

Penicillin grew on the lemon that was kept warm and moist, but not on the one in the refrigerator. A warm, moist environment is better than a cold, moist one for growing penicillin mold.

Details

Observation Report **395**

Word Choice Precise, descriptive language creates vivid images for readers and helps them picture the process used in the experiment.

Sentence Fluency A variety of sentence types and structures gives writing energy and flow. The writing is a pleasure to read.

Conventions The letter is carefully edited prior to publishing. There are no mistakes in grammar, usage, mechanics, and spelling to confuse the reader or obscure the author's purpose.

Analyze
the Model

Week 1 • Day 2

Student Objectives

- Read a model observation report. *(p. 395)*

Read the Model

Have students read the observation report on page 395. Before they read, remind students to look for the writing traits outlined on page 394.

Elements of an Observation Report

Use the notes on the model to discuss how Mark Volk has written an effective observation report. Ask:

- Why does it make sense for Mark to use first-person point of view? (He is describing observations he made.)

- How do the headings help you follow the report? (They tell what type of information I'll find in each section.)

Point out the underlined details and ask:

- Why does Mark include such vivid details in the report. (Possible response: Helping readers visualize the lemons in the experiment makes it clear to them why Mark reached his conclusions.)

You may wish to have students refer back to What's in an Observation Report? on page 368 for review.

CCSS Common Core State Standards
R/Inf.6.1: Cite textual evidence to support analysis of what the text says explicitly as well as inferences drawn from the text. **R/Inf.6.5:** Analyze how a particular sentence, paragraph, chapter, or section fits into the overall structure of a text and contributes to the development of the ideas.

Analyze the Model

Week 1 • Day 3

Student Objectives

- Learn to read a rubric. (pp. 396–397)

Use the Rubric

Explain the Rubric Explain that a rubric is a tool that helps you plan, improve, and evaluate a piece of writing. A rubric also helps a writer focus on key elements, or traits, in writing (**Ideas, Organization, Voice, Word Choice, Sentence Fluency, Conventions,** and **Presentation**).

The 6-point rubric on pages 396 and 397 is based on the Descriptive Writing Traits that students read on page 394. Draw students' attention to the six columns to explain how the scoring system works. Explain that the column under the numeral 6 describes a very good observation report, one that has received the highest score in all categories.

Discuss the Rubric Guide the students in a discussion of the rubric. Read the descriptors that go with each trait. Note how the descriptors vary as you move from column to column. Remind students to keep the rubric in mind when they write their own observation reports and again when they revise them.

Online Writing Center

Provides a variety of **interactive rubrics,** including 4-, 5-, and 6-point models.

T396 Descriptive Writing

Rubric

Use this 6-point rubric to plan and score an observation report.

	6	5	4	
Ideas	Information is thorough and complete. Details in diagrams or charts enhance information.	Information is thorough. Details in diagrams or charts are useful.	The information may be missing a few details. Diagrams and charts are included.	
Organization	Steps are presented in a logical order. A variety of transitions accurately conveys the sequence of events.	The text structure makes sense. Transitions convey the sequence of events.	The organization is easy to follow. Transitions indicate the sequence of events, but some transitions are repetitive.	
Voice	First-person point of view is used consistently throughout to connect strongly to the audience.	First-person point of view connects to the audience.	First-person point of view is not used in a few places.	
Word Choice	Precise language, such as strong verbs, makes the process clear.	Several strong verbs are used, and precise language describes the process.	Most of the verbs are strong and help the reader follow the process.	
Sentence Fluency	Sentence variety is striking. The writing is pleasurable to read.	Sentences are varied in length and beginnings. The writing has a smooth flow.	There is some variety in sentence length and beginnings. A few are choppy or too long.	
Conventions	Apostrophes are used to form possessive nouns and contractions.	Apostrophes are used correctly for the most part. There are a few errors that are hard to spot.	Noticeable errors with apostrophes and other conventions don't affect meaning.	

✛Presentation Text features, such as headings, and visuals are integrated thoughtfully.

396 Descriptive Writing

CCSS Common Core State Standards

Observation Report

Writing in the Descriptive mode can engage the Common Core State Standards for both Narrative and Informative/Explanatory writing. The rubric and writing strategies for Ideas are drawn from informative/explanatory standard **W.6.2.b** and narrative standard **W.6.3.d,** which focus on developing a topic with solid, relevant details. The rubric and writing strategies for Organization are grounded in informative/explanatory standard **W.6.2.a** and narrative standard **W.6.3.a,** both of which highlight the importance of organizing the writing in a logical, natural way. Organization is also supported by informative/explanatory standard **W.6.2.c** and narrative standard **W.6.3.c,** which emphasize the importance of transitions. The rubric and writing strategies for Voice reflect language standard **L.6.3.b,** which calls for the writer to maintain a consistent

3	2	1	
Some information may be inaccurate or missing. Diagrams and charts may be incomplete or unclear.	Information is incomplete or may be inaccurate. Visuals are also incomplete or not included.	The information is inaccurate, and no visuals are included. The writer clearly knows very little about the topic.	**Ideas**
The organization needs attention to follow. Some transitions are missing.	The writing is hard to follow. Transitions are missing or unclear.	Lack of organization is confusing for the reader. No transitions are present.	**Organization**
First-person point of view is used inconsistently, and the writing sometimes fails to connect to the audience.	Point of view switches back and forth often. The reader is confused.	No voice is present in the writing. The writer does not connect with the audience.	**Voice**
Some verbs are weak, making the process harder to follow in places.	Many verbs are weak. The steps are not clearly described.	Verbs are missing. The steps are unclear.	**Word Choice**
Sentence beginnings are the same. There is little variety in length. The writing is readable but choppy.	There is little variety in sentence length and beginnings. Many sentences are incorrect.	Sentences are incomplete or incorrect. The writing takes work to read.	**Sentence Fluency**
Noticeable errors with apostrophes may slow down reading.	Errors with apostrophes and other conventions are distracting and interrupt the message.	The report has not been edited. There are many errors in spelling, grammar, and punctuation.	**Conventions**

See Appendix B for 4-, 5-, and 6-point descriptive rubrics.

style and tone. The rubric and writing strategies for Word Choice focus on precise language per both informative/explanatory standard **W.6.2.d** and narrative standard **W.6.3.d**. Like standard **L.6.3.a,** the rubrics and writing strategies for Sentence Fluency highlight the importance of varying sentence types in writing. The language standards **L.6.1** and **L.6.2,** which focus on command of the conventions of grammar, usage, capitalization, spelling, and punctuation, are evident in Conventions. Woven throughout the unit are writing standards **W.6.4–W.6.6** and **W.6.10,** which focus on writing appropriately for the task, the purpose, and the audience; using technology; and writing routinely over extended time frames. Presentation is based on Informative/explanatory standard **W.6.2.a,** with its emphasis on using visuals.

Apply the Rubric

Assign Groups Assign a small group of students to check the model for one trait. One person in each group should be responsible for recording one or two strong examples of the trait as described by the rubric.

Reassemble the Class Bring the class together and ask one person from each group to report the group's findings to the class. The point of this exercise is less to score the model than it is to practice identifying and evaluating the traits within a piece of writing.

Additional Rubrics Appendix B includes 4-, 5-, and 6-point rubrics that can be used with any piece of descriptive writing. The rubrics are also available as blackline masters in the back of this Teacher Edition, beginning on page T525.

CCSS Common Core State Standards

SL.6.1: Engage effectively in a range of collaborative discussions (one-on-one, in groups, and teacher-led) with diverse partners on *grade 6 topics, texts, and issues,* building on others' ideas and expressing their own clearly. **SL.6.1.a:** Come to discussions prepared, having read or studied required material; explicitly draw on that preparation by referring to evidence on the topic, text, or issue to probe and reflect on ideas under discussion. **SL.6.1.b:** Follow rules for collegial discussions, set specific goals and deadlines, and define individual roles as needed.

Analyze
the Model

Week 1 • Day 4

Student Objectives

- Read a model observation report. *(p. 395)*
- Use the observation report rubric. *(pp. 396–397)*
- Use the model observation report to study Ideas, Organization, and Voice. *(pp. 398–399)*

Study the Model

Assess the Model Once students have read pages 398 and 399, ask them whether they agree or disagree with Denise's assessment of the model on each point. For example, do students feel that Mark gave enough details for students to understand his conclusion? Use questions such as the following to discuss the model and the traits with students.

- What other visuals could Mark have used to help clarify his explanations? (Possible responses: drawings of the two lemons at the end of the experiment; a chart with descriptions of the lemons each day of the experiment)

Strategies for Writers Online

Go to **www.sfw.z-b.com** for additional online resources for students and teachers.

Observation Report

Using the Rubric to Study the Model

Did you notice that the model on page 395 points out some key elements of an observation report? As he wrote "Growing Paintbrush Mold," Mark Volk used these elements to help him describe an observation. He also used the 6-point rubric on pages 396–397 to plan, draft, revise, and edit the writing. A rubric is a great tool for evaluating writing during the writing process.

Now let's use the same rubric to score the model. To do this, we'll focus on each trait separately, starting with Ideas. We'll use the top descriptor for each trait (column 6), along with examples from the model, to help us understand how the traits work together. How would you score Mark on each trait?

 Ideas

- Information is thorough and complete.
- Details in diagrams or charts enhance information.

The information in Mark's report is complete, from Procedure to Observations to Conclusion. Mark described the mold and included a picture that enhances the reader's understanding of why penicillin is named for the Latin word that means "brush."

[from the writing model]

It resembled a cluster of stems with feathery ends—something like a paintbrush.

398 Descriptive Writing

English Language Learners

BEGINNING

First-Person Point of View Review usage of the first-person pronouns *I, we, me, us, my,* and *our.* Give several simple examples, such as *We eat dinner together every night. Our favorite meal is spaghetti. Mom makes a special dessert for us, too.* Write other examples on the board, but do not include the pronouns. Have students fill in the appropriate pronouns.

INTERMEDIATE

Sensory Details Briefly review the five senses. Present students with something familiar, such as a lemon or an apple. Have partners complete an Observation Chart for the object, making sure to include at least one idea for each of the five senses.

Organization

- Steps are presented in a logical order.
- A variety of transitions accurately conveys the sequence of events.

Mark numbers each of the steps and describes them in order. In Step 4, notice how he uses the transition phrase *At the end of the two weeks* to keep the process clear for the reader.

> [from the writing model]
>
> **Step 3:** For the next two weeks, I checked the lemons every day, took notes in my observation log, and made several color sketches.
> **Step 4:** At the end of the two weeks, one lemon was covered with green mold.

Voice

- First-person point of view is used consistently throughout to connect strongly to the audience.

Mark is consistent about using first-person point of view throughout the report. This helps keep the reader focused on following the information in the experiment.

> [from the writing model]
>
> **Step 1:** First, I rubbed two lemons on the floor to roughen up their skin. Then I left them on the kitchen table overnight.

Observation Report **399**

- What time-order transitions does Mark use in the Observations section? How do they help the reader? (*During the whole experiment, By the end of the experiment, By the end of two weeks;* They tell the reader when Mark made his observations of the lemons.)

- How does Mark's use of first-person point of view help you connect with his writing? (Possible response: It sounds as if he's speaking directly to me when he tells about his observations.)

ADVANCED

Organizing Details Review the meaning of *sequence* and discuss the importance of proper sequence in an observation report. Talk students through a process, such as making a bowl of cereal. Have them complete a Sequence Chain to identify the important steps. Then have them trade graphic organizers with another pair who will verify that the correct details were included and in the correct sequence.

ADVANCED HIGH

Transition Words Write the steps for a simple process on the board, but mix up the order of the steps. Have students put the steps of the process in order. Then have students suggest transition words and phrases that can be used to help the information flow, such as *first, then,* and *after that*. Add them to the story, and have a volunteer reread it.

CCSS **C**ommon **C**ore **S**tate **S**tandards

R/Inf.6.5: Analyze how a particular sentence, paragraph, chapter, or section fits into the overall structure of a text and contributes to the development of the ideas. **R/Inf.6.6:** Determine an author's point of view or purpose in a text and explain how it is conveyed in the text. **SL.6.1.b:** Follow rules for collegial discussions, set specific goals and deadlines, and define individual roles as needed. **SL.6.1.d:** Review the key ideas expressed and demonstrate understanding of multiple perspectives through reflection and paraphrasing.

Analyze
the Model

Week 1 • Day 5

Student Objectives

- Read a model observation report. *(p. 395)*
- Use the observation report rubric. *(pp. 396–397)*
- Use the model observation report to study Word Choice, Sentence Fluency, and Conventions. *(pp. 400–401)*

Continue Discussing the Traits

Use questions such as the following to discuss the traits analyzed on pages 400 and 401:

- Find other examples of strong verbs in the report. (Possible responses: *affect, rubbed, roughen, resembled*)

- How does Mark create sentence variety in the Observations section? (He uses sentences with different lengths and structures and includes a question.)

- How do you know Mark carefully edited his writing? (Possible response: I couldn't find any spelling or grammar mistakes.)

 **Strategies for Writers Online**
Go to **www.sfw.z-b.com** for additional online resources for students and teachers.

 **Word Choice** • Precise language, such as strong verbs, makes the process clear.

Several strong verbs describe the action in the experiment and help the reader picture the process in Mark's report. I think the verbs in these sentences are especially good choices for making the process clear.

> **[from the writing model]**
>
> **Step 2:** . . . Then I repeated this process . . .
> **Step 3:** For the next two weeks, I checked the lemons every day . . .
> **Step 4:** . . . I scraped a little of this mold . . . Then I sketched the slide for my observation log.

Sentence Fluency • Sentence variety is striking. The writing is pleasurable to read.

Mark's description of his experiment could have sounded dull, but he made sure that didn't happen. He includes interesting questions and exclamations to make the writing flow. See how he does that in his opening paragraph?

> **[from the writing model]**
>
> *Penicillium notatum* is a green mold that grows on cheese, bread, and fruit. This disgusting mold is the source of penicillin, an antibiotic! I already knew that mold grows better in a moist environment. How would temperature affect this mold's growth? My prediction was that the mold would grow better in a warm, moist environment than in a cold, moist environment.

400 Descriptive Writing

Technology Tip for 21st Century Literacies

Observing over time requires capturing and making meaning of specific data. Using Google Spreadsheets allows writers to construct a document for recording data and sharing it with a larger set of users. Consider opening this assignment to a group of peer collaborators so students must design a spreadsheet that works for multiple participants and helps capture a range of useful, purposeful observations. This tool builds in options for an embedded chat and other opportunities for collaboration across the user group.

See **www.sfw.z-b.com** for further information about and links to these websites and tools.

Conventions

- Apostrophes are used correctly to form possessive nouns and contractions.

Mark always uses apostrophes correctly. Read the two sentences below. One shows how he correctly punctuated a contraction. The second sentence includes a possessive noun, with the apostrophe placed correctly.

[from the writing model]

During the whole experiment, the lemon in the refrigerator didn't change much.

[from the writing model]

I already knew that mold grows better in a moist environment. How would temperature affect this mold's growth?

✚ Presentation

Text features, such as headings, and visuals are integrated thoughtfully.

Now it's my turn! I'm going to write an observation report that follows the rubric and good writing strategies. Read along and see how I do it!

Observation Report **401**

Differentiating Instruction

ENRICHMENT

Analyze Reports Challenge students to read and analyze observation reports of experiments from scientific magazines, informational books, or textbooks. Make a photocopy of several for students to analyze. Ask them to look for and number the steps in the process, explain how charts and diagrams add to the report, and underline any time-order words. Then have students assess the observation reports using the rubric.

REINFORCEMENT

Reinforce Procedure Find examples of simple step-by-step instructions, such as short recipes, and share them with students. Discuss how each step describes a separate action. Have students list the steps of an everyday activity such as making a bowl of cereal and milk or getting lunch in the lunchroom.

Presentation Explain that in an observation report, visuals can play a key role in helping readers understand the experiment and results. Tell students that as they write, they should be thinking about what types of diagrams or charts would best illustrate their results. Headings are another useful text feature students should plan to incorporate. Encourage students to write their observations on a computer and take advantage of its features to create clear headings and incorporate useful visuals.

Think About the Traits Now ask students which traits they think are most important in an observation report. Explain that all traits are important in every piece of writing, but some stand out more in some genres than in others. Some students may feel that **Organization** is very important because the reader needs to be able to follow the sequence of steps in order to understand the experiment. Others may think that **Word Choice** is important because precise words and phrases help the reader visualize the procedure and results.

CCSS Common Core State Standards

SL.6.1.b: Follow rules for collegial discussions, set specific goals and deadlines, and define individual roles as needed. **SL.6.1.c:** Pose and respond to specific questions with elaboration and detail by making comments that contribute to the topic, text, or issue under discussion. **SL.6.1.d:** Review the key ideas expressed and demonstrate understanding of multiple perspectives through reflection and paraphrasing. **W.6.6:** Use technology, including the Internet, to produce and publish writing as well as to interact and collaborate with others; demonstrate sufficient command of keyboarding skills to type a minimum of three pages in a single sitting.

Observation Report T401

Write
an Observation Report

Week 2 • Day 1

Student Objectives

• Read and understand a prewriting strategy. *(p. 402)*

Prewrite

Focus on ⬭Ideas⬭

Gather Information Discuss how Denise and her partner found and chose this experiment for her report. Ask volunteers to give other ideas for places where they could search for experiment ideas, and write the ideas on the board. **(Possible responses: the Internet, science magazines, books of science experiments for young people)** If you do not wish to have students research experiments, supply a list of experiments or specific sources from which they will choose. If you do have students research their own experiments, tell them they must get your approval before they conduct the experiments.

Ask students what they notice about Denise's notes. **(Possible responses: They include the question she and her partner are trying to answer and their prediction of the answer. The notes are brief but very specific. They are divided into categories.)**

Online Writing Center

 Provides **interactive graphic organizers** as well as a variety of graphic organizers in PDF format.

Prewrite   Focus on ⬭Ideas⬭

The Rubric Says	Information is thorough and complete.
Writing Strategy	Observe and take notes.

Our teacher asked us to work with partners for this assignment. One partner will do an experiment, and the other one will write an observation report on the experiment. Lisa, my partner, and I found a book in the library that has experiments in speed. One experiment shows how gravity affects acceleration (how fast an object starts to move). We decided that Lisa would do the experiment, and I would write the report.

My Notes on the Acceleration Experiment

• **Our question:** How would attaching weights to a toy car affect its acceleration?

• **Our prediction:** Each additional weight would increase the car's acceleration.

• **What we did:** attached paper clip hook to car with string; put one weight (washer) on hook and hung it over edge of table; held car 2.5 ft from edge; let car go and started timing with stopwatch; stopped timing when car hit cardboard bumper; recorded time in log; averaged time over 3 runs; repeated with more weights.

• **The results (averages):** 1 weight: car hit bumper in 2.6 seconds; 2 weights: car hit in 1.8 seconds; 3 weights: 1.4 seconds; 4 weights: 1.1 seconds; 5 weights: 0.7 seconds

• **Conclusion:** Our prediction is correct. More weights mean a faster acceleration rate.

Apply

Conduct or observe an experiment. Take notes on what you observed.

402   Descriptive Writing

English Language Learners

BEGINNING/INTERMEDIATE

Observation Report Vocabulary Perform a simple task to show a process for doing something. As you do, introduce vocabulary that students may use as headings for their reports, such as *materials, process, observations,* and *conclusions.* As you teach each word, write it on the board and have students repeat. If applicable, convey the meaning of the verb form of the word; for example, you can use the word *observe* to teach *observations.*

ADVANCED/ADVANCED HIGH

Diagrams and Charts Have several examples of diagrams and charts available to introduce to students. Tell them that a *diagram* often is a visual representation of a process. Write the word and have students say it. Similarly, tell them that a *chart* often shows data associated with a process. Write *chart* and have students say the word.

Prewrite

Focus on Organization

The Rubric Says Steps are presented in a logical order.

Writing Strategy Make a Sequence Chain of the steps in the experiment.

Writer's Term

Sequence Chain
A **Sequence Chain** shows steps or events in the order they happen.

According to the rubric, I need to explain the steps in our experiment in the order we did them. A Sequence Chain is a good way to do that.

Sequence Chain

Step 1: To set up the experiment, we
  a) made a paper clip into a hook.
  b) used tape to mark a starting line 2.5 ft from the edge of a table.
  c) taped a cardboard bumper to the edge of the table to stop the car; made a hole at the bottom of the bumper for the string.
  d) cut 3 ft of string; tied one end to the car's axle and the other end to the hook.
  e) pushed the hook through the hole in the bumper.

Step 2: Lisa put one weight on the hook.

Step 3: Next, she held the weight over the edge of the table.

Step 4: With her other hand, she put the car at the starting line.

Step 5: She let the weight fall, and I started the stopwatch.

Step 6: I stopped timing when the car hit the bumper. I recorded the time.

Step 7: We repeated Steps 2–6 two more times. Then we averaged the times.

Step 8: We repeated Steps 2–7 with 2, 3, 4, and 5 weights. We recorded and averaged the times.

Reflect

Is the Sequence Chain logical and complete? How will it help Denise write a well-organized report?

Apply

Organize your notes by using a Sequence Chain.

Observation Report 403

Conferencing

PEER TO PEER Have partners exchange Sequence Chains with another pair of students. Each pair reviews the other pair's organizer and points out any gaps they see in the sequence of events.

PEER GROUPS Have groups of three or four pairs pass their Sequence Chains around the group. The pairs discuss and write down one question about each Sequence Chain that might help clarify the steps of the experiment.

TEACHER-LED Work with pairs to improve their Sequence Chains. Compare the students' notes to their Sequence Chains and ask questions about any gaps or discrepancies you see.

Write
an Observation Report

Week 2 • Day 2

Student Objectives

- Use a Sequence Chain to organize the steps of the experiment. *(p. 403)*

Prewrite

Focus on  Organization

Make a Sequence Chain Explain that the steps in the Sequence Chain will probably mirror the steps in the experiment's instructions. The difference is that the steps in the Sequence Chain tell what happened as students performed the experiment. Explain that students will have to take careful, detailed notes as they conduct their experiments in order to create a thorough Sequence Chain like Denise's.

Writer's Term

Sequence Chain While a Sequence Chain is an excellent tool for preparing to write an observation report, it does not cover every part of an experiment. It can be helpful to add brief statements detailing the question the experiment is designed to answer and the results of the experiment.

CCSS Common Core State Standards

W.6.2.b: Develop the topic with relevant facts, definitions, concrete details, quotations, or other information and examples. **W.6.3.d:** Use precise words and phrases, relevant descriptive details, and sensory language to convey experiences and events.

Observation Report T403

Write
an Observation Report

Week 2 • Day 3

Student Objectives

• Begin writing the steps in a logical order. *(p. 404)*

Draft

Focus on Organization

Begin a Draft Review the purpose of a draft. Note that the draft is a temporary form of a piece of writing that should be changed and corrected several times before it is finished. Then have students read page 404.

Point out that Denise refers to the rubric as she completes this step in the writing process. Remind students to get into the habit of referring to the rubric so they fully understand its use as a tool for shaping their writing.

Online Writing Center

 Provides student eBooks with an **interactive writing pad** for drafting, revising, editing, and publishing.

Draft   Focus on **Organization**

The Rubric Says	Steps are presented in a logical order.
Writing Strategy	Introduce the experiment in the introduction and use numbered steps to show the order.

Now it's time to write my report. My parents, my classmates, and their parents are going to read it. The rubric says that the steps have to be in order. Since I am describing something that happened, time (chronological) order makes sense. Just like in the model, I can use headings and numbers to highlight the order of steps in the experiment.

I also have to think about organizing the whole report. It needs an introduction, a body, and a conclusion. I'll tell the steps of the experiment in the body of my report.

As for spelling and grammar, I will do my best now and check for mistakes later. Right now, I need to get my draft on paper. You can read part of my draft on the next page. I still have to write the observations and conclusions sections.

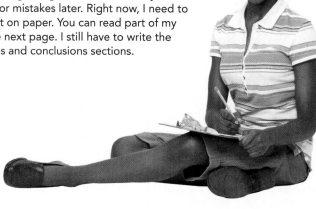

404 Descriptive Writing

Differentiating Instruction

ENRICHMENT

Add Research Have students research some of the scientific principles behind the experiment they conducted. Students should use this information to add possible explanations or clarifications of the results they recorded and to expand their conclusions.

REINFORCEMENT

Partner Writing Have students divide up the job of drafting the observation report with their experiment partner. One can write the introduction and first steps, while the other can write the later steps and conclusion. Then, as students go through the revising and editing stages, they can work together to review and improve the report as a whole.

[DRAFT]

[introduction]

How Gravity Affects Acceleration

Gravity is one of Earths forces. It keeps everything from floating off into space. Lisa and I did an experiment with a model car to see how gravity affects aceleration—how fast the car starts to move. We decided to attach a weight to one end of a string, tie the other end to the car, and drop the weight over the ege of a table. As gravity pulled the weight down, the weight would pull the car across the table. Lisa and I predickted that as we added more weights, the car would accelerate faster.

PROCEDURE ← [heading]

[steps in procedure]

Step 1: Lisa twisted a paper clip into a hook. She used tape to mark a starting line on a table 2.5 ft from the edge. She taped a bumper, a piece of heavy cardboard, to the edge of the table. This bumper would stop the car from falling off the table. She made a small opening at the bottom of the bumper for the string to slide through. I cut 3 ft of string. Lisa tied one end to the cars axel and the other end to the hook.

Reflect

Think about the draft. Is the report organized so that it's easy to read?

Apply

Write a draft using your Sequence Chain to help you. Be sure to include an introduction, observations, and a conclusion. Use headings to make your report easier to read.

Observation Report 405

Conferencing

PEER TO PEER Have pairs exchange drafts with another pair. The pairs comment on the sequence of steps in each other's drafts and point out any places where information seems to be missing or out of sequence.

PEER GROUPS Have pairs pass their drafts around the group. Each pair writes one suggestion on each draft for clarifying the sequence of steps.

TEACHER-LED Work with pairs individually. Read the draft and then facilitate a discussion between the two students about what information they could add to make their draft more complete.

Write
an Observation Report

Week 2 • Day 4

Student Objectives

• Complete a draft. (p. 405)

Finish the Draft Have students read Denise's draft excerpt on page 405. Discuss how the headings help her organize her draft and how they will make it easier for readers to skim it to find the sections they most want to read. Ask students which trait on the rubric is supported by the use of headings. (organization) Ask:

• Why is it helpful to number the steps in an observation report? (Possible response: Numbering the steps helps the writer make sure the reader won't get lost in following the procedure.)

• What type of information is included in the introduction? (Possible responses: the purpose of the experiment; the reason the writer is conducting the experiment)

Instruct students to keep their Sequence Chains in front of them as they draft, to ensure that they do not miss a step or place a step out of order.

CCSS Common Core State Standards

W.6.2.a: Introduce a topic; organize ideas, concepts, and information, using strategies such as definition, classification, comparison/contrast, and cause/effect; include formatting (e.g., headings), graphics (e.g., charts, tables), and multimedia when useful to aiding comprehension. W.6.3.a: Engage and orient the reader by establishing a context and introducing a narrator and/or characters; organize an event sequence that unfolds naturally and logically.

Write an Observation Report

Week 2 • Day 5

Student Objectives

• Revise to maintain consistency in style and tone. (p. 406)

Revise

Focus on Voice

Keep the Tone Consistent If necessary, begin by making sure students understand that first-person point of view means the writer is using the pronouns *I, me, we,* and *us* to describe his or her own experiences. Read aloud the draft excerpt, first without the revisions and then with the revisions. Ask:

• How does the passage sound without the revisions? (Possible response: a bit stiff and formal)

• How does it sound with the revisions? (Possible response: more direct, less formal)

• Which version of the draft makes a better connection with the reader? (the revised version)

You may wish to point out that the sentences in the original draft are in the passive voice. Although sentences written in the passive voice are correct, overuse of the passive voice can make the writing sound stiff and artificial.

Strategies for Writers Online

Go to **www.sfw.z-b.com** for additional online resources for students and teachers.

Revise Focus on Voice

The Rubric Says — First-person point of view is used consistently throughout to connect strongly to the audience.

Writing Strategy — Maintain consistency in style and tone.

I was really involved with the gravity experiment I did with Lisa, from setting it up to writing the observation log. In my report, I wanted to show how engaged I was with each step. So I used first person throughout the report. I see one step, however, where the point of view doesn't match up with the rest of the report. I'll revise that now to maintain first person throughout my writing.

[DRAFT]

Step 6: ~~The~~ stopwatch ~~was stopped~~ I stopped the when the car hit the bumper. Actually,
~~it took~~ I had to practice several times before ~~it was done~~ this I could do it right.

Apply

Make sure you use first-person point of view to show your involvement with your subject.

406 Descriptive Writing

English Language Learners

BEGINNING/INTERMEDIATE

Using Precise Words Illustrate the importance of using precise words. Write the following sentence frame: _____ *is very good.* Point to the blank and ask, *What word should go here?* Students might offer *The teacher, The cake, The movie,* and so on. Change *good* to *tasty.* Ask, *Now what can go in the blank?* Students should understand that *tasty* is used only to describe foods. Repeat for other adjectives, such as *kind* or *boring.*

ADVANCED/ADVANCED HIGH

Question-Answer Format For variety, students might use a question-answer format in their writing. Tell students that they can use a question as the introduction of a topic, and the answer is the supporting details. For example, each question could be a heading for part of the Observations section of their reports.

Revise

The Rubric Says	Precise language, such as strong verbs, makes the process clear.
Writing Strategy	Choose words and phrases to convey ideas precisely.

I want my report to be clear and easy to follow so my reader will understand all the parts of my experiment. The rubric says using precise words—especially strong verbs—will help me make the process clear. I'll look for places where there are weak verbs that I can replace with stronger ones. Look at how I strengthened Step 2 by putting in a stronger, more descriptive verb.

[DRAFT]

Step 2: Lisa ~~put~~ *slipped* one weight on the hook.

Reflect

How does the stronger verb help you to better follow the process?

Apply

Look for weak verbs and replace them with strong ones to make the process clear.

Observation Report **407**

Conferencing

PEER TO PEER Have each pair exchange drafts with another pair of students. The pairs review each other's drafts and underline in pencil up to four words they think could be replaced with a more precise term.

PEER GROUPS Have one member of each pair read their draft aloud for the group. Other group members comment on places where first-person point of view may be lacking or where precise words are needed.

TEACHER-LED Meet with partners. Read the observation report aloud to the partners and have them note places where voice or word choice could be improved. If necessary, offer suggestions.

Write
an Observation Report

Week 3 • Day 1

Student Objectives

- Revise to use precise words and phrases. (p. 407)

Revise

Focus on **Word Choice**

Use Precise Words Write the following words on the board: *went, ate, reported, scurried, saw, delicious, glimpsed, painful, said, devoured, good,* and *bad.* Beside the words, write the headings *Precise* and *Vague.* Ask volunteers to tell you which words belong in each category and copy the words under the correct headings. (Precise: reported, scurried, delicious, glimpsed, painful, devoured; Vague: went, ate, saw, said, good, bad) Have volunteers draw lines between the related words in each category (e.g., *devoured/ate*).

Explain that part of what makes the meaning of a word precise is the connotation that the reader brings to a piece of text. Ask students to compare and contrast someone devouring a meal with someone eating a meal. How do their images differ?

Instruct students to review their reports for vague words that should be replaced with precise ones.

CCSS Common Core State Standards

W.6.2.d: Use precise language and domain-specific vocabulary to inform about or explain the topic. **L.6.3.b:** Maintain consistency in style and tone. **L.6.5.c:** Distinguish among the connotations (associations) of words with similar denotations (definitions) (e.g., *stingy, scrimping, economical, unwasteteful, thrifty*).

Write an Observation Report

Week 3 • Day 2

Student Objectives

• Revise to include questions and exclamations. (p. 408)

Revise

Focus on  Sentence Fluency

Use Different Sentence Types

Discuss the value of using a variety of sentence types. Ask students how questions and exclamations make writing easier to read. (Possible responses: Question-answer format engages the readers. The variety keeps readers' interest.)

Explain that reading aloud a piece of writing often makes it easier to evaluate sentence fluency. Sometimes it is easier to hear the flow of language than to see it. Have a volunteer read aloud the draft excerpts without the revisions and then with the revisions. Discuss the differences in sentence flow and energy. Ask students whether the questions and exclamations help them connect to the writing.

Online Writing Center

 Provides **interactive proofreading activities** for each genre.

Revise — Focus on Sentence Fluency

The Rubric Says — Sentence variety is striking. The writing is pleasurable to read.

Writing Strategy — Blend questions and exclamations into the report.

The rubric says I should use different types of sentences to make my writing a pleasure to read. As I read through my report, I noticed that I had used only statements. I also noticed a sentence that was too long and dull. Look at how I changed two sections of my report to make my writing flow better.

[DRAFT]

[added question]

[broke up long, boring sentence]

But how does gravity affect aceleration?

Gravity is one of Earths forces. It keeps everything from floating off into space. Lisa and I did an experiment with a model car to see how gravity affects aceleration—how fast the car starts to move.

about that question, using a ⊙We wanted

[DRAFT]

Step 4: She put the car at the starting line and held it their. Thats when we figured out that I would have to work the stopwatch ~~since Lisa~~ Lisa already had her hands full! ~~was busy with the car~~

[added exclamation]

Apply

Are your sentences all statements? Add some questions and exclamations to make your report more enjoyable.

408 Descriptive Writing

Optional Revising Lessons

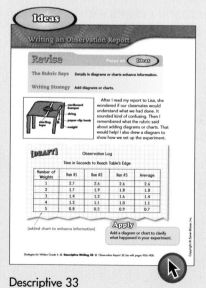

Descriptive 33

Descriptive 34

 Strategies for Writers Grade 6 CD-ROM

Edit

Focus on Conventions

The Rubric Says	Apostrophes are used correctly to form possessive nouns and contractions.
Writing Strategy	Be sure apostrophes are used correctly in possessive nouns and contractions.

Writer's Term___

Apostrophes
Apostrophes are used in possessive nouns and contractions. A possessive noun shows ownership. A contraction is a word formed from two words, such as *I'm (I am)* and *didn't (did not)*.

My last step is to check for spelling, grammar, and punctuation errors. The rubric reminds me to make sure I used apostrophes correctly in possessive nouns and contractions.

[DRAFT]

[apostrophe in a contraction]

[apostrophe to show possession]

It's clear. The numbers say it all. Adding weights increased gravity's pull on the weights. The more weight's we added, the faster the car [no apostrophe for plural] accelerated across the table. Our prediction was correct.

Reflect

Is the report more interesting with the added questions and exclamations? Do any more errors need to be corrected?

Apply Conventions

Edit your draft for spelling, punctuation, and capitalization. Be sure to fix any errors with apostrophes.

For more practice with apostrophes, use the exercises on the next two pages.

Observation Report **409**

Related Grammar Practice___

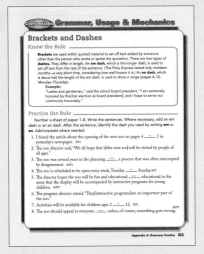

Student Edition page 513

Go to ➡ **Appendix A: Grammar Practice**

Write
an Observation Report

Student Objectives

- Edit for correct use of apostrophes in possessive nouns and contractions. *(p. 409)*

Edit

Focus on Conventions

Check Apostrophes Remind students that unedited writing can be hard to understand. Apostrophes should be used correctly in contractions and in possessives.

If students have trouble with apostrophes or frequently confused words, teach the mini-lessons on pages T410 and T411 and have students complete pages 410 and 411.

Writer's Term___

Apostrophes In contractions, the apostrophe shows where letters have been left out in the joined words. In possessives, the position of the apostrophe indicates whether the possessive noun is singular or plural.

CCSS **C**ommon **C**ore **S**tate **S**tandards
L.6.1: Demonstrate command of the conventions of standard English grammar and usage when writing or speaking. **L.6.1.a:** Ensure that pronouns are in the proper case (subjective, objective, possessive). **L.6.2:** Demonstrate command of the conventions of standard English capitalization, punctuation, and spelling when writing.

Observation Report **T409**

Mini-Lesson

Student Objectives

- Learn to use apostrophes correctly. *(p. 410)*

Apostrophes

To practice apostrophes, write the following sentences on the board:

- *My friend's cat likes to sit next to the heater.*
- *We keep our dogs' bowls in the kitchen.*

Have students identify which sentence has a singular possessive and which has a plural possessive. Then have volunteers come to the board and write sentences that have singular and plural possessive nouns.

To practice contractions, write the following on the board: *We are thrilled with our new car.* Ask students to form a contraction by combining the words *we* and *are.* (we're) Then write the following sentences on the board and have students write the correct contraction(s) for each sentence.

- *I will not be allowed to drive it until I am older.* (won't, I'm)
- *My brother will be able to drive the car because he is 18.* (he's)
- *My uncle does not like the new car.* (doesn't)
- *He says he would not like to have such a small car.* (wouldn't)

 Online Writing Center

Provides **interactive grammar games** and **practice activities** in student eBook.

Apostrophes

Know the Rule

To form the **possessive** of a singular noun, add an apostrophe and *s.*
Example: My brother**'s** hobby is racing slot cars.

To form the **possessive** of a plural noun that ends in *s,* just add an apostrophe.
Example: He joined a slot car racers**'** club.

To form the **possessive** of a plural noun that does not end in *s,* add an apostrophe and *s.*
Example: The club has a large men**'s** group and a small women**'s** group.

To form a **contraction,** use an apostrophe to replace dropped letters.
Example: They**'re** crazy about this hobby.

Practice the Rule

Number a sheet of paper 1–10. Write the correct form of the words in parentheses on your paper.

1. One (dictionary's/dictionarys') definition says a slot car is "an electric toy racing car with a pin underneath that fits into a groove on a track."
2. The (car's/cars') bodies are made of plastic or metal.
3. A slot (car's/cars') power is transmitted through steel rails in the track.
4. My (dad's/dads') oldest track layout is from the 1960s.
5. (It's/Its') a two-lane plastic track that snaps together.
6. (American's/Americans') interest in slot cars grew in the 1960s.
7. Slot cars are (children's/childrens') toys, but adults like Dad enjoy them, too.
8. (I've/Iv'e) played with the slot cars a few times myself.
9. I (do'nt/don't) think I will ever enjoy them as much as Dad and my brother do.
10. (People's/Peoples') interest in slot cars has decreased in the last several decades.

Related Grammar Practice

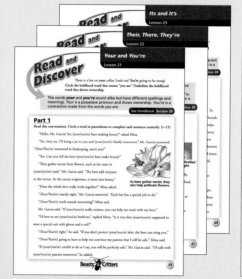

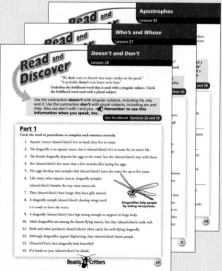

Pages 59, 61, 63, 69, 71, 119

Go to ⇒ G.U.M. Student Practice Book

Frequently Confused Words

Know the Rule

Some words are easily confused. Be sure you use these words correctly in your writing.
- ***Your*** is a possessive pronoun and shows ownership.
  - **Example:** Our teacher said, "**Your** research report is due on Friday."
- ***You're*** is a contraction made from *you* and *are*.
  - **Example: You're** supposed to be finished with the experiment by now.
- ***Their*** is a possessive pronoun and means "belonging to them."
  - **Example:** The students keep **their** observation logs on the bookshelf.
- ***There*** is an adverb and usually means "in that place."
  - **Example:** The moldy lemons are over **there** in the paper bag.
- ***They're*** is a contraction of *they are*.
  - **Example: They're** ready to do the last step of the experiment.

Practice the Rule

Number a sheet of paper 1–10. Write the correct form of the words in parentheses on your paper.

1. You can feed (your/you're) backyard birds in the winter with sunflower seeds.
2. Some insects leave (their/there/they're) eggs to hibernate under leaves.
3. If you see hibernating spider eggs around your windows, leave them (their/there/they're).
4. When (your/you're) out in the snow, look for animal tracks of birds and deer.
5. Even if skunks and raccoons are hibernating, (their/there/they're) likely to wake up to eat in mild weather.
6. You might see squirrels around (your/you're) house all winter.
7. Many birds migrate to (their/there/they're) nesting grounds in warm climates.
8. Migrating birds may find a flight path because (their/there/they're) using the sun and moon, or possibly Earth's magnetic field.
9. Earthworms move deep into the soil in the winter because it isn't frozen (their/there/they're).
10. If (your/you're) looking at a hibernating animal, it might be in such a deep sleep that it looks dead!

Observation Report 411

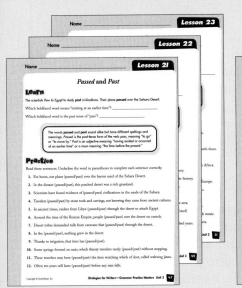

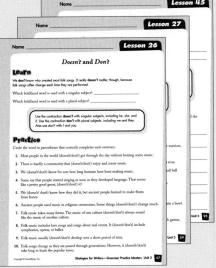

Pages 47, 49, 51, 57, 59, 95

Go to ➡ *Grammar Practice Masters*

Mini-Lesson

Student Objectives

- Learn to distinguish among frequently confused words. *(p. 411)*

Frequently Confused Words

Read the Know the Rule box with students. Write the following sentences on the board, and have volunteers write *your* or *you're* in the blanks:

- _____ *going to the movie Friday, right?* (You're)
- *That's* _____ *coat; mine is over there.* (your)

Then write the following on the board and have volunteers choose the correct form of *their/they're/there* for each sentence:

- *The phone is* _____, *under the table.* (there)
- *My parents are looking for* _____ *keys.* (their)
- _____ *tired and want to sleep late.* (They're)

If necessary, continue practicing with additional sentences before students complete the page.

CCSS Common Core State Standards
L.6.1: Demonstrate command of the conventions of standard English grammar and usage when writing or speaking. **L.6.1.a:** Ensure that pronouns are in the proper case (subjective, objective, possessive). **L.6.2:** Demonstrate command of the conventions of standard English capitalization, punctuation, and spelling when writing.

Write
an Observation Report

Student Objectives

- Discuss preparation for publishing and presentation. *(p. 412)*
- Use a final editing checklist to publish their work. *(p. 412)*

Publish +Presentation

Publishing Strategy Ask students if they like Denise's choice for sharing her observation report. Have students suggest other ways Denise could share her report. Discuss what they feel are the benefits of publishing an observation report on Family Night.

Note that Denise and her partner are using a checklist based on the Conventions and Presentation rubrics they have learned about. Remind students to review their drafts against their own checklists to be sure that they have included everything they need to include. Students' checklists can be tailored to cover errors that they make frequently.

Strategies for Writers Online

Go to **www.sfw.z-b.com** for additional online resources for students and teachers.

Writing an Observation Report

Publish +Presentation

Publishing Strategy	Display your report on Family Night.
Presentation Strategy	Include headings in dark print and visuals.

Our class decided to display our observation reports during Family Night. We wanted them to look nice for the occasion. Lisa and I used the computer to format headings so the reader will see how we organized our report. To make the steps visually clear and reinforce the information, we also added a diagram. Before Lisa and I turned in our report, we checked it using our final checklist.

My Final Checklist

Did I—

✔ check that apostrophes are used correctly for possessive nouns and contractions?

✔ use the right word—*your* or *you're*, and *there*, *their*, or *they're*?

✔ include headings in dark print and visuals to make the report easier to read and understand?

✔ check my spelling, grammar, and punctuation?

Apply

Check your observation report against your checklist. Then make a final copy to publish.

Differentiating Instruction

ENRICHMENT

Create a Slide Show Have students present their observation reports as slide shows, using presentation software. Students should try to include diagrams or other visuals on several slides as appropriate. They may also add sound and video clips. Students may create their own visuals or search online for visuals that illustrate a point or concept featured in their reports.

REINFORCEMENT

Support Computer Skills Have an older student or the technology instructor give students a short course in creating visuals and inserting them in a document. Create a text document students can use to practice their newly learned skills before they work on inserting visuals into their observation reports.

How Gravity Affects Acceleration

by Lisa and Denise

Gravity is one of Earth's forces. It keeps everything from floating off into space. But how does gravity affect acceleration? Lisa and I did an experiment about that question, using a model car. We wanted to see how gravity affects acceleration—how fast the car starts to move. We decided to attach a weight to one end of a string, tie the other end to the car, and drop the weight over the edge of a table. As gravity pulled the weight down, the weight would pull the car across the table. Lisa and I predicted that as we added more weights, the car would accelerate faster.

PROCEDURE

Step 1: To begin setting up the experiment, Lisa twisted a paper clip into a hook. Next, she used tape to mark a starting line on a table 2.5 feet from the edge of the table. Then she taped a bumper, a piece of heavy cardboard, to the edge of the table. This bumper would stop the car from falling off the table. She made a small opening at the bottom of the bumper for the string to slide through. Meanwhile, I cut 3 feet of string. Lisa tied one end to the car's axle and the other end to the hook. To finish setting up, she pushed the hook through the opening at the bottom of the bumper.

Step 2: Lisa slipped one weight on the hook.

Step 3: Then she held the weight over the edge of the table.

Step 4: She put the car at the starting line and held it there. That's when we figured out that I would have to work the stopwatch. Lisa already had her hands full!

Step 5: Lisa let the weight fall, and I started the stopwatch.

Observation Report **413**

Technology Tip — for 21st Century Literacies

QR codes, or quick response codes, are squares of information that direct a reader equipped with a smart phone or webcam to online content. Challenge students to create their own QR code, posted to their print observation report, that will lead readers to additional resources and enrich their understanding of the report. To use a QR code generator such as Splash, students need the URL they want to link to and a document on which to post the code.

See **www.sfw.z-b.com** for further information about and links to these websites and tools.

Write
an Observation Report

Student Objectives

- Use an observation report rubric. *(pp. 396–397)*
- Share a published observation report. *(pp. 413–415)*

Presentation Strategy Remind students that the formatting of their observation reports will help readers navigate through them and the visuals will help readers understand the procedures and results. The headings must be set in bold type and set apart so that readers can find them easily. The visuals should be placed near the text that relates to them and inserted neatly into the document, with sufficient space around them so that they do not clash with the text. Emphasize that the visuals should support the text, not contradict it.

Point out that all the usual rules of good presentation apply as well: Margins should be sufficient, typing should be neat and accurate, and each step should start a new paragraph.

CCSS **Common Core State Standards**

W.6.4: Produce clear and coherent writing in which the development, organization, and style are appropriate to task, purpose, and audience. **W.6.5:** With some guidance and support from peers and adults, develop and strengthen writing as needed by planning, revising, editing, rewriting, or trying a new approach. **W.6.6:** Use technology, including the Internet, to produce and publish writing as well as to interact and collaborate with others; demonstrate sufficient command of keyboarding skills to type a minimum of three pages in a single sitting. **SL.6.5:** Include multimedia components (e.g., graphics, images, music, sound) and visual displays in presentations to clarify information.

Reflecting on an Observation Report

Ask students to return to the rubric on pages 396 and 397 to evaluate Denise's observation report. Have students work in groups to decide how to score the writing on each of the six traits and then ask the groups to present their scores to the class. Encourage students to support their opinions with examples.

Ask students to reflect on the experience of writing an observation report. Ask:

- What did you enjoy most about writing your report?

- Did the results of your experiment surprise you?

- Which part of writing an observation report was the most difficult for you?

- What did you learn about writing from this experience?

Have students write their responses in a personal writing journal or discuss them as a class or in small groups.

 Strategies for Writers Online

Go to **www.sfw.z-b.com** for additional online resources for students and teachers.

Step 6: I stopped the stopwatch when the car hit the bumper. Actually, I had to practice this several times before I could do it right. That car moved fast!

Step 7: Lisa and I timed the car with one weight on it two more times. Then I added the times and divided by 3 to get the average. I wrote that in our observation log.

Step 8: Then we repeated the whole process with 2, 3, 4, and 5 weights hanging on the hook. We did each number of weights 3 times and averaged the speed.

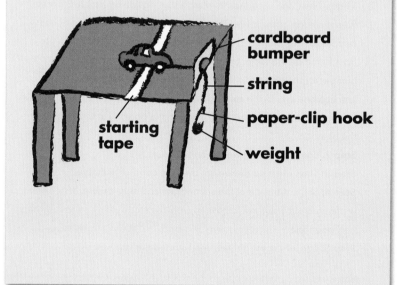

414 Descriptive Writing

Books for Professional Development

Atwell, Nancie. *Lessons That Change Writers.* Portsmouth, NH. Heinemann, 2002. In this book, the author focuses on the mini-lesson as a vehicle for helping students improve their writing. Over 100 writing lessons are included.

National Writing Project. *Writing for a Change: Boosting Literacy and Learning Through Social Action.* San Francisco. Jossey-Bass, 2006. This book shows teachers how to engage students in real-world problem-solving activities that can help them acquire voice, authority, and passion for both reading and writing practices. In collaboration with the Center for Social Action in England, the book describes innovative strategies for encouraging students to collaborate on problems.

OBSERVATIONS

When I looked at our observation log, I didn't see a pattern at first, but Lisa pointed it out. As the number of weights increased, the time decreased.

Observation Log
Time in Seconds to Reach Table's Edge

Number of Weights	Run #1	Run #2	Run #3	Average
1	2.7	2.6	2.6	2.6
2	1.7	1.9	1.8	1.8
3	1.4	1.2	1.6	1.4
4	1.2	1.1	1.0	1.1
5	0.8	0.5	0.9	0.7

CONCLUSION

It's clear. The numbers say it all. Adding weights increased gravity's pull on the weights. The more weights we added, the faster the car accelerated across the table. Our prediction was correct.

Reflect

What do you think? Do all the traits of a good observation report appear in the writing? Check it against the rubric. Then check your own observation report with the rubric.

Peha, Steve, and Margot Carmichael Lester. *Be a Better Writer: Power Tools for Young Writers!* Bend, OR. The Leverage Factory, 2006. This fun, easy-to-use guide is packed with practical tips and techniques to help young writers build a solid foundation. Students learn how to generate interesting ideas, how to use descriptive detail, and how to beat writer's block. They also learn how to perform the five most important types of revision.

Cole, Ardith Davis. *Right-Answer Writing: An All-in-One Resource to Help Students Craft Better Responses.* Portsmouth, NH. Heinemann, 2006. In this book, Cole describes a simple, powerful, step-by-step procedure for responding to prompts. From a single, unified paragraph to a multiple-paragraph response, students are taught a reliable procedure for writing answers to test questions.

CCSS **C**ommon **C**ore **S**tate **S**tandards

W.6.4: Produce clear and coherent writing in which the development, organization, and style are appropriate to task, purpose, and audience. **W.6.5:** With some guidance and support from peers and adults, develop and strengthen writing as needed by planning, revising, editing, rewriting, or trying a new approach. **W.6.6:** Use technology, including the Internet, to produce and publish writing as well as to interact and collaborate with others; demonstrate sufficient command of keyboarding skills to type a minimum of three pages in a single sitting.

Descriptive Article Planner

WEEK 1

Day 1
Introduce
a Descriptive Article

Student Objectives
- Review the elements of a descriptive article.
- Consider purpose and audience.
- Learn the traits of descriptive writing.

Student Activities
- Read and discuss **What's in a Descriptive Article?** (p. 416)
- Read and discuss **Why Write a Descriptive Article?** (p. 417)
- Read **Linking Descriptive Writing Traits to a Descriptive Article.** (p. 418)

Day 2
Analyze
Read a Descriptive Article

Student Objectives
- Read a model descriptive article.

Student Activities
- Read **"Neighborhood Notes."** (p. 419)

Day 3
Analyze
Introduce the Rubric

Student Objectives
- Learn to read a rubric.

Student Activities
- Review **"Neighborhood Notes."** (p. 419)
- Read and discuss the **Descriptive Article Rubric.** (pp. 420–421)

WEEK 2

Day 1
Write
Prewrite: Ideas

Student Objectives
- Read and understand a prewriting strategy.

Student Activities
- Read and discuss **Prewrite: Focus on Ideas.** (p. 426)
- Apply the prewriting strategy.

Day 2
Write
Prewrite: Organization

Student Objectives
- Use a Five-Senses Chart to organize the notes.

Student Activities
- Read and discuss **Prewrite: Focus on Organization.** (p. 427)
- Reflect on the model Five-Senses Chart.
- Apply the prewriting strategy to create a Five-Senses Chart.
- Participate in a peer conference.

Day 3
Write
Draft: Voice

Student Objectives
- Begin writing, using first-person point of view.

Student Activities
- Read and discuss **Draft: Focus on Voice.** (p. 428)
- Apply the drafting strategy by using a Five-Senses Chart to write a draft.

WEEK 3

Day 1
Write
Revise: Word Choice

Student Objectives
- Revise to avoid clichés.

Student Activities
- Read and discuss **Revise: Focus on Word Choice.** (p. 431)
- Participate in a peer conference.

Day 2
Write
Revise: Sentence Fluency

Student Objectives
- Revise to use a repeated sentence pattern for emphasis.

Student Activities
- Read and discuss **Revise: Focus on Sentence Fluency.** (p. 432)

Note: Optional Revising Lessons appear on the *Strategies for Writers* CD-ROM.

Day 3
Write
Edit: Conventions

Student Objectives
- Edit to correct inappropriate shifts in verb tense.

Student Activities
- Read and discuss **Edit: Focus on Conventions.** (p. 433)

Note: Teach the Conventions mini-lessons (pp. 434–435) if needed.

Day 4

Analyze
Ideas, Organization, and Voice

Student Objectives
- Read a model descriptive article.
- Use the descriptive article rubric.
- Use the model descriptive article to study Ideas, Organization, and Voice.

Student Activities
- Review **"Neighborhood Notes."** (p. 419)
- Review the rubric. (pp. 420–421)
- Read and discuss **Using the Rubric to Study the Model.** (pp. 422–423)

Day 5

Analyze
Word Choice, Sentence Fluency, and Conventions

Student Objectives
- Read a model descriptive article.
- Use the descriptive article rubric.
- Use the model descriptive article to study Word Choice, Sentence Fluency, and Conventions.

Student Activities
- Review **"Neighborhood Notes."** (p. 419)
- Review the rubric. (pp. 420–421)
- Read and discuss **Using the Rubric to Study the Model.** (pp. 424–425)

Day 4

Write
Draft

Student Objectives
- Complete a draft.

Student Activities
- Finish the draft. (p. 429)
- Participate in a peer conference.

Day 5

Write
Revise: Ideas

Student Objectives
- Revise to add sensory details.

Student Activities
- Read and discuss **Revise: Focus on Ideas.** (p. 430)
- Reflect on a model draft.
- Apply the revising strategy.

Day 4

Write
Publish: +Presentation

Student Objectives
- Discuss preparation for publishing and presentation.
- Use a final editing checklist to publish their work.

Student Activities
- Read and discuss **Publish: +Presentation.** (p. 436)
- Apply the publishing strategy.

Day 5

Write
Publish: +Presentation

Student Objectives
- Use a descriptive article rubric.
- Share a published descriptive article.

Student Activities
- Share their work.
- Use the rubric to reflect upon and evaluate the model and their own writing. (pp. 420–421, 437)

To complete the chapter in fewer days, combine the learning objectives and activities in a way that supports students as they write.

Grammar, Usage & Mechanics

Differentiating Instruction

For additional Differentiating Instruction activities, see Strategies for Writers *Extensions Online at* **www.sfw.z-b.com.**

English Language Learners

Conferencing

Technology Tip

 Connection Letter
Reproducible letter (in English and Spanish) appears on the *Strategies for Writers* CD-ROM and at **www.sfw.z-b.com.**

Online Writing Center

Provides IWB resources, interactive games and practice activities, videos, eBooks, and a virtual file cabinet.

 Strategies for Writers Online
Go to **www.sfw.z-b.com** for free online resources for students and teachers.

Student Objectives

- Review the elements of a descriptive article. *(p. 416)*
- Consider purpose and audience. *(p. 417)*
- Learn the traits of descriptive writing. *(p. 418)*

What's a Descriptive Article?

Ask students to identify the five senses. Write them on the board as headings. (sight, hearing, taste, touch, smell) Next have students name a place near where they live and contribute sensory details about the place. Have them tell you in which column to place the details. Point out that students could use these details to write an article for the local paper or a visitor's guide. Such an article would be an example of a descriptive article.

What's in a Descriptive Article?

Read and discuss the elements of a descriptive article. Point out that these are similar to the elements of a descriptive essay but that one element—audience appeal—is unique to descriptive articles, which are meant to be published for a larger audience to read.

 Strategies for Writers Online

Go to **www.sfw.z-b.com** for additional online resources for students and teachers.

What's a Descriptive Article?

A descriptive article gives a clear, detailed picture of a person, a place, a thing, or an event. This sounds just like the definition of a descriptive essay, doesn't it? The difference is that a descriptive article is meant to inform the readers of a newspaper, magazine, brochure, or another publication. I think this kind of writing will make me feel like a professional writer!

What's in a Descriptive Article?

Vivid Imagery
I want my readers to see, smell, hear, touch, and taste whatever I'm describing. Using sensory details and clear descriptions will make my subject seem real to my audience!

Point of View
A descriptive article can be written in third person or first person. Either way, it must give a clear picture that shows the writer has actual experience with the subject.

Lively Language
Lively language helps breathe life into a subject. I'll use interesting sentence patterns to keep my audience reading. Instead of clichés, my article will have fresh and appealing phrases!

Audience Appeal
It's always good to think about your audience when you write, but it's especially important with a descriptive article. The article will be published for a specific audience, so it needs to be interesting and informative to those readers!

Descriptive Text Exemplars (Descriptive Article)

Hynson, Colin. *Ancient Rome.* **Gareth Stevens Publishing, 2004.** One of several from the *Historic Civilizations* series, this book includes details about the language, religion, art, and politics of ancient Rome. The information is presented in the form of several articles within the book, making it a factual yet manageable read.

"Space Probe." Astronomy & Space: From the Big Bang to the Big Crunch. **Edited by Phillis Engelbert. Gale Cengage Learning, 2009.** **CCSS** This article explains the purpose of space probes and provides examples of many of their important voyages. While some of the earliest space probes traveled to the moon, current probes are actually aimed at leaving the solar system and entering interstellar space.

Why write a Descriptive Article?

I've been thinking about reasons to write a descriptive article. Here are some of my ideas. I'm still trying to decide about my own descriptive article.

Informing
A descriptive article can give readers a lot of information about its subject. Readers get plenty of details, and they can learn about something they haven't experienced personally.

Reflecting
Writing a descriptive article makes me stop and think. Taking time to reflect on the subject I'm describing can help me appreciate it and what it means to me.

Entertaining
A descriptive article is entertaining for me and for my readers! I think it's fun to describe something so clearly that other people can experience it. And my audience can escape awhile with some fun reading!

Sharing
It's a great feeling to share something in my life with other people. A descriptive article gives me a good way to do that.

As students practice their own writing, it is helpful to remind them that all writing has a purpose and that learning the different genres of writing will help them become better writers. These authentic purposes also help shape their writing.

Review the reasons listed on the page with students. Ask what type of tone students would use for each purpose. For example, if the principal goal of an article is to inform the audience, the writer would probably use a matter-of-fact, straightforward tone. Point out Denise's words at the top of the page and explain that once she has chosen her reason—or reasons—and the topic of her article, she can set the appropriate tone.

Miller, Gary. "Flat Sharks." *National Geographic Explorer,* **May 2011.** "Flat Sharks" focuses on a species of fish called the ray. The ray's body structure and movement, as well as its methods of survival and eating habits, are all detailed in this informative article.

Wedner, Diane. "Far-Out Foods." *National Geographic Explorer,* **Nov.–Dec. 2010.** Diane Wedner describes the many fascinating insects people eat around the world. From termites and ants to grasshoppers and water bugs, these six-legged creatures not only taste good but are nutritious, too. Besides insects, some daring eaters also enjoy the taste of the foul-smelling durian fruit, the poisonous manioc root, and the deadly fugu.

CCSS Common Core State Standards

SL.6.1: Engage effectively in a range of collaborative discussions (one-on-one, in groups, and teacher-led) with diverse partners on *grade 6 topics, texts, and issues,* building on others' ideas and expressing their own clearly. **SL.6.1.a:** Come to discussions prepared, having read or studied required material; explicitly draw on that preparation by referring to evidence on the topic, text, or issue to probe and reflect on ideas under discussion. **SL.6.1.b:** Follow rules for collegial discussions, set specific goals and deadlines, and define individual roles as needed.

Introduce
a Descriptive Article

Linking Descriptive Writing Traits to a Descriptive Article

Explain to students that they will follow Denise as she models using the writing process and the traits together. As they follow Denise through the writing process, students will see how the Descriptive Writing Traits have been adapted and applied to writing a descriptive article. They will see that a descriptive article has many factors in common with other types of descriptive writing. However, the particular audience and purpose of a descriptive article determine how the traits are used.

Linking Descriptive Writing Traits to a Descriptive Article

In this chapter, you will write a detailed description of a person, a place, a thing, or an event. This type of descriptive writing is called a descriptive article. Denise will guide you through the stages of the writing process: Prewrite, Draft, Revise, Edit, and Publish. In each stage, Denise will show you important writing strategies that are linked to the Descriptive Writing Traits below.

Descriptive Writing Traits

 Ideas
- a clear topic that is supported and enhanced by specific sensory details

 **Organization**
- well-organized paragraphs that follow the order of the description, whether by time, location, or another order

 Voice
- a voice and tone that are appropriate for the purpose and audience

 Word Choice
- precise, descriptive words, possibly with figurative language, that create an accurate picture for the reader

 Sentence Fluency
- sentences that vary in length and type to add flow to the writing

 **Conventions**
- no or few errors in grammar, usage, mechanics, and spelling

Before you write, read Adam Riley's descriptive article on the next page. Then use the descriptive article rubric on pages 420–421 to decide how well he did. (You might want to look back at What's in a Descriptive Article? on page 416, too!)

Descriptive Writing Traits in a Descriptive Article

 **Ideas** The writer maintains focus on the topic throughout the report. Plentiful sensory details allow the reader to visualize the descriptions easily and accurately.

 **Organization** Each paragraph focuses on one main idea, and the overall structure of the article is logical and easy to follow.

 **Voice** The writer consistently uses first-person point of view to express himself or herself. The voice connects with the audience.

Neighborhood Notes
by Adam Riley

Lively language

Growling cars crawl down Main Street. Happy customers swarm the stores. Luscious aromas float out of restaurants. Our little town is bustling as usual. This is a wonderful place to live, but do you ever wish you could slip away to someplace quiet?

Audience appeal

I do! Luckily, I found the perfect location for a little escape just steps away from Main Street. My family and I love it so much, you'll find us picnicking there almost every weekend.

First-person point of view

To get to our almost-secret spot, we walk behind the town hall and toward the dense patch of woods that borders the lawn. There's a secluded path back there that few people have discovered. As soon as we step onto the path, the sounds of town begin to fade. The leaves above us whisper hushed hellos, and unseen birds warble a friendly welcome. After a short walk, we hear a gurgling noise, like a cheerful baby is playing somewhere nearby. That's Buck Creek, of course!

Lively language

Suddenly the flickering shadows of the woods give way to the bright sunshine of a large, grassy clearing. The path winds past an old fire pit and down a slope. We see sun sparks dancing on the flowing waters of the creek.

We plop down on the soft grass under the old tree—but only for a moment. In no time, we've stripped off our shoes and socks and raced down to the creek to wade in the cool water.

Vivid imagery

After playing in the water awhile, we relax under the big oak. Even though we're actually still in town, the air smells fresher here. Sometimes the sharp scent of an evergreen blows our way on a gentle breeze.

There's nothing like the first bite of homemade fried chicken, crisp and warm and juicy! Add the creamy tang of coleslaw and the salty crunch of chips, and you're in picnic heaven! Cold, sweet iced tea washes it all down.

We pack up and head back home feeling like new people. We're relaxed. We're refreshed. We're ready to face our busy lives.

Audience appeal

Won't you join us sometime, neighbor?

Descriptive Article 419

Word Choice Precise, descriptive language creates vivid images for readers and helps them put themselves into the scenes described. The language is fresh and fun to read.

Sentence Fluency A variety of sentence types and structures gives writing energy and flow. The writer occasionally makes effective use of repeated sentence structures for emphasis.

Conventions The letter is carefully edited prior to publishing. There are no mistakes in grammar, usage, mechanics, and spelling to confuse the reader or obscure the author's purpose.

Analyze
the Model

Week 1 • Day 2

Student Objectives

- Read a model descriptive article. *(p. 419)*

Read the Model

Have students read the descriptive article on page 419. Before they read, remind students to look out for the writing traits outlined on page 418.

Elements of a Descriptive Article

Use the notes on the model to discuss how Adam Riley has written an effective descriptive article. Ask:

- Why does it make sense for Adam to use first-person point of view? (He is describing an experience he had.)

Point out the underlined vivid images and ask:

- How does appealing to multiple senses help readers appreciate the article? (Possible response: It helps readers imagine the scene.)

You might wish to have students refer to What's in a Descriptive Article? on page 416 for review.

CCSS Common Core State Standards

R/Inf.6.1: Cite textual evidence to support analysis of what the text says explicitly as well as inferences drawn from the text. **R/Inf.6.5:** Analyze how a particular sentence, paragraph, chapter, or section fits into the overall structure of a text and contributes to the development of the ideas. **SL.6.1.b:** Follow rules for collegial discussions, set specific goals and deadlines, and define individual roles as needed.

Analyze
the Model

Week 1 • Day 3

Student Objectives

- Learn to read a rubric. (pp. 420–421)

Use the Rubric

Explain the Rubric Explain that a rubric is a tool that helps you plan, improve, and evaluate a piece of writing. A rubric also helps a writer focus on key elements, or traits, in writing (**Ideas, Organization, Voice, Word Choice, Sentence Fluency, Conventions,** and **Presentation**).

The 6-point rubric on pages 420 and 421 is based on the Descriptive Writing Traits that students read on page 418. Explain that column 6 describes a very good descriptive article, one that has received the highest score in all categories. This is what students should strive for in their own writing.

Discuss the Rubric Guide the students in a discussion of the rubric. Read the descriptors that go with each trait. Note how the descriptors vary as you move from column to column. Remind students to keep the rubric in mind when they write their own descriptive article and again when they revise it.

Online Writing Center

Provides a variety of **interactive rubrics,** including 4-, 5-, and 6-point models.

Descriptive Article

Rubric

Use this 6-point rubric to plan and score a descriptive article.

	6	5	4
Ideas	The writing engages the reader with a clear, focused topic. Relevant, sensory details create a vivid picture for the reader.	The topic is focused. Sensory details are mostly relevant and create strong images for the reader.	The topic is fairly focused. Some details are interesting, but some are irrelevant.
Organization	The structure of the writing enhances the reader's understanding. Each paragraph presents one main idea.	The organization fits the writing and the order makes sense. Most paragraphs are organized around one main idea.	The organization of the writing works most of the time. The focus of some paragraphs is unclear.
Voice	First-person point of view reveals the writer's personality and connects with the reader.	The writer uses first-person point of view and connects with the reader most of the time.	First-person point of view is used inconsistently at times. The writer tries to connect to the audience.
Word Choice	The writer's fresh and interesting phrases make the writing appealing and fun to read.	Some striking words and phrases engage and entertain the reader.	Some of the descriptions are ordinary but convey the writer's message.
Sentence Fluency	Repetitive sentence patterns are used to emphasize a point.	Sentence patterns are repeated for effect.	The writer tries to use repeated sentence patterns for effect but does not always succeed.
Conventions	Verb tenses are consistent throughout. The writing is easy to read and understand.	Verb tenses are consistent. The reader has to hunt to find a few errors.	Verb tenses switch back and forth sometimes, confusing the reader.
⁺Presentation	The page is designed for visual appeal.		

CCSS Common Core State Standards

Descriptive Article

Writing in the Descriptive mode can engage the Common Core State Standards for both Narrative and Informative/Explanatory writing. The rubric and writing strategies for Ideas are drawn from informative/explanatory standard **W.6.2.b** and narrative standard **W.6.3.d,** which focus on developing a topic with relevant and sensory details. The rubric and writing strategies for Organization are grounded in informative/explanatory standard **W.6.2.a** and narrative standard **W.6.3.a,** both of which highlight the importance of organizing the writing in a way that supports understanding. The rubric and writing strategies for Voice reflect language standard **L.6.3.b,** which calls for the writer to maintain a

3	2	1	
The topic is not clear. The details are general. There are few images for the reader.	The topic is not clear. Details are limited. The reader cannot form images from the details.	The writing lacks details. It reads like a list of thoughts.	**Ideas**
The organizational structure is hard to identify. Several paragraphs are unfocused.	The organization is very hard to follow; the reader feels lost. The paragraphs have no main idea.	The writing has no order. The article is not organized into paragraphs.	**Organization**
Point of view is inconsistent in places. The writer only sometimes connects to the audience.	The voice is weak and point of view is inconsistent throughout the article. The writer does not connect with the reader.	The writing has no voice. The writer is unaware of the reader.	**Voice**
Some of the words and phrases are vague or ordinary. They do not grab the reader.	Many vague and general words confuse the meaning. The writing may be dull to read.	Words are consistently vague and general. The reader has to work to get meaning.	**Word Choice**
Repeated sentence patterns are used, but they may not emphasize a point.	Repeated sentence patterns make the writing choppy and do not help the writer make a point.	There are many sentence problems (incomplete, run-ons), and there is too much repetition.	**Sentence Fluency**
Noticeable verb tense errors slow down the reader.	Many errors with verb tenses make reading this article difficult.	The writing is filled with serious verb-tense errors. It is difficult to read out loud.	**Conventions**

See Appendix B for 4-, 5-, and 6-point descriptive rubrics.

Descriptive Article **421**

Apply the Rubric

Evaluate a Descriptive Article

Find a descriptive article in a print or online magazine or newspaper that is appropriate for your class. The travel or lifestyle sections are good places to look. Share the sample article with the class. Ask students to use the rubric to score the article on each of the traits. Be sure that students can offer examples from the article to support each score.

Once the class has reached a consensus on the scores, ask these follow-up questions:

- Which trait is strongest in the article? Why do you think so?
- Does the article fit the audience and the purpose? How?

Additional Rubrics Appendix B includes 4-, 5-, and 6-point rubrics that can be used with any piece of descriptive writing. The rubrics are also available as blackline masters in the back of this Teacher Edition, beginning on page T525.

consistent style and tone. The emphasis on precise language in the rubric and writing strategies for Word Choice comes from both informative/explanatory standard **W.6.2.d** and narrative standard **W.6.3.d**. The language standards **L.6.1** and **L.6.2**, which focus on command of the conventions of grammar, usage, capitalization, spelling, and punctuation, are evident in Conventions. Woven throughout the unit are writing standards **W.6.4–W.6.6** and **W.6.10**, which focus on writing appropriately for the task, the purpose, and the audience; using technology; and writing routinely over extended time frames.

CCSS **Common Core State Standards**

SL.6.1: Engage effectively in a range of collaborative discussions (one-on-one, in groups, and teacher-led) with diverse partners on *grade 6 topics, texts, and issues,* building on others' ideas and expressing their own clearly. **SL.6.1.a:** Come to discussions prepared, having read or studied required material; explicitly draw on that preparation by referring to evidence on the topic, text, or issue to probe and reflect on ideas under discussion. **SL.6.1.b:** Follow rules for collegial discussions, set specific goals and deadlines, and define individual roles as needed.

Analyze
the Model

Week 1 • Day 4

Student Objectives

- Read a model descriptive article. *(p. 419)*
- Use the descriptive article rubric. *(pp. 420–421)*
- Use the model descriptive article to study Ideas, Organization, and Voice. *(pp. 422–423)*

Study the Model

Assess the Model Once students have read pages 422 and 423, ask them whether they agree or disagree with Denise's assessment of the model on each point. For example, did students feel that Adam's personality really came through in his writing? Use questions such as the following to discuss the model and the traits with students.

- What is the strongest sensory detail in the article? What makes it strong? (Possible response: *The leaves above us whisper hushed hellos, and unseen birds warble a friendly welcome.* The description gives me a feeling that's both peaceful and welcoming.)

Strategies for Writers Online
Go to **www.sfw.z-b.com** for additional online resources for students and teachers.

Descriptive Article
Using the Rubric to Study the Model

Did you notice that the model on page 419 points out some key elements of a descriptive article? As he wrote "Neighborhood Notes," Adam Riley used these elements to help him describe a special place. He also used the 6-point rubric on pages 420–421 to plan, draft, revise, and edit the writing. A rubric is a great tool for evaluating writing during the writing process.

Now let's use the same rubric to score the model. To do this, we'll focus on each trait separately, starting with Ideas. We'll use the top descriptor for each trait (column 6), along with examples from the model, to help us understand how the traits work together. How would you score Adam on each trait?

Ideas

- The writing engages the reader with a clear, focused topic.
- Relevant, sensory details create a vivid picture for the reader.

This article has a focused topic—a secret spot in the neighborhood—and lots of sensory details that make the reader see a vivid picture. I can easily picture myself walking down the path with Adam!

[from the writing model]

Suddenly the flickering shadows of the woods give way to the bright sunshine of a large, grassy clearing. The path winds past an old fire pit and down a slope. We see sun sparks dancing on the flowing waters of the creek.

English Language Learners

BEGINNING
Article Show students a magazine. Say, *magazine,* and have students repeat. Point out an article that has colorful, vivid pictures. Say, *This is an article.* Write *article,* and have students repeat. Introduce or review the meanings of *describe* and *descriptive.*

INTERMEDIATE
Audience Show students a photo of a theater full of spectators. Point to the audience and say, *The audience watches and listens.* Have students repeat. Write *audience* on the board. Point to a magazine article. Ask, *Who is the audience?* Allow students time to brainstorm ideas.

Organization

- The structure of the writing enhances the reader's understanding.
- Each paragraph presents one main idea.

Adam has organized his article so that each paragraph focuses on one of the senses. This makes his reading easy to follow. I understand Adam's experience because he leads me through it one sense at a time.

[from the writing model]

After playing in the water awhile, we relax under the big oak. Even though we're actually still in town, the air smells fresher here. Sometimes the sharp scent of an evergreen blows our way on a gentle breeze.

Voice

- First-person point of view reveals the writer's personality and connects with the reader.

I can easily relate to Adam's descriptions. Using first-person point of view, he seems to be speaking directly to me. See where he uses the words *I* and *us* to draw the reader in.

[from the writing model]

I do! Luckily, I found the perfect location for a little escape just steps away from Main Street. My family and I love it so much, you'll find us picnicking there almost every weekend.

Descriptive Article 423

- How does Adam use sensory details to make his point in the first paragraph? (Possible response: Sensory details about the sounds of cars and delicious smells make the town sound like a busy, pleasant place.)

- Based on his writing, how would you describe Adam's personality? (Possible responses: positive, upbeat, enthusiastic)

ADVANCED

Imagery Write the word *imagery* and ask for volunteers to guess its meaning. If needed, write *image* and *imagine*, too. Once students understand that *imagery* is creating pictures with words, have them brainstorm some ways they can include imagery in their writing. Discuss descriptive details, figurative language, and powerful verbs.

ADVANCED HIGH

Vivid Imagery Have students close their eyes and listen closely to figure out what you are describing. Say, *Her face is suntanned and deeply wrinkled, but it is still silky smooth when I touch it. Her fluffy white hair smells like jasmine. I can't wait to taste the sweet orange cake she has lovingly baked for me.* Ask a volunteer to guess whom you described. Ask them what words helped paint a vivid picture.

CCSS **Common Core State Standards**
R/Inf.6.5: Analyze how a particular sentence, paragraph, chapter, or section fits into the overall structure of a text and contributes to the development of the ideas. **R/Inf.6.6:** Determine an author's point of view or purpose in a text and explain how it is conveyed in the text. **SL.6.1.b:** Follow rules for collegial discussions, set specific goals and deadlines, and define individual roles as needed. **SL.6.1.d:** Review the key ideas expressed and demonstrate understanding of multiple perspectives through reflection and paraphrasing.

Analyze
the Model

Week 1 • Day 5

Student Objectives

- Read a model descriptive article. (p. 419)
- Use the descriptive article rubric. (pp. 420–421)
- Use the model descriptive article to study Word Choice, Sentence Fluency, and Conventions. (pp. 424–425)

Continue Discussing the Traits

Use questions such as the following to discuss the traits analyzed on pages 424 and 425:

- Choose another word or phrase you found original and appealing. (Possible response: *We see sun sparks dancing on the flowing waters of the creek.*)

- Find another example of sentence repetition in the article. What is the effect of this repetition? (*We're relaxed. We're refreshed. We're ready to face our busy lives.* The repetition emphasizes Adam's point about how good his family feels after the picnic.)

- Why is it important that Adam carefully checked his use of verb tenses? (Possible response: The article would be confusing to read if verb tenses were used incorrectly.)

Strategies for Writers Online
Go to **www.sfw.z-b.com** for additional online resources for students and teachers.

Word Choice

- The writer's fresh and interesting phrases make the writing appealing and fun to read.

Adam could have used worn-out phrases and old clichés in his descriptive article, but he keeps his writing fresh. For example, in the sentences below, he could have said that the leaves rustled, the birds sang, and the creek babbled. Instead, he used fresh ways to describe these things.

[from the writing model]

The leaves above us whisper hushed hellos, and unseen birds warble a friendly welcome. After a short walk, we hear a gurgling noise, like a cheerful baby is playing somewhere nearby.

Sentence Fluency

- Repetitive sentence patterns are used to emphasize a point.

It's usually a good idea to vary sentence patterns to keep your writing interesting, but repetition has its place too. Adam sometimes repeats sentence patterns to make a point. For example, he starts his article with repetitive sentences that felt as busy as his little town.

[from the writing model]

Growling cars crawl down Main Street. Happy customers swarm the stores. Luscious aromas float out of restaurants.

Technology Tip — for 21st Century Literacies

Writing for a global audience requires a prompt that not only engages students' interest but also beckons to readers of student writing. Sometimes in building lessons that integrate social media, we get caught up in planning where to post, which classrooms to connect with, and how to facilitate students' thinking and online writing. In the process, the importance of offering students a relevant and purposeful reason to write can be forgotten. Keep writing at the forefront—technology is just the delivery.

Conventions
- Verb tenses are consistent throughout. The writing is easy to read and understand.

Adam does a great job being consistent in his use of verb tenses. All his descriptions are in the present tense, which helps me imagine I'm in his favorite spot right now. When it's appropriate, he does use the past and future tenses.

[from the writing model]

We pack up and head back home feeling like new people. We're relaxed. We're refreshed. We're ready to face our busy lives.

Won't you join us sometime, neighbor?

➕**Presentation** The page is designed for visual appeal.

I'm going to write a descriptive article about one of my favorite places. I'll follow the rubric and use good writing strategies. Read on to see how I do it!

Differentiating Instruction

ENRICHMENT
Explore Figures of Speech Have students who are already familiar with metaphors and similes research three figures of speech that are new to them (e.g., litotes, hyperbole, synecdoche, onomatopoeia). Have them use each figure of speech to describe the scene in the model article.

REINFORCEMENT
Analyze Articles Find two examples of short descriptive articles at an appropriate reading level. In one article, underline sensory details and other elements from the rubric. Discuss whether these elements are used effectively in the article. Give students copies of the second article and have them find and underline examples of two or three elements from the descriptive article rubric. Discuss how to score the examples using the rubric.

Presentation Explain that visual appeal is an important part of writing. Text that is neat, makes good use of white space, and is generally easy on the eyes will be more appealing to readers and easier to access. Students should resist the temptation to use excessively ornate fonts, which can be appealing in small doses but give a crowded feel when used for an entire page or more. Students may wish to type their article on a computer and set it in two columns, as Adam did in the model. In that case, they should pay attention to the margin settings in their word-processing program to make sure there is enough space between and around the columns.

Think About the Traits Now ask students which traits they think are most important in a descriptive article. Explain that all traits are important in every piece of writing, but some stand out more in some genres than in others. Some students may feel that **Word Choice** is important because precise words and phrases are the key to helping readers visualize the description. Others may feel that **Voice** is important because readers will engage with the article if they feel a connection with the writer.

CCSS **C**ommon **C**ore **S**tate **S**tandards
SL.6.1.b: Follow rules for collegial discussions, set specific goals and deadlines, and define individual roles as needed. **SL.6.1.c:** Pose and respond to specific questions with elaboration and detail by making comments that contribute to the topic, text, or issue under discussion. **SL.6.1.d:** Review the key ideas expressed and demonstrate understanding of multiple perspectives through reflection and paraphrasing. **W.6.6:** Use technology, including the Internet, to produce and publish writing as well as to interact and collaborate with others; demonstrate sufficient command of keyboarding skills to type a minimum of three pages in a single sitting.

Write
a Descriptive Article

Week 2 • Day 1

Student Objectives

• Read and understand a prewriting strategy. *(p. 426)*

Prewrite

Focus on Ideas

Gather Information Remind students that when you first met Denise, you learned that one of her interests is cooking. It's not surprising, then, that Denise chooses her grandmother's kitchen to write about for this assignment. Ask students why they think she will write an article on this subject and what her interest in cooking will bring to the article. (Possible responses: Because she likes cooking, she will be able to talk knowledgeably about cooking in the kitchen or about the smells and tastes of her grandmother's cooking. She is very familiar with her grandmother's kitchen and will be able to describe it in detail.) Remind students that they should choose a topic that interests them and that they know something about.

Have students choose their topics and write down as many sensory details as they can about it.

Online Writing Center

Provides **interactive graphic organizers** as well as a variety of graphic organizers in PDF format.

Prewrite

Focus on Ideas

The Rubric Says	The writing engages the reader with a clear, focused topic. Relevant, sensory details create a vivid picture for the reader.
Writing Strategy	Jot down some notes that appeal to the senses.

When I got my assignment, I decided to write about one of my favorite places—my grandmother's kitchen. To get started, I jotted down the sights, sounds, feelings, smells, and tastes of Grandma's kitchen. Here are my notes.

My Notes on Grandma's Kitchen

Family uses back door, goes right into kitchen.
African violets in crusty pots on windowsill
Good smells on back porch, something baking, meat
Kitchen is tiny.
She always fixes me something to eat!
Stuff bubbling on stove
White cabinets, green walls like kiwi
We can sit and be quiet or sit and talk.
Mmmm . . . fresh cookies, melted chocolate chips
Volcano chili—hot as fire!
Grandma tells about old times in low husky voice.
House creaks.
Grandma—big smile, twinkling eyes, strong hands, busy
What she makes is always special.
Refrigerator hums.
Wash dishes in warm, soapy water.
Dry hands on crisp towel.
Can still feel hug after she lets go.

Apply

Choose your favorite spot, and jot down some notes about it. Remember to cover the five senses.

426 Descriptive Writing

English Language Learners

BEGINNING/INTERMEDIATE

Sensory Details Review the five senses. Show students a photo of a fair or an amusement park. Describe how the place looks (bright, colorful); how it smells (like cotton candy); how it feels (many people pushing, wind rushing); how it sounds (happy children laughing); and how it tastes (ice cream, salty pretzels). Then have students draw a picture of their favorite place and describe it to a partner using sensory details.

ADVANCED/ADVANCED HIGH

Five-Senses Chart Briefly review the five senses. Talk about a local gathering place. Have partners imagine the sights, sounds, smells, and tastes associated with the place, in addition to what they might feel when they are there. Have them fill in a Five-Senses Chart. Then have them trade with another pair who should try to guess what place is described by the details in the chart.

Prewrite
Focus on Organization

The Rubric Says	The structure of the writing enhances the reader's understanding.
Writing Strategy	Use a Five-Senses Chart to organize the notes.

✏️ Writer's Term___

Five-Senses Chart
A **Five-Senses Chart** organizes descriptive words according to the five senses.

It looks like I have some good ideas for my article, but I have to get things organized. I can use a Five-Senses Chart to do that. I'll divide a sheet of paper into five parts, one for each sense. Then I'll rewrite my notes in the right spaces. This will help me organize my thoughts and keep me from forgetting anything important.

Five-Senses Chart

Smell: on back porch
something baking
meat
delicious!

Sight:
Kitchen—back door leads to kitchen
tiny, cheery, bright
kiwi-green walls
fresh white cabinets
square wooden table in corner
two purple chairs
deep purple African violets in
crusty pots on windowsill
Grandma—wide smile
twinkling eyes
strong, busy hands

Taste: fresh, homemade cookies, melted
chocolate chips
volcano chili—hot as fire
everything she makes is special

Sound: stuff bubbling on stove
house creaks
refrigerator hums
Grandma's low, husky voice
Grandma's sympathetic sounds

Touch: warm, soapy dishwater
dry hands on crisp, cotton towel
Grandma's arms, soft, warm, strong
can still feel hug when she lets go

Reflect
How does Denise's chart look? Are the notes well organized?

Apply
Organize your notes with a Five-Senses Chart.

Descriptive Article 427

Conferencing

PEER TO PEER Have students exchange Five-Senses Charts with a partner. Each partner asks a question about a detail from each of the senses to elicit clarifications or additional details.

PEER GROUPS Have students pass their Five-Senses Charts around the group. Each student underlines in pencil the detail he or she thinks is most interesting or appealing in each chart and writes one question about one of the details in the chart.

TEACHER-LED Work with pairs of students. Have students exchange charts, and have each student give a brief verbal description of his or her topic. Then coach students in asking each other questions to elicit more details for the charts.

Write
a Descriptive Article

Week 2 • Day 2

Student Objectives

• Use a Five-Senses Chart to organize the notes. *(p. 427)*

Prewrite

Focus on Organization

Make a Five-Senses Chart Ask students which sense in Denise's chart has the largest number of details. **(sight)** Explain that writers usually have the easiest time coming up with sight details and that, while there is nothing wrong with including many sight details, they should make an effort to think of details for the other senses as well. Point out also that students may find themselves thinking of additional details when they copy their notes into the charts.

✏️ Writer's Term___

Five-Senses Chart A Five-Senses Chart is a good way to make sure a writer includes a variety of sensory details, not just those pertaining to sight. With a quick glance, the writer can tell whether there are enough details for all senses.

CCSS Common Core State Standards
W.6.2.a: Introduce a topic; organize ideas, concepts, and information, using strategies such as definition, classification, comparison/contrast, and cause/effect; include formatting (e.g., headings), graphics (e.g., charts, tables), and multimedia when useful to aiding comprehension. **W.6.2.b:** Develop the topic with relevant facts, definitions, concrete details, quotations, or other information and examples. **W.6.3.d:** Use precise words and phrases, relevant descriptive details, and sensory language to convey experiences and events.

Write
a Descriptive Article

Week 2 • Day 3

Student Objectives

- Begin writing, using first-person point of view. *(p. 428)*

Draft

Focus on  Voice

Begin a Draft Review what it means to write a draft. Note that the draft is a temporary form of a piece of writing that should be changed and corrected several times before it is finished.

Explain that students will need to decide which point of view to use before they start writing so that it will be used consistently throughout the article. If they choose to follow Denise and write in first person, then students establish themselves as the narrator of the article, and the reader will know that everything will be filtered through the eyes of the writer/narrator.

Writer's Term

Point of View Writers decide which point of view to use depending on the purpose for writing and the audience. If the purpose is to share personal experiences, then first-person point of view makes sense.

Online Writing Center

Provides student eBooks with an **interactive writing pad** for drafting, revising, editing, and publishing.

Draft

Focus on **Voice**

The Rubric Says   First-person point of view reveals the writer's personality and connects with the reader.

Writing Strategy   Use first-person point of view.

Writer's Term

Point of View
When you write using the pronouns **I, me, my, we,** or **us,** you are writing in the first person. A first-person narration allows the writer to make a personal connection with the reader. However, it limits the action to only what the narrator experiences.

Now I'll use my Five-Senses chart as I write my draft. The rubric says to use first-person point of view, which shows that it's me right there in my description. When I share my thoughts and feelings with my reader that way, my writing sounds personal, and the reader can connect to what I'm saying.

I'll do my best with spelling and grammar, but I know I can check things over later and correct any mistakes. I mostly want to concentrate on getting my description down on paper.

428 Descriptive Writing

Differentiating Instruction

ENRICHMENT

Experiment With Point of View Have students rewrite the first few paragraphs of the model, first using second- and then third-person points of view. Once writing is complete, have small groups of students read the paragraphs aloud and discuss how each point of view affected both the writing and listening experience.

REINFORCEMENT

Review Point of View Write the following sentences on the board: *I absolutely love chocolate chip ice cream! You love the flavor rocky road. She loves good old-fashioned vanilla.* Point out the point of view in each sentence. (first, second, third) Discuss how each point of view affects the reader's connection with the statement.

Cooking Up Love   **[DRAFT]**

Nobody in our family goes to my grandmother's front door. The shed is in the back. We all use the back door, the family entrance. It leads straight to her kitchen—and right into her heart!

It's good to visit often since we live on the same street. Every time you step onto Grandma's porch, something smells wonderful. Sometimes, something is baking. At other times, something chocolate promises a sweet surprise. If it's near suppertime, I'll smell meat or something else delicious!

[first-person point of view]

Grandma greets me with a wide smile and twinkling eyes. Usually her strong hands are chopping or stirring something, so I give her a sideways hug. The kitchen has fresh, white cabinets and green walls that make the place cheery and bright. As soon as I sit down, she fixes me something to eat!

Sometimes she gives me fresh, homemade cookies with melted chocolate chips. Or she might give me a bowl of her volcano chili. It's as hot as fire, but I love it. Whatever she makes is special.

Reflect

How does Denise make you "see" her grandmother's kitchen? How has her Five-Senses Chart guided her writing?

Apply

Write a draft using your Five-Senses Chart. Be sure to make your descriptions vivid!

Descriptive Article 429

Conferencing

PEER TO PEER Have partners exchange drafts. Have students look for any lapses in point of view in their partner's draft and suggest places where a first-person sentence could be added to help connect with the reader.

PEER GROUPS Have students read their drafts aloud to the group. Each listening student comments on one place in the article where he or she feels first-person point of view is used effectively and makes one suggestion for using first person to make a stronger connection to the reader.

TEACHER-LED Work with individual students. Read the draft, and then discuss the student's use of first-person point of view with him or her. Point out places in the article that could be strengthened, and encourage the student to think of ideas for improvement.

Write
a Descriptive Article

Student Objectives

• Complete a draft. *(p. 429)*

Finish the Draft Have students read the draft excerpt on page 429. Point out the highlighted phrases and ask students to find other examples of first-person point of view in the excerpt. (*Grandma greets me; I give her a sideways hug; As soon as I sit down, she fixes me something to eat; Sometimes she gives me fresh, homemade cookies; Or she might give me a bowl of her volcano chili.*) Discuss how Denise's use of first-person point of view affects readers. (Possible response: It makes them feel closer to her, because she seems to be speaking directly to them.)

Mention to students that writers often start with a strong, clear point of view but then allow it to become weaker as the writing progresses. Encourage them to think about keeping their voice and point of view consistently strong throughout their article.

CCSS **Common Core State Standards**

W.6.3.a: Engage and orient the reader by establishing a context and introducing a narrator and/or characters; organize an event sequence that unfolds naturally and logically. **W.6.4:** Produce clear and coherent writing in which the development, organization, and style are appropriate to task, purpose, and audience. **L.6.3.b:** Maintain consistency in style and tone.

Write
a Descriptive Article

Week 2 • Day 5

Student Objectives

- Revise to add sensory details. (p. 430)

Revise

Focus on Ideas

Use Sensory Details Remind students of the meaning of sensory details. Look at the changes Denise made to her draft. Ask students why they think she added the word *roasting* to describe the meat. (Possible response: It appeals to the readers' sense of smell.) Ask students if they feel that Denise's changes have made her draft more appealing for readers.

Before students revise their own descriptive articles, have them practice with sensory details by thinking of ones they could add to the draft excerpt. Ask:

- What do you think Denise sees inside Grandma's kitchen? (Possible response: gleaming white countertops)

- What does she hear? (Possible response: Grandma's scratchy voice calling out a greeting)

- What does she feel? (Possible response: Grandma's stiff apron between them as Grandma gives Denise a hug)

 Strategies for Writers Online
Go to **www.sfw.z-b.com** for additional online resources for students and teachers.

T430 Descriptive Writing

Revise   Focus on ⟨Ideas⟩

The Rubric Says	Relevant, sensory details create a vivid picture for the reader.
Writing Strategy	Add sensory details.

After I wrote my draft, I looked at the rubric again. It says I should use sensory details throughout my article to create a vivid picture for the reader. I tried to do that, but there are places where I didn't appeal to the senses as much as I could. Look at how I improved the paragraph below by adding more sensory details. Can you imagine how the food smells?

[DRAFT]

It's good to visit often since we live on the same street. Every time you step onto Grandma's porch, something smells wonderful. Sometimes, ~~something is baking.~~ At other times, ~~something~~ chocolate mouth-watering roasting promises a sweet surprise. If it's near suppertime, I'll smell meat zesty spices, or ~~or~~ something else delicious!

[added sensory details]

the home-baked scents of vanilla and cinnamon welcome me

Apply

Do you see some parts of your article that could use more sensory details? Add some, and make your subject come alive for your readers.

430 Descriptive Writing

English Language Learners

BEGINNING/INTERMEDIATE

Editing Remind students that if they draft on every other line, they will have room to make edits later. Review the proofreading marks. Have students review their drafts and look for one type of error. Then have them read the draft again and search for another type of error. Monitor that students are using the proper proofreading marks as they find any errors.

ADVANCED/ADVANCED HIGH

Repetition Ask a student what *repeat* means. Use this information to introduce the terms *repetition* and *repetitive*. Then review the Sentence Fluency trait on page 424. Tell students that using repetition in their writing is helpful for creating a vivid picture for readers.

Revise

The Rubric Says The writer's fresh and interesting phrases make the writing appealing and fun to read.

Writing Strategy Replace clichés with interesting phrases.

✏ Writer's Term____

Clichés

A **cliché** is a familiar word or phrase that has been used so much that its original meaning is lost. In addition, clichés, such as **a ton of homework,** are boring.

Now it's time to make sure my word choice is interesting. I looked at my draft again, and I thought that some sections sounded dull and stale. I need to get rid of any clichés and make sure that all my language is appealing and fresh! Look at how I livened up this paragraph.

[DRAFT]

[added fresh language]

oven-warm

Sometimes she gives me ~~fresh, homemade~~ cookies with melted

chocolate chips. Or she might give me a bowl of her volcano chili.

It's so hot it makes me want to dunk my whole face in the creek

~~It's as hot as fire,~~ but I love it! Whatever she makes is special.

[replaced cliché]

Reflect

Did the changes make the language fresher and more lively? Are there other clichés in the descriptive article that should be replaced?

Apply

Read through your draft and replace any tired, old language with fresh, interesting words and phrases. Replace any clichés with fresh phrases as well.

Descriptive Article 431

Conferencing

PEER TO PEER Have partners exchange drafts. Each student circles his or her favorite sensory detail in the partner's draft and explains why he or she likes that detail. Students should also underline any clichés they see in the drafts.

PEER GROUPS Have students pass their drafts around the group. On each draft, students should either underline a cliché and offer a suggestion for replacing it or suggest a sensory detail that could be added to the draft.

TEACHER-LED Meet with pairs of students. Have students read each other's drafts, and facilitate a conversation in which they offer constructive criticism on each other's use of sensory details and fresh language.

Write
a Descriptive Article

Week 3 • Day 1

Student Objectives

• Revise to avoid clichés. *(p. 431)*

Revise

Focus on

Eliminate Clichés Have students read the definition of *clichés* in the Writer's Term box. Explain that in this step of the revising process, Denise is looking for ways to make her writing more appealing. One way writers can make their writing more enjoyable for readers is by replacing clichés and uninteresting language. Ask students why fresh and interesting language is important in a descriptive article. **(Possible response: Readers won't be bored by the descriptions if they're new and different.)** Encourage students to look through their drafts and replace clichés and uninteresting descriptions with fresh, original descriptions.

✏ Writer's Term____

Clichés Phrases become clichés through overuse. Writers need to judge whether a phrase they want to use has become too common and is considered a cliché.

CCSS **C**ommon **C**ore **S**tate **S**tandards

W.6.2.b: Develop the topic with relevant facts, definitions, concrete details, quotations, or other information and examples. **W.6.2.d:** Use precise language and domain-specific vocabulary to inform about or explain the topic. **W.6.3.d:** Use precise words and phrases, relevant descriptive details, and sensory language to convey experiences and events.

Write
a Descriptive Article

Week 3 • Day 2

Student Objectives

- Revise to use a repeated sentence pattern for emphasis. (p. 432)

Revise

Focus on  **Sentence Fluency**

Repeat a Sentence Pattern for Emphasis Point out that writers can emphasize a point by repeating a sentence pattern. Read the draft excerpt aloud, once without the revisions and once with the revisions. Ask:

- How do the revisions change the rhythm and flow of the sentences? (Possible response: The sentences have a similar rhythm.)

- How does the rhythm created by the repeated sentence pattern draw readers' attention? (Possible responses: It relates the sentences to each other. It separates them from the surrounding sentences.)

Ask students why they think Denise has decided to repeat the sentence pattern for that part of her article. (Possible responses: The similarity of the rhythm of the sentences mimics the ticking of a clock. Denise wants readers to feel as though time is passing as she and her grandmother notice what's going on around them.)

Online Writing Center

 Provides **interactive proofreading activities** for each genre.

Revise

Focus on Sentence Fluency

The Rubric Says   Repetitive sentence patterns are used to emphasize a point.

Writing Strategy   Repeat a sentence pattern to emphasize a point.

The rubric says to repeat a sentence pattern to emphasize a point. At first, I didn't understand how to do that because I've always tried to use a variety of sentences for flow. Then I understood that a repetitive pattern could help strengthen a point in the paragraph below. Does the repetition make you feel that time is passing as Grandma and I sit there quietly?

[DRAFT]

While I eat, Grandma sits with me and drinks a cup of coffee.

Sometimes we're quiet. We listen to whatever's bubbling on the stove. ~~We hear~~ its one-note song. The refrigerator hums, ~~and the old house creaks~~. It's a nice, comfortable quiet.

[repeated sentence pattern] → We notice the creaks the old house makes as it settles.

Apply

Use a repetitive sentence pattern to emphasize one of your points.

432 Descriptive Writing

Optional Revising Lessons

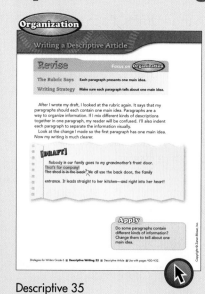

Descriptive 35

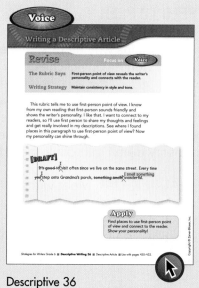

Descriptive 36

Go to → *Strategies for Writers Grade 6 CD-ROM*

Edit

Focus on **Conventions**

The Rubric Says   Verb tenses are consistent throughout. The writing is easy to read and understand.

Writing Strategy   Recognize and correct inappropriate shifts in verb tense.

✏️ Writer's Term_

Verb Tense

Verb tenses tell whether an action is taking place in the past, present, or future. Most past- and present-tense verbs are formed by adding *-s, -ed, -en,* or *-ing.* Most future-tense verbs are formed by placing the helping verb *will* in front of the verb.

The rubric says to use the proper tense for verbs. If I make the verb tenses consistent, my reader will be able to understand when things happen. Sometimes I have a hard time keeping present, past, and future tenses straight. You can see some of my edits below.

[DRAFT]

[correct present-tense verb]

Usually
~~Usually,~~ we talk. Grandma's voice is low and husky and I ~~liked~~ **like** to

listen to her tell stories about how she lived back in the day. When I'm

sympathetic
talking, Grandma makes ~~simpathetic~~ noises. I feel like she understands

care
me, and she'll always ~~cared~~ about me.   [correct future-tense verb]

Reflect

How can repeating a sentence pattern strengthen a point? How do Denise's edits help the reader better understand her article?

Apply   Conventions

Edit your draft for spelling, grammar, and punctuation. Be sure to fix any errors in verb tense.

For more practice with verb tenses, use the exercises on the next two pages.

Descriptive Article   433

Related Grammar Practice _____

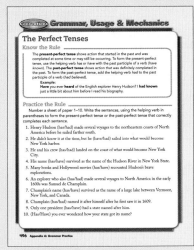

Student Edition page 496

Go to ➡️ **Appendix A: Grammar Practice**

Student Objectives

- Edit to correct inappropriate shifts in verb tense. *(p. 433)*

Edit

Focus on **Conventions**

Check Verb Tenses Have students read the page and remind them that it is important to use verb tenses correctly so that readers can understand when events happen in relationship to one another.

Instruct students to edit their own descriptive articles for spelling, grammar, punctuation, and capitalization. If students find verb tenses confusing, teach the mini-lessons on pages T434 and T435. Then have students complete the exercises on pages 434 and 435. Review the answers as a class.

✏️ Writer's Term_____

Verb Tense Regular verbs are formed using the endings listed in the Writer's Term box. Irregular verbs such as *eat, say, be, see,* and *bring* form the past tense in different ways, which must be learned separately. The future tense is formed the same way for all verbs.

CCSS **Common Core State Standards**

L.6.1: Demonstrate command of the conventions of standard English grammar and usage when writing or speaking. **L.6.2:** Demonstrate command of the conventions of standard English capitalization, punctuation, and spelling when writing. **L.6.2.b:** Spell correctly.

Student Objectives

- Learn to recognize present-, past-, and future-tense verbs. (p. 434)

Present, Past, and Future Tenses

Have students read the Know the Rule box. Point out the rules for forming verbs in the past and future tenses. Write the following on the board: *She lifts her arms up in the air to stretch.* Ask students whether the sentence uses a present- or a past-tense verb. (present) Have a volunteer rewrite the sentence so that it is in the past tense. (*She lifted her arms up in the air to stretch.*) Ask another volunteer to rewrite the sentence in the future tense. (*She will lift her arms up in the air to stretch.*)

Write the following sentence on the board: *He kicked the ball hard toward the goal.* Ask students what tense the verb is in. (past) Have them rewrite the sentence in the present and future tenses. (*He kicks the ball hard toward the goal; He will kick the ball hard toward the goal.*) Provide additional practice sentences if necessary.

Online Writing Center

GAMES Provides **interactive grammar games** and **practice activities** in student eBook.

Present, Past, and Future Tenses

Know the Rule

A **present-tense verb** is used to indicate that something happens regularly or is true now.

> **Example:** Our family **holds** a reunion every summer.

A **past-tense verb** tells about something that has already happened. Regular verbs form the past tense by adding *-ed*.

> **Example:** Mom and I **created** a scrapbook to take to this year's reunion.

Irregular verbs change their spelling in the past tense.

> **Example:** The scrapbook **took** hours and hours of work.

A **future-tense verb** tells what is going to happen. Add the helping verb *will* to the present-tense form of a verb to form the future tense.

> **Example:** Everyone **will enjoy** looking at the family scrapbook.

Practice the Rule

Copy the sentences onto a sheet of paper. Underline each past-tense verb, circle each present-tense verb, and draw a box around each future-tense verb.

1. We started the scrapbook six months before the reunion.
2. Mom and I take our time with projects.
3. First we looked through all our boxes of old photos.
4. An old family photo really brings back memories!
5. Someone labeled most of the photos, but we will never know all the people in the really old pictures.
6. From now on, we will label all our photos for future generations.
7. That way everyone will know the names of family members who came before them.
8. I look forward to this family reunion!
9. We will all look at the photos together.
10. Maybe Grandpa will know the names of some of the people in the older pictures.

Related Grammar Practice

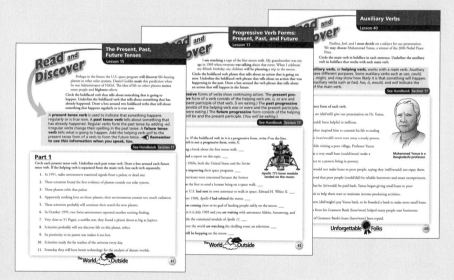

Pages 41, 45, 103

Go to ▷ G.U.M. Student Practice Book

Present-Perfect and Past-Perfect Tenses

Know the Rule

The **perfect tenses** are made with the helping verb *has, have,* or *had* and the past participle of a verb.

- The **present-perfect tense** shows action that started in the past and was recently completed or is still happening.
  - Example: I **have helped** my grandmother cook since I was little.
- The **past-perfect tense** shows action that was definitely completed in the past.
  - Example: I **had learned** about spices from Grandma before I cooked my first meal by myself.

Practice the Rule

Read the following sentences. Complete each sentence by writing the present-perfect or the past-perfect form of the verb in parentheses.

1. Every summer my sister and I (help) my dad plant his vegetable garden. have helped
2. Before we started last summer, I (read) a new book about gardening. had read
3. I (learn) to use organic methods to produce the best vegetables. have learned
4. This summer I (choose) to plant broccoli and carrots. have chosen
5. My sister (want) to plant corn before my dad told her our garden isn't big enough. had wanted
6. My dad (enjoy) planting small gardens since he was my age. has enjoyed
7. His family (own) a farm for two generations before my grandfather sold it. had owned
8. My dad says that if he (like) farming, we would be living on a farm now. had liked
9. I'm glad my dad (teach) us to appreciate planting and tending a vegetable garden each summer. has taught
10. I (eat) our own tasty vegetables since I was a baby! have eaten

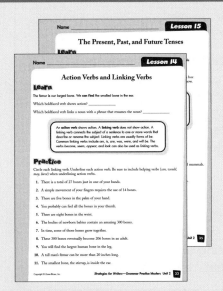
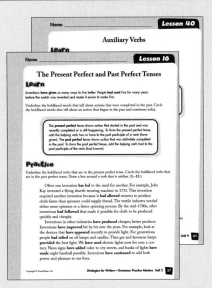

Pages 33, 35, 37, 85

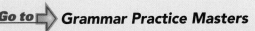

Go to → *Grammar Practice Masters*

Student Objectives

- Learn to correctly use verbs in the present-perfect and past-perfect tenses. *(p. 435)*

Present-Perfect and Past-Perfect Tenses

Write the following sentences on the board. Ask students to name the tense of each verb:

- *I had just eaten when Uncle Bob showed up.* (past perfect)
- *I have known Uncle Bob all my life.* (present perfect)
- *He has lived in the neighborhood for a few years now.* (present perfect)
- *He had bought a puppy and wanted to show it to me.* (past perfect)

Ask students to make up sentences in the present-perfect tense to describe activities they do or sports they play. (Possible responses: I have played hockey since I was six years old. I have taken drama classes for three years now.) Ask students to make sentences in the past-perfect tense about something that happened this morning or last night. (Possible responses: I had finished my breakfast by the time my sister got up. I had finished my homework the night before.)

CCSS **Common Core State Standards**

L.6.1: Demonstrate command of the conventions of standard English grammar and usage when writing or speaking. L.6.2: Demonstrate command of the conventions of standard English capitalization, punctuation, and spelling when writing.

Write
a Descriptive Article

Week 3 • Day 4

Student Objectives

- Discuss preparation for publishing and presentation. (p. 436)
- Use a final editing checklist to publish their work. (p. 436)

Publish +Presentation

Publishing Strategy Ask students why they think Denise has chosen to publish her paper in a family scrapbook. (Possible response: It's a subject her family would be interested in reading about. Someday she might want to remember her visits to her grandmother.) Have students brainstorm other ideas for publishing their descriptive articles. (Possible responses: create a class magazine, submit the articles for publication in a youth magazine or website, read the articles aloud to the class)

Point out that Denise uses a checklist to review her use of conventions and her presentation. Instruct students to create checklists of their own to help them review their articles one last time. Suggest that students incorporate errors they make frequently into their checklists.

 Strategies for Writers Online

Go to **www.sfw.z-b.com** for additional online resources for students and teachers.

Publish +Presentation

Publishing Strategy	Publish your article in a family scrapbook.
Presentation Strategy	Use the computer to prepare a neat and attractive article.

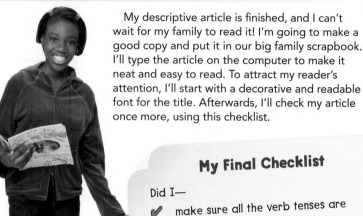

My descriptive article is finished, and I can't wait for my family to read it! I'm going to make a good copy and put it in our big family scrapbook. I'll type the article on the computer to make it neat and easy to read. To attract my reader's attention, I'll start with a decorative and readable font for the title. Afterwards, I'll check my article once more, using this checklist.

My Final Checklist

Did I—

✓ make sure all the verb tenses are consistent?

✓ use present perfect and past perfect tenses correctly?

✓ make sure the article is designed for visual appeal?

✓ check my spelling, punctuation, and grammar?

Apply

Make a checklist for a final check of your descriptive article. Then make a final copy to publish.

436 Descriptive Writing

Differentiating Instruction

ENRICHMENT

Submit an Article for Publication Help students research publications, such as youth-oriented magazines or websites or the community newspaper, that might accept their descriptive articles for publication. Guide them in obtaining the submission requirements, writing a cover letter, and submitting their articles.

REINFORCEMENT

Support Presentation Have an older student or the technology assistant work with students to learn or practice word-processing skills. Student should practice setting margins and line spacing, choosing appropriate fonts, and centering the title to create a neat, readable text.

Cooking Up Love

by Denise

Nobody in our family goes to my grandmother's front door. That's for company! We all use the back door, the family entrance. It leads straight to her kitchen—and right into her heart!

I visit often since we live on the same street. Every time I step onto Grandma's back porch, I smell something wonderful. Sometimes, the home-baked scents of vanilla and cinnamon welcome me. At other times, mouth-watering chocolate promises a sweet surprise. If it's near suppertime, I'll smell roasting meat, zesty spices, or something else delicious!

Grandma greets me with a wide smile and twinkling eyes. Usually her strong hands are chopping or stirring something, so I give her a sideways hug. The kitchen has fresh, white cabinets and green walls that make the place cheery and bright. As soon as I sit down, she fixes me something to eat!

Sometimes she gives me oven-warm cookies with melted chocolate chips. Or she might give me a bowl of her volcano chili. It's so hot it makes me want to dunk my whole face in the creek, but I love it! Whatever she makes is special.

While I eat, Grandma sits with me and drinks a cup of coffee. Sometimes we're quiet. We listen to whatever's bubbling on the stove. We hear the refrigerator hum its one-note song. We notice the creaks the old house makes as it settles. It's a nice, comfortable quiet.

Usually, we talk. Grandma's voice is low and husky, and I like to listen to her tell stories about how she lived back in the day. When I'm talking, Grandma makes sympathetic noises. I feel like she understands me, and she'll always care about me.

When it's time to go, I wash my dishes in warm, soapy water and dry my hands on a crisp, cotton towel. Then Grandma wraps me tightly in her arms, soft and warm and strong. After she lets go, it feels like she's still holding me. I hurry home, full of good food and Grandma's love!

Reflect

Do you see all the traits of a good descriptive article in Denise's writing? Check it against the rubric. Don't forget to use the rubric to check your own descriptive article.

Descriptive Article **437**

Technology Tip for 21st Century Literacies

One strategy for helping students learn about how their written text is navigated by readers is to have students be silent participants in a small group discussion of that work. Invite readers outside of the classroom to a backchannel discussion, such as TodaysMeet, in which participants engage in an asynchronous chat. In addition to the range of participants and perspectives, another benefit of this forum is that the student writer can return to the archive of the chat as a resource during the revision process.

See **www.sfw.z-b.com** for further information about and links to these websites and tools.

Write
a Descriptive Article

Week 3 • Day 5

Student Objectives

- Use a descriptive article rubric. (pp. 420–421)
- Share a published descriptive article. (p. 437)

Presentation Strategy Remind students that a neat and appealing presentation is almost as important as the content of the article when it comes to attracting readers. Even a well-written article will be a chore to read if it is sloppy, with hard-to-read fonts and poor line spacing. Using a computer is the best way to create a neat article with clean, consistent margins and spacing and an attractive placement on the page.

Reflecting on a Descriptive Article

Take time for students to review the process of writing a descriptive article. Use these questions to generate reflection and discussion:

- How did the rubric help you plan, write, revise, and edit your descriptive article?
- What advice would you give to someone about to write a descriptive article?

CCSS Common Core State Standards

W.6.4: Produce clear and coherent writing in which the development, organization, and style are appropriate to task, purpose, and audience. **W.6.5:** With some guidance and support from peers and adults, develop and strengthen writing as needed by planning, revising, editing, rewriting, or trying a new approach. **W.6.6:** Use technology, including the Internet, to produce and publish writing as well as to interact and collaborate with others; demonstrate sufficient command of keyboarding skills to type a minimum of three pages in a single sitting.

Poem Planner

Day 1

WEEK 1

Day 1

Introduce
a Poem

Student Objectives
- Review the elements of a poem.
- Consider purpose and audience.
- Learn the traits of descriptive writing.

Student Activities
- Read and discuss **What's in a Poem?** (p. 438)
- Read and discuss **Why Write a Poem?** (p. 439)
- Read **Linking Descriptive Writing Traits to a Poem.** (p. 440)

Day 2

Analyze
Read a Poem

Student Objectives
- Read model poems.

Student Activities
- Read **"Haiku."** (p. 441)

Day 3

Analyze
Introduce the Rubric

Student Objectives
- Learn to read a rubric.

Student Activities
- Review **"Haiku."** (p. 441)
- Read and discuss the **Poem Rubric.** (pp. 442–443)

WEEK 2

Day 1

Write
Prewrite: Ideas

Student Objectives
- Read and understand a prewriting strategy.

Student Activities
- Read and discuss **Prewrite: Focus on Ideas.** (p. 448)
- Apply the prewriting strategy.

Day 2

Write
Prewrite: Organization

Student Objectives
- Use a Web to organize the notes.

Student Activities
- Read and discuss **Prewrite: Focus on Organization.** (p. 449)
- Reflect on the model Web.
- Apply the prewriting strategy to create a Web.
- Participate in a peer conference.

Day 3

Write
Draft: Word Choice

Student Objectives
- Begin writing, choosing words and phrases for effect.

Student Activities
- Read and discuss **Draft: Focus on Word Choice.** (p. 450)
- Apply the drafting strategy by using a Web to write a draft.

WEEK 3

Day 1

Write
Revise: Organization

Student Objectives
- Revise to make sure each line or stanza conveys one idea.

Student Activities
- Read and discuss **Revise: Focus on Organization.** (p. 453)
- Participate in a peer conference.

Day 2

Write
Revise: Sentence Fluency

Student Objectives
- Revise for line breaks.

Student Activities
- Read and discuss **Revise: Focus on Sentence Fluency.** (p. 454)

Note: Optional Revising Lessons appear on the *Strategies for Writers* CD-ROM.

Day 3

Write
Edit: Conventions

Student Objectives
- Edit for correct use of comparative and superlative adjectives and adverbs.

Student Activities
- Read and discuss **Edit: Focus on Conventions.** (p. 455)

Note: Teach the Conventions mini-lessons (pp. 456–457) if needed.

Day 4	Day 5
Analyze Ideas, Organization, and Voice	**Analyze** Word Choice, Sentence Fluency, and Conventions
Student Objectives • Read model poems. • Use the poem rubric. • Use the model poems to study Ideas, Organization, and Voice.	**Student Objectives** • Read model poems. • Use the poem rubric. • Use the model poems to study Word Choice, Sentence Fluency, and Conventions.
Student Activities • Review **"Haiku."** (p. 441) • Review the rubric. (pp. 442–443) • Read and discuss **Using the Rubric to Study the Model.** (pp. 444–445)	**Student Activities** • Review **"Haiku."** (p. 441) • Review the rubric. (pp. 442–443) • Read and discuss **Using the Rubric to Study the Model.** (pp. 446–447)

Day 4	Day 5
Write Draft	**Write** Revise: Ideas
Student Objectives • Complete a draft.	**Student Objectives** • Revise to add vivid details.
Student Activities • Finish the draft. (p. 451) • Participate in a peer conference.	**Student Activities** • Read and discuss **Revise: Focus on Ideas.** (p. 452) • Reflect on a model draft. • Apply the revising strategy.

Day 4	Day 5
Write Publish: +Presentation	**Write** Publish: +Presentation
Student Objectives • Discuss preparation for publishing and presentation. • Use a final editing checklist to publish their work.	**Student Objectives** • Use a poem rubric. • Share a published poem.
Student Activities • Read and discuss **Publish: +Presentation.** (p. 458) • Apply the publishing strategy.	**Student Activities** • Share their work. • Use the rubric to reflect upon and evaluate the model and their own writing. (pp. 442–443, 459)

To complete the chapter in fewer days, combine the learning objectives and activities in a way that supports students as they write.

Resources at-a-Glance

Grammar, Usage & Mechanics

Differentiating Instruction

For additional Differentiating Instruction activities, see Strategies for Writers Extensions Online at **www.sfw.z-b.com.**

English Language Learners

Conferencing

Technology Tip

 Connection Letter
Reproducible letter (in English and Spanish) appears on the *Strategies for Writers* CD-ROM and at **www.sfw.z-b.com.**

Online Writing Center

Provides IWB resources, interactive games and practice activities, videos, eBooks, and a virtual file cabinet.

 Strategies for Writers Online

Go to **www.sfw.z-b.com** for free online resources for students and teachers.

Introduce
a Poem

Week 1 • Day 1

Student Objectives

- Review the elements of a poem. (p. 438)
- Consider purpose and audience. (p. 439)
- Learn the traits of descriptive writing. (p. 440)

What's a Poem?

Ask students to name some poems they have read in school or on their own. Ask volunteers to mention their favorite poems and explain why they like them.

What's in a Poem?

Discuss with students the differences between a poem and prose. Point out the definition of *line* on page 438. Help students compare lines and stanzas in poetry to sentences and paragraphs in prose. Next point out the definition of *figurative language.* Ask students whether they have ever used figurative language in prose writing. Explain that while figurative language can be used in just about any type of writing, it is used often in poetry because more meaning can be packed into fewer words.

Read aloud some examples of haiku. Discuss the images found in the poems and how they made students feel.

Strategies for Writers Online

Go to **www.sfw.z-b.com** for additional online resources for students and teachers.

What's a Poem?

A poem is a piece of writing that expresses thoughts, feelings, and ideas. It's a creative way to describe any topic or emotion.

What's in a Poem?

Haiku
A haiku is a form of Japanese poetry that is often about nature. It contains three unrhymed lines with five, seven, and five syllables, respectively.

Line
The words of a poem are grouped in lines. A word, phrase, or complete sentence can form one line in a poem. Lines have a rhythmic flow to them, sometimes rhyming and sometimes not. The lines of a poem are grouped in stanzas.

Figurative Language
Figurative language, or figures of speech, help paint a picture in the reader's mind. Poets use figurative language—such as metaphor, simile, personification, and alliteration—to make their topic come alive for readers.

438 Descriptive Writing

Descriptive Text Exemplars (Poem)

Lazarus, Emma. "The New Colossus." *Favorite Poems Old and New.* **Doubleday, 1957.** CCSS "The New Colossus" is a poem about the millions of immigrants who came to the United States. It is engraved on a bronze plaque mounted inside the Statue of Liberty.

Thayer, Ernest Lawrence. "Casey at the Bat." *Favorite Poems Old and New.* **Doubleday, 1957.** CCSS "Casey at the Bat" is a poem about baseball. In the last inning, the mighty Casey is at the bat, but the ending is not what you might expect.

Why write a Poem?

There are many reasons to write a poem. I can think of three good ones. What other ideas can you think of?

Description
I can write a poem to describe any subject I choose. A creative description allows readers to see a topic more clearly or in a different light. In a poem, I can describe and share my feelings.

Personal Reflection
Writing a poem is a great way to reflect on what something means to me personally. How I feel about something, how I'm affected, or what I'm thinking can all be expressed in a poem.

Understanding
A poem can help readers gain a new understanding of the subject I'm describing. Not only can a poem help my readers gain new insights, but the process of writing poetry also helps me appreciate and understand the work of a poet.

Poem **439**

Mora, Pat. "Words Free as Confetti." *Confetti: Poems for Children.* Lee and Low, 1999. **CCSS** "Words Free as Confetti" is a poem about language. The author compares words to confetti in this playful poem.

Dickinson, Emily. "A Bird Came Down the Walk." *The Complete Poems of Emily Dickinson.* Little, Brown, 1960. **CCSS** In this delightful poem, the author describes watching a bird come down the walk. By providing details of the bird eating a worm and drinking from dew, the author shows that there is poetry and beauty in everyday life.

Why write a Poem?

As students practice their own writing, it is helpful to remind them that all writing has a purpose and that learning the different genres of writing will help them become better writers. These authentic purposes also help shape their writing.

Review the reasons listed on the page with students. Refer to the haiku examples you presented to students or to a poem you have read in class. Discuss whether the poem was written for one or more of the reasons Denise listed. Can students think of other reasons why the poet chose to write the poem?

CCSS Common Core State Standards

SL.6.1: Engage effectively in a range of collaborative discussions (one-on-one, in groups, and teacher-led) with diverse partners on *grade 6 topics, texts, and issues*, building on others' ideas and expressing their own clearly. **SL.6.1.a:** Come to discussions prepared, having read or studied required material; explicitly draw on that preparation by referring to evidence on the topic, text, or issue to probe and reflect on ideas under discussion. **SL.6.1.b:** Follow rules for collegial discussions, set specific goals and deadlines, and define individual roles as needed.

Introduce

a Poem

Linking Descriptive Writing Traits to a Poem

Explain to students that they will follow Denise as she models using the writing process and the traits together. As they follow Denise through the writing process, students will see how the Descriptive Writing Traits have been adapted and applied to writing a poem. They will see that a poem has many factors in common with other types of descriptive writing. However, the particular audience and purpose as well as the special format of a poem determine how the traits are used.

Linking Descriptive Writing Traits to a **Poem**

In this chapter, you will write a three-line poem about something in nature or another topic of your choosing. This type of descriptive writing is a form of poem called a haiku. Denise will guide you through the stages of the writing process: Prewrite, Draft, Revise, Edit, and Publish. In each stage, Denise will show you important writing strategies that are linked to the Descriptive Writing Traits below.

Descriptive Writing Traits

	• a clear topic that is supported and enhanced by specific sensory details
	• well-organized paragraphs that follow the order of the description, whether by time, location, or another order
	• a voice and tone that are appropriate for the purpose and audience
	• precise, descriptive words, possibly with figurative language, that create an accurate picture for the reader
	• sentences that vary in length and type to add flow to the writing
	• no or few errors in grammar, usage, mechanics, and spelling

Before you write, read Taylor Spinelli's poems (three haiku) on the next page. Then use the poem rubric on pages 442–443 to decide how well he did. (You might want to look back at What's in a Poem? on page 438, too!)

Descriptive Writing Traits in a Poem

 Ideas The writer maintains focus on the topic throughout the poem. Original, engaging details support and develop the topic.

 **Organization** Each line or stanza focuses on one main idea, and the overall structure of the poem is logical and easy to follow.

 **Voice** The writer consistently uses voice that is appropriate for the topic and tone of the poem and that connects strongly with the reader.

Haiku
By Taylor Spinelli

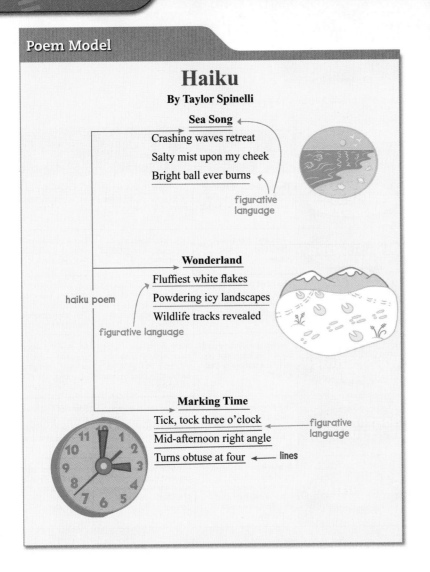

Sea Song ← haiku poem

Crashing waves retreat
Salty mist upon my cheek
Bright ball ever burns ← figurative language

Wonderland

Fluffiest white flakes
Powdering icy landscapes
Wildlife tracks revealed

figurative language

Marking Time

Tick, tock three o'clock ← figurative language
Mid-afternoon right angle
Turns obtuse at four ← lines

Poem **441**

Word Choice Precise, descriptive language and well-chosen figures of speech create vivid images for readers. The language is creative and striking.

Sentence Fluency The lines have an engaging rhythm and flow, and breaks are in such a way as to enhance this effect. Ideas are introduced at a good pace.

Conventions The poem is carefully edited prior to publishing. There are no mistakes in grammar, usage, mechanics, and spelling to confuse the reader or obscure the author's purpose.

Analyze
the Model

Week 1 • Day 2

Student Objectives

• Read model poems. *(p. 441)*

Read the Model

Have students read the poems on page 441. Before they read, remind students to look for the writing traits outlined on page 440.

Elements of a Poem

Use the notes on the model to discuss the three haiku. Ask:

• How can you tell each poem is a haiku? (Possible response: In English, haiku is usually presented with three lines of 5, 7, and 5 syllables, respectively.)

• What types of figurative language does Taylor use? (metaphors, onomatopoeia)

• What is the *bright ball* in the first haiku? (the sun)

• Why is this metaphor effective? (Possible response: It gives a clear image of the sun and reminds the reader that it is always there.)

Discuss the other images in the three poems. You may wish to have students refer back to What's in a Poem? on page 438 for review.

CCSS Common Core State Standards
R/Lit.6.1: Cite textual evidence to support analysis of what the text says explicitly as well as inferences drawn from the text. **R/Lit.6.5:** Analyze how a particular sentence, chapter, scene, or stanza fits into the overall structure of a text and contributes to the development of the theme, setting, or plot.

Poem **T441**

Analyze
the Model

Week 1 • Day 3

Student Objectives

- Learn to read a rubric. *(pp. 442–443)*

Use the Rubric

Explain the Rubric Explain that a rubric is a tool that helps you plan, improve, and evaluate a piece of writing. A rubric also helps a writer focus on key elements, or traits, in writing (**Ideas, Organization, Voice, Word Choice, Sentence Fluency, Conventions,** and **Presentation**).

The 6-point rubric on pages 442 and 443 is based on the Descriptive Writing Traits that students read on page 440. Explain that column 6 describes a very good poem, one that has received the highest score in all categories. This is what students should strive for in their own writing.

Discuss the Rubric Guide the students in a discussion of the rubric. Read the descriptors that go with each trait. Note how the descriptors vary as you move from column to column. Remind students to keep the rubric in mind when they write their own poem and again when they revise it.

Online Writing Center

Provides a variety of **interactive rubrics**, including 4-, 5-, and 6-point models.

Poem

Rubric

Use this 6-point rubric to plan and score a poem.

	6	5	4	
Ideas	The topic is presented in an original, creative way. Descriptive details are vivid.	The topic is presented in an original, creative way. Details are descriptive.	The topic is presented in a creative way. A couple of details are descriptive.	
Organization	Lines and stanzas, if used, organize the ideas.	Lines and stanzas, if used, organize most of the ideas.	Lines and stanzas, if used, organize many of the ideas.	
Voice	The poet's voice sets the tone and mood of the piece. It connects with the audience.	The poet's voice sets the tone and mood of the piece. It connects with the audience most of the time.	The poet's voice sets the tone and mood at first but then fades. The connection is inconsistent.	
Word Choice	Precise vocabulary and figurative language are used purposefully and effectively.	Most words are used purposefully. One example of figurative language could be more effective.	Most of the words are used purposefully. Several examples of figurative language could be more effective.	
Sentence Fluency	The lines and stanzas, if used, convey ideas at a good pace. The line breaks establish the rhythm and flow.	Most of the lines and stanzas, if used, flow well. One or two line breaks interrupt the rhythm.	Some of the lines and stanzas, if used, flow well. Several line breaks interrupt the rhythm.	
Conventions	The writing has been carefully edited. Comparative and superlative forms of modifiers are used correctly.	Minor errors are present but do not interfere with meaning. Modifiers are used correctly.	A few errors cause confusion. One or two modifiers may be misspelled. (Ex. "joyful or joyfully")	
+ Presentation	Visuals and audio are integrated effectively.			

442 Descriptive Writing

CCSS Common Core State Standards
Poem

Writing in the Descriptive mode can engage the Common Core State Standards for both Narrative and Informative/Explanatory writing. The rubric and writing strategies for Ideas are drawn from informative/explanatory standard **W.6.2.a,** which focuses on introducing the topic clearly, and informative/explanatory standard **W.6.2.b** and narrative standard **W.6.3.d,** which focus on developing the topic with effective descriptive details. The rubric and writing strategies for Organization are grounded in informative/explanatory standard **W.6.2.a** and narrative standard **W.6.3.a,** both of which highlight the importance of organizing the writing in a way that supports understanding. The rubric and writing

3	2	1	
The topic is presented. Most details are ordinary or dull.	The topic is incomplete. Details are vague or weak.	The topic is not clear. Details may be unrelated or inaccurate.	**Ideas**
Lines and stanzas, if used, organize some of the ideas.	Lines and stanzas do not organize the ideas well.	Ideas are listed but not organized as verse.	**Organization**
The poet's voice sets a tone that may not be appropriate. A connection is not maintained.	The voice is very weak. The connection is very weak.	The voice is absent. A connection is not established.	**Voice**
Some of the words are used purposefully. Figurative language may be unclear.	Many words are ordinary or overused. Figurative language is unclear or absent.	Words are very basic and limited. Several words may be used incorrectly.	**Word Choice**
Lines do not flow well. Line breaks impede the pace and rhythm.	Lines do not flow well. Line breaks do not establish a rhythm.	Poetic lines are not established.	**Sentence Fluency**
Many errors are repeated and cause confusion. Modifiers may be used incorrectly. (Ex. "more joyfuller")	Serious errors interfere with meaning. Modifiers may be used incorrectly.	The writing has not been edited.	**Conventions**

See Appendix B for 4-, 5-, and 6-point descriptive rubrics.

Apply the Rubric

Evaluate a Poem Find a poem in a book or an online resource that is appropriate for your class. A haiku would be ideal, but any kind of poem will do. Share the sample poem with the class. Ask students to use the rubric to score the poem on each of the traits. Be sure that students can offer examples from the poem to support each score.

Once the class has reached a consensus on the scores, ask these follow-up questions:

• Which trait is strongest in the poem? Why do you think so?

• Does the poem fit the audience and the purpose? How?

Additional Rubrics Appendix B includes 4-, 5-, and 6-point rubrics that can be used with any piece of descriptive writing. The rubrics are also available as blackline masters in the back of this Teacher Edition, beginning on page T525.

strategies for Voice reflect language standard **L.6.3.b**, which calls for the writer to maintain a consistent style and tone. The emphasis on precise language in the rubric and writing strategies for Word Choice comes from informative/explanatory standard **W.6.2.d** and narrative standard **W.6.3.d**. The language standards **L.6.1** and **L.6.2**, which focus on command of the conventions of grammar, usage, capitalization, spelling, and punctuation, are evident in Conventions. Woven throughout the unit are writing standards **W.6.4–W.6.6** and **W.6.10**, which focus on writing appropriately for the task, the purpose, and the audience; using technology; and writing routinely over extended time frames.

CCSS **C**ommon **C**ore **S**tate **S**tandards
SL.6.1: Engage effectively in a range of collaborative discussions (one-on-one, in groups, and teacher-led) with diverse partners on *grade 6 topics, texts, and issues*, building on others' ideas and expressing their own clearly. **SL.6.1.a:** Come to discussions prepared, having read or studied required material; explicitly draw on that preparation by referring to evidence on the topic, text, or issue to probe and reflect on ideas under discussion. **SL.6.1.b:** Follow rules for collegial discussions, set specific goals and deadlines, and define individual roles as needed.

Analyze
the Model

Student Objectives

- Read model poems. *(p. 441)*
- Use the poem rubric. *(pp. 442–443)*
- Use the model poems to study Ideas, Organization, and Voice. *(pp. 444–445)*

Study the Model

Assess the Model Once students have read pages 444 and 445, ask them whether they agree or disagree with Denise's assessment of the model on each point. For example, do they feel the ideas in the poems are clearly organized in the lines? Use questions such as the following to discuss the model and the traits with students.

- Which poem do you think was most creative in its presentation of its topic? (Possible response: "Sea Song"; the image of the sea and the sun was very striking.)

Strategies for Writers Online

Go to **www.sfw.z-b.com** for additional online resources for students and teachers.

Using the Poem Rubric to Study the Model

Did you notice that the model on page 441 points out some key elements of a haiku poem? As he wrote "Sea Song," "Wonderland," and "Marking Time," Taylor Spinelli used these elements to help him describe the sea, snow, and angles. He also used the 6-point rubric on pages 442–443 to plan, draft, revise, and edit the writing. A rubric is a great tool to evaluate writing during the writing process.

Now let's use the same rubric to score the model. To do this, we'll focus on each trait separately, starting with Ideas. We'll use the top descriptor for each trait (column 6), along with examples from the model, to help us understand how the traits work together. How would you score Taylor on each trait?

Ideas
- The topic is presented in an original, creative way.
- Descriptive details are vivid.

In "Marking Time," Taylor chose to discuss types of angles in a creative way. I never thought about a clock having so many angles! The details are vivid because I can hear the sound of the clock ticking, and I can picture the arms turning. Can you picture it?

[from the writing model]

Tick, tock three o'clock
Mid-afternoon right angle
Turns obtuse at four

English Language Learners

BEGINNING
Alliteration Ask students to tell a name that begins with the letter *T*. Then ask for other words beginning with *T*, including a verb, a noun, and an adjective that describes the noun. Then put the words together in a sentence. For example, *Tommy tells terrible tales.* Underline each letter *t* to illustrate the idea of alliteration. Have students create other examples with different letters.

INTERMEDIATE
Elements of a Haiku Point out the model haiku poetry on page 441. Clarify any vocabulary students may not know, such as *retreat, powdering,* or *obtuse.* Then identify the following elements of the poems: lines, syllables, figurative language, and rhythm.

Organization
- Lines and stanzas, if used, organize the ideas.

The three lines of "Marking Time" follow the 5-7-5 syllable format of a haiku, and each line addresses an aspect of angles. The ideas are organized clearly so that in the second line, I can picture the right angle, and in the next, the wider obtuse angle.

[from the writing model]

Tick, tock three o'clock
Mid-afternoon right angle
Turns obtuse at four

Voice
- The poet's voice sets the tone and mood of the piece.
- It connects with the audience.

In "Wonderland," Taylor has carefully chosen certain words to create a carefree tone. *Wonderland* is a light and carefree word. It makes me think of *winter* wonderland, and that reminds me of my home here in Minnesota, where I've seen a lot of beautiful, snow-covered landscapes. By using other light and carefree words such as *fluffiest* and *powdering*, Taylor creates a captivating mood.

[from the writing model]

Fluffiest white flakes
Powdering icy landscapes
Wildlife tracks revealed

Poem 445

- Which idea does each line present in "Marking Time"? (Possible responses: line 1—The clock shows three o'clock; line 2—Three-o'clock is a right angle on a clock face; line 4—When the time changes, the angle changes.)

- How would you describe the tone in "Sea Song"? (Possible responses: awestruck, reflective)

ADVANCED
Descriptive Details Have students use a Web graphic organizer to write down ideas about their selected nature concepts. Each "branch" of the web should contain an aspect of the concept that they want to explore. For each aspect, have students list words they can use to accurately and creatively describe it. Then have them include examples for each.

ADVANCED HIGH
Haiku Offer several examples of haiku or have students read the examples on page 441. Have partners read the poems and identify similarities among them. If they need help, ask the following questions: *How many lines does each poem have? How many syllables are in the first line of each poem? The second line? The third line? What is each poem about?* Say *haiku* and have students repeat.

CCSS Common Core State Standards
R/Inf.6.5: Analyze how a particular sentence, paragraph, chapter, or section fits into the overall structure of a text and contributes to the development of the ideas. **R/Inf.6.6:** Determine an author's point of view or purpose in a text and explain how it is conveyed in the text. **SL.6.1.b:** Follow rules for collegial discussions, set specific goals and deadlines, and define individual roles as needed. **SL.6.1.d:** Review the key ideas expressed and demonstrate understanding of multiple perspectives through reflection and paraphrasing.

Analyze
the Model

Week 1 • Day 5

Student Objectives

- Read model poems. *(p. 441)*
- Use the poem rubric. *(pp. 442–443)*
- Use the model poems to study Word Choice, Sentence Fluency, and Conventions. *(pp. 446–447)*

Continue Discussing the Traits

Use questions such as the following to discuss the traits analyzed on pages 446 and 447:

- Choose an example of a figure of speech from a different haiku that struck you as precise and vivid. Why did this image appeal to you? (Possible response: *Powdering icy landscapes* reminded me of powdered sugar dusting a cake.)

- Read one of the haiku aloud. How does this help you appreciate the rhythm of the poem? (Possible response: It's easier to hear the "beats" when the poem is read aloud.)

- Why is it important that Taylor correctly used the superlative form of the first adjective in "Wonderland"? (Possible response: The meaning of the poem would have been confusing if he had used the wrong form.)

▶ Strategies for Writers Online

Go to **www.sfw.z-b.com** for additional online resources for students and teachers.

Word Choice
- Precise vocabulary and figurative language are used purposefully and effectively.

I like how Taylor chooses words that paint a picture in my mind. In "Sea Song," the use of *crashing* shows the fierce action of the waves. Taylor could have said *moving waves*, but *crashing waves* shows a sharper contrast between how the waves come in and how they go out, or *retreat*, a softer action. The alliteration in line three—the repetition of the *b* sound in *Bright ball ever burns*—is a good example of figurative language. The repeated sound puts emphasis on the image of the sun (the "bright ball"), making the description stand out and come alive for the reader. Not only that, but line three uses a metaphor, as it compares the sun to a bright ball burning. That's a lot of rich language in one short poem!

[from the writing model]

Crashing waves retreat
Salty mist upon my cheek
Bright ball ever burns

Sentence Fluency
- The lines and stanzas, if used, convey ideas at a good pace.
- The line breaks establish the rhythm and flow.

I like how Taylor introduces ideas one at a time in "Sea Song." First we hear the rhythm of the waves, next we taste and feel the salty sensation, and last we see the burning sun. Each image flows nicely into the next. Taylor has also followed the appropriate syllable counts for each line. Five for the first, seven for the second, and five for the third. This creates the classic flow of a haiku.

[from the writing model]

Crashing waves retreat
Salty mist upon my cheek
Bright ball ever burns

Technology Tip — for 21st Century Literacies

Sharing with a global community requires knowing how to find readers/collaborators/experts with whom to work. Help students participate in community-building using networks of engaged teachers and students (e.g., ePals). For this activity, work with students to create a community of student poets who will collaborate in responding to one another's poetry. Have discussions about how the community supports student work, what voices are needed, how and when students participate, and so on. Keep in mind that this doesn't have to be bound to these pieces of writing.

See **www.sfw.z-b.com** for further information about and links to these websites and tools.

Conventions

- The writing has been carefully edited.
- Comparative and superlative forms of modifiers are used correctly.

I didn't come across any mistakes, so I know Taylor did a careful job when he edited. Also the superlative adjective *fluffiest* is used correctly. It appropriately compares many snowflakes. If Taylor were comparing just two snowflakes, he would have used the word *fluffier*.

[from the writing model]

Fluffiest white flakes
Powdering icy landscapes
Wildlife tracks revealed

✛ Presentation Visuals and audio are integrated effectively.

Now it's my turn to write a poem. I'll use the rubric and good writing strategies to help me. Follow along to see how I do it.

Poem **447**

Differentiating Instruction

ENRICHMENT

Learn About Haiku Have students use books, encyclopedias, and the Internet to research the haiku form of poetry. Students should find information about the origins and history of the form and examples of well-known haiku poems. Allow students to work individually or in pairs to write short reports about their findings and present them to the class.

REINFORCEMENT

Analyze the Form Give students one or two additional examples of haiku. Read the poems aloud and help students practice counting the syllables. Discuss with students what the haiku have in common, in addition to the syllable count: focus on a single idea or image and creative, figurative language.

Presentation Explain that adding visuals and audio to a poem can greatly enhance the reader's—and listener's—appreciation of the poem. These elements have to be integrated seamlessly and effectively with the poem. The visuals must be relevant and help develop the images found in the poet's language. The audio should also flow from the images in the poem and appeal to the reader's senses without distracting from the pleasure of hearing the poem read aloud. Point out that even if students are reading their work aloud to the class, the poems should be neatly typed and attractively placed on the page.

Think About the Traits Now ask students which traits they think are most important in a poem. Explain that all traits are important in every piece of writing, but some stand out more in some genres than in others. Some students may feel that **Word Choice** is important because figurative language is crucial to creating the images in a poem. Others may feel that **Sentence Fluency** is important because a good rhythm makes a poem enjoyable to read.

CCSS Common Core State Standards

SL.6.1.b: Follow rules for collegial discussions, set specific goals and deadlines, and define individual roles as needed. **SL.6.1.c:** Pose and respond to specific questions with elaboration and detail by making comments that contribute to the topic, text, or issue under discussion. **SL.6.1.d:** Review the key ideas expressed and demonstrate understanding of multiple perspectives through reflection and paraphrasing. **W.6.6:** Use technology, including the Internet, to produce and publish writing as well as to interact and collaborate with others; demonstrate sufficient command of keyboarding skills to type a minimum of three pages in a single sitting.

Write
a Poem

Week 2 • Day 1

Student Objectives

- Read and understand a prewriting strategy. *(p. 448)*

Prewrite

Focus on Ideas

Gather Information Point out that Denise has stayed close to home in her choice of topics for her poems. She has chosen places and a person who are very familiar to her and that she can easily visualize when they are not present. Advise students to choose topics that they know well for their own poems. They should be able to easily think of several descriptive details for each topic; if they have to struggle to think of details, then they will find themselves struggling when it comes time to write the poems.

Encourage students to jot down more details than they know they will be able to include in the haiku. At this stage, they should be brainstorming. When they begin to draft their poems, they will have the chance to review their ideas and select the most descriptive or unique details.

Prewrite

Focus on Ideas

The Rubric Says The topic is presented in an original, creative way. Descriptive details are vivid.

Writing Strategy Choose a topic. Make a list of descriptive details.

My assignment is to write a haiku. My teacher said we could write more than one. Since a traditional Japanese haiku is about something in nature, I'll jot down ideas and descriptions about some of my favorite outdoor spots. I'll write down ideas about other subjects that appeal to me, too. I'll also need to keep in mind that my final haiku will consist of three unrhymed lines. The first line will have five syllables, the next seven, and the last five.

Notes on topics for haiku

Notes about visiting my favorite pond

Water is still, calm, serene.
Water is high after a heavy rain and there's hardly any beach.
Surface of the water has a glare from the sun.

Notes about my garden

Tomatoes, peppers, cucumbers
Green and leafy, grow and grow
Need plenty of water and sunlight
Flowers form, fruits grow

Notes about my neighbor's baby

Always looking around with wide eyes
Loves to be cuddled
Learns to clap hands
Mother takes good care of him

Apply

Choose something in nature or another topic that interests you. Write down some notes about it.

English Language Learners

BEGINNING/INTERMEDIATE

Similes and Metaphors Write this sentence: *Her eyes twinkle like stars.* After clarifying any words students may not know, underline *like*. Point out that this word helps create a simile. Write *simile* and have students repeat it. Repeat with other examples. Teach *metaphor* in the same way using the sentence *Her eyes are twinkling stars.*

ADVANCED/ADVANCED HIGH

Figurative Language Describe personification, simile, and metaphor to students. Write the following sentences on the board: *The wind whispered my name. The cool breeze is like a playful child. The cool breeze is a playful child.* Have students tell what type of figurative language is used in each sentence. Then have students revise one portion of haiku to include figurative language.

Online Writing Center

Provides **interactive graphic organizers** as well as a variety of graphic organizers in PDF format.

Prewrite

Focus on Organization

The Rubric Says Lines and stanzas, if used, organize the ideas.

Writing Strategy Use a Web to plan the poem.

Writer's Term
Web
A **Web** is a way to organize ideas around a topic. The topic is in the center. Attached to each topic are related categories. Attached to each category are related details.

To organize my ideas I'll use a graphic organizer called a Web. I have a few ideas that I'd like to use as the topics for the haiku I'm going to write. A haiku does not have stanzas. However, the Web will help me organize my notes so I can figure out the ideas I want to include in each line.

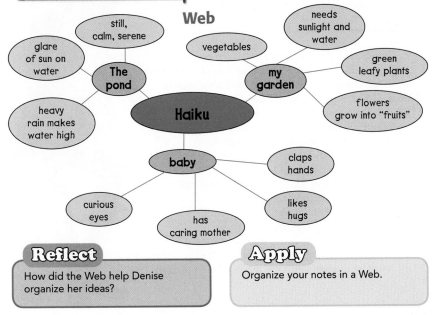

Web

Reflect
How did the Web help Denise organize her ideas?

Apply
Organize your notes in a Web.

Poem 449

Conferencing

PEER TO PEER Have students exchange Webs and then give a brief verbal description of one of the haiku topics. The partner compares the Web to the verbal description and points out any interesting details that were in the description but not in the Web.

PEER GROUPS Have students pass their Webs around the group. Each student underlines in pencil the detail he or she thinks is most interesting or appealing in one of the topic areas and explains why he or she likes that detail.

TEACHER-LED Work with pairs of students. Have students exchange Webs. Guide students in asking each other questions that might elicit additional details about the haiku topics (e.g., *What did the prairie grasses look like in that meadow?*).

Write
a Poem

Student Objectives

• Use a Web to organize the notes. *(p. 449)*

Prewrite

Focus on Organization

Make a Web Explain that making a Web will help students organize their notes and decide which details to include in their poems.

Point out that students do not have to pick out precisely three details for each haiku at this point. They should include in their Webs all the relevant details from their notes. Looking at the details laid out in a Web will help students decide which ones to include, which ones to leave out, and which ones to combine.

Writer's Term
Web A Web is ideal for organizing writing, such as a poem, that does not have a defined or hierarchical structure. In a Web, the details are linked by their themes, rather than by sequence, order of importance, or cause and effect.

CCSS Common Core State Standards
W.6.2.b: Develop the topic with relevant facts, definitions, concrete details, quotations, or other information and examples. **W.6.3.d:** Use precise words and phrases, relevant descriptive details, and sensory language to convey experiences and events.

Write
a Poem

Week 2 • Day 3

Student Objectives

• Begin writing, choosing words and phrases for effect. (p. 450)

Draft

Focus on Word Choice

Begin a Draft Review what it means to write a draft. Note that the draft is a temporary form of a piece of writing that should be changed and corrected several times before it is finished. Like Denise, students should focus on getting their ideas on paper in haiku form. They can refine the poem and correct errors in spelling and grammar during the revision and editing stages of the writing process.

Even as they draft, students should be aware of using figurative language in their poems. Denise explores personification and alliteration. Students might want to explore other types of figurative language.

Point out that Denise refers to the rubric as she completes this step in the writing process. Remind students to get into the habit of referring to the rubric so they fully understand its use as a tool for shaping their writing.

Online Writing Center

Provides student eBooks with an **interactive writing pad** for drafting, revising, editing, and publishing.

Draft   Focus on Word Choice

The Rubric Says   Precise vocabulary and figurative language are used purposefully and effectively.

Writing Strategy   Choose words and phrases for effect.

> **Writer's Term**
>
> **Personification and Alliteration**
> **Personification** makes writing come alive by giving human qualities to things or animals. **Alliteration** is repeating a consonant sound within a sentence or phrase. It can give a poem rhythm and emphasize an idea by drawing the reader's attention.

The words I choose for my haiku are especially important because there will be so few of them. Each word has important work to do! I will also have to take into account the words' syllables because the 5-7-5 count is essential to a haiku. Using descriptive language and adjectives and adverbs will help readers "see" what I'm describing.

I want the words I use to paint a picture in your mind. Figurative language is another great way to do this. One type of figurative language is called personification. Personification gives human qualities to things or animals. I'll also use alliteration in my poem titles to make them stand out.

As I write, I'll try to avoid making mistakes in grammar and spelling, but I know I can fix my mistakes later when I edit my work. Here's my draft.

450 Descriptive Writing

Differentiating Instruction

ENRICHMENT
Focus on Figurative Language Challenge students to make one type of figurative language the focus of each haiku. For example, one haiku can have personification at its core, another can make intensive use of alliteration, and the third can focus on simile, metaphor, or another type of figurative language (e.g., synecdoche, metonymy).

REINFORCEMENT
Limit the Task Have students write just one haiku, choosing the topic from their Webs that interests them most. In addition, have students work with a writing partner throughout the process. Each partner writes his or her own poem, but the students work through the revising and editing stages together. Guide them in reading each other's drafts, as well as their own, to offer ideas and suggestions.

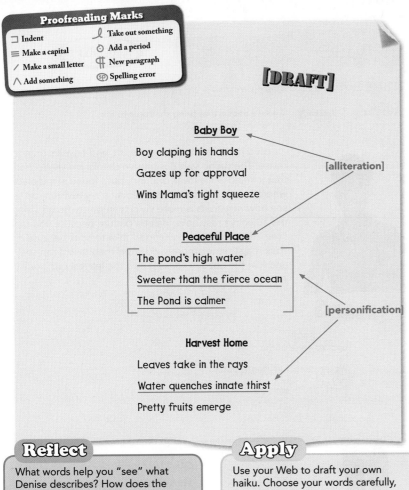

[DRAFT]

Baby Boy

Boy claping his hands

Gazes up for approval

Wins Mama's tight squeeze

[alliteration]

Peaceful Place

The pond's high water

Sweeter than the fierce ocean

The Pond is calmer

[personification]

Harvest Home

Leaves take in the rays

Water quenches innate thirst

Pretty fruits emerge

Reflect

What words help you "see" what Denise describes? How does the figurative language make the poem come alive?

Apply

Use your Web to draft your own haiku. Choose your words carefully, because every word counts!

Poem **451**

Conferencing

PEER TO PEER Have partners exchange drafts. Students should point out an example of figurative language or a sensory detail in their partner's draft that they like and explain why they like it.

PEER GROUPS After each student reads his or her draft aloud to the group, the student mentions a part of the poem that he or she struggled with. The group discusses these points and offers suggestions.

TEACHER-LED Work with individual students. Read the draft aloud to the student so that he or she can listen. Ask the student where he or she feels the figurative language is present and effective. Discuss together how to solve any issues.

Write
a Poem

Week 2 • Day 4

Student Objectives

• Complete a draft. (p. 451)

Finish the Draft Have students read the draft on page 451. Use the underlined words and phrases to discuss the poems. Discuss how the alliteration in the titles draws the reader's attention. Do students feel that alliteration makes the titles more appealing? What is the point of the personification in "Peaceful Place"? (Possible response: It compares the pond to a kind, calm person.)

Writer's Term

Personification and Alliteration
Personification and alliteration are highly effective, but they can cause frustration or unwanted amusement when they are excessively or incorrectly used. Carrying alliteration through several lines of a poem makes the rhythm choppy and distracts the reader's attention from the message of the poem. Poorly thought-out personifications, such as *the arms of the sun gathered us into its warmth*, create odd, off-putting, or comical mental images.

CCSS **Common Core State Standards**

W.6.2.d: Use precise language and domain-specific vocabulary to inform about or explain the topic. **W.6.3.d:** Use precise words and phrases, relevant descriptive details, and sensory language to convey experiences and events. **W.6.4:** Produce clear and coherent writing in which the development, organization, and style are appropriate to task, purpose, and audience.

Poem **T451**

Write
a Poem

Week 2 • Day 5

Student Objectives

- Revise to add vivid details. (p. 452)

Revise

Focus on Ideas

Use Details That Bring the Topic to Life Look at the draft excerpt with students. Note that the new words have the same number of syllables as the original ones, allowing Denise to maintain the typical haiku form in her revisions.

Ask:

- Which other writing trait, in addition to **Ideas,** is improved by Denise's revisions? (Word Choice)

Explain that the writing traits are not completely independent from one another—often two traits support each other. In this instance, Denise used stronger, more original words to create more vivid details for her haiku.

Strategies for Writers Online
Go to **www.sfw.z-b.com** for additional online resources for students and teachers.

Writing a Poem

Revise   Focus on (Ideas)

The Rubric Says   Descriptive details are vivid.

Writing Strategy   Choose details that bring the topic to life.

I used my notes to write my draft, and now it's time to revise. The rubric says descriptive details are vivid. I had that in mind while I was drafting, but I found some places where I could make improvements. In my revision, do you see how *rosy fruits* is more vivid than *pretty fruits*? Using the adjective *rosy* helps paint a picture because you can "see" that color. I also changed *take* to *soak* because *soak* is a stronger, more vivid word than *take*. I can see and feel the hot sun *soaking* into the leaves! Can you?

[DRAFT]

                                    [replaced weaker verb]
          soak
Leaves ~~take~~ in the rays

     Water quenches innate thirst
Rosy
~~Pretty~~ fruits emerge
     ^

[replaced dull description]

Apply

Look through your draft in search of descriptions needing improvement. Can you make details any stronger to make your poem more vivid?

452 Descriptive Writing

English Language Learners

BEGINNING/INTERMEDIATE

Vivid Details Show students a pale color, such as pink. Then show the vivid version of the color, such as red. Point to red and say, *This is a vivid color.* Have students repeat the word *vivid.* Teach the words *mumble, whisper, scream, wail.* Let students know that while all of the words are ways that someone might talk, they describe the talking more vividly.

ADVANCED/ADVANCED HIGH

Vivid Details Introduce the concept of vivid details. Write: *Grand coconut tree/Your tropical fruit whispers,/"Sip my sweet juices."* Read the sentences, and have students repeat. Ask, *Which words give vivid detail?* Have partners work together to revise their haiku to include more vivid words.

Revise

Focus on Organization

The Rubric Says   Lines and stanzas, if used, organize the ideas.

Writing Strategy   Make sure each line or stanza conveys one clear idea.

As I revise, I need to look again at how I have organized my ideas. The way a poem is organized affects how the reader experiences the poem. I want my reader to "see" a short series of crystal-clear images in each haiku. That means each line should focus on one precisely described idea.

As I look at my writing, I notice that the second two lines of "Peaceful Place" blend images of the Pond and the ocean. I think my poem will convey my thoughts more clearly to the reader if I use a separate line to describe each body of water.

[DRAFT]

The pond's high water
Glistens most calmly and sweetly
~~Sweeter than the fierce ocean~~
   Than the fierce, rushing ocean
~~The Pond is calmer~~

Reflect

How did Denise's revision help the organization and flow of ideas in the poem?

Apply

Check the lines of your poem to see that ideas are grouped logically.

Poem 453

Conferencing

PEER TO PEER Have partners exchange drafts. After students have read the poem through once, have them state the idea in each line. Then have them point out any lines in their partners' drafts that have unclear ideas.

PEER GROUPS Have students take turns reading their drafts aloud to the group. Group members each point out one detail they think is especially vivid or one detail that could be made clearer or livelier.

TEACHER-LED Meet with pairs of students. Have students read each other's drafts and facilitate a conversation in which they offer constructive criticism on adding vivid details or making sure each line conveys one clear idea.

Write
a Poem

Student Objectives

• Revise to make sure each line or stanza conveys one idea. *(p. 453)*

Revise

Focus on  Organization

Check Lines and Ideas Remind students that when they write prose pieces, they are careful to focus each paragraph on one clearly stated idea. In poetry, each line or stanza should do the same. Since haiku do not have stanzas, students should make sure each line conveys a clear, distinct image or idea.

Have a volunteer read aloud the draft excerpt without the revisions and another volunteer read the excerpt aloud with the revisions. Compare the two versions. Ask:

• How are they different in the way they express Denise's ideas? (Possible response: In the original draft, the idea that the pond is calmer than the ocean is spread across two lines. In the revision, the calm of the pond is featured in the second line, and the fierceness of the ocean is featured in the third.)

CCSS **Common Core State Standards**

W.6.2.b: Develop the topic with relevant facts, definitions, concrete details, quotations, or other information and examples. **W.6.3.d:** Use precise words and phrases, relevant descriptive details, and sensory language to convey experiences and events.

Poem T453

Write
a Poem

Week 3 • Day 2

Student Objectives

• Revise for line breaks. (p. 454)

Revise

Focus on  Sentence Fluency

Check Syllables and Line Breaks

Have students follow Denise's example and read aloud their poems to count the syllables. Students should make revisions if they find that any of their lines have an incorrect number of syllables.

Explain that line breaks should not only define the rhythm of the poem, but they should also be placed logically in terms of the poem's content; that is, lines should break at the end of a complete phrase or idea. The line in the draft excerpt, for example, clearly expresses one idea about the pond—that it is shiny and calm. Refer students to page 453 for more information about the importance of expressing one idea per line and explain that this is a good example of the way two writing traits (**Organization, Sentence Fluency**) support each other.

Revise

Focus on Sentence Fluency

The Rubric Says	The lines and stanzas, if used, convey ideas at a good pace. The line breaks establish the rhythm and flow.
Writing Strategy	Place line breaks where they make sense.

As you can see, the flow of ideas in the lines of a poem is important. Equally important is the flow of the lines themselves. The lines are what give poetry its rhythm, and the syllable counts in each line of a haiku give it the form and feel of a haiku. The lines also determine which words will be read together or apart. A good trick I use to make sure the lines of my haiku sound okay and have the correct number of syllables is to read the lines aloud, counting out the syllables for 5-7-5.

As I did this for my haiku, I noticed that a line that is supposed to have seven syllables has eight. See it in line two? I didn't catch it when I was revising that same line for organization. I thought up another word with the same feel as *glistens*, since *glistens* fits with the flow of ideas for that line. Have a look at what I did.

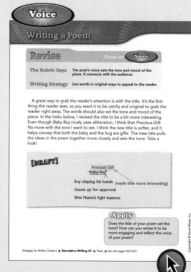

[DRAFT]

[adjusted syllable count]

Gleams

~~Glistens~~ most calmly and sweetly

Apply

Read your lines aloud to hear how they sound to you. Pay attention to rhythm and flow.

Optional Revising Lessons

Voice

Writing a Poem

Revise

Focus on Voice

The Rubric Says	The poet's voice sets the tone and mood of the piece. It connects with the audience.
Writing Strategy	Use words in original ways to appeal to the reader.

A great way to grab the reader's attention is with the title. It's the first thing the reader sees, so you want it to be catchy and original to grab the reader right away. The words should also set the tone and mood of the piece. In the haiku below, I revised the title to be a bit more interesting. Even though *Baby Boy* nicely uses alliteration, I think that *Precious Gift* fits more with the tone I want to set. I think the new title is softer, and it helps convey that both the baby and the hug are gifts. The new title pulls the ideas in the poem together more closely and sets the tone. Take a look!

[DRAFT]

Precious Gift
~~Baby Boy~~

Boy clapping his hands   [made title more interesting]

Gazes up for approval

Wins Mama's tight squeeze

Apply

Does the title of your poem set the tone? How can you revise it to be more engaging and reflect the voice of your poem?

Strategies for Writers Grade 6 ■ Descriptive Writing 37 ■ Poem ■ Use with pages 452–454.

Descriptive 37

Word Choice

Writing a Poem

Revise

Focus on Word Choice

The Rubric Says	Precise vocabulary and figurative language are used purposefully and effectively.
Writing Strategy	Replace vague, general words with precise words.

The words in a poem, especially in a haiku, are especially important because there are so few of them. It's better to use a word that gives a lot of information than to use several that don't tell much. In the haiku below, I want my readers to know that I am talking about a baby, or more specifically an infant, not just a boy, especially since the original title has been revised. Infant is more precise than boy, and it more accurately describes the subject of my haiku. I also double-checked the syllable count after I made this revision, and I found out I needed to make another adjustment! Look at my revisions to see how I fixed the problem.

[DRAFT]

Precious Gift

Infant   [adjusted syllable count]
~~Boy~~ clapping his hands

Gazes up for approval

Wins Mama's tight squeeze

[added precise vocabulary]

Apply

Look over the words you have chosen in your writing. How can you make any vague words more precise?

Strategies for Writers Grade 6 ■ Descriptive Writing 38 ■ Poem ■ Use with pages 452–454.

Descriptive 38

Go to **Strategies for Writers Grade 6 CD-ROM**

Edit — Focus on **Conventions**

The Rubric Says	The writing has been carefully edited. Comparative and superlative forms of modifiers are used correctly.
Writing Strategy	Check the use and form of comparative and superlative adjectives and adverbs.

Writer's Term

Comparative and Superlative Forms
The **comparative form** of an adjective or adverb compares two items. The **superlative form** is used to compare three or more items. For example, "This book is funnier than that book." (comparative) "This book is the funniest of all." (superlative)

Now I need to double-check my spelling, grammar, and punctuation. The rubric also says to use comparative and superlative forms correctly. I may have to use a dictionary for the tricky ones! Here are some corrections I made. I need to use the comparative form instead of the superlative since I'm comparing two things, the pond and the ocean.

[DRAFT]

more ← [used correct comparative form]

Gleams ~~most~~ calmly and sweetly

Than the fierce, rushing ocean

Reflect

How do the edits Denise made affect her poem?

Apply — **Conventions**

Edit your draft for spelling, punctuation, and comparative and superlative forms.

For more practice with comparative and superlative forms of adjectives and adverbs, use the exercises on the next two pages.

Poem 455

Related Grammar Practice

Student Edition page 498

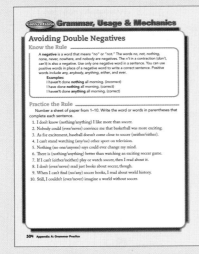

Student Edition page 504

Go to ▷ Appendix A: Grammar Practice

Write
a Poem

Student Objectives

- Edit for correct use of comparative and superlative adjectives and adverbs. (p. 455)

Edit

Focus on **Conventions**

Check Adjectives and Adverbs
Remind students that writing that has poor grammar, spelling, and punctuation is frustrating to read and hard to understand. It is important to use comparative and superlative forms of adjectives and adverbs correctly in order to avoid confusion.

If students find comparative and superlative adjectives and adverbs confusing, teach the mini-lessons on pages T456 and T457. Then have students complete the exercises on pages 456 and 457. Review the answers as a class.

Writer's Term

Comparative and Superlative Forms Sometimes it is hard to know when to add an ending (*-er*, *-est*) and when not to. Use *more* or *most* with adjectives that have two or more syllables, except two-syllable adjectives that end in *y* (*silly*) or an unstressed vowel sound (*yellow*). Use *more* or *most* with most adverbs.

CCSS Common Core State Standards
L.6.1: Demonstrate command of the conventions of standard English grammar and usage when writing or speaking. **L.6.2:** Demonstrate command of the conventions of standard English capitalization, punctuation, and spelling when writing. **L.6.2.b:** Spell correctly.

Mini-Lesson

Student Objectives

- Learn to use the comparative and superlative forms of adjectives correctly. (p. 456)

Comparative and Superlative Adjectives

Have students read the Know the Rule box. Write the following on the board and have students identify whether each word or phrase is in the comparative or superlative form:

taller (comparative)

most surprising (superlative)

more interesting (comparative)

sillier (comparative)

smallest (superlative)

most tempting (superlative)

Have students practice creating comparative and superlative forms. Show pairs or groups of objects and have volunteers say sentences about them. Begin with an example: Show two pencils and say, *This pencil is shorter than that one.*

Online Writing Center

Provides **interactive grammar games** and **practice activities** in student eBook.

Conventions Grammar, Usage & Mechanics

Comparative and Superlative Adjectives

Know the Rule

The **comparative form** of an adjective compares two people, places, or things. Add -er to short adjectives to create the comparative form. Use the word *more* before long adjectives to create the comparative form.

The **superlative form** compares three or more people, places, or things. Add -est to create the superlative form. Use the word *most* before long adjectives to create the superlative form.

Practice the Rule

Number a sheet of paper 1–10. Write the correct form of the adjective in parentheses.

1. The second poem was (funny) than the first poem. funnier
2. The first poem was (serious) than the second poem. more serious
3. Of the three poems that Taylor wrote, I think "Sea Song" is the (descriptive). most descriptive
4. Reading funny poems is (enjoyable) than reading serious ones. more enjoyable
5. Sometimes I have a (hard) time than my friends when I am thinking up vivid descriptions. harder
6. Choosing the right words to describe your ideas can be the (hard) work of all! hardest
7. A poem may not use as many words as a story, so that means the poem's words are (important). more important
8. To create the (thoughtful) haiku, choose your words carefully and don't forget to count those syllables. most thoughtful
9. His poem was the (fine) one in the whole book. finest
10. His poem was also the (long) one in the whole book! longest

Related Grammar Practice

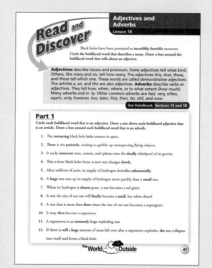

Page 47

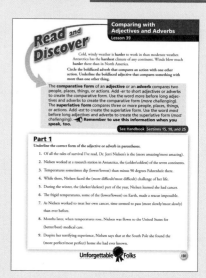

Page 101

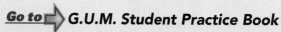

Comparative and Superlative Adverbs

Know the Rule

The **comparative form** of an adverb compares two actions. Add *-er* to short adverbs to create the comparative form. Use the word *more* before long adverbs to create the comparative form.

The **superlative form** compares three or more actions. Add *-est* to create the superlative form. Use the word *most* before long adverbs to create the superlative form. Most of the time, you will use *more* or *most*.

Practice the Rule

Number a sheet of paper 1–10. Write the correct form of the adverb in parentheses.

1. The first poem read (smoothly) than the second poem. more smoothly
2. The second poem read (awkwardly) than the first poem. more awkwardly
3. Out of the whole class, Jake read his haiku the (seriously). most seriously
4. Emma revised her poem (fast) than I did because I needed more time to choose a better word for my description. faster
5. Out of the whole class, I worked the (slowly). most slowly
6. My hard work paid off, though. My haiku described mountains (beautifully) than the teacher's poem! more beautifully
7. I may have worked (slowly) than others, but it was worth it. more slowly
8. You might say I worked on my haiku the (hard)! hardest
9. Jake read his poem aloud (clearly) than Emma did. more clearly
10. Kavitha was the last one to read aloud, so she had to wait the (long). longest

Poem **457**

Go to ➡ **Grammar Practice Masters**

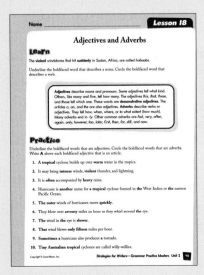

Page 41

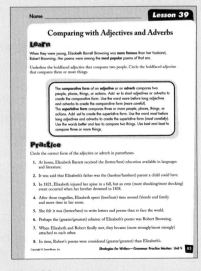

Page 83

Mini-Lesson

Student Objectives

- Learn to use the comparative and superlative forms of adverbs correctly. *(p. 457)*

Comparative and Superlative Adverbs

Make sure students understand the difference between an adjective and an adverb. (An adjective modifies a noun or a pronoun; an adverb modifies a verb, an adjective, or another adverb.)

Write the following sentences on the board and have volunteers underline the adverbs:

- *The people on the sidelines cried, "Run fast!"*
- *The runners swiftly crossed the finish line.*

For each adverb, have students write one sentence using the comparative form and one sentence using the superlative form. (Possible responses: Noah ran faster than Mark. Eli ran fastest of all. A horse runs more swiftly than a turtle. A cheetah runs the most swiftly of all the animals.)

If necessary, provide more sentences with adverbs for students to identify and have them make up more sentences using comparative and superlative adverbs.

CCSS Common Core State Standards

L.6.1: Demonstrate command of the conventions of standard English grammar and usage when writing or speaking. **L.6.2:** Demonstrate command of the conventions of standard English capitalization, punctuation, and spelling when writing.

Poem **T457**

Write
a Poem

Week 3 • Day 4

Student Objectives

- Discuss preparation for publishing and presentation. (p. 458)
- Use a final editing checklist to publish their work. (p. 458)

Publish ✛Presentation

Publishing Strategy Ask students what they think of Denise's ideas for audio to include with her haiku. Ask:

- What audio clips might Denise choose to accompany "Peaceful Place" and "Harvest Home"? (Possible responses: "Peaceful Place"—sounds of wind and splashing water; "Harvest Home"—sounds of rain)

- How else can our class publish the poems? (Possible responses: on a bulletin board, accompanied by illustrations; in an illustrated book; at a poetry slam)

Point out that Denise uses her checklist to make sure that her poem is ready to be presented. Instruct students to create checklists of their own to help them review their poems one last time. Students should tailor their checklists to cover errors that they make frequently.

▶ Strategies for Writers Online
Go to **www.sfw.z-b.com** for additional online resources for students and teachers.

Publish ✛Presentation

Publishing Strategy	Present your poem in a multimedia presentation.
Presentation Strategy	Choose video and audio that enhances the poem.

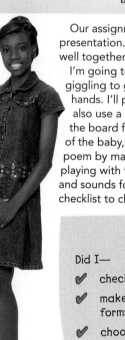

Our assignment is to showcase our poetry in a multimedia presentation. I'll need to choose images and sounds that work well together to enhance and support the ideas in my poems. I'm going to tape record my neighbor's baby playing and giggling to go along with the haiku about him clapping his hands. I'll play that for the class while I read the haiku. I will also use a computer to project the lines of my haiku on the board for the class to see, and I'll include a photograph of the baby, too. These sights and sounds will enhance my poem by making my readers feel like they are right there playing with the baby. I'll also choose appropriate images and sounds for my other two poems. But first, I'll use my final checklist to check over my poems.

My Final Checklist

Did I—

✔ check my spelling, grammar, and punctuation?

✔ make sure I used comparative and superlative forms of adjectives and adverbs correctly?

✔ choose visuals and sounds that will enhance the audience's experience of my poem?

Apply
Make a final checklist and use it to create the final copy of your poetry.

458 Descriptive Writing

Differentiating Instruction

ENRICHMENT
Create a Multimedia Presentation Have students create a slide-show presentation of all the class's poems, including audio and visuals. Students should decide how to organize the poems and pace the presentation. They may also include transitions between poems or groups of poems. Students may seek the poets' permission to include additional images and sound clips with their poems.

REINFORCEMENT
Technology Support Have the technology assistant give students a lesson in using presentation software to present their poems and to include audio and video clips. A more experienced student can help those who are less tech-savvy to find images and audio clips online to include in the presentations.

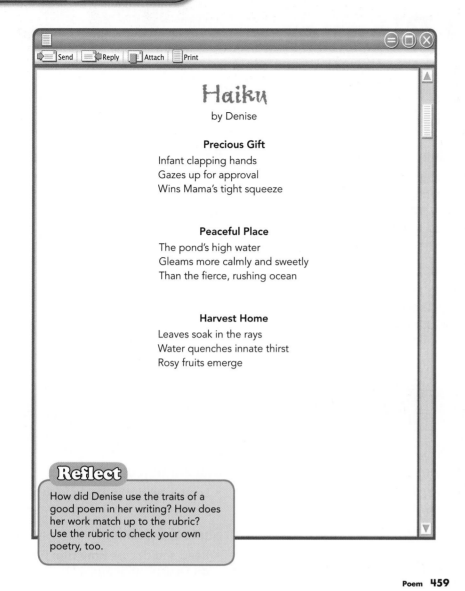

Send   Reply   Attach   Print

Haiku
by Denise

Precious Gift
Infant clapping hands
Gazes up for approval
Wins Mama's tight squeeze

Peaceful Place
The pond's high water
Gleams more calmly and sweetly
Than the fierce, rushing ocean

Harvest Home
Leaves soak in the rays
Water quenches innate thirst
Rosy fruits emerge

Reflect

How did Denise use the traits of a good poem in her writing? How does her work match up to the rubric? Use the rubric to check your own poetry, too.

Poem **459**

Technology Tip for 21ˢᵗ Century Literacies

Publishing student writing can take multiple forms. Sometimes it works best to distribute print copies. Other times it is more effective to post to a weblog or a wiki. When formatting is an important component of the text (e.g., writing a shape poem) but it helps to still have a URL to share with an audience, consider using a document sharing tool like Ge.tt or iPaper. Keep in mind that these are tools to help with file sharing but will require some other mechanism for securing feedback or knowing who has accessed the document.

See **www.sfw.z-b.com** for further information about and links to these websites and tools.

Write
a Poem

Week 3 • Day 5

Student Objectives

- Use a poem rubric. (pp. 442–443)
- Share a published poem. (p. 459)

Presentation Strategy Remind students that the audio and visuals they choose must complement the poem without overwhelming it. All audio and visuals should be clearly relevant—if the listener takes time to wonder why a certain clip or image was used, the impact of the short poem will be lost. Point out that Denise has typed her haiku neatly and placed them attractively on the page. Explain that a neat, clean paper is important, even if students are to present their poems aloud.

Reflecting on a Poem

Take time for students to review the process of writing a poem. Use these questions to generate reflection and discussion:

- What was the most challenging part of writing a poem?
- What advice would you give to someone about to write a poem?

CCSS Common Core State Standards

W.6.4: Produce clear and coherent writing in which the development, organization, and style are appropriate to task, purpose, and audience. **W.6.5:** With some guidance and support from peers and adults, develop and strengthen writing as needed by planning, revising, editing, rewriting, or trying a new approach. **W.6.6:** Use technology, including the Internet, to produce and publish writing as well as to interact and collaborate with others; demonstrate sufficient command of keyboarding skills to type a minimum of three pages in a single sitting. **SL.6.5:** Include multimedia components (e.g., graphics, images, music, sound) and visual displays in presentations to clarify information.

Descriptive Test Planner

WEEK 1

Day 1
Introduce
Descriptive Test Writing

Student Objectives
- Learn the components of the writing prompt.

Student Activities
- Discuss the components of the writing prompt. *(pp. 460–461)*

Day 2
Analyze
Introduce the Scoring Guide

Student Objectives
- Recognize the relationship of the scoring guide to the rubric and the six traits of writing.
- Read a writing prompt response model.

Student Activities
- Read and discuss **Writing Traits in the Scoring Guide.** *(p. 462)*
- Read the writing prompt response model. *(p. 463)*

Day 3
Analyze
Apply the Scoring Guide

Student Objectives
- Apply the scoring guide to the writing prompt response model.

Student Activities
- Read and discuss **Using the Scoring Guide to Study the Model.** *(pp. 464–465)*

WEEK 2

Day 1
Write
Prewrite: Ideas

Student Objectives
- Read a writing prompt for descriptive writing.
- Apply the six traits of writing to the writing prompt.

Student Activities
- Read and discuss **Prewrite: Focus on Ideas.** *(pp. 468–469)*

Day 2
Write
Prewrite: Ideas

Student Objectives
- Learn how to respond to the task in the writing prompt.

Student Activities
- Read and discuss **Prewrite: Focus on Ideas.** *(p. 470)*

Day 3
Write
Prewrite: Organization

Student Objectives
- Learn how to choose a graphic organizer for the writing prompt.

Student Activities
- Read and discuss **Prewrite: Focus on Organization.** *(p. 471)*

WEEK 3

Day 1
Write
Revise: Organization

Student Objectives
- Revise to organize information into paragraphs.

Student Activities
- Read and discuss **Revise: Focus on Organization.** *(p. 476)*

Day 2
Write
Revise: Voice

Student Objectives
- Revise to use a casual tone.

Student Activities
- Read and discuss **Revise: Focus on Voice.** *(p. 477)*

Day 3
Write
Revise: Word Choice

Student Objectives
- Revise for lively and interesting language.

Student Activities
- Read and discuss **Revise: Focus on Word Choice.** *(p. 478)*

Note: Optional Revising Lessons appear on the *Strategies for Writers* CD-ROM.

Analyze
Apply the Scoring Guide

Student Objectives
- Continue to apply the scoring guide to the writing prompt response model.

Student Activities
- Read and discuss **Using the Scoring Guide to Study the Model.** (p. 466)

Analyze
Time Management

Student Objectives
- Learn how to plan their time during a writing test.

Student Activities
- Read and discuss **Planning My Time.** (p. 467)

Write
Prewrite: Organization

Student Objectives
- Learn how to check the graphic organizer against the scoring guide.

Student Activities
- Read and discuss **Prewrite: Focus on Organization.** (pp. 472–473)

Write
Draft: Ideas

Student Objectives
- Draft a descriptive writing test using relevant sensory details.

Student Activities
- Read and discuss **Draft: Focus on Ideas.** (pp. 474–475)
- Draft a descriptive writing test.

Write
Edit: Conventions

Student Objectives
- Edit the writing test for proper grammar, spelling, punctuation, and capitalization.

Student Activities
- Read and discuss **Edit: Focus on Conventions.** (pp. 479–480)

Review
Test Tips

Student Objectives
- Review tips for writing for a test.

Student Activities
- Read and discuss the **Test Tips.** (p. 481)

To complete the chapter in fewer days, combine the learning objectives and activities in a way that supports students as they write.

Resources at-a-Glance

Differentiating Instruction

Using the Scoring
   Guide T464–T465
Planning T467
Prewrite T470–T471
Revise T476–T477
Edit T479
For additional Differentiating Instruction activities, see Strategies for Writers *Extensions Online at* **www.sfw.z-b.com.**

English Language Learners

Scoring Guide T462–T463
Prewrite T468–T469
Draft T474–T475

 Connection Letter
Reproducible letter (in English and Spanish) appears on the *Strategies for Writers* CD-ROM and at **www.sfw.z-b.com**.

Online Essay Grader and Writing Tutor

Powered by Vantage Learning's MY Access!®, includes writing prompts and ongoing feedback for students as they write. Available for Grades 5–8.

Online Writing Center

Provides IWB resources, interactive games and practice activities, videos, eBooks, and a virtual file cabinet.

 Strategies for Writers Online

Go to **www.sfw.z-b.com** for free online resources for students and teachers.

Introduce
Descriptive Test Writing

Week 1 • Day 1

Student Objectives

• Learn the components of the writing prompt. *(pp. 460–461)*

Read the Writing Prompt

Descriptive Test Writing Tell students that they are going to apply what they have learned about descriptive writing to writing a descriptive test. Note that when they write for a test, they will receive a writing prompt and a certain amount of time in which to write. Then their writing will be evaluated, as with any test. Assure students that the skills they have already practiced will help them do a good job. You might wish to refer to pages T368–T391 if you have already taught the descriptive essay form.

Direct students' attention to the three parts of the writing prompt.

Setup The setup does just what its name says: It sets the writer up to do a good job. The setup gets writers to think about the writing topic in general before they choose a narrow topic.

Strategies for Writers Online
Go to **www.sfw.z-b.com** for additional online resources for students and teachers.

Descriptive
test writing

Read the Writing Prompt

When you take a writing test, you'll be given a writing prompt. Most writing prompts have three parts:

Setup This part of the writing prompt gives you the background information you need to get ready to write.

Task This part of the writing prompt tells you exactly what you are supposed to write: a descriptive essay.

Scoring Guide This section tells how your writing will be scored. To do well on the test, you should make sure your writing does everything on the list.

Remember the rubrics you used earlier in the unit? When you take a writing test, you don't always have all of the information that's on a rubric. However, the scoring guide is a lot like a rubric. It lists everything you need to think about to write a good paper. Like the rubrics you've used in this unit, many scoring guides are based upon the six important traits of writing:

Ideas Organization Voice

Word Choice Sentence Fluency Conventions

460 Descriptive Writing

Online Essay Grader and Writing Tutor

Powered by Vantage Learning's MY Access!®, this tool gives students

• immediate, ongoing, sentence-by-sentence feedback.

• helpful suggestions to improve their draft.

• a holistic score and a trait-specific score on their final draft.

• unlimited response submissions to the prompts.

Think about a place that's very special to you. Maybe it's your room or a favorite park you like to visit.

Write an essay describing this place in detail.

Be sure your writing

- includes relevant, sensory details that create a vivid picture for the reader.

- is organized so that all the related information is together.

- has a voice that matches the audience and purpose.

- creates a picture with descriptive words and figurative language.

- contains sentences that flow smoothly.

- contains correct grammar, punctuation, capitalization, and spelling.

Descriptive Test Writing 461

Task The task tells students not only what to write about but also what kind of writing to do: narrative, descriptive, informative/explanatory, or opinion. Tell students that the best-written test will not receive a strong grade if it misses the topic or uses a form of writing other than the assigned form. Students must follow the instructions in the task.

Scoring Guide The scoring guide helps students plan and evaluate their writing. Tell students that the scoring guide is similar to the rubrics they have seen. They should read it carefully before writing and refer to it as they draft and revise their tests. Help students understand how the scoring guide is similar to the rubrics by asking these questions:

- Which trait corresponds to the first bullet? (Ideas)

- Which trait corresponds to the fourth bullet? (Word Choice)

- Which trait corresponds to the last bullet? (Conventions)

CCSS **Common Core State Standards**

W.6.4: Produce clear and coherent writing in which the development, organization, and style are appropriate to task, purpose, and audience. **W.6.10:** Write routinely over extended time frames (time for research, reflection, and revision) and shorter time frames (a single sitting or a day or two) for a range of discipline-specific tasks, purposes, and audiences.

Analyze
the Scoring Guide

Week 1 • Day 2

Student Objectives

- Recognize the relationship of the scoring guide to the rubric and the six traits of writing. *(p. 462)*
- Read a writing prompt response model. *(p. 463)*

Writing Traits in the Scoring Guide

Scoring Guide as a Rubric
Remind students how they used rubrics to guide, evaluate, and improve their writing for other assignments. Point out that in a writing test, the scoring guide acts as a rubric. Read the scoring guide and discuss why each trait is important in good descriptive writing.

Tell students that they will sometimes use writing prompts that do not include guidance for each of the six traits by name. However, students can use their writing experience to remember the main requirements for descriptive writing, as described on page 462.

Writing Traits
in the Scoring Guide

The scoring guide in the prompt on page 461 has been made into this chart. Does it remind you of the rubrics you've used? Not all prompts include all of the writing traits, but this one does. Use them to do your best writing. Remember to work neatly and put your name on each page.

 **Ideas** • Be sure your writing includes relevant, sensory details that create a vivid picture for the reader.

 **Organization** • Be sure your writing is organized so that all the related information is together.

 **Voice** • Be sure your writing has a voice that matches the audience and purpose.

 **Word Choice** • Be sure your writing creates a picture with descriptive words and figurative language.

 **Sentence Fluency** • Be sure your writing contains sentences that flow smoothly.

 **Conventions** • Be sure your writing contains correct grammar, punctuation, capitalization, and spelling.

Look at Daniel Maloney's essay on the next page. Did he follow the scoring guide?

462 Descriptive Writing

English Language Learners

BEGINNING

The Writing Process Review the steps in the writing process using simple words. Use the following words to substitute for *prewrite, draft, revise, edit,* and *publish: about/plan, write, change, fix,* and *show.* Remind students to follow all of these steps during a writing test.

INTERMEDIATE

Sensory Details Prepare a set of index cards with words associated with a place such as schools, for example, *loud bell, students rushing, cafeteria food,* and so on. Draw a Spider Map with the label *School.* As you introduce a word on an index card, ask students to tell which category the word belongs with on the Spider Map. It is possible for a word to fit in more than one category.

Sitting on the Dock

by Daniel Maloney

I really didn't want to spend my summer vacation with my family at Bass Lake—I wanted to stay home with my friends. But by the end of our vacation, my parents practically had to drag me away from what had quickly become my favorite place. You see, Bass Lake, with its calm, crystal-blue morning water and its choppy, loud, and fun-filled afternoons, is a truly magnificent place.

On our last day there, I got up early and walked the few steps from our rented log cabin to the dock on the lake for a final goodbye. At this hour, the lake was still. The water, a deep navy blue, had a glassy sheen to it that I hated to disturb. As I walked to the end of the dock, the wood planks creaked and gave slightly, causing small ripples in the water below.

Two small boats were tied to the dock—an old, messy rowboat and a speed boat ready to take its passengers for water-skiing adventures after dawn turned to day. On either side, not far from my dock, were other similar docks, quietly waiting for the day to begin. Homes old and new, large and small, lined the shore and rose up into the hills above it. In the distance, I heard a dog bark and thought it must be eager for its morning swim. Across the vast lake there were no homes, just pine trees bunched together thickly, leaving a dark impression of their outline in the water.

I took a deep breath, inhaling the strong scent of pine and the slightly fishy smell of the water. I also smelled the faint odor of fuel from the boat. Though the sun was quickly rising, the air was still crisp, and my toes caught a chill when I took off my shoes. I wanted to get one last feel of the lake's cool, clean water, a final reminder of my visit. I could see rocks below the surface of the lake as I carefully stuck my toe into its chilly bath. The rocks became blurry and faded from my view with the movement of the water, and I got up to leave for the last time.

Descriptive Test Writing **463**

Read the Model

Writing Prompt Response Have students read "Sitting on the Dock." Tell them to keep the requirements of the scoring guide in mind as they follow along. After reading the story aloud, ask questions such as the following:

- How is the descriptive essay organized? (Each paragraph describes a different aspect of the lake.)

- What sensory details make the essay come alive for you? (Possible responses: *loud, and fun-filled afternoons; glassy sheen; strong scent of pine and the slightly fishy smell of the water*)

- What figurative language does Daniel use to help paint a clear picture of the lake? (Possible response: *chilly bath*)

- What does Daniel mean by using this word or phrase? (Possible response: *The water is cold.*)

ADVANCED

Using Precise Words Write a generic word such as *like* on the board. Use the Web graphic organizer to brainstorm other words that have the same meaning or stronger meanings as *like*. Tell students to use this idea when choosing words for their descriptive writing.

ADVANCED HIGH

Using Appropriate Voice Write the topic *School* on the board. Below it, write several introductory words, phrases, or sentences for a report about school. For example, *Ding! Clang! The class doors burst open and chattering children fill the hallway. Can you smell the delicious aroma coming from the kitchen?* Ask students to rank the introductions according to how interesting they are. To keep readers interested, students can use simple phrases, questions, or single words.

CCSS Common Core State Standards

R/Inf.6.4: Determine the meaning of words and phrases as they are used in a text, including figurative, connotative, and technical meanings. R/Inf.6.5: Analyze how a particular sentence, paragraph, chapter, or section fits into the overall structure of a text and contributes to the development of the ideas. SL.6.1.a: Come to discussions prepared, having read or studied required material; explicitly draw on that preparation by referring to evidence on the topic, text, or issue to probe and reflect on ideas under discussion.

Analyze
the Model

Student Objectives

• Apply the scoring guide to the writing prompt response model. (pp. 464–465)

Using the Scoring Guide to Study the Model

Review the Scoring Guide
Remind students that the scoring guide is the tool that an evaluator—a teacher or another professional—will use to score the writing test. Students are given the scoring guide so they will know the criteria on which the writing will be judged. They should use the scoring guide as they write to make sure they meet all requirements.

Use the Scoring Guide Have students use the Writing Traits in the Scoring Guide chart on page 462 to evaluate the model test response on page 463. The chart is based on the scoring guide to the writing prompt.

Find More Examples Explain that pages 464–466 show how the writing model on page 463 meets all six writing traits. Have students read pages 464–465 and look for additional examples of **Ideas, Organization, Voice,** and **Word Choice** in the model.

 Strategies for Writers Online
Go to **www.sfw.z-b.com** for additional online resources for students and teachers.

Using the Scoring Guide to Study the Model

Now let's use the scoring guide to check Daniel's writing test, "Sitting on the Dock." Let's see how well his essay meets each of the six writing traits.

 Ideas
• The writing includes relevant, sensory details that create a vivid picture for the reader.

Daniel does a good job providing details that are both relevant and sensory. For instance, he talks about how still the lake was. He even describes what it smelled like outside.

> At this hour, the lake was still. The water, a deep navy blue, had a glassy sheen to it that I hated to disturb.

> I took a deep breath, inhaling the strong scent of pine and the slightly fishy smell of the water. I also smelled the faint odor of fuel from the boat.

 **Organization**
• The writing is organized so that all the related information is together.

Daniel takes care to describe stepping in the water in great detail. He puts information about the crisp air, cool water, and rocks under the surface—all related details—together in the same paragraph.

> Though the sun was quickly rising, the air was still crisp, and my toes caught a chill when I took off my shoes. I wanted to get one last feel of the lake's cool, clean water, a final reminder of my visit. I could see rocks below the surface of the lake as I carefully stuck my toe in to its chilly bath.

464 Descriptive Writing

Differentiating Instruction

ENRICHMENT
Explore Vivid Writing Ask students to think about how writing can be made more vivid and interesting. Have them look through books, magazines, or websites to find descriptive essays or articles in which the writing seems especially vivid and engaging. Ask them to bring a paragraph from the article or story to class and read it aloud to the group. Have students note the words or descriptions in the paragraph that made them decide it serves as an example of good writing. Have students compare their paragraphs to the scoring guide on page 462.

- The writing has a voice that matches the audience and purpose.

Daniel uses first-person point of view because his purpose is to share a personal experience. He connects with his audience right from the start by explaining why he loves Bass Lake.

> But by the end of our vacation, my parents practically had to drag me away from what had quickly become my favorite place. You see, Bass Lake, with its calm, crystal-blue morning water and its choppy, loud, and fun-filled afternoons, is a truly magnificent place.

- The writing creates a picture with descriptive words and figurative language.

Daniel makes his writing more interesting by using colorful, descriptive words. I know, for instance, that docks can't wait for the day to begin, but it helps to give the reader a clearer picture when Daniel uses figurative language like this.

> On either side, not far from my dock, were other similar docks, quietly waiting for the day to begin. Homes old and new, large and small, lined the shore and rose up into the hills above it. In the distance, I heard a dog bark and thought it must be eager for its morning swim. Across the vast lake there were no homes, just pine trees bunched together thickly, leaving a dark impression of their outline in the water.

Think About the Traits Once students have thoroughly discussed the model descriptive essay, ask them which traits they think are most important in a descriptive essay. Of course, all the traits are important in every piece of writing, but some of the traits stand out more in some types of writing than in others. Students might say, for example, that the trait of **Ideas** is important because the sensory details make the writer's descriptions come alive for the reader. Or, they may say that **Word Choice** is important because precise, memorable words convey an accurate picture of the person, place, or experience being described.

REINFORCEMENT

Reinforce Figurative Language Make sure students understand the meaning of the term *figurative language*. Explain that when a writer uses a comparison to create an image for the reader, he or she is using figurative language. In a simile, the comparison is signaled by the word *like* or *as* (e.g., the grass was like a cool, green carpet). In other figurative language, such as metaphors, the comparison is implicit (e.g., a wispy mare's tail of cloud trailed across the sky). Give students a story or an article to read that features figurative language. Have students read the piece and underline examples of figurative language.

CCSS **C**ommon **C**ore **S**tate **S**tandards

R/Inf.6.1: Cite textual evidence to support analysis of what the text says explicitly as well as inferences drawn from the text. **SL.6.1:** Engage effectively in a range of collaborative discussions (one-on-one, in groups, and teacher-led) with diverse partners on *grade 6 topics, texts, and issues,* building on others' ideas and expressing their own clearly. **SL.6.1.a:** Come to discussions prepared, having read or studied required material; explicitly draw on that preparation by referring to evidence on the topic, text, or issue to probe and reflect on ideas under discussion.

Analyze
the Model

Week 1 • Day 4

Student Objectives

- Continue to apply the scoring guide to the writing prompt response model. *(p. 466)*

Analyze the Model Ask students to choose another passage that has a good variety of sentence lengths and types. (Possible response: *On our last day there, I got up early and walked the few steps from our rented log cabin to the dock on the lake for a final goodbye. At this hour, the lake was still. The water, a deep navy blue, had a glassy sheen to it that I hated to disturb.*) Have students analyze the sentences types in the passage and explain why they give the writing a good flow. (Possible response: The first sentence includes several prepositional phrases. The second sentence is simple and short. The third sentence is longer and structured with an appositive in the middle.)

Remind students that using conventions correctly is crucial to making their writing accessible to readers. Ask students to think about areas of grammar, spelling, or punctuation where they often make mistakes. Have them look for examples of those conventions being used correctly in the model.

 Strategies for Writers Online
Go to **www.sfw.z-b.com** for additional online resources for students and teachers.

T466 Descriptive Writing

Using the Scoring Guide to Study the Model

 **Sentence Fluency**

- The writing contains sentences that flow smoothly.

Daniel's sentences flow smoothly because he's careful to vary their lengths and structures. I never got lost trying to follow a series of too-long sentences or confused by too many short, choppy sentences together. Look how well these sentences flow.

> On our last day there, I got up early and walked the few steps from our rented log cabin to the dock on the lake for a final goodbye. At this hour, the lake was still. The water, a deep navy blue, had a glassy sheen to it that I hated to disturb.

 **Conventions**

- The writing contains correct grammar, punctuation, capitalization, and spelling.

I didn't notice any mistakes in Daniel's writing. When you take a test, it's important to check for mistakes in your work, including errors in grammar, punctuation, capitalization, and spelling. Be sure to go through and edit your work before you turn it in!

466 Descriptive Writing

Planning My Time

Before giving us a writing test prompt, my teacher tells us how much time we'll have to complete the test. Since I'm already familiar with the writing process, I can think about how much total time I have and then divide it up into the different parts of the writing process. If the test takes an hour, here's how I can organize my time. Planning your time will help you, too!

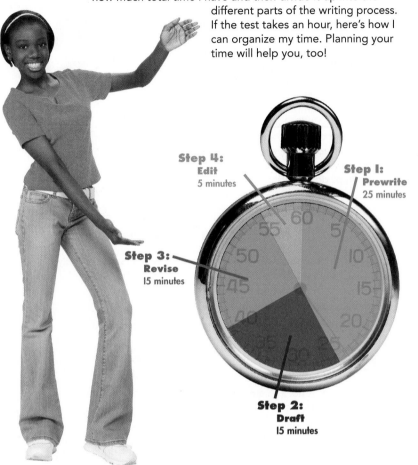

Step 4:
Edit
5 minutes

Step 1:
Prewrite
25 minutes

Step 3:
Revise
15 minutes

Step 2:
Draft
15 minutes

Descriptive Test Writing **467**

Differentiating Instruction

REINFORCEMENT

Reinforce Time Management For students who have trouble visualizing analog time, do a sample conversion to digital time. Tell students, for example, that if a test starts at 11:00, the testing period will break down as follows: Prewrite: 11:00–11:25; Draft: 11:25–11:40; Revise: 11:40–11:55; Edit: 11:55–12:00. Have students create a writing schedule for a one-hour test that starts at 10:30. Tell students that when they take a writing test, they should take a moment at the beginning to jot down a writing schedule like this, so that they can keep track as they move through the writing process. The moment it takes to jot down the schedule will be time well invested.

Student Objectives

• Learn how to plan their time during a writing test. *(p. 467)*

Planning My Time

Time Management Explain to students that when they write for a test, they must complete all the steps of the writing process quickly. Students may be surprised that the student guide, Denise, has allotted so much of the writing time—25 minutes out of 60—to prewriting. Ask students why this time is necessary. (Without a plan for writing, students may write a draft that does not respond to the task. Then they will not have time to write another draft.)

Remind students also that revising is part of the writing task. Drafting and revising together take a little more time—30 minutes—than prewriting; five minutes remain to edit. Tell students that when they have a shorter or longer time in which to write a test, they can use a similar time plan: about the same amount of time for prewriting and for drafting/revising, with a shorter time left for editing.

CCSS **C**ommon **C**ore **S**tate **S**tandards
R/Inf.6.1: Cite textual evidence to support analysis of what the text says explicitly as well as inferences drawn from the text. **W.6.10:** Write routinely over extended time frames (time for research, reflection, and revision) and shorter time frames (a single sitting or a day or two) for a range of discipline-specific tasks, purposes, and audiences.

Write
a Descriptive Test

Week 2 • Day 1

Student Objectives

- Read a writing prompt for descriptive writing. *(p. 468)*
- Apply the six traits of writing to the writing prompt. *(p. 469)*

Prewrite

Focus on Ideas

Study the Writing Prompt Have a volunteer read Denise's step-by-step instructions for studying and marking the writing prompt. Ask students to identify the words Denise circled and discuss why she made those choices. Discuss other words in the instructions that students might want to circle or underline. When they begin to take a test, students should mark the scoring guide to highlight instructions they often overlook in their writing. Ask students to share which sections of the scoring guide they would choose to highlight.

Strategies for Writers Online
Go to **www.sfw.z-b.com** for additional online resources for students and teachers.

Prewrite

Focus on **Ideas**

Writing Strategy   Study the writing prompt to find out what to do.

When I am handed a test, the first thing I do is study the writing prompt so I will know what to do. The writing prompt usually has three parts. The parts probably won't be labeled, so you'll have to identify them on your own, like I did with my writing prompt. Locate and label the setup, task, and scoring guide on your writing prompt. Circle key words in the setup and the tasks that tell what kind of writing you need to do and who your audience will be. Here, I circled the setup in blue and the task in orange. I'm going to write my test for my teacher, since the writing prompt doesn't identify who the reader is.

My Writing Test Prompt

Setup — Think about an ⟨event that you attended or witnessed⟩ that really stands out in your mind.

Task — Write an ⟨essay describing the event in detail.⟩

Be sure your writing

Scoring Guide
- includes relevant, sensory details that create a vivid picture for the reader.
- is organized so that all the related information is together.
- has a voice that matches the audience and purpose.
- creates a picture with descriptive words and figurative language.
- contains sentences that flow smoothly.

468 Descriptive Writing

English Language Learners

BEGINNING

Writing Prompt Give students a copy of the standard descriptive test writing prompt. Have them look at each word in the prompt and circle the words they do not know. Then teach the most important words, such as *essay, event, witnessed, relevant, sensory details, vivid picture.* You might have a higher-level ELL work with a lower-level ELL to review the meanings of these words.

INTERMEDIATE

Writing Prompt Have students read the descriptive test writing prompt and write down words they do not know. Review how to ask for help, such as *What does* vivid *mean? Does* vivid *mean "clear"?* Have them practice asking and answering with two other students. Finally, ask students to write their answers; for example, *If something is vivid, it is clear and bright.* Review as a class.

Let's think about how the scoring guide for my descriptive writing test relates to the writing traits you've studied in the rubrics. All of the traits might not be included in every scoring guide, but you need to remember them all to write a good essay.

Ideas
- Be sure your writing includes relevant, sensory details that create a vivid picture for the reader.

My descriptions should include sensory details that are relevant and create a clear mental image.

Organization
- Be sure your writing is organized so that all the related information is together.

I'll put information that goes together in the same paragraph so my reader won't be confused.

Voice
- Be sure your writing has a voice that matches the audience and purpose.

I'll use first-person point of view and a personal tone to share my thoughts and impressions.

Word Choice
- Be sure your writing creates a picture with descriptive words and figurative language.

My writing will be more interesting if I use colorful words and figurative language that give the reader a clear picture of my descriptions.

Sentence Fluency
- Be sure your writing contains sentences that flow smoothly.

I'll check that my sentences flow easily and do not repeat the same structure or length too many times.

Conventions
- Be sure your writing contains correct grammar, punctuation, capitalization, and spelling.

Editing my work for grammar and spelling mistakes is really important!

Descriptive Test Writing **469**

Have students take turns reading the bullet points on page 469. Discuss Denise's responses and encourage students to add their own thoughts. For example, ask why sensory details will help Denise provide a good description of an experience she had. What type of voice do students think will match the purpose and audience for a descriptive essay such as this one?

You also may wish to use this opportunity to further reinforce the connection between bullet points on the scoring guide and their corresponding writing traits. For instance, ask which writing trait corresponds to the first bullet point. (Ideas) Encourage students to ask any questions they have about the scoring guide and the traits. Call on volunteers to answer the questions before you provide answers yourself.

ADVANCED
Writing Prompt Make a few copies of the descriptive writing prompt. Cut apart the sentences in the scoring guide. Have partners work together to assign the sentences to one of the rubric writing traits—Ideas, Organization, Voice, Word Choice, Sentence Fluency, and Conventions. Remind students that they must address all of the writing traits during a writing test.

ADVANCED HIGH
Writing Prompt Have students read the descriptive writing prompt and write down no more than three words in each part of the prompt that they think are most important. Then have them compare with a partner and discuss the differences.

CCSS Common Core State Standards
SL.6.1.a: Come to discussions prepared, having read or studied required material; explicitly draw on that preparation by referring to evidence on the topic, text, or issue to probe and reflect on ideas under discussion. **SL.6.1.b:** Follow rules for collegial discussions, set specific goals and deadlines, and define individual roles as needed. **SL.6.1.c:** Pose and respond to specific questions with elaboration and detail by making comments that contribute to the topic, text, or issue under discussion.

Descriptive Test Writing **T469**

Write
a Descriptive Test

Week 2 • Day 2

Student Objectives

• Learn how to respond to the task in the writing prompt. *(p. 470)*

Prewrite

Focus on Ideas

Gather Information Remind students that they have written descriptive pieces in the past and will be using writing strategies that they've already practiced. Assure them that this descriptive essay will share many traits with pieces they have already written. Point out that the step on page 470 is similar to the first step in any other writing assignment—think of a topic to write about and jot down details.

Discuss how Denise chose her topic. Note that she picked an episode from her life that made a strong impression on her. She won't have to spend a lot of time trying to think of details because the event was very exciting for her—and therefore memorable.

Point out that Denise is thinking about time management right from the start. Tell students they should do the same when they find themselves in a testing situation.

Online Writing Center

Provides **interactive graphic organizers** as well as a variety of graphic organizers in PDF format.

T470 Descriptive Writing

Prewrite

Focus on **Ideas**

Writing Strategy Respond to the task.

I know that good writers prepare to write even before they put their pens to paper. Before I begin writing my essay, I'll gather information and take notes. The writing prompt provides me with a lot of information, so I'll start by looking at that. First, look at the task to find out what you are supposed to write. Then think about how you'll respond to the task before you start writing. Since you don't get much time when you write for a test, these steps are helpful.

The task that I identified from my writing prompt is to write a descriptive essay about an event that stands out in my mind. The thing that comes to my mind is my brother's first football game at his high school—it was really exciting. I'll quickly jot down some notes to get started.

Task —— [Write an essay describing the event in detail.

Notes

✔ Wow, it was loud!

✔ The stands were full of people of all ages.

✔ The team ran through the banner to get on the field.

Apply

Think about how you are going to respond to the task before you start writing. Then you can write notes to help you gather information.

470 Descriptive Writing

Differentiating Instruction

ENRICHMENT

Include Dialogue Explain that dialogue is a great way to bring characters to life and help the reader picture the action in a scene. Challenge students to include at least three pieces of dialogue in their descriptive essays. They do not need to include fully written-out dialogue in their notes or graphic organizers, but they should include dialogue fragments in their notes and indicate in their graphic organizers where they plan to include the dialogue.

Prewrite

Focus on **Organization**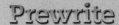

Writing Strategy — Choose a graphic organizer.

Now I need to start organizing my ideas with the help of a graphic organizer. A graphic organizer will help me gather ideas and organize them at the same time. That will help, since my time is limited! A Spider Map will help me remember and organize all the details and ideas I want to include.

TOPIC: first football game of year

Where I was
- My brother's first football game was at the high school.
- My grandmother, my mom, and I were all excited!
- The stadium is next to the school.

What I saw
- Lights were on, so it looked like daylight on the field.
- The team came running out, tearing through a banner held by cheerleaders.
- The stands were filled with people of all ages and the band in their uniforms.
- People were wearing green and yellow to support the Eagles, our team.
- I spotted my brother, Number 67.

What I smelled
- Popcorn and hot dogs were being sold at the stadium.

What I heard
- Everyone stood up and yelled and shouted as the team ran through the banner to the field.
- The band was playing team fight songs.
- It was loud as the team took to the field to play.

What I felt
- Even though it was cold, all the excitement kept me warm.
- From my seat, I could feel the rumble of the crowd, stomping feet, and yelling.

Reflect
Does the Spider Map list enough details for a complete essay?

Apply
Choose a graphic organizer that will help you organize the details you want to include in your essay.

Descriptive Test Writing 471

REINFORCEMENT

Support Graphic Organizer Options Provide more explicit guidance for students in choosing a graphic organizer for their descriptive essays. Give students copies of a blank Spider Map, Sequence Chain (p. 403), Five-Senses Chart (p. 427), Web (p. 449), and any other graphic organizers you feel are appropriate. Briefly explain how each organizer works. Tell students they may use a Spider Map like the one on page 471, or they can choose to use one of the organizers you have shown them. Work with individual students to choose a graphic organizer. Have students briefly tell you about their experiences and then help them determine which organizer will work best.

Student Objectives

- Learn how to choose a graphic organizer for the writing prompt. (p. 471)

Prewrite

Focus on **Organization**

Remind students that during a writing test, they will not be told what kind of graphic organizer to use. Instead, they must think about how they have used graphic organizers in the past, and they must decide which one will be the most useful in helping them fulfill the test prompt.

A Spider Map is one appropriate graphic organizer for a descriptive essay. Ask students what other organizers might work well for this genre. (**Possible responses: Web, Sequence Chain, Five-Senses Chart**) Tell students they may use a Spider Map, or they may choose a different organizer for their test writing.

Analyze the Spider Map with students. Ask:

- What categories did Denise choose to include? (**the five senses**)

CCSS **Common Core State Standards**

W.6.2.a: Introduce a topic; organize ideas, concepts, and information, using strategies such as definition, classification, comparison/contrast, and cause/ effect; include formatting (e.g., headings), graphics (e.g., charts, tables), and multimedia when useful to aiding comprehension. **W.6.2.b:** Develop the topic with relevant facts, definitions, concrete details, quotations, or other information and examples. **W.6.3.d:** Use precise words and phrases, relevant descriptive details, and sensory language to convey experiences and events.

Write
a Descriptive Test

Week 2 • Day 4

Student Objectives

- Learn how to check the graphic organizer against the scoring guide. (pp. 472–473)

Prewrite

Focus on  Organization

Check the Graphic Organizer

Ask students why they think Denise is not yet ready to write, even though she has finished her graphic organizer. (Possible response: First, she needs to check her graphic organizer against the scoring guide.) Explain to students that it is essential to check their work against the scoring guide before they move from prewriting to drafting. That way, if they find that the graphic organizer is lacking some elements according to the scoring guide, they can go back and make some quick adjustments to the graphic organizer before proceeding to write their drafts.

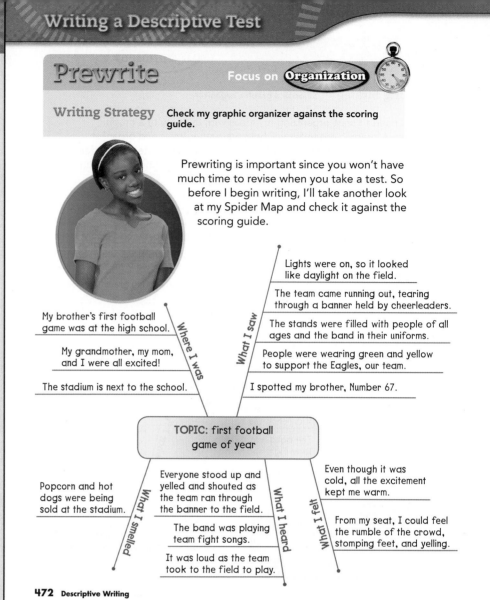

Prewrite

Focus on **Organization**

Writing Strategy Check my graphic organizer against the scoring guide.

Prewriting is important since you won't have much time to revise when you take a test. So before I begin writing, I'll take another look at my Spider Map and check it against the scoring guide.

Where I was
My brother's first football game was at the high school.
My grandmother, my mom, and I were all excited!
The stadium is next to the school.

What I saw
Lights were on, so it looked like daylight on the field.
The team came running out, tearing through a banner held by cheerleaders.
The stands were filled with people of all ages and the band in their uniforms.
People were wearing green and yellow to support the Eagles, our team.
I spotted my brother, Number 67.

TOPIC: first football game of year

What I smelled
Popcorn and hot dogs were being sold at the stadium.

What I heard
Everyone stood up and yelled and shouted as the team ran through the banner to the field.
The band was playing team fight songs.
It was loud as the team took to the field to play.

What I felt
Even though it was cold, all the excitement kept me warm.
From my seat, I could feel the rumble of the crowd, stomping feet, and yelling.

472 Descriptive Writing

Strategies for Writers Online

Go to **www.sfw.z-b.com** for additional online resources for students and teachers.

- Be sure your writing includes relevant, sensory details that create a vivid picture for the reader.

I included lots of sensory details in my Spider Map to choose from. Using them will help my reader "see" what I am describing.

- Be sure your writing is organized so that all the related information is together.

My Spider Map helped me get my ideas organized so information that goes together will be in the same paragraph in my essay.

- Be sure your writing has a voice that matches the audience and purpose.

I want to give my readers a feel for all the excitement of the big game. Using first-person point of view will really help me connect.

- Be sure your writing creates a picture with descriptive words and figurative language.

I'll try to use colorful words and figurative language to describe things as I write.

- Be sure your writing contains sentences that flow smoothly.

Using my Spider Map as a guide, I'll write a variety of sentence structures that flow smoothly.

Conventions

- Be sure your writing contains correct grammar, punctuation, capitalization, and spelling.

After I complete my draft, I will be sure to thoroughly edit it so that I don't have any mistakes.

Reflect

How will Denise's Spider Map help her write a descriptive and well-organized essay?

Apply

Reviewing your graphic organizer against the scoring guide will help you determine what you're going to write even before you start writing.

Descriptive Test Writing 473

Prepare to Draft Students may not see the value in checking all six writing traits at this point in the writing process. After all, the Spider Map won't help students vary sentences or use precise language, and there is no draft to edit for conventions yet. Ask students to consider why Denise checks all the writing traits at this point—even those that don't apply to prewriting. (Possible response: Denise is not only checking the work she's done so far, but she's also reminding herself of what to do as she starts to draft.) Because time is short, Denise needs to remember the kind of draft she wants to write—well organized and full of precise, descriptive language. Remembering these goals now will help her write a better draft in the short time she has.

CCSS **C**ommon **C**ore **S**tate **S**tandards

W.6.2.a: Introduce a topic; organize ideas, concepts, and information, using strategies such as definition, classification, comparison/contrast, and cause/effect; include formatting (e.g., headings), graphics (e.g., charts, tables), and multimedia when useful to aiding comprehension. **W.6.2.b:** Develop the topic with relevant facts, definitions, concrete details, quotations, or other information and examples. **W.6.3.d:** Use precise words and phrases, relevant descriptive details, and sensory language to convey experiences and events.

Write
a Descriptive Test

Week 2 • Day 5

Student Objectives

- Draft a descriptive writing test using relevant sensory details. (*pp. 474–475*)

Draft

Focus on Ideas

Tips for Test Writing Ask students what they notice about how Denise has written her draft. (Denise has written on every other line to leave room for later changes. She has written neatly so that she can read her work.) Remind students that the drafting stage is not the time to try to produce a perfect essay. In fact, perfect writing takes so much time that it's rarely possible during a test. The goal of drafting is to get words on paper quickly, following the organization that students decided on during prewriting and including details that support the topic.

Ask students how much time they will have to write this draft. (15 minutes) As students begin their drafts, remind them to write as neatly as they can on every other line of paper. This way, they will have space to make changes while revising and editing.

Online Writing Center

Provides student eBooks with an **interactive writing pad** for drafting, revising, editing, and publishing.

Draft

Focus on Ideas

Writing Strategy Include relevant sensory details.

The scoring guide says to use details that are both sensory and relevant. I want my reader to picture everything in my essay, so I'll choose details that will make it easy for them to imagine they are right there at the game with me. I'll be sure all my details relate to the topic so I don't confuse the reader.

[DRAFT]

Go, Eagles!
by Denise

The crowd roars. The cheerleaders kick and yell cheers. The band plays team songs to get us in the spirit. Eagle stadium is about to hold its first game of the season, and the crowd is going wild!

Along with my mother and my grandmother. I have come to watch the Eagles, the team that which my brother plays defense, compete. As we enter the stadium just before the game begins, I can feel the energy of the crowd! Even though it's a cold fall night, the excitement inside the stadium makes it seem warm.

We make our way to seats in the stands that surround the stadium. The smell of popcorn and hot dogs comes drafting through the stands as we walk up the steps. It even smells like a football game! Popcorn is one of my very favorite foods. As I look around, I see a green and

474 Descriptive Writing

English Language Learners

BEGINNING

What Is Friendly? Show a photo of two people who are talking and smiling. Say, *They are friendly.* Repeat for other photos, including photos of unhappy or unfriendly-looking people. Then check students' understanding by showing a photo and asking, *Are they friendly?* As students' understanding allows, have them act out friendliness or unfriendliness. Tell students their writing should sound friendly, too.

INTERMEDIATE

Editing Remind students that if they draft on every other line, they will have room to make edits later. Review the proofreading marks. Have students review their drafts and look for one type of error. Then have them read the draft again and search for another type of error. Monitor that students are using the proper proofreading marks as they find any errors.

Proofreading Marks

⌐ Indent   ℓ Take out something
≡ Make a capital   ⊙ Add a period
/ Make a small letter   ⌗ New paragraph
∧ Add something   ⓢⓟ Spelling error

yellow blur, with fans of all ages—students, parents, grandparents, and members of the community sporting the Eagles green and yellow colors and waving handheld pompons to show their spirit. The band in their ornate uniforms and hats were seen sitting on the bleachers near the field. They were heard playing a team song as the cheerleaders on the field in their green and yellow skirts and sweaters could be seen opening up a huge paper banner that reads, "Go, eagles!"

Although it's after dark, the huge lights illuminate the field so that it looks like daytime. Across the field I sea the stands filled with blue and black and more people. Their there to support the opposing team, the Panthers.

I know it must be time for the team to come on the field. The stands start to vibrate with all the stomping, and then almost all at once, the Eagles fans rise to their feet.

Our team comes running through the Banner the cheerleaders are holding, ripping it as they cross, and the sound of the crowd is almost defening. I finally spot Number 67, my brother, runs onto the field and over to the sidelines. My mom and grandma and I yell even louder. The game is about to begin!

Reflect

How does the essay capture the excitement for the reader?

Apply

It's important to think about and write for your audience whenever you write for a test.

Descriptive Test Writing 475

ADVANCED

Using Strong Descriptors After students have written their first drafts, have them circle all the adjectives and adverbs they used in the first paragraph. Then have them trade with a partner who will read the paragraph and change each of the circled words to a more descriptive one. Next have the partners discuss why they made each change. Monitor that students' changes were appropriate.

ADVANCED HIGH

Peer Review After students have drafted their descriptive essays, have them trade with another student. Partners should review the draft and look for specific details. Students should point out weak voice and suggest more descriptive words their partners could use. As you monitor, identify two or three examples of weak words or sentences, and discuss ways to strengthen them as a class.

Support the Topic With Relevant Sensory Details Discuss the draft on pages 474–475. What sensory details does Denise use to describe her experience at the football game? (Possible responses: the sounds of the crowd, cheerleaders, and band; the smell of popcorn and hot dogs; the stands vibrating) What senses do these details appeal to? (Possible responses: sound, smell, touch) Discuss how these sensory details help the reader share the experience.

Instruct students to begin drafting their essays. Tell them to keep these questions in mind as they write:

- Does each detail relate clearly to the topic?

- Does each detail help the reader experience some aspect of the topic through the senses?

- Does each detail relate well to the other details in the paragraph?

Remind students that they are not obligated to include every detail that appears in their graphic organizers. Students may find as they write that one or two details seem less important or relevant than they did at first.

CCSS Common Core State Standards

W.6.2.b: Develop the topic with relevant facts, definitions, concrete details, quotations, or other information and examples. **W.6.3.d:** Use precise words and phrases, relevant descriptive details, and sensory language to convey experiences and events.

Write
a Descriptive Test

Week 3 • Day 1

Student Objectives

• Revise to organize information into paragraphs. *(p. 476)*

Revise

Focus on  Organization

Time Management Point out that students have about fifteen minutes to revise their drafts and that there are three revision tasks. (If you are using the Optional Revising Lessons, you will need to plan accordingly. See page T478.)

Use Paragraphs Effectively Ask students why the deleted sentence does not fit with the rest of the paragraph. (Denise's feelings about popcorn do not tell the reader anything about the scene.)

Tell students to review their drafts and look for details that do not fit into their paragraphs. Have students ask themselves the following questions:

• Can I change this detail so that it will fit better with the paragraph?

• Can this detail be moved to a different paragraph where it will fit better?

Once students have answered these questions, they can decide what to do about stray details.

 Strategies for Writers Online
Go to **www.sfw.z-b.com** for additional online resources for students and teachers.

Revise   Focus on Organization

Writing Strategy   Organize the information into paragraphs.

I know that all the sentences in a paragraph need to be about the same topic. Any details that aren't relevant to the topic of the paragraph must be removed, because they might confuse my reader. I'll go through my story again looking for any sentences that are off topic. I see one I can delete!

[DRAFT]

[deleted off-topic sentence]

We make our way to seats in the stands that surround the stadium. The smell of popcorn and hot dogs comes drafting through the stands, as we walk up the steps. It even smells like a football game! ~~Popcorn is one of my very favorite foods~~. As I look around, I see a green and yellow blur, with fans of all ages—students, parents, grandparents, and members of the community sporting the Eagles green and yellow colors and waving handheld pompons to show their spirit.

Apply

Read your story to see if any sentences do not relate to the topic of the paragraph.

476 Descriptive Writing

Differentiating Instruction

ENRICHMENT

Selecting Details Encourage students to check over the details to make sure that they are the best ones for the writing assignment. Tell students to identify weak details and replace them with details that will lift the paper beyond ordinary.

Revise

Focus on **Voice**

Writing Strategy Use a casual tone.

My story will be judged on how well I connect to my reader as I describe the event. When I talk about a personal event that I have attended myself, I need to use an appropriate casual tone, like I am talking in a friendly way to my reader. See these changes I made to add a more casual tone.

[DRAFT]

On the bleachers near the field sits the band in their ornate uniforms and hats. They're playing a team song as the cheerleaders on the field in their green and yellow skirts and sweaters open

~~The band in their ornate uniforms and hats were seen sitting on the bleachers near the field. They were heard playing a team song as the cheerleaders on the field in their green and yellow skirts and sweaters could be seen opening~~ up a huge paper banner that reads, "Go, eagles!"

Apply

A casual tone is appropriate to describe a personal event. Look for places where you can use more friendly language. Imagine you're talking to your reader.

Descriptive Test Writing 477

REINFORCEMENT

Focused Editing When it comes time to edit, instruct students to select just two or three items to check for and then to check for only one item at a time. If students try to cover too much, they will run out of time and become frustrated.

Write
a Descriptive Test

Week 3 • Day 2

Student Objectives

• Revise to use a casual tone. (p. 477)

Revise

Focus on **Voice**

Use a Friendly Tone Read the draft excerpt aloud, once without the revisions and once with the revisions, to help students hear the difference in tone. Discuss the differences between the two versions.

• What gives the revised version its friendlier, more casual tone? (Possible reason: Denise sounds more like she's speaking directly to me, the reader, and she uses a contraction—*they're*.)

If students do not note it themselves, point out that the sentences Denise replaced are in the passive voice. (If necessary, explain that in the passive voice, the subject is acted upon.) Explain that students should use passive voice only when it is effective or necessary. When used inappropriately, the passive voice gives a stiff, distanced feeling to writing. Using the active voice gives writing more energy and allows the writer to make a direct connection with the reader.

CCSS **C**ommon **C**ore **S**tate **S**tandards

W.6.2.b: Develop the topic with relevant facts, definitions, concrete details, quotations, or other information and examples. **W.6.3.d:** Use precise words and phrases, relevant descriptive details, and sensory language to convey experiences and events. **L.6.3.b:** Maintain consistency in style and tone.

Write
a Descriptive Test

Week 3 • Day 3

Student Objectives

• Revise for lively and interesting language. (p. 478)

Revise

Focus on  Word Choice

Use Interesting Words Read the draft excerpt with students. Discuss Denise's revisions and how they help create more vivid images for readers. Remind students that the purpose of a descriptive essay is to give readers a clear, accurate description. Ask:

• How does lively, interesting language support that purpose? (Possible response: Lively, interesting language helps readers feel like they can actually see and feel the scene that's being described.)

Have students read their essays to look for statements that contain words such as *big, small, nice, interesting, pretty,* and *cool* that do not convey precise images to the reader. Tell students to think of more interesting and vivid words or phrases to replace vague expressions such as these.

Online Writing Center

Provides **interactive proofreading activities** for each genre.

Revise   Focus on Word Choice

Writing Strategy   Use lively and interesting language.

The scoring guide says that I should use writing that's lively and interesting. I'm going to read through my essay again to see if any of my descriptions are boring. I notice a few areas where the words I use don't really convey what I am trying to explain. I can jazz it up with more personal language.

[DRAFT]   [added colorful and interesting language]

Along with my mother and grandmother. I have come to watch the
Eagles, the team ~~that~~ which my brother plays defense, on ~~compete~~. show their might against the Panthers As we
enter the stadium just before the game begins, I can feel the energy of
the crowd! Even though it's a cold fall night, the excitement inside the , and it feels electrifying
stadium makes it ~~seem warm~~. feel like a warm summer day

Reflect

Do the added words make the story read better?

Apply

Boring words and phrases will make your essay seem uninteresting. You can make your descriptions stand out by using words that are lively and exciting.

478 Descriptive Writing

Optional Revising Lessons

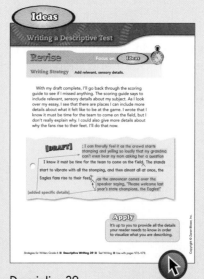

Descriptive 39

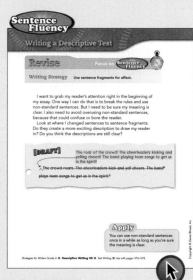

Descriptive 40

Go to ➤ *Strategies for Writers Grade 6 CD-ROM*

Edit   Focus on Conventions

Writing Strategy Check the grammar, punctuation, capitalization, and spelling.

Now I need to do a final edit on my test. I don't want to have any mistakes!

[FINAL DRAFT]   Go, Eagles!
by Denise

The roar of the crowd! The cheerleaders kicking and yelling cheers! The band playing team songs to get us in the spirit!
~~The crowd roars. The cheerleaders kick and yell cheers. The band plays team songs to get us in the spirit.~~ Eagle stadium is about to hold its first game of the season, and the crowd is going wild!

Along with my mother and my grandmother, I have come to watch the
                                                    show their might against the Panthers
Eagles, the team ~~that~~ on which my brother plays defense, ~~compete.~~ As we

enter the stadium just before the game begins, I can feel the energy of
, and it feels electrifying
the crowd! Even though it's a cold fall night, the excitement inside the
                    feel like a warm summer day
stadium makes it ~~seem warm.~~

We make our way to seats in the stands that surround the stadium.
                                                    drifting
The smell of popcorn and hot dogs comes ~~drafting~~ through the stands

Apply

It's important to check your grammar, punctuation, capitalization, and spelling every time you write for a test.

Descriptive Test Writing 479

Differentiating Instruction

ENRICHMENT
Early Finishers Some students often finish tests early and fall into the habit of simply waiting for the testing period to be over. If students have revised for writing traits and checked for conventions once, instruct them to reread the writing prompt on page 468 and carefully read their essays one more time while keeping the writing traits and the writing task in mind.

REINFORCEMENT
Support Editing Have students practice editing by writing sample sentences for correction on the board. Then ask them to take turns using the appropriate editing marks from page 475 to edit the sentences. Tailor the sentences to focus on the conventions that give students the most trouble.

Student Objectives

• Edit the writing test for proper grammar, spelling, capitalization, and punctuation. *(pp. 479–480)*

Edit

Focus on Conventions

Edit the Test Tell students that it's very hard to write a perfect descriptive essay in an hour, but they should use the five minutes they have for editing to find and correct as many errors as they can. Remind students that proofreading marks are shown on page 475.

Some students may feel that they should rewrite their drafts so that the test graders can read them easily. Explain that time spent rewriting is time spent *not* writing. Graders understand that test essays will be a little messy, with deletions, insertions, and crossed-out text. They are looking for good content, not for perfectly neat writing. Encourage students to use every minute given to strengthen content.

CCSS Common Core State Standards

W.6.3.d: Use precise words and phrases, relevant descriptive details, and sensory language to convey experiences and events. **L.6.1:** Demonstrate command of the conventions of standard English grammar and usage when writing or speaking. **L.6.2:** Demonstrate command of the conventions of standard English capitalization, punctuation, and spelling when writing. **L.6.2.b:** Spell correctly.

Review
Test Tips

Student Objectives

- Review tips for writing for a test. (p. 481)

Test Tips

Reviewing Test Writing Read and discuss each of the test tips with students. Incorporate the following thoughts:

- Remind students to always read the writing prompt carefully and completely and to make no assumptions about what the prompt might require.

- Before writing, they should look for and label the three key parts of the prompt—setup, task, and scoring guide. Also stress that not all writing test prompts will include the six traits of writing. Nevertheless, students should keep all the traits in mind as they write.

- Remind students that a writing prompt may include an illustration. Urge students to use the illustration as another clue to understanding the task.

- In addition to circling key words in the task, encourage students to mark their scoring guides, highlighting instructions they often overlook in their writing.

Strategies for Writers Online
Go to **www.sfw.z-b.com** for additional online resources for students and teachers.

[FINAL DRAFT]

On the bleachers near the field sits the band in their ornate uniforms and hats. They're playing a team song as the cheerleaders on the field in their green and yellow skirts and sweaters open as we walk up the steps. It even smells like a football game! ~~Popcorn is one of my very favorite foods.~~ As I look around, I see a green and yellow blur, with fans of all ages—students, parents, grandparents, and members of the community sporting the Eagles green and yellow colors and waving handheld pompons to show their spirit. ~~The band in their ornate uniforms and hats were seen sitting on the bleachers near the field. They were heard playing a team song as the cheerleaders on the field in their green and yellow skirts and sweaters could be seen opening~~ up a huge paper banner that reads, "Go, Eagles!"

Although it's after dark, the huge lights illuminate the field so that it looks like daytime. Across the field I ~~sea~~ see the stands filled with blue and black and more people. ~~Their~~ They're there to support the opposing team, the Panthers. ; I can literally feel it as the crowd starts stamping and yelling so loudly that my grandma can't even hear my mom asking her a question I know it must be time for the team to come on the field. The stands start to vibrate with all the stomping, and then almost all at once, the Eagles fans rise to their feet, as the announcer comes over the speaker saying, "Please welcome last year's state champions, the Eagles!" Our team comes running through the banner the cheerleaders are holding, ripping it as they cross, and the sound of the crowd is almost ~~defening~~ deafening I finally spot Number 67, my brother, as he runs onto the field and over to the sidelines. My mom and grandma and I yell even louder. The game is about to begin!

Reflect

This is your last chance! Take one more look at the scoring guide to be sure you didn't miss anything.

That's it! We've finished the test. Pretty easy, don't you think? Here are some helpful tips to remember when you write for a test.

TEST TIPS

1. **Study the writing prompt before you start to write.** Most writing prompts have three parts: the setup, the task, and the scoring guide. The parts probably won't be labeled. You'll have to figure them out for yourself!

2. **Make sure you understand the task before you start to write.**
   - Read all three parts of the writing prompt carefully.
   - Circle key words in the task part of the writing prompt that tell what kind of writing you need to do. The task might also identify your audience.
   - Make sure you know how you'll be graded.
   - Say the assignment in your own words to yourself.

3. **Keep an eye on the clock.** Decide how much time you will spend on each part of the writing process and try to stick to your schedule. Don't spend so much time prewriting that you don't have enough time left to write.

4. **Reread your writing. Compare it to the scoring guide at least twice.** Remember the rubrics you have used all year? A scoring guide on a writing test is like a rubric. It can help you keep what's important in mind.

5. **Plan, plan, plan!** You don't get much time to revise during a test, so planning is more important than ever.

6. **Write neatly.** Remember: If the people who score your test can't read your writing, it doesn't matter how good your essay is!

Descriptive Test Writing 481

Tell students that while remaining aware of their time is important, they should focus primarily on the test itself. Advise them not to worry if some students seem to finish ahead of time. They should stay focused on their own work. Similarly, remind students who do finish early to use the time to read through their writing test once more and make any last changes or corrections.

Finally, urge students who experience anxiety in test situations to keep a positive attitude and to stay relaxed throughout the test. Remind them that they have been learning and practicing the skills and strategies necessary to complete the test successfully. If any students begin to feel nervous, suggest they sit back, take a few deep breaths, relax and refocus, then resume the test. The benefits will be well worth the few seconds this takes.

CCSS **C**ommon **C**ore **S**tate **S**tandards
W.6.10: Write routinely over extended time frames (time for research, reflection, and revision) and shorter time frames (a single sitting or a day or two) for a range of discipline-specific tasks, purposes, and audiences.

Grammar Practice The mini-lessons in this section are designed to reinforce targeted grammar, usage, and mechanics skills that students can transfer to their writing. These pages are referenced throughout the Teacher Edition in the Related Grammar section. Or you may wish to use the Table of Contents on this page to choose specific lessons that will benefit your students. To provide valuable additional practice, follow up each mini-lesson with an exercise from **More Practice,** which begins on page 514.

Appendix A
Grammar Practice

Simple Sentences

Know the Rule

A **simple sentence** expresses a complete thought. It has a simple subject and a simple predicate. Helping verbs may or may not be part of the simple predicate.
Examples:
Tomás's **watch needed** repairs. (The simple subject is *watch*. The simple predicate is the verb *needed*.)
He will take his watch to a jewelry store tomorrow. (The simple subject is *He*. The simple predicate is *will take*.)

Practice the Rule

Number a sheet of paper 1–10. Copy the sentences. Underline the simple subject of each sentence once. Underline the simple predicate twice.

1. Tomás took his watch to a jewelry store.
2. The owner of the store examined Tomás's watch.
3. She suggested a new battery for the watch.
4. Two girls had entered the store before Tomás.
5. They were looking at bracelets and earrings.
6. An assistant removed the bracelets from the showcase.
7. Tomás's repairs to his watch cost five dollars.
8. He paid the owner with a ten-dollar bill.
9. His mother had given Tomás the money for the repair.
10. Tomás will give the change to his mother.

Appendix A: Grammar Practice **483**

Mini-Lesson

Student Objectives

- Identify the simple subject and simple predicate in simple sentences. *(p. 483)*

Simple Sentences

A simple sentence expresses a complete thought and has a simple subject and a simple predicate. The simple subject is the main word in the complete subject. Helping verbs, such as *were* and *will*, may be part of the simple predicate.

Display these simple sentences. Have students identify the simple subjects and simple predicates.

- *Yesterday my uncle was telling me about his hiking experiences.* **(uncle, was telling)**

- *Hiking in state parks can be great fun.* **(Hiking, can be)**

Remind students that a simple subject can also be a group of words. Display this sentence, and have students identify the simple subject and simple predicate.

- *Carlsbad Caverns is a national park in New Mexico.* **(Carlsbad Caverns, is)**

Explain that simple sentences help writers express thoughts completely and clearly. For more practice with simple sentences, see page T514.

CCSS **Common Core State Standards**
L.6.1: Demonstrate command of the conventions of standard English grammar and usage when writing or speaking.

Appendix A: Grammar Practice **T483**

Mini-Lesson

Student Objectives

• Identify predicate nouns and the subjects they rename. *(p. 484)*

Predicate Nouns

A predicate noun renames the subject of a sentence. Predicate nouns always follow linking verbs. A linking verb does not show action but links the subject of a sentence to another word in the predicate. The most common linking verb is *be*, whose forms include *is, are, was,* and *were*. Other verbs that may act as linking verbs include *become, seem, feel, taste, look,* and *appear*.

Display the following sentences. Help students identify the simple subject, the linking verb, and the predicate noun in each sentence.

- *Abraham Lincoln was the president of this country during the Civil War.* (Abraham Lincoln, was, president)

- *Bruce Catton is my grandfather's favorite Civil War historian.* (Bruce Catton, is, historian)

Explain to students that using predicate nouns enables them to include important information about the subject in a sentence. For more practice with predicate nouns, see page T514.

CCSS **Common Core State Standards**

L.6.1: Demonstrate command of the conventions of standard English grammar and usage when writing or speaking.

Predicate Nouns

Know the Rule

A **predicate noun** follows a linking verb and renames the subject of the sentence. A linking verb does not show action. Rather, it "links" a subject with another noun in the sentence. The forms of the verb *be* (*is, are, was, were*) are commonly used as linking verbs. Other verbs that may be linking verbs include *become, seem, feel, taste, look,* and *appear*. In the sentence below, the predicate noun *goalie* follows the linking verb *is* and describes the simple subject *Janice*.

> **Example:**
> **Janice** is the **goalie** on the soccer team.

Practice the Rule

Number a sheet of paper 1–10. Find the subject and the predicate noun in each sentence. Then write them in this form: **Janice=goalie**.

1. Devon's favorite sport is soccer. sport=soccer
2. His sister is the captain of our school soccer team. sister=captain
3. Her goal in yesterday's game was a controversial event. goal=event
4. It was the fatal blow to the opposing team's hope for victory. It=blow
5. Devon was certainly the most enthusiastic spectator at the game. Devon=spectator
6. By contrast, golf seems a really dull sport. golf=sport
7. My uncle, however, is an excellent golfer. uncle=golfer
8. He was the winner of this year's county championship. He=winner
9. The championship has become an annual competition. championship=competition
10. Generally, though, my friends are not fans of golf. friends=fans

Predicate Adjectives

Know the Rule

A **predicate adjective** follows a linking verb and describes the subject. In the sentence below, the predicate adjective *dull* follows the linking verb *seems* and describes the simple subject *book*.

Example:
This **book** about the environment seems **dull**.

Practice the Rule

Number a sheet of paper 1–10. Find the subject and the predicate adjective in each sentence. Then write them in this form: **book=dull**.

1. The first chapter about oil spills in the ocean seemed interesting. chapter=interesting
2. One company was responsible for an oil spill in the Gulf of Mexico. company=responsible
3. The first attempts at stopping the oil leak were unsuccessful. attempts=unsuccessful
4. Plumes of oil in the water appeared endless. Plumes=endless
5. Many residents along the Gulf of Mexico coast became angry about the company's failures. residents=angry
6. The effects of the spilled oil on coastal wildlife seemed devastating. effects=devastating
7. The damage from the oil was similar to a large spill back in 1989. damage=similar
8. After that spill, the future of fishing in part of Alaska looked bleak. future=bleak
9. After an oil spill, many people become more aware of their energy use. people=aware
10. We should always be careful about how much energy we use. we=careful

Conventions

Mini-Lesson

Student Objectives

- Identify and use predicate adjectives. *(p. 485)*

Predicate Adjectives

A predicate adjective follows a linking verb and describes the simple subject of a sentence. Remind students that *be* is a common linking verb. Other verbs that may act as linking verbs include *become, seem, feel, sound, taste, look,* and *appear.*

Display these sentences on the board. Have students identify the simple subject, the linking verb, and the predicate adjective in each.

- *My first attempt at writing poetry was terrible.* (attempt, was, terrible)

- *The rhyme in your poem seems successful.* (rhyme, seems, successful)

Then display this sentence starter. Have students suggest predicate adjectives to complete it.

- *The last book I read was _____ .* (Possible responses: boring, great, funny)

Explain to students that using predicate adjectives adds descriptive details about the subject to their sentences. For more practice with predicate adjectives, see page T514.

CCSS **C**ommon **C**ore **S**tate **S**tandards
L.6.1: Demonstrate command of the conventions of standard English grammar and usage when writing or speaking.

Conventions

Mini-Lesson

Student Objectives

• Identify dependent clauses and independent clauses. (p. 486)

Clauses

An independent clause contains a subject and a verb and expresses a complete thought. A dependent clause also contains a subject and a verb, but it does not express a complete thought. Dependent clauses usually begin with words such as *although, as, because,* and *when.* A dependent clause combined with an independent clause forms a complex sentence. Note that when a dependent clause begins a sentence, it is followed by a comma.

Display these complex sentences. Have students identify the clauses.

- *When the soccer game began, the weather was warm and sunny.* (dependent clause/independent clause)

- *The match was soon postponed because a thunderstorm moved quickly into the area.* (independent clause/dependent clause)

Explain to students that using complex sentences allows them to show the connections between closely related ideas and adds variety and flow to their writing. For more practice with clauses, see page T515.

CCSS **Common Core State Standards**
L.6.3: Use knowledge of language and its conventions when writing, speaking, reading, or listening.
L.6.3.a: Vary sentence patterns for meaning, reader/listener interest, and style.

Conventions — Grammar, Usage & Mechanics

Clauses

Know the Rule

An **independent clause** makes sense by itself and can be written as a sentence. A **dependent clause** has a subject and a verb, but it does not make complete sense by itself. It needs to be used with an independent clause. A **complex sentence** is made up of a dependent clause and an independent clause. Dependent clauses usually begin with a subordinating conjunction, such as *although, because, if, as, when,* or *unless.* At the beginning of a sentence, a dependent clause is followed by a comma.

Examples:
Abraham Lincoln was elected President of the United States in 1860. (independent clause written as a simple sentence)
Because Lincoln was against slavery, his election enraged many people in the South. (complex sentence beginning with a dependent clause followed by an independent clause)

Practice the Rule

Number a sheet of paper 1–8. Copy each sentence. Underline each dependent clause twice. Circle the subordinating conjunction. Underline each independent clause once.

1. Although I have read about the American Civil War, I am not sure about its causes.
2. Because southern plantation owners depended upon the continued practice of slavery, they opposed all attempts by the U.S. government to end it.
3. Many southern states threatened to form a separate country unless they were allowed to continue the practice of slavery.
4. People from the South and North were sharply divided over the issue of slavery as the war began.
5. When the Civil War finally ended, slaves in all the states of the union had gained their freedom.
6. Although enslaved people had gained their freedom, many were not truly free.
7. The war was hard on the whole country because more than 600,000 people had died in the war.
8. If I ever have to write a report about the Civil War, I will already know a lot of the facts.

Compound Sentences

Know the Rule

A **compound sentence** is made of two closely related independent clauses. The two clauses can be joined by a comma and a conjunction (*and, but, or*) or by a semicolon (;).

Examples:

Service dogs help people in many ways, **but** not everyone knows very much about them.

Uncle Nate uses a service dog; he is very fond of the dog.

Practice the Rule

Number a sheet of paper 1–8. Read each sentence pair. Combine the sentences in 1–3 with a semicolon. Combine the rest of the sentences with a comma and a conjunction.

1. Dogs that help individuals with disabilities are called service dogs. ^{dogs} Dogs that help farmers and law enforcement officials are called working dogs.

2. One kind of service dog is a guide dog that helps blind people. ^{another} Another valuable service dog is a signal dog that helps deaf people.

3. A signal dog can help deaf people know when the telephone rings. ^{it} It can also alert the person when a smoke alarm goes off.

4. Service dogs often help people with physical disabilities. ^{and they} They can also help people with psychological disabilities, such as autism.

5. A person does not need a special certificate or license for a service dog. ^{but the} The person who uses a service dog may require some special training.

6. Golden retrievers and Labrador retrievers make the best service dogs. ^{but there} There are exceptions.

7. People who enjoy working with animals train service dogs. ^{but not} Not all people who love animals are capable of training them.

8. Training a dog for service takes a long time. ^{and a} A person has to be willing to work many hours.

Appendix A: Grammar Practice **487**

Conventions

Mini-Lesson

Student Objectives

- Combine sentences to form compound sentences. (*p. 487*)

Compound Sentences

A compound sentence is made by combining two closely related independent clauses. Join the two clauses by adding a comma and a coordinating conjunction (*and, but, or*) or a semicolon (;). Display these pairs of independent clauses. Work with students to combine each pair to form a compound sentence.

- *I have never visited Niagara Falls. I have seen photographs of it.* (Possible response: *I have never visited Niagara Falls, but I have seen photographs of it.*)

- *My aunt has traveled to several African countries. She has also traveled to Europe.* (Possible response: *My aunt has traveled to several African countries; she has also traveled to Europe. Or … countries, and she …*)

Explain to students that being able to form different kinds of sentences will make their writing more interesting to the readers. For more practice with compound sentences, see page T515.

CCSS **Common Core State Standards**

L.6.3: Use knowledge of language and its conventions when writing, speaking, reading, or listening. **L.6.3.a:** Vary sentence patterns for meaning, reader/listener interest, and style.

Conventions

Mini-Lesson

Student Objectives

- Correct dangling and misplaced modifiers. *(p. 488)*

Dangling and Misplaced Modifiers

A dangling modifier is a verbal phrase (a phrase that contains an *-ing* or *-ed* form of a verb) that does not refer to any word in a sentence. To correct a dangling modifier, you must revise the sentence.

A misplaced modifier seems to describe the wrong word or words in a sentence. Correcting misplaced modifiers usually requires moving them closer to the word or words they modify.

Display these sentences. Have students identify the problems and suggest ways to fix them.

- *While walking home, a motorcycle roared past us.* (Dangling: While walking home, we heard a motorcycle roar past us.)

- *I watched a movie with my friend called* Star Wars. (Misplaced: I watched a movie called *Star Wars* with my friend.)

Explain that dangling modifiers and misplaced modifiers can confuse the readers. For more practice with dangling and misplaced modifiers, see page T516.

CCSS **C**ommon **C**ore **S**tate **S**tandards
L.6.1: Demonstrate command of the conventions of standard English grammar and usage when writing or speaking.

Dangling and Misplaced Modifiers

Know the Rule

Modifying phrases must always refer to a noun or a pronoun in the main part of a sentence. **Dangling modifiers** are phrases that do not refer to any particular word in the sentence.

Examples:
While eating supper, the phone rang. (incorrect)
While eating supper, I heard the phone ring. (correct)

Misplaced modifiers are words or phrases that seem to describe the wrong part of the sentence.

Examples:
It took only me five minutes to change my clothes. (not clear)
It took me only five minutes to change my clothes. (clear)

Practice the Rule

Number a sheet of paper 1–10. Identify the sentences that are correct (have no dangling modifier) by writing **Correct**.

1. Hoisting the main sail, the boat was prepared for sailing.
2. The passengers boarded the boat wearing life jackets.
3. Sitting at the tiller, the captain guided the boat among the other boats. **Correct**
4. The captain almost looked out to see the whole bay.
5. While heading away from the shore, the stars began to twinkle in the sky.
6. Silently gliding over the water, the boat moved swiftly across the bay. **Correct**
7. Leaping from the boat onto the dock, the boat was secured with a rope by a crew member.
8. The only passengers were on the boat for an hour, but they had a great time.
9. Standing on the dock, several passengers watched the boat glide away. **Correct**
10. The passengers told each other goodbye while holding their souvenirs. **Correct**

Direct Objects

Know the Rule

The **direct object** is the noun or pronoun that receives the action of the verb. Only action verbs can take a direct object. To find the direct object, say the verb and then ask "What?" or "Whom?"

Examples:

Our neighbor keeps her **books** in a separate room. (Ask: The neighbor keeps "what"? Answer: The neighbor keeps books. The direct object is *books*.)

Once in a while, her friends ask **her** for an interesting book. (Ask: Her friends ask "whom"? Her friends ask her. The direct object is *her*.)

Practice the Rule

Number a sheet of paper 1–10. Write the action verb in each sentence. Then write the direct object.

1. My cousin Raphael collects stamps.   collects; stamps
2. He cuts them from mailed letters and postcards.   cuts; them
3. Raphael owns several books about stamp collecting.   owns; books
4. He really loves his hobby.   loves; hobby
5. Aunt Janelle owned a valuable collection of coins.   owned; collection
6. My family often visited her on weekends.   visited; her
7. She once gave an old coin to me as a present.   gave; coin
8. I keep her gift in a small box under my bed.   keep; gift
9. My grandfather collected electric toy trains.   collected; trains
10. He built an elaborate track for his trains.   built; track

Conventions

Mini-Lesson

Student Objectives

• Identify direct objects. *(p. 489)*

Direct Objects

A direct object is a noun or pronoun that receives the action of an action verb. To identify the direct object in a sentence, say the verb and then ask *What* or *Whom*.

Display these sentences. Have students first identify the action verb in each. Then have them identify the direct object.

• *Today in class, Rachel presented her report on chipmunks.* (presented; report)

• *Afterwards, we complimented her on her interesting research.* (complimented; her)

Explain that a sentence may have more than one direct object. Display this sentence, and have students identify the action verb and the direct objects.

• *Chipmunks eat seeds and nuts.* (eat; seeds, nuts)

Explain to students that they can add important details to their sentences by using direct objects. For more practice with direct objects, see page T516.

CCSS **C**ommon **C**ore **S**tate **S**tandards

L.6.1: Demonstrate command of the conventions of standard English grammar and usage when writing and speaking.

Conventions

Mini-Lesson

Student Objectives

• Distinguish between concrete nouns and abstract nouns. (p. 490)

Concrete Nouns and Abstract Nouns

A concrete noun names a person, place, or thing that can be touched or recognized through the senses (*shoe, cheese, music*). An abstract noun names a feeling, an idea, or a quality (*excitement, democracy, kindness*). Display these sentences. Have students identify the concrete nouns in each sentence. Then have them identify the abstract nouns.

• *My friend talked about his love of swimming.* (friend, swimming; love)

• *Our teacher talked about her interest in ants.* (teacher, ants; interest)

Have students name some concrete nouns that name objects in the classroom. (Possible responses: chalk, books, chair, desk, aquarium) Then have them name some other abstract nouns they know (Possible responses: patriotism, sadness, anger).

Explain that using concrete nouns and abstract nouns enables them to give specific details and to talk about ideas in their writing. For more practice with this skill, see page T516.

CCSS **Common Core State Standards**
L.6.1: Demonstrate command of the conventions of standard English grammar and usage when writing or speaking.

Concrete and Abstract Nouns

Know the Rule

A **concrete noun** (*teacher, library, clarinet*) names a person, a place, or a thing that can be touched or recognized through the senses. An **abstract noun** (*joy, dream, trust*) names a feeling, an idea, or a quality.

Practice the Rule

Number a sheet of paper 1–10. Copy each sentence. Underline the concrete nouns. Circle the abstract nouns.

1. My friends and I had fun at the picnic.
2. We played soccer before lunch.
3. The excitement of the game exhausted us.
4. Our teachers barbecued hamburgers on a grill.
5. Later in the afternoon, we hiked along paths through the park.
6. The girl walking beside me stubbed her toe on the root of a tree.
7. We saw turtles along the banks of a pond.
8. Their shells glistened in the bright sunlight.
9. The day provided me with many great memories.
10. I will always remember the beauty of the sunset that night.

Singular and Plural Nouns

Know the Rule

A **singular noun** names one person, place, thing, or idea. A **plural noun** names more than one. Most nouns add *-s* or *-es* to form the plural. The spelling of some nouns changes when *-es* is added to form the plural (*puppy/puppies; life/lives*). Some nouns do not add *-s* or *-es* to form the plural; instead, they change spelling (*cactus/cacti*). Other nouns have the same form in the singular and plural (*fish*).

Examples:
Many of the **children** in the fourth grade class have **pets**.
Two **girls** own pet **mice**.
Birds can make the **lives** of their **owners** more musical.
Geese would probably not make good **pets**.

Practice the Rule

Number your paper 1–12. Copy the following chart. Give the missing singular or plural form of each noun.

Singular Nouns	Plural Nouns
1. country	countries
2. classmate	classmates
3. child	children
4. sheep	sheep
5. city	cities
6. tooth	teeth
7. man	men
8. body	bodies
9. echo	echoes
10. deer	deer
11. party	parties
12. dance	dances

Conventions

Mini-Lesson

Student Objectives

- Spell singular and plural nouns correctly. (p. 491)

Singular Nouns and Plural Nouns

A singular noun names one person, place, thing, or idea. A plural noun names more than one. Most nouns add *–s* or *–es* to form the plural (*building/buildings; fox/foxes*).

The spelling of some nouns changes when *–es* is added to form the plural (*knife/knives; country/countries*). A few nouns do not add *–s* or *–es* to form the plural; they just change spelling (*mouse/mice*). A few other nouns have the same form in the singular and plural (*sheep/sheep*).

Display these singular nouns. Have students spell the plural of each noun.

leaf (leaves)	*fly* (flies)
dress (dresses)	*woman* (women)
deer (deer)	*child* (children)
chair (chairs)	*enemy* (enemies)

Encourage students to memorize the plural forms of nouns or check a dictionary if they are uncertain.

Explain that using singular and plural nouns makes writing more precise. For more practice with singular and plural nouns, see page T517.

CCSS **C**ommon **C**ore **S**tate **S**tandards
L.6.2: Demonstrate command of the conventions of standard English capitalization, punctuation, and spelling when writing. **L.6.2b:** Spell correctly.

Conventions

Mini-Lesson

Student Objectives

• Form the possessive of singular nouns and plural nouns. *(p. 492)*

Possessive Nouns

Possessive nouns show ownership. To form the possessive of a singular noun, add an apostrophe and -*s* (*man/man's*). To form the possessive of most plural nouns ending with -*s*, add an apostrophe after the -*s* (*bears/bears'*). To form the possessive of plurals that don't end in -*s* (*women, geese*), add an apostrophe and -*s* (*women's, geese's*).

Display these phrases. Have students revise each phrase to use the possessive of the underlined noun.

• *the legs of the <u>table</u>* (the table's legs)

• *the coats of the <u>ladies</u>* (the ladies' coats)

• *the nest of the <u>mice</u>* (the mice's nest)

Display this sentence. Have students form the possessive of the noun in parentheses: *I helped clean up the (children) mess.* (children's)

Explain that using possessive nouns adds variety to writing and sometimes avoids awkward wording. For more practice with possessive nouns, see page T517.

CCSS **Common Core State Standards**
L.6.2: Demonstrate command of the conventions of standard English capitalization, punctuation, and spelling when writing. **L.6.2b:** Spell correctly.

Possessive Nouns

Know the Rule

A **possessive noun** shows ownership. To form the possessive of a singular noun, add an apostrophe and -*s* (*girl/girl's*). To form the possessive of most plural nouns that end with -*s*, add an apostrophe after the -*s* (*raccoons/raccoons'*). To form the possessive of plurals that don't end in -*s* (*children, mice*) add an apostrophe and -*s* (*children's, mice's*).

> **Examples:**
> the **man's** car
> the **students'** test results
> the **women's** shoes

Practice the Rule

Number a sheet of paper 1–5. Rewrite each phrase to use a possessive noun.

1. the attitude of the boy the boy's attitude
2. the experiences of other children other children's experiences
3. the parents of her friends her friends' parents
4. the jokes of his brothers his brothers' jokes
5. the instructions of his mother his mother's instructions

Number your paper 6–10. Write each sentence using the correct possessive form of the singular or plural noun in parentheses.

6. Samantha picked up the (kittens) toys and put them in a box. kittens'
7. Next she helped with her (brother) school project. brother's
8. After that, she helped to straighten her (mother) office. mother's
9. She wondered if other (women) offices had as many piles of paper. women's
10. That night, her (parents) praise made Samantha feel good about having finished her chores. parents'

Personal Pronouns

Know the Rule

A pronoun can take the place of a noun. Use the **personal pronouns** *I, me, we,* and *us* and the **compound personal pronouns** *myself* and *ourselves* to speak or write about yourself. Use the personal pronouns *she, her, it, he, him, you, they,* and *them* and the compound personal pronouns *herself, himself, itself, yourself, yourselves,* and *themselves* to refer to other people and things.

> **Example:**
> The **coach** asked **herself** what **she** needed to do to inspire **her** team. (The compound personal pronoun *herself* and the personal pronouns *she* and *her* refer to the noun *coach*.)

Practice the Rule

Number a sheet of paper 1–10. Write the personal pronouns you find in each sentence.

1. Joel asked himself how he could best help his team win the relay race. himself, he, his
2. He wondered if he should run before Dina or after her. he, her
3. Joel was not sure how fast she could run. she
4. Joel and Dina had never tested themselves against one another. themselves
5. Mr. Strand asked the two runners, "Have you two ever timed yourselves in a fifty-yard dash?" you, yourselves
6. Joel said, "My sister timed me last week." me
7. Dina said, "I timed myself during practice yesterday." I, myself
8. Mr. Strand told Joel and Dina to prepare themselves for a short race. themselves
9. Dina's friends urged her on as she shot from the starting line. her, she
10. The race itself proved nothing because the two runners crossed the finish line at the same time. itself

Conventions

Mini-Lesson

Student Objectives

- Use personal pronouns and compound personal pronouns. (p. 493)

Personal Pronouns

Explain that pronouns must reflect the nouns themselves (whether they are masculine, feminine, or neutral) and how the nouns are used (as subjects or objects).

Display these sentences. Have students first identify any personal pronouns and then compound personal pronouns in each sentence.

- *I myself feel prepared for the test.* (I; myself)

- *Dawn wondered if she herself could pass the test.* (she; herself)

Point out that the compound personal pronouns are used here as intensive pronouns. An intensive pronoun emphasizes its antecedent and cannot be used to replace a personal pronoun. Note that the sentence still makes sense with the removal of the intensive pronoun. For more practice with personal pronouns, see page T517.

CCSS Common Core State Standards

L.6.1.a: Ensure that pronouns are in the proper case (subjective, objective, possessive). **L.6.1.b:** Use intensive pronouns (e.g., *myself, ourselves*). **L.6.1.c:** Recognize and correct inappropriate shifts in pronoun number and person.

Conventions

Mini-Lesson

Student Objectives

- Use possessive pronouns. (p. 494)

Possessive Pronouns

Display the following sentences. Have students choose the possessive pronoun that can be used to replace each underlined word.

- *Amalia can't find <u>Amalia's</u> library card.* (her)

- *Jack returned <u>Jack's</u> overdue books.* (his)

Then display these incomplete sentences. Have students choose the possessive pronoun that completes each.

- *Two librarians ate _____ lunch in the park.* (their)

- *Lilly and I were eating _____ lunch on a bench nearby.* (our)

Advise students to watch out for common errors in their writing, such as using *their* in combination with a singular antecedent and omitting a clear antecedent for the possessive pronoun. For more practice with possessive pronouns, see page T517.

CCSS **Common Core State Standards**

L.6.1a: Ensure that pronouns are in the proper case (subjective, objective, possessive). **L.6.1.d:** Recognize and correct vague pronouns (i.e., ones with unclear or ambiguous antecedents).

Possessive Pronouns

Know the Rule

The **possessive pronouns** *my, your, her, his, its, our,* and *their* show possession. They can replace possessive nouns.

Examples:

Tyrell will play a trumpet as part of <u>Tyrell's</u> report on music.

Tyrell will play a trumpet as part of **his** report on music.

Tyrell and Mona carry <u>Tyrell's and Mona's</u> instruments in leather cases.

Tyrell and Mona carry **their** instruments in leather cases.

Practice the Rule

Number a sheet of paper 1–10. Write the possessive pronoun from the box that best completes each sentence.

my	your	her	his	its	our	their

1. Kyle and Caitlyn are working on _____ project about classical music. **their**
2. Kyle created a timeline as part of _____ contribution to the project. **his**
3. The timeline showed the births and deaths of famous composers as well as the dates of _____ important compositions. **their**
4. Caitlyn drew a portrait of the composers Mozart and Beethoven as part of _____ contribution to the project. **her**
5. You might choose to write about twentieth-century classical music for _____ report. **your**
6. In the public library, we found a book about the Spanish composer Joaquín Rodrigo as well as CDs of _____ music. **his**
7. Everyone in _____ class was excited about hearing a real classical music concert. **our**
8. Before the concert, the conductor asked us to name _____ favorite instruments. **our**
9. I told him that the clarinet was _____ favorite. **my**
10. I don't know why I chose the clarinet; I guess that I just like _____ sound. **its**

Relative and Interrogative Pronouns

Know the Rule

When the pronouns *who, whom, whose, which,* and *that* are used to introduce an adjective clause, they are called **relative pronouns**. A relative pronoun always follows the noun that the adjective clause is describing. When the pronouns *who, whom, whose, which,* and *what* are used to begin a question, they are called **interrogative pronouns**.

Examples:
Our homeroom teacher, **who** made us feel comfortable on our first day, is Mr. Streep.
What kinds of new things do sixth graders encounter as they begin middle school?

Practice the Rule

Number a sheet of paper 1–5. Write the relative pronoun or interrogative pronoun in each sentence. Then write **relative** or **interrogative** to identify the kind of pronoun each is.

1. <u>What</u> do you think are the issues facing American students today? interrogative
2. The practice of bullying is one problem <u>that</u> I think must be solved. relative
3. <u>Which</u> concern does Kasha think is most important to today's students? interrogative
4. The problem <u>that</u> Kasha has is how to score well on standardized tests. relative
5. Anyone <u>who</u> takes standardized tests knows how hard they can be. relative

Number your paper 6–10. Write the relative pronoun or interrogative pronoun that completes each sentence.

6. _____ is that boy waving his hand in the air at the back of the class? Who
7. His name is Todd, a boy _____ always has something to say about everything. who
8. _____ makes him so interested in all sorts of different topics? What
9. He reads only books _____ give information. that
10. _____ magazines do you read for information or for fun? What or Which

Conventions

Mini-Lesson

Student Objectives

- Identify relative pronouns and interrogative pronouns. *(p. 495)*

Relative and Interrogative Pronouns

An adjective clause always follows the noun it describes. When the clause is nonrestrictive (not necessary), it is set off by commas.

When the pronouns *who, whom, whose, which,* and *what* begin a question, they are called interrogative pronouns.

Display these sentences. Have students identify each underlined word as a relative pronoun or an interrogative pronoun and explain their answers.

- *<u>Who</u> was the third president of the United States?* (interrogative; It begins a question.)

- *Thomas Jefferson is the president <u>whom</u> you are asking about.* (relative; It begins an adjective clause.)

Being able to use relative pronouns and interrogative pronouns enables writers to add information to their sentences and to vary sentence structures. For more practice with relative and interrogative pronouns, see page T518.

CCSS **C**ommon **C**ore **S**tate **S**tandards
L.6.2.a: Use punctuation (commas, parentheses, dashes) to set off nonrestrictive/parenthetical elements. **L.6.3.a:** Vary sentence patterns for meaning, reader/listener interest, and style.

Conventions

Mini-Lesson

Student Objectives

- Identify perfect tense verbs. (p. 496)

The Perfect Tenses

The present-perfect tense shows action that started in the past and was completed at some time or may still be occurring. To form the present perfect, use the helping verb *has* or *have* with the past participle of a verb. (*I have known Aidan for two years.*) The past-perfect tense shows action that was definitely completed in the past. To form the past perfect, use *had* with the past participle. (*I thought I had locked the door.*) Other words can come between the helping verb and the past participle. (*I have never liked carrots.*)

Display these sentences. Have students identify each verb phrase and its tense.

- *Jack had rarely used a dictionary.* (had used, past-perfect tense)

- *We have now learned the value of dictionaries.* (have learned, present-perfect tense)

The perfect tenses enable writers to describe precisely when an action occurred. For more practice with the perfect tenses, see page T518.

CCSS Common Core State Standards
L.6.1: Demonstrate command of the conventions of standard English grammar and usage when writing or speaking.

Conventions Grammar, Usage & Mechanics

The Perfect Tenses

Know the Rule

The **present-perfect tense** shows action that started in the past and was completed at some time or may still be occurring. To form the present-perfect tense, use the helping verb *has* or *have* with the past participle of a verb (*have known*). The **past-perfect tense** shows action that was definitely completed in the past. To form the past-perfect tense, add the helping verb *had* to the past participle of a verb (*had believed*).

Example:
Have you ever **heard** of the English explorer Henry Hudson? I **had known** just a little bit about him before I read his biography.

Practice the Rule

Number a sheet of paper 1–10. Write the sentences, using the helping verb in parentheses to form the present-perfect tense or the past-perfect tense that correctly completes each sentence.

1. Henry Hudson (has/had) made several voyages to the northeastern coasts of North America before he sailed farther south.
2. He didn't know it at the time, but he (have/had) sailed into what would become New York harbor.
3. He and his crew (has/had) landed on the coast of what would become New York City.
4. His name (has/have) survived as the name of the Hudson River in New York State.
5. Many books and Hollywood movies (has/have) recounted Hudson's brave explorations.
6. An explorer who also (has/had) made several voyages to North America in the early 1600s was Samuel de Champlain.
7. Champlain's name (has/have) survived as the name of a large lake between Vermont, New York, and Canada.
8. Champlain (has/had) named it after himself after he first saw it in 1609.
9. Only one president (has/have) had a state named after him.
10. (Has/Have) you ever wondered how your state got its name?

496 Appendix A: Grammar Practice

Transitive and Intransitive Verbs

Know the Rule

Action verbs may or may not take an object to complete the action of the verb. An action verb that has an object is called a **transitive verb**. A verb that expresses action without an object is called an **intransitive verb**. Many verbs can be either transitive or intransitive, depending on how they are used in the sentence.

Examples:
The pitcher **threw** a wild **pitch**. (transitive verb with the direct object *pitch*)
The batter **ducked**. (intransitive verb, no object needed)
Luckily, the ball **missed** the **batter**. (transitive verb with the direct object *batter*)
The fans **yelled**. (intransitive verb, no object needed)
They **yelled** threats at the pitcher. (transitive verb with the object *threats*)

Practice the Rule

Number a sheet of paper 1–10. Write the action verb in each sentence. Label it **transitive** or **intransitive**. If the verb is a transitive verb, write the object that goes with it.

1. The umpire <u>raised</u> his hands, signaling time out. transitive; hands
2. He <u>explained</u> the rules to the managers of both teams. transitive; rules
3. They <u>listened</u> carefully. intransitive
4. Both managers <u>shrugged</u> their shoulders. transitive; shoulders
5. After the brief dispute, the game <u>resumed</u>. intransitive
6. The next batter <u>swung</u> the bat hard. transitive; bat
7. The ball <u>rolled</u> out of play. intransitive
8. Then the rain <u>began</u>. intransitive
9. The ground crew <u>covered</u> the field with a tarp. transitive; field
10. At the end of the game, the fans <u>cheered</u>. intransitive

---

Mini-Lesson

Student Objectives

- Identify transitive and intransitive verbs. (*p. 497*)

Transitive Verbs and Intransitive Verbs

A transitive verb is an action verb that takes an object, a noun or pronoun that shows *who* or *what* is affected by the action. An intransitive verb is an action verb that does not take an object. Many verbs can be transitive or intransitive, depending on how they are used in a sentence.

- *Lily <u>misunderstood</u> my question.* (transitive)
- *Shawn <u>misunderstood</u>.* (intransitive)

Display these sentences. Have students identify the action verb in each and tell whether the verb is transitive or intransitive. Then have them identify the object of the transitive verb.

- *The mayor delivered her speech at the town hall meeting.* (delivered, transitive; speech)
- *Everyone listened carefully.* (listened, intransitive)

Tell students that knowing if a verb is transitive or intransitive helps them write and speak more clearly. For more practice with transitive and intransitive verbs, see page T518.

CCSS **C**ommon **C**ore **S**tate **S**tandards

L.6.1: Demonstrate command of the conventions of standard English grammar and usage when writing or speaking.

Mini-Lesson

Student Objectives
• Identify articles. (*p. 498*)

Articles

The words *a, an,* and *the* are special adjectives called articles. Use *the* when referring to a specific noun, whether singular or plural (*the highway, the cars*). Use *a* or *an* when referring to a general noun (*a bus, an airplane*).

An article can come before a noun or another adjective. Use *a* before a word that begins with a consonant sound and *an* before a word that begins with a vowel sound (*a wrecked car, an old train*).

Display the following sentences. Have students identify the articles in each sentence.

- *An empty train approached the subway station.* **(An, the)**
- *A passenger asked the conductor for a map.* **(A, the, a)**

Explain to students that using articles correctly enables them to communicate information about nouns more accurately. For more practice with articles, see page T519.

CCSS **Common Core State Standards**

L.6.1: Demonstrate command of the conventions of standard English grammar and usage when writing or speaking.

Articles

Know the Rule

Adjectives describe nouns. The words *a, an,* and *the* are adjectives called **articles**. Use *a* or *an* to refer to a general noun. Use *a* before a singular word that begins with a consonant sound and *an* before a singular word that begins with a vowel sound. Use *the* when you refer to a specific noun, whether singular or plural.

Examples:
Mom needs **a** new computer.
Her computer is **an** old model.
The computer we have at home is broken.
Unfortunately, **the** computers we've seen in stores are expensive.

Practice the Rule

Number a sheet of paper 1–10. Write each sentence, using the correct article or articles in parentheses. Then underline the word it modifies.

1. (A/An) computer is (a/an) machine that receives and stores information.
2. The first electronic computers were about the size of (a/an) room.
3. Today people can carry (a/an) computer easily.
4. Adults and children use computers for (a/an) number of purposes.
5. (A/An) child might use (a/an) computer to play (a/an) game or to write (a/an) essay for school.
6. Almost everyone has used some sort of electronic device to write (a/an) e-mail or another kind of message.
7. The world of today almost requires that (a/an) individual own (a/an) cell phone and (a/an) computer.
8. The scientists who created computers probably did not foresee (a/an) world like ours.
9. If you could create (a/an) invention, what would it be?
10. Remember, the person who first thought of computers started out as (a/an) kid just like everyone else.

Interjections

Know the Rule

An **interjection** expresses emotion and is not related grammatically to any of the other words in a sentence. Words like *hurray, oh, ah, wow,* and *hush* are interjections because they exclaim, protest, or command. An interjection usually appears at the beginning of a sentence. An exclamation mark or a comma may follow it. When you write, choose the punctuation for the effect that you want to convey.

Examples:

Hey! Why are we going to the museum's dinosaur room?

Hush, just listen to me and you'll find out

Practice the Rule

Number a sheet of paper 1–10. Write the interjection in each sentence. Then add the appropriate punctuation after the interjection.

1. Wow __!__ Look at this great dinosaur skeleton!
2. Ah __,__ that's all you ever want to see when we visit the museum.
3. Oh __,__ I don't think that's true at all.
4. Hey __!__ Check out this dinosaur footprint preserved in tar.
5. Good grief __!__ There must be more interesting things in the museum!
6. Well __,__ let's try to find the animal habitat displays.
7. Okay __!__ Now you're talking about something that interests me!
8. Whew __,__ I thought I'd never find anything that you liked.
9. Oh, no __!__ The guard says that the animal habitats are closed for repairs.
10. Hurray __!__ It's back to the dinosaurs we go!

Mini-Lesson

Student Objectives

• Identify and use interjections. (p. 499)

Interjections

An interjection is a word that expresses emotion. Words like *hurray, oh, ah, wow,* and *hush* are interjections. They usually appear at the beginning of a sentence. An exclamation mark or a comma may follow the interjection. When you write, choose the punctuation for the effect that you want to convey. An exclamation mark shows stronger emotion than a comma.

Display these sentences. Have students identify the interjection in each and the punctuation that follows it.

• *Wow! That's a beautiful poster.* (Wow, exclamation mark)

• *Oh, do you really like it?* (Oh, comma)

Point out that when an exclamation mark follows an interjection, the next word begins with a capital letter.

Explain to students that using interjections now and then enables them to express strong emotions in their writing, especially in dialogue. For more practice with interjections, see page T519.

CCSS Common Core State Standards

L.6.2: Demonstrate command of the conventions of standard English capitalization, punctuation, and spelling when writing.

Conventions

Mini-Lesson

Student Objectives

- Identify and use subordinating conjunctions. *(p. 500)*

Subordinating Conjunctions

Subordinating conjunctions tell how a clause in a sentence is related to the rest of the sentence. Some commonly used subordinating conjunctions are *although, as, because, before, if, since, unless, until,* and *when.* Subordinating conjunctions begin adverb clauses (which are dependent clauses). A comma comes at the end of an adverb clause when the clause begins a sentence.

Display the following sentences. Help students identify the adverb clause in each sentence and the subordinating conjunction that begins each clause.

- *Although rain had fallen for days,* the river had not flooded. **(Although)**

- *People in town became anxious as the level of the river's water rose.* **(as)**

A sentence that contains an adverb clause is a complex sentence. Knowing how to form different kinds of sentences allows students to include important information in their writing and create a variety of sentences. For more practice with subordinating conjunctions, see page T519.

CCSS **Common Core State Standards**

L.6.3: Use knowledge of language and its conventions when writing, speaking, reading, or listening. **L.6.3.a:** Vary sentence patterns for meaning, reader/listener interest, and style.

Conventions **Grammar, Usage & Mechanics**

Subordinating Conjunctions

Know the Rule

> **Subordinating conjunctions,** such as *although, because, before, if, since,* and *so that,* show how one clause is related to another. Subordinating conjunctions are used at the beginning of adverb clauses. Notice that a comma is used at the end of the adverb clause when it comes first in a sentence.
>
> **Examples:**
> **If** Chante had not been assigned the report, she would not have learned about wind power.
> She and her group members went to the library **so that** they could research the topic.

Practice the Rule

Number a sheet of paper 1–10. Choose a subordinating conjunction from above to complete each sentence.

1. Chanté was looking for articles on wind power _____ she was working on a group project on that topic for class. **because**

2. She did not know how wind turbines worked, _____ she had seen some turning in a field. **although**

3. _____ wind power became popular among environmentalists, solar power had been promoted as the best renewable energy. **Because**

4. _____ wind power has become popular, a lot of controversy has surrounded it. **Since**

5. Some people don't want wind turbines near them _____ they are noisy. **because**

6. Other people wonder what will happen _____ we don't use more renewable energy sources. **if**

7. Chanté tried to find out as much as she could _____ she gave her report. **before**

8. You can look on a website about wind power _____ you want to know more about it. **if**

9. _____ she began her report, Chanté had never thought about wind power. **Before**

10. Chanté has become a believer in wind power _____ she did her report. **since**

Compound Personal Pronouns

Know the Rule

The **compound personal pronouns** are these: *myself, yourself, himself, herself, itself, ourselves, yourselves,* and *themselves.* Depending on how they are used in a sentence, they are also known as **reflexive** or **intensive pronouns.**

- A reflexive pronoun reflects back on the subject.
   Example:
   Grandpa and Grandma built their house **themselves.**

- An intensive pronoun emphasizes the subject. It often appears right after the subject.
   Example:
   Grandma **herself** put on all the shingles.

Practice the Rule

Number a sheet of paper 1–10. Write each sentence with the correct compound personal pronoun. Underline the antecedent (the word or words to which the pronoun refers) for each sentence.

1. I _____ had a tough time finding a quiet place to do my homework last night. myself
2. My older sister was doing homework _____, too. herself
3. She and one of her friends closed _____ in her room. themselves
4. Suddenly, the bedroom door seemed to open all by _____. itself
5. The noise from my sister's TV was so loud that I couldn't hear _____ think. myself
6. My sister should know better than to distract _____ with noise while doing homework. herself
7. She _____ always tells me to keep quiet when she's studying. herself
8. I asked my father for help, but he said we should settle the problem _____. ourselves
9. My father _____ prefers to have some quiet time in the evening. himself
10. Finally, everyone had settled _____ down for the rest of the evening. themselves

Appendix A: Grammar Practice 501

Conventions

Mini-Lesson

Student Objectives

- Identify and use compound personal pronouns. *(p. 501)*

Compound Personal Pronouns

The compound personal pronouns are *myself, yourself, himself, herself, itself, ourselves, yourselves,* and *themselves.* Depending on how they are used, they are also known as reflexive pronouns or intensive pronouns. A reflexive pronoun reflects back on the subject. *(Maria forces herself to read one book each month.)* An intensive pronoun emphasizes the subject; it can be removed from a sentence without affecting the meaning. *(Ms. Taylor herself donated some books to the library.)*

Display the following incomplete sentences. Have students choose the compound personal pronoun that completes each and explain how the pronoun is used.

- *Jason reminded _____ to call Devon after school.* (himself, reflexive pronoun)

- *The players _____ decided to practice for an extra hour.* (themselves, intensive pronoun)

Using compound personal pronouns enables writers to add important information to sentences. For more practice with compound personal pronouns, see page T519.

CCSS **C**ommon **C**ore **S**tate **S**tandards

L.6.1: Demonstrate command of the conventions of standard English grammar and usage when writing or speaking. **L.6.1.b:** Use intensive pronouns (e.g., *myself, ourselves*).

Conventions

Mini-Lesson

Student Objectives

- Use words correctly. (p. 502)

Using the Right Word

Some words are often misused in writing. Words such as *coarse* and *course* sound the same but have different meanings. Other words, such as *between* and *among*, have similar meanings but different uses. Using words correctly is characteristic of standard English.

Some other commonly misused words include these pairs:

accept/except	*affect/effect*
beside/besides	*bring/take*
good/well	*or/nor*

Display these sentences. Have students choose the word in parentheses that should be used to complete each sentence.

- *May I (bring/take) this book back to my desk?* **(take)**

- *Neither Douglas (or/nor) Julia liked this book.* **(nor)**

- *Tina played really (good/well) in today's basketball game.* **(well)**

Explain to students that using words correctly in their writing improves their expression and use of conventional language. For more practice with using the right word, see page T520.

CCSS **C**ommon **C**ore **S**tate **S**tandards

L.6.1.e: Recognize variations from standard English in their own and others' writing and speaking, and identify and use strategies to improve expression in conventional language. **L.6.2.b:** Spell correctly.

Conventions Grammar, Usage & Mechanics

Using the Right Word

Know the Rule

Some words are often misused in writing. Some words, such as *new* and *knew*, sound the same but have different meanings. Other words, such as *fewer* and *less*, have similar meanings but different uses. It is important to know how to use the right word so your readers will not be confused.

Examples:

I cannot **accept** the invitation to the party.
I'm free every night **except** the night of the party.

Practice the Rule

Number a sheet of paper 1–10. Write each sentence, using the correct word in parentheses. Check the meanings of the words in a dictionary if necessary.

1. Please (bring/take) these color markers back to your desk.
2. Would you please (bring/take) your report up to my desk?
3. We have (fewer/less) minutes between classes this year than we had last year.
4. This means that we have (fewer/less) time to talk with friends in the hallways.
5. I had to build something from wood for my art (coarse/course).
6. I used a (coarse/course) piece of sandpaper to work on my birdfeeder.
7. Hearing about natural disasters, such as floods, usually (affects/effects) people in different ways.
8. The newspaper article described the damaging (affects/effects) of the tornado.
9. Each student was (allowed/aloud) just five minutes to present his or her oral report.
10. As part of her report, Janelle read (allowed/aloud) some poems she had written.

Irregular Verbs

Know the Rule

Many commonly used verbs are **irregular;** the past tense of these verbs is not formed by adding *-ed*. The chart lists some irregular verbs.

Present	Past	With *has, have,* or *had*
begin	began	begun
become	became	become
draw	drew	drawn
keep	kept	kept

Practice the Rule

Number a sheet of paper 1–10. Write each sentence, using the correct form of the irregular verb in parentheses.

1. A professional artist (speak) to our class yesterday. spoke
2. She (tell) us about an artist named Pablo Picasso. told
3. I had (hear) of Picasso before from my older brother. heard
4. Picasso (begin) painting when he was seven years old. began
5. By the age of twenty-five, Picasso had (become) a famous artist. become
6. Last year Jon always (draw) the best pictures. drew
7. The school (keep) most of his drawings on display. kept
8. Jon (become) interested in drawing when he visited the art museum. became
9. After his visit, he (begin) to draw pencil sketches. began
10. Eventually he (become) interested in working with charcoal. became

Appendix A: Grammar Practice 503

Conventions

Mini-Lesson

Student Objectives

- Identify and use irregular verbs. (p. 503)

Irregular Verbs

Many verbs in English are irregular verbs. The past tense of these verbs is not formed by adding *-ed*. The best way to learn the forms of irregular verbs is to memorize them. The chart lists some irregular verbs and their past-tense forms.

Present	**Past**	**With *has, have,* or *had***
break	*broke*	*broken*
choose	*chose*	*chosen*
hear	*heard*	*heard*
know	*knew*	*known*

Display these sentences. Have students identify the irregular verb in each. Then have students give the other forms of the verb.

- *We rode to a restaurant last night in my dad's truck.* (rode; ride, have ridden)

- *We have eaten at the restaurant many times.* (have eaten; eat, ate)

Tell students that using irregular verbs correctly will help them improve their expression in conventional language. For more practice with irregular verbs, see page T520.

CCSS Common Core State Standards

L.6.1.e: Recognize variations from standard English in their own and others' writing and speaking, and identify and use strategies to improve expression in conventional language. **L.6.2.b:** Spell correctly.

Mini-Lesson

Student Objectives

- Avoid using double negatives. (p. 504)

Avoiding Double Negatives

The words *no, not, nothing, none, never, nowhere,* and *nobody* are called *negatives.* The *n't* in contractions (*don't*) is also a negative. In standard English, only one negative is used in a sentence.

To correct a double negative (the use of two negatives in one sentence), you can replace one of the negatives with a positive word, such as *any, anybody, anything, either,* and *ever.* Sometimes taking out one negative solves the problem.

Display these sentences. Have students identify each double negative and suggest how to correct it.

- *My sister and I don't never watch television at night.* (don't never; don't ever or My sister and I never watch ...)

- *Julian didn't want none of the soup.* (didn't ... none; didn't want any or Julian wanted none ...)

Avoiding double negatives improves expression and the use of conventional language. For more practice with avoiding double negatives, see page T520.

CCSS Common Core State Standards
L.6.1: Demonstrate command of the conventions of standard English grammar and usage when writing or speaking. **L.6.1e:** Recognize variations from standard English in their own and others' writing and speaking, and identify and use strategies to improve expression in conventional language.

Avoiding Double Negatives

Know the Rule

A **negative** is a word that means "no" or "not." The words *no, not, nothing, none, never, nowhere,* and *nobody* are negatives. The *n't* in a contraction (*don't, can't*) is also a negative. Use only one negative word in a sentence. You can use positive words in place of a negative word to write a correct sentence. Positive words include *any, anybody, anything, either,* and *ever.*

Examples:
I have**n't** done **nothing** all morning. (incorrect)
I have done **nothing** all morning. (correct)
I have**n't** done **anything** all morning. (correct)

Practice the Rule

Number a sheet of paper 1–10. Write the word or words in parentheses that complete each sentence.

1. I don't know (nothing/anything) I like more than soccer.
2. Nobody could (ever/never) convince me that basketball was more exciting.
3. As for excitement, baseball doesn't come close to soccer, (neither/either).
4. I can't stand watching (any/no) other sport on television.
5. Nothing (no one/anyone) says could ever change my mind.
6. There is (nothing/anything) better than watching an exciting soccer game.
7. If I can't (either/neither) play or watch soccer, then I read about it.
8. I don't (ever/never) read books just about soccer.
9. When I can't find (no/any) soccer books, I read about world history.
10. Still, I couldn't (ever/never) imagine a world without soccer.

Subject-Verb Agreement

Know the Rule

The **subject** and its **verb** must **agree** in number. That is, a singular subject takes a singular verb. A plural subject takes a plural verb. There are special rules for certain kinds of subjects. A **collective noun,** such as *family, country, team,* or *herd,* names more than one person or object acting together as one group. These nouns are almost always considered singular. (*The country is changing its form of money.*) Most indefinite pronouns, including *everyone, nobody, nothing,* and *anything,* are considered singular. (*Not everyone is happy about the change.*) A few **indefinite pronouns,** such as *many* and *several,* are considered plural. (*Many plan to protest.*)

Practice the Rule

Number a sheet of paper 1–10. Write each sentence, using the verb in parentheses that agrees in number with the subject. Then underline the simple subject in the sentence.

1. Many people (use/uses) spices when cooking meals.
2. Spices (add/adds) flavor to food.
3. Also, several (appear/appears) in certain perfumes and cosmetic products.
4. One of the more common spices (are/is) pepper.
5. Everyone (sprinkle/sprinkles) a little pepper on scrambled eggs.
6. Cinnamon trees (grow/grows) in Southeast Asia, Africa, and South America.
7. The spice (come/comes) from the bark of the cinnamon tree.
8. Nothing (taste/tastes) better than cinnamon in applesauce!
9. The production of spices (is/are) a huge business around the world.
10. Many (lose/loses) their fragrance and taste after a year on a kitchen shelf.

Appendix A: Grammar Practice **505**

Mini-Lesson

Student Objectives

- Understand subject-verb agreement. *(p. 505)*

Subject-Verb Agreement

The subject and the verb in a sentence must agree in number. A singular subject takes a singular verb. A plural subject takes a plural verb.

A collective noun (*family, club*) names a group. These nouns are often considered singular. (*The club meets every Friday.*) Most indefinite pronouns, including *everyone, nobody, nothing,* and *anything* are considered singular. (*Everyone wants a carnival ticket.*) A few indefinite pronouns, such as *many* and *several,* are considered plural. (*Several prefer basketball to baseball.*)

Display these sentences. Have students identify the simple subject and choose the verb in parentheses that agrees in number with the subject.

- *My class (enjoys/enjoy) field trips.* **(class, enjoys)**
- *Nothing in school (is/are) more fun than a field trip.* **(Nothing, is)**

Explain that using proper subject-verb agreement improves expression in writing. For more practice with subject-verb agreement, see page T521.

CCSS **C**ommon **C**ore **S**tate **S**tandards
L.6.1: Demonstrate command of the conventions of standard English grammar and usage when writing or speaking.

Mini-Lesson

Student Objectives

- Use capitalization and punctuation in sentences correctly. *(p. 506)*

Writing Sentences Correctly

A declarative sentence makes a statement and ends with a period. An interrogative sentence asks a question and ends with a question mark. An imperative sentence gives a command and ends with a period or an exclamation point. An exclamatory sentence shows excitement and ends with an exclamation point. Every sentence begins with a capital letter.

Display these sentences without capitals or end marks. Have students correct the sentences.

- *are you and your friend in the same class* (Are, ?)

- *tell me the subjects you like best* (Tell, .)

- *math is probably my favorite class* (Math, .)

- *recess is the very best time of the day* (Recess, ! or .)

Tell students that correctly written sentences are much clearer and easier to understand. For more practice with writing sentences correctly, see page T521.

CCSS **Common Core State Standards**
L.6.2: Demonstrate command of the conventions of standard English capitalization, punctuation, and spelling when writing.

Writing Sentences Correctly

Know the Rule

Begin every sentence with a capital letter. A **declarative sentence** makes a statement and ends with a period. An **interrogative sentence** asks a question and ends with a question mark. An **imperative sentence** gives a command and ends with a period or an exclamation point. An **exclamatory sentence** shows excitement and ends with an exclamation point. When you write, choose the punctuation that is right for the effect you want to convey.

Examples:

Have you ever watched a silent movie**?** (interrogative sentence)

We don't know what a silent movie is**.** (declarative sentence)

Wow! I can't believe you've never heard of silent movies**!** (exclamatory sentence)

Tell me what they are**.** (imperative sentence)

Practice the Rule

Number a sheet of paper 1–10. Write each sentence correctly. Use capital letters and appropriate punctuation marks.

1. before the 1920s, most movies did not have sound .
2. how could you tell what was going on in the movie ?
3. captions that the audience had to read were inserted in the movie .
4. good grief! watching a movie back then must have been really boring !
5. come with me to the library .
6. does the library have any silent movies that we could check out ?
7. you bet! the library probably has a hundred silent movies !
8. tell me the titles of a few famous silent movies .
9. was D. W. Griffith a famous silent movie director ?
10. we want to learn more about silent movies .

Capitalization

Know the Rule

Begin the following with a capital letter: proper noun (*India*), proper adjective (*Boston baked beans*), title of respect (*Doctor Johnson*), initial (*J. S. Bach*), first word in a sentence, month (*April*), and day of the week (*Saturday*).

Practice the Rule

Number a sheet of paper 1–5. Write each phrase using capital letters correctly.

1. the first monday in october
2. my dentist doctor Sanchez
3. the asian country of vietnam
4. our neighbor pastor kim
5. my birthday in june

Number your paper 6–10. Write each sentence, using capital letters correctly.

6. robert louis stevenson is a famous scottish author.
7. he was born in november 1850 in the city of edinburgh.
8. edinburgh is the capital of scotland.
9. the author who created the character peter pan, j. m. barrie, admired stevenson's work.
10. this friday, I am going to get some of r. l. stevenson's books from the public library.

Conventions

Mini-Lesson

Student Objectives

- Use capitalization correctly. (p. 507)

Capitalization

Capitalize the first word in a sentence and important words in titles, including the first and last words. Always capitalize proper nouns and proper adjectives.

Proper nouns name geographical places, holidays, organizations, and historical documents. The word *the* that comes before some proper nouns is usually not capitalized (*the Civil War*). Proper adjectives usually are forms of a proper noun (*Europe/European*).

Write the following phrases. Have students capitalize where appropriate.

- *the european country of italy* (European, Italy)
- *the last friday in december* (Friday, December)
- *the famous science fiction writer h. p. lovecraft* (H.P. Lovecraft)
- *the justices on the united states supreme court* (United States Supreme Court)

Capitalization helps a word serve a purpose or distinguishes a word from surrounding text. For more practice with capitalization, see page T521.

CCSS **C**ommon **C**ore **S**tate **S**tandards
L.6.2: Demonstrate command of the conventions of standard English capitalization, punctuation, and spelling when writing.

Mini-Lesson

Student Objectives

- Understand abbreviations. (p. 508)

Initials and Abbreviations

An abbreviation is a shortened form of a word. Abbreviations usually begin with a capital letter and end with a period. Explain that abbreviations are not appropriate in formal writing. They are appropriately used for letters and envelopes and in e-mail and texting.

An initial can replace part of a person's name (*C. S. Lewis/Clive Staples Lewis*).

Display these abbreviations. Have students identify the word each stands for.

Sen. (Senator)
Wed. (Wednesday)
Ave. (Avenue)
Corp. (Corporation)
Rev. (Reverend)
Sept. (September)

Tell students that they should learn standard abbreviations so they can use them when appropriate. For more practice with abbreviations, see page T522.

CCSS **Common Core State Standards**
L.6.2: Demonstrate command of the conventions of standard English capitalization, punctuation, and spelling when writing.

Initials and Abbreviations

Know the Rule

An **abbreviation** is a shortened form of a word. **Titles of respect** are often abbreviated (*Dr., Rev.*). So are words in **addresses,** such as Street (*St.*), Road (*Rd.*), and Apartment (*Apt.*). **Days** (*Fri.*), some **months** (*Nov.*), and parts of **business names** (*Co.* for Company) are often abbreviated in informal notes. Abbreviations usually begin with a capital letter and end with a period. An **initial** can replace the name of a person or place. An initial is written as a capital letter followed by a period (*W. S. Merwin for William Stanley Merwin*).

Practice the Rule

Number a sheet of paper 1–5. Write the word that each abbreviation stands for.

1. Mr. **Mister**
2. Oct. **October**
3. Ave. **Avenue**
4. Thurs. **Thursday**
5. Gov. **Governor**

Number your paper 6–10. Write each item using initials and abbreviations where possible.

6. the waiting room of Doctor Kelly's office **Dr. Kelly's**
7. a magazine article about General Patton **Gen. Patton**
8. the poet Thomas Stearns Eliot **T. S. Eliot**
9. the last Sunday in August **Sun.; Aug.**
10. 280 75th Street, Apartment 2 **St.; Apt.**

Titles

Know the Rule

When writing, underline the **titles** of longer works, such as **books, magazines, newspapers,** and **movies**. In printed texts, such as papers that you prepare on the computer, these titles appear in italics. Use quotation marks around the titles of shorter works, such as **songs, stories,** and **poems**. Capitalize the first word and the last word in titles. Capitalize all other words except articles, short prepositions, and coordinating conjunctions. Also, capitalize short verbs, such as *is* and *are*.

Practice the Rule

Number a sheet of paper 1–5. Rewrite each sentence, punctuating and capitalizing each title correctly.

1. I have never seen the movie batman returns.
2. You could probably find a review of it at the website for a major newspaper, such as the washington post.
3. You could also check the websites for the magazines time and newsweek.
4. I found the Robert Frost poem stopping by woods on a snowy evening online.
5. The lyrics of the star-spangled banner (our national anthem) can also be found online.

Number your paper 6–10. Write each title correctly.

6. america the beautiful (song)
7. the emperor of ice cream (poem)
8. the dallas morning news (newspaper)
9. maniac magee (novel)
10. the legend of sleepy hollow (short story)

Conventions

Mini-Lesson

Student Objectives

- Write titles correctly. *(p. 509)*

Titles

When writing by hand, underline the titles of long works (books, magazines, newspapers, and movies). When writing on a computer, style these titles in italics. Whether writing by hand or on a computer, place quotation marks around the titles of shorter works (songs, stories, and poems).

Capitalize the first word and the last word as well as all nouns, verbs, adjectives, adverbs, and other words that have more than three letters. Do not capitalize articles, short prepositions (three letters or fewer), or coordinating conjunctions.

Display these titles. Have students capitalize each and explain how the title should appear when handwritten and written on a computer.

- *the twilight saga: eclipse* (movie) (*The Twilight Saga: Eclipse;* underlined, italic)

- *just dance* (pop song) ("Just Dance"; quotation marks)

- *a wrinkle in time* (novel) (*A Wrinkle in Time;* underlined, italic)

For more practice with titles, see page T522.

CCSS **C**ommon **C**ore **S**tate **S**tandards

L.6.2: Demonstrate command of the conventions of standard English capitalization, punctuation, and spelling when writing.

Conventions

Mini-Lesson

Student Objectives
• Use commas in a series. *(p. 510)*

Commas

A series is a list of three or more words or phrases in a sentence. Commas are used to separate items in a series. Each item in a series might consist of one word or a longer phrase. The last comma in a series goes before the conjunction (*and, or*).

Display these sentences. Have students tell where commas are needed and identify the conjunction used.

• *Records tapes and CDs seem old-fashioned to us kids.* **(Records, tapes, and CDs; and)**

• *Did Megan Kelvin Lynn or Joel lose a cell phone?* **(Megan, Kelvin, Lynn, or Joel; or)**

Remind students that a comma acts as a short pause in sentences. Have volunteers read aloud the example sentences, pausing at the commas.

Explain that using commas in a series can help prevent confusion in writing. For more practice with commas, see page T522.

CCSS **C**ommon **C**ore **S**tate **S**tandards
L.6.2: Demonstrate command of the conventions of standard English capitalization, punctuation, and spelling when writing.

Commas

Know the Rule

A series is a list of three or more words or phrases. **Commas** are used to separate items in a series. Each item in a series might consist of one word or a longer phrase. The last comma in a series goes before the conjunction (*and, or*).

Examples:

My **friend,** my friend's **parents,** and **I** went to a baseball game last week.

Did you have a **pizza,** a **hot dog,** or just a **soda** for a snack?

Practice the Rule

Number a sheet of paper 1–10. Rewrite each sentence, adding commas where appropriate. Underline the conjunction used in each series.

1. My favorite player hit a single, a double, and a home run.
2. My friends Dina, Miguel, and Felix also attended the game.
3. The batter, the catcher, and the umpire got into a heated argument.
4. Is your favorite sport baseball, football, basketball, or soccer?
5. Should we play baseball at the park on Thursday, Friday, or Saturday?
6. My friends and I will play summer league baseball in June, July, and August.
7. Florida, Texas, and Ohio each have two Major League baseball teams.
8. The teams in Toronto, Phoenix, and Tampa play indoors.
9. Five California cities have baseball teams: San Francisco, Oakland, Anaheim, Los Angeles, and San Diego.
10. Dina, Miguel, Felix, and I think it would be fun to see baseball games in different cities.

More Commas

Know the Rule

A **comma** is used to separate an **introductory word** from the rest of the sentence (*Hey, wait for me! Bob, tell me where you were born.*). Commas are also used to set off information that is useful but not necessary to a sentence (*Next year, when I am 13, I will probably get braces.*). Nonessential information is called *nonrestrictive*. A comma is also used between the name of a city or town and state (*My aunt lives in Asheville, North Carolina.*).

Practice the Rule

Number a sheet of paper 1–10. Write each sentence, adding commas where appropriate.

1. Mom, can you tell me what time of the day I was born?
2. Well, I think you were born around midnight.
3. Have we always lived in Fort Worth, Texas?
4. Yes, but your father and I were not born here.
5. He and I grew up in Lexington, Kentucky.
6. Oh, is that where the Kentucky Derby is run?
7. No, that race is run in Louisville, Kentucky.
8. In 1999, a year before you were born, we moved to Texas.
9. Eliot, who happens to be my best friend, was born in Tucson, Arizona.
10. Last year, just as he was about to start middle school, Eliot moved here.

Appendix A: Grammar Practice **5II**

Mini-Lesson

Student Objectives

• Use commas in sentences. *(p. 511)*

More Commas

Remind students that a comma indicates a pause in a sentence.

Display these sentences. Have students add commas where appropriate and explain why.

- *Emma have you visited a railroad museum?* (after *Emma*; introductory word)

- *Railroad museums which are really cool are in many states.* (after *museums* and after *cool*; unnecessary information)

- *The National Railroad Museum is in Green Bay Wisconsin.* (after *Green Bay*; separate city and state)

Explain to students that both placing commas incorrectly and omitting commas can cause confusion for the readers. For more practice with commas, see page T523.

CCSS **Common Core State Standards**

L.6.2: Demonstrate command of the conventions of standard English capitalization, punctuation, and spelling when writing. **L.6.2.a:** Use punctuation (commas, parentheses, dashes) to set off nonrestrictive/parenthetical elements.

Conventions

Mini-Lesson

Student Objectives

- Use semicolons and colons in sentences. (p. 512)

Semicolons and Colons

A semicolon can separate two related independent clauses. The second clause does not begin with a capital letter. Display this example: *We met after school to practice the play; we practiced for two hours.*

You can use a colon to separate two independent clauses when the second clause states a direct result of the first. Display this example: *The many hours of rehearsal paid off: Our class play was a huge success.*

Display these sentences. Have students explain where a semicolon or colon can be used to separate the clauses.

- *A century ago, many Americans worked on farms. This is not true today.* (farms; this)

- *Corporations took over the farming industry. Many small farmers lost their farms.* (industry: Many)

Combining sentences with semicolons and colons can add sentence variety to writing. For more practice with semicolons and colons, see page T523.

CCSS Common Core State Standards
L.6.2: Demonstrate command of the conventions of standard English capitalization, punctuation, and spelling when writing.

Semicolons and Colons

Know the Rule

A **semicolon** can be used instead of a comma and a conjunction to separate independent clauses in a compound sentence. A **colon** can be used to separate two independent clauses when the second clause states something that is a direct result of the first.

Examples:

Almost everyone does some traveling at some point; knowing a few basic things about packing can make the trip more enjoyable. I once forgot to pack a toothbrush: I had to buy one at a store in the airport.

Practice the Rule

Number a sheet of paper 1–10. Combine each pair of sentences, using a semicolon or a colon as appropriate. Possible answers

1. Pack only essential items when you go to camp or on a long trip; light packing makes traveling a lot easier.
2. No one likes to carry a lot of luggage on a trip; the bags are heavy and clumsy when you have to move through a crowd of people.
3. Most camps provide you with a list of items; this list usually includes the suggested number of each item.
4. Parents often drive their children to camp; Doing so cuts down a bit on the lugging of suitcases.
5. Sometimes the campers all travel together on a bus; This is a great way to get to know the kids you'll be camping with.
6. Find out where the bus stops; the bus does not go to every town or city.
7. Children come from all over; Last year children came from ten different states.
8. Camp can be hard at first; it's worth adjusting because it can be a great experience.
9. My sister went to camp last summer; she hasn't stopped talking about it.
10. Be sure to register early; Many camps fill up quickly.

Brackets and Dashes

Know the Rule

Brackets are used within quoted material to set off text added by someone other than the person who wrote or spoke the quotation. There are two types of **dashes.** They differ in length. An **em dash,** which is the longer dash, is used to set off text from the rest of the sentence. *(The Pony Express lasted only nineteen months—a very short time, considering how well known it is.)* An **en dash,** which is about half the length of the em dash, is used to show a range *(pages 4–10, Monday–Thursday).*

> **Example:**
> "Ladies and gentlemen," said the school board president, "I am extremely honored by this [her election as board president], and I hope to serve our community honorably."

Practice the Rule

Number a sheet of paper 1–8. Write the sentences. Where necessary, add an em dash or an en dash. After the sentence, identify the dash you used by writing **em** or **en.** Add brackets where needed.

1. I found the article about the opening of the new zoo on pages 4 —–— 5 in yesterday's newspaper. **en**
2. The zoo director said, "We all hope that it[the new zoo]will be visited by people of all ages."
3. The zoo was several years in the planning —–— a process that was often interrupted by disagreement. **em**
4. The zoo is scheduled to be open every week, Tuesday —–— Sunday.**en**
5. The director hopes the zoo will be fun and educational —–— educational in the sense that the display will be accompanied by interactive programs for young children. **em**
6. The program director stated, "They[interactive programs]are an important part of the zoo."
7. Activities will be available for children ages 2 —–— 12. **en**
8. The zoo should appeal to everyone —–— unless, of course, something goes wrong. **em**

Appendix A: Grammar Practice **513**

Mini-Lesson

Student Objectives

- Use brackets and dashes correctly in sentences. *(p. 513)*

Brackets and Dashes

Use brackets to set off explanations within direct quotations when the explanation is added by someone else and is not part of the quotation.

There are two types of dashes. An em dash is the longer of the two dashes. Use it to set off text in a sentence. An en dash, the shorter dash, is used to show a range *(May–July, chapters 2–4)*.

Display these sentences. Have students suggest where brackets, an em dash, or an en dash should be used.

- *"My fellow students," said Ernie, "I would be honored Ernie is running for student council to serve my class."* ([Ernie … council])

- *Jean read the novel a book of three hundred pages in two weeks.* (—a … pages—)

Brackets and dashes enable writers to include additional information in sentences that is interesting but not essential. For more practice with brackets and dashes, see page T523.

CCSS **C**ommon **C**ore **S**tate **S**tandards
L.6.2a: Use punctuation (commas, parentheses, dashes) to set off nonrestrictive/parenthetical elements.

More Practice

Simple Sentences

Copy the sentences. Underline the simple subject of each sentence. Then circle the simple predicate.

1. Lions (live) on the plains of Africa and Asia.
2. A male (can weigh) over five hundred pounds.
3. The females usually (survive) longer than the males.
4. A mane of long hair around its neck (distinguishes) the male lion.
5. Lions (travel) in large groups called prides.

Predicate Nouns

Write the subject in each sentence. Then write the predicate noun that renames it.

1. Florida is a state in the southeastern United States.
2. The capital of the state is Tallahassee.
3. Florida's northern neighbor is Georgia.
4. Tourism is the largest industry in the state.
5. The Atlantic is the ocean that borders the eastern coast of Florida.

Predicate Adjectives

Copy the sentences. Underline the simple subject of each sentence. Then circle the predicate adjective that describes the subject.

1. Last summer my sister became (interested) in collecting butterflies.
2. Her collection is now pretty (extensive).
3. The wings of butterflies are usually very (beautiful).
4. Catching butterflies is very (difficult).
5. Butterflies are very (delicate).

CCSS **C**ommon **C**ore **S**tate **S**tandards

L.6.1: Demonstrate command of the conventions of standard English grammar and usage when writing or speaking.

More Practice

Clauses

Copy the sentences. Underline each independent clause once. Underline each dependent clause twice. Circle the subordinating conjunction that begins each dependent clause.

1. (Whenever) I have some free time, I like to play electronic games.
2. I play the games (until) my mother tells me to quit.
3. My older sister sometimes tells me to turn off the computer (because) the noise annoys her.
4. (When) I grow up, I think I will still like electronic games.
5. (Unless) I get a better idea, my career will be designing electronic games.

Compound Sentences

Combine each pair of sentences with a comma and a conjunction to make a compound sentence.

1. Should we do our own research on rivers of the world? ~~or should~~ Should we ask our teacher or the librarian for help locating resources?
2. The Mississippi River begins in Minnesota. ~~and many~~ Many other smaller rivers feed into it as it flows toward the Gulf of Mexico.
3. I always thought that the Amazon River was the longest river in the world. ~~but~~ I recently learned that the Nile River in Africa is longer.
4. Rivers have many important uses. ~~and this~~ This is one reason why many of the important cities on Earth are located near major rivers.
5. Rivers can provide many fun activities. ~~but they~~ They can also be extremely dangerous.

CCSS **Common Core State Standards**
L.6.3: Use knowledge of language and its conventions when writing, speaking, reading, or listening. **L.6.3.a:** Vary sentence patterns for meaning, reader/listener interest, and style.

More Practice

Dangling and Misplaced Modifiers

Select the sentence in each pair that is written correctly (has no dangling or misplaced modifiers).

1a. Supporting unpopular issues, many people disliked the candidate for mayor.

(b.) As a candidate supporting unpopular issues, he was disliked by many people.

2a. Having been in office for a year, those same people liked him.

(b.) Having been in office for a year, he was liked by some people.

(3a.) People stood outside the mayor's office carrying signs of protest.

b. Carrying signs of protest, the mayor's office had people standing outside.

(4a.) Having learned about politics in class, I now know how important voting is.

b. Having learned about politics in class, voting is very important.

(5a.) My only sister is 18 years old, so she can vote in the next election.

b. My sister is only 18 years old, so she can vote in the next election.

Direct Objects

Write each sentence. Underline the direct object and draw an arrow from it to the transitive verb.

1. At the concert, the band played their most popular songs.

2. The audience loved the performance.

3. I framed my ticket as a souvenir.

4. My brother downloaded the band's most recent release.

5. I played the song on repeat for hours.

Concrete and Abstract Nouns

Copy the sentences. Underline the concrete nouns. Circle the abstract nouns.

1. The article I read about the human brain was a pure joy.

2. Our brain controls our breathing and contains our memories.

3. At night, our brains generate our dreams.

4. I have an illustration of the human body on the wall of my bedroom.

5. Of all the parts of the human body, I find the brain most interesting.

CCSS **Common Core State Standards**
L.6.1: Demonstrate command of the conventions of standard English grammar and usage when writing or speaking.

More Practice

Singular and Plural Nouns

Copy the following chart. Give the missing singular or plural form of each noun.

Singular Nouns	Plural Nouns
1. knife	knives
2. woman	women
3. goose	geese
4. sheep	sheep
5. wolf	wolves

Possessive Nouns

Write the possessive form of the noun in parentheses that correctly completes each sentence.

1. The (children) theater will present a play this Saturday. **children's**
2. Have you picked up your (parents) tickets yet? **parents'**
3. My (brother) seat is in the front row. **brother's**
4. I helped design the (actors) costumes for the play. **actors'**
5. My (grandparents) video camera will capture the entire play. **grandparents'**

Personal and Compound Personal Pronouns

Write the pronoun in parentheses that correctly completes each sentence.

1. Mary and (me/Ⓘ) have set a personal goal for (ourself/ⓞurselves).
2. (Us/Ⓦe) both intend to read two books every month.
3. Some friends of ours think (us/ⓦe) have a good idea.
4. They are going to try reading a book every week (ourselves/ⓣhemselves).
5. If (ⓦe/us) meet our goal, (ⓦe/us) are going to celebrate!

Possessive Pronouns

Write the possessive pronoun that could replace each possessive noun.

1. Roberto's notebook **his**
2. Ms. Greene's desk **her**
3. the car's tires **its**
4. the players' celebration **their**
5. the bird's nest **its**

CCSS **C**ommon **C**ore **S**tate **S**tandards

L.6.1: Demonstrate command of the conventions of standard English grammar and usage when writing or speaking. **L.6.1.a:** Ensure that pronouns are in the proper case (subjective, objective, possessive). **L.6.1.b:** Use intensive pronouns (e.g., *myself, ourselves*). **L.6.1.c:** Recognize and correct inappropriate shifts in pronoun number and person. **L.6.1.d:** Recognize and correct vague pronouns (i.e., ones with unclear or ambiguous antecedents). **L.6.2:** Demonstrate command of the conventions of standard English capitalization, punctuation, and spelling when writing. **L.6.2.b:** Spell correctly.

More Practice

Relative and Interrogative Pronouns

Identify each underlined pronoun as a **relative** or an **interrogative**.

1. <u>Who</u> from your class is on the Student Council? interrogative
2. Tell me about some of the issues <u>that</u> the Student Council is working on. relative
3. One issue, <u>which</u> I think is very important, concerns the elimination of free periods. relative
4. <u>Which</u> solution to this problem do you favor? interrogative
5. <u>Which</u> points of the argument do you find most convincing? interrogative

The Perfect Tenses

Write each sentence using the correct helping verb to form the present-perfect tense or past-perfect tense of the verb.

1. Pakistan (has/had) experienced severe flooding.
2. (Have/Had) you known anything about Pakistan before we began studying it in class?
3. Countries around the world (has/have) offered emergency assistance.
4. The Pakistani government (has/had) stated that the country will take years to recover.
5. (Has/Have) your school done anything to help out people in need in times of emergency?

Transitive and Intransitive Verbs

Write the action verb in each sentence. Label it **transitive** or **intransitive**. If the verb is a transitive verb, write the object that goes with it.

1. My father <u>quit</u> smoking last week. transitive, smoking
2. He <u>threw</u> his cigarettes in the garbage can. transitive, cigarettes
3. Since quitting, he <u>runs</u> two miles every day. intransitive
4. Have your parents <u>quit</u> yet? intransitive
5. Some people <u>develop</u> health problems from secondhand smoke. transitive, problems

CCSS **C**ommon **C**ore **S**tate **S**tandards

L.6.1: Demonstrate command of the conventions of standard English grammar and usage when writing or speaking. **L.6.2.a:** Use punctuation (commas, parentheses, dashes) to set off nonrestrictive/paren-thetical elements. **L.6.3.a:** Vary sentence patterns for meaning, reader/listener interest, and style.

More Practice

Articles

Write each sentence, using the correct article in parentheses. Underline the article *the* each time it appears and the word to which it refers.

1. Last summer I worked part-time in (a/**an**) orchard.
2. I swept <u>the</u> store <u>area</u> with (**a**/an) long broom.
3. <u>The</u> <u>job</u> involved working only (**a**/an) few hours each week.
4. As (**a**/an) perk of <u>the</u> <u>job</u>, I could eat (a/**an**) apple whenever I wanted one.
5. One day, I ate so many apples I got (**a**/an) stomachache!

Interjections

Use the interjections *Wow, Hey, Ah, Ick,* and *Well* to complete the sentences. Use each interjection only once. Use the appropriate punctuation after the interjection.

1. _____ would you like to go swimming today? **Hey,**
2. _____ I have a little homework to do before I can go. **Well,**
3. _____ You do homework on Saturdays? **Wow!**
4. _____ the water feels so refreshing. **Ah,**
5. _____ There's a bug in the water. **Ick!**

Subordinating Conjunctions

Write the subordinating conjunction in parentheses that correctly completes each sentence.

1. (**Although**/If) the war was unpopular with the people, the president and his staff thought that it was necessary.
2. (Before/**If**) people disagree with an elected official's actions, they can choose not to vote for him or her in the next election.
3. Voters should learn as much as they can about candidates (although/**before**) they vote for one or another.
4. My parents read newspapers and watch TV news shows (**because**/if) they want to be well informed about issues.
5. Some voters develop strong opinions about the candidates (**before**/if) they vote.

CCSS **Common Core State Standards**

L.6.1: Demonstrate command of the conventions of standard English grammar and usage when writing or speaking. **L.6.2:** Demonstrate command of the conventions of standard English capitalization, punctuation, and spelling when writing. **L.6.3:** Use knowledge of language and its conventions when writing, speaking, reading, or listening. **L.6.3.a:** Vary sentence patterns for meaning, reader/listener interest, and style.

More Practice

Using the Right Word

Write each sentence, using the correct word in parentheses.

1. (Among/**Between**) you and me, we have a lot of baseball cards.
2. I have most of the cards I want (accept/**except**) for Derek Jeter's rookie card.
3. Who is standing (**beside**/besides) the manager on that team card?
4. My uncle knows a (hole/**whole**) lot about baseball players.
5. He even (**knew**/new) Babe Ruth's real first name.

Irregular Verbs

Write each sentence, using the correct form of the irregular verb in parentheses.

1. Our class has (begin) a unit on the Holocaust. begun
2. We learned about a girl who (keep) a diary while hiding from the Nazis. kept
3. Her book later (become) very famous. became
4. I had never (hear) of Anne Frank before. heard
5. Since learning about the Holocaust in class, I have (read) several books on the topic. read

Avoiding Double Negatives

Write each sentence, using the correct word in parentheses to avoid a double negative.

1. Haven't you (**ever**/never) learned to swim?
2. People who can't swim don't have (no/**any**) business wading in a river.
3. They shouldn't wander into the deep end of a pool (neither/**either**).
4. I can't think of (**anything**/nothing) more important than learning to swim.
5. I don't know if there's (**anything**/nothing) better than swimming on a hot summer day.

CCSS **Common Core State Standards**

L.6.1: Demonstrate command of the conventions of standard English grammar and usage when writing or speaking. **L.6.1.e:** Recognize variations from standard English in their own and others' writing and speaking, and identify and use strategies to improve expression in conventional language. **L.6.2.b:** Spell correctly.

More Practice

Subject-Verb Agreement

Write the verb in parentheses that agrees with the subject of the sentence. Then identify the verb as a singular verb or plural verb.

1. Our country (has/have) many people from other countries living in it. singular
2. Not everyone (agree/agrees) that this is a good policy. singular
3. Many strongly (oppose/opposes) America's immigration laws. plural
4. Others (believe/believes) in the fairness of the laws. plural
5. Many senators (has/have) tried to pass new laws. singular

Writing Sentences Correctly

Write **declarative, interrogative, imperative,** or **exclamatory** to identify the type of each sentence.

1. What are the three branches of the United States government? interrogative
2. The legislative, judicial, and executive branches make up our government. declarative
3. Tell me who the head of the executive branch is. imperative
4. Everyone knows that the president heads the executive branch! exclamatory
5. What is the main function of the executive branch? interrogative

Capitalization

Write each phrase, using capitalization where needed.

1. the end of december the end of December
2. the british author j. k. rowling the British author J. K. Rowling
3. the capital of puerto rico the capital of Puerto Rico
4. vice president biden Vice President Biden
5. dr. matthew perez of houston medical center Dr. Matthew Perez of Houston Medical Center

CCSS **C**ommon **C**ore **S**tate **S**tandards

L.6.1: Demonstrate command of the conventions of standard English grammar and usage when writing or speaking. **L.6.2:** Demonstrate command of the conventions of standard English capitalization, punctuation, and spelling when writing.

More Practice

Initials and Abbreviations

Write the abbreviation of each word.

1. Monday Mon.
2. February Feb.
3. Doctor Dr.
4. Street St.
5. California CA, Calif., or Cal.

Titles

Write each sentence. Use correct punctuation and capitalization for titles.

1. Have you ever heard the Beatles' song something? "Something"
2. What about the song here comes the sun? "Here Comes the Sun"
3. No, but I've seen the movie yellow submarine, which is based on the group's music. Yellow Submarine
4. I saw Paul McCartney's picture in a magazine called newsweek. Newsweek
5. You can read about pop stars in the entertainment section of the houston chronicle. The Houston Chronicle

Commas

Write the sentences, using commas where needed.

1. My family feeds finches, chickadees, and cardinals in the winter.
2. We don't put out birdseed in the spring, summer, or fall.
3. Chipmunks will eat unsalted peanuts, dried corn, and other kinds of seeds.
4. My friends Debbie, Shauna, and Cory like to watch the animals with me.
5. We eat snacks like popcorn, cereal, and fruit as we watch the animals nibble on birdseed.

CCSS **Common Core State Standards**

L.6.2: Demonstrate command of the conventions of standard English capitalization, punctuation, and spelling when writing.

More Practice

More Commas

Write each sentence, using commas where needed.

1. Pedro, can you tell me where the ballpark for the Texas Rangers is located?

2. The Rangers ballpark is in Arlington, Texas.

3. Arlington, which is located between Fort Worth and Dallas, is also the home of a theme park.

4. Two rivers, one of which is the Trinity River, flow through the city.

5. Mary, can you tell me any of facts about the city of Arlington, Texas?

Semicolons and Colons

Use a semicolon or a colon to combine each pair of sentences.   **Possible answers**

1. Forests are valuable resources in nature.; People should protect forests when they can.

2. Forests provide habitats for many animals and insects.; Thousands of different plants also live in forests.

3. Logging and urban sprawl are two ways humans affect forests.; Disease and weather are two natural conditions that affect forests.

4. Too often campers are careless about their use of fire.; Resulting fires have destroyed millions of acres of forests.

5. Campers must take precautions when using fire.; Making sure coals are completely dead before going to sleep is one way to prevent forest fires.

Brackets and Dashes

Write each sentence, using brackets and em dashes or en dashes where needed. Identify the dashes you used by writing **em** or **en**.

1. My homeroom period is 7:24 A.M. —— 7:58 A.M. each morning. **en**

2. During her morning address, our principal Ms. Weinstein said, "There will be a change in this policy —[— roaming freely through the hallways after lunch —]— starting tomorrow."

3. Then the class read pages 36 —— 42 in our history textbook. **en**

4. The upcoming spring break —— and a very welcome break it is —— falls in April. **em**

5. I will be going to the Bahamas with my family April 4 —— 10 for vacation. **en**

CCSS **C**ommon **C**ore **S**tate **S**tandards

L.6.2: Demonstrate command of the conventions of standard English capitalization, punctuation, and spelling when writing. **L.6.2.a:** Use punctuation (commas, parentheses, dashes) to set off nonrestrictive/parenthetical elements.

Transitions

Certain words and phrases can help make the meaning of your writing clearer. Below are lists of words and phrases that you can use to help readers understand more completely what you are trying to say.

Time Order

about	first	today	later
after	second	tomorrow	finally
at	to begin	until	then
before	yesterday	next	as soon as
during	meanwhile	soon	in the end

Cause and Effect

and so	as a result	because	besides
consequently	once	since	so
therefore			

Compare and Contrast

Compare:

also	as	both
in the same way	like	likewise
one way	similarly	

Contrast:

although	but	even though
however	still	on the other hand
otherwise	yet	

Words and phrases that can show location:

above	across	around	behind
below	beneath	beside	between
down	in back of	in front of	inside
near	next to	on top of	outside
over	under		

Words and phrases that can conclude or summarize:

finally	in conclusion	in the end	lastly
therefore	to conclude		

524 Appendix A: Grammar Practice

Appendix B
Rubrics

Mode-Specific Rubrics This section contains 4-, 5-, and 6-point rubrics that can be used with any piece of Narrative, Informative/Explanatory, Opinion/Argument, and Descriptive writing. Rubrics based on the six traits of writing can help students identify their writing goals and better understand the expectations of each writing assignment. Rubrics also provide valuable self-assessment for students during the revising process.

Narrative Writing Rubric

	4	3	2	1
Ideas	An engaging topic, experience, or series of events is supported by relevant details. Memorable descriptions develop the narrative. Carefully selected ideas completely satisfy the reader.	Most of the details are relevant and supportive. Descriptions are adequate. The ideas selected by the author frequently meet the needs of the reader.	The narrative is not supported by enough relevant details. Descriptions are inadequate. The ideas selected by the author sometimes meet the needs of the reader.	The topic is not clear. Details are unrelated to the topic.
Organization	The narrative has an engaging beginning and an ending that leaves the reader thinking or feeling. Events are logically and creatively sequenced. A variety of effective transition words, phrases, and clauses signifies shifts in the setting and plot.	The beginning and the conclusion are functional, but one may be stronger than the other. The sequence of events is logical, but may have a flaw or two. More or better transitions may be needed to guide the reader.	The beginning does not get the reader's attention, or the ending does not satisfy. Some events are out of order. Transitions are needed.	The writing is not organized into a beginning, middle, and ending.
Voice	The voice, mood, and tone are perfect for the purpose and audience. Dialogue, if used, is realistic and fits all the characters.	The voice, mood, and tone are appropriate in places, but inconsistent. Dialogue, if used, usually fits the characters.	The voice sounds disinterested. Mood and tone are weak. Dialogue, if used, is unrealistic or does not fit the characters.	Voice, mood, and tone are not established.
Word Choice	Clear and precise nouns and verbs consistently capture the imagery and action of the story. Descriptive language clearly conveys the experiences and events. Modifiers are strong.	Some nouns and verbs are strong, but others are weak. Descriptive language conveys most of the imagery, experiences, and events. Modifiers are satisfactory.	Many nouns and verbs do not capture the imagery or action of the story. The descriptive language is overly dependent on modifiers, and many of these are weak.	Words are overused, very weak, or incorrect. Descriptive language is not used.
Sentence Fluency	A variety of sentence structures and sentence beginnings makes the narrative flow smoothly. To read this paper aloud with inflection and feeling is effortless.	A few sentences share the same structures, lengths, or beginnings. The writing flows reasonably well. It is possible to read this writing aloud with inflection and feeling.	Many sentences have the same structures, lengths, or beginnings. The writing is robotic or rambling. It is difficult to read this writing aloud with inflection and feeling.	Sentences are incorrectly written or incomplete. The writing is difficult to follow.
Conventions	The narrative has been carefully edited. Grammar, usage, and mechanics are correct.	The narrative contains some minor errors that may distract the reader, but meaning remains clear.	The narrative contains many errors. Line-by-line editing in specific places is needed.	The writing has not been edited. Serious errors affect or alter the meaning.

Informative/Explanatory Writing Rubric

	4	3	2	1
Ideas	The topic is introduced clearly. It is developed and supported with relevant facts and concrete details. If included, quotations are relevant, accurate, and insightful. Carefully selected ideas completely answer the reader's main questions.	The topic is introduced adequately. Some facts, details, and quotations (if included) support the topic adequately. The reader's main questions are frequently answered.	The topic is introduced. Facts, details, and quotations (if included) do not develop and support the topic effectively. A few of the reader's questions are answered.	The topic is not clear. The topic is not supported by facts and details. The author did not think about what questions the reader might have.
Organization	The ideas, concepts, and information are organized into a strong introduction, body, and conclusion. Varied, appropriate, and unique transitions connect and clarify relationships among ideas.	The ideas, concepts, and information are organized into an introduction, body, and conclusion. More or better transitions may be needed.	An introduction, body, and conclusion are present. Some transitions may be inappropriate or incorrect.	The text is not organized into an introduction, body, and conclusion. It is hard or impossible to follow the ideas.
Voice	The writer's voice is appropriate for the purpose and audience. The tone is informative, respectful, and consistent.	The writer's voice is mostly appropriate for the purpose and audience. The tone is mostly informative and respectful, but may be too informal in some places.	The writer's voice is not very appropriate for the purpose or audience. The tone is inconsistent.	The writer's voice is very weak or absent. The tone is not established.
Word Choice	The language is exact and concise. Domain-specific vocabulary is used correctly and explained, as needed. Nouns and verbs are clear and precise, supported by a few carefully selected modifiers.	Some of the language is exact, but some is too general or vague. Some domain-specific vocabulary is used but not explained. Some nouns and verbs are weak, requiring too much help from modifiers. Modifiers are satisfactory.	Some language is confusing. Domain-specific vocabulary may be used incorrectly. Nouns and verbs lack clarity and precision. Too many or too few modifiers are used, and many of these are weak.	Many words are repeated or used incorrectly. Domain-specific vocabulary is not used.
Sentence Fluency	The sentences vary greatly in length and structure, adding style and interest. Almost all sentences begin differently. The text flows smoothly and is effortlessly read aloud with inflection.	Sentence length and structure vary somewhat, with some sentences adding style or interest. Some sentence beginnings are repeated. Parts of the text flow smoothly. The paper can be read aloud with inflection.	In many places, the writing does not flow smoothly because sentences are the same length or begin the same way. The paper is difficult to read aloud with inflection.	Sentences are incomplete or incorrect. The text does not flow smoothly.
Conventions	The text has been carefully edited. Grammar, usage, and mechanics are correct.	The text contains some minor errors that may distract the reader, but meaning remains clear.	Many errors are repeated. Line-by-line editing in specific places is needed. The errors interfere with meaning in some places.	The text has not been edited. Serious errors affect or alter the meaning.

Argument Writing Rubric

	4	3	2	1
Ideas	The writer's claim is stated clearly. Counterclaims are anticipated and addressed very well. Accurate reasons and evidence from reliable sources support the claim.	The writer's claim is stated adequately. The author may fail to anticipate or address one or more common counterclaims. One or two reasons or pieces of evidence may not be from reliable sources.	A claim is stated. Counterclaims are not anticipated or are not addressed well. There is little accurate support for the writer's claim.	The writer does not state a claim. Reasons and evidence are not provided.
Organization	The argument is organized logically, including a strong introduction. A compelling conclusion restates the thesis and includes a call to action. Clear and unique transitions clarify the relationships between the claim, reasons, supporting evidence, and counterclaims.	The argument is organized logically, including an introduction. The conclusion may not restate the thesis or may not include a call to action. More or better transitions may be needed to clarify the relationships between the claim, reasons, supporting evidence, and counterclaims.	The argument is not organized logically. The introduction or conclusion is missing (or problematic). Transitions are not appropriate or effective. Counterclaims are not addressed effectively.	The writing is not organized as an argument. The introduction and conclusion are missing. Transitions are not used. Counterclaims are not addressed.
Voice	The voice strongly supports the writer's purpose and consistently connects with the audience. A respectful, confident tone is maintained.	The voice mostly supports the writer's purpose. The tone is mostly respectful and confident, but may be too informal in some places.	The voice is fairly weak or passive throughout the piece and fails to connect with the audience. The tone is inconsistent.	The voice is flat or absent.
Word Choice	Compelling language conveys the writer's ideas and engages the reader. Nouns and verbs are clear and precise, supported by a few carefully selected modifiers.	Some of the language is compelling, but some is vague or ineffective. Some nouns and verbs are strong, but others are weak, requiring too much help from modifiers. Modifiers are satisfactory.	Much of the language is vague or ineffective. Nouns and verbs lack clarity or precision. Too many or too few modifiers are used, and many of these are weak.	The language is not compelling. Words are weak, negative, or used incorrectly.
Sentence Fluency	The sentences vary greatly in length and structure, adding style and interest. Almost all sentences begin differently. The text flows smoothly and is effortlessly read aloud with inflection.	Sentence length and structure vary somewhat, with some sentences adding style or interest. Some sentence beginnings are repeated. Parts of the text flow smoothly. The paper can be read aloud with inflection.	In many places, the writing does not flow smoothly because sentences are the same length or begin the same way. The paper is difficult to read aloud with inflection.	Sentences are incomplete or incorrect. Sentence beginnings are repeated over and over again. The text does not flow smoothly.
Conventions	The writing has been carefully edited. Grammar, usage, and mechanics are correct.	The writing contains some minor errors that may distract the reader, but meaning remains clear.	Many errors are repeated. Line-by-line editing in specific places is needed. The errors interfere with meaning in some places.	The writing has not been edited. Serious errors affect or alter the meaning.

Descriptive Writing Rubric

	4	3	2	1
Ideas	The topic is focused and exactly the right size. Sensory details clearly develop, describe, and reveal the subject. Carefully chosen ideas help the reader to completely experience what is being described.	The topic may need to be more carefully focused. Some sensory details reveal the subject. The author's ideas sometimes help the reader experience what is being described.	The topic is not well focused. Too few sensory details reveal the subject. The ideas fail to consistently help the reader experience what is being described.	The topic is unfocused or unclear. Details are random or missing. The ideas do not support the reader's experience of the topic.
Organization	The description is organized logically and creatively, including an engaging introduction and a thoughtfully crafted conclusion. Varied and appropriate transitions clarify relationships between ideas.	The description is organized logically, including a functional introduction and conclusion. More or better transitions may be needed to clarify relationships between ideas.	The description is not well organized. The introduction or the conclusion is weak or missing. Transitions are weak or confusing. Some of the ideas are hard to follow.	The writing is not organized. The introduction and the conclusion are missing. Transitions are not used.
Voice	An authentic, clear voice conveys the writer's purpose and connects with the reader. The mood is perfect, and the tone conveys respect for the subject and the audience.	The voice connects with the reader in some places. The tone is appropriate but inconsistent. An appropriate mood is somewhat established.	The voice may convey purpose but does not connect with the reader. The mood and tone may not be appropriate.	The voice is weak or absent. Mood and tone are not established.
Word Choice	Precise, descriptive words (including nouns, verbs, and modifiers) bring the subject to life. Figurative language and comparisons create a clear, coherent picture.	Some words are precise and descriptive, but others are not. Some nouns and verbs may rely too heavily on modifiers for clarity. Figurative language and/ or comparisons sometimes create a clear picture.	Nouns and verbs lack precision and clarity. Too many or too few modifiers are used, and many of these are weak. Figurative language and/or comparisons do not create a clear picture.	Words are basic and very limited. Figurative language and comparisons are not used.
Sentence Fluency	A variety of sentences and/or lines adds interest and energy to the description. The writing flows very smoothly. Reading this aloud with inflection and feeling is effortless.	Some sentences and/or lines are varied and interesting. The writing flows smoothly some of the time. It can be read aloud with inflection and feeling.	Many sentences and/or lines are not varied or interesting. Most of the writing does not flow smoothly. It is difficult to read aloud with inflection or feeling.	Sentences and/or lines are incomplete or incorrect. The writing does not flow.
Conventions	The description has been carefully edited. Grammar, usage, and mechanics are correct.	The description contains some minor errors that may distract the reader, but meaning remains clear.	Many errors are repeated. Line-by-line editing in specific places is needed. Errors interfere with meaning in places.	The writing has not been edited. Serious errors affect or alter the meaning.

Narrative Writing Rubric

	5	4	3	2	1
Ideas	An engaging topic, experience, or series of events is supported by relevant details. Memorable descriptions develop the narrative. Carefully selected ideas completely satisfy the reader.	Most of the details are relevant and supportive. Most descriptions are memorable. Carefully selected ideas satisfy most of the reader's needs.	Some of the details may be unrelated or marginally supportive, but descriptions are adequate. The ideas selected by the author sometimes meet the needs of the reader.	The narrative is not supported by enough relevant details. Descriptions are inadequate. The ideas selected by the author frequently meet the needs of the reader.	The topic is not clear. Details are unrelated to the topic.
Organization	The narrative has an engaging beginning and an ending that leaves the reader thinking or feeling. Events are logically and creatively sequenced. A variety of effective transition words, phrases, and clauses signifies shifts in the setting and plot.	The narrative has an interesting beginning and satisfying ending. Events are logically sequenced. Most transitions are effective, especially as they signify shifts in the setting and plot.	The beginning and the conclusion are functional, but one may be stronger than the other. The sequence of events is logical, but may have a flaw or two. More or better transitions may be needed to guide the reader.	The beginning does not get the reader's attention, or the ending does not satisfy. Some events are out of order. Transitions are needed.	The writing is not organized into a beginning, middle, and ending.
Voice	The voice, mood, and tone are perfect for the purpose and audience. Dialogue, if used, is realistic and fits all the characters.	The voice, mood, and tone are appropriate. Dialogue, if used, is realistic and usually fits the characters well.	The voice, mood, and tone are appropriate in places, but inconsistent. Dialogue, if used, sometimes fits the characters.	The voice sounds disinterested. Mood and tone are weak. Dialogue, if used, is unrealistic or does not fit the characters.	Voice, mood, and tone are not established.
Word Choice	Clear and precise nouns and verbs consistently capture the imagery and action of the story. Descriptive language clearly conveys the experiences and events. Modifiers are strong.	Most of the nouns and verbs are clear, capturing the imagery and action of the story. Descriptive language conveys the experiences and events well. The majority of the modifiers are strong.	Some nouns and verbs are strong, but others are weak. Descriptive language conveys most of the imagery, experiences, and events. Modifiers are satisfactory.	Many nouns and verbs do not capture the imagery or action of the story. The descriptive language is weak, or action is weak or incorrect. The writing is difficult to read.	Words are overused, very weak, or incorrect. Descriptive language is not used.
Sentence Fluency	A variety of sentence structures and sentence beginnings makes the narrative flow smoothly. To read this paper aloud with inflection and feeling is effortless.	Most sentence structures and sentence beginnings are varied and flow well. Most of the sentences are well crafted. It is easy to read this writing aloud with inflection and feeling.	A few sentences share the same structures, lengths, or beginnings. The writing flows reasonably well. It is possible to read this writing aloud with inflection and feeling.	Many sentences have the same structures, lengths, or beginnings. The flow is robotic or rambling. It is difficult to read this writing aloud with inflection and feeling.	Sentences are incorrectly written or incomplete. The writing is difficult to follow.
Conventions	The narrative has been carefully edited. Grammar, usage, and mechanics are correct.	The narrative contains one or two minor errors that are easily corrected.	The narrative contains some minor errors that may distract the reader, but meaning remains clear.	The narrative contains many errors. Line-by-line editing in specific places is needed.	The writing has not been edited. Serious errors affect or alter the meaning.

Informative/Explanatory Writing Rubric

	5	4	3	2	1
Ideas	The topic is introduced clearly. It is developed and supported with relevant facts and concrete details. If included, quotations are relevant, accurate, and insightful. Carefully selected ideas completely answer the reader's main questions.	The topic is introduced well. Almost all the facts and details support the topic well. If included, quotations are relevant and accurate. Almost all of the reader's main questions are answered.	The topic is introduced adequately. Some facts, details, and quotations (if included) support the topic adequately. The reader's main questions are frequently answered.	The topic is introduced. Facts, details, and quotations (if included) do not develop and support the topic effectively. A few of the reader's questions are answered.	The topic is not clear. The topic is not supported by facts and details. The author did not think about what questions the reader might have.
Organization	The ideas, concepts, and information are organized into a strong introduction, body, and conclusion. Varied, appropriate, and unique transitions connect and clarify relationships among ideas.	The ideas, concepts, and information are organized into an introduction, body, and conclusion. Most transitions are appropriate and helpful.	The ideas, concepts, and information are organized into an introduction, body, and conclusion. More or better transitions may be needed.	An introduction, body, and conclusion are present. Some transitions may be inappropriate or incorrect.	The text is not organized into an introduction, body, and conclusion. It is hard or impossible to follow the ideas.
Voice	The writer's voice is appropriate for the purpose and audience. The tone is informative, respectful, and consistent.	The writer's voice is appropriate for the purpose and audience most of the time. The tone is almost always informative and respectful.	The writer's voice is mostly appropriate for the purpose and audience. The tone is mostly informative and respectful, but may be too informal in some places.	The writer's voice is not very appropriate for the purpose or audience. The tone is inconsistent.	The writer's voice is very weak or absent. The tone is not established.
Word Choice	The language is exact and concise. Domain-specific vocabulary is used correctly and explained, as needed. Nouns and verbs are clear and precise, supported by a few carefully selected modifiers.	Most of the language is exact and concise. Domain-specific vocabulary is used correctly and usually explained, as needed. Most nouns and verbs are clear and precise. Most modifiers are carefully selected.	Some of the language is exact, but some is too general or vague. Some domain-specific vocabulary is used but not explained. Some nouns and verbs are weak, requiring too much help from modifiers. Modifiers are satisfactory.	Some language is confusing. Domain-specific vocabulary may be used incorrectly. Nouns and verbs lack clarity and precision. Too many or too few modifiers are used, and many of these are weak.	Many words are repeated or used incorrectly. Domain-specific vocabulary is not used.
Sentence Fluency	The sentences vary greatly in length and structure, adding style and interest. Almost all sentences begin differently. The text flows smoothly and is effortlessly read aloud with inflection.	Most of the sentences vary in their beginnings, lengths, and structures. Several add style or interest. Most of the text flows smoothly and is easy to read aloud with inflection.	Sentence length and structure vary somewhat, with some sentences adding style or interest. Some sentence beginnings are repeated. Parts of the text flow smoothly. The paper can be read aloud with inflection.	In many places, the writing does not flow smoothly because sentences are the same length or begin in the same way. The paper is difficult to read aloud with inflection.	Sentences are incomplete or incorrect. The text does not flow smoothly.
Conventions	The text has been carefully edited. Grammar, usage, and mechanics are correct.	The text contains one or two minor errors, but the meaning remains clear.	The text contains some minor errors that may distract the reader, but meaning remains clear.	Many errors are repeated. Line-by-line editing in specific places is needed. The errors interfere with meaning in some places.	The text has not been edited. Serious errors affect or alter the meaning.

Argument Writing Rubric

	5	4	3	2	1
Ideas	The writer's claim is stated clearly. Counterclaims are anticipated and addressed very well. Accurate reasons and evidence from reliable sources support the claim.	The writer's claim is stated clearly. Counterclaims are anticipated and addressed. Most of the reasons and evidence are accurate and from reliable sources.	The writer's claim is stated adequately. The author may fail to anticipate or address one or more common counterclaims. One or two reasons or pieces of evidence may not be from reliable sources.	A claim is stated. Counterclaims are not anticipated or are not addressed well. There is little accurate support for the writer's claim.	The writer does not state a claim. Reasons and evidence are not provided.
Organization	The argument is organized logically, including a strong introduction. A compelling conclusion restates the thesis and includes a call to action. Clear and unique transitions clarify the relationships between the claim, reasons, supporting evidence, and counterclaims.	The argument is organized logically, including a good introduction. The conclusion restates the thesis and may include a call to action. Most transitions clarify the relationships between the claim, reasons, supporting evidence, and counterclaims.	The argument is organized logically, including an introduction. The conclusion may not restate the thesis or may not include a call to action. More or better transitions may be needed to clarify the relationships between the claim, reasons, supporting evidence, and counterclaims.	The argument is not organized logically. The introduction or conclusion is missing (or problematic). Transitions are not appropriate or effective. Counterclaims are not addressed effectively.	The writing is not organized as an argument. The introduction and conclusion are missing. Transitions are not used. Counterclaims are not addressed.
Voice	The voice strongly supports the writer's purpose and consistently connects with the audience. A respectful, confident tone is maintained.	The voice supports the writer's purpose and almost always connects with the audience. A respectful, confident tone is maintained.	The voice mostly supports the writer's purpose. The tone is mostly respectful and confident, but may be too informal in some places.	The voice is fairly weak or passive throughout the piece and fails to connect with the audience. The tone is inconsistent.	The voice is flat or absent.
Word Choice	Compelling language conveys the writer's ideas and engages the reader. Nouns and verbs are clear and precise, supported by a few carefully selected modifiers.	Most of the language is compelling. Nouns and verbs are mostly clear and precise. Most modifiers are carefully selected.	Some of the language is compelling, but some is vague or ineffective. Some nouns and verbs are strong, but others are weak, requiring too much help from modifiers. Modifiers are satisfactory.	Much of the language is vague or ineffective. Nouns and verbs lack clarity or precision. Too many or too few modifiers are used, and many of these are weak.	The language is not compelling. Words are weak, negative, or used incorrectly.
Sentence Fluency	The sentences vary greatly in length and structure, adding style and interest. Almost all sentences begin differently. The text flows smoothly and is effortlessly read aloud with inflection.	The sentences vary in their beginnings, lengths, and structures. Several add style and interest. Most of the text flows smoothly and is easy to read aloud with inflection.	Most of the sentences vary somewhat, with some sentences adding style or interest. Some sentence beginnings are repeated. Parts of the text flow smoothly. The paper can be read aloud with inflection.	Sentence length and structure vary somewhat, with some sentences adding style and interest. Some sentences are the same length or begin the same way. The paper is difficult to read aloud with inflection.	In many places, the writing does not flow smoothly because sentences are the same length or repeated over and over again. The text does not flow smoothly.
Conventions	The writing has been carefully edited. Grammar, usage, and mechanics are correct.	The writing contains one or two minor errors, but the meaning remains clear.	The writing contains some minor errors that may distract the reader, but meaning remains clear.	Many errors are repeated. Line-by-line editing in specific places is needed. The errors interfere with meaning in some places.	Sentences are incomplete or incorrect. Sentence beginnings are repeated. Serious errors affect or alter the meaning. The writing has not been edited. Serious errors affect or alter the meaning.

Descriptive Writing Rubric

	5	4	3	2	1
Ideas	The topic is focused and exactly the right size. Sensory details clearly develop, describe, and reveal the subject. Carefully chosen ideas help the reader to completely experience what is being described.	The topic is focused and the right size. Many sensory details develop, describe, and reveal the subject. The ideas selected usually enable the reader to experience what is being described.	The topic may need to be more carefully focused. Some sensory details reveal the subject. The author's ideas sometimes help the reader experience what is being described.	The topic is not well focused. Too few sensory details reveal the subject. The ideas fail to consistently help the reader experience what is being described.	The topic is unfocused or unclear. Details are random or missing. The ideas do not support the reader's experience of the topic.
Organization	The description is organized logically and creatively, including an engaging introduction and a thoughtfully crafted conclusion. Varied and appropriate transitions clarify relationships between ideas.	The description is organized logically, including a strong introduction and a strong conclusion. Most of the transitions clarify relationships between ideas.	The description is organized logically, including a functional introduction and conclusion. More or better transitions may be needed to clarify relationships between ideas.	The description is not well organized. The introduction or the conclusion is weak or missing. Transitions are weak or confusing. Some of the ideas are hard to follow.	The writing is not organized. The introduction and the conclusion are missing. Transitions are not used.
Voice	An authentic, clear voice conveys the writer's purpose and connects with the reader. The mood is perfect, and the tone conveys respect for the subject and the audience.	The voice is clear and connects with the reader most of the time. The mood is appropriate, and the tone conveys respect for the subject and audience most of the time.	The voice connects with the reader in some places. The tone is appropriate but inconsistent. An appropriate mood is somewhat established.	The voice may convey purpose but does not connect with the reader. The mood and tone may not be appropriate.	The voice is weak or absent. Mood and tone are not established.
Word Choice	Precise, descriptive words (including nouns, verbs, and modifiers) bring the subject to life. Figurative language and comparisons create a clear, coherent picture.	Most words (including nouns, verbs, and modifiers) are precise and descriptive. Figurative language and comparisons create a clear, coherent picture most of the time.	Some words are precise and descriptive, but others are not. Some nouns and verbs may rely too heavily on modifiers for clarity. Figurative language and/or comparisons sometimes create a clear picture.	Nouns and verbs lack precision and clarity. Too many or too few modifiers are used, and many of these are weak. Figurative language and/or comparisons do not create a clear picture.	Words are basic and very limited. Figurative language and comparisons are not used.
Sentence Fluency	A variety of sentences and/or lines adds interest and energy to the description. The writing flows smoothly. Reading this aloud with inflection and feeling is effortless.	Most sentences and/or lines are varied and interesting. The writing flows smoothly most of the time. It is easy to read aloud with inflection and feeling.	Some sentences and/or lines are varied and interesting. The writing flows smoothly some of the time. It can be read aloud with inflection and feeling.	Many sentences and/or lines are not varied or interesting. Most of the writing does not flow smoothly. It is difficult to read aloud with inflection or feeling.	Sentences and/or lines are incomplete or incorrect. The writing does not flow.
Conventions	The description has been carefully edited. Grammar, usage, and mechanics are correct.	The description contains one or two minor errors that are easily corrected. Meaning is clear.	The description contains some minor errors that may distract the reader, but meaning remains clear.	Many errors are repeated. Line-by-line editing in specific places is needed. Errors interfere with meaning in places.	The writing has not been edited. Serious errors affect or alter the meaning.

Narrative Writing Rubric

	6	5	4	3	2	1
Ideas	An engaging topic, experience, or series of events is supported by relevant details. Memorable descriptions develop the narrative. Carefully selected ideas completely satisfy the reader.	Most of the details are relevant and supportive. Most descriptions are memorable. Carefully selected ideas satisfy most of the reader's needs.	Some of the details may be unrelated or marginally supportive, but descriptions are adequate. The ideas selected by the author frequently meet the needs of the reader.	The narrative is not supported by enough relevant details. Descriptions are inadequate. The ideas selected by the author sometimes meet the needs of the reader.	The topic may not be clear. Many details are unrelated. The author did not consider the needs of the reader.	The topic is not clear. Details are unrelated to the topic.
Organization	The narrative has an engaging beginning and an ending that leaves the reader thinking or feeling. Events are logically and creatively sequenced. A variety of effective transition words, phrases, and clauses signifies shifts in the setting and plot.	The narrative has an interesting beginning and satisfying ending. Events are logically sequenced. Most transitions are effective, especially as they signify shifts in the setting and plot.	The beginning and the conclusion are functional, but one may be stronger than the other. The sequence of events is logical, but may have a flaw or two. More or better transitions may be needed to guide the reader.	The beginning does not get the reader's attention, or the ending does not satisfy. Some events are out of order. Transitions are needed.	The beginning and ending are weak. The sequence of events is seriously flawed. Transitions are not used.	The writing is not organized into a beginning, middle, and ending.
Voice	The voice, mood, and tone are perfect for the purpose and audience. Dialogue, if used, is realistic and fits all the characters.	The voice, mood, and tone are appropriate. Dialogue, if used, is realistic and usually fits the characters well.	The voice, mood, and tone are appropriate in places, but inconsistent. Dialogue, if used, sometimes fits the characters.	The voice sounds disinterested. Mood and tone are weak. Dialogue, if used, is unrealistic or does not fit the characters.	The voice, mood, and tone are inappropriate for the audience. Dialogue, if used, is unrealistic.	Voice, mood, and tone are not established.
Word Choice	Clear and precise nouns and verbs consistently capture the imagery and action of the story. Descriptive language clearly conveys the experiences and events. Modifiers are strong.	Most of the nouns and verbs are clear, capturing the imagery and action of the story. Descriptive language conveys the experiences and events well. The majority of the modifiers are strong.	Some nouns and verbs are strong, but others are weak. Descriptive language conveys most of the imagery, experiences, and events. Modifiers are satisfactory.	Many nouns and verbs do not capture the imagery or action of story. The descriptive language is overly dependent on modifiers, and many of these are weak.	Words are not powerful or precise. Descriptive language is not used.	Words are overused, very weak, or incorrect.
Sentence Fluency	A variety of sentence structures and sentence beginnings makes the narrative flow smoothly. To read this paper aloud with inflection and feeling is effortless.	Most sentence structures and sentence beginnings are varied and flow well. Most of the sentences are well crafted. It is easy to read this writing aloud with inflection and feeling.	A few sentences share the same structures, lengths, or beginnings. The writing flows reasonably well. It is possible to read this writing aloud with inflection and feeling.	Many sentences have the same structures, lengths, or beginnings. The flow is robotic or rambling. It is difficult to read this writing aloud with inflection and feeling.	Sentences have little variation. The narrative does not flow well.	Sentences are incorrectly written or incomplete. The writing is difficult to follow.
Conventions	The narrative has been carefully edited. Grammar, usage, and mechanics are correct.	The narrative contains one or two minor errors that are easily corrected.	The narrative contains some minor errors that may distract the reader, but meaning remains clear.	The narrative contains many errors. Line-by-line editing in specific places is needed.	Serious errors affect or alter the meaning.	The writing has not been edited.

Informative/Explanatory Writing Rubric

	6	5	4	3	2	1
Ideas	The topic is introduced clearly. It is developed and supported with relevant facts and concrete details. If included, quotations are relevant, accurate, and insightful. Carefully selected ideas completely answer the reader's main questions.	The topic is introduced well. Almost all the facts and details support the topic well. If included, quotations are relevant and accurate. Almost all of the reader's main questions are answered.	The topic is introduced adequately. Some facts, details, and quotations (if included) support the topic adequately. The reader's main questions are frequently answered.	The topic is introduced. Facts, details, and quotations (if included) do not develop and support the topic effectively. A few of the reader's questions are answered.	The topic is not introduced, or more than one topic is introduced. Details are not relevant. Facts are not included. The author did not think about what questions the reader might have.	The topic is not clear. The topic is not supported by facts and details.
Organization	The ideas, concepts, and information are organized into a strong introduction, body, and conclusion. Varied, appropriate, and unique transitions connect and clarify relationships among ideas.	The ideas, concepts, and information are organized into an introduction, body, and conclusion. Most transitions are appropriate and helpful.	The ideas, concepts, and information are organized into an introduction, body, and conclusion. More or better transitions may be needed.	An introduction, body, and conclusion are present. Some transitions may be inappropriate or incorrect.	The text is not well organized. The introduction and conclusion are weak or missing. Transitions are not used.	The text is not organized into an introduction, body, and conclusion. It is hard or impossible to follow the ideas.
Voice	The writer's voice is appropriate for the purpose and audience. The tone is informative, respectful, and consistent.	The writer's voice is appropriate for the purpose and audience. The tone is almost always informative and respectful.	The writer's voice is mostly appropriate for the purpose and audience. The tone is mostly informative and respectful, but may be too informal in some places.	The writer's voice is not very appropriate for the purpose or audience. The tone is inconsistent.	The writer's voice is not appropriate. The tone is too informal.	The writer's voice is very weak or absent. The tone is not established.
Word Choice	The language is exact and concise. Domain-specific vocabulary is used correctly and explained, as needed. Nouns and verbs are clear and precise, supported by a few carefully selected modifiers.	Most of the language is exact and concise. Domain-specific vocabulary is used correctly and usually explained, as needed. Most nouns and verbs are clear and precise. Most modifiers are carefully selected.	Some of the language is exact, but some is too general or vague. Some domain-specific vocabulary is used but not explained. Some nouns and verbs are weak, requiring too much help from modifiers. Modifiers are satisfactory.	Some language is confusing. Domain-specific vocabulary may be used incorrectly. Nouns and verbs lack clarity and precision. Too many or too few modifiers are used, and many of these are weak.	The language is very basic and limited. Domain-specific vocabulary is used incorrectly. Nouns and verbs are vague, unclear, or confusing. Modifiers may be missing.	Many words are repeated or used incorrectly. Domain-specific vocabulary is not used.
Sentence Fluency	The sentences vary greatly in length and structure, adding style and interest. Almost all sentences begin differently. The text flows smoothly and is effortlessly read aloud with inflection.	Most of the sentences vary in their beginnings, lengths, and structures. Several add style or interest. Most of the text flows smoothly and is easy to read aloud with inflection.	Sentence length and structure vary somewhat, with some sentences adding style or interest. Some sentence beginnings are repeated. Parts of the text flow smoothly. The paper can be read aloud with inflection.	In many places, the writing does not flow smoothly because sentences are the same length or begin the same way. The paper is difficult to read aloud with inflection.	Most sentences are the same length and structure. Sentence beginnings are repeated over and over again. The flow is too robotic or rambling.	Sentences are incomplete or incorrect. The text does not flow smoothly.
Conventions	The text has been carefully edited. Grammar, usage, and mechanics are correct.	The text contains one or two minor errors, but the meaning remains clear.	The text contains some minor errors that may distract the reader, but meaning remains clear.	Many errors are repeated. Line-by-line editing in specific places is needed. The errors interfere with meaning in some places.	Serious errors affect or alter the meaning.	The text has not been edited.

Argument Writing Rubric

	6	5	4	3	2	1
Ideas	The writer's claim is stated clearly. Counterclaims are anticipated and addressed very well. Accurate reasons and evidence from reliable sources support the claim.	The writer's claim is stated clearly. Counterclaims are anticipated and addressed well. Most of the reasons and evidence are accurate and from reliable sources.	The writer's claim is stated adequately. The author may fail to anticipate or address one or more common counterclaims. One or two pieces of evidence may not be from reliable sources.	A claim is stated. Counterclaims are not stated clearly. Counterclaims are not addressed well. Reasons and evidence are unrelated or inaccurate.	The writer's claim is not stated clearly. Counterclaims are not addressed. Reasons and evidence are not provided.	The writer does not state a claim. Reasons and evidence are not provided.
Organization	The argument is organized logically, including a strong introduction. A compelling conclusion restates the thesis and includes a call to action. Clear and unique transitions clarify the relationships between the claim, reasons, supporting evidence, and counterclaims.	The argument is organized logically, including a good introduction. The conclusion restates the thesis and may include a call to action. Most transitions clarify the relationships between the claim, reasons, supporting evidence, and counterclaims.	The argument is organized logically, including an introduction. The conclusion may not restate the thesis or may not include a call to action. More or better transitions may be needed to clarify the relationships between the claim, reasons, supporting evidence, and counterclaims.	The argument is not organized logically. The introduction or conclusion is missing (or problematic). Transitions are not used. Transitions are missing. Counterclaims are not used.	The argument is not organized logically. The introduction and conclusion are not effective. Counterclaims are not addressed.	The writing is not organized as an argument.
Voice	The voice strongly supports the writer's purpose and consistently connects with the audience. A respectful, confident tone is maintained.	The voice supports the writer's purpose and almost always connects with the audience. A respectful, confident tone is maintained.	The voice mostly supports the writer's purpose. The tone is mostly respectful and confident, but may be too informal in some places.	The voice is fairly weak or passive throughout the piece and fails to connect with the audience. The tone is inconsistent.	The voice is weak or inappropriate for the purpose and audience. A respectful, confident tone is not established.	The voice is flat or absent.
Word Choice	Compelling language conveys the writer's ideas and engages the reader. Nouns and verbs are clear and precise, supported by a few carefully selected modifiers.	Most of the language is compelling. Nouns and verbs are mostly clear and precise. Most modifiers are carefully selected.	Some of the language is compelling, but some is vague or ineffective. Some nouns and verbs are strong, but others are weak, requiring too much help from modifiers. Modifiers are satisfactory.	Much of the language is vague or ineffective. Nouns and verbs lack clarity or precision. Too many or too few modifiers are used, and many of these are weak.	The language is not compelling. Many words are very basic. Nouns and verbs are weak. Modifiers may be missing.	Words are weak, negative, or used incorrectly.
Sentence Fluency	The sentences vary greatly in length and structure, adding style and interest. Almost all sentences begin differently. The text flows smoothly and is effortless to read aloud with inflection.	Most of the sentences vary in their beginnings, lengths, and structures. Several add style or interest. Most of the text flows smoothly and is easy to read aloud with inflection.	Sentence length and structure vary somewhat, with some sentences adding style or interest. Some sentence beginnings are repeated. Parts of the text flow smoothly. The paper can be read aloud with inflection.	In many places, the writing does not flow smoothly because sentences are the same length or begin the same way. The paper is difficult to read aloud with inflection.	Most sentences are the same length and structure. Sentence beginnings are repeated over and over again. The flow is too robotic or rambling.	Sentences are incomplete or incorrect. The text does not flow smoothly.
Conventions	The writing has been carefully edited. Grammar, usage, and mechanics are correct.	The writing contains one or two minor errors, but the meaning remains clear.	The writing contains some minor errors that may distract the reader, but meaning remains clear.	The writing contains some minor errors. Line-by-line editing is needed. The errors interfere with meaning in some places.	Many errors are repeated. Line-by-line editing in specific places is needed. The errors interfere with meaning in some places.	Serious errors affect or alter the meaning. The writing has not been edited.

Strategies for Writers. Copyright © Zaner-Bloser, Inc. This page may be duplicated for classroom use.

Descriptive Writing Rubric

	6	5	4	3	2	1
Ideas	The topic is focused and exactly the right size. Sensory details clearly develop, describe, and reveal the subject. Carefully chosen ideas help the reader to completely experience what is being described.	The topic is focused and the right size. Many sensory details develop, describe, and reveal the subject. The ideas selected usually enable the reader to experience what is being described.	The topic may need to be more carefully focused. Some sensory details reveal the subject. The author's ideas sometimes help the reader experience what is being described.	The topic is not well focused. Too few sensory details reveal the subject. The ideas fail to consistently help the reader experience what is being described.	The topic is not focused. Details are scarce, or may relate to more than one subject. The ideas do not support the reader's experience of the topic.	The topic is unfocused or unclear. Details are random or missing.
Organization	The description is organized logically and creatively, including an engaging introduction and a thoughtfully crafted conclusion. Varied and appropriate transitions clarify relationships between ideas.	The description is organized logically, including a strong introduction and a strong conclusion. Most of the transitions clarify relationships between ideas.	The description is organized logically, including a functional introduction and conclusion. More or better transitions may be needed to clarify relationships between ideas.	The description is not well organized. The introduction or the conclusion is weak or missing. Transitions are weak or confusing. Some of the ideas are hard to follow.	The description is not organized. The introduction and the conclusion are missing. Transitions are incorrect or missing. The ideas are hard to follow.	The writing is not organized. Transitions are not used.
Voice	An authentic, clear voice conveys the writer's purpose and connects with the reader. The mood is perfect, and the tone conveys respect for the subject and the audience.	The voice is clear and connects with the reader most of the time. The mood is appropriate, and the tone conveys respect for the subject and audience most of the time.	The voice connects with the reader in some places. The tone is appropriate but inconsistent. An appropriate mood is somewhat established.	The voice may convey purpose but does not connect with the reader. The mood and tone may not be appropriate.	The voice does not convey purpose or connect with the reader. The mood and tone are inappropriate.	The voice is weak or absent. Mood and tone are not established.
Word Choice	Precise, descriptive words (including nouns, verbs, and modifiers) bring the subject to life. Figurative language and comparisons create a clear, coherent picture.	Most words (including nouns, verbs, and modifiers) are precise and descriptive. Figurative language and comparisons create a clear, coherent picture most of the time.	Some words are precise and descriptive, but others are not. Some nouns and verbs may rely too heavily on modifiers for clarity. Figurative language and/or comparisons sometimes create a clear picture.	Nouns and verbs lack precision and clarity. Too many or too few modifiers are used, and many of these are weak. Figurative language and/or comparisons do not create a clear picture.	Words are vague or confusing. Figurative language or comparisons are incomplete or missing.	Words are basic and very limited. Figurative language and comparisons are not used.
Sentence Fluency	A variety of sentences and/or lines adds interest and energy to the description. The writing flows very smoothly. Reading this aloud with inflection and feeling is effortless.	Most sentences and/or lines are varied and interesting. The writing flows smoothly most of the time. It is easy to read aloud with inflection and feeling.	Some sentences and/or lines are varied and interesting. The writing flows smoothly some of the time. It can be read aloud with inflection and feeling.	Many sentences and/or lines are not varied or interesting. Most of the writing does not flow smoothly. It is difficult to read aloud with inflection or feeling.	Sentences and/or lines are very basic, limited, or repetitive. The writing is predictable and dull.	Sentences and/or lines are incomplete or incorrect. The writing does not flow.
Conventions	The description has been carefully edited. Grammar, usage, and mechanics are correct.	The description contains one or two minor errors that are easily corrected. Meaning is clear.	The description contains some minor errors that may distract the reader, but meaning remains clear.	Many errors are repeated. Line-by-line editing in specific places is needed. Errors interfere with meaning in places.	Serious errors affect or alter the meaning.	The writing has not been edited.

Scope and Sequence

	Grade 5	Grade 6	Grade 7
Conferencing	Z14–Z15, T17, T19, T22, T43, T45, T47, T69, T71, T73, T95, T97, T99, T144, T147, T149, T169, T171, T173, T191, T193, T195, T213, T215, T217, T261, T263, T265, T285, T287, T289, T307, T309, T311, T329, T331, T333, T377, T379, T381, T399, T401, T403, T423, T425, T427, T445, T447, T449	Z14–Z15, T15, T17, T19, T41, T43, T45, T65, T67, T69, T89, T91, T93, T141, T143, T145, T165, T167, T169, T191, T193, T195, T215, T217, T219, T265, T267, T269, T289, T291, T293, T311, T313, T315, T333, T335, T337, T381, T383, T385, T403, T405, T407, T427, T429, T431, T449, T451, T453	Z14–Z15, T17, T19, T21, T41, T43, T45, T66, T70, T73, T95, T97, T99, T145, T147, T149, T170, T174, T178, T203, T205, T207, T227, T229, T231, T275, T277, T279, T297, T299, T301, T323, T325, T327, T347, T349, T351, T395, T397, T399, T417, T419, T421, T441, T444, T467, T469, T471
Differentiated Instruction	Z12–Z13, T15, T18, T28, T41, T44, T52, T67, T70, T78, T93, T96, T104, T112, T113, T118, T119, T127, T128, T141, T146, T154, T167, T170, T178, T189, T192, T200, T211, T214, T222, T230, T231, T233, T236, T237, T245, T246, T259, T262, T270, T283, T286, T294, T305, T308, T316, T327, T330, T338, T344, T346, T347, T350, T359, T375, T378, T386, T397, T400, T408, T421,	Z12–Z13, T13, T16, T24, T39, T42, T50, T63, T66, T74, T87, T90, T98, T106, T107, T108, T109, T112, T113, T118, T119, T121, T122, T137, T142, T150, T161, T166, T174, T187, T192, T200, T213, T216, T224, T232, T233, T235, T238, T239, T244, T245, T247, T261, T266, T274, T287, T290, T298, T309, T312, T320, T331, T334, T342, T348, T349, T351, T354, T355, T360, T361,	Z12–Z13, T15, T18, T26, T39, T42, T50, T63, T78, T93, T96, T104, T114, T115, T117, T120, T121, T126, T127, T129, T143, T146, T154, T167, T184, T199, T204, T212, T225, T228, T236, T244, T245, T246, T247, T250, T251, T259, T273, T276, T295, T298, T306, T321, T324, T332, T345, T348, T356, T364, T365, T366, T367, T370, T379, T380, T393, T396, T404, T415, T418, T426,

For a complete program Scope and Sequence, go to **www.sfw.z-b.com**.

	Grade 5	Grade 6	Grade 7
Differentiated Instruction (con't)			
	T424, T432, T443, T446, T454, T460, T461, T463, T466, T467, T475, T476	T363, T377, T382, T390, T401, T404, T412, T425, T428, T436, T447, T450, T458, T464, T465, T467, T470, T471, T476, T477, T479	T437, T424, T452, T465, T468, T476, T482, T483, T485, T488, T489, T497, T498
English Language Learners			
	Z13, T12, T13, T16, T20, T21, T38, T39, T42, T46, T64, T65 T68, T72, T90, T91, T94, T98, T110, T111, T116, T117, T122, T123, T138 T139, T142, T143, T148, T164, T165, T168, T172, T186, T187, T190, T194 T208, T209, T212, T216, T228, T229, T234, T235, T240, T241, T256, T257, T260, T264, T280, T281, T284, T288, T302, T303, T306, T310, T324, T325, T328, T332, T342, T343, T348, T349, T354, T355, T372, T373, T376, T380, T394, T395, T398, T402, T418, T419, T422, T426, T440, T441, T444, T448, T458, T459, T464, T465, T470, T471	Z13, T10, T11, T14, T18, T36, T37, T40, T44, T60, T61, T64, T68, T84, T85, T88, T92, T104, T105, T110, T111, T116, T117, T134, T135, T138, T139, T144, T158, T159, T162, T163, T168, T184, T185, T188, T189, T194, T210, T211, T214, T218, T230, T231, T236, T237, T242, T243, T258, T259, T262, T263, T268, T284, T285, T288, T292, T306, T307, T310, T314, T328, T329, T332, T336, T346, T347, T352, T353, T358, T359, T374, T375, T378, T379, T384, T398, T399, T402, T406, T422, T423, T426, T430, T444, T445, T448, T452, T462, T463, T468, T469, T474, T475	Z13, T12, T13, T16, T20, T36, T37, T40, T44, T60, T61, T64, T72, T90, T91, T94, T98, T112, T113, T118, T119, T124, T125, T140, T141, T144, T148, T164, T165, T168, T176, T177, T196, T197, T200, T201, T206, T222, T223, T226, T230, T242, T248, T249, T254, T270, T271, T274, T278, T292, T293, T296, T300, T318, T319, T322, T326, T342, T343, T346, T350, T362, T363, T368, T369, T374, T390, T391, T394, T398, T412, T413, T416, T420, T434, T435, T438, T439, T445, T462, T463, T466, T470, T480, T481, T486, T487, T492, T493

Scope and Sequence (continued)

	Grade 5	Grade 6	Grade 7
Grammar, Usage, and Mechanics			
abbreviations	T152, T293	T199, T508, T522	T182
action verbs	T514	T96	
active and passive voice		T70, T187, T192, T193, T339, T341	
adjective and adverb clauses		T192, T193, T339, T341	T474, T475, T506, T507, T533, T534
adjectives	T177, T313, T314, T315, T385, T484, T487, T512, T513	T197, T199, T389, T455, T456, T485, T498, T514, T519	T182, T450–T451, T503, T516, T529, T537
adverbs	T313, T314, T485, T512	T455, T457	T450–T451
apostrophes	T77, T383, T384, T507, T519	T409, T410	T143, T152
appositives	T219, T220, T502, T517	T387, T388	T282
articles	T385, T484, T512	T498, T519	T450, T515, T536
auxiliary verbs			T234, T526
brackets and dashes		T513, T523	T531, T541
capitalization	T151, T152, T153, T176, T505, T518	T197, T198, T199, T507, T508, T509, T521, T522	T76, T167, T170, T181, T182, T183
colons	T506, T519	T512, T523	T331, T530, T541
comma splices	T483, T511	T22	T24, T508
commas	T26, T103	T49, T273, T510, T511, T522, T523	T24, T76, T282, T475, T505, T528, T529, T541
comparative adjectives	T177	T455, T456	T451
complex sentences	T428, T511	T271, T272	T103
compound personal pronouns	T494, T515	T501, T517	T512, T535
compound sentences	T25, T26, T103, T428	T22, T49, T487, T515	T15, T23, T102, T153, T330, T530

	Grade 5	Grade 6	Grade 7
Grammar, Usage, and Mechanics (cont.)			
conjunctions	T25, T26, T27, T334, T428, T503, T517	T22, T23, T272, T500, T519	T24, T25, T102, T103, T522, T523, T539
demonstrative pronouns and adjectives	T487, T513		T516, T537
dependent and independent clauses	T103, T197, T198	T23, T271, T272, T486, T515	T505, T533
direct and indirect objects	T481, T510	T489, T516	T502, T532
direct quotations	T75, T76	T47, T48	T76
frequently confused words	T495, T496, T515	T411, T502	T356
helping verbs	T488, T513		T354, T356
homophones	T495, T496, T515	T317–T319	T354, T355
hyphens			T77
indefinite pronouns		T71, T73, T505, T521	T283
infinitive phrases			T305
initials	T293	T199, T508, T523	T181, T182
interjections	T489, T513		
irregular verbs	T197, T199, T497, T516	T173, T340, T503, T520	T235, T524, T539
kinds of sentences	T102	T506, T521	
linking verbs	T490, T491, T514	T96	T450, T503
negatives	T50	T504, T520	T303, T304
nouns	T103, T151, T152, T188, T315, T383, T384, T486, T505, T512, T518	T49, T197, T198, T199, T389, T409, T410, T484, T490, T491, T492, T505, T514, T516, T517	T182
parentheses	T219, T221, T508, T519		T77
personal pronouns	T269	T72, T493, T501, T517	T21, T511, T512, T535

	Grade 5	Grade 6	Grade 7
Grammar, Usage, and Mechanics (cont.)			
plural nouns	T383, T384	T198, T491, T517	T425, T510, T534
possessive pronouns	T269	T72, T492, T517	T210, T513, T536
predicate nouns and adjectives		T389, T484, T485, T514	T503, T532
prepositional phrases	T14, T481, T510	T220, T221, T222, T223	T403
prepositions	T481, T510	T221–T223	T403, T517, T537
present perfect tense	T452, T453, T504	T435, T496, T518	
pronoun antecedents	T268	T268, T296, T495	T210
relative pronouns and adverbs		T297, T495, T518	T514, T536
run-on sentences	T25, T26	T21, T22	T23, T24, T508, T534
semicolons	T26, T509, T519	T22, T512, T523	T330, T530, T541
sentence fragments	T291, T292	T21, T22, T272	T23, T24, T25
subject and object pronouns	T335, T336	T171, T172	T210, T211, T511, T512
subject and predicate	T479, T480, T510	T22	T501, T532
subject-verb agreement	T405, T406	T147, T148, T505, T522	T424–T425, T525, T540
superlative adjectives	T177	T455, T456	
titles	T175, T176, T293	T509	T183, T527, T540
transitive and instransitive verbs		T497, T518	T521, T538
using the right word	T495, T496, T515	T411, T502, T520	T354, T355, T356
verb tenses	T453, T492, T504	T95, T97, T433, T434, T435, T496, T518	T48, T49, T518, T519, T520, T537, T538, T539
verbals and verbal phrases			T305, T402
Writing Modes and Genres			
Argument Essay		T278A–T299	
Argument/Opinion Writing	T248A–T361	T250A–T365	T262A–T381

Writing Modes and Genres (cont.)	Grade 5	Grade 6	Grade 7
Biographic Sketch/Biography	T412A–T433	T76A–T101	T384A–T405
Book Review/Report	T250A–T273	T252A–T277	
Cause-and-Effect Report		T152A–T175	T134A–T155
Compare-and-Contrast Essay	T158A–T179		
Descriptive Article		T416A–T437	
Descriptive Paragraph/Essay	T364A–T387	T368A–T391	T428A–T455
Descriptive Writing	T362A–T477	T366A–T481	T382A–T499
Editorial			T264A–T285
E-Mail			T30A–T51
Explananatory Essay	T202A–T225	T204A–T227	
Eyewitness Account		T4A–T27	
Fable	T32A–T55		
Geographic Description			T428A–T455
Historical Episode		T28A–T53	T52A–T81
How-To Essay	T180A–T201		
Informative/Explanatory Writing	T130A–T247	T124A–T249	T132A–T261
Letters: Friendly, Business	T274A–T295	T300A–T321	T286A–T309
Literary Analysis			T336A–T359
Mystery	T56A–T81		
Narrative Writing	T2A–T129	T2A–T123	T2A–T131
Observation Report	T388A–T411	T392A–T415	T406A–T427
Opinion Essay	T296A–T317		
Opinion Speech	T318A–T339		
Personal Narrative	T4A–T31		T4A–T29
Play	T82A–T107		T82A–T109
Poem	T434A–T455	T438A–T459	T456A–T477
Problem Solution Essay			T214A–T239

Scope and Sequence (continued)

	Grade 5	Grade 6	Grade 7
Writing Modes and Genres (con't)			
Research Report	T132A–T157	T176A–T203	T156A–T187
Response to Literature	T250A–T273	T252A–T277	T336A–T359
Short Story		T54A–T75	
Speech		T322A–T343	
Summary		T126A–T151	T188A–T213
Test Writing	T108A–T129, T226A–T247, T340A–T361, T456A–T477	T102A–T123, T228A–T249, T344A–T365, T460A–T481	T110A–T131, T240A–T261, T360A–T381, T478A–T499
Website Review			T310A–T335
Graphic Organizers			
5 W's Chart		T15, T113	T17, T121
Argument Map		T333	T297, T371
Biography Map		T89	
Cause-and-Effect Chain	T43	T164, T165	T145, T251
Character Chart			T395
Concept Map	T329		
Five-Column Chart			
Five-Senses Chart		T427	
K-W-S Chart			T168
Main-Idea Table			T41, T203
Network Tree	T307, T399, T445	T289, T355	
Observation Chart			T417, T489
Order-of-Importance Organizer		T311	
Outline	T285	T191	T171
Paragraph Organizer			T347
Problem-Solution Frame			T227, T275
Pros-and-Cons Chart	T261		T323

	Grade 5	Grade 6	Grade 7
Graphic Organizers (con't)			
Sequence Chain	T119, T191, T237	T403	
Spider Map	T377, T467	T139, T239, T380, T381, T471	
Story Map	T69, T95	T41	T67, T95
Storyboard	T17	T65	
Support Pattern	T144, T213, T351		
Timeline			
Venn Diagram		T264–T265	
Web	T423	T215, T449	T441, T467
Listening and Speaking			
	T28, T52, T78, T104, T154, T178, T200, T222, T270, T294, T316, T338, T386, T408, T432, T454	T24, T50, T74, T98, T150, T174, T200, T224, T274, T298, T320, T342, T390, T412, T436, T458	T26, T50, T104, T154, T184, T212, T236, T284, T306, T332, T356, T404, T426, T452, T476
Publish & Presentation			
	T28, T52, T78, T104, T154, T178, T200, T222, T270, T294, T316, T338, T386, T408, T432, T454	T24, T50, T98, T150, T174, T200, T224, T274, T298, T320, T342, T390, T412, T436, T458	T26, T50, T78, T104, T154, T184, T212, T236, T284, T306, T332, T356, T404, T426, T452, T476
Rubrics			
	Z10, T10–T15, T36–T41, T62–T67, T88–T93, T136–T141, T162–T167, T184–T189, T206–T211, T254–T259, T278–T283, T300–T305, T322–T327, T370–T375, T392–T397, T416–T421, T438–T443, T522–T533	Z10, T8–T13, T34–T39, T58–T63, T82–T87, T132–T137, T156–T161, T182–T187, T208–T213, T256–T261, T282–T287, T304–T309, T326–T331, T372–T377, T396–T401, T420–T425, T442–T447, T526–T537	Z10, T10–T15, T34–T39, T58–T63, T88–T93, T138–T143, T162–T167, T194–T199, T220–T225, T268–T273, T290–T295, T316–T321, T340–T345, T388–T393, T410–T415, T432–T437, T460–T465, T544–T555

Scope and Sequence (continued)

	Grade 5	Grade 6	Grade 7
Technology	Z6–Z7, T2C, T14, T29, T40, T53, T66, T79, T92, T105, T130C, T140, T155, T166, T179, T188, T201, T210, T223, T248C, T258, T271, T282, T295, T304, T317, T326, T339, T362C, T374, T387, T396, T409, T420, T433, T442, T455	Z6–Z7, T2C, T12, T25, T38, T51, T62, T75, T86, T99, T124C, T136, T151, T160, T175, T186, T201, T212, T225, T250C, T275, T286, T299, T308, T321, T330, T343, T366C, T376, T391, T400, T413, T424, T437, T446, T459	Z6–Z7, T2C, T14, T27, T38, T51, T62, T79, T92, T105, T132C, T142, T155, T166, T185, T198, T213, T224, T237, T262C, T272, T382C, T285, T294, T307, T320, T333, T344, T357, T382C, T392, T405, T414, T427, T436, T453, T477
Text Exemplars	T4–T5, T32–T33, T56–T57, T82–T83, T132–T133, T158–T159, T180–T181, T202–T203, T250–T251, T274–T275, T296–T297, T318–T319, T364–T365, T388–T389, T412–T413, T434–T435	T4–T5, T28–T29, T54–T55, T76–T77, T126–T127, T152–T153, T176–T177, T204–T205, T252–T253, T278–T279, T300–T301, T322–T323, T368–T369, T392–T393, T416–T417, T438–T439	T4–T5, T30–T31, T52–T53, T82–T83, T134–T135, T156–T157, T188–T189, T214–T215, T264–T265, T286–T287, T310–T311, T336–T337, T384–T385, T406–T407, T428–T429, T456–T457
Traits	Z9, T6, T34, T58, T84, T110, T134, T160, T182, T204, T228, T252, T276, T298, T320, T342, T366, T390, T414, T436, T458	Z9, T6, T30, T56, T78, T104, T128, T154, T178, T206, T230, T254, T280, T302, T324, T346, T370, T394, T418, T440, T462	Z9, T6, T32, T54, T84, T112, T136, T158, T190, T216, T242, T266, T288, T312, T338, T362, T386, T408, T430, T458, T480

	Grade 5	Grade 6	Grade 7
Writing Across the Curriculum			
	Z16, T82A–T107, T202A–T225, T318A–T335, T434A–T455	Z16, T76A–T101, T204A–T227, T322A–T343, T438A–T459	Z16, T82A–T109, T214A–T239, T336A–T359, T428A–T455
Writing Process			
Prewrite	T16, T17, T42, T43, T68, T69, T94, T95, T116–T121, T142–T145, T168–T169, T190, T191, T212, T213, T234–T239, T260, T261, T284, T285, T306, T307, T328, T329, T348–T353, T376, T377, T398, T399, T422, T423, T444, T445, T464–T469	T14, T15, T40, T41, T64, T65, T88, T89, T110–T115, T138–T141, T162–T165, T188–T191, T214–T215, T236–T241, T262–T265, T288–T289, T310–T311, T332–T333, T352–T357, T378–T381, T402–T403, T426–T427, T448–T449, T468–T473	T16, T17, T40, T41, T64–T67, T94, T95, T118–T123, T144, T145, T168–T171, T200–T203, T226, T227, T248–T253, T274, T275, T296, T297, T322, T323, T346, T347, T368–T373, T394, T395, T416, T417, T438–T441, T466, T467, T486–T491
Draft	T18–T19, T44–T45, T70–T71, T96–T97, T122, T123, T146–T147, T170–T171, T192–T193, T214–T215, T240–T241, T262–T263, T286–T287, T308–T309, T330–T331, T354–T355, T378–T379, T400–T401, T424–T425, T446–T447, T470–T471	T16–T17, T42–T43, T66–T67, T90–T91, T116–T117, T142–T143, T166–T167, T192–T193, T216–T217, T242–T243, T266–T267, T290–T291, T312–T313, T334–T335, T358–T359, T382–T383, T404–T405, T428–T429, T450–T451, T474–T475	T18–T19, T42–T43, T68–T71, T96–T97, T124–T125, T146–T147, T172–T175, T204–T205, T228–T229, T254–T255, T276–T277, T298–T299, T324–T325, T348–T349, T374–T375, T396–T397, T418–T419, T442–T445, T468–T469, T492–T493

	Grade 5	Grade 6	Grade 7
Writing Process (cont.)			
Revise	T20–T24, T46–T48, T72–T74, T98–T100, T124–T126, T148–T150, T172–T174, T194–T196, T216–T218, T242–T244, T264–T266, T288–T290, T310–T312, T332–T334, T356–T358, T380–T382, T402–T404, T426–T428, T448–T450, T472–T474	T18–T20, T44–T46, T68–T70, T92–T94, T118–T120, T144–T146, T168–T170, T194–T196, T218–T220, T244–T246, T268–T270, T292–T294, T314, T316, T336–T338, T360–T362, T384–T386, T406–T408, T430–T432, T452–T454, T476–T478	T20–T22, T44–T46, T72–T74, T98–T100, T126–T128, T148–T150, T176–T180, T206–T208, T230–T232, T256–T258, T278–T280, T300–T302, T326–T328, T350–T352, T376–T378, T398–T400, T420–T422, T446–T448, T470–T472, T494–T496
Edit	T25, T49, T75, T101, T127–T128, T151, T175, T197, T219, T245–T246, T267, T291, T313, T335, T359–T360, T383, T405, T429, T451, T475–T476	T21, T47, T71, T95, T121–T122, T147, T171, T197, T221, T247–T248, T271, T295, T317, T339, T363–T364, T387, T409, T433, T455, T479–T480	T23, T47, T75, T101, T129–T130, T151, T181, T209, T233, T259–T260, T281, T303, T329, T353, T379–T380, T401, T423, T449, T473, T497–T498
Publish	T28, T52, T78, T104, T154, T178, T200, T222, T270, T294, T316, T338, T386, T408, T432, T454	T24, T50, T74, T98, T150, T174, T200, T224, T274, T298, T320, T342, T390, T412, T436, T458	T26, T50, T78, T104, T154, T184, T212, T236, T284, T306, T332, T356, T404, T426, T452, T476

Index